# APPLYING ANTHROPOLOGY

## *An Introductory Reader*

TENTH EDITION

Aaron Podolefsky
*Buffalo State University (SUNY)*

Peter J. Brown
*Emory University*

Scott M. Lacy
*Fairfield University*

APPLYING ANTHROPOLOGY: AN INTRODUCTORY READER, TENTH EDITION

Published by McGraw-Hill, a business unit of The McGraw-Hill Companies, Inc., 1221 Avenue of the Americas, New York, NY 10020. 

This book is printed on recycled, acid-free paper containing 10% postconsumer waste.

1 2 3 4 5 6 7 8 9 0 QDB/QDB 1 0 9 8 7 6 5 4 3 2 1

ISBN 978-0-07-811704-6
MHID 0-07-811704-6

Vice President & Editor-in-Chief: *Michael Ryan*
Vice President of Specialized Publishing: *Janice M. Roerig-Blong*
Editorial Director: *William Glass*
Senior Sponsoring Editor: *Debra B. Hash*
Marketing Manager: *Patrick Brown*
Project Manager: *Melissa M. Leick*
Design Coordinator: *Margarite Reynolds*
Cover Designer: *Studio Montage, St. Louis, Missouri*
Cover Image: *Royalty-Free/CORBIS*
Buyer: *Sherry L. Kane*
Media Project Manager: *Sridevi Palani*
Compositor: *Laserwords Private Limited*
Typeface: *10/12 PalatinoLTStd-Roman*
Printer: *Quad/Graphics*



**Library of Congress Cataloging-in-Publication Data**

Applying anthropology : an introductory reader / [edited by] Aaron Podolefsky,
Peter J. Brown, Scott M. Lacy.—10th ed.
p. cm.
ISBN 978-0-07-811704-6 (alk. paper)
1. Applied anthropology. 2. Anthropology. I. Podolefsky, Aaron.
II. Brown, Peter J. III. Title.
GN397.5.A67 2012
301—dc23

2011036666

www.mhhe.com

*There are things I couldn't have known when Peter and I began developing the ideas for this book during the late 1980s. I could not predict its growth and development nor how grateful I now am that the numerous editions have brought enlightenment to so many students over the years. In a similar way, my sons—young boys at the time—were also works in progress and at the start of their own lives. Looking back I reflect with great joy, pride, and satisfaction as I have watched these young boys blossom into men of character and wisdom.*

*This book is dedicated to my sons, Noah and Isaac, who have grown to be men since our first edition eighteen years ago.*

*—Aaron Podolefsky*

# Contents

## PART III *Linguistic Anthropology* *157*



## PART IV *Cultural Anthropology* *197*

### FIELDWORK

# Theme Finder for Chapters

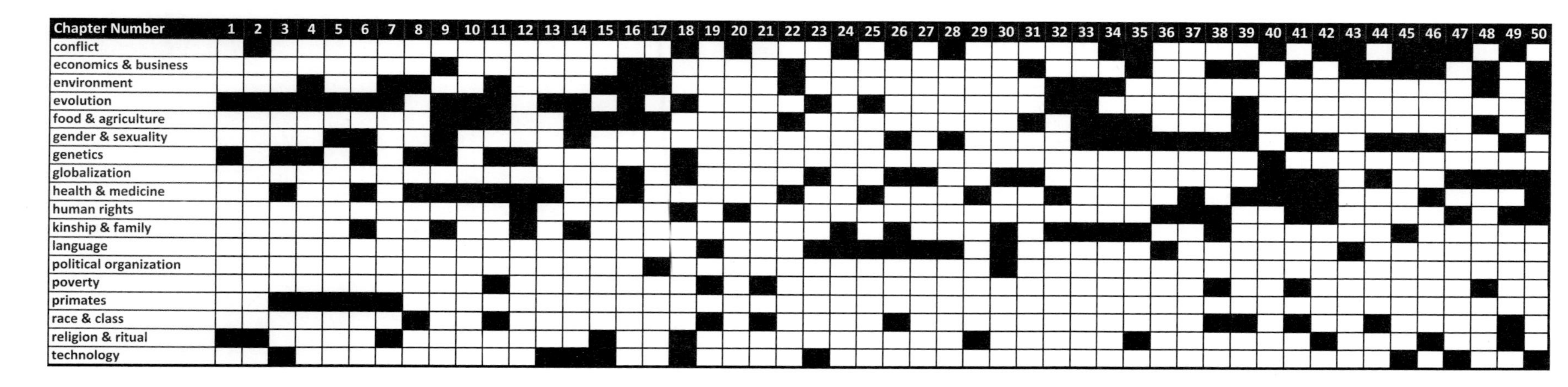

| Chapter Number | 1 | 2 | 3 | 4 | 5 | 6 | 7 | 8 | 9 | 10 | 11 | 12 | 13 | 14 | 15 | 16 | 17 | 18 | 19 | 20 | 21 | 22 | 23 | 24 | 25 | 26 | 27 | 28 | 29 | 30 | 31 | 32 | 33 | 34 | 35 | 36 | 37 | 38 | 39 | 40 | 41 | 42 | 43 | 44 | 45 | 46 | 47 | 48 | 49 | 50 |
|---|---|---|---|---|---|---|---|---|---|---|---|---|---|---|---|---|---|---|---|---|---|---|---|---|---|---|---|---|---|---|---|---|---|---|---|---|---|---|---|---|---|---|---|---|---|---|---|---|---|---|
| conflict |  | ■ |  |  |  |  |  |  |  |  |  |  |  |  |  |  |  | ■ |  | ■ |  |  |  | ■ |  | ■ |  | ■ |  |  |  |  |  | ■ | ■ |  |  |  |  | ■ |  | ■ | ■ |  | ■ | ■ | ■ |  | ■ |  |
| economics & business |  |  |  |  |  |  |  |  | ■ |  |  |  |  |  |  | ■ | ■ |  |  |  |  | ■ |  |  |  |  |  |  |  |  | ■ |  |  |  | ■ |  |  | ■ | ■ |  | ■ |  | ■ | ■ | ■ | ■ |  | ■ |  | ■ |
| environment |  |  |  | ■ |  |  | ■ | ■ |  |  | ■ |  |  |  | ■ | ■ | ■ |  |  |  |  | ■ |  |  |  |  |  |  |  |  |  | ■ | ■ | ■ |  |  |  |  |  |  |  |  |  |  |  |  |  | ■ |  | ■ |
| evolution | ■ | ■ | ■ | ■ | ■ | ■ | ■ |  | ■ | ■ | ■ |  | ■ | ■ |  | ■ |  | ■ |  |  |  |  | ■ |  | ■ |  |  |  |  |  |  | ■ | ■ |  |  |  |  |  | ■ |  |  |  |  |  |  |  |  |  |  | ■ |
| food & agriculture |  |  |  |  |  |  |  |  | ■ | ■ | ■ |  |  | ■ | ■ | ■ | ■ |  |  |  |  | ■ |  |  |  |  |  |  |  |  | ■ |  | ■ | ■ | ■ |  |  |  | ■ |  |  |  |  |  |  |  |  | ■ |  | ■ |
| gender & sexuality |  |  |  |  | ■ | ■ |  |  | ■ |  |  |  |  | ■ |  |  |  |  |  |  |  |  |  |  |  | ■ |  | ■ |  |  |  |  | ■ | ■ | ■ | ■ | ■ | ■ | ■ |  | ■ | ■ |  | ■ | ■ | ■ |  |  | ■ |  |
| genetics | ■ |  | ■ | ■ |  | ■ |  | ■ | ■ |  | ■ | ■ |  |  |  |  |  | ■ |  |  |  |  |  |  |  |  |  |  |  |  |  |  |  |  |  |  |  |  |  | ■ |  |  |  |  |  |  |  |  |  |  |
| globalization |  |  |  |  |  |  |  |  |  |  |  |  |  |  |  | ■ |  | ■ |  |  |  |  | ■ |  |  | ■ | ■ |  |  | ■ | ■ |  |  |  |  |  |  |  |  | ■ | ■ | ■ |  | ■ |  |  | ■ | ■ | ■ | ■ |
| health & medicine |  |  | ■ |  |  | ■ |  | ■ | ■ | ■ | ■ | ■ | ■ |  |  | ■ |  |  |  |  |  | ■ |  |  | ■ |  |  |  | ■ |  |  | ■ |  |  |  |  | ■ |  | ■ | ■ | ■ | ■ |  |  |  | ■ |  |  |  | ■ |
| human rights |  |  |  |  |  |  |  |  |  |  |  | ■ |  |  |  |  |  | ■ |  | ■ |  |  |  |  |  |  |  |  |  |  |  |  |  |  |  | ■ | ■ | ■ |  |  | ■ | ■ |  |  |  |  | ■ |  | ■ | ■ |
| kinship & family |  |  |  |  |  | ■ |  |  | ■ |  |  | ■ |  | ■ |  |  |  |  |  |  |  |  |  | ■ |  | ■ |  |  |  | ■ |  | ■ | ■ | ■ | ■ |  |  | ■ |  |  |  |  |  |  | ■ |  |  |  |  |  |
| language |  |  |  |  |  |  |  |  |  |  |  |  |  |  |  |  |  |  | ■ |  |  |  | ■ | ■ | ■ | ■ | ■ | ■ |  | ■ |  |  |  |  |  | ■ |  |  |  |  |  |  | ■ |  |  |  |  |  |  |  |
| political organization |  |  |  |  |  |  |  |  |  |  |  |  |  |  |  |  | ■ |  |  |  |  |  |  |  |  |  |  |  |  | ■ |  |  |  |  |  |  |  |  |  |  |  |  |  |  |  |  |  |  |  |  |
| poverty |  |  |  |  |  |  |  |  |  |  | ■ |  |  |  |  |  |  |  | ■ |  | ■ |  |  |  |  |  |  |  |  |  |  |  |  |  |  |  |  | ■ |  |  | ■ |  |  |  |  |  |  | ■ |  |  |
| primates |  |  | ■ | ■ | ■ | ■ | ■ |  |  |  |  |  |  |  |  |  |  |  |  |  |  |  |  |  |  |  |  |  |  |  |  |  |  |  |  |  |  |  |  |  |  |  |  |  |  |  |  |  |  |  |
| race & class |  |  |  |  |  |  |  | ■ |  |  | ■ |  |  |  |  |  |  |  | ■ |  | ■ |  |  |  |  | ■ |  |  |  |  |  |  |  |  |  |  |  | ■ | ■ |  | ■ |  |  | ■ |  |  |  |  | ■ |  |
| religion & ritual | ■ | ■ |  |  |  |  | ■ |  |  |  |  |  |  |  | ■ |  |  | ■ |  |  |  |  |  |  |  |  |  |  | ■ |  |  |  |  |  | ■ |  |  |  |  |  |  | ■ |  |  |  | ■ |  |  | ■ |  |
| technology |  |  | ■ |  |  |  |  |  |  |  |  |  | ■ | ■ | ■ |  |  | ■ |  |  |  |  | ■ |  |  |  |  |  |  |  |  |  |  |  |  |  |  |  |  |  |  |  |  |  | ■ |  | ■ |  |  | ■ |

■ Denotes theme present in chapter

# To the Student

An introductory course in any discipline is full of new terminology, concepts, and facts. Sometimes students forget that these new ideas and vocabulary are actually intellectual tools that can be put to work for analyzing and solving problems. In preparing this book, we have selected readings that will show you how anthropological concepts, discoveries, and methods can be applied in today's world.

The study of anthropology can help you view the world in a completely different way than you ever have before. You can come to appreciate the great diversity of human cultures and the interrelatedness of economic, sociopolitical, and religious systems. Anthropology can give you a broad perspective on humanity and help you understand other people's beliefs and customs. In doing so, it can help you become a better citizen in an increasingly global society. But your motivation need not be completely altruistic—there are many examples in this book of how cross-cultural awareness can improve performances in business, negotiations, and clinical medicine.

The fascinating side of anthropology seems obvious to most educated people, but there is also a lesser-known practical side of the discipline. The readings we have selected demonstrate that practical, applied side. Many of the articles depict anthropological ideas and research methods in action—as they are used to understand and solve practical problems. We have included articles on anthropologists working outside the academic setting to show how they are applying anthropology. We believe that the fundamental lessons of anthropology can be applied to many careers and all areas of human endeavor.

To benefit from the study of anthropology, you need to study effectively. Over the years, we have found that students often read assignments without planning, and this actually makes studying less efficient. Before you read a selection, spend a few moments skimming it to get an idea of what it is about, where it is going, and what you should look for. This kind of preliminary reading is a poor idea for mystery novels but is essential for academic assignments. Without this preparation, the article may become a hodgepodge of facts and figures; details may be meaningless because you have missed the big picture. By planning your reading, you can see how the details are relevant to the central themes of an article.

To help you plan your reading, at the beginning of each article we have included questions and a list of glossary terms. Looking at these questions in advance, you may gain an idea of what is to come and why the article is important. This will help make the time you spend reading more fruitful. Most of the questions highlight the central themes of the selection or draw your attention to interesting details. Some of the questions, however, do not have straightforward answers—they are food for thought and topics for debate. Some of the selections refer directly to current discussions of HIV, migration, obesity, gender diversity, and drug use. Our idea is to challenge you to think about how anthropology can be applied to your own life and education.

These articles have been selected with you, the student, in mind. We hope they convey our excitement about the anthropological adventure, and we trust that you will find them both enjoyable and thought-provoking.

"Applied anthropology" most often refers to a situation in which a client hires an anthropologist to do research that will help the client resolve a particular problem. Some applied anthropologists run their own research companies that bid and win research contracts from clients and funding agencies; other applied anthropologists work directly for corporations. Applied anthropologists write their reports specifically for their clients. A good place to find out about applied anthropology is at the society for applied anthropology's Web site, www.sfaa.net. There are many master's degree programs in this field. You may also run across the term "public anthropology" in your studies. This refers to anthropological research and writing that engages important public issues (like many of those addressed in this book) and whose audience is the lay educated public. As "public scholars," anthropologists want to communicate their perspective on contemporary issues and influence public opinion and policy. A good place to find out what is happening in public anthropology is through the Web site of the American Anthropological Association (www.aaanet.org) or the Public Anthropology Web site (www.publicanthropology.org).

If you are interested in reading more about applied anthropology, there are several excellent books available, such as *Applied Anthropology: A Practical Guide,* by Erve Chambers; *Applied Anthropology: An Introduction,* by John van Willigen; *Anthropological Praxis: Translating Knowledge into Action,* by Robert M. Wulff and Shirley J. Fiske; *Applied Anthropology in America,* by Elizabeth M. Eddy and William L. Partridge; and *Making Our Research Useful,* by John van Willigen, Barbara Rylko-Bauer, and Anne McElroy. If you are interested in medical matters, you may want to consult *Understanding and Applying Medical Anthropology,* by Peter J. Brown, or *Anthropology and Public Health,* by Robert Hahn. You may also want to look at the journals *Human Organization* and *Practicing Anthropology,* both of which are published by the Society for Applied Anthropology. The National Association of Practicing Anthropologists (NAPA) also publishes interesting works on specific fields such as medical anthropology.

# To the Instructor

Introductory anthropology has become an established part of the college curriculum, and through this course our profession communicates with a large and diverse undergraduate audience. Members of that audience differ in experience, academic concentration, and career aspirations. For those students considering anthropology as a major, we need to provide (among other things) a vision of the future, a view of anthropological work to be done in the public domain as well as within academia. For them, we need to provide some answers to the question, what can I do with a degree in anthropology? For students majoring in other areas, such as business, engineering, or psychology, we need to address the question, how can anthropological insights or research methods help me understand and solve human problems? If we can provide such a service, we increase the likelihood that students will find creative solutions to the professional problems that await them, and we brighten the future for our anthropology majors by underscoring the usefulness of an anthropological perspective in attempts to solve the practical problems of today's world.

Over the years we have found that many introductory texts do little more than include a chapter on applied anthropology at the end of the book. This suggests, at least to students, that most of anthropology has no relevance to their lives. Such treatment also implies that the application of anthropological knowledge is a tangent or afterthought—at best an additional subject area, such as kinship or politics.

We disagree. We believe that the applications of anthropology cut across and infuse all the discipline's subfields. This book is a collection of articles that provide examples of both basic and applied research in all four fields of anthropology.

One of our primary goals is to demonstrate some of the ways our discipline is used outside the academic arena. We want anthropology to be seen as a field that is intellectually compelling as well as relevant to the real world. Like the public at large, students seem well aware that the subject matter of anthropology is fascinating, but they seem unaware of both the fundamental questions of humanity addressed by anthropologists and the practical applications of the field. Increased public awareness of the practical contributions of anthropology is a goal that we share with many in the profession. In fact, this is a major long-term goal of the American Anthropological Association.

Since we first started editing these readers in 1989, the general field of anthropology has changed in precisely this direction of emphasizing public relevance. "Public anthropology" refers to anthropological research and writing that engages important public issues (like many of those addressed in this book) and whose audience is the lay educated public. Our discipline has a long history in this regard, as in the work of Franz Boas on racial discrimination and Margaret Mead's famous articles in *Redbook* magazine. As "public scholars," anthropologists must communicate their perspective on contemporary issues and influence public opinion and policy. In this age of globalization and increased cultural intolerance often linked to religious fundamentalism, the basic messages of public anthropology are more important than ever. Being an effective public anthropologist is just being a great teacher in a larger classroom. A good place to find out what is happening in public anthropology is through the Web site of the American Anthropological Association (www.aaanet.org) or the Public Anthropology Web site (www.publicanthropology.org).

Although people distinguish between basic and applied research, much of anthropology falls into a gray area, having elements of both. Many selections in this book fall into that gray zone—they are brief ethnographic accounts that contain important implications for understanding and resolving problems. We could have included a large number of articles exemplifying strictly applied research—an evaluation report of agency performance, for example. Although this sort of research is fascinating and challenging to do, it is usually not exciting for students to read. We have selected articles that we believe are fascinating for students and convey the dual nature (basic/applied) of social science research. We think that it is not the scholarly writing style that is most important, but rather the content of the research as a way to get students to think and to challenge their own assumptions about the world.

Anthropological research is oriented by certain basic human values. These include being against ethnocentrism, racism, and ignorance. Anthropology is about understanding and appreciating human similarities and differences. Such an understanding can lead students to new attitudes—such as tolerance for cultural differences, commitment to human equality, stewardship of the environment, appreciation of the past, and personal dedication to the continued and honest pursuit of knowledge.

Any student who completes an introductory course in anthropology should learn that anthropological work, in its broadest sense, may include (or at least contribute to) international business, epidemiology, program evaluation, social impact studies, conflict resolution, organizational analysis, market research, and nutrition research, even though their introductory anthropology texts make no mention of those fields. The selections in this book should help students understand why anthropology is important in today's world and also make the course more memorable and meaningful.

## FEATURES OF THIS EDITION

- To spark student discussion and thinking about controversial issues and issues of public policy, we have included selections dealing with contemporary topics like globalization, HIV/AIDS, racism, cell phones, gender diversity, migration, obesity, intelligent design, and the U.S. military in Afghanistan and Iraq. These selections are clearly anthropological in perspective and approach. When students are able to relate the concepts and examples of anthropology to current debates, they recognize the value of their education.
- We chose readings that complement typical courses in introductory anthropology. The sequence of articles follows the organization of standard anthropology textbooks, grouped under headings with terms such as kinship, gender, marriage, and conflict, rather than headings based on areas of applied anthropology like medical anthropology or the anthropology of development. At the same time, we include headings such as globalization and health and medicine, reflecting growth and development in the anthropological discipline and purview.

  Had we meant this book as a reader on applied anthropology, our organization would have been different. Although this book could be used by students in upper-level courses on applied anthropology (as earlier editions have been), those students are not our intended audience. For this reason, we have not provided extensive discussion of the history or definition of applied anthropology.
- For students interested in pursuing applied anthropology on their own, there are a number of fine books. These include *Applied Anthropology: A Practical Guide*, by Erve Chambers; *Applied Anthropology: An Introduction*, by John van Willigen; *Anthropological Praxis: Translating Knowledge into Action*, by Robert M. Wulff and Shirley J. Fiske; *Applied Anthropology in America*, by Elizabeth M. Eddy and William L. Partridge; and *Making Our Research Useful*, by John van Willigen, Barbara Rylko-Bauer, and Anne McElroy. Students interested in medical matters may want to consult *Understanding and Applying Medical Anthropology*, by Peter J. Brown, or *Anthropology and Public Health* by Robert Hahn.
- To emphasize how anthropology can be put to work in different settings, we include examples of anthropologists whose careers involve applying anthropology outside the university setting.
- To help students better understand the subject matter, we include a number of pedagogical aids: introductions, a list of glossary terms, and guiding questions for each article; a world map that pinpoints the locations of places and peoples discussed in the articles; and, for easy reference, an extensive glossary and index.
- A Theme Finder follows the table of contents to help instructors and students identify critical cross-chapter themes, including gender, environment, globalization, human rights, poverty, race and class, and technology.

## NEW TO THIS EDITION

In this edition, we continue to juxtapose "classic" anthropological articles with selections that highlight contemporary issues and cutting-edge methodologies. One such juxtaposition is the enduring issue of the biological theory of evolution as opposed to creationism, which has been reborn as "intelligent design." Because the corpus of fossil evidence for human evolution has become so large and ever more complex for undergraduates, we added a new chapter that explains how paleontology, genetics, and the digital scanning and virtual reconstruction of fossils have revealed exciting new details about lives and physiology of our earliest human ancestors.

There are eleven new articles that refer to contemporary social issues such as the changing cultural norms of patriarchy and respecting elders in South Africa. The new selections also deal with hot-button issues such as the indigenous control of archaeological research and artifacts, and the sociolinguistic roots of male–female conflict.

To bring more balance to our representation of the four-field approach of American anthropology, we slightly increased our coverage of linguistic anthropology and archaeology. We also organized the biological anthropology section into three subsections to clearly distinguish chapters that focus on human evolution, primatology, and human biology.

We uphold our enduring commitment to the critical discussion of race as a salient topic for introductory anthropology. We added a new biological anthropology selection that separates fact from fiction in terms of the relationship between race and biology, but we placed nearly all of the other articles about race within the cultural anthropology section because race is a cultural construction, not a biological fact. In this regard, students need to understand that whiteness, as a cultural construction, brings with it certain privileges despite progress since the emergence of the civil rights movement. Racism, sexism, homophobia, severe economic inequality, and intolerance for cultural differences are continuing problems of our society; as such, anthropology and its four subfields provide essential perspectives for cross-cultural understanding.

## ACKNOWLEDGMENTS

We thank the following reviewers of this edition for their helpful comments and suggestions: Jason Antrosio, Hartwick College; Mary Theresa Bonhage-Freund, Alma College; John Coggeshall, Clemson University; Garrett Cook, Baylor University; Christa Craven, College of Wooster; Amy DeWys, Henry Ford Community College; Julie Ernstein, Northwestern State University; Lynne Goldstein, Michigan State University; P. Nick Kardulias, College of Wooster; Jennifer Price, Foothill College; Kendall Thu, Northern Illinois University; and LuAnn Wandsnider, University of Nebraska–Lincoln.

*Aaron Podolefsky*
*Peter J. Brown*
*Scott M. Lacy*

# INTRODUCTION

## *Understanding Humans and Human Problems*

To the uninitiated, the term *anthropology* conjures up images of mummies' tombs, Indiana Jones, and treks through steaming jungles or over high alpine peaks. Anthropologists agree that their chosen field is exciting, that they have been places and seen things that few experience firsthand, and that they have been deeply and emotionally involved in understanding the human condition. At the same time, however, the vision of anthropology presented by Hollywood has probably done more to obscure the true nature of the profession than it has to enlighten the public about what we really do.

Providing an accurate image of anthropology and anthropological work is both simple and complex. Essentially, anthropology is the study of people, or more properly, of humankind. But, you may say, many disciplines study people: psychology, sociology, history, biology, medicine, and so on. True, but anthropology is different in that it seeks to integrate these separate and perhaps narrower views of humanity. To understand ourselves, we need to join these disparate views into a single framework, a process that begins with our biological and evolutionary roots, explores the development of culture through the prehistoric and historical periods, probes the uniquely human ability to develop culture through communication, and examines the diversity of recent and present-day cultures that inhabit the globe.

From this conception of the *holistic* and *comparative* study of humankind emerge what are termed the four fields of anthropology: biological (or physical) anthropology, archaeology, anthropological linguistics, and cultural anthropology. Some universities offer an introductory course that covers all four subfields. Other schools cover the subfields in two or three separate introductory courses. Each approach has its advantage. The former may more fully integrate the biocultural and historical dimensions of humanity; the latter allows students to explore each subfield in greater depth. This book introduces you to the four fields of anthropology and how they are used in today's world.

Another way to divide the discipline—in fact almost any discipline—is into *basic* and *applied* research. These categories are important in this reader because we would like students to appreciate both the basic and the applied sides of anthropology.

A survey of natural and social scientists and engineers conducted by the U.S. Census Bureau for the National Science Foundation used the following definitions of these fundamental concepts: *Basic research* is study directed toward gaining scientific knowledge primarily for its own sake. *Applied research* is study directed toward gaining scientific knowledge in an effort to meet a recognized need.

Anthropology is a discipline concerned primarily with basic research. It asks "big" questions concerning the origins of humankind, the roots of human nature, the development of civilization, and the functions of our major social institutions (such as marriage and religion). Nevertheless, anthropologists have put the methods and skills developed in basic research to use in solving human problems and fulfilling the needs of society. Anthropologists have, for example, worked with medical examiners in the identification of skeletal remains. They have also helped communities preserve their cultural heritage and businesses and government agencies understand the social impact of programs or development projects.

Although the application of anthropology has a long history, it has, until recent years, remained in the shadows of pure or basic research. The past few decades have seen a change. Anthropologists have moved beyond their traditional roles in universities and museums and now work in a broad range of settings. They are employed in many government agencies, in the private sector, and in a variety of nonresearch capacities (such as administrators, evaluators, or policy analysts). Profiles of anthropologists in nonacademic careers (high-tech industry) can be found in this book.

In response to the growing opportunities for anthropologists outside academia and to the demands of students, an increasing number of master's degree and doctoral programs provide training specifically in the applications of anthropology. This is not to say that the classified ads list jobs titled "anthropologist." Rather, for those interested in anthropology, there are increasing opportunities to find careers that draw on anthropological training and skills. At the same time, studies have shown that there will be increasing job opportunities for anthropologists in universities and colleges during the next decade and beyond.

In this era of multiculturalism, there is increasing recognition that our society—indeed, our world—is a culturally diverse social mosaic. Living in a multicultural society presents real challenges stemming from chronic ethnocentrism and persistent social tension. But it also brings a cultural richness, even luxuriance, of diversity in art, food, language, values, and beliefs.

Applications of anthropology are found in all four fields and include the identification of skeletal remains (forensics); the study of size and fit for the design of clothing, furniture, or airplane cockpits (ergonomics); exploration of the patterns and causes of disease (epidemiology); evaluation of the effectiveness of programs (from Third World development to crime prevention); assessment of community needs; prediction of the social impact of change; analysis of organizations such as businesses and government agencies; market research; and research into health and nutrition—just to name a few. School administrators, engineers, doctors, business leaders, lawyers, medical researchers, and government officials now recognize that the knowledge, unique perspective, and research skills of anthropologists are applicable to practical problems—in the United States and elsewhere in the world.

As we explore anthropology, keep in mind the interplay between and interdependence of basic cultural research and the applications of anthropological knowledge and research methods to the solution of human problems.

# PART I

# *Biological Anthropology*

To understand ourselves, we must first understand the human animal. Fundamentally, humans are flesh-and-blood biological beings. Although we are qualitatively different from the other animals, anthropology nonetheless takes the position that we must begin our understanding of humanity by examining our biological heritage. *Biological anthropology* (also known as *physical anthropology*) has the goal of increasing the knowledge about our species, *Homo sapiens sapiens,* by examining the evolutionary roots of our biology and behavior. There are three primary ways in which this evolutionary story is studied: In *paleoanthropology,* anthropologists discover and analyze the fossil remains of our ancestors; in *primatology,* anthropologists examine the survival strategies, social organization, and behavior of the nonhuman primates; and in *human biology,* anthropologists explore variations in the physical characteristics of human populations, which represent genetic differences shaped by environmental conditions through the processes of evolution.

Anthropological research in all these areas, particularly human biology, can have important applications for understanding and solving today's human problems. Much of the applied work in biological anthropology is related to health problems. Through the study of genetics, anthropologists study hereditary predispositions to particular diseases like obesity or Tay-Sachs. Through the study of human anatomy, anthropologists study skeletal disorders, bone development, and the relationship between poor nutrition and health. Biological anthropologists also examine the physiological adaptations of humans to environmental stressors like extreme temperatures or high altitude. They also describe the variations in the human life cycle—childhood, puberty, reproduction, and aging. One of the major tools of biological anthropology is *anthropometry,* the measurement of the human body. Anthropometry is used in the design of clothing and furniture; it is also used to assess the health of a prehistoric population as well as to identify human remains after an accident or murder.

Although the ongoing research in paleoanthropology, for example, is *basic science*—the search for fundamental knowledge not necessarily related to solving specific problems—the detailed study of the fossil record can reveal much about human nature and about what Melvin Konner has called "biological constraints on the human spirit."

When we study ourselves, we need to remember that the human animal is the product of millions of years of evolutionary history. The genes that we inherit from our parents (and that we pass to our children) are exact duplicates of the genes of our ancestors passed down through countless generations. The biology of our own bodies (and that of all our fellow humans) represents thousands of centuries of natural selection in action, that is, interaction between people and the environment affecting patterns of survival and reproduction. Natural selection is no trivial concept. It signifies nothing less than the cumulative effects of the lives and deaths of our ancestors. The scientific study of our evolutionary heritage might therefore be motivated as much by a respect for our own unnamed ancestors as by our curiosity about what happened in the distant past. Yet in the United States today, the study of our own evolutionary history has been attacked, and many students are deprived of the opportunity to learn about the evolutionary heritage of all humanity.

Evolution is a central concept in all of anthropology because humans adapt through both biology and culture. *Culture,* the learned patterns of thought and behavior characteristic of a social group, is the primary reason for the amazing success of our species.

The story of human evolution is still unfolding. Important new fossils are discovered almost every year, and their interpretation is often the subject of vigorous scholarly debate. These debates are a normal part of the scientific enterprise. However, bones do not tell the whole story. To answer questions about the evolution of behavior, anthropologists sometimes make analogies with the behavior of nonhuman primates. The comparison of humans with nonhuman primates is important for both basic and applied research. Fundamental aspects of social organization, like the social alliances between "friends" in a baboon troop described by Barbara Smuts in Selection 5, can be understood only after thousands of hours of observation of the animals in their natural setting. Similarly, research on the sex lives of Bonobo chimpanzees may shed light on the nonreproductive functions of sex in human societies. Such research can help in understanding principles of social behavior and can serve as a model of the evolutionary past.

Primatological research may also have practical applications. For example, apes have been shown to have the ability to learn nonverbal human languages using symbols from American Sign Language or artificial languages (Yerkish). One spin-off of these discoveries is the development of new tools for enabling mentally and physically disabled people to communicate. Similarly, studies of peacemaking among primates may help in identifying fundamental keys for maintaining social relations.

Anthropologists have lived with and studied people whose economy is based on food foraging—a combination of hunting and gathering wild foods. Their culture might be thought of as the original human lifestyle. Only a few groups of people in today's world primarily hunt and collect their food, and they have been displaced to marginal environments. No doubt their lives have also been influenced by the farming groups who may live near them. Nevertheless, the study of hunters and gatherers can serve as a model or analogy for understanding the lives of prehistoric peoples. One mistake that anthropologists made in the past was to overemphasize the role of male-dominated hunting in early prehistory. Anthropologists now argue that women played a key role in the evolutionary story through food gathering, food sharing, and the creation of social cooperation.

Some of the lessons we learn from studying the culture and lifestyle of food foragers and other traditional societies may help us understand our own health. The diet of Paleolithic people, for example, might be considered an ideal diet for the prevention of certain diseases of civilization, like hypertension, diabetes, cardiovascular disease, and obesity, to name a few. Western medicine has borrowed many of the fundamental drugs in our modern pharmacopoeia from technologically simple peoples. In recent years, some anthropologists have begun to examine health and illness from a Darwinian perspective of the pathogen as well as the human host. This work is leading to the development of Darwinian medicine, as described by Elizabeth Whitaker in Selection 9.

A central concern of biological anthropology has been the description of (and explanation for) biological differences between ethnic groups. Some of the physical differences between groups are evolutionarily interesting, and some have important medical ramifications. The scientific study of these differences—of what was once called *race*—must be understood in the context of two basic facts: We are all members of a single human species, and all humans are unique individuals. Human variation may be described in terms of morphological characteristics (stature, skin color, and so on) or underlying genetic characteristics. Both techniques have led anthropologists to conclude that much of human biology is influenced by an environment that is in turn shaped by culture.

Applied biological anthropology is associated with a wide variety of career opportunities. Research techniques originally developed to describe and analyze long-buried human remains unearthed by the archaeologist or paleontologist, for example, can be used to identify remains from a disaster or crime. This application of anthropological knowledge is called *forensic anthropology* because it is used in courts of law.

Other biological anthropologists have worked in forensic settings by using genetic lab techniques to untangle legal questions of identity.

The relevance of biological anthropology to down-to-earth human problems is evident. Using knowledge of human morphology and human variation, physical anthropologists have, for example, worked in the field of human factors engineering, designing uniforms, aircraft seats, and other equipment. Biological anthropologists have also studied complex problems like malnutrition and child growth in Third World nations, the interaction of malnutrition and infection, and the effect of high-altitude living on work performance. Biological anthropologists have discovered how particular patterns of breast-feeding result in natural four-year birth spacing in some societies like the food-foraging !Kung. They are also discovering that newer reproductive patterns may result in high rates of breast cancer. Moreover, biological anthropologists have helped untangle the phenomenon of sudden infant death syndrome (SIDS).

The contribution of anthropologists to understanding practical human problems extends beyond the collection of data on human biological variation. The research and discoveries of biological anthropology are being applied to the solution of those problems.

# 1

# Teaching Theories

## *The Evolution-Creation Controversy*

*Robert Root-Bernstein and Donald L. McEachron*

At the beginning of a book of readings on anthropology as a biosocial science, we can appropriately concern ourselves with defining science and scientific explanation. When asked, most people describe science by naming disciplines: "Oh, science, let's see, that's physics, chemistry, biology, and so on." However, science is more than a list of subjects or particular fields of study. Rather, it is a process for drawing conclusions. Stated differently, science is a particular way of knowing. We have, of course, many ways of knowing things. For example, one might see something in a dream and be convinced that it is true. One might be told some fact or theory by a teacher (such as what goes up must come down) and accept it based on the teacher's authority. In this case, the student has learned a scientific principle but has not participated in hypothesis testing or theory building.

In their work, scientists give special definitions to some common, everyday words. Words such as *validity, reliability, random, hypothesis,* and *theory* take on meanings that are precise and often significantly different from their everyday counterparts. These meanings can lead to serious misunderstandings as scientists try to communicate with the public.

In recent years, questions about the nature of science have been at the root of public debate over the teaching of human evolution in the public schools. As anthropologists, we respect and value the belief systems of other people, and we recognize that many of the cultures of the world have their own beliefs about creation. Yet the only scientific model that can explain the fossil and genetic record is evolution.

***As you read this selection, ask yourself the following questions:***

- How is the term *theory* used differently by scientists and nonscientists?
- Why is it so important that scientific theories be testable and correctable?
- What does the phrase "scientific skepticism" mean to you?
- Who do you think should decide what is science and what is not?
- Why has the evolution versus creationism debate been such an emotional issue in some sectors of American society?

***The following terms discussed in this selection are included in the Glossary at the back of the book:***

*contingent truths*
*creationism*
*evolution*
*hypothesis*
*natural selection*
*religion*
*scientific theory*

In recent years, a controversy has developed in the United States over the teaching of evolutionism and creationism in the public schools. The controversy, while nominally a scientific one, also has philosophical, historical, religious, and legal implications as well. Since some twenty state legislatures or courts are presently considering or have considered legislation and lawsuits concerning the controversy, we believe that it is in the best interest of the voting public to be informed of the issues.

We believe that there are four basic issues: (1) What is a scientific theory? (2) What is a religious belief? (3) Who has the right to decide these issues? (4) How do one's answers to the previous three questions affect one's view on whether evolutionism and creationism are scientific and should be taught in public schools?

Very briefly, a controversy has arisen between evolutionists and creationists because they disagree on

Root-Bernstein, Robert & McEachron, Donald L. "Teaching Theories: The Evolution-Creation Controversy." From *The American Biology Teacher*, October 1982. Reprinted with permission of the National Assoc. of Biology Teachers.

all four basic issues. Evolutionists generally believe: (1) that evolutionism is a valid scientific theory, whereas creationism is not; (2) that evolutionism is not a religious belief, whereas creationism is; and (3) that the validity of a religious belief should be decided by religious believers. In consequence, evolutionists conclude (4) that since evolutionism is a valid scientific theory, it should be taught in the public schools; whereas, since creationism is not a scientific theory, it should not be taught as science in the public schools.

Creationists disagree completely. Creationists generally believe (1) that evolutionism is not a valid scientific theory, whereas creationism is; (2) that evolutionism is a dogmatic, secular religion, whereas "scientific creationism" is not; and (3) that the state (that is, either the legislature or the courts) has the right to decide whether any theory is scientifically valid or not. Thus, creationists argue (4) that the state has the right to decide that evolutionism must be censored as a dogmatic religious belief and equal time given to creationism as a valid scientific theory. Creationists argue that either both should be taught in the public schools, or neither.

Clearly, to decide between these two positions, one must understand what a scientific theory is and how it differs from a religious belief. It is our purpose to explore these issues in this essay.

## WHAT IS A SCIENTIFIC THEORY?

Begin by considering the question, "What is a scientific theory?" There is nothing mysterious about the answer; a scientific theory is a simple, *testable,* and *correctable* explanation of *observable* phenomena that yields *new information* about nature in answer to a set of pre-existing problems. While this definition may sound complicated or imposing, in practice it is not. All of us use scientific theories in our daily thinking. Consider the following situation as an example.

You come home one evening, open the front door, and turn on the light switch. The lights do not come on. This is an *observation.* One compares this observation to memories of observations made under similar circumstances: every other time you've turned on the light switch, the lights have come on. One has an *anomaly*—that is, something that should work the same as always, but doesn't. Why do the lights not come on? This is your *problem.*

How do you resolve your problem? First, it occurs to you that something about the electrical system is different tonight. You consider possible differences: perhaps the light switch isn't working properly. You've invented an *hypothesis.* Can you *test* it? Sure. You jiggle the switch. Nothing happens. Your hypothesis is probably wrong. You reject it. But you still have your problem. Can there be some other explanation? Yes. Maybe the fuse has burned out. Another hypothesis. Can it be tested? Easily. You go turn on the light switch in the next room and the lights in there go on. So your problem isn't the fuse. There must be some other explanation.

But wait a minute: you've made an *assumption* about the fuse that may not be correct! What if the two rooms are controlled by two different fuses? Then the fact that the lights work in the second room proves nothing at all about the first fuse. The manner in which you've tested your hypothesis about the fuse being burned out is not valid. If your *assumption* about both rooms being controlled by a single fuse is wrong, then the test is useless. Thus, one must be careful to test not only one's hypothesis, but the assumptions upon which it rests as well. This is a very important point to which we will return later.

Checking your fuses, you find that all are fine. So, still in the dark, you hypothesize that the bulb is burned out. You take out the bulb, put in a new one, throw the switch, and, lo and behold—light! So you conclude that your third hypothesis was correct. The reason the light would not go on was because it was burned out.

But wait! You've made another assumption, haven't you? You've assumed the light bulb is burned out, but have you tested the light bulb in another socket to see whether it really *is* burned out? If you are acting scientifically, you must not only test your hypothesis; you must also test your assumptions. So, you screw the light bulb into another socket and—much to your surprise—it lights! Your last hypothesis was wrong! And just think—if you hadn't bothered testing your assumption, you would never have known you were wrong. Indeed, you would have thrown away a perfectly good light bulb.

Now, how do you explain why the light bulb failed to light before? It wasn't burned out. The power was on. The fuse was fine. The switch works. Logically, there seems to be only one other likely explanation of all these observations: perhaps the light bulb wasn't screwed in properly. This is your new hypothesis.

As with any scientific hypothesis, you ask once again: Is it testable? But this time your answer is both yes and no. Yes, one may test the general hypothesis that an unscrewed light bulb won't light. That's easy to do: just loosen any light bulb in its socket and you can verify that it doesn't go on when you turn the switch. However, one cannot test the *particular* hypothesis that the cause of your problem tonight was a loose bulb; you've already removed the bulb from its socket. There is now no way to tell whether the bulb was loose or not. One concludes that it had to have been loose because one cannot think of any other *test hypothesis.*

Note that one accepts one's *particular* hypothesis only when *two* conditions are met: (1) that its corresponding *general* hypothesis is testable; and (2) when no other *testable* hypothesis is available to explain the problem. If one's explanation meets these criteria, then it is a scientific theory. But note also that one's theory is not actually *true*—it is only *probable.* It is only probable because there might be another testable hypothesis that might explain the collection of observations better; or there might be a test that demonstrates that one's theory is wrong. One might, for example, someday discover that one's lights go out sporadically because a mouse causes short circuits by gnawing on the wires in the wall. But, if you don't know you have a mouse then you are unlikely to think of this hypothesis and even less likely to test it by looking for the mouse. In consequence, theories are always tentative, even when tested and found correct. For, as you saw when you thought your problem was a burned-out bulb, it sometimes takes only one more simple test to reveal your error.

Now, we may draw several important conclusions about scientific theories from this example. Most important of these is the fact that scientific theories can never be proven absolutely. A mouse may always be hiding, unknown, in some wall waiting to be discovered, thereby disproving your loose-light-bulb theory. The same is true of *any* scientific theory. Science is not, therefore, truth—at best it is the unending *search* for truth. The conclusions reached by science are only *contingent* truths—truths contingent upon man's limited knowledge of himself and the world around him.[1]

Now, one may ask what good is a theory if it is not true? A theory is good because it is *useful* and it is *fruitful of new knowledge.* Scientific methods have explained more of the empirical world than any alternative approaches including religion. Science allows man to work in the universe as no other system of knowledge does. It allows one to do things that one could not otherwise do, and it allows one to learn things one would otherwise not learn. For example, Faraday's theory of electricity allowed him to invent the first electric motor. Pasteur's germ theory has allowed the control of innumerable diseases. The laws of thermodynamics allowed atomic power to be harnessed by mankind. The list could go on almost indefinitely. So, scientific theories are important because they give mankind knowledge of this world and the ability to act wisely in this world. In our case, it gave us knowledge of the electrical system and thus the ability to fix the light.

Man's ability to act usefully from the predictions of a theory, however, depend upon his ability to test the predictions made by the theory. The process of testing, as we saw with the light bulb, is more important than the theory itself. For even when the theory was wrong, the test yielded new information that was used to invent the next theory. Thus, right or wrong, a testable theory always yields new information about the problem it claims to resolve. This new information is *cumulative.* It adds up. First we tested the switch and found that it worked. So, we knew the problem was not the switch. Then we tested the fuse, and found that the fuse worked. So we knew the problem was not the fuse or the switch. Then we tested the light bub . . . and so on. The more we tested, the more we learned. And the more we learned, the fewer the possible explanations left to try. We knew more, and our ignorance was less. We were converging on the correct answer. All good scientific theories work this way. Thus, although scientific truths are always contingent ones, the method by which they are advanced and tested ensures their improvement.

In short, the power of scientific theories results from the fact that they are *correctable.* They may be tested. Whether the theory is right or wrong, these tests yield new information about the world. And, if the theory is wrong, then this new information can be used to invent a new and better theory. Thus, while scientific theories are never perfect, they become better and better with time. And, as theories become better, mankind knows more, can act more wisely, and can solve more problems.

## CAN GOD BE USED IN A SCIENTIFIC THEORY?

One further explanation of our light problem remains to be discussed before considering whether evolutionism and creationism are scientific theories. One might explain the failure of the light by saying that "It was God's will." Indeed, it might have been. "God's will" cannot, however, be part of a *scientific* explanation.

Three reasons preclude the use of God, or other supernatural agencies, in scientific theories. First, scientific theories must be *bounded.* That is, they must apply only to a particular field of inquiry. A simple analogy can be made to sports. Each sport has its own rules that are valid only for that sport. And every sport is played within an area *bounded* by sidelines, goals, or a defined course. In this sense, science is the attempt to discover the rules by which nature plays its various "games" and the boundaries within which each different "game" is played. In our light bulb example, we concluded that a rule must exist that says: the light will not go on if the bulb is not screwed in properly. This is a *bounded* explanation that applies to all light bulbs, but which could not, for example, be used to explain other natural events such as a flood or a death. "God's will" is, on the other hand, an *unbounded* explanation. It can be used to explain the light problem, floods, deaths, and anything else imaginable. In consequence, "God's will" and other supernatural powers cannot be invoked in a scientific theory because they would make the theory *unbounded.* The rules of science would not apply, just as the rules of baseball do not apply to tennis.

Unbounded explanations have a second problem. They cannot be tested. As we stated above, all theories must be testable. Testability, in turn, is necessary if a theory is to be correctable. To be testable, and therefore correctable, a theory must state *how* an event occurs. Because God's actions are beyond man's knowledge, we cannot know *how* He works His will. The same is true of any supernatural explanation. Supernatural, by definition, means beyond man's comprehension. Since God's power is supernatural, He is capable of doing anything. Thus, there is no test imaginable that could disprove an hypothesis stating that an event occurred because of "God's will." In consequence, there would be no way to discover if one's hypothesis were wrong, and no way to correct one's error.

Untestable explanations present a third difficulty. They can neither be harnessed to useful ends nor to the discovery of new knowledge. Explaining the light bulb problem as "God's will," for example, does not enable us to correct the problem. On the contrary, it places the problem beyond our comprehension. By proposing that the light bulb failed to light because it was unscrewed, we could correct the problem immediately. Further, we would be able to recognize and solve that problem if it ever arose again. Thus, we have learned something new. We have acquired new knowledge. Invoking "God's will" does not yield the same sort of new and useful knowledge.

One must not conclude from the foregoing that science is anti-religious. On the contrary, scientific and religious explanations can be completely compatible. What the light bulb problem shows us is that scientific explanations are simply a very select subset of all possible explanations. Religious, or supernatural, explanations form another subset. Sometimes these two subsets overlap. Then, something may be "God's will" and also have a scientific explanation. In these cases, one should be able to explain *how* "God's will" was implemented. If one can do this, then science and religion are in harmony. If not, then they represent two irreconcilable views of the problem. On this point, Pope John Paul II recently quoted the following conclusion from the Vatican II Ecumenical Council: "research performed in a truly scientific manner can never be in contrast with faith because both profane and religious realities have their origin in the same God." Religious leaders of almost all religious denominations agree.

## EVOLUTION: SCIENCE OR RELIGION?

Now, how does the light bulb example illuminate the question of whether evolution is a scientific explanation of nature? First of all, as in the light bulb example, one must have a *problem* to address. The problem evolutionists face is to explain *how* the living organisms that exist on the earth today developed through history, and *how* they achieved the forms and distributions characteristic of each species, alive or extinct. Many hypotheses have been proposed to resolve these problems during the 2,000 years of man's recorded history. Each has been found wanting. Perhaps the best known of these was Lamarck's idea that organisms could modify their structures by force of will. Lamarck's idea did not pass the test of observation and its assumptions were never verified. Thus, it, like our hypothesis concerning the fuses, was retired to scientific purgatory. Not until Darwin invented the concept of evolution by natural selection of the fittest organisms was an hypothesis suggested that explained all of the data accumulated during tests of previous hypotheses. It did so in a simple, harmonious, and verifiable way. Thus, if one looks at the history of science, one finds that Darwin's is neither the first nor the only theory to attempt to explain the history and development of life. It is the culmination of 2,000 years of theory building. In this, evolution is analogous to our loose-light-bulb hypothesis: it is the end product of a long chain of hypothesizing and testing. It is the best theory so far devised.

Darwin's basic hypothesis was that only the best-adapted organisms survive the competition for food, the ravages of disease, and the attacks of natural predators to reproduce themselves. The weeding out of weaker organisms creates a steady change in the adaptive characteristics of the individual organisms comprising each species. As the individual characteristics change, so does the profile of the whole species. Thus, evolution.

Is evolution a scientific theory? Just as with the light bulb example, the first question that must be asked about the Darwinian hypothesis is whether it is testable. In this case, as in the case of the loose-light-bulb hypothesis, one must answer both yes and no. Yes, the *general* mechanism of natural selection is testable because it is operating today. No, the specific application of natural selection to extinct species is not directly testable because they, like the light bulb in our analogy, have (metaphorically) already been taken out of the socket. Like the light bulb taken out of its socket, however, fossil remains provide enough information to disprove all hypotheses so far invented *other than* evolution by natural selection. Thus, just as in the light bulb example, one accepts evolution as a valid scientific theory for two reasons: (1) its corresponding *general* hypothesis is testable; and (2) no other *testable hypothesis* is available to explain the problem. It is, of course, always possible that a better theory will be invented in the future.

It was stated above that the general mechanism of natural selection is testable. Since many creationists have denied this conclusion, we present two examples here. Everyone knows that germs cause disease and that various insects, such as mosquitoes, can transmit diseases to man. Natural selection has been observed, occurring in both germs and insects. The selection process has even been controlled in the laboratory by means of antibiotics and pesticides. The invention of antibiotics has virtually allowed man to wipe out certain diseases. The few disease germs that have survived man's ingenuity, however, have developed into antibiotic-resistant strains which man can no longer easily control. The same thing has happened with insects sprayed repeatedly with insecticides. The hardiest have survived to reproduce new races of insects that are insecticide-resistant. Thus, in some areas of the world, diseases like yellow fever and malaria are once again becoming major health problems. Even in the United States, farmers are faced with crop-eating insects that are harder and harder to eliminate. Direct observation leaves no doubt that natural selection does occur. The fittest do survive, and they breed new populations of better-adapted individuals.

It is not sufficient to test just the hypothesis of natural selection. One must, as we pointed out repeatedly in our light bulb example, also test one's assumptions. Several assumptions underlie evolutionary theory. One assumption is that there is a mechanism for creating a spectrum of different individuals within a species so that natural selection can weed out the weakest. Another assumption is that some mechanism exists by which those individuals that survive can pass their adaptive traits on to future generations. And finally, evolution by natural selection assumes sufficient time for new species to be formed by the accumulation of adaptive traits. Each of these assumptions has been questioned, doubted, and tested. Each assumption is correct to the best of current scientific knowledge.

The primary mechanism for producing genetic variability in evolving organisms is mutation. Mutation theory has been given a firm experimental basis by numerous scientists including Nobel Laureates T. H. Morgan and J. H. Mueller. Geneticists, such as Barbara McClintock, have evidence that rearrangements of whole genes and even chromosomes may also play a role in creating genetic variability.

The mechanism of genetic inheritance of mutations and rearrangements is also well understood. Despite early fears by nineteenth-century biologists that adaptive variations would blend out of existence like a drop of ink in a gallon of paint, Gregor Mendel and his successors established that inheritance is not blending—it is particulate. The ink spot does not blend into the paint in genetics. Rather, it stays separate and definable, like a water drop in oil. If the water-based ink is better adapted than the oil-based paint, then the ink will reproduce faster than the paint and so come to dominate the mixture. Thus, beneficial mutations, while rare, are not lost from the population. Mendel's "laws" and the population genetics of R. A. Fisher, J. B. S. Haldane, and their colleagues explain the rules by which such populations evolve. James Watson and Sir Francis Crick, two more Nobel Laureates, have explained the details of the inheritance process itself at the molecular level of DNA.

Finally, astronomers, physicists, and geologists have established that the earth is definitely old enough to make evolution by natural selection plausible. One hundred years ago, scientific opinion was just the opposite. Physicists such as Lord Kelvin calculated that the age of the earth was only a few million years—too short to allow evolution. Even Darwin was worried by his arguments. But Kelvin's calculation turned out to be incorrect, for it was based on a faulty hypothesis. Kelvin *assumed* that there was no internal source of energy heating the earth because he knew of none. In fact, his assumption was incorrect. In this case there was a metaphorical "mouse in the wall" called radioactivity. Kelvin did not know about radioactivity because it was discovered after he died. Once other physicists took the heating effects of radioactivity into account in new calculations, it became clear that the earth was billions, not millions, of years old. Astronomers measuring the age of the solar system and geologists dating rocks and fossils have reached the same conclusion. There has been sufficient time for evolution to have occurred.

In short, evolution by natural selection is a valid scientific theory because it and its underlying assumptions have been tested and validated by observation or experiment. Further, anyone who has walked through a modern research library or flipped through a general science magazine will not fail to realize the amount of new knowledge this theory has evoked. Much of this new knowledge has even been useful, especially in the production of new breeds of farm animals and hybrid crops. Evolution by natural selection has thus fulfilled the requirements of a scientific theory superbly. To what degree it may someday need to be modified by new discoveries, only the future will tell.

## CREATIONISM: SCIENCE OR RELIGION?

Now, is "scientific creationism" also a scientific theory? "Scientific" creationists claim to be interested in solving the same problems that evolutionists address: how does one explain the forms of living organisms and their geological and geographical distribution? In place of evolution by natural selection, creationists postulate the existence of a supernatural "God," "Creator" or "Intelligence" who created the earth and all of the living organisms on it and in it. They claim that this supernatural agent produced the earth and its life within a period of thousands of years. The question we must address is whether or not the "creation explanation" is a scientific one. In other words, is it testable? Is it correctable? Have its assumptions been tested and verified? And is it fruitful of new or useful information concerning nature?

It is important to point out that our criteria for evaluating scientific theories are identical to those used by creationists such as Robert Kofahl, Kelly Segraves, Duane Gish, and Henry Morris in the course of this controversy. We are not, therefore, asking of "creation science" any more than the creationists ask of science itself.

Can "scientific" or "special" creationism be tested? Creationist scientists themselves admit that it cannot be. Gish, for example, writes in his book *Evolution? The Fossils Say No!* that

> . . . we do not know how God created, what processes He used, for God used processes which are not now operating anywhere in the natural universe. This is why we refer to divine creation as special creation. We cannot discover by scientific investigations anything about the creative processes used by God.

Instead, creationists maintain that the Creator used catastrophic or supernatural means to His end. The Noahic Flood is an example of such a supernatural catastrophe. But, Morris, Director of the Institute for Creation Research (ICR), has written in his book *Biblical Cosmology and Modern Science,* "the main trouble with catastrophist theories is that there is no way of subjecting them to empirical test." Thus, the scientific methods of hypothesis followed by testing, which were so useful in solving our light bulb problem, are totally useless for solving the problems addressed by creationists.

The second characteristic of a theory is that it is correctable. Once again, creationist scientists admit that the creation explanation fails to possess this characteristic. Morris, for example, lists 23 predictions from Genesis 1–11 in his book. His own conclusion is that all 23 predictions are contradicted by the past century of geological research. Does he therefore treat Genesis 1–11 as a scientific hypothesis in need of correction? No. On the contrary, Morris states that "no geological difficulties, *real or imagined,* can be allowed to take precedence over the clear statements and necessary inferences of Scriptures." In short, creationism is uncorrectable.

Indeed, another creationist scientist, John N. Moore of the ICR, has written in several pamphlets that the major advantage creationism has over evolution is that creationism is "the *only unchanging* explanation of origins." It is so unchanging that "scientific creationism" is essentially identical to the prescientific form of Biblical creationism espoused by Jews over 2,000 years ago. This makes creationism one of the oldest surviving explanations for anything. No doubt this intellectual stability is comforting in these times of rapid change, but is stability, in and of itself, necessarily good?

Think back a moment to our light bulb analogy. Would an unchanging, uncorrectable explanation of our problem have been an advantage to us there? Certainly not. Just imagine the depths of our ignorance had we stuck with our first light bulb hypothesis no matter what the evidence indicated. Instead of accumulating new knowledge through the testing of new hypotheses until we discovered that the light bulb was loose, we would still be standing at the light switch wondering what in Heaven's name could be wrong. After a while, no doubt, we would conclude that whatever it is, it is beyond our comprehension. Unfortunately, this is exactly what the creationists have concluded.

All creationist literature falls back, at some point, upon the assumption that a supernatural, omniscient, omnipotent God, Creator, or Intelligence must exist to direct the creative process. Some creationists make this assumption explicit. Others, especially those writing public school texts, do not. These others believe that if they leave God out of the text, then it will be "less religious" and "more scientific." Their belief is unfounded. As we have demonstrated with examples both from the light bulb analogy and from evolutionary theory, all assumptions must be tested whether they are stated explicitly or not. Failure to state an assumption simply makes the explanation less scientific because it is then harder to test it. In this case, whether one explicitly states that God is the Creator or one leaves the Creator unidentified, Someone or Something must cause Creation. These assumed causes (or mechanisms) have been identified and tested for evolution. They must also be identified and tested for creationism if it is to be considered scientific.

Unfortunately, creation scientists are on the horns of a scientific dilemma. If they leave the Creator out of their explanations, they provide no testable mechanism for creation. This form of the creation explanation is therefore unscientific. On the other horn, if they identify the Creator with God or other supernatural powers, then they are also being unscientific. As the great and pious astronomer Sir Isaac Newton said more than a century before Darwin was born, the use of any final cause such as God automatically takes the explanation out of the realm of science. Morris and A. E. Wilder-Smith of ICR and Kofahl and Segraves of the Creation Research Center (CRC) consistently and blatantly identify the Creator as a final cause in their textbooks. But, "God's will," as we discussed with regard to our light bulb analogy, cannot be used as a *scientific* explanation of anything.

Nonetheless, the "scientific creationists" attempt to do just that. Morris and Gish of ICR, Kofahl and Segraves of CRC, and the hundreds of members of the Creation Research Society have all stated that the Creator is the God of the Bible and that the Creation itself occurred exactly as described in Genesis. These same individuals also admit that, to use Morris' words from his textbook *Scientific Creationism,*

> . . . it is impossible to devise a scientific experiment to describe the creation process, or even to ascertain whether such a process can take place. The Creator does not create at the whim of a scientist.

So we come to the crux of the evolution-creation debate. Science depends upon observation, testing, and control. Religion depends upon faith in the existence of an unobservable, untestable, uncontrollable God. As scientists, we can turn off and on a light at will; we can create mutations and breed new varieties of plants and animals at will; we can observe the natural processes of evolution in fossils, fields, forests, and laboratories—at will. How different is creationism. No one can turn off or on the Creator at will. No one can cause Him to create new varieties of plants or animals at will. No one can observe any of the processes by which He creates. Creationism, because it depends upon the existence of such an unobservable, untestable, uncorrectable Creator can not be a scientific theory.

Indeed, the attempt to use a Creator as a scientific explanation only promotes *scientific* ignorance. Invoking "God's will" did not help us to understand or fix our light problem. Invoking "God's will" as the cause of Creation is no more enlightening. "God's will," because it is not testable or correctable, yields no new or useful knowledge concerning nature. Thus, creationism fails to possess the final characteristic required of all scientific theories: that it be fruitful of new scientific knowledge. Creationism is not *scientifically* fruitful.

There are two ways of demonstrating this. The first is to search the historical record since Darwin to determine whether creationism has been used in the formulation of any major scientific discovery. The history of science shows that it has not. On the contrary, almost all important discoveries made during the last century in biology and geology either stem from or add to our understanding of evolution.

This conclusion may be verified in a second manner. Reference to the numerous sources cited by the creationists themselves demonstrates that their conclusions are almost entirely dependent upon research carried out by evolutionists. Only in the rarest instances have the creationist scientists created any of their own data. This is a sorry state of affairs for an explanation that is hundreds and thousands of years older than evolutionary theory. Yet, it makes sense when you think about it. Science, as we pointed out initially, is based upon recognizing and answering new questions or problems. Creationists have no new problems. Accepting the Biblical account of Creation as the True Word of God, creationists can assert, as Kofahl and Segraves have done in their book *The Creation Explanation,* that "the Genesis record [already] provides the answers." For creationists, nothing more can be known; nothing more needs to be known.

## CONCLUSION: SCIENCE AND RELIGION

In summary, we have argued that evolution qualifies as a valid scientific theory while creationism does not. We have also argued that evolutionary theory is not a religious explanation while creationism is. We do not conclude thereby that evolution is "true" and creationism "false," nor can the opposite conclusion be maintained. We conclude only that evolution and creationism are two totally different sorts of explanations of nature. They should not be confused.

It is also clear to us that evolution, as the best available scientific explanation of nature, deserves to be taught as a scientific theory in science classes. Creationism, since it is not a scientific theory, should not be taught as science in science classes. On the other hand, we have no objection to seeing creationism taught as a *religious* explanation of nature. Although religion is constitutionally banned from the public schools, perhaps some time could be made available for the teaching of creationism in its proper historical and philosophical context. Such an arrangement would teach students the differences between scientific and religious explanations that have been summarized here.

We believe that it is particularly important that students do learn the differences between scientific and religious beliefs. Indeed, we believe that it is the confusion between the two that has caused the present controversy. Despite the rhetoric used by the creationists, their view is not scientific, nor is science a religion. Yet "scientific creationists" have made both claims. Historically, this is nothing new. Fundamentalists have created the same confusion ever since Darwin first published *On the Origin of Species* in 1859. Harvey Cox, Professor of Divinity at the Harvard Divinity School, has recently written that

> . . . the notorious nineteenth century "Warfare Between Science and Religion" arose from mistaken notions of what religion and science are. Although there are still occasional border skirmishes, most theologians and scientists now recognize that religion overstepped its boundaries when—at least in the West—it tried to make geological and biological history into matters of revelation.

We can only regret that a small group of fundamentalists believe it necessary once again to overstep the boundaries differentiating science from religion. The result is needless confusion, confusion that could be eliminated by proper teaching of what science is, what religion is, and how they differ.

Science and religion, as Cox pointed out, need not be at war. They can be, as we pointed out initially, complementary. It is only when science poses as religion or religion as science that controversy erupts. Otherwise faith and reason are compatible. In fact, the English clergyman Charles Kingsley pointed this compatibility out to Darwin in a letter written in 1860. Kingsley wrote:

> I have gradually learnt to see that it is just as noble a conception of Deity to believe that He created animal forms capable of self-development into all forms needful . . . as to believe that He required a fresh act of intervention to supply the lacunae which He Himself made. I question whether the former be not the loftier thought.

Whether one agrees with Kingsley's view or not, it illustrates an important point. There are many possible conceptions of the relationship between science and religion. It does not seem appropriate to us that any group, such as the creationists, should attempt to legislate their particular view of this relationship into law. Our Constitution guarantees freedom of religious choice. We believe that an equal guarantee exists for all intellectual choices, including those involving science. Thus, just as the courts and legislatures may not judge the validity of various religious beliefs or impose one in preference to another, neither should courts and legislatures be involved in determining the validity of scientific ideas nor should they impose one in preference to another. Just as religious practice is left to the individual religious practitioner, so should scientific research be left to the individual scientist. To do otherwise infringes upon the rights of individuals to decide for themselves the relationship between scientific ideas and religious beliefs. To do otherwise is thus not only an abridgment of intellectual freedom, but of religious freedom as well.

It may strike some people as odd that we equate protection of religion with protection of science. There is good reason for the equation. Several governments in the past have usurped to themselves the control of science. They are not commendable examples to follow: Nazi Germany, Soviet Russia, and Communist Red China. Science, religion, and liberty suffered hand-in-hand in these countries. Let us not begin the journey down their road by harnessing science to legislatures and courts. On the other hand, let us learn from the evolutionism-creationism controversy that dogmatism, be it scientific or religious, is best left out of the classroom. Dogmatism teaches only narrow-mindedness at a time when it is clear that better understanding of the issues is what is needed. We must teach the best of man's knowledge to the best of our ability. But we must also teach how we can recognize it as best. And we must always remain humbly aware that we may be ignorant of something better. That is the lesson of science.

## NOTE

1. The authors of this article used the term *man* to refer to humanity in general. This term is not used by modern anthropologists because, to many people, it reflects an unconscious sexist bias in language and rhetoric. At the time that this article was written, however, the generalized *man* was a common convention in writing. In the interest of historical accuracy we have not changed the wording in this article, but students should be aware that nonsexist terms (*humans, people, Homo sapiens,* and so on) are preferred.—The Editors.

## REFERENCES

Barbour, I. 1966. *Issues in science and religion.* New York: Harper and Row.

Baum, R. M. 1982. Science confronts creationist assault. *Chemical and Engineering News* 12(26): 19.

Beckner, M. 1968. *The biological way of thought.* Berkeley and Los Angeles: University of California Press.

Clark, H. W. 1968. *Fossils, flood and fire.* Escondido, Calif.: Outdoor Picture Press.

Colloms, B. 1975. *Charles Kingsley.* London: Constable; New York: Barnes and Noble.

Cox, H. 1981. Religion. In Villoldo, A., and Dychtwald, K. (eds.). *Millennium: Glimpses into the 21st century.* Los Angeles: J. P. Tarcher.

Eldredge, N. 1981. The elusive eureka. *Natural History* August 24–26.

Gillispie, C. C. 1959. *Genesis and geology.* New York: Harper and Row.

Gish, D. T. 1978. *Evolution? The fossils say no!* San Diego: Creation-Life Publishers.

______. n.d. *Have you been brainwashed?* San Diego: Creation-Life Publishers.

______. 1981. Letter to the editor. *Science Teacher* 48: 20.

Gould, S. J. 1982. On paleontology and prediction. *Discover* July 56–57.

Hardin, G. 1959. *Nature and man's fate.* New York: Holt, Rinehart and Winston.

Huxley, T. H. 1892. *Essays on controverted questions.* London and New York: Macmillan and Co.

Kofahl, R. E., and Segraves, K. L. 1975. *The creation explanation.* Wheaton, Ill.: Shaw.

Lammerts, W. (ed.) 1970. *Why not creation?* Phillipsburg, NJ Presbyterian and Reformed Publishing Co.

______. 1971. *Scientific studies in special creation.* Phillipsburg, NJ Presbyterian and Reformed Publishing Co.

Lewin, R. 1982. Where is the science in creation science? *Science* 215: 142–146.

Moore, J. R. 1979. *The post-Darwinian controversies.* Cambridge and New York: Cambridge University Press.

Morris, H. M. 1975. *Introducing scientific creationism into the public schools.* San Diego: Institute for Creation Research.

______. 1970. *Biblical cosmology and modern science.* Nutley, N.J.: Craig Press.

Overton, W. R. 1982. Creationism in schools: The decision in *McLean versus the Arkansas Board of Education* [Text of 5 January 1982 Judgment]. *Science* 215: 934–943.

Peacocke, A. R. 1979. *Creation and the world of science.* Oxford: The Clarendon Press.

Pupin, M. (ed.) 1969. *Science and religion.* Freeport, N.Y.: Books for Libraries Press.

Root-Bernstein, R. S. 1982. On defining a scientific theory: Creationism considered. In Montagu, A. (ed.) *Evolution and creationism.* Oxford: The University Press.

______. 1982. Ignorance versus knowledge in the evolutionist creationist controversy. Paper presented June 22 at the symposium, "Evolutionists Confront Creationists," American Association for the Advancement of Science, Pacific Division, Santa Barbara, Calif.

Ruse, M. 1982. A philosopher at the monkey trial. *New Scientist* 317–319.

Skoog, G. 1980. The textbook battle over creationism. *Christian Century* 97: 974–976.

______. 1982. We must not succumb to specious arguments for equal time. *Education Week* 1(18): 19.

Zimmerman, P. A. (ed.) 1970. *Rock strata and the Bible record.* St. Louis: Concordia Publishing House.

# 2

# Re-reading Root-Bernstein and McEachron in Cobb County, Georgia

## *A Year Past and Present*

*Benjamin Z. Freed*

The following selection is a recent update of the important issues raised in the first article by Root-Bernstein and McEachron. As a holistic science that looks at many different aspects of the human condition over time, anthropology incorporates different approaches to data collection and interpretation. Some areas of anthropology, such as biological and physical anthropology, primatology, and archaeology, generally adhere to the tenets of hypothetico-deductive science. In other words, anthropologists in these fields propose theories that can be tested using empirical data.

Insights into how living organisms function and how they change over time have been generated by a set of concepts and theories collectively known as evolutionary theory. Modern biology, from the understanding of cells to populations of animals, relies heavily on evolutionary theory for explanations about why living things are the way they are. As discussed in the following article, evolutionary theory provides an explanatory backdrop for understanding biological phenomena, much as any explanation of physical movement or a chemical reaction should be compatible with the laws of physics and chemistry.

Although it is almost universally accepted by the scientific community, some people (particularly fundamentalist groups) have seen evolutionary theory as incompatible with Christian beliefs. The past two decades have seen a resurgence of popular debate over evolutionary theory, especially as it is taught in high schools in the United States. There has been a push in some religiously conservative communities to have evolutionary theory removed from schools, or to have its teaching presented as mere theory rather than scientific fact. One alternative explanation of complex biological mechanisms has been proposed called "intelligent design."

In this selection, the author re-examines many of the principles in the first article. He looks at the religious underpinnings of creationist beliefs and then examines the supposedly "scientific" intelligent design theory. Using basic criteria for the evaluation of scientific theory, he concludes that intelligent design fails to qualify as hypothetico-deductive science. He then goes on to discuss how anthropology both suggests a need to understand the religious motivation for attacks on evolutionary theory and, at the same time, provides a strong impetus for anthropologists who work on evolution to defend the teaching of evolution on the basis of its scientific merit.

***As you read this selection, ask yourself the following questions:***

- Why did the Cobb County, Georgia, school board decide to put warning stickers inside every high school biology textbook that contained material on evolution?
- Why does the author, himself a biological anthropologist and a Cobb County resident, find the stickers objectionable?
- What does the author mean when he says that science is not monolithic?
- Why haven't the claims of intelligent design been tested and reviewed according to the usual rules and procedures of science?
- Are religion and science compatible? Is this even a reasonable question to ask? Why or why not?

***The following terms discussed in this selection are included in the Glossary at the back of the book:***

*creationism*
*evolution*
*hypothesis*
*hypothetico-deductive method*
*intelligent design*
*natural selection*
*peer review*

This article was written especially for *Applying Anthropology* 10th ed.

In 1984 I took a graduate course on the history of biology. In preparation for that seminar I read Root-Bernstein & McEachron's (RBM) treatise on what is a scientific theory. Little did I realize that the article would later catch up to my everyday life some twenty years later.

I am now an anthropologist at Emory University, and I live in the suburban Atlanta, Georgia community of Cobb County—a place that has recently been in the news because of debates concerning the teaching of evolution in public schools. I not only must write about my results on lemur ecology, behavior, and evolution, but I must also transfer the information to the general public, especially within my community. In my case, I give guest lectures at schools, provide workshops for teachers, and talk with parents and students at coffee shops and PTA meetings. Moore and Kraemer (2005) have shown that teachers face many issues if and when they teach evolution. Many teachers have had to learn to come to terms with teaching evolution. Kyzer (2004) found that teachers with different beliefs, training, community involvement, and comfort were likely to teach evolutionary biology much differently, in terms of time and content. From these and other studies, I have seen that, without direct contact and further training from universities, teachers in my own community could have remained isolated, and would have been less likely to communicate the core principle in modern biology. Workshops and discussions provided teachers a convenient way to keep up with materials, to generate new lessons, and to address lingering questions. More importantly, by discussing biological anthropology with teachers, I gave them better ways of understanding how relevant evolutionary biology is to understanding our own biology. We continue to discuss primates, fossils, human variation, disease, health, and many other topics.

In the 1990s and early 2000s, anti-evolution proponents from Kansas, Ohio, Pennsylvania, and Georgia (Cobb County) brought their arguments to local school boards, state legislatures, and even the national political stage. For example, prior to 2002, Cobb public school students' exposure to evolutionary biology was limited. The subject had been excised from some lessons and books, and students whose classes and books did deal with the subject had the choice of opting out of those lessons. Three primary effects were observed by many of us at local universities: 1) relatively few students went on to major in the biological sciences; 2) students were at a disadvantage in intro-level college biology when asked to compete with other students who had received high school evolutionary biology instruction; and 3) students continued to misunderstand and underappreciate science, especially biology.

In 2002, the Cobb County school board approved a college-compatible biology textbook. Shortly afterwards, a creationist-led petition was announced and the board soon after began affixing in each biology textbook stickers that read: "This textbook contains material on evolution. Evolution is a theory, not a fact, regarding the origin of living things. This material should be approached with an open mind, studied carefully and critically considered." Likewise, similar moves were raised elsewhere under the banners of "critical consideration," "teach the controversy," "alternative scientific views," and "theory, not fact" legislation. Soon after the Cobb stickers, anti-evolution proponents in Dover, Pennsylvania required that "intelligent design" (ID) objections to evolution be raised before science lessons on evolutionary biology.

## WHY WOULD A SCIENTIST, SUCH AS MYSELF, GET UPSET OVER A SUCH A STICKER?

Strictly speaking, the stickers confound student comprehension of evolution in several ways. First, evolution is fact AND scientific theory, overwhelmingly observed and discussed in the peer-reviewed, scientific literature. To those who claim that evolution has never been observed, I point to peer-reviewed research on Anolis lizards, tomatoes, and North American fossil primates, among numerous other topics. Secondly, evolution is not a hunch, a guess, or a theory, as the term is used in the common vernacular. To conflate scientific theory (as described by RBM) and the vernacular use of the term "theory" is to confound student comprehension of the strengths and limitations of the scientific method. Thirdly, evolution is NOT a scientific theory about origins of life. It is a well-substantiated scientific explanation for critical aspects of origins, such as its timing, but primarily evolution is about biological change over time. Fourthly, facts themselves are mutable; they are subject to re-evaluation as techniques and accuracy improve. Finally, the school board singled out evolution. No other scientific theories (e.g., gravity, germ theory, plate tectonics) needed to be approached with an open mind, studied carefully, and granted critical consideration. The board went out of its way to have students be wary of one scientific theory, the theory at the core of modern biology.

To be clear, the school board's stickers were completely at odds with RBM's article and the scientific literature. Twenty years after my initiation into anti-evolutionist arguments, here I was faced with a sticker and policy that showed no comprehension as to what is science, theory, and evolution, the very topics discussed in RBM. To me, as a scientist, the sticker was technically inaccurate, misleading, and confusing. It was typical of a new wave of anti-evolutionism.

## DOES THIS VERSION OF ANTI-EVOLUTIONISM, INCLUDING ID, MEET THE STANDARD OF SCIENCE AS DEFINED IN RBM?

RBM's article was written during the early 1980s, when biologists, legal scholars, and historians dealt with the first legal wave of modern creationism. After a resounding series of legal decisions against this religious-based movement, a new wave of anti-evolution approaches emerged under the name "Intelligent Design" (ID). ID is a belief that a so-called irreducible complexity of living forms is too great to be explained by evolution. To this movement's proponents, only an "intelligence" (e.g., an omnipotent deity) could account for the origin and diversity of life. Strictly speaking, intelligent design can be traced to early nineteenth century theologian William Paley. Like 1980s creationism, ID represents a belief about a scientific issue rather than a scientific view of the same issue.

In recent years, biochemist Michael Behe, mathematician William Dembski, and other proponents of ID have called into question Darwinian natural selection's ability to explain origins and evolution of organisms. For instance, they point to developments in the field of molecular biology, which have shown cells to be much more complex than once suspected (Behe, 1996). At the cellular level, ID supporters suggest that a bacterium's flagellum, or propeller-like tail, could not have evolved independently of all the complex cellular structures which move the tail. They argue that, because all of these complex parts must 'fit' together to function, like the parts of a mousetrap, no one element could evolve independent of the others, and so they must be evidence for an intelligent designer. Other proponents of intelligent design point to mathematical models that suggest Darwinian selection might not be any better than random accumulations of changes, and is unlikely to explain complex living organisms.

Fortunately, evolutionary theory is up to these challenges. So-called irreducibly complex structures can evolve from non-irreducible complexity if a structure evolves with one function and is then co-opted for another. Moreover, a species does not evolve in a vacuum, but rather co-evolves alongside other species that are also evolving—a condition left unaccounted for by the mathematical models of evolution.

Biologists, such as Miller (1996, 1999, 2004) and Padian (2002), have shown serious scientific flaws with ID. Miller (2004) noted that the bacterial flagellum is not as irreducibly complex as people have been led to believe. ID is not considered science by anyone actually studying evolutionary biology (see discussions in Pennock, 2001; Larson, 2003; Scott, 2004) because it does not fulfill basic requirements of scientific endeavor. Many scientific theories have proven wrong in whole or part, but they are scientific nevertheless because they can be tested against empirical data. If one re-examines RBM, an ID proponent would have to relax at least two tenets of the scientific method: the need for testable and falsifiable hypotheses, and the reliance on above-nature forces. Evolution by natural selection is built on scientific evaluation of testable and falsifiable hypotheses of natural phenomena without the invocation of above-nature forces. ID fails on all of these criteria. For that reason, evolutionary theory has generated a wealth of research in which hypotheses are tested and confirmed, while ID has produced no such research programs or scholarship.

## THEN WHY HAVE SO MANY PEOPLE TAKEN TO ID AND OTHER FORMS OF ANTI-EVOLUTION?

To many people ID is a satisfying rubric or explanation. The notion of an "intelligence" matches many religious viewpoints or world views of a single, omnipotent deity. Forrest and Gross (2004), for example, noted the religious ties between ID and creationism. As part of a long series of surveys of people's beliefs in pseudoscience, Eve (2004) and Harrold and Eve (1987) surveyed creationists, Wiccans, and university students, and found strong evidence that adherence to creationism was more strongly related to social beliefs, attitudes, and politics than to actual scientific literacy. Belief in creationism was more a matter of the ways that people use to judge "truth claims" about evidence of the ancient human past. In an ethnography of a creationist study group (which included scientists), Toumey (1994) found that these people were often well-read. What I personally have seen is that a person who is willing to suspend acceptance of scientific principles may choose to ignore overwhelming scientific evidence. Such a person may choose to believe spectacular and pseudoscientific claims that more closely match his or her own belief system (see recent discussions in Plavcan 2007).

I suspect what Eve found occurs in my community as well. Few people readily access the scientific literature. Many anti-evolutionists incorrectly, but readily equate evolution, natural selection, and Darwin. By doing so, Darwin has been made into a strawman, one that is viewed as being opposed to local religious beliefs. To many people, science is used to support religious beliefs. If it cannot do so, it must be viewed with great skepticism. Many of these people turn to internet accessible, readily available opinion, political, and religious pieces to confirm their views. Science is viewed as an opposing monolith that directly contradicts and opposes religious belief.

## AS MANY IN MY COMMUNITY HAVE ASKED ME, HOW DOES SCIENCE CRITICIZE ITS THEORIES? OR IS SCIENCE A MONOLITH?

Science criticizes itself primarily through peer-review. In peer-review, a manuscript is sent to a journal's editor, who then solicits evaluations from independent scientists. These reviewers receive no payment for their time and effort. Each manuscript is checked for its authenticity, overall scientific merit, adherence to professional, ethical, and scientific guidelines, and accuracy in review of previous works. Based on the reviewers' comments, the editor decides whether or not to publish the article, and whether revisions or clarifications are required before publication. In this way, peer-review affords the reader the assurance that an article has fulfilled its overall scientific mission, and contributed to the overall understanding about a topic. If a scientist takes issue with an article, the scientist may write a response in the publication.

This is the level of scholarship that scientists have come to expect. I suspect that the public expects no less of science. Responsible? Yes. Tough? You bet. Manuscripts get rejected all the time. We revise and re-submit. Democratic? Not necessarily. Scientists don't vote in opinion polls or cast ballots about each item, but at least scientists have a way to "critically consider" material. If an ID follower wanted to write a scientific research article, the peer-review process would yield an evaluation of the article's scientific merits, ethics, and scholarship, just like any scientific manuscript. Science is no monolith.

To many of us in evolutionary biology and anthropology, ID followers have not only failed to show clear scientific merit in method, they have yet to show true scholarship. Reviewing the peer-reviewed scientific literature, one finds no research articles nor any evidence that ID is being used to explain biology. ID has not been shown to be a best-fit or useful scientific explanation for understanding nature. In Cobb, anti-evolution material that was not vetted by scientific peer-review was introduced to the public access television, and the local op-ed pages. Many people could not then understand why this material shouldn't be available for science classes. Padian & Gishlick (2002), however, have cited numerous flaws in the science and scholarship of this material. Rennie (2002) and Young and Edis (2004) have also discussed many of the most frequent claims (see more recent discussions in Petto and Godfrey 2007). Position statements against ID proponents' claims have also been brought forth by the American Institute of Biological Sciences, the American Association for the Advancement of Science, the National Science Teachers Association, and many other scientific organizations, including those from anthropology.

In Cobb, local parents sued the school board, seeing an unnecessary intrusion of religion into government. Scientists from the region's major colleges spoke up, submitted affidavits, in some cases testified, and worked with local parents, educators, and students to explain more about the scientific method. Initially, a district judge decision forced the school board to remove the stickers from the texts. Although the board appealed the decision, the case was sent back to the original judge. Before the case was re-tried (more than four years after the stickers went into the books), the board settled with the plaintiffs. In doing so, the board promised never again to interfere as it had with the teaching of evolution. Although the scientist in me wished the board had finally comprehended the scientific merits, the decision to settle may have had little to do with the actual science. The board had been through an arduous and costly legal process, lived through several protracted political battles with its superintendent and chair (unrelated to the sticker), and had just lost one sticker-supporting member in an election. The decision to settle also came after resounding legal decisions elsewhere, particularly in Dover, PA. Likewise, shortly after the settlement, the legal firm of the initial creationist petitioner was subsumed by the board's own legal firm. People on the board wanted to make a fresh start, devoid of divisive public issues.

Similar anti-evolution tactics and claims were repeated elsewhere, most notably in Dover, Pennsylvania. The school board tried to diminish evolution and to provide alternate scientific theory discussion for its science classrooms. Parents in the district sued the school board, arguing an unnecessary religious intrusion into biology lessons. Proponents of evolutionary biology and ID provided testimony before a federal judge. In December 2005 the judge ruled that the tactics, claims, and literature of anti-evolution proponents were not divorced from religious motives. In some cases, what was presented as an alternate scientific view was thinly-veiled creationism. The proposed alternative scientific views, including ID, were not science. The effect of the board's policy was to diminish evolutionary biology education, and to presuppose in students' minds that alternate scientific views exist. The overall effect of Dover has had a profound impact throughout the country. Although ID is not dead, the various forms of creationism are changing along with the times (see Scott 2007). Creationism is evolving.

On the bright side, both Cobb and Dover have forced educators at all levels to think more about what is science. In Cobb, scientists and educators have begun to interact more directly with the general public and with each other. The school district science administration has also formed a unique partnership with businesses and educators to improve science outreach, to establish greater links between teachers and college educators, and to foster greater student interest in science. Many of us are now re-reading and discussing philosophy of science papers. Perhaps most important, in the midst of the Cobb issue, scientists, teachers, and politicians were able to work together to strengthen the state's science standards. Evolution is now a firm part of the state's biology curriculum; student comprehension of it is tested. Teachers and students question me thoroughly whenever I see them. It's refreshing to go into a public biology classroom on an off day from my college duties.

In Cobb, it's not a question of whether or not students and teachers believe in evolution. Scientists don't *believe* in it; they *accept* this overarching scientific theory. The overall goal in education is to be sure that students and teachers comprehend it. Do they make proper sense of it? Does it relate to the world around them? People are starting to focus on these goals.

## WHAT IS THE VIEW OF GENERAL ANTHROPOLOGY?

As a rule, anthropologists are trained to respect the fact that different groups of people possess vastly different worldviews. Indeed, the variation among different ways of seeing, understanding, and making sense of the world lies at the root of many anthropologists' curiosity about humanity and human experience. While anthropology teaches respect and appreciation for such diversity, it also teaches that respect does not equal agreement. A North American anthropologist, for instance, may be fascinated by the origin myths or healing rituals of aboriginal peoples in Australia, Central Africa, or the Amazonian rainforest. But he can be respectful of cultural differences and still insist on taking antimalarial drugs to prevent infection, or refuse to participate in a healing ceremony involving traditional surgery even if the host community is convinced that it would help.

As a biological anthropologist trained in the scientific method, I can appreciate the fact that some belief systems are rooted in stories about the nature and origins of life that are fundamentally distinct from—and even contradict—the basic tenets of scientific research and scholarship. Anthropology does, however, help demonstrate that different systems of knowledge address different questions. Some knowledge systems, like religious traditions, address questions about the ultimate meaning and purpose of the human life and of the world as we know it. As RBM so clearly describe it, science is designed to address a different set of concerns. Rather than seeking answers to questions of ultimate meaning, science seeks explanations for how the natural world operates, and for how it has come to exist as we observe it today. Science uses tools, methods of gathering and evaluating knowledge, and methods for determining the validity, reliability, and relevance of such knowledge that differ markedly from those of the world's myriad religious systems. These tools, methods, and procedures are the very hallmarks of science, and they are what allow scientists across the globe to communicate and evaluate one another's work through a common language.

Religious beliefs, like those motivating the ID movement, often have profound meaning and significance for proponents. We must, nonetheless, keep in mind the fundamental distinction between forms of religious belief and scientifically validated forms of knowledge. While evolutionary biologists and biological anthropologists may be deeply frustrated by the challenges the ID movement poses for science education and scientific literacy in the United States, this frustration does not come from a sense of disrespect for ID advocates' religious beliefs. Rather it stems from an overriding commitment to the fact that different kinds of questions demand different kinds of information, different methods of evaluation, and different criteria for establishing what is "true." Ultimately, anthropology teaches that religion and science aim to define and establish different kinds of truth about humanity, human life, and the world we live in.

Looking back, the RBM article has helped me refocus and analyze science as it relates to my community and my students. For those of us who view science as a way of explaining many critical aspects of life, we find an overwhelming preponderance of peer-reviewed evidence for evolution. For anthropologists, evolution is the best-fit scientific explanation for the genetic and paleontological record, and it offers us much understanding about medicine, ecology, and ourselves. Scientists have thorough and responsible scholarly debates on many aspects about evolution, such as its mechanisms, effects, and pace. To many of us in science, evolution is a tremendous theory, one that holds power in explaining the available scientific evidence, and the vast data yet to be discovered. Theories are powerful and wonderful; they're not just hunches.

## REFERENCES


Behe, M. 1996. *Darwin's Black Box.* New York: The Free Press.

Eve, R. 2004. "Creationism, evolution, and a struggle for the means of cultural reproduction," American Anthropological Association meetings. Atlanta, GA, December, 19, 2004.

Forrest, B., and Gross, P. 2004. *Creationism's Trojan Horse: The Wedge of Intelligent Design.* Oxford University Press.

Harrold F. B. and Eve R. A. 1987. Patterns of creationist belief among college students. In *Cult archaeology and creationism: Understanding pseudoscientific beliefs about the past,* eds. Harrold, F. B., and Eve, R. A. Iowa City: University of Iowa Press. 6: 68–90.

Kyzer P. M. 2004. Three Southern high school biology teachers' perspectives on teaching evolution: Sociocultural influences. PhD thesis. University of Alabama. pp. 244

Larson, E. 2003. *Trial and error: The American controversy over creation and evolution.* 3rd ed. Oxford: Oxford University Press.

Miller, K. R. 1996. "A review of Darwin's Black Box," *Creation/Evolution* 16: 36–40.

Miller, K. R. 1999. *Finding Darwin's God.* Harper Collins.

Miller, K. R. 2004. The flagellum unspun: The collapse of irreducible complexity, In *Debating design: From Darwin to DNA,* eds. Dembski, W. and Ruse, M. 81–97. Cambridge University Press.

Moore, R. and Kraemer, K. 2005. The teaching of evolution and creationism in Minnesota. *Am. Biol. Teach.* 67: 457–466.

Padian, K. 2002. "Waiting for the watchmaker," *Science* 295: 2373–2374.

Padian, K., and Gishlick, A. 2002. "The talented Mr. Wells," *Quarterly Review of Biology* 77(1): 33–37.

Pennock, R. T. 2001. *Intelligent design creationism and its critics: Philosophical, theological, and scientific perspectives.* Cambridge University Press.

Petto, A. J., and, Godfrey, L. R. (eds.). 2007. *Scientists confront creationism: Intelligent design and beyond.* New York: WW Norton.

Plavcan, J. M. 2007. The invisible Bible: The logic of creation science. In *Scientists confront creationism: Intelligent design and beyond,* eds. Petto, A. J., and Godfrey, L. R., 361–380. New York: WW Norton.

Rennie, J. 2002. "15 answers to creationist nonsense," *Scientific American* 287(1): 78–85.

Scott, E. 2004. *Evolution vs. creationism: An introduction.* Greenwood Press.

Scott E. C. 2007. Creation science lite: "Intelligent Design" as the new anti-evolutionism. In *Scientists confront creationism: Intelligent design and beyond,* eds. Petto, A. J., and Godfrey, L. R., 59–109. New York: WW Norton.

Toumey, C. P. 1994. *God's own scientists: Creationists in a secular world.* New Brunswick, NJ: Rutgers University Press.

Young, M. and Edis, T. (eds.). 2004. *Why intelligent design fails: A scientific critique of the new creationism.* Rutgers University Press.

# 3

# Great Mysteries of Human Evolution

*Carl Zimmer*

Paleoanthropology—the discovery, description, and analysis of the fossil evidence of human evolution—is an important branch of biological anthropology. The methods of paleontology and skeletal biology are used to understand the distant biological prehistory of our hominid ancestors. The fossils of hominids are relatively hard to find compared to, for example, the fossils of other species like horses. In fact, paleontologists have traced the evolution of the modern horse throughout the Cenozoic era (the age of mammals) in great detail. Although it might be easier to study the evolution of other species, it seems "natural" that we are more interested in the prehistory of humans. Human evolution has been a subject surrounded by controversy—not only because of religious beliefs as seen in Selection 1, but also because there have been so many debates about the interpretation of the fossils. There has been an incredible increase in the number of hominid fossils found in recent years. These are facts—hard as stone—that provide clues for understanding the distant past. As in all areas of science, the more we discover, the more questions we can generate about the complexities of our biological history.

This selection considers some of the serious questions that continue to puzzle paleoanthropologists about our hominid origins. Despite the tremendous increase in the number of fossil hominids, the origins and evolutionary history of the human line are still unclear. These discoveries have shown that hominid evolution was a complicated process and not a unilinear stairway of species on their way to becoming modern *Homo sapiens.* We know about humans' upright posture; their large, modern brains; and their use of tools; but we do not necessarily understand why or how those adaptations arose. The author considers eight mysteries about what makes us human, and the paleoanthropological evidence that exists to answer those questions.

***As you read this selection, ask yourself the following questions:***

- Why do people like to think that human evolution is a grand story of linear progression rather than a complex history of multiple species?
- Why does the author think questions about human origins are important? Why are they so difficult to answer?
- How, and why, does the author think humans are so different from other primates?
- What arguments does the author offer to explain why *Homo sapiens* ultimately emerged as the sole remaining hominid species?

***The following terms discussed in this selection are included in the Glossary at the back of the book:***

*adaptations*
*Australopithecus afarensis*
*bipedal*
*FOXP2*
*Homo erectus*
*Homo ergaster*
*Homo neanderthalensis (Neaderthals)*
*Sahelanthropus tchadensis*

Everything you do has a history. You wake up each morning and get out of bed using an anatomy that allowed your ancestors to stand upright at least 4 million years ago. You go to the kitchen and eat cereal with a bowl and spoon that are part of a toolmaking tradition at least 2.5 million years old. As you munch your cereal, you page through the newspaper, which you can understand thanks to a brain capable of language, abstract thought, and prodigious memory—a brain that has been expanding for 2 million years.

Until a few decades ago, most of that evolutionary history was hidden from science's view. But these days hardly a month goes by without news of a significant discovery. Paleoanthropologists keep digging up new

Zimmer, Carl. "Great Mysteries of Human Evolution." *Discover* Magazine (Sept. 2003):34–43. Reprinted with permission of the author.

fossils of our ancestors, and some of those fossils have even yielded DNA fragments. Meanwhile, geneticists have compiled a veritable encyclopedia of evolution—the sequenced human genome—and within a few years they'll be able to compare it with the genome of one of our closest living relatives, the common chimpanzee. Still, what we don't know about our evolution vastly outweighs what we do know. Age-old questions defy a full accounting, and new discoveries introduce new questions. That's not unusual for any field of science, but the eight mysteries on the following pages are intimate ones, because understanding our origins is key to understanding ourselves.

## WHO WAS THE FIRST HOMINID?

Time travel would make everything so much easier. Imagine that you could drop down by an African lake some 7 million years ago and watch the parade of aardvarks, antelopes, and elephants pass by until, sooner or later, you caught sight of a group of apes. They'd probably look something like chimpanzees—about the same height, with the same coat of hair—but their flat faces and the other odd proportions of their bodies would indicate that they belong to a different species. Perhaps they would turn your way and look you in the eye—a gaze from your most distant hominid ancestors, the first primates to split off from the other apes and begin the family that produced us. Such are the daydreams paleoanthropologists indulge in as they endure blazing heat, merciless sandstorms, and years of fruitless fieldwork.

If the earliest hominids were anything like chimps, bonobos, and other living apes, each species may have numbered in the hundreds of thousands, even millions. But few left fossils behind. Most of their bones were scavenged and scattered by hyenas or other animals, and what little remained rotted. When it comes to early hominids, paleoanthropologists have to make do with a few teeth or skull fragments.

Yet paleoanthropologists are learning a lot about our origins. Not long ago, the oldest known hominid was *Australopithecus afarensis*, a species that walked the savannas of East Africa around 3.6 million years ago and is best known from one well-preserved female skeleton found in Ethiopia in 1974 and nicknamed Lucy. In recent years, paleoanthropologists have found perhaps as many as five species that are older than *A. afarensis*—in some cases much older. Just last year, Michel Brunet of the University of Poitiers, in France, and his team of explorers announced that amid the sand dunes of the Sahara they had found a species between 6 million and 7 million years old: *Sahelanthropus tchadensis.*

These new fossils have thrown cherished orthodoxies into question. "We saw human evolution as a nice, straight line," says Leslie Aiello of University College London. Now some researchers are arguing that human evolution looked more like a bush, with lots of species branching off in different directions.

No new orthodoxy has gained enough strength yet to take over the old one. Instead, there's lots of debate. Some paleoanthropologists, for example, have declared *Sahelanthropus* to be on the line that led to gorillas, not humans. "That's crazy," replies Brunet, who points to small teeth and other key traits that link the creature with hominids rather than apes. But while Brunet is confident he has discovered the oldest known hominid, he doesn't think it's possible yet to make grand pronouncements about the shape of the hominid tree and its various branches. "You can't say that it's bushy," he says. "Maybe it is; we don't know. Our story has just doubled in time, and we're just beginning to understand it."

## WHY DO WE WALK UPRIGHT?

For millions of years, the earliest hominids were a lot like other apes. They were short, had tiny brains compared with modern humans, and could not speak or fashion a spear. But there was a profound difference that set them apart: They could stand up and walk. Bipedalism was the first great transformation of our ancestors, coming long before the evolution of all the other things that make us uniquely human.

The answer to the question of how our ancestors evolved into bipeds seemed pretty clear for decades. "The long-standing idea was that we became bipedal because we moved out of the forest and onto the savanna, either because we had to look over tall grass or get to isolated stands of trees," says Craig Stanford, a primatologist at the University of Southern California's Jane Goodall Research Center.

But in recent years new evidence has thrown that scenario into doubt. "The time-honored idea that a weakling hominid left the safety of the forest for the dangerous savanna and had to live by its wits and stood upright is a nice story, but it's probably fiction," says Stanford. As researchers have looked closer at the older hominid sites, many have concluded that the areas were not savannas at all but a variety of lightly to densely wooded landscapes. Hominids may not have lived in savannas until 2 million to 2.5 million years ago—2.5 million to 3 million years after the earliest known hominids walked on two legs.

Now scientists are trying to figure out what evolutionary pressure led hominids to become bipedal in the forest. To answer that question, they have to figure out what upright walking evolved from. Fossils offer some clues, but opinion is divided over what the clues mean. Some paleoanthropologists studying Lucy's skeleton say she walked much as we do, for example, while others say she moved awkwardly on the ground and spent a lot of time in trees. Paleoanthropologists can say even less about the oldest hominids, because they've found hardly anything below the skull.

The best clues to our upright origins may come from living apes, although no one knows for sure how much chimpanzees have evolved from the last common ancestor they shared with us. Some primatologists are conducting lab studies of how modern apes knuckle-walk and clamber through trees to see which movements are most like human walking. Other researchers, like Craig Stanford, watch apes in the wild. "Chimpanzees may stand upright on a big limb of a fig tree and pluck figs just overhead," Stanford says. "And when they're on the ground, they'll stand up to pull down branches." He backs a hypothesis originally devised by Kevin Hunt of Indiana University: The earliest hominids may have become specialists in getting food by standing up for short spells, both in the trees or on the ground. It may not seem as heroic as striding out into the savanna, but then again, many great chapters in the book of evolution have been built from such modest changes.

## WHY ARE OUR BRAINS SO BIG?

Our brains are not just big—they're grotesquely huge. A typical mammal our size would have a brain one-seventh as large as ours. And big brains are relatively new for hominids. From 7 million to 2 million years ago, our ancestors had brains about the size of a modern chimpanzee's. Hominid brains only began to increase 2 million years ago, and they continued to balloon, in fits and starts, until they neared their present size at least 160,000 years ago.

When it comes to explaining this explosion in brain size, scientists agree on one thing: It must have offered a powerful evolutionary advantage. "It costs you an awful lot in terms of energy," says Aiello. "You don't evolve large and expensive organs unless there's a reason."

But paleoanthropologists are divided about that reason. One possibility is that bigger brains gave hominids extra information-processing power they could use to make better tools. After all, stone tools unlocked new supplies of food, and so better tool users could support more offspring. Another possibility is that the driving force was hominid social life. Primates living in big groups tend to have bigger brains, possibly because there's an evolutionary advantage to keeping track of other members of your group. And certainly the human brain has evolved into an awesome social computer, able to draw subtle clues about other people's thoughts from their faces in a fraction of a second.

On the other hand, big brains may have prompted humans to become more social. For one thing, big brains made children helpless. Hominid kids, then as now, needed years to develop large brains, during which time they depended on adults for high-energy foods. It's possible that the basic shape of the human family as a group of parents, siblings, and grandparents formed to feed the brains of their children.

## WHEN DID WE FIRST USE TOOLS?

It is hard to imagine life without tools—finding food with our bare hands, eating it raw with our teeth, seeking a cave or a tree for shelter. In fact, our reliance on tools is reflected in our brains and bodies. The areas of our brains responsible for things like controlling our hands are enlarged compared with other primates. Our hands themselves are different, with proportionately longer thumbs and other anatomic changes that allow us to touch our fingertips and hold tools with more skill. The dawn of tool use was a crucial turning point in human history: It let our ancestors take control of their lives by finding food in places that were off-limits to their ancestors. But scientists still have hardly any clues to how that evolutionary transition took place.

The most reliable record of our technological history comes from the tools themselves. The oldest known hominid tools date back 2.5 million years, to a collection of chipped rocks in Ethiopia. They don't look like much, but with them hominids could butcher an elephant or crack open a wildebeest's bones and suck out the marrow. Mentally, they're also a big accomplishment: They require a brain capable of looking at an untouched rock and seeing a tool hiding within it.

In recent years, however, some hints have emerged that human technology may have roots reaching back millions of years further into the past. For one thing, chimpanzees and other apes have proved surprisingly gifted at making tools. In order to walk across thorn-covered ground, chimpanzees can fashion sandals out of leaves. In order to eat termites, they can strip sticks to create fishing tools. Unfortunately, a leaf-sandal doesn't leave a fossil. But some researchers believe that the hands of hominids may shed some light on the mystery of tools. For example, Lucy and her *A. afarensis* fellows lived a million years before the oldest tools. Despite having curved, chimplike fingers, this hominid also had an elongated thumb that could make contact with its fingertips. "There's nothing to say that these creatures couldn't make crude stone tools," says

Bernard Wood of George Washington University. It's possible that hominids had already become skilled with wood and other materials 3.5 million years ago, paving the way to mental breakthroughs for making stone tools.

As intriguing as this hypothesis may be, however, many researchers think there's not enough evidence to say anything definitive about the evolution of tool use. Tim White, a paleoanthropologist at the University of California at Berkeley, says any speculations "would be strictly *X-Files.*"

## HOW DID WE GET MODERN MINDS?

Walking upright, growing a big brain, and even making tools are not enough to make an ape truly human. Consider *Homo ergaster,* a species that lived in Africa between 1.7 million and 600,000 years ago and probably gave rise to our own species. *H. ergaster* stood up to six feet tall, had a medium-size brain, and could survive even in arid grasslands thanks to an impressive kit of stone axes and other tools. Despite all that, this species' brain didn't work like ours. For hundreds of thousands of years, *H. ergaster* was content to use the same set of tools, with few modifications. Putting a stone axe on the end of a stick to make a spear would have allowed these hominids to become much better hunters, and yet this simple idea apparently never occurred to them. Such an idea seems simple only to our modern minds, which can see new possibilities in the world, discover hidden connections, and think and communicate with symbols.

Scientists don't yet know how that modern mind came into existence. The question is particularly hard to answer because they can't get into the brain of *H. ergaster* or any of our other ancestors. Instead, they have to infer what those ancient minds were like by looking at the things they made. The people who painted pictures of mammoths and woolly rhinos in French caves almost 32,000 years ago must have already had minds much like our own. Archaeologists have documented an explosion of expressions of the modern mind after roughly 50,000 years ago, in the form of jewelry, elaborate graves, bone-tipped spears, and other new kinds of tools. The bones of the people who made these things look like our own. They were members of *Homo sapiens,* complete with long, slender arms and legs, a flat face, a jutting chin, and a high forehead that fronted a big brain. But they were hardly the first people with our anatomy. *H. sapiens* fossils have been found in Africa from at least 160,000 years ago, and some experts argue that the earliest members of our species may have existed over 200,000 years ago.

Richard Klein, a paleoanthropologist at Stanford University, has offered a controversial theory: The modern mind is the result of a rapid genetic change. He puts the date of the change at around 50,000 years ago, pointing out that the rise of cultural artifacts comes after that date, as does the spread of modern humans from Africa. The evolution of the modern mind allowed humans to thrive as never before, Klein argues, and soon even a continent as huge as Africa could not contain their expanding population.

Many other paleoanthropologists beg to differ. Sally McBrearty, an archaeologist at the University of Connecticut, believes the evidence shows that the technology and artistic expression of modern humans emerged slowly over hundreds of thousands of years, as humans gradually moved into new habitats and increased their population. She points to a long list of tantalizing clues in Africa that predate Klein's 50,000-year milestone. Humans may have been grinding pigments 250,000 years ago, for example, and researchers have found barbed bone fishing hooks in Central Africa that they estimate are 90,000 years old. Last year scientists in South Africa discovered stones covered with geometrical cross-hatching dating back 77,000 years.

Klein dismisses the evidence for such slow-fuse change as paltry and misleading. "It's a little bit here, it's a little bit there. Most sites don't have anything like this at all, but when you get to 50,000 years ago, they all do. Then you get real art—not stuff you can argue about whether it shows some form of symbolism—and elaborate graves and houses and the rest of it."

A resolution to this debate may be waiting in Africa, at archaeological sites scattered across the continent. "We know what we'd like to find and where we ought to look for it," says McBrearty. "But are we going to have the money and the perseverance to mount the assault and come up with the goods?"

## WHY DID WE OUTLIVE OUR RELATIVES?

Humans today are driving other species toward extinction at a disturbing pace—a quarter of all mammal species, for example, are officially listed as threatened. But the evidence from fossils suggests that this wave of extinctions has been rising for thousands of years. And there's a grim irony in the possibility that two of the first species to fall victim to us may have been our closest relatives.

Studies on human mitochondrial DNA indicate that all humans alive today can trace their ancestry back to members of *Homo sapiens* who lived in Africa roughly 150,000 years ago. At the time, there were two other hominid species. Members of *Homo neanderthalensis* (Neanderthals), who lived in Europe, have a reputation as lumbering brutes, but they had brains as big as or bigger than those of humans and awesome hunting skills that helped them survive cyclic ice ages for half a million years or more. In Asia, *Homo erectus* survived for about 1.5 million years. And yet not long after *H. sapiens* spread from Africa, both of these species vanished. Our close kinship with these hominids makes their disappearance all the more puzzling. "It's very difficult to get your head around the idea that there could be another species so closely related to us, but isn't us," says McBrearty.

It wasn't very long ago, geologically speaking, when our ancestors came face to face with these other species, and yet scientists still know little about the encounter. About *H. erectus,* all they can say is that the youngest *H. erectus* fossils, Indonesian skulls from perhaps 50,000 years ago, come from a time when our own species had already settled in Asia and moved on to Australia. "We don't know what the hell is going on there," says Klein. "We need more fossils with good dates. It'll come—within a decade we'll know something more about this." Neanderthals left behind more hints, although the picture is still far from clear. Scientists have isolated six fragments of Neanderthal DNA and have concluded that the Neanderthal did not interbreed much—if at all—with *H. sapiens.* Neanderthals appear to have clung to existence for 15,000 years after encountering our own species in Europe. But over time they became rarer and rarer, until they could be found only in isolated mountain valleys. And then they could be found nowhere at all.

Over the years, scientists have tried to explain the disappearance of Neanderthals and *H. erectus* with everything from warfare to exotic viruses that their *H. sapiens* relatives brought with them from Africa. But the cause of their demise could have been far more subtle. Even if our species had just a slight evolutionary edge over the other hominids, the effect could have been devastating, given enough time. It's possible, for example, that humans benefited from long-distance trade and better tools, allowing them to withstand droughts, ice ages, and other hard times better than their competitors. Our ancestors may have had just a few more children in each generation, and gradually they took over the best places for hunting and living. After a few hundred generations, they unwittingly squeezed their cousins out of existence.

"It may have been something as simple as modern humans having better clothing," says Leslie Aiello.

## WHAT GENES MAKE US HUMAN?

In April 2003, geneticists finished sequencing the human genome, and now they're well on their way to decoding the genome of one of our closest relatives, the common chimpanzee. The sight of these two sequences placed side by side is astonishing. For thousands of positions at a stretch, their codes are identical. Recently Morris Goodman, a biologist at the Wayne State University School of Medicine, and his colleagues analyzed the portions of DNA that are responsible for the structure of proteins. In this crucial part of the genome, humans and chimps were 99.4 percent identical. In other words, much of what makes us uniquely human may be found in just .6 percent of our genome.

That tiny fraction will be the focus of a huge amount of research in years to come. "There will be a gold mine of information," predicts Sean Carroll, a geneticist at the University of Wisconsin and an investigator with the Howard Hughes Medical Institute. As the differences between humans and chimps come to light, for instance, medicine will be revolutionized. Scientists hope to find the genetic differences that explain why chimpanzees don't get AIDS, Alzheimer's, and other diseases that plague humans.

Scientists will also be searching the two genomes for clues to how and why humans evolved traits that distinguish us from chimpanzees, including a bipedal body, a big brain, and language. A taste of things to come is the recent study of a gene called *FOXP2.* People who inherit mutant forms of *FOXP2* have trouble speaking and understanding grammar. Scientists have reconstructed the evolutionary history of the gene by comparing the subtle variations in *FOXP2* that different people carry. The researchers found that in the past 200,000 years, the gene underwent an intense burst of evolutionary selection. It's possible that changes to this gene may have helped prompt the transformation of simple apelike grunts into language.

But it would be a mistake to think that any single gene will tell us much about human nature, or even just the ability to talk. "We're just not going to have two or three speech genes and that's the end of the story," says Carroll. "It's going to be much more subtle than that."

The early evidence already suggests that perhaps several thousand human genes have undergone intense natural selection since our ancestors split with the chimp lineage. And those genes can only build a modern human being by cooperating with one another rather than working alone. This comes as no surprise to scientists who have studied the evolution of other animals. "We look for simple answers, but we almost always find a mess," says Carroll.

## HAVE WE STOPPED EVOLVING?

It has been an amazing run: over 7 million years our lineage has evolved from diminutive apes to the planet's dominant species. We've evolved brains that are capable of things never achieved on our planet, and perhaps in the universe. Why shouldn't we continue evolving more powerful brains? It's easy to think that we'll just keep marching ahead, that in another million years we'll have gigantic brains like out of some episode of *Star Trek.* But scientists can't say where we're headed. It's even possible that we've reached an evolutionary dead end.

Consider the fact that the human brain hasn't expanded all that much in at least 160,000 years. You might think that if bigger brains meant more intelligence, natural selection would still be inflating them today. But big brains have their drawbacks. Like an expanding computer network, a growing brain needs more and more wiring to connect its processors together. The human brain may be reaching the edge of this computational limit. Big brains also make a lot of demands on the human body—particularly the bodies of pregnant women. A woman's birth canal has to be wide enough for a big-brained baby to get out. But there's a limit to how wide the female pelvis can become: If it became too wide, women would struggle to walk upright. That constraint may make it impossible for the human brain to get any bigger.

The only way to know the answer to this particular question, however, may be to wait for the future to become the past. "One of the reasons why people are fascinated with human evolution is because it's about where we came from and where we're going," says Aiello. "But we don't know where we're going. It's too much of a lottery."

# 4

# A New Kind of Ancestor: *Ardipithecus* Unveiled

*Ann Gibbons*

Sixty-six years after the publication of Darwin's *Origin of Species*, Tennessee biology teacher John Scopes was found guilty of teaching evolution in defiance of state law. Political cartoons from the era mocked the idea of evolution as pseudo-science and as a threat to law and order. One cartoon shows a scientist unleashing evolution as a monstrous, club-wielding genie from a bottle labeled "Darwinism"; another one titled *Ancestor Worship* portrays a tuxedo-clad man praying to a chimpanzee atop an altar.

While many objected to Darwin's theory of evolution on religious or philosophical grounds, one secular reasons cited for the existence of laws against the teaching of evolution was the absence of a convincing fossil record. As lawyers presented their arguments in the Dayton, Tennessee, courthouse, that same year anthropologist Raymond Dart published his revolutionary analysis of a 2.5 million-year-old human-like skull that he claimed was an unknown species. His discovery may not have been enough to sway the Scopes jury, but it marked the first of many more fossil finds in the twentieth century. Piece by piece, bone fragment by bone fragment, the emerging fossil record started revealing the inner workings of human evolution.

As discussed in chapter two by Freed, debates on teaching evolution in public schools endure to the present, but with one major difference. The fossil record has grown considerably since the days of Darwin and the Scopes trial. After the remarkable 1974 discovery of Lucy, for example, anthropologists had the convincing fossil evidence that Darwin could only dream of. Lucy's partial skeleton taught us that our upright, bipedal ancestors dated back to at least 3.2 million years ago. Lucy's discovery, however, generated as many questions as it answered, and anthropologists immediately sought to uncover the remains of even earlier ancestral humans In this chapter, Ann Gibbons describes a thrilling recent discovery that gives us the best picture yet of our earliest human ancestors.

***As you read this selection, consider the following questions:***

- When and where did *Ardipithecus ramidus* and *Ardipithecus kadabba* live?
- How does *Ardipithicus ramidus* differ from apes and chimpanzees, and what do these differences tell us about the last common ancestor shared by humans and other primates?
- How, when, and where were the first *Ardipithicus ramidus* fossils found?
- What evidence leads Dr. White and his team to the conclusion that *Ardipithicus ramidus* was a facultative biped?

***The following terms discussed in this selection are included in the Glossary at the back of the book:***

*Ardipithicus ramidus*
*Ardipithecus kadabba*
*facultative biped*
*hominin*
*Orrorin tugenensis*

Every day, scientists add new pages to the story of human evolution by deciphering clues to our past in everything from the DNA in our genes to the bones and artifacts of thousands of our ancestors. But perhaps once each generation, a spectacular fossil reveals a whole chapter of our prehistory all at once. In 1974, it was the famous 3.2-million-year-old skeleton "Lucy," who proved in one stroke that our ancestors walked upright before they evolved big brains.

Ever since Lucy's discovery, researchers have wondered what came before her. Did the earliest members of the human family walk upright like Lucy or on their knuckles like chimpanzees and gorillas? Did they swing through the trees or venture into open

Gibbons, Ann. "A New Kind of Ancestor: *Ardipithecus* Unveiled." *Science* 326, no. 5949 (2 Oct. 2009):36–40. Reprinted with permission from AAAS.

grasslands? Researchers have had only partial, fleeting glimpses of Lucy's own ancestors—the earliest hominins, members of the group that includes humans and our ancestors (and are sometimes called hominids). Now, a multidisciplinary international team have uncovered the oldest known skeleton of a potential human ancestor, 4.4 million year-old *Ardipithecus ramidus* from Aramis, Ethiopia.

This remarkably rare skeleton is not the oldest putative hominin, but it is by far the most complete of the earliest specimens. It includes most of the skull and teeth, as well as the pelvis, hands, and feet—parts that the authors say reveal an "intermediate" form of upright walking, considered a hallmark of hominins. "We thought Lucy was the find of the century but, in retrospect, it isn't," says paleoanthropologist Andrew Hill of Yale University. "It's worth the wait."

To some researchers' surprise, the female skeleton doesn't look much like a chimpanzee, gorilla, or any of our closest living primate relatives. Even though this species probably lived soon after the dawn of humankind, it was not transitional between African apes and humans. "We have seen the ancestor, and it is not a chimpanzee," says paleoanthropologist Tim White of the University of California, Berkeley, co-director of the Middle Awash research group, which discovered and analyzed the fossils.

Instead, the skeleton and pieces of at least 35 additional individuals of *Ar. ramidus* reveal a new type of early hominin that was neither chimpanzee nor human. Although the team suspects that *Ar. ramidus* may have given rise to Lucy's genus, *Australopithecus*, the fossils "show for the first time that there is some new evolutionary grade of hominid that is not *Australopithecus*, that is not *Homo*," says paleontologist Michel Brunet of the College de France in Paris.

In 11 papers published in this issue and online, the team of 47 researchers describes how *Ar. ramidus* looked and moved. The skeleton, nicknamed "Ardi," is from a female who lived in a woodland, stood about 120 centimeters tall, and weighed about 50 kilograms. She was thus as big as a chimpanzee and had a brain size to match. But she did not knuckle-walk or swing through the trees like living apes. Instead, she walked upright, planting her feet flat on the ground, perhaps eating nuts, insects, and small mammals in the woods.

She was a "facultative" biped, say the authors, still living in both worlds—upright on the ground but also able to move on all fours on top of branches in the trees, with an opposable big toe to grasp limbs. "These things were very odd creatures," says paleoanthropologist Alan Walker of Pennsylvania State University, University Park. "You know what Tim [White] once said: If you wanted to find something that moved like these things, you'd have to go to the bar in *Star Wars*."

Most researchers, who have waited 15 years for the publication of this find, agree that Ardi is indeed an early hominin. They praise the detailed reconstructions needed to piece together the crushed bones. "This is an extraordinarily impressive work of reconstruction and description, well worth waiting for," says paleoanthropologist David Pilbeam of Harvard University. "They did this job very, very well," agrees neurobiologist Christoph Zollikofer of the University of Zurich in Switzerland.

But not everyone agrees with the team's interpretations about how *Ar. ramidus* walked upright and what it reveals about our ancestors. "The authors . . . are framing the debate that will inevitably follow," because the description and interpretation of the finds are entwined, says Pilbeam. "My first reaction is to be skeptical about some of the conclusions," including that human ancestors never went through a chimpanzee-like phase. Other researchers are focusing intently on the lower skeleton, where some of the anatomy is so primitive that they are beginning to argue over just what it means to be "bipedal." The pelvis, for example, offers only "circumstantial" evidence for upright walking, says Walker. But however the debate about Ardi's locomotion and identity evolves, she provides the first hard evidence that will inform and constrain future ideas about the ancient hominin bauplan.

## DIGGING IT

The first glimpse of this strange creature came on 17 December 1992 when a former graduate student of White's, Gen Suwa, saw a glint among the pebbles of the desert pavement near the village of Aramis. It was the polished surface of a tooth root, and he immediately knew it was a hominin molar. Over the next few days, the team scoured the area on hands and knees, as they do whenever an important piece of hominin is found, and collected the lower jaw of a child with the milk molar still attached. The molar was so primitive that the team knew they had found a hominin both older and more primitive than Lucy. Yet the jaw also had derived traits—novel evolutionary characters—shared with Lucy's species, *Au. afarensis*, such as an upper canine shaped like a diamond in side view.

The team reported 15 years ago in *Nature* that the fragmentary fossils belonged to the "long-sought potential root species for the Hominidae." (They first called it *Au. ramidus*, then, after finding parts of the skeleton, changed it to *Ar. ramidus*—for the Afar words for "root" and "ground.") In response to comments that he needed leg bones to prove *Ar. ramidus* was an upright hominin, White joked that he would be delighted with more parts, specifically a thigh and an intact skull, as though placing an order.

Within 2 months, the team delivered. In November 1994, as the fossil hunters crawled up an embankment, Berkeley graduate student Yohannes Haile-Selassie of Ethiopia, now a paleoanthropologist at the Cleveland Museum of Natural History in Ohio, spotted two pieces of a bone from the palm of a hand. That was soon followed by pieces of a pelvis; leg, ankle, and foot bones; many of the bones of the hand and arm; a lower jaw with teeth—and a cranium. By January 1995, it was apparent that they had made the rarest of rare finds, a partial skeleton. It is one of only a half-dozen such skeletons known from more than 1 million years ago, and the only published one older than Lucy.

It was the find of a lifetime. But the team's excitement was tempered by the skeleton's terrible condition. The bones literally crumbled when touched. White called it road kill. And parts of the skeleton had been trampled and scattered into more than 100 fragments; the skull was crushed to 4 centimeters in height. The researchers decided to remove entire blocks of sediment, covering the blocks in plaster and moving them to the National Museum of Ethiopia in Addis Ababa to finish excavating the fossils.

It took three field seasons to uncover and extract the skeleton, repeatedly crawling the site to gather 100% of the fossils present. At last count, the team had cataloged more than 110 specimens of *Ar. ramidus*, not to mention 150,000 specimens of fossil plants and animals. "This team seems to suck fossils out of the earth," says anatomist C. Owen Lovejoy of Kent State University in Ohio, who analyzed the post-cranial bones but didn't work in the field. In the lab, he gently unveils a cast of a tiny, pea-sized sesamoid bone for effect. "Their obsessiveness gives you—this!"

White himself spent years removing the silty clay from the fragile fossils at the National Museum in Addis Ababa, using brushes, syringes, and dental tools, usually under a microscope. Museum technician Alemu Ademassu made a precise cast of each piece, and the team assembled them into a skeleton.

Meanwhile in Tokyo and Ohio, Suwa and Lovejoy made virtual reconstructions of the crushed skull and pelvis. Certain fossils were taken briefly to Tokyo and scanned with a custom micro–computed tomography (CT) scanner that could reveal what was hidden inside the bones and teeth. Suwa spent 9 years mastering the technology to reassemble the fragments of the cranium into a virtual skull. "I used 65 pieces of the cranium," says Suwa, who estimates he spent 1000 hours on the task. "You go piece by piece."

Once he had reassembled the pieces in a digital reconstruction, he and paleoanthropologist Berhane Asfaw of the Rift Valley Research Service in Addis Ababa compared the skull with those of ancient and living primates in museums worldwide. By March of this year, Suwa was satisfied with his 10th reconstruction. Meanwhile in Ohio, Lovejoy made physical models of the pelvic pieces based on the original fossil and the CT scans, working closely with Suwa. He is also satisfied that the 14th version of the pelvis is accurate. "There was an *Ardipithecus* that looked just like that," he says, holding up the final model in his lab.

## PUTTING THEIR HEADS TOGETHER

As they examined Ardi's skull, Suwa and Asfaw noted a number of characteristics. Her lower face had a muzzle that juts out less than a chimpanzee's. The cranial base is short from front to back, indicating that her head balanced atop the spine as in later upright walkers, rather than to the front of the spine, as in quadrupedal apes. Her face is in a more vertical position than in chimpanzees. And her teeth, like those of all later hominins, lack the daggerlike sharpened upper canines seen in chimpanzees. The team realized that this combination of traits matches those of an even older skull, 6-million to 7-million-year-old *Sahelanthropus tchadensis*, found by Brunet's team in Chad. They conclude that both represent an early stage of human evolution, distinct from both *Australopithecus* and chimpanzees. "Similarities with *Sahelanthropus* are striking, in that it also represents a first-grade hominid," agrees Zollikofer, who did a three-dimensional reconstruction of that skull.

Another, earlier species of *Ardipithecus*—Ar. kadabba, dated from 5.5 million to 5.8 million years ago but known only from teeth and bits and pieces of skeletal bones—is part of that grade, too. And *Ar. kadabba's* canines and other teeth seem to match those of a third very ancient specimen, 6-million-year-old *Orrorin tugenensis* from Kenya, which also has a thighbone that appears to have been used for upright walking (*Science*, 21 March 2008, p. 1599). So, "this raises the intriguing possibility that we're looking at the same genus" for specimens now put in three genera, says Pilbeam. But the discoverers of O. *tugenensis* aren't so sure. "As for Ardi and *Orrorin* being the same genus, no, I don't think this is possible, unless one really wants to accept an unusual amount of variability" within a taxon, says geologist Martin Pickford of the College de France, who found *Orrorin* with Brigitte Senut of the National Museum of Natural History in Paris.

Whatever the taxonomy of *Ardipithecus* and the other very ancient hominins, they represent "an enormous jump to *Australopithecus*," the next hominin in line, says australopithecine expert William Kimbel of Arizona State University, Tempe. For example, although Lucy's brain is only a little larger than that of *Ardipithecus,* Lucy's species, *Au. afarensis*, was an adept biped. It walked upright like humans, venturing increasingly into more diverse habitats, including grassy savannas. And it had lost its opposable big toe, as seen in 3.7-million-year-old footprints at Laetoli, Tanzania, reflecting an irreversible commitment to life on the ground.

Lucy's direct ancestor is widely considered to be *Au. anamensis*, a hominin whose skeleton is poorly known, although its shinbone suggests it walked upright 3.9 million to 4.2 million years ago in Kenya and Ethiopia. *Ardipithecus* is the current leading candidate for *Au. anamensis*'s ancestor, if only because it's the only putative hominin in evidence between 5.8 million and 4.4 million years ago. Indeed, *Au. anamensis* fossils appear in the Middle Awash region just 200,000 years after Ardi.

## MAKING STRIDES

But the team is not connecting the dots between *Au. anamensis* and *Ar. ramidus* just yet, awaiting more fossils. For now they are focusing on the anatomy of Ardi and how she moved through the world. Her foot is primitive, with an opposable big toe like that used by living apes to grasp branches. But the bases of the four other toe bones were oriented so that they reinforced the forefoot into a more rigid lever as she pushed off. In contrast, the toes of a chimpanzee curve as flexibly as those in their hands, say Lovejoy and co-author Bruce Latimer of Case Western Reserve University in Cleveland. *Ar. ramidus* "developed a pretty good bipedal foot while at the same time keeping an opposable first toe," says Lovejoy.

The upper blades of Ardi's pelvis are shorter and broader than in apes. They would have lowered the trunk's center of mass, so she could balance on one leg at a time while walking, says Lovejoy. He also infers from the pelvis that her spine was long and curved like a human's rather than short and stiff like a chimpanzee's. These changes suggest to him that *Ar. ramidus* "has been bipedal for a very long time."

Yet the lower pelvis is still quite large and primitive, similar to African apes rather than hominins. Taken with the opposable big toe, and primitive traits in the hand and foot, this indicates that *Ar. ramidus* didn't walk like Lucy and was still spending a lot of time in the trees. But it wasn't suspending its body beneath branches like African apes or climbing vertically, says Lovejoy. Instead, it was a slow, careful climber that probably moved on flat hands and feet on top of branches in the midcanopy, a type of locomotion known as palmigrady. For example, four bones in the wrist of *Ar. ramidus* gave it a more flexible hand that could be bent backward at the wrist. This is in contrast to the hands of knuckle-walking chimpanzees and gorillas, which have stiff wrists that absorb forces on their knuckles.

However, several researchers aren't so sure about these inferences. Some are skeptical that the crushed pelvis really shows the anatomical details needed to demonstrate bipedality. The pelvis is "suggestive" of bipedality but not conclusive, says paleoanthropologist Carol Ward of the University of Missouri, Columbia. Also, *Ar. ramidus* "does not appear to have had its knee placed over the ankle, which means that when walking bipedally, it would have had to shift its weight to the side," she says. Paleoanthropologist William Jungers of Stony Brook University in New York state is also not sure that the skeleton was bipedal. "Believe me, it's a unique form of bipedalism," he says. "The postcranium alone would not unequivocally signal hominin status, in my opinion." Paleoanthropologist Bernard Wood of George Washington University in Washington, D.C., agrees. Looking at the skeleton as a whole, he says, "I think the head is consistent with it being a hominin, . . . but the rest of the body is much more questionable." All this underscores how difficult it may be to recognize and define bipedality in the earliest hominins as they began to shift from trees to ground. One thing does seem clear, though: The absence of many specialized traits found in African apes suggests that our ancestors never knuckle-walked.

That throws a monkey wrench into a hypothesis about the last common ancestor of living apes and humans. Ever since Darwin suggested in 1871 that our ancestors arose in Africa, researchers have debated whether our forebears passed through a great-ape stage in which they looked like proto-chimpanzees (*Science*, 21 November 1969, p. 953). This "troglodytian" model for early human behavior (named for the common chimpanzee, *Pan troglodytes*) suggests that the last common ancestor of the African apes and humans once had short backs, arms adapted for swinging, and a pelvis and limbs adapted for knuckle walking. Then our ancestors lost these traits, while chimpanzees and gorillas kept them. But this view has been uninformed by fossil evidence because there are almost no fossils of early chimpanzees and gorillas.

Some researchers have thought that the ancient African ape bau-plan was more primitive, lately citing clues from fragmentary fossils of apes that lived from 8 million to 18 million years ago. "There's been growing evidence from the Miocene apes that the common ancestor may have been more primitive," says Ward. Now *Ar. ramidus* strongly supports that notion. The authors repeatedly note the many ways that *Ar. ramidus* differs from chimpanzees and gorillas, bolstering the argument that it was those apes that changed the most from the primitive form.

But the problem with a more "generalized model" of an arboreal ape is that "it is easier to say what it wasn't than what it was," says Ward. And if the last common ancestor, which according to genetic studies lived 5 million to 7 million years ago, didn't look like a chimp, then chimpanzees and gorillas evolved their numerous similarities independently, after gorillas diverged from the chimp/human line. "I find [that] hard to believe," says Pilbeam.

As debate over the implications of *Ar. ramidus* begins, the one thing that all can agree on is that the new papers provide a wealth of data to frame the issues for years. "No matter what side of the arguments you come down on, it's going to be food for thought for generations of graduate students," says Jungers. Or, as Walker says: "It would have been very boring if it had looked half-chimp."

# 5

# What Are Friends For?

*Barbara Smuts*

In tracing the evolution of humanity, anthropologists are concerned with both biological features and sociocultural forms. Some people believe that a prerequisite for culture was the emergence of more permanent relationships between men and women and the formation of families. How this actually occurred in evolution has been the subject of controversy. The traditional view centered on dominant males who, as mighty hunters, put the proverbial meat on the table, selected females, and, through protection of the helpless females and their offspring, ensured the transmission of their genes to future generations. The conventional wisdom left little room for the role of women in human adaptation. This is no longer the case.

In recent years, much research has helped to revise and refine our understanding of ancestral lifeways. In this selection, Barbara Smuts examines sex and friendship among baboons. The implications for the origin of male–female relations and the role of female choice are fascinating.

***As you read this selection, ask yourself the following questions:***

- Why do some anthropologists study monkeys and apes to better understand human behavior?
- Why do females prefer some males over others?
- Who forms the core membership of a baboon troop?
- What criteria does the author use to determine friendship?
- Do the bonds between adult male baboons and infants arise from paternity or from a relationship with the infant's mother?
- In what three ways does this article challenge the conventional wisdom about the origin of the nuclear family?

***The following terms discussed in this selection are included in the Glossary at the back of the book:***

| | |
|---|---|
| *aggression* | *grooming* |
| *dominance* | *paternity* |
| *estrus* | *primatology* |

Virgil, a burly adult male olive baboon, closely followed Zizi, a middle-aged female easily distinguished by her grizzled coat and square muzzle. On her rump Zizi sported a bright pink swelling, indicating that she was sexually receptive and probably fertile. Virgil's extreme attentiveness to Zizi suggested to me—and all rival males in the troop—that he was her current and exclusive mate.

Zizi, however, apparently had something else in mind. She broke away from Virgil, moved rapidly through the troop, and presented her alluring sexual swelling to one male after another. Before Virgil caught up with her, she had managed to announce her receptive condition to several of his rivals. When Virgil tried to grab her, Zizi screamed and dashed into the bushes with Virgil in hot pursuit. I heard sounds of chasing and fighting coming from the thicket. Moments later Zizi emerged from the bushes with an older male named Cyclops. They remained together for several days, copulating often. In Cyclops's presence, Zizi no longer approached or even glanced at other males.

Primatologists describe Zizi and other olive baboons (*Papio cynocephalus anubis*) as promiscuous, meaning that both males and females usually mate with several members of the opposite sex within a short period of time. Promiscuous mating behavior characterizes many of the larger, more familiar primates, including chimpanzees, rhesus macaques, and gray langurs, as well as olive, yellow, and chacma baboons, the three subspecies of savanna baboon. In colloquial usage, promiscuity often connotes wanton and random sex, and several early studies of primates supported this

---

Smuts, Barbara. "What Are Friends For?" from *Natural History* (Feb. 1987):36, 38–44; copyright © Natural History Magazine, Inc. 1987. Reprinted with permission.

stereotype. However, after years of laboriously recording thousands of copulations under natural conditions, the Peeping Toms of primate fieldwork have shown that, even in promiscuous species, sexual pairings are far from random.

Some adult males, for example, typically copulate much more often than others. Primatologists have explained these differences in terms of competition: the most dominant males monopolize females and prevent lower-ranking rivals from mating. But exceptions are frequent. Among baboons, the exceptions often involve scruffy, older males who mate in full view of younger, more dominant rivals.

A clue to the reason for these puzzling exceptions emerged when primatologists began to question an implicit assumption of the dominance hypothesis—that females were merely passive objects of male competition. But what if females were active arbiters in this system? If females preferred some males over others and were able to express these preferences, then models of mating activity based on male dominance alone would be far too simple.

Once researchers recognized the possibility of female choice, evidence for it turned up in species after species. The story of Zizi, Virgil, and Cyclops is one of hundreds of examples of female primates rejecting the sexual advances of particular males and enthusiastically cooperating with others. But what is the basis for female choice? Why might they prefer some males over others?

This question guided my research on the Eburru Cliffs troop of olive baboons, named after one of their favorite sleeping sites, a sheer rocky outcrop rising several hundred feet above the floor of the Great Rift Valley, about 100 miles northwest of Nairobi, Kenya. The 120 members of Eburru Cliffs spent their days wandering through open grassland studded with occasional acacia thorn trees. Each night they retired to one of a dozen sets of cliffs that provided protection from nocturnal predators such as leopards.

Most previous studies of baboon sexuality had focused on females who, like Zizi, were at the peak of sexual receptivity. A female baboon does not mate when she is pregnant or lactating, a period of abstinence lasting about eighteen months. The female then goes into estrus, and for about two weeks out of every thirty-five-day cycle, she mates. Toward the end of this two-week period she may ovulate, but usually the female undergoes four or five estrous cycles before she conceives. During pregnancy, she once again resumes a chaste existence. As a result, the typical female baboon is sexually active for less than 10 percent of her adult life. I thought that by focusing on the other 90 percent, I might learn something new. In particular, I suspected that routine, day-to-day relationships between males and pregnant or lactating (nonestrous) females might provide clues to female mating preferences.

Nearly every day for sixteen months, I joined the Eburru Cliffs baboons at their sleeping cliffs at dawn and traveled several miles with them while they foraged for roots, seeds, grass, and occasionally, small prey items, such as baby gazelles or hares (see "Predatory Baboons of Kekopey," *Natural History,* March 1976). Like all savanna baboon troops, Eburru Cliffs functioned as a cohesive unit organized around a core of related females, all of whom were born in the troop. Unlike the females, male savanna baboons leave their natal troop to join another where they may remain for many years, so most of the Eburru Cliffs adult males were immigrants. Since membership in the troop remained relatively constant during the period of my study, I learned to identify each individual. I relied on differences in size, posture, gait, and especially facial features. To the practiced observer, baboons look as different from one another as human beings do.

As soon as I could recognize individuals, I noticed that particular females tended to turn up near particular males again and again. I came to think of these pairs as friends. Friendship among animals is not a well-documented phenomenon, so to convince skeptical colleagues that baboon friendship was real, I needed to develop objective criteria for distinguishing friendly pairs.

I began by investigating grooming, the amiable simian habit of picking through a companion's fur to remove dead skin and ectoparasites (see "Little Things That Tick Off Baboons," *Natural History,* February 1984). Baboons spend much more time grooming than is necessary for hygiene, and previous research had indicated that it is a good measure of social bonds. Although eighteen adult males lived in the troop, each nonestrous female performed most of her grooming with just one, two, or occasionally three males. For example, of Zizi's twenty-four grooming bouts with males, Cyclops accounted for thirteen, and a second male, Sherlock, accounted for all the rest. Different females tended to favor different males as grooming partners.

Another measure of social bonds was simply who was observed near whom. When foraging, traveling, or resting, each pregnant or lactating female spent a lot of time near a few males and associated with the others no more often than expected by chance. When I compared the identities of favorite grooming partners and frequent companions, they overlapped almost completely. This enabled me to develop a formal definition of friendship: any male that scored high on both grooming and proximity measures was considered a friend.

Virtually all baboons made friends; only one female and the three males who had most recently joined the troop lacked such companions. Out of more than 600 possible adult female–adult male pairs in the troop, however, only about one in ten qualified as friends; these really were special relationships.

Several factors seemed to influence which baboons paired up. In most cases, friends were unrelated to each other, since the male had immigrated from another troop. (Four friendships, however, involved a female and an adolescent son who had not yet emigrated. Unlike other friends, these related pairs never mated.) Older females tended to be friends with older males; younger females with younger males. I witnessed occasional May–December romances, usually involving older females and young adult males. Adolescent males and females were strongly rule-bound, and with the exception of mother–son pairs, they formed friendships only with one another.

Regardless of age or dominance rank, most females had just one or two male friends. But among males, the number of female friends varied greatly from none to eight. Although high-ranking males enjoyed priority of access to food and sometimes mates, dominant males did not have more female friends than low-ranking males. Instead it was the older males who had lived in the troop for many years who had the most friends. When a male had several female friends, the females were often closely related to one another. Since female baboons spend a lot of time near their kin, it is probably easier for a male to maintain bonds with several related females at once.

When collecting data, I focused on one nonestrous female at a time and kept track of her every movement toward or away from any male; similarly, I noted every male who moved toward or away from her. Whenever the female and a male moved close enough to exchange intimacies, I wrote down exactly what happened. When foraging together, friends tended to remain a few yards apart. Males more often wandered away from females than the reverse, and females, more often than males, closed the gap. The female behaved as if she wanted to keep the male within calling distance, in case she needed his protection. The male, however, was more likely to make approaches that brought them within actual touching distance. Often, he would plunk himself down right next to his friend and ask her to groom him by holding a pose with exaggerated stillness. The female sometimes responded by grooming, but more often, she exhibited the most reliable sign of true intimacy: she ignored her friend and simply continued whatever she was doing.

In sharp contrast, when a male who was not a friend moved close to a female, she dared not ignore him. She stopped whatever she was doing and held still, often glancing surreptitiously at the intruder. If he did not move away, she sometimes lifted her tail and presented her rump. When a female is not in estrus, this is a gesture of appeasement, not sexual enticement. Immediately after this respectful acknowledgement of his presence, the female would slip away. But such tense interactions with nonfriend males were rare, because females usually moved away before the males came too close.

These observations suggest that females were afraid of most of the males in their troop, which is not surprising: male baboons are twice the size of females, and their canines are longer and sharper than those of a lion. All Eburru Cliffs males directed both mild and severe aggression toward females. Mild aggression, which usually involved threats and chases but no body contact, occurred most often during feeding competition or when the male redirected aggression toward a female after losing a fight with another male. Females and juveniles showed aggression toward other females and juveniles in similar circumstances and occasionally inflicted superficial wounds. Severe aggression by males, which involved body contact and sometimes biting, was less common and also more puzzling, since there was no apparent cause.

An explanation for at least some of these attacks emerged one day when I was watching Pegasus, a young adult male, and his friend Cicily, sitting together in the middle of a small clearing. Cicily moved to the edge of the clearing to feed, and a higher-ranking female, Zora, suddenly attacked her. Pegasus stood up and looked as if he were about to intervene when both females disappeared into the bushes. He sat back down, and I remained with him. A full ten minutes later, Zora appeared at the edge of the clearing; this was the first time she had come into view since her attack on Cicily. Pegasus instantly pounced on Zora, repeatedly grabbed her neck in his mouth and lifted her off the ground, shook her whole body, and then dropped her. Zora screamed continuously and tried to escape. Each time, Pegasus caught her and continued his brutal attack. When he finally released her five minutes later she had a deep canine gash on the palm of her hand that made her limp for several days.

This attack was similar in form and intensity to those I had seen before and labeled "unprovoked." Certainly, had I come upon the scene after Zora's aggression toward Cicily, I would not have understood why Pegasus attacked Zora. This suggested that some, perhaps many, severe attacks by males actually represented punishment for actions that had occurred some time before.

Whatever the reasons for male attacks on females, they represent a serious threat. Records of fresh injuries indicated that Eburru Cliffs adult females received canine slash wounds from males at the rate of one for every female each year, and during my study, one female died of her injuries. Males probably pose an even greater threat to infants. Although only one infant was killed during my study, observers in Botswana and Tanzania have seen recent male immigrants kill several young infants.

Protection from male aggression, and from the less injurious but more frequent aggression of other females and juveniles, seems to be one of the main advantages of friendship for a female baboon. Seventy times I observed an adult male defend a female or her offspring against aggression by another troop member, not infrequently a high-ranking male. In all but six of these cases, the defender was a friend. Very few of these confrontations involved actual fighting; no male baboon, subordinate or dominant, is anxious to risk injury by the sharp canines of another.

Males are particularly solicitous guardians of their friends' youngest infants. If another male gets too close to an infant or if a juvenile female plays with it too roughly, the friend may intervene. Other troop members soon learn to be cautious when the mother's friend is nearby, and his presence provides the mother with a welcome respite from the annoying pokes and prods of curious females and juveniles obsessed with the new baby. Male baboons at Gombe Park in Tanzania and Amboseli Park in Kenya have also been seen rescuing infants from chimpanzees and lions. These several forms of male protection help to explain why females in Eburru Cliffs stuck closer to their friends in the first few months after giving birth than at any other time.

The male–infant relationship develops out of the male's friendship with the mother, but as the infant matures, this new bond takes on a life of its own. My co-worker Nancy Nicolson found that by about nine months of age, infants actively sought out their male friends when the mother was a few yards away, suggesting that the male may function as an alternative caregiver. This seemed to be especially true for infants undergoing unusually early or severe weaning. (Weaning is generally a gradual, prolonged process, but there is tremendous variation among mothers in the timing and intensity of weaning. See "Mother Baboons," *Natural History*, September 1980.) After being rejected by the mother, the crying infant often approached the male friend and sat huddled against him until its whimpers subsided. Two of the infants in Eburru Cliffs lost their mothers when they were still quite young. In each case, their bond with the mother's friend subsequently intensified, and—perhaps as a result—both infants survived.

A close bond with a male may also improve the infant's nutrition. Larger than all other troop members, adult males monopolize the best feeding sites. In general, the personal space surrounding a feeding male is inviolate, but he usually tolerates intrusions by the infants of his female friends, giving them access to choice feeding spots.

Although infants follow their male friends around rather than the reverse, the males seem genuinely attached to their tiny companions. During feeding, the male and infant express their pleasure in each other's company by sharing spirited, antiphonal grunting duets. If the infant whimpers in distress, the male friend is likely to cease feeding, look at the infant, and grunt softly, as if in sympathy, until the whimpers cease. When the male rests, the infants of his female friends may huddle behind him, one after the other, forming a "train," or, if feeling energetic, they may use his body as a trampoline.

When I returned to Eburru Cliffs four years after my initial study ended, several of the bonds formed between males and the infants of their female friends were still intact (in other cases, either the male or the infant or both had disappeared). When these bonds involved recently matured females, their long-time male associates showed no sexual interest in them, even though the females mated with other adult males. Mothers and sons, and usually maternal siblings, show similar sexual inhibitions in baboons and many other primate species.

The development of an intimate relationship between a male and the infant of his female friend raises an obvious question: Is the male the infant's father? To answer this question definitely we would need to conduct genetic analysis, which was not possible for these baboons. Instead, I estimated paternity probabilities from observations of the temporary (a few hours or days) exclusive mating relationships, or consortships, that estrous females form with a series of different males. These estimates were apt to be fairly accurate, since changes in the female's sexual swelling allow one to pinpoint the timing of conception to within a few days. Most females consorted with only two or three males during this period, and these males were termed likely fathers.

In about half the friendships, the male was indeed likely to be the father of his friend's most recent infant, but in the other half he was not—in fact, he had never been seen mating with the female. Interestingly, males who were friends with the mother but not likely fathers nearly always developed a relationship with her infant, while males who had mated with the female but were not her friend usually did not. Thus friendship with the mother, rather than paternity, seems to mediate the development of male–infant bonds. Recently, a similar pattern was documented for South American capuchin monkeys in a laboratory study in which paternity was determined genetically.

These results fly in the face of a prominent theory that claims males will invest in infants only when they are closely related. If males are not fostering the survival of their own genes by caring for the infant, then why do they do so? I suspected that the key was female choice. If females preferred to mate with males who had already demonstrated friendly behavior, then friendships with mothers and their infants might pay off in the future when the mothers were ready to mate again.

To find out if this was the case, I examined each male's sexual behavior with females he had befriended before they resumed estrus. In most cases, males consorted considerably more often with their friends than with other females. Baboon females typically mate with several different males, including both friends and nonfriends, but prior friendship increased a male's probability of mating with a female above what it would have been otherwise.

This increased probability seemed to reflect female preferences. Females occasionally overtly advertised their disdain for certain males and their desire for others. Zizi's behavior, described above, is a good example. Virgil was not one of her friends, but Cyclops was. Usually, however, females expressed preferences and aversions more subtly. For example, Delphi, a petite adolescent female, found herself pursued by Hector, a middle-aged adult male. She did not run away or refuse to mate with him, but whenever he wasn't watching, she looked around for her friend Homer, an adolescent male. When she succeeded in catching Homer's eye, she narrowed her eyes and flattened her ears against her skull, the friendliest face one baboon can send another. This told Homer she would rather be with him. Females expressed satisfaction with a current consort partner by staying close to him, initiating copulations, and not making advances toward other males. Baboons are very sensitive to such cues, as indicated by an experimental study in which rival hamadryas baboons rarely challenged a male–female pair if the female strongly preferred her current partner. Similarly, in Eburru Cliffs, males were less apt to challenge consorts involving a pair that shared a long-term friendship.

Even though females usually consorted with their friends, they also mated with other males, so it is not surprising that friendships were most vulnerable during periods of sexual activity. In a few cases, the female consorted with another male more often than with her friend, but the friendship survived nevertheless. One female, however, formed a strong sexual bond with a new male. This bond persisted after conception, replacing her previous friendship. My observations suggest that adolescent and young adult females tend to have shorter, less stable friendships than do older females. Some friendships, however, last a very long time. When I returned to Eburru Cliffs six years after my study began, five couples were still together. It is possible that friendships occasionally last for life (baboons probably live twenty to thirty years in the wild), but it will require longer studies, and some very patient scientists, to find out.

By increasing both the male's chances of mating in the future and the likelihood that a female's infant will survive, friendship contributes to the reproductive success of both partners. This clarifies the evolutionary basis of friendship-forming tendencies in baboons, but what does friendship mean to a baboon? To answer this question we need to view baboons as sentient beings with feelings and goals not unlike our own in similar circumstances. Consider, for example, the friendship between Thalia and Alexander.

The affair began one evening as Alex and Thalia sat about fifteen feet apart on the sleeping cliffs. It was like watching two novices in a singles bar. Alex stared at Thalia until she turned and almost caught him looking at her. He glanced away immediately, and then she stared at him until his head began to turn toward her. She suddenly became engrossed in grooming her toes. But as soon as Alex looked away, her gaze returned to him. They went on like this for more than fifteen minutes, always with split-second timing. Finally, Alex managed to catch Thalia looking at him. He made the friendly eyes-narrowed, ears-back face and smacked his lips together rhythmically. Thalia froze, and for a second she looked into his eyes. Alex approached, and Thalia, still nervous, groomed him. Soon she calmed down, and I found them still together on the cliffs the next morning. Looking back on this event months later, I realized that it marked the beginning of their friendship. Six years later, when I returned to Eburru Cliffs, they were still friends.

If flirtation forms an integral part of baboon friendship, so does jealousy. Overt displays of jealousy, such as chasing a friend away from a potential rival, occur occasionally, but like humans, baboons often express their emotions in more subtle ways. One evening a colleague and I climbed the cliffs and settled down near Sherlock, who was friends with Cybelle, a middle-aged female still foraging on the ground below the cliffs. I observed Cybelle while my colleague watched Sherlock, and we kept up a running commentary. As long as Cybelle was feeding or interacting with females, Sherlock was relaxed, but each time she approached another male, his body would stiffen, and he would stare intently at the scene below. When Cybelle presented politely to a male who had recently tried to befriend her, Sherlock even made threatening sounds under his breath. Cybelle was not in estrus at the time, indicating that male baboon jealousy extends beyond the sexual arena to include affiliative interactions between a female friend and other males.

Because baboon friendships are embedded in a network of friendly and antagonistic relationships, they inevitably lead to repercussions extending beyond the pair. For example, Virgil once provoked his weaker rival Cyclops into a fight by first attacking Cyclops's friend Phoebe. On another occasion, Sherlock chased Circe, Hector's best friend, just after Hector had chased Antigone, Sherlock's friend.

In another incident, the prime adult male Triton challenged Cyclops's possession of meat. Cyclops grew increasingly tense and seemed about to abandon the prey to the younger male. Then Cyclops's friend Phoebe appeared with her infant Phyllis. Phyllis wandered over to Cyclops. He immediately grabbed her, held her close, and threatened Triton away from the prey. Because any challenge to Cyclops now involved a threat to Phyllis as well, Triton risked being mobbed by Phoebe and her relatives and friends. For this reason, he backed down. Males frequently use the infants of their female friends as buffers in this way. Thus, friendship involves costs as well as benefits because it makes the participants vulnerable to social manipulation or redirected aggression by others.

Finally, as with humans, friendship seems to mean something different to each baboon. Several females in Eburru Cliffs had only one friend. They were devoted companions. Louise and Pandora, for example, groomed their friend Virgil and no other male. Then there was Leda, who, with five friends, spread herself more thinly than any other female. These contrasting patterns of friendship were associated with striking personality differences. Louise and Pandora were unobtrusive females who hung around quietly with Virgil and their close relatives. Leda seemed to be everywhere at once, playing with infants, fighting with juveniles, and making friends with males. Similar differences were apparent among the males. Some devoted a great deal of time and energy to cultivating friendships with females, while others focused more on challenging other males. Although we probably will never fully understand the basis of these individual differences, they contribute immeasurably to the richness and complexity of baboon society.

Male–female friendships may be widespread among primates. They have been reported for many other groups of savanna baboons, and they also occur in rhesus and Japanese macaques, capuchin monkeys, and perhaps in bonobos (pygmy chimpanzees). These relationships should give us pause when considering popular scenarios for the evolution of male–female relationships in humans. Most of these scenarios assume that, except for mating, males and females had little to do with one another until the development of a sexual division of labor, when, the story goes, females began to rely on males to provide meat in exchange for gathered food. This, it has been argued, set up new selection pressures favoring the development of long-term bonds between individual males and females, female sexual fidelity, and as paternity certainty increased, greater male investment in the offspring of these unions. In other words, once women began to gather and men to hunt, presto—we had the nuclear family.

This scenario may have more to do with cultural biases about women's economic dependence on men and idealized views of the nuclear family than with the actual behavior of our hominid ancestors. The nonhuman primate evidence challenges this story in at least three ways.

First, long-term bonds between the sexes can evolve in the absence of a sexual division of labor or food sharing. In our primate relatives, such relationships rest on exchanges of social, not economic, benefits.

Second, primate research shows that highly differentiated, emotionally intense male–female relationships can occur without sexual exclusivity. Ancestral men and women may have experienced intimate friendships long before they invented marriage and norms of sexual fidelity.

Third, among our closest primate relatives, males clearly provide mothers and infants with social benefits even when they are unlikely to be the fathers of those infants. In return, females provide a variety of benefits to the friendly males, including acceptance into the group and, at least in baboons, increased mating opportunities in the future. This suggests that efforts to reconstruct the evolution of hominid societies may have overemphasized what the female must supposedly do (restrict her mating to just one male) in order to obtain male parental investment.

Maybe it is time to pay more attention to what the male must do (provide benefits to females and the young) in order to obtain female cooperation. Perhaps among our ancestors, as in baboons today, sex and friendship went hand in hand. As for marriage—well, that's another story.

# 6

# Mothers and Others

## *Sarah Blaffer Hrdy*

Ethnocentrism is everywhere; it affects our views of human nature. In North America and the West, we have grown up with beliefs about our species' emergence as mighty hunters. As such, there is a cultural self-image of "man the hunter" as master of nature. Similarly, we have cultural ideas of the original human society as characterized by the division of labor in two spheres of primordial importance: subsistence (bringing home the bacon) and breeding, nourishing, and nurturing (homemaking). Our imaginary view of our ancestors, shaped by our self-image, can result in depictions like *The Flintstones*. For example, we have assumed that women stayed at home by their campfires nurturing the young while men set off to hunt big game and make war on their neighbors—other bands of "primitive" hunters. We have typically assumed that prehistoric men hunted in groups, whereas women, despite cooperation in communal food gathering, individually nursed and otherwise nourished their children.

But is this Western-style nuclear family, with our traditional division of labor between mothers and fathers or between mothers and neighbors, the natural human adaptation that emerged from our biological heritage? Or does the evolutionary record, and observations of our closest biological kin, point in other directions?

Theories and observations of both nonhuman primates as well as hunter-gatherer societies may cast doubt on our long-held ideas about the past. This selection examines both biological and cultural mechanisms that engender *cooperation* in child rearing. The argument presented here emphasizes the importance of social cooperation in child rearing both for individuals and for society as a whole.

This is a new way of thinking about our "human nature." Thinking about humans and some other primates as "cooperative breeders" has fascinating implications for child rearing and gender roles, the critical importance of kin groups, and the practices and policies for our ever-expanding day-care system.

***As you read this selection, ask yourself the following questions:***

- In what ways do human infants and children differ from the young of nonhuman primates such as chimpanzees, gorillas, and orangutans?
- How do Western habits of child care in individual nuclear families differ from the practices of many other cultures? Do we put too much pressure on individual mothers to do everything as the so-called supermom?
- How does the belief in *partible paternity* affect cultural beliefs about sex and marriage and increased support for children?
- According to Hrdy, what are three ways that humans are motivated to protect and care for babies?
- How are hormones affected by nurturing, even in fathers and other males?
- What does this theory suggest about day-care policies? Extended families? Supermoms? Child abuse?

***The following terms discussed in this selection are included in the Glossary at the back of the book:***

| | |
|---|---|
| *gestation* | *Pleistocene* |
| *matrilineal* | *primate* |
| *parturient* | *sociobiology* |

Mother apes—chimpanzees, gorillas, orangutans, humans—dote on their babies. And why not? They give birth to an infant after a long gestation and, in most cases, suckle it for years. With humans, however, the job of providing for a juvenile goes on and on. Unlike all other ape babies, ours mature slowly and reach independence late. A mother in a foraging society may give birth every four years or so, and her first few children remain dependent long after each new baby arrives; among nomadic foragers, grown-ups may provide food to children for eighteen or more years.

"Mothers and Others" by Sarah Blaffer Hrdy from *Co-operation, Empathy, and the Needs of Human Infants*. Delivered as a Tanner Lecture on Human Values. Printed with permission of the Tanner Lectures on Human Values, a Corporation, University of Utah, Salt Lake City, Utah.

To come up with the 10–13 million calories that anthropologists such as Hillard Kaplan calculate are needed to rear a young human to independence, a mother needs help.

So how did our prehuman and early human ancestresses living in the Pleistocene Epoch (from 1.6 million until roughly 10,000 years ago) manage to get those calories? And under what conditions would natural selection allow a female ape to produce babies so large and slow to develop that they are beyond her means to rear on her own?

The old answer was that fathers helped out by hunting. And so they do. But hunting is a risky occupation, and fathers may die or defect or take up with other females. And when they do, what then? New evidence from surviving traditional cultures suggests that mothers in the Pleistocene may have had a significant degree of help—from men who thought they just might have been the fathers, from grandmothers and great-aunts, from older children.

These helpers other than the mother, called allomothers by sociobiologists, do not just protect and provision youngsters. In groups such as the Efe and Aka Pygmies of central Africa, allomothers actually hold children and carry them about. In these tight-knit communities of communal foragers—within which men, women, and children still hunt with nets, much as humans are thought to have done tens of thousands of years ago—siblings, aunts, uncles, fathers, and grandmothers hold newborns on the first day of life. When University of New Mexico anthropologist Paula Ivey asked an Efe woman, "Who cares for babies?" the immediate answer was, "We all do!" By three weeks of age, the babies are in contact with allomothers 40 percent of the time. By eighteen weeks, infants actually spend more time with allomothers than with their gestational mothers. On average, Efe babies have fourteen different caretakers, most of whom are close kin. According to Washington State University anthropologist Barry Hewlett, Aka babies are within arm's reach of their fathers for more than half of every day.

Accustomed to celebrating the antiquity and naturaleness of mother-centered models of child care, as well as the nuclear family in which the mother nurtures while the father provides, we Westerners tend to regard the practices of the Efe and the Aka as exotic. But to sociobiologists, whose stock in trade is comparisons across species, all this helping has a familiar ring. It's called cooperative breeding. During the past quarter century, as anthropologists and sociobiologists started to compare notes, one of the spectacular surprises has been how much allomaternal care goes on, not just within various human societies but among animals generally. Evidently, diverse organisms have converged on cooperative breeding for the best of evolutionary reasons.

A broad look at the most recent evidence has convinced me that cooperative breeding was the strategy that permitted our own ancestors to produce costly, slow-maturing infants at shorter intervals, to take advantage of new kinds of resources in habitats other than the mixed savanna-woodland of tropical Africa, and to spread more widely and swiftly than any primate had before. We already know that animal mothers who delegate some of the costs of infant care to others are thereby freed to produce more or larger young or to breed more frequently. Consider the case of silver-backed jackals. Patricia Moehlman, of the World Conservation Union, has shown that for every extra helper bringing back food, jackal parents rear one extra pup per litter. Cooperative breeding also helps various species expand into habitats in which they would normally not be able to rear any young at all. Florida scrub-jays, for example, breed in an exposed landscape where unrelenting predation from hawks and snakes usually precludes the fledging of young; survival in this habitat is possible only because older siblings help guard and feed the young. Such cooperative arrangements permit animals as different as naked mole rats (the social insects of the mammal world) and wolves to move into new habitats and sometimes to spread over vast areas.

What does it take to become a cooperative breeder? Obviously, this lifestyle is an option only for creatures capable of living in groups. It is facilitated when young but fully mature individuals (such as young Florida scrub-jays) do not or cannot immediately leave their natal group to breed on their own and instead remain among kin in their natal location. As with delayed maturation, delayed dispersion of young means that teenagers, "spinster" aunts, real and honorary uncles will be on hand to help their kin rear young. Flexibility is another criterion for cooperative breeders. Helpers must be ready to shift to breeding mode should the opportunity arise. In marmosets and tamarins—the little South American monkeys that are, besides us, the only full-fledged cooperative breeders among primates—a female has to be ready to be a helper this year and a mother the next. She may have one mate or several. In canids such as wolves or wild dogs, usually only the dominant, or alpha, male and female in a pack reproduce, but younger group members hunt with the mother and return to the den to regurgitate predigested meat into the mouths of her pups. In a fascinating instance of physiological flexibility, a subordinate female may actually undergo hormonal transformations similar to those of a real pregnancy: her belly swells, and she begins to manufacture milk and may help nurse the pups of the alpha pair. Vestiges of cooperative breeding crop up as well in domestic dogs, the distant descendants of wolves. After undergoing a pseudopregnancy, my neighbors'

Jack Russell terrier chased away the family's cat and adopted and suckled her kittens. To suckle the young of another species is hardly what Darwinians call an adaptive trait (because it does not contribute to the surrogate's own survival). But in the environment in which the dog family evolved, a female's tendency to respond when infants signaled their need—combined with her capacity for pseudopregnancy—would have increased the survival chances for large litters born to the dominant female.

According to the late W. D. Hamilton, evolutionary logic predicts that an animal with poor prospects of reproducing on his or her own should be predisposed to assist kin with better prospects so that at least some of their shared genes will be perpetuated. Among wolves, for example, both male and female helpers in the pack are likely to be genetically related to the alpha litter and to have good reasons for not trying to reproduce on their own: in a number of cooperatively breeding species (wild dogs, wolves, hyenas, dingoes, dwarf mongooses, marmosets), the helpers do try, but the dominant female is likely to bite their babies to death. The threat of coercion makes postponing ovulation the better part of valor, the least-bad option for females who must wait to breed until their circumstances improve, either through the death of a higher-ranking female or by finding a mate with an unoccupied territory.

One primate strategy is to line up extra fathers. Among common marmosets and several species of tamarins, females mate with several males, all of which help rear her young. As primatologist Charles T. Snowdon points out, in three of the four genera of Callitrichidae (*Callithrix, Saguinus,* and *Leontopithecus*), the more adult males the group has available to help, the more young survive. Among many of these species, females ovulate just after giving birth, perhaps encouraging males to stick around until after babies are born. (In cotton-top tamarins, males also undergo hormonal changes that prepare them to care for infants at the time of birth.) Among cooperative breeders of certain other species, such as wolves and jackals, pups born in the same litter can be sired by different fathers.

Human mothers, by contrast, don't ovulate again right after birth, nor do they produce offspring with more than one genetic father at a time. Ever inventive, though, humans solve the problem of enlisting help from several adult males by other means. In some cultures, mothers rely on a peculiar belief that anthropologists call partible paternity—the notion that a fetus is built up by contributions of semen from all the men with whom women have had sex in the ten months or so prior to giving birth. Among the Canela, a matrilineal tribe in Brazil studied for many years by William Crocker of the Smithsonian Institution, publicly sanctioned intercourse between women and men other than their husbands—sometimes many men—takes place during villagewide ceremonies. What might lead to marital disaster elsewhere works among the Canela because the men believe in partible paternity. Across a broad swath of South America—from Paraguay up into Brazil, westward to Peru, and northward to Venezuela—mothers rely on this convenient folk wisdom to line up multiple honorary fathers to help them provision both themselves and their children. Over hundreds of generations, this belief has helped children thrive in a part of the world where food sources are unpredictable and where husbands are as likely as not to return from the hunt empty-handed.

The Bari people of Venezuela are among those who believe in shared paternity, and according to anthropologist Stephen Beckerman, Bari children with more than one father do especially well. In Beckerman's study of 822 children, 80 percent of those who had both a "primary" father (the man married to their mother) and a "secondary" father survived to age fifteen, compared with 64 percent survival for those with a primary father alone. Not surprisingly, as soon as a Bari woman suspects she is pregnant, she accepts sexual advances from the more successful fishermen or hunters in her group. Belief that fatherhood can be shared draws more men into the web of possible paternity, which effectively translates into more food and more protection.

But for human mothers, extra mates aren't the only source of effective help. Older children, too, play a significant role in family survival. University of Nebraska anthropologists Patricia Draper and Raymond Hames have just shown that among !Kung hunters and gatherers living in the Kalahari Desert, there is a significant correlation between how many children a parent successfully raises and how many older siblings were on hand to help during that person's own childhood.

Older matrilineal kin may be the most valuable helpers of all. University of Utah anthropologists Kristen Hawkes and James O'Connell and their UCLA colleague Nicholas Blurton Jones, who have demonstrated the important food-gathering role of older women among Hazda hunter-gatherers in Tanzania, delight in explaining that since human life spans may extend for a few decades after menopause, older women become available to care for—and to provide vital food for—children born to younger kin. Hawkes, O'Connell, and Blurton Jones further believe that dating from the earliest days of *Homo erectus,* the survival of weaned children during food shortages may have depended on tubers dug up by older kin.

At various times in human history, people have also relied on a range of customs, as well as on coercion, to line up allomaternal assistance—for example, by using slaves or hiring poor women as wet nurses. But all the helpers in the world are of no use if they're not motivated to protect, carry, or provision babies. For both humans and nonhumans, this motivation arises in three main ways: through the manipulation of information about kinship; through appealing signals coming from the babies themselves; and, at the heart of it all, from the endocrinological and neural processes that induce individuals to respond to infants' signals. Indeed, all primates and many other mammals eventually respond to infants in a nurturing way if exposed long enough to their signals. Trouble is, "long enough" can mean very different things in males and females, with their very different response thresholds.

For decades, animal behaviorists have been aware of the phenomenon known as priming. A mouse or rat encountering a strange pup is likely to respond by either ignoring the pup or eating it. But presented with pup after pup, rodents of either sex eventually become sensitized to the baby and start caring for it. Even a male may gather pups into a nest and lick or huddle over them. Although nurturing is not a routine part of a male's repertoire, when sufficiently primed he behaves as a mother would. Hormonal change is an obvious candidate for explaining this transformation. Consider the case of the cooperatively breeding Florida scrub-jays studied by Stephan Schoech, of the University of Memphis. Prolactin, a protein hormone that initiates the secretion of milk in female mammals, is also present in male mammals and in birds of both sexes. Schoech showed that levels of prolactin go up in a male and female jay as they build their nest and incubate eggs and that these levels reach a peak when they feed their young. Moreover, prolactin levels rise in the jays' nonbreeding helpers and are also at their highest when they assist in feeding nestlings.

As it happens, male, as well as immature and nonbreeding female, primates can respond to infants' signals, although quite different levels of exposure and stimulation are required to get them going. Twenty years ago, when elevated prolactin levels were first reported in common marmoset males (by Alan Dixson, for *Callithrix jacchus*), many scientists refused to believe it. Later, when the finding was confirmed, scientists assumed this effect would be found only in fathers. But based on work by Scott Nunes, Jeffrey Fite, Jeffrey French, Charles Snowdon, Lucille Roberts, and many others—work that deals with a variety of species of marmosets and tamarins—we now know that all sorts of hormonal changes are associated with increased nurturing in males. For example, in the tufted-eared marmosets studied by French and colleagues, testosterone levels in males went down as they engaged in caretaking after the birth of an infant. Testosterone levels tended to be lowest in those with the most paternal experience.

The biggest surprise, however, has been that something similar goes on in males of our own species. Anne Storey and colleagues in Canada have reported that prolactin levels in men who were living with pregnant women went up toward the end of the pregnancy. But the most significant finding was a 30 percent drop in testosterone in men right after the birth. (Some endocrinologically literate wags have proposed that this drop in testosterone levels is due to sleep deprivation, but this would probably not explain the parallel testosterone drop in marmoset males housed with parturient females.) Hormonal changes during pregnancy and lactation are, of course, indisputably more pronounced in mothers than in the men consorting with them, and no one is suggesting that male consorts are equivalent to mothers. But both sexes are surprisingly susceptible to infant signals—explaining why fathers, adoptive parents, wet nurses, and day-care workers can become deeply involved with the infants they care for.

Genetic relatedness alone, in fact, is a surprisingly unreliable predictor of love. What matters are cues from infants and how these cues are processed emotionally. The capacity for becoming emotionally hooked—or primed—also explains how a fully engaged father who is in frequent contact with his infant can become more committed to the infant's well-being than a detached mother will.

But we can't forget the real protagonist of this story: the baby. From birth, newborns are powerfully motivated to stay close, to root—even to creep—in quest of nipples, which they instinctively suck on. These are the first innate behaviors that any of us engage in. But maintaining contact is harder for little humans to do than it is for other primates. One problem is that human mothers are not very hairy, so a human mother not only has to position the baby on her breast but also has to keep him there. She must be motivated to pick up her baby even *before* her milk comes in, bringing with it a host of hormonal transformations.

Within minutes of birth, human babies can cry and vocalize just as other primates do, but human newborns can also read facial expressions and make a few of their own. Even with blurry vision, they engage in eye-to-eye contact with the people around them. Newborn babies, when alert, can see about eighteen inches away. When people put their faces within range, babies may reward this attention by looking back or even imitating facial expressions. Orang and chimp babies, too, are strongly attached to and interested in their mothers' faces. But unlike humans, other ape mothers and infants do not get absorbed in gazing deeply into each other's eyes.

To the extent that psychiatrists and pediatricians have thought about this difference between us and the other apes, they tend to attribute it to human mental agility and our ability to use language. Interactions between mother and baby, including vocal play and babbling, have been interpreted as protoconversations: revving up the baby to learn to talk. Yet even babies who lack face-to-face stimulation—babies born blind, say—learn to talk. Furthermore, humans are not the only primates to engage in the continuous rhythmic streams of vocalization known as babbling. Interestingly, marmoset and tamarin babies also babble. It may be that the infants of cooperative breeders are specially equipped to communicate with caretakers. This is not to say that babbling is not an important part of learning to talk, only to question which came first—babbling so as to develop into a talker, or a predisposition to evolve into a talker because among cooperative breeders, babies that babble are better tended and more likely to survive.

If humans evolved as cooperative breeders, the degree of a human mother's commitment to her infant should be linked to how much social support she herself can expect. Mothers in cooperatively breeding primate species can afford to bear and rear such costly offspring as they do only if they have help on hand. Maternal abandonment and abuse are very rarely observed among primates in the wild. In fact, the only primate species in which mothers are anywhere near as likely to abandon infants at birth as mothers of our own species are the other cooperative breeders. A study of cotton-top tamarins at the New England Regional Primate Research Center showed a 12 percent chance of abandonment if mothers had older siblings on hand to help them rear twins, but a 57 percent chance when no help was available. Overburdened mothers abandoned infants within seventy-two hours after birth.

This new way of thinking about our species' history, with its implications for children, has made me concerned about the future. So far, most Western researchers studying infant development have presumed that living in a nuclear family with a fixed division of labor (mom nurturing, dad providing) is the normal human adaptation. Most contemporary research on children's psychosocial development is derived from John Bowlby's theories of attachment and has focused on such variables as how available and responsive the mother is, whether the father is present or absent, and whether the child is in the mother's care or in day care. Sure enough, studies done with this model in mind always show that children with less responsive mothers are at greater risk.

It is the baby, first and foremost, who senses how available and how committed its mother is. But I know of no studies that take into account the possibility that humans evolved as cooperative breeders and that a mother's responsiveness also happens to be a good indicator of her social supports. In terms of developmental outcomes, the most relevant factor might not be how securely or insecurely attached to the mother the baby is—the variable that developmental psychologists are trained to measure—but rather how secure the baby is in relation to *all* the people caring for him or her. Measuring attachment this way might help explain why even children whose relations with their mother suggest they are at extreme risk manage to do just fine because of the interventions of a committed father, an older sibling, or a there-when-you-need-her grandmother.

The most comprehensive study ever done on how nonmaternal care affects kids is compatible with both the hypothesis that humans evolved as cooperative breeders and the conventional hypothesis that human babies are adapted to be reared exclusively by mothers. Undertaken by the National Institute of Child Health and Human Development (NICHD) in 1991, the seven-year study included 1,364 children and their families (from diverse ethnic and economic backgrounds) and was conducted in ten different U.S. locations. This extraordinarily ambitious study was launched because statistics showed that 62 percent of U.S. mothers with children under age six were working outside the home and that the majority of them (willingly or unwillingly) were back at work within three to five months of giving birth. Because this was an entirely new social phenomenon, no one really knew what the NICHD's research would reveal.

The study's main finding was that both maternal and hired caretakers' sensitivity to infant needs was a better predictor of a child's subsequent development and behavior (such traits as social "compliance," respect for others, and self-control were measured) than was actual time spent apart from the mother. In other words, the crucial variable was not the continuous presence of the mother herself but rather how secure infants felt when cared for by someone else. People who had been convinced that babies need full-time care from mothers to develop normally were stunned by these results, while advocates of day care felt vindicated. But do these and other, similar findings mean that day care is not something we need to worry about anymore?

Not at all. We should keep worrying. The NICHD study showed only that day care was better than mother care if the mother was neglectful or abusive. But excluding such worst-case scenarios, the study showed no detectable ill effects from day care *only* when infants had a secure relationship with parents to begin with (which I take to mean that babies felt wanted) and *only* when the day care was of high quality. And in this study's context, "high quality" meant that the facility had a high ratio of caretakers to babies, that it had the same caretakers all the time, and that the caretakers were sensitive to infants' needs—in other words, that the day care staff acted like committed kin.

Bluntly put, this kind of day care is almost impossible to find. Where it exists at all, it's expensive. Waiting lists are long, even for cheap or inadequate care. The average rate of staff turnover in day care centers is 30 percent per year, primarily because these workers are paid barely the minimum wage (usually less, in fact, than parking-lot attendants). Furthermore, day care tends to be age-graded, so even at centers where staff members stay put, kids move annually to new teachers. This kind of day care is unlikely to foster trusting relationships.

What conclusion can we draw from all this? Instead of arguing over mother-care versus "other care," we need to make day care better. And this is where I think today's evolution-minded researchers have something to say. Impressed by just how variable child-rearing conditions can be in human societies, several anthropologists and psychologists (including Michael Lamb, Patricia Draper, Henry Harpending, and James Chisholm) have suggested that babies are up to more than just maintaining the relationship with their mothers. These researchers propose that babies actually monitor mothers to gain information about the world they have been born into. Babies ask, in effect, Is this world filled with people who are going to provide for me and help me survive? Can I count on them to care about me? If the answer to those questions is yes, they begin to sense that developing a conscience and a capacity for compassion would be a great idea. If the answer is no, they may then be asking, Can I not afford to count on others? Would I be better off just grabbing what I need, however I can? In this case, empathy, or thinking about others' needs, would be more of a hindrance than a help.

For a developing baby and child, the most practical way to behave might vary drastically, depending on whether the mother has kin who help, whether the father is around, whether foster parents are well-meaning or exploitative. These factors, however unconsciously perceived by the child, affect important developmental decisions. Being extremely self-centered or selfish, being oblivious to others or lacking in conscience—traits that psychologists and child-development theorists may view as pathological—are probably quite adaptive traits for an individual who is short on support from other group members.

If I am right that humans evolved as cooperative breeders, Pleistocene babies whose mothers lacked social support and were less than fully committed to infant care would have been unlikely to survive. But once people started to settle down—10,000 or 20,000 or perhaps 30,000 years ago—the picture changed. Ironically, survival chances for neglected children increased. As people lingered longer in one place, eliminated predators, built walled houses, stored food—not to mention inventing things such as rubber nipples and pasteurized milk—infant survival became decoupled from continuous contact with a caregiver.

Since the end of the Pleistocene, whether in preindustrial or industrialized environments, some children have been surviving levels of social neglect that previously would have meant certain death. Some children get very little attention, even in the most benign of contemporary homes. In the industrialized world, children routinely survive caretaking practices that an Efe or a !Kung mother would find appallingly negligent. In traditional societies, no decent mother leaves her baby alone at any time, and traditional mothers are shocked to learn that Western mothers leave infants unattended in a crib all night.

Without passing judgment, one may point out that only in the recent history of humankind could infants deprived of supportive human contact survive to reproduce themselves. Certainly there are a lot of humanitarian reasons to worry about this situation: one wants each baby, each child, to be lovingly cared for. From my evolutionary perspective, though, even more is at stake.

Even if we manage to survive what most people are worrying about—global warming, emergent diseases, rogue viruses, meteorites crashing into earth—will we still be human thousands of years down the line? By that I mean human in the way we currently define ourselves. The reason our species has managed to survive and proliferate to the extent that 6 billion people currently occupy the planet has to do with how readily we can learn to cooperate when we want to. And our capacity for empathy is one of the things that make us good at doing that.

At a rudimentary level, of course, all sorts of creatures are good at reading intentions and movements and anticipating what other animals are going to do. Predators from gopher snakes to lions have to be able to anticipate where their quarry will dart. Chimps and gorillas can figure out what another individual is likely to know or not know. But compared with that of humans this capacity to entertain the psychological perspective of other individuals is crude.

The capacity for empathy is uniquely well developed in our species, so much so that many people (including me) believe that along with language and symbolic thought, it is what makes us human. We are capable of compassion, of understanding other people's "fears and motives, their longings and griefs and vanities," as novelist Edmund White puts it. We spend time and energy worrying about people we have never even met, about babies left in dumpsters, about the existence of more than 12 million AIDS orphans in Africa.

Psychologists know that there is a heritable component to emotional capacity and that this affects the development of compassion among individuals. By fourteen months of age, identical twins (who share all genes) are more alike in how they react to an experimenter who pretends to painfully pinch her finger on a clipboard than are fraternal twins (who share only half their genes). But empathy also has a learned component, which has more to do with analytical skills. During the first years of life, within the context of early relationships with mothers and other committed caretakers, each individual learns to look at the world from someone else's perspective.

And this is why I get so worried. Just because humans have evolved to be smart enough to chronicle our species' histories, to speculate about its origins, and to figure out that we have about 30,000 genes in our genome is no reason to assume that evolution has come to a standstill. As gene frequencies change, natural selection acts on the outcome: the expression of those genes. No one doubts, for instance, that fish benefit from being able to see. Yet species reared in total darkness—as are the small cave-dwelling characin of Mexico—fail to develop their visual capacity. Through evolutionary time, traits that are unexpressed are eventually lost. If populations of these fish are isolated in caves long enough, youngsters descended from those original populations will no longer be able to develop eyesight at all, even if reared in sunlight.

If human compassion develops under particular rearing conditions, and if an increasing proportion of the species survives to breeding age without developing compassion, it won't make any difference how useful this trait was among our ancestors. It will become like sight in cave-dwelling fish.

No doubt our descendants thousands of years from now (should our species survive) will still be bipedal, symbol-generating apes. Most likely they will be adept at using sophisticated technologies. But will they still be human in the way we, shaped by a long heritage of cooperative breeding, currently define ourselves?

# 7

# Apes, Hominids, and the Roots of Religion

*Barbara J. King*

Around 28,000 years ago a group of Neandertals buried two children approximately 125 miles north of present-day Moscow. The older child, a teenage boy, was adorned with nearly 5,000 beads and a belt decorated with 250 polar fox teeth. To his right, they placed a long ivory lance, and under his left shoulder a mammoth sculpture made of ivory. The younger child was a girl with more than 5,000 beads covering her body. Why did the survivors bury these children with beads and ivory lances, and why did they place a mammoth sculpture under the boy's left shoulder versus the small ivory disc near the young girl's head?

Under specific circumstances such as the death of a child, human and non-human primates typically display empathy and compassion. In his book *The Age of Empathy*, behavioral biologist Frans de Waal describes empathy as a shared behavior common throughout the animal kingdom. Compassion may have been an evolutionarily advantageous behavior for our primate ancestors, but could it also be an origin of the human religious experience?

Apart from our empathetic imagination, we will never truly understand the full significance of a mammoth sculpture placed beneath a Neandertal shoulder, but the attentive, aesthetic details of this Paleolithic burial suggest a compassionate and shared, emotional experience among the survivors. In this chapter, primatologist Barbara King argues that empathy, decorative burials, and shared emotional experiences may be the evolutionary roots of contemporary religion.

***As you read this selection, consider the following questions:***

- According to the author, human religious practices may be rooted in which particular behaviors of our primate ancestors?
- What is "belongingness" and why does the author argue that it is a viable evolutionary explanation for the origins of religious practices?
- What can the study of primate behavior contribute to our understanding of the origins of human religion?
- What evidence supports the presence of emotional connections and (pre)religious behaviors of Neandertals?

***The following terms discussed in this selection are included in the Glossary at the back of the book:***

*agency detection*
*cognitive empathy*
*French Neandertal Mask*
*religion*

For many years, Bibi and Ernie, zoo gorillas, are mates and close friends. Together they weather the rare transfers to new environments and the routine challenges of life. When Bibi, the older of the two apes, begins to decline, Ernie, who as a brash young male stole her sleeping nests from her, offers his own soft nest for her to use. As Bibi weakens, Ernie refuses to leave her side. When she dies, Ernie visibly, and audibly, grieves.

Two male chimpanzees enter into a screaming, arm-waving altercation, a conflict that verges on the violent. Afterwards, the loser, nursing a bad bite, sits alone, hunched and quiet. A third chimpanzee walks up and lays a consoling hand on his shoulder.

In what is now France, a group of Neandertals clusters around a freshly dug hole in the earth. Group members lower the body of a companion into the grave, laying it atop a series of stones. They cover the body with a slab of rock on which they place tools and a worked bear bone. With an elk antler, they mark the grave and light a flame there.

On the walls of caves in Africa and Europe, early *Homo sapiens* artists paint images that occasionally

King, Barbara J. "Apes, Hominids, and the Roots of Religion." Reproduced by permission of the American Anthropological Association from *General Anthropology: Bulletin of the General Anthropology Division*, Volume 16, Issue 2, pp. 1–8, September 2009. Not for sale or further reproduction. King's blog and information about her recent work on human-animal bonds are featured on www.barbarajking.com.

**Note the tone of certainty of these high-profile reports:**

> "Large agreement is emerging that selective pressures over the course of human evolution can explain the wide cross-cultural recurrence, historical persistence, and predictable cognitive structures of religious beliefs and behaviors. The tendency to detect agency in nature likely supplied the cognitive template that supports the pervasive belief in supernatural agents." (Norenzayan and Shariff 2008, p. 58).

> "The data support [this] conclusion: religious thoughts seem to be an emergent property of our standard cognitive capacities," including the agency-detection capacity. (Boyer 2008, p. 1039, see also Boyer 2001.)

If the judgment of "large agreement" is an accurate reflection of today's scholarship, I am not in the majority! In the spirit of a good quote, I offer the following response: "The expansion of belongingness to a spiritual realm emerged from mutuality and from hominids' talent for constructing their lives around emotional engagement with others" (King 2007:183).

In other words, my view is that the drumbeat of *cognitive, cognitive, cognitive* in the agency-detection theorizing misses the explanatory importance of belongingness in the origins of religion. In my work I offer, as Robert Sloan Wilson does in his, in a somewhat different way, an alternative to ideas that cede primacy to non-social processes in religion's origins. We anthropologists need, and should thrive on, alternative ideas about the origins of behaviors so lost to us in time. It's as much in our cross-talk about our ideas, as it is in publishing those ideas in the first place, that we will move forward in understanding our past.

It is challenging to test predator detection versus belongingness hypotheses against the paleoanthropological "on the job," for the elderly or unwell who grew tired as the group traversed long distances. This isn't some feel-good, woo-woo school of paleoanthropology: record. However, evidence that indicates our ancestors came together in highly emotional, highly dynamic rituals that verge on the supernatural (see Mithen 2005) supports a focus on belongingness over a focus only on evolved agency detection capabilities. The belongingness ideas predict more findings like the ones that I have laid out in my new book *Being With Animals*—half human, half animal hybrid images in cave paleo-art of France (with possible parallels to shamanism), spectacular temples meant as regional gathering places for worship as found in Gobekli Tepe in today's Turkey, and rich animal-human double burials across a number of continents and time periods. In short, belongingness is a good candidate as an evolutionary explanation for the deepest roots of human religiosity.

## REFERENCES


Armstrong, K. 2006. *The Great Transformation: The Beginning of our Religious Traditions*. New York: Alfred A. Knopf.

Bekoff, M. and J. Pierce. 2009. *Wild Justice: The Moral Lives of Animals*. Chicago: University of Chicago Press.

Boesch, C. and H. Boesch-Achermann. 2000. *The Chimpanzees of Tai Forest: Behavioural Ecology and Evolution*. Oxford, England: Oxford University Press.

Boyer, C. 2008. Religion: bound to believe? *Nature* 455:1038–1039.

——. 2001. *Religion Explained*. New York: Basic Books.

Durkheim, E. 2001. *The Elementary Forms of the Religious Life*. Carol Cosman, trans. Oxford: Oxford University Press.

Geertz, C. 1973. *The Interpretation of Cultures*. New York: Basic Books.

Goodall, J. 2007. The Dance of Awe. In Waldau, P. and Patton, K. (eds.) *A Communion of Subjects: Animals in Religion, Science, and Ethics*. New York: Columbia University Press.

King, B.J. 2007. *Evolving God: A Provocative View on the Origins of Religion*. New York: Doubleday.

—. 2010. *Being With Animals: Why We are Obsessed with the Furry, Scaly, Feathery Creatures Who Populate Our World*. New York: Doubleday.

Mithen. S.J. 2005. *The Singing Neanderthals: The Origins of Music, Language, Mind, and Body*. London: Weidenfeld and Nicolson.

Norenzayan, A. and Shariff, A.F. 2008. The Origin and Evolution of Religious Prosociality. *Science* 322:58-62.

Rappaport, Roy. 1999. *Ritual and Religion in the Making of Humanity*. Cambridge: Cambridge University Press.

de Waal, F.M.B. 2007. *Our Inner Ape: A Leading Primatologist Explains Why We Are Who We Are*. New York: Riverhead.

Wilson, D.S. 2002. *Darwin's Cathedral: Evolution, Religion, and the Nature of Society*. Chicago: University of Chicago Press.

Wright, R. 2009. *The Evolution of God*. New York: Little, Brown, and Co.

# 8

# How Race Becomes Biology: Embodiment of Social Inequality

*Clarence C. Gravlee*

One hundred years ago, the father of American Anthropology, Franz Boas, demonstrated that the "bodily forms" of Italian immigrants in New York City were quite different than their American-born offspring. The children of immigrants were taller and had larger "cranial capacities." Boas was arguing against theories of racial determinism—that there are genetically based inequalities between social groups; such ideas later became the intellectual basis of Nazi ideology and the Holocaust. Boas was showing that human biology is not fixed but is sensitive to local environmental circumstances like diet. Although anthropologists have shown that the concept of race is "bad biology," the simplistic thinking about genetics as the cause of health inequalities still persists.

In this selection, Clarence Gravlee explains how socially defined race becomes biology through biocultural processes of stress in reaction to racist social interactions and discrimination. These complex processes, which involve multiple levels of causation, are best understood with the concept of embodiment. The health inequalities between socially defined groups continue from one generation to the next because the embodiment of race causes low-birth-weight babies and chronic adult diseases. Gravlee demonstrates that the simplistic logic of race and health is based on three fundamental mistakes: that race equals human biological variation, that biology equals genetics, and that race is a myth. His argument combines both biological and cultural anthropological approaches for understanding human differences. This topic continues to be very important for American society.

***As you read this selection, ask yourself the following questions:***

- What are the three classic anthropological critiques of the race concept?
- What is the difference between the "phenotype of skin pigmentation" and the "cultural significance of skin color"?
- What is intellectually appealing about the notion that "race equals genetic variation"? Why is this a theme in medical research?
- How did the tragedy of September 11, 2001, affect the health of mothers and children with Arab surnames in the United States?
- What does the author mean when he says that there is more genetic variation within races than between races?

***The following terms discussed in this section are included in the Glossary in the back of the book:***

*cultural construction*
*embodiment*
*epidemiology*
*phenotype*
*racism*

A recent cover story in *Scientific American* posed a question that has gained new life: "Does race exist?" (Bamshad and Olson, 2003). For decades, there seemed to be broad agreement among anthropologists and geneticists that the answer was "no," but some observers suggest that the consensus is unraveling (e.g., Leroi, 2005). Indeed, in both the scientific literature and the popular press, there is renewed debate over the magnitude and significance of genetic differences between racially defined groups (Jorde and Wooding, 2004; Keita et al., 2004; Ossorio and Duster, 2005; Bakalar, 2007; Drexler, 2007).

Gravlee, Clarence C. "How Race Becomes Biology: Embodiment of Social Inequality." *American Journal of Physical Anthropology* 139 (2009):47–57. 

Yet much of the debate falters on the question—does race exist?—because it can be interpreted in different ways. The implicit question is usually whether race exists as a natural biological division of humankind. This question is important but incomplete. We should also ask in what ways race exists as a sociocultural phenomenon that has force in people's lives—one with biological consequences.

In this article, I take up these questions in the context of the current interdisciplinary debate over racial inequalities in health (Dressler et al., 2005a). This debate is important for three reasons. First, the magnitude of racial inequalities in health demands attention. In the United States, where debate over race is most intense, the risk of morbidity and mortality from every leading cause is patterned along racial lines (Keppel et al., 2002). The burden of poor health is especially high for African Americans: Between 1945 and 1999, more than 4.3 million African Americans died prematurely, compared to their white counterparts (Levine et al., 2001). This inequality needs to be explained and addressed.

Second, debate over race and health provides an important opportunity to advance scientific and public understanding of race, racism, and human variation. In recent years, several high-profile journals have devoted special issues to race; in each case, racial inequalities in health were a major focus of debate (*Nature Genetics*, 2004; *American Journal of Public Health*, 2005; *American Psychologist*, 2005). Moreover, when research on race and human variation makes the news, it often has to do with race, medicine, and disease (e.g., Wade, 2002, 2004; Bakalar, 2007; Drexler, 2007). Thus, if anthropologists want to reconcile race for anyone other than ourselves, we have to engage the debate over racial inequalities in health.

Third, the association between race and health exposes the inadequacy of the conventional critique of race in anthropology and other social sciences. Social scientists often dismiss race as a cultural construct, not a biological reality (e.g., Palmié, 2007; Shaw, 2007). However, this position requires more nuance. If race is not biology, some may ask, why are there such clear differences among racially defined groups in a range of biological phenomena? This question highlights the need to move beyond "race-as-bad-biology" (Goodman, 1997, p 22) to explain *how race becomes biology*.

There are two senses in which race becomes biology. First, the sociocultural reality of race and racism has biological consequences for racially defined groups. Thus, ironically, biology may provide some of the strongest evidence for the persistence of race and racism as sociocultural phenomena. Second, epidemiological evidence for racial inequalities in health reinforces public understanding of race as biology; this shared understanding, in turn, shapes the questions researchers ask and the ways they interpret their data—reinforcing a racial view of biology. It is a vicious cycle: Social inequalities shape the biology of racialized groups, and embodied inequalities perpetuate a racialized view of human biology.

In this article, I address both ways that race becomes biology. To establish the significance of the problem, I begin with a brief review of the epidemiologic evidence regarding racial inequalities in health and show that these inequalities are commonly interpreted as evidence of fundamental, genetic differences between "races." Then, given the persistence of racial–genetic determinism, I argue that it is necessary to clarify and refine the critique of race in three ways: 1) to reiterate why race is insufficient for describing human genetic diversity, 2) to promote a more complex, biocultural view of human biology, and 3) to take seriously the claim that race is a cultural construct that profoundly shapes life chances. Drawing on social epidemiology and allied fields, I propose a model for anthropological research on racial inequalities in health that emphasizes the development and intergenerational transmission of racial health disparities across multiple levels of analysis. This model improves on the standard critique, which dismissed race as bad biology without offering a constructive framework for explaining biological differences among racially defined groups. It also entails a shift in how we articulate the critique of race as bad biology.

## WHAT IS RACE?

Debate about race often founders on ambiguity in the definition of race. Following Smedley (2007, p 18), I define race as a worldview: "a culturally structured, systematic way of looking at, perceiving, and interpreting" reality. In North America, a central tenet of the racial worldview is that humans are naturally divided into a few biological subdivisions. These subdivisions, or races, are thought to be discrete, exclusive, permanent, and relatively homogenous (Keita and Kittles, 1997; Banton, 1998; Smedley, 2007). The race concept also implies that the superficial traits used to distinguish races reflect more fundamental, innate biological differences (Smedley, 2007). This definition should not be taken to mean that race is merely a bad idea. Race emerged from unique material circumstances in English North America (Harris, 1964), and racism remains embedded in social, political, and economic structures in the United States (Feagin, 2006).

Some researchers (e.g., Long and Kittles, 2003) distinguish between folk and scientific definitions of race. This distinction may be misleading, because scientists have played a pivotal role in constructing and legitimating race for centuries (Brace, 2005). The key elements of the racial worldview persisted in anthropology well into the twentieth century (Caspari, 2003), and it still shapes much research on race and health.

## RACE AND HEALTH: EPIDEMIOLOGICAL EVIDENCE

There is abundant evidence of health inequalities among racially defined groups in many societies (e.g., Brockerhoff and Hewett, 2000; Cutter et al., 2001; Pan American Health Organization, 2001; Nazroo et al., 2007; Harding et al., 2008). Here, I focus on the United States, where epidemiological data has reflected and reinforced scientific thinking about race for more than 200 years (Krieger, 1987).

Epidemiological evidence in the United States shows that there are substantial racial inequalities in morbidity and mortality across multiple biological systems. The mortality profile is bleakest for African Americans: In 2004, the overall age-adjusted death rate for black Americans was more than 30 percent higher than it was for white Americans; for some leading causes of death, the disparity was substantially higher. Age-adjusted death rates from diabetes, septicemia, kidney disease, and hypertension and hypertensive renal disease were all more than two times higher among African Americans than among whites (Minin˜ o et al., 2007). Cardiovascular disease accounts for the largest share of black–white difference in mortality (34.0 percent), but there are also substantial contributions from infections (21.1 percent), trauma (10.7 percent), diabetes (8.5 percent), renal disease (4.0 percent), and cancer (3.4 percent) (Wong et al., 2002).

Similar inequalities exist in infant mortality and life expectancy. From 1990 to 2004, infant mortality declined by 26 percent (9.2 to 6.8 per 1,000 live births) for the United States as a whole, but the gap between black and white Americans remained approximately the same (see Figure. 1). In 2004, the infant mortality rate among African Americans was 2.4 times the rate of other groups, as compared to 2.3 in 1990 (Keppel et al., 2002; Mathews and MacDorman, 2007). Black–white inequalities in life expectancy at birth narrowed dramatically in the early twentieth century—from 17.8 years in 1903 to less than seven in 1995—but changed relatively little in the second half of the century (Figure. 2). In 1995, the black–white gap in life expectancy was the same as it was 40 years earlier—6.9 years. Only recently has the gap narrowed to its historic low of just over 5 years (National Center for Health Statistics, 2007).

Much of the epidemiological literature focuses on such black–white comparisons. This focus is justified on grounds of the magnitude and historical depth of inequalities between black and white Americans, but crude black–white comparisons are limited in at least three ways. First, they conceal variation in morbidity and mortality profiles within racial categories. Second, they neglect the changing racial demography of the United States, where African Americans are no longer the largest ethnic minority group (Smelser et al., 1999). Third, they imply that race per se is an important cause of health inequalities, rather than focusing on the specific causal factors that shape racial inequalities in health (Kaufman and Cooper, 1995). Both genetic and social epidemiologists are developing new approaches to overcome these limitations (Gonzalez Burchard et al., 2005; Krieger et al., 2005; Murray et al., 2006), but much of the debate is still framed in black and white.

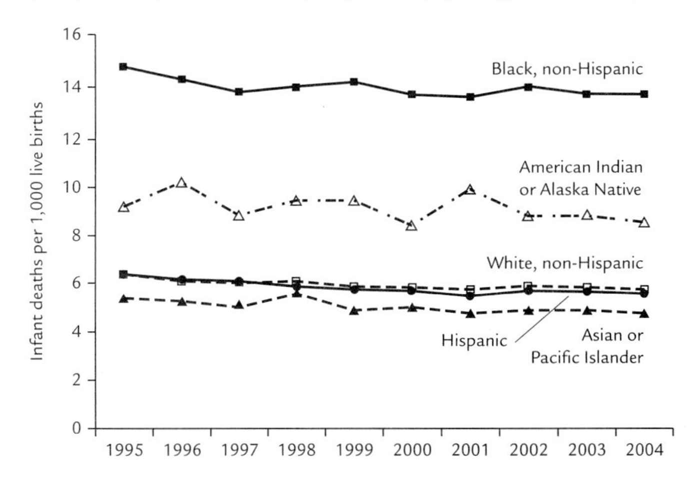


FIGURE. 1. Infant mortality in the United States, 1995–2004, by race and ethnicity (Data source: National Center for Health Statistics. 2007. Health, United States, 2007. Hyattsville: National Center for Health Statistics).

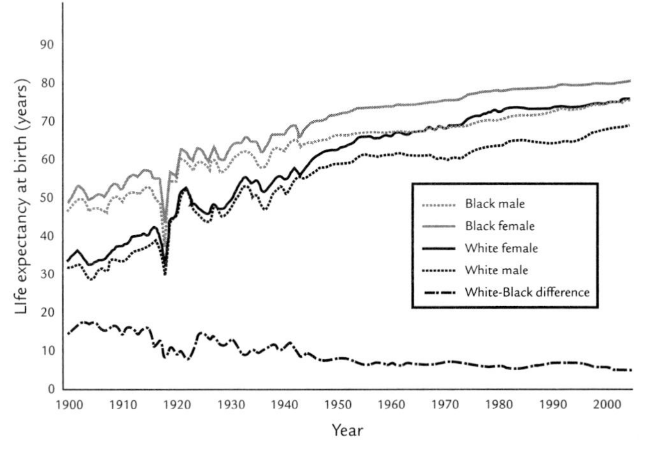


FIGURE. 2. Life expectancy at birth in the United States, 1900–2004, by race and ethnicity (Data source: Arias E. 2006. United States life tables, 2003. Natl Vital Stat Rep 54:1–40; National Center for Health Statistics, 2007).

based on susceptibility alleles (Jorde and Wooding, 2004). Fourth, in racially stratified societies like the United States, continental ancestry is likely to be confounded with many environmental factors; consequently, reported associations between genetic ancestry and disease may be mediated through unmeasured environmental mechanisms (Kaufman and Cooper, 2008). These considerations imply that researchers should test specific hypotheses about the mechanisms linking ancestry and disease and remain cognizant that complex disease involves the interaction of many genetic and environmental influences.

To be clear, the critique of race is neither a denial of human biodiversity, nor a claim that genes are irrelevant to racial inequalities in health. Rather, the central argument is that the race concept is inadequate for describing the complex structure of human genetic variation. Clearly, there is geographic structure to human genetic variation. This structure is most consistent with a model of serial founder effects beginning with a single African origin of our species. Relatively low levels of genetic differentiation across major barriers to gene flow (e.g., Himalayas, the Sahara desert) appear to produce minor discontinuities that can be detected by clustering algorithms (Rosenberg et al., 2005), but to emphasize clustering at the expense of clinal variation and within-region diversity—the dominant signals—is to privilege a typological view of human genetic variation with pre- Darwinian roots (Caspari, 2003).

## Biology ≠ Genetics

The argument that race does not correspond to global patterns of human genetic variation has come to dominate the critique of race. Yet, as important as the genetic evidence is, it understates the case against race. Indeed, the emphasis on genetic evidence may undermine the critique, because it tacitly accepts the primacy of genes in describing and explaining human biological variation. Thus, it is important to expand the critique of race by rejecting naïve reductionism and replacing it with a more complex view of human biology that acknowledges the interplay of organisms and environments over the life course.

This goal may require a shift in the way we articulate the critique of race. Often the critique is condensed to the idea that "race is not biology." Sometimes, this idea appears in the context of more subtle arguments about the complexity of human biology (e.g., Goodman, 2000), but more often it stands alone as a ritual repudiation of the race myth. Despite its popularity in scholarly circles, this ritual has failed to sway public understanding of race. As one observer put it, "Clearly for mainstream popular culture, the idea that race is not biology is still 'surprising' news" (Caminero-Santangelo, 2004, p 207).

The debate over racial inequalities in health brings this problem into sharp relief. Epidemiologic evidence shows that, in a very certain sense, race *is* biology. There are, in fact, well-defined differences between racially defined groups for a range of biological outcomes—cardiovascular disease, diabetes, renal failure, cancer, stroke, and birth outcomes, to name a few. In the face of this evidence, the refrain that race is not biology is impotent at best, counterproductive at worst. The challenge is to move beyond the pat assertion that race is not biology to explain how race *becomes* biology.

This shift in emphasis suggests that we may need to devote as much attention to revising our conception of biology as we do to our conception of race. Some observers may be uneasy with talk of biological differences among racially defined groups. They may worry—with good cause—that such talk reinforces the perception of intrinsic, genetic differences between alleged races. This well-founded concern is important, because it reveals how deeply entrenched the twin assumptions of reductionism and genetic determinism are in our understanding of race (Caspari, 2003) and biology in general (Lewontin, 2000). The idea that it is politically dangerous to discuss biological differences among racially defined groups makes sense only if we (or our audience) implicitly reduce biology to genetics and minimize or ignore the causal influence of external, environmental factors on human biology. The tacit conflation of genes and biology in the conventional critique of race unwittingly perpetuates this form of reductionism.

Recent research on racial inequalities in health provides a counterweight to reductionism and lends support for renewed attention to phenotypic plasticity and a complex view of human biology as biocultural. One influential model is Krieger's ecosocial theory for social epidemiology (Krieger, 1994, 2001). To comprehend humans' dual status as biological organisms and social beings, Krieger proposes the construct of *embodiment*:

> a concept referring to how we literally incorporate, biologically, the material and social world in which we live, from conception to death; a corollary is that no aspect of our biology can be understood absent knowledge of history and individual and societal ways of living (Krieger, 2005, p 352).

There is an obvious affinity between *embodiment* and a century of anthropological research on human biology in the context of culture. Indeed, Franz Boas might be seen as a pioneer in the study of embodiment. His demonstration that descendants of immigrants

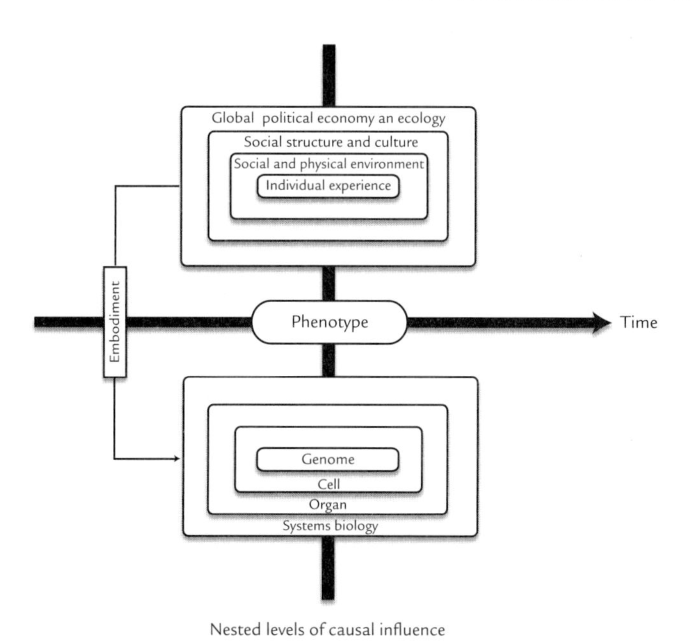


**FIGURE. 3.** Conceptual model for the study of multilevel and developmental influences on phenotype.

embodied the new American environment (Boas, 1912) established plasticity as a central construct in human biology and turned the tide against biological determinism in anthropology (Gravlee et al., 2003). Yet the construct of *embodiment* does work that *plasticity* alone does not. In particular, Krieger's model reflects an emerging consensus that the next wave of research needs to integrate 1) multiple levels of analysis with 2) developmental and life-course perspectives. The conceptual model in Figure 3 illustrates the approach, drawing on previous recommendations for research on the social patterning of health (e.g., Kaplan, 2004; Glass and McAtee, 2006; Diez Roux, 2007; Krieger, 2008).

A key feature of this model is that it situates phenotype at the intersection of two axes. The first (horizontal) axis represents time. This axis may reflect life-course, developmental processes at an individual level or historical change at a population level (Glass and McAtee, 2006). The second (vertical) axis represents the nested hierarchy of causal influences on phenotypes, ranging from the genome to global political economy and ecology. The line depicting embodiment represents the direct and indirect influences of sociocultural context at multiple scales and levels (Krieger, 2008) on gene expression and biological functioning. Although the model draws on current developments in health-related social sciences, the main elements and connections are also recognized in anthropology (e.g., Baker, 1997; Goodman and Leatherman, 1998; Kuzawa and Pike, 2005).

The model applies to population health in general, but a growing body of evidence establishes its importance for explaining racial inequalities in health in particular. First, recent research on the health effects of racism points to direct and indirect effects of racism across multiple levels of analysis. At an individual level, the experience of unfair treatment or interpersonal discrimination has a wide range of embodied consequences (Krieger, 1999). Researchers in several societies have linked self-reported experiences of discrimination to elevated blood pressure (Steffen et al., 2003; Brondolo et al., 2008), breast cancer (Taylor et al., 2007), coronary artery calcification (Lewis et al., 2006), body mass index (Gee et al., 2008), abdominal adiposity (Vines et al., 2007), preterm birth (Dole et al., 2004), low birth weight (Mustillo et al., 2004), depression (Williams et al., 2003; Borrell et al., 2006; Kelaher et al., 2008), and other aspects of mental and physical health and health-related behaviors (Harris et al., 2006; Borrell et al., 2007; Chae et al., 2008; Ryan et al., 2008).

At a higher level of analysis, studies show that institutionalized racism contributes to racial disparities in health, above and beyond individual factors. In particular, Williams and Collins (2001) argue that racial residential segregation is a fundamental cause of racial inequalities in health, because it a) constrains opportunities for success on traditional markers of individual SES such as education, occupational status, or income, and b) creates pathogenic social contexts that influence the distribution of disease. Recent studies bear out this argument. Residential segregation has been associated with overweight and obesity (Chang, 2006), low birth weight (Grady, 2006), fetal growth restriction (Bell et al., 2006), cardiovascular disease (Cooper et al., 2001), tuberculosis (Acevedo-Garcia, 2000), and all-cause mortality (Inagami et al., 2006). A related body of research links a variety of neighborhood conditions to health, independent of individual- level risk factors (Ellen et al., 2001; Sampson et al., 2002; Diez Roux, 2003; Kawachi and Berkman, 2003; Zenk et al., 2005; Cozier et al., 2007; Primack et al., 2007; O'Campo et al., 2008). One recent study in Chicago, for example, found that the unadjusted odds of hypertension were 80 percent higher for African Americans than for whites; controlling for individual-level factors reduced the disparity only slightly, but adding neighborhood- level variables completely eliminated the black- white gap in prevalence of hypertension (Morenoff et al., 2007).

There is also evidence that structures and events at even higher levels of analysis reverberate to the individual level. A recent study of birth outcomes before and after September 11, 2001, provides a dramatic example. Lauderdale (2006) examined birth certificate data for all California births during the 6 months after September 2001, compared to the same period 1 year earlier. They found that women with Arabic names—and *only* women with Arabic names—experienced a

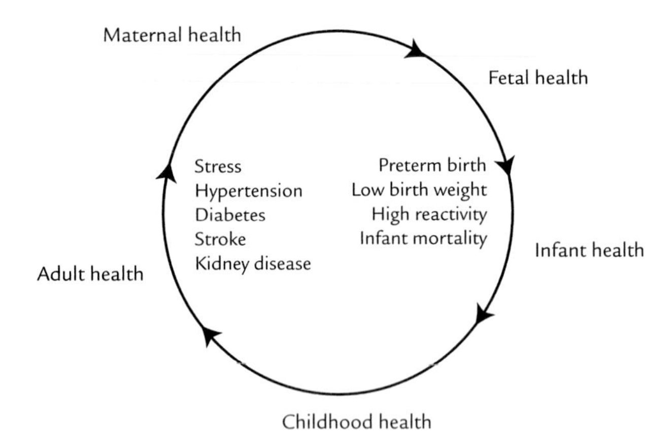


**FIGURE. 4.** Conceptual model for the emergence and persistence of health inequalities over the life course and across generations [adapted from Kuzawa (2008)].

34 percent increased in the likelihood of having a low birth weight infant after 9/11. Moreover, the effect appeared to be moderated by parents' strength of ethnic identification: Infants who were given ethnically distinctive Arabic names had twice the risk of low birth weight after the attacks of September 2001, compared to 1 year earlier. This finding hints at how events structured by global political–economic forces may have embodied consequences that are often hidden from view (Krieger, 2008).

Second, a growing body of research addresses the time axis (see Figure. 3) and suggests that inequalities across multiple levels of analysis have lingering effects across the life course and even from one generation to the next. This body of work draws on life course epidemiology (Davey Smith, 2003; Kuh and Shlomo, 2004) and on recent developments in evolutionary and developmental biology (West-Eberhard, 2003; Gluckman and Hanson, 2005; Jablonka and Lamb, 2005). The synthesis of these fields has the potential to produce a minor revolution in how we think about racial differences in biology, because it identifies the biological—but not genetic—pathways through which social disadvantage may be transmitted from one generation to the next (Schell, 1997; Drake and Walker, 2004; Gluckman et al., 2007).

Figure 4, adapted from Kuzawa (2008), illustrates the general model. The toxic effects of exposure to racism in one's own lifetime include a higher risk of hypertension, diabetes, stroke, and other conditions (Williams, 1999; Geronimus, 2001). These conditions, in turn, affect the health of the next generation, because they alter the quality of the fetal and early postnatal environment. The immediate consequence of this intergenerational effect is a higher risk of adverse birth outcomes (Rosenberg et al., 2002; Collins et al., 2004; Mustillo et al., 2004; Giscombe´ and Lobel, 2005; Bell et al., 2006; Dominguez et al., 2008), but there is also a lingering effect into adulthood, as adult chronic diseases like heart disease and diabetes can be traced in part to prenatal and early life conditions (Barker, 2004; Adair and Dahly, 2005; Cruickshank et al., 2005; Pollitt et al., 2005; Junien and Nathanielsz, 2007). Thus, the cycle begins again.

David and Collins (2007) provide an elegant example of how these life course and intergenerational processes unfold. They first compared birth weights across three groups of women who gave birth in Illinois during 1980–1995: U.S.-born black women, African-born black women, and U.S.-born white women. Contrary to the racial–genetic model, the distribution of birth weight for infants of African-born black women was almost identical to that for U.S.-born white women. By contrast, the entire distribution was shifted downward for U.S.-born black women (David and Collins, 1997). Within a single generation, however, the relative advantage of African and Caribbean-born women began to disappear. The first generation of girls born in the United States to mothers of African descent grew up to have girls of their own with lower mean birth weights—a trend that shifted the distribution toward that of U.S.-born black women (Collins et al., 2002).

This example brings us full circle to the roots of the critique of race in anthropology (Boas, 1912). The major elements of that critique still apply, but it is increasingly clear that we need new ways to articulate the failures of race. The common assertion that "race is not biology" may be correct in spirit, but it is too crude and imprecise to be effective. It does not adequately challenge the reductionism and genetic determinism of contemporary biomedical science or popular culture, and it blinds us to the biological consequences of race and racism as sociocultural phenomena.

## Race ≠ Myth

The counterpart to the assertion that "race is not biology" is the mantra that "race is a cultural construct." As a growing number of cultural anthropologists recognize, this element of the critique also needs to be reexamined. The central problem is that, when biological anthropologists declared race a "myth" (Montagu, 1997), the concept lost its place in anthropology. The rise of "no-race" anthropology (Harrison 1995) came to mean not only that there were no biological races of humankind but also that there was no *discussion* of race in anthropology. Only in the last decade have race and racism reemerged as a major areas of research in cultural anthropology (Mukhopadhyay and Moses 1997; Mullings, 2005).

In advancing this line of research, I suggest that the conceptualization of race as a cultural construct needs to be refined in two ways. First, it cannot be—or appear to be—a wholesale dismissal of human biological diversity. In a recent invited commentary in *American Ethnologist*, Shaw (2007, p 236) laments that anthropology's view of race as "locally variable and socially constructed never captured the popular imagination in the United States":

> For decades, anthropologists have tried to teach the world that commonly used racial categories have little or no biological validity and that race is a social idea used in practices and institutions to give people differential access to opportunities and resources. More recently, amid reports of the Human Genome Project, anthropologists have joined others in trumpeting the homogeneity of the genetic makeup of people around the globe (Shaw, 2007, p 236).

Shaw rightly attributes the staying power of race to deeply embedded political and economic structures that sustain racial thinking and oppose "trumpeting the homogeneity" of humankind, but she does not appear to consider that there may be something wrong with the trumpet: Part of the reason people are not convinced by the claim of homogeneity is that it is false. We are indeed a less variable species than are our closest relatives, but genetic variation exists. Moreover, as current defenders of race emphasize, variation is structured in such a way that there are detectable genetic differences between people who self-identify with conventional racial categories (Risch et al., 2002; Tang et al., 2005). The denial of human genetic variation is, therefore, both false and strategically shortsighted, because it opens the door for a straightforward empirical defense of race.

Second, the view of race as a cultural construct needs to become a starting point for empirical research, rather than an end point in the dismissal of race. To say that race is a cultural construct is not to say it does not exist; cultural constructs have an objective reality despite their reliance on human thought (Searle, 2006). Two avenues for research on racial inequalities in health follow from this observation. The first—an anthropology *of* medicine (Foster, 1974)—examines the cultural construction of race in biomedical research and clinical practice. There is already important work in this area, which shows how hidden assumptions about race shape the formulation of research questions and interpretation of data (e.g., Fullwiley, 2007; Lee, 2007; Montoya, 2007; Hunt and Megyesi, 2008). It would be valuable to have more ethnography of race and racism in clinical settings, especially given evidence for systematic racial bias in the delivery of health care (Braveman and Tarimo, 2002; Smedley et al., 2002; Bhopal, 2007).

Another avenue for research—an anthropology in medicine—is to contribute to explaining the origin and persistence of racial inequalities in health. Chapman and Berggren (2005) argue that anthropologists have an important role to play through the "radical contextualization" of racial inequalities in health. In particular, a major thrust of current research in cultural anthropology is to understand how global political–economic structures shape the local context of people's lives and become embodied in individual sickness and suffering (Nguyen and Peschard, 2003; Farmer, 2004). Integrating this approach with the model in Figure 3 has potential to elucidate the pathways of embodiment through which race becomes biology.

In addition, cultural anthropologists can contribute to interdisciplinary research by developing measurement strategies that take seriously the view of race as a cultural construct. My work on the relationship between skin color and blood pressure illustrates this point (Gravlee and Dressler, 2005; Gravlee et al., 2005). Previous researchers had showed that, within the African Diaspora, people with darker skin had higher average blood pressures than did their lighter skinned counterparts. Some researchers interpreted this pattern as evidence of a racial–genetic predisposition for high blood pressure; others suggested that it may reflect sociocultural factors. Yet previous studies had not tested these alternatives directly, because they conflated two dimensions of skin color: the *phenotype of skin pigmentation and the cultural significance of skin color* as a criterion of social classification.

The distinction between cultural and biological dimensions of skin color requires a measurement strategy that incorporates the cultural meaning of skin color. In Puerto Rico, I adopted a two-phase approach (cf. Dressler et al., 2005b). I first conducted a systematic ethnographic study of the cultural model of *color* (Gravlee, 2005). The ethnography shed light on local ways of talking about skin color and on how *color* shapes Puerto Ricans' exposure to racism and other social stressors. Systematic ethnographic methods (Romney et al., 1986) made it possible to test the assumption that people shared a coherent cultural model of *color*. Colleagues and I then developed a survey measure that explicitly linked respondents to ethnographic data on the cultural model of *color* to estimate how they would be perceived by other Puerto Ricans in everyday social interaction. In a small epidemiologic survey, we compared blood pressure to *color*, as defined by the local cultural model, and to skin pigmentation, as measured by reflectometry. The key finding was that both self-rated and culturally ascribed *color*—but not skin pigmentation—were associated with blood pressure through an interaction with income and education (Gravlee and Dressler, 2005;

Gravlee et al., 2005). This finding suggests that empirical research on *how* race is culturally constructed better positions us to identify the biological consequences of cultural constructs like *race* in the United States or *color* in Puerto Rico.

## CONCLUSION

Race has played a pivotal yet tortured role in the history of anthropology. In the nineteenth and early twentieth century, anthropologists were central in legitimating race as a framework for understanding human biological variation. By the mid-twentieth century, most anthropologists rejected race as biology, and the view of race as a cultural construct came to dominate the social sciences. However, the anthropological critique of race has had only partial success. In particular, current debate over racial inequalities in health exposes important weaknesses in the usual framing of the critique and points the way toward a more constructive approach to the links between race, biology, and culture.

The specific challenge is to explain *how race becomes biology*. Our response to this challenge must deal with two senses in which race becomes biology: Systemic racism becomes embodied in the biology of racialized groups and individuals, and embodied inequalities reinforce a racialized understanding of human biology. To break this cycle, I propose that the conventional critique of race needs to be refined in three ways: 1) to clarify why recent genetic findings do not warrant a return to racial thinking, 2) to promote a more complex, biocultural view of human biology, and 3) to revise the conceptualization of race so that it becomes more than a mantra.

These three claims inform a conceptual model for research on the multilevel and developmental influences on racial inequalities in health. This model crosses old fault lines and lays the groundwork for more productive collaboration between the social and biological sciences. The model does not promote a focus on social and cultural factors to the exclusion of genetic ones; rather, it implies that the embodiment of social inequality passes through biological systems regulated by genes. It does not deny human biological variation; rather, it claims that the pattern and causes of human biological variation are more complex than the race concept allows. It does not claim that race is a myth; rather, it treats race as deeply embedded in sociocultural systems. Research on the biological consequences of race and racism can help to reinvigorate the critique of race by offering a constructive framework for explaining biological differences between racially defined groups.

## ACKNOWLEDGMENTS

My thanks go to Heather Edgar and Keith Hunley for organizing and inviting me to participate in the symposium at the University of New Mexico on which this article is based. Connie Mulligan offered helpful comments on my review of literature in population genetics.

## LITERATURE CITED

Acevedo-Garcia D. 2000. Residential segregation and the epidemiology of infectious diseases. Soc Sci Med 51:1143–1161.

Adair L, Dahly D. 2005. Developmental determinants of blood pressure in adults. Annu Rev Nutr 25:407–434.

American Journal of Public Health. 2005. Special issue on "race, genetics, and health disparities." Am J Public Health 95.

American Psychologist. 2005. Special issue on "genes, race, and psychology in the genome era." Am Psychol 60.

Anderson MR, Moscou S. 1998. Race and ethnicity in research on infant mortality. Fam Med 30:224–227.

Bach PB, Schrag D, Brawley OW, Galaznik A, Yakren S, Begg CB. 2002. Survival of black and whites after a cancer diagnosis. JAMA 287:2106–2113.

Bakalar N. 2007. Study points to genetics in disparities in preterm births. New York Times, February 27, 2007, p F5.

Baker PT. 1997. The Raymond Pearl memorial lecture, 1996: the eternal triangle—genes, phenotypes, and environment. Am J Hum Biol 9:93–101.

Bamshad MJ, Olson SE. 2003. Does race exist? Sci Am 289:78–85.

Bamshad MJ, Wooding S, Salisbury BA, Stephens JC. 2004. Deconstructing the relationship between genetics and race. Nat Rev Genet 5:598–609.

Bamshad MJ, Wooding S, Watkins WS, Ostler CT, Batzer MA, Jorde LB. 2003. Human population genetic structure and inference of group membership. Am J Hum Genet 72:578–589.

Banton M. 1998. Racial theories, 2nd ed. Cambridge: Cambridge University Press.

Barbujani G, Belle EMS. 2006. Genomic boundaries between human populations. Hum Hered 61:15–21.

Barker DJP. 2004. The developmental origins of adult disease. J Am Coll Nutr 23:588S–595S.

Barnholtz-Sloan JS, McEvoy B, Shriver MD, Rebbeck TR. 2008. Ancestry estimation and correction for population stratification in molecular epidemiologic association studies. Cancer Epidemiol Biomarkers Prev 17:471.

Bell JF, Zimmerman FJ, Almgren GR, Mayer JD, Huebner CE. 2006. Birth outcomes among urban African-American women: a multilevel analysis of the role of racial residential segregation. Soc Sci Med 63:3030–3045.

Bhopal RS. 2007. Racism in health and health care in Europe: reality or mirage? Eur J Public Health 17:238–241.

Biffl WL, Myers A, Franciose RJ, Gonzalez RJ, Darnell D. 2001. Is breast cancer in young Latinas a different disease? Am J Surg 182:596–600.

Boas F. 1912. Changes in bodily form of descendants of immigrants. New York: Columbia University Press.

Borrell LN, Jacobs DR Jr, Williams DR, Pletcher MJ, Houston TK, Kiefe CI. 2007. Self-reported racial discrimination and substance use in the Coronary Artery Risk Development in Adults Study. Am J Epidemiol 166:1068–1079.

Borrell LN, Kiefe CI, Williams DR, Diez-Roux AV, Gordon-Larsen P. 2006. Self-reported health, perceived racial discrimination, and skin color in African Americans in the CARDIA study. Soc Sci Med 63:1415–1427.

Brace CL. 2005. "Race" is a four-letter word: the genesis of the concept. New York: Oxford University Press.

Braun L. 2006. Reifying human difference: the debate on genetics, race, and health. Int J Health Serv 36:557–573.

Braveman P, Tarimo E. 2002. Social inequalities in health within countries: not only an issue for affluent nations. Soc Sci Med 54:1621–1635.

Brockerhoff M, Hewett P. 2000. Inequality of child mortality among ethnic groups in sub-Saharan Africa. Bull World Health Organ 78:30–41.

Brondolo E, Libby DJ, Denton E-G, Thompson S, Beatty DL, Schwartz J, Sweeney M, Tobin JN, Cassells A, Pickering TG, Gerin W. 2008. Racism and ambulatory blood pressure in a community sample. Psychosom Med 70:49–56.

Brown RA, Armelagos GJ. 2001. Apportionment of racial diversity: a review. Evol Anthropol 10:34–40.

Caminero-Santangelo M. 2004. "Puerto Rican negro": defining race in Piri Thomas's Down These Mean Streets. MELUS 29:205(22).

Caspari R. 2003. From types to populations: a century of race, physical anthropology, and the American Anthropological Association. Am Anthropol 105:63–74.

Chae DH, Takeuchi DT, Barbeau EM, Bennett GG, Lindsey J, Krieger N. 2008. Unfair treatment, racial/ethnic discrimination, ethnic identification, and smoking among Asian Americans in the National Latino and Asian American Study. Am J Public Health 98:485–492.

Chang VW. 2006. Racial residential segregation and weight status among US adults. Soc Sci Med 63:1289–1303.

Chapman RR, Berggren JR. 2005. Radical contextualization: contributions to an anthropology of racial/ethnic health disparities. Health 9:145–167.

Collins JW Jr, David RJ, Handler A, Wall S, Andes S. 2004. Very low birthweight in African American infants: the role of maternal exposure to interpersonal racial discrimination. Am J Public Health 94:2132–2138.

Collins JW Jr, Wu S-Y, David RJ. 2002. Differing intergenerational birth weights among the descendants of US-born and foreign-born Whites and African Americans in Illinois. Am J Epidemiol 155:210–216.

Comstock RD, Castillo EM, Lindsay SP. 2004. Four-year review of the use of race and ethnicity in epidemiologic and public health research. Am J Epidemiol 159:611–619.

Cooper RS, Kaufman JS, Ward R. 2003. Race and genomics. N Engl J Med 348:1166–1170.

Cooper RS, Kennelly JF, Durazo-Arvizu R, Oh HJ, Kaplan G, Lynch J. 2001. Relationship between premature mortality and socioeconomic factors in black and white populations of US metropolitan areas. Public Health Rep 116:464–473.

Corander J, Waldmann P, Marttinen P, Sillanpaa MJ. 2004. BAPS 2: enhanced possibilities for the analysis of genetic population structure. Bioinformatics 20:2363–2369.

Cozier YC, Palmer JR, Horton NJ, Fredman L, Wise LA, Rosenberg L. 2007. Relation between neighborhood median housing value and hypertension risk among black women in the United States. Am J Public Health 97:718–724.

Cruickshank JK, Mzayek F, Liu L, Kieltyka L, Sherwin R, Webber LS, Srinivasan SR, Berenson GS. 2005. Origins of the "black/white" difference in blood pressure: roles of birth weight, postnatal growth, early blood pressure, and adolescent body size: the Bogalusa Heart Study. Circulation 111: 1932–1937.

Cutter J, Tan BY, Chew SK. 2001. Levels of cardiovascular disease risk factors in Singapore following a national intervention programme. Bull World Health Organ 79:908–915.

Davey Smith, G. 2003. Health inequalities: lifecourse approaches. Bristol: Policy Press.

David RJ, Collins JW Jr. 1997. Differing birth weight among infants of U.S.-born Blacks, African-born Blacks, and U.S.-born Whites. N Engl J Med 337:1209–1214.

David RJ, Collins JW Jr. 2007. Disparities in infant mortality: what's genetics got to do with it? Am J Public Health 97:1191–1197.

Diez Roux AV. 2003. Residential environments and cardiovascular risk. J Urban Health 80:569–589.

Diez Roux AV. 2007. Integrating social and biologic factors in health research: a systems view. Ann Epidemiol 17:569–574.

Dole N, Savitz DA, Siega-Riz AM, Hertz-Picciotto I, McMahon MJ, Buekens P. 2004. Psychosocial factors and preterm birth among African American and White women in central North Carolina. Am J Public Health 94:1358–1365.

Dominguez TP, Dunkel-Schetter C, Glynn LM, Hobel C, Sandman CA. 2008. Racial differences in birth outcomes: the role of general, pregnancy, and racism stress. Health Psychol 27:194–203.

Drake AJ, Walker BR. 2004. The intergenerational effects of fetal programming: non-genomic mechanisms for the inheritance of low birth weight and cardiovascular risk. J Endocrinol 180:1–16.

Dressler WW, Oths KS, Gravlee CC. 2005a. Race and ethnicity in public health research: models to explain health disparities. Annu Rev Anthropol 34:231–252.

Dressler WW, Borges CD, Balieiro MC, dos Santos JE. 2005b. Measuring cultural consonance: examples with special reference to measurement theory in anthropology. Field Methods 17:331–355.

Drevdahl D, Taylor JY, Phillips DA. 2001. Race and ethnicity as variables in Nursing Research, 1952–2000. Nurs Res 50:305–313.

Drexler M. 2007. How racism hurts—literally. Boston Globe, July 15, 2007, p E1.

Ellen IG, Mijanovich T, Dillman K-N. 2001. Neighborhood effects on health: exploring the links and assessing the evidence. J Urban Aff 23:391–408.

Farmer P. 2004. An anthropology of structural violence. Curr Anthropol 45:305–317.

Feagin JR. 2006. Systemic racism: a theory of oppression. New York: Routledge.

Foster GM. 1974. Medical anthropology: some contrasts with medical sociology. Med Anthropol Newsl 6:1–6.

Frank R. 2007. What to make of it? The (Re)emergence of a biological conceptualization of race in health disparities research. Soc Sci Med 64:1977–1983.

Fullwiley D. 2007. The molecularization of race: institutionalizing human difference in pharmacogenetics practice. Sci Cult (Lond) 16:1–30.

Gee GC, Ro A, Gavin A, Takeuchi DT. 2008. Disentangling the effects of racial and weight discrimination on body mass index and obesity among Asian Americans. Am J Public Health 98:493–500.

Geronimus AT. 2001. Understanding and eliminating racial inequalities in women's health in the United States: the role of the weathering conceptual framework. J Am Med Womens Assoc 56:133–136, 149–150.

Giscombe´ CL, Lobel M. 2005. Explaining disproportionately high rates of adverse birth outcomes among African Americans: the impact of stress, racism, and related factors in pregnancy. Psychol Bull 131:662–683.

Glass TA, McAtee MJ. 2006. Behavioral science at the crossroads in public health: extending horizons, envisioning the future. Soc Sci Med 62:1650–1671.

Gluckman P, Hanson M. 2005. The fetal matrix: evolution, development and disease. New York: Cambridge University Press.

Gluckman PD, Hanson MA, Beedle AS. 2007. Non-genomic transgenerational inheritance of disease risk. BioEssays 29: 145–154.

Gonzalez Burchard E, Borrell LN, Choudhry S, Naqvi M, Tsai H-J, Rodriguez-Santana JR, Chapela R, Rogers SD, Mei R, Rodriguez-Cintron W, Arena JF, Kittles R, Perez-Stable EJ, Ziv E, Risch N. 2005. Latino populations: a unique opportunity for the study of race, genetics, and social environment in epidemiological research. Am J Public Health 95:2161–2168.

Gonzalez Burchard E, Ziv E, Coyle N, Gomez SL, Tang H, Karter AJ, Mountain JL, Perez-Stable EJ, Sheppard D, Risch N. 2003. The importance of race and ethnic background in biomedical research and clinical practice. N Engl J Med 348:1170–1175.

Goodman AH. 1997. Bred in the bone? Sciences 37:20–25.

Goodman AH. 2000. Why genes don't count (for racial differences in health). Am J Public Health 90:1699–1702.

Goodman AH, Leatherman TL. 1998. Building a new biocultural synthesis: political-economic perspectives on human biology. Ann Arbor: University of Michigan Press.

Grady SC. 2006. Racial disparities in low birthweight and the contribution of residential segregation: a multilevel analysis. Soc Sci Med 63:3013–3029.

Gravlee CC. 2005. Ethnic classification in southeastern Puerto Rico: the cultural model of "color." Soc Forces 83:949–970.

Gravlee CC, Bernard HR, Leonard WR. 2003. Heredity, environment, and cranial form: a re-analysis of Boas's immigrant data. Am Anthropol 105:125–138.

Gravlee CC, Dressler WW. 2005. Skin pigmentation, self-perceived color, and arterial blood pressure in Puerto Rico. Am J Hum Biol 17:195–206.

Gravlee CC, Dressler WW, Bernard HR. 2005. Skin color, social classification, and blood pressure in southeastern Puerto Rico. Am J Public Health 95:2191–2197.

Gravlee CC, Sweet E. 2008. Race, ethnicity, and racism in medical anthropology, 1977–2002. Med Anthropol Q 22:27–51.

Handley LJL, Manica A, Goudet J, Balloux F. 2007. Going the distance: human population genetics in a clinal world. Trends Genet 23:432–439.

Harding S, Teyhan A, Maynard MJ, Cruickshank JK. 2008. Ethnic differences in overweight and obesity in early adolescence in the MRC DASH study: the role of adolescent and parental lifestyle. Int J Epidemiol 37:162–172.

Harris M. 1964. Patterns of race in the Americas. Westport, CT: Greenwood Press.

Harris R, Tobias M, Jeffreys M, Waldegrave K, Karlsen S, Nazroo J. 2006. Racism and health: the relationship between experience of racial discrimination and health in New Zealand. Soc Sci Med 63:1428–1441.

Harrison FV. 1995. The persistent power of "race" in the cultural and political economy of racism. Annu Rev Anthropol 24:47–74.

Hunt LM, Megyesi MS. 2008. The ambiguous meanings of the racial/ethnic categories routinely used in human genetics research. Soc Sci Med 66:349–361.

Inagami S, Borrell LN, Wong MD, Fang J, Shapiro MF, Asch SM. 2006. Residential segregation and Latino, black and white mortality in New York City. J Urban Health 83:406–420.

Jablonka E, Lamb MJ. 2005. Evolution in four dimensions: genetic, epigenetic, behavioral, and symbolic variation in the history of life. Cambridge, MA: The MIT Press.

Jorde LB, Wooding SP. 2004. Genetic variation, classification and 'race.' Nat Genet 36:S28–S33.

Junien C, Nathanielsz P. 2007. Report on the IASO Stock Conference 2006: early and lifelong environmental epigenomic programming of metabolic syndrome, obesity and type II diabetes. Obes Rev 8:487–502.

Kaplan GA. 2004. What's wrong with social epidemiology, and how can we make it better? Epidemiol Rev 26:124–135.

Kaufman JS, Cooper RS. 1995. In search of the hypothesis. Public Health Rep 110:662–666.

Kaufman JS, Cooper RS. 2008. Race in epidemiology: new tools, old problems. Ann Epidemiol 18:119–123.

Kawachi I, Berkman LF. 2003. Neighborhoods and health. New York: Oxford University Press.

Keita SO, Kittles RA. 1997. The persistence of racial thinking and the myth of racial divergence. Am Anthropol 99:534–544.

Keita SO, Kittles RA, Royal CD, Bonney GE, Furbert-Harris P, Dunston GM, Rotimi CN. 2004. Conceptualizing human variation. Nat Genet 36:S17–S20.

Kelaher M, Paul S, Lambert H, Ahmad W, Paradies Y, Davey Smith G. 2008. Discrimination and health in an English study. Soc Sci Med 66:1627–1636.

Keppel KG, Pearcy JN, Wagener DK. 2002. Trends in racial and ethnic-specific rates for the Health Status Indicators: United States, 1990–1998. Healthy People 2000 Stat Notes 23:1–16.

Kistka ZA-F, Palomar L, Lee KA, Boslaugh SE, Wangler MF, Cole FS, DeBaun MR, Muglia LJ. 2007. Racial disparity in the frequency of recurrence of preterm birth. Am J Obstet Gynecol 196:131.e1–131.e6.

Krieger N. 1987. Shades of difference: theoretical underpinnings of the medical controversy on black/white differences in the United States, 1830–1870. Int J Health Serv 17:259 278.

Krieger N. 1994. Epidemiology and the web of causation: has anyone seen the spider? Soc Sci Med 39:887–903.

Krieger N. 1999. Embodying inequality: a review of concepts, measures, and methods for studying health consequences of discrimination. Int J Health Serv 29:295–352.

Krieger N. 2001. Theories for social epidemiology in the 21st century: an ecosocial perspective. Int J Epidemiol 30:668–677.

Krieger N. 2005. Embodiment: a conceptual glossary for epidemiology. J Epidemiol Community Health 59:350–355.

Krieger N. 2008. Proximal, distal, and the politics of causation: what's level got to do with it? Am J Public Health 98:221–230.

Krieger N, Chen JT, Waterman PD, Rehkopf DH, Subramanian SV. 2005. Painting a truer picture of US socioeconomic and racial/ethnic health inequalities: the Public Health Disparities Geocoding Project. Am J Public Health 95:312–323.

Kuh D, Shlomo YB. 2004. A life course approach to chronic diseases epidemiology. Oxford: Oxford University Press.

Kuzawa CW. 2008. The developmental origins of adult health: intergenerational inertia in adaptation and disease. In: Trevathan WR, McKenna JJ, editors. Evolutionary medicine and health: new perspectives. New York: Oxford University Press. p 325–349.

Kuzawa CW, Pike IL. 2005. Introduction. Fetal origins of developmental plasticity. Am J Hum Biol 17:1–4.

Lauderdale DS. 2006. Birth outcomes for Arabic-named women in California before and after September 11. Demography 43:185–201.

Lee SS-J. 2007. The ethical implications of stratifying by race in pharmacogenomics. Clin Pharmacol Ther 81:122–125.

Leroi, AM. 2005. A family tree in every gene. The New York Times, March 14, 2005, p A21.

Levine RS, Foster JE, Fullilove RE, Fullilove MT, Briggs NC, Hull PC, Husaini BA, Hennekens CH. 2001. Black–white inequalities in mortality and life expectancy, 1933–1999: implications for healthy people 2010. Public Health Rep 116:474–483.

Lewis TT, Everson-Rose SA, Powell LH, Matthews KA, Brown C, Karavolos K, Sutton-Tyrrell K, Jacobs E, Wesley DM. 2006. Chronic exposure to everyday discrimination and coronary artery calcification in African American women: the SWAN Heart Study. Psychosom Med 68:362–368.

Lewontin RC. 2000. The triple helix: gene, organism, and environment. Cambridge, MA: Harvard University Press.

Lewontin RC. 1972. The apportionment of human diversity. Evol Biol 6:381–398.

Li JZ, Absher DM, Tang H, Southwick AM, Casto AM, Ramachandran S, Cann HM, Barsh GS, Feldman M, Cavalli-Sforza LL, Myers RM. 2008. Worldwide human relationships inferred from genome-wide patterns of variation. Science 319:1100 1104.

Lin SS, Kelsey JL. 2000. Use of race and ethnicity in epidemiologic research: concepts, methodological issues, and suggestions for research. Epidemiol Rev 22:187–202.

Livingstone FB. 1962. On the non-existence of human races. Curr Anthropol 3:279–281.

Long JC, Kittles RA. 2003. Human genetic diversity and the nonexistence of biological races. Hum Biol 75:449–471.

Manica A, Prugnolle F, Balloux F. 2005. Geography is a better determinant of human genetic differentiation than ethnicity. Hum Genet 118:366–371.

Mathews TJ, MacDorman MF. 2007. Infant mortality statistics from the 2004 period linked birth/infant death data set. Natl Vital Stat Rep 55:1–32.

Miniño AM, Heron MP, Murphy SL, Kochanek KD. 2007. Deaths: final data for 2004. Natl Vital Stat Rep 55:1–120.

Montagu A. 1997. Man's most dangerous myth: the fallacy of race, 6th ed. Walnut Creek, CA: AltaMira Press.

Montoya MJ. 2007. Bioethnic conscription: genes, race, and Mexicana/o ethnicity in diabetes research. Cult Anthropol 22:94–128.

concept of the autonomous individual denies it. After childbirth, the separation between mother and child is complete, and the physiological interrelationship in breast-feeding is obscured by a focus on the infant's nutritional and psychological independence. This has notable health outcomes for both mothers and infants, some of which we will now examine in light of an evolutionary perspective.

## BREAST CANCER

Until the nineteenth century, European medical philosophers observed that well-off women who lived in cities were much more susceptible to breast cancer than women who lived in the countryside. They attributed this difference to the abandonment of breast-feeding, which, they noted, caused numerous other maladies and grave health effects. Even today, not only is breast cancer more common in affluent societies, but within them it is more frequent among the wealthier classes.

The decline in breast-feeding has been part of a broad change in reproductive and child-rearing patterns since the Industrial Revolution. Urban women were the first to undergo the *secular trend* of earlier maturation and greater achieved stature. They experienced earlier puberty, delayed marriage and first birth, fewer pregnancies, and reduced or forsaken breast-feeding. Over time, these patterns diffused through the entire population.

Many of the things we consider "natural" are therefore more like aberrations or deviations from what evolution has produced. To illustrate, a typical woman of a foraging or pre-industrial society reaches puberty and her first menstrual period *(menarche)* at the age of 16 to 18. She becomes pregnant within three or four years, breast-feeds for three or four years, and has a subsequent child four or five years after the first. This sequence repeats itself between four and six times before she reaches menopause at around the age of 45. As a result, she has about 150 ovulations in her lifetime, taking account of non-ovulatory cycles at the near and far end of her reproductive years. Periodic nutritional and exercise stress reduce the number of ovulations even more. Because only half of her children survive long enough to reproduce, population grows very slowly, as was the case until historical times. Lactation has represented humankind's main method of birth control for most of our existence.

In contrast, Western women enjoy a stable food supply, including foods concentrated in fat, protein, and calories, and experience very little stress from exercise and exposure. Over the past centuries, this has caused them, and men, to reach higher stature and lower age at puberty. Girls arrive at menarche at the age of 12 or 13, while menopause is delayed to 50 or 55 years. Significantly, the first birth is postponed for 13 or 14 years, to the age of 25 or 26, and the average number of births is reduced to two or three. The average Western woman breast-feeds for a few months, if at all. Because she spaces feedings at long intervals and supplements with other foods, breast-feeding does not inhibit ovulation for long. As a result, population growth was very rapid in Europe for several centuries (and in many developing countries today) not only because mortality rates were falling but also because women did not have a long interval of infertility associated with lactation.

If she does not take oral contraceptives, the average woman will ovulate around 450 times over her lifetime. Ovulation will rarely be suppressed due to physiological constraints associated with nutritional or exercise stress. This amounts to three or four times as many ovulations over the life-span, and some scholars have suggested that the proportion may be as high as nine times.

The differences in reproductive patterns between women in foraging as opposed to affluent societies match some of the currently known risk factors for women's reproductive cancers (breast, endometrium, ovary), including age at menarche and menopause, *parity* (number of births), and breast-feeding. Differences in diet and physical activity, as well as body composition, also agree with identified non-reproductive risk factors such as fat intake and percent body fat. Together with other factors, they give Western women, especially below the age of 60, at least 20 times the risk of reproductive cancer. The risk for breast cancer may be more than 100 times higher. In nonhuman primates, these cancers are extremely rare.

For all three cancers, earlier age at menarche and later age at menopause increase risk, while greater parity reduces risk. Like these factors, breast-feeding is protective against ovarian cancer because it inhibits ovulation. This reduces the monthly mechanical injury to the ovarian epithelium and the release of hormones by the follicle, which are considered the main elements in the etiology of ovarian cancer. For breast cancer, lactation and earlier first birth are also protective factors.

The breast's susceptibility to carcinogenesis is directly related to the rate of epithelial cell proliferation. Consequently, the lengthening of the period between menarche and first birth widens the window of time in which undifferentiated structures destined to become secretory glands are vulnerable to carcinogenic agents and therefore the initiation of tumors. In breast tissue, cell proliferation is promoted by exposure to estrogen, apparently in concert with progesterone, and cell division rates are highest during the first five years after menarche. With pregnancy and lactation, these structures differentiate and develop, devoting themselves less ardently to cell proliferation. Their cell cycle is longer, and they are more resistant to chemical carcinogens. Subsequent pregnancies may also be protective because they increase the proportion of fully differentiated secretory lobules, until in advanced age pregnancy increases risk by favoring the expansion of initiated tumors.

While the age at first pregnancy seems to be of primary importance and may even modulate the protective effect of breast-feeding and later pregnancies, breast-feeding in itself provides protection against breast cancer in step with the number of children breast-fed and the cumulative duration of breast-feeding. The reason some studies have found no effect or a weak one is that they were based upon the experiences of Western women, who do not generally conform to the ancient pattern of breast-feeding at close intervals for at least a year. Short periods of breast-feeding may in fact provide very little protection.

At the level of the breast fluid, there are lower levels of a potential carcinogen, cholesterol-epoxide, as well as cholesterol, in breast-feeding women, a reduction that persists for two years after childbirth or lactation. Estrogen levels are also lower, protecting the breast tissue directly as opposed to systemically through variations in blood estrogen levels. Breast-feeding also affects the turnover rate of substances in the breast fluid, so that prolonged breast-feeding reduces exposure of the breast epithelial tissue to potential exogenous carcinogens.

Exercise, high consumption of dietary fiber, and low fat consumption and percent body fat are all protective against breast and other cancers. High dietary levels of fat and protein (especially from animal sources) and total calories are associated with higher levels of breast cancer across populations and within subpopulations of single countries. Animal studies have shown that dietary protein promotes tumor development while restriction of protein intake inhibits tumor growth. The enzymes in adipose tissue convert precursor adrenal hormones into active estrogens. Dietary fat raises serum estrogen levels and promotes tumor development and may also play a role in originating tumors. In contrast to Western women, women in foraging societies have low serum estrogen levels.

Western women's skinfold thickness (a measure of the proportion of body fat) is almost twice that of pre-agricultural women. Compared to college athletes, women who are not athletic in college (and less active in adolescence and somewhat less active after college) have two to five times the rates of breast, uterine, and ovarian cancer. Women in affluent societies consume 40 percent or more of their calories in the form of fat, against 20 percent to 25 percent among pre-agricultural women, but only 20 as opposed to 100 grams of fiber per day. Dietary fiber is protective because it reduces free estrogen levels in the blood. It helps to prevent bowel dysfunction, which has been associated with breast cancer, and the severe constipation which can lead to the migration of mutagenic substances from the gastrointestinal tract to the breast fluid.

The protective effect of breast-feeding goes beyond the current generation to the next one, for early nutritional influences seem to have an important effect on later susceptibility to cancer. Breast-feeding contributes to the development and regulation of the immune system, which plays a central role in suppressing the initiation and growth of tumors. It prevents over-consumption of fat, protein, and calories. This influences body size and composition, the baseline against which nutrition works throughout life. That is, breast-feeding prevents the accelerated growth of muscles and fat stores associated with breast cancer risk factors: faster growth rates, earlier menarche, and greater achieved stature and size. Women who have been breast-fed themselves are less likely to develop breast cancer.

We have seen that breast-feeding benefits both the mother and child with respect to prevention of breast cancer. In the mother, breast-feeding according to the ancient pattern influences systemic hormone levels and the micro-environment of the breast tissue, reducing exposure to exogenous and endogenous carcinogens. In the child, breast-milk provides an appropriate balance of nutrients that prevents over-nutrition, rapid growth, and early maturation. This circular interaction of factors expresses and can be predicted by the concept of the mother-infant dyad as a biological interacting pair.

## SUDDEN INFANT DEATH SYNDROME

From a global perspective, Western society's expectation that infants should sleep alone for long hours away from their parents stands out as anomalous, even if it fits well in its cultural context. One unfortunate consequence is that the diffusion of lone infant sleep over the past several generations may be related to the rise in the frequency of infant death from the Sudden Infant Death Syndrome (SIDS).

The meaning of reproduction and child-rearing changed with the emergence of industrial society and its predominance of small, simple families (couples plus children). In this kind of society, the crib symbolizes the child's place and is usually placed in a separate room. By contrast, in rural pre-industrial Europe and in a survey of over 90 contemporary non-Western societies, infants invariably slept in the same bed or room as their parents. SIDS does not appear to exist in these societies, nor is it found among non-human primates or other mammals. In many Western societies, SIDS is the major cause of infant death, though rates are very low among sub-populations in which there is co-sleeping and nocturnal breast-feeding. Peak mortality is between the ages of two and four months, with 90 percent of all deaths occurring before the age of six months.

While there seem to be many intrinsic and secondary factors that affect infants in different ways to bring about SIDS events, one common factor is that SIDS usually happens during sleep. While breast-feeding in itself reduces risk, it is the frequent, intensive, prolonged breast-feeding implying mother–infant co-sleeping that may provide the best environment for avoiding the disease.

Co-sleeping infants lie on their backs or sides with their heads turned toward the breast and feed through the night, often without waking their mothers. Even newborns and very young infants are able to attach to the breast on their own, provided it is within reach. In non-industrialized societies, it is rare for infants younger than one year to sleep long hours with only a few arousals or feedings. They do not increase the length of their longest sleep episode within the first few months, nor do they stop feeding at night, as parents in Western societies expect.

These same patterns are observed in sleep laboratories, where mothers report waking up and feeding their child many times fewer than the number recorded on the monitors. They and their infants move through the various stages of sleep in synchrony, shifting between them more frequently and spending less time in the deep sleep which makes arousal more difficult. If in the laboratory the breast-feeding mother spends the night in a separate room from her child, on average she breast-feeds less than half as often. She also tends to put the child on its stomach when leaving it to sleep alone. Notably, breast-feeding mothers who routinely sleep in a separate room from their infants actually sleep for a shorter amount of time during the night, even though they feed their infants less often and for a shorter overall time period than mothers who co-sleep.

One factor common to a majority of cases is that the infant had been placed on its stomach to sleep: the opposite of the position used by infants who sleep with their mothers and breast-feed throughout the night. This may be due to suffocation because the child is unable to move out of pockets of its own carbon dioxide in puffy mattresses or bean bag cushions. It also may be the result of developmental changes related to a shift in the position of the larynx (windpipe) which takes place at four to six months.

At birth, the larynx is in contact with the back of the palate, allowing air inhaled by the nostrils to go by its own route to the lungs. It then begins to descend in the throat to a position below the back of the tongue, so that the two openings leading to the lungs and stomach lie side by side (which is why food sometimes "goes down the wrong tube"). During this shift, problems can occur if breathing through the nose (which infants greatly prefer) is impeded by a cold or other factor. Breathing through the mouth can be blocked by the uvula (the fleshy structure hanging over the back of the tongue) if it enters the descending larynx, especially if the child is lying at the wrong angle. Huge reductions in SIDS rates have taken place over the past decade in many European countries and the United Kingdom since the initiation of campaigns against the face-down position, and the U.S. is also beginning to show rapid improvement in SIDS rates.

There is more to the story than sleep position, which itself inculpates the crib since co-sleeping is associated with the safer position. More directly, the crib implies isolated, prolonged, deep sleep. Like adults, infants are able to fall into deep sleep, but they are less equipped to arouse themselves out of it. All people have temporary lapses in breathing during the night, but their brains generally respond to them appropriately. Infants are different, for they are born at a much earlier stage of neurological development than other primates, even our closest relatives.

During sleep, infants may need frequent arousals to allow them to emerge from episodes of apnea or cardiorespiratory crisis. External stimuli and parental monitoring from co-sleeping and breast-feeding give them practice at doing so, and keep them from spending long periods of time in deep stages of sleep. SIDS deaths peak at the same age at which the amount of deep sleep relative to REM sleep increases dramatically, at two to three months. Moreover, at this time infants begin to exercise more voluntary control of breathing, as parents notice in their more expressive cries. This is a step toward the speech breathing they will use later, but may complicate breathing in the short term.

The rhythm of sound and silence in the mother's breathing gives the infant auditory stimulation, while contact with her body provides tactile stimulation. The carbon dioxide which her breathing releases into the air they share induces the infant to breathe. Frequent waking for breast-feeding is a behavior common to primates and prevents hypoglycemia, which has been implicated in some SIDS deaths. Human milk also provides immunological protection against several infectious organisms (and preparations of them given as immunizations) considered responsible for some deaths. This protection is especially needed after two months, when inherited maternal antibodies become scarce but the infant's own immune system is not yet developed. Breast-feeding and constant physical contact prevent overheating and the exhausting crying spells which seem to be factors in the disease. In addition, the infant is sensitive to other aspects of its micro-environment, including temperature, humidity, and odors.

While many experts and parents advise against or avoid co-sleeping because they fear suffocating the infant, in fact this risk is very low, especially where people sleep on hard bedding or the floor. Modern bedding is dangerous because of the conformation of bed frames and the use of soft mattresses and heavy coverings. Yet, these factors are at least as relevant to cribs as parents' beds. On the other hand, some parents should not sleep with their infants, such as those who go to bed affected by drugs or alcohol. Cigarette smoke in the sleeping room could cancel the benefit of co-sleeping.

While isolated infant sleep may be consistent with parents' desires and the primacy of the conjugal bond and other Western values, it is a new behavioral norm in human history and does not represent a "natural" need. It is neither in the infant's best interest nor in conformity with behavioral patterns and biological conditions established long before our time. By contrast, parent–infant co-sleeping matches evolutionary considerations such as the need for temperature regulation, frequent nutrition, and protection from predators and disease. There may be some wisdom to the popular term, "crib death," or "cot death," for it points to the crib and the Western concept of infant independence as major factors in the disease.

## SOCIAL AND CULTURAL INTERVENTION

We have seen that mothers and infants are physiologically bound together from conception to weaning, not just conception to birth. The Western ideal of the autonomous individual, even the neonate, is not shared by other societies today or by those of the past. The biocultural model shows that evolution has favored frequent, exclusive, and prolonged breast-feeding in humans. This entails constant physical contact, parent–infant co-sleeping, and nighttime breast-feeding. It leads to postpartum infertility and protects against SIDS and breast and other reproductive system cancers. Breast-feeding, therefore, has significant health outcomes, beyond the usual benefits of breast-milk, which have been popularized in recent years.

Unfortunately, the health benefits of breast-feeding, especially for mothers, are generally overshadowed by assertions regarding the supposed convenience of bottle feeding and the nutritional adequacy of artificial milk. Even the promotion of breast-feeding on the basis of the milk's value to infants does not always induce women to breast-feed, since there is little if any mention of a benefit to them. To the contrary, there are many disincentives to breast-feeding, such as beliefs that it causes the breasts to sag and makes it difficult to lose weight, or that it makes the husband feel jealous and left out. The lack of familiarity with breast-feeding which has resulted from a couple of generations of preference for the bottle also discourages it. Many people have never seen a woman breast-feed, and would prefer not to.

The degree to which our culture has come to favor intervention in the fundamental relationship between nurslings and mothers is evident in the nearly universal use of pacifiers. This has been promoted by the notion, sanctioned by professional medicine, that infants need to suckle, and better a scientifically designed object than the thumb or finger (the nipple is not even among the choices). However, in evolutionary perspective, a pacifier is completely unnecessary since infants who are breast-fed according to the ancient pattern are allowed to suckle to their heart's content. Not surprisingly, pacifier use has been found to reduce the duration of breast-feeding.

The birthing process is focused upon the infant, while the mother is considered and often treated as an impediment to the physician's efforts to extract the child. Afterward, the medical care of the two is split between obstetricians and pediatricians, reflecting the conceptual splitting of the mother–infant relationship at birth. There is little or no breast-feeding (in the United States, only one half of all infants begin life feeding at the breast). Weaning takes place within a few months and almost always within the first year, and the mother resumes her menstrual cycle within a few months. Mothers are strongly encouraged to put their children on feeding schedules and eliminate nighttime feeding as quickly as possible, and to teach them to get to sleep and stay asleep on their own, in their own bed and room. Instead of being carried and cuddled throughout the day and night, infants are left in cribs, strollers, and playpens and are touched relatively rarely. They are expected to cry and left to do so, sometimes for hours. Often, the door to their room is closed at nap time and during the night.

On a social-structural level, cultural interference in breast-feeding seems to be more common in societies which are based upon vertical inheritance and the simple family structure, than societies in which families are wide and inheritance is lateral. In the former, the institution of marriage is emphasized over kin relationships. Women's sexual and conjugal duties take precedence over their role as kinswomen and mothers, while children are considered heirs rather than links in a kinship network. These conditions can make breast-feeding seem to interfere with sexuality, and pit the husband against the child in competition over the woman's sexualized breast.

Notably, our culture describes breasts as "secondary *sexual* characteristics," highlighting a tendency to regard them as objects of display rather than functional organs. In medieval to modern Europe, the post-partum taboo against sex during lactation was circumvented among the elite classes by wet-nursing, so that women could be available to their husbands instead of breast-feeding. This was subsequently replaced by formula feeding and practiced by a much wider segment of the population.

The rise of the modern nation-state over the past two centuries meanwhile has brought an expansion of the authority of medical experts. Beginning with early industrialization, the state and its emerging medical system sought to shape public morality and oppose traditional authority by reaching into the private, intimate world of the family. As a result, reproduction and child-rearing became medicalized well before professional medicine had much legitimate knowledge or expertise in these areas. As multiple families broke up due to socioeconomic changes, families became more dependent upon outside experts in areas which had previously been handled by older relatives or other authorities such as midwives and clerics.

By now, it is rare for anyone to question the authority of the medical community in questions such as birth control or infant feeding. This phenomenon has emerged hand-in-hand with the notion of the autonomous individual. By considering fetuses and infants as beings independent of their mothers, Western society has allowed and welcomed experts into the life of the dyad and granted them predominant authority in decisions regarding the care and upbringing of the young. Mothers are not encouraged to think of themselves as competent or knowledgeable enough to breast-feed without expert intervention and surveillance. This is reinforced by the regimen of ever-more numerous obstetric and pediatric examinations before and after childbirth, and the literature directed at mothers by the medical and pharmaceutical communities.

In contrast to agricultural and foraging societies, in ours breast-feeding does not easily fit into women's work or social lives. Few professions allow women much flexibility in time scheduling, and there is a deep, underlying expectation that the new mother will immediately be independent from her child. Many working women are forced to pump their milk in bathrooms, often in secrecy. Women who do not work outside the home are targeted by formula manufacturers, who capitalize on cultural values such as work and efficiency by suggesting that formula feeding with an increasingly complex array of products demonstrates a woman's capability in scientific mothering.

Firms that sell formula, pacifiers, and other infant care products distribute samples and coupons through hospitals and physicians' offices, lending their products a medical stamp of approval that appeals to many parents. Often, they are able to "hook" babies even before they leave the hospital because the staff supplements the mother's milk with formula or sugar water, and the infant comes to prefer the easier flow of the bottle.

Thus, even when breast-feeding is promoted and women feel committed to it, social and cultural obstacles can make it difficult. A biocultural understanding of breast-feeding as an evolved, two-way process could help to make conditions more favorable. It would highlight the fact that women are normally able to breast-feed without medical approval, surveillance, and intervention and reduce the public's receptiveness to industrially produced formula and baby foods. Most importantly, the biocultural perspective would foster an appreciation of the intricate mechanisms linking mothers and infants together in a dynamic system of nutrition that benefits them both.

## SUGGESTED READING

Cohen, Mark Nathan. 1989. *Health and the Rise of Civilization.* New Haven: Yale University Press.

Daly, S. E. J., and P. E. Hartmann. 1995. Infant Demand and Milk Supply. *Journal of Human Lactation* 11(1): 21–37.

Dettwyler, Katherine. 1995. A Time to Wean. In *Breast-feeding: Biocultural Perspectives,* eds. Patricia Stuart-Macadam and Katherine Dettwyler. New York: Aldine de Gruyter.

Eaton, S. Boyd, Melvin Konner, and Marjorie Shostak. 1988. *The Paleolithic Prescription.* New York: Harper and Row.

Eaton, S. Boyd, et al. 1994. Women's Reproductive Cancers in Evolutionary Perspective. *The Quarterly Review of Biology* 69(3): 353–367.

Ellison, Peter. 1995. Breast-feeding, Fertility, and Maternal Condition. In *Breast-feeding: Biocultural Perspectives,* eds. Patricia Stuart-Macadam and Katherine Dettwyler. New York: Aldine de Gruyter.

Ewald, Paul W. 1994. *Evolution of Infectious Disease.* New York: Oxford University Press.

Konner, Melvin, and Marjorie Shostak. 1987. Timing and Management of Birth among the !Kung. *Cultural Anthropology* 2(1): 11–28.

Konner, Melvin, and Carol Worthman. 1980. Nursing Frequency, Gonadal Function, and Birth Spacing among !Kung Hunter-Gatherers. *Science* 207: 788–791.

Maher, Vanessa (ed.). 1992. *The Anthropology of Breast-feeding.* Oxford: Berg.

McKenna, James. 1986. An Anthropological Perspective on the Sudden Infant Death Syndrome (SIDS): The Role of Parental Breathing Cues and Speech Breathing Adaptations. *Medical Anthropology* 10(1): 9–53.

McKenna, James, and Sarah Mosko. 1990. Evolution and the Sudden Infant Death Syndrome (SIDS). Part 3: Infant Arousal and Parent–Infant Co-Sleeping. *Human Nature* 1(3): 291–330.

Micozzi, Marc. 1995. Breast Cancer, Reproductive Biology, and Breast-feeding. In *Breast-feeding: Biocultural Perspectives,* eds. Patricia Stuart-Macadam and Katherine Dettwyler. New York: Aldine de Gruyter.

Nesse, Randolph M., and George C. Williams. 1994. *Why We Get Sick: The New Science of Darwinian Medicine.* New York: Random House.

Riordan, Jan, and Kathleen Auerbach. 1993. *Breast-feeding and Human Lactation.* Boston: Jones and Bartlett.

Scheper-Hughes, Nancy, and Margaret Lock. 1987. The Mindful Body: A Prolegomenon to Future Work in Medical Anthropology. *Medical Anthropology Quarterly* 1(1): 6–41.

Stuart-Macadam, Patricia. 1995. Breast-feeding in Prehistory. In *Breast-feeding: Biocultural Perspectives,* eds. Patricia Stuart-Macadam and Katherine Dettwyler. New York: Aldine de Gruyter.

Williams, George C., and Randolph M. Nesse. 1991. The Dawn of Darwinian Medicine. *The Quarterly Review of Biology* 66(1): 1–22.

Wood, James W. et al. 1985. Lactation and Birth Spacing in Highland New Guinea. *Journal of Biosocial Sciences, Supplement* 9: 159–173.

Woolridge, Michael W. 1995. Baby-Controlled Breast-feeding. In *Breast-feeding: Biocultural Perspectives,* eds. Patricia Stuart-Macadam and Katherin Dettwyler. New York: Aldine de Gruyter.

# 10

# Ancient Genes and Modern Health

*S. Boyd Eaton and Melvin Konner*

The best available evidence about prehistory is that early humans were scavengers and gatherers of wild plants, not mighty hunters. This idea might at first seem far removed from the daily worries of people in complex societies like the United States. What do the food-getting methods of prehistoric people have to do with us and our world?

Two points are relevant here. First, anthropologists believe that food-getting and food-producing systems have been important factors in historical change, as we will see in Selection 16, "Disease and Death at Dr, Dickson's Mounds." Second, a major problem confronting Western society has been the rise in particular chronic illnesses—sometimes called the diseases of civilization—that ultimately kill most Americans. In this article, S. Boyd Eaton and Melvin Konner demonstrate how information from paleoanthropology and the study of contemporary hunters and gatherers can shed new light on the origins of some present-day health problems.

***As you read this selection, ask yourself the following questions:***

- What is the difference between biological and cultural evolution?
- Do biological culture and cultural evolution advance at the same rate? If not, what sorts of things might happen as cultural changes occur faster than biological changes?
- What was the diet of our Paleolithic ancestors?
- What sort of nutritional changes accompanied the development of agriculture?
- What sorts of illnesses are found in the West but not among hunter-gatherers?
- In addition to diet, what other lifestyle differences are related to chronic illness in the Western world?

***The following terms discussed in this selection are included in the Glossary at the back of the book:***

*agricultural development*
*Cro-Magnon*
*cultural evolution*
*dental anthropology*
*epidemiology*
*foraging*
*hunter-gatherers*
*Paleolithic*
*paleontology*
*prehistoric*

For the past ten years we have been investigating the proposition that the major chronic illnesses which afflict humans living in affluent industrialized Western nations are promoted by a mismatch between our genetic constitution and a variety of lifestyle factors which have bioenvironmental relevance. The diseases include atherosclerosis with its sequels of heart attacks, strokes, and peripheral vascular disease; adult-onset diabetes; many important forms of cancer; hypertension (high blood pressure); emphysema; and obesity. The main lifestyle variables are diet, exercise patterns and exposure to abusive substances—chiefly alcohol and tobacco. We have taken the basic position that the genetic constitution of humanity, which controls our physiology, biochemistry, and metabolism, has not been altered in any fundamental way since *Homo sapiens sapiens* first became widespread. In contrast, cultural evolution during the relatively brief period since the appearance of agriculture has been breathtakingly rapid, so that genes selected over the preceding geologic eras must now function in a foreign and, in many ways, hostile Atomic Age milieu.

In order to better understand our current lifestyle/genetic discord and to appreciate what steps might be taken to eliminate its harmful etiologic consequences, we needed to determine, as best we could, the actual constituents of our ancestral lifestyle. For most people speculation about our Stone Age ancestors exerts a strong fascination: How did they live, what did they look like, how did they differ from us and how were

Eaton, S. Boyd & Melvin Konner. "Ancient Genes and Modern Health." Courtesy of the Leakey Foundation.

they similar? For us, the effort to characterize their nutritional practices and the exercise patterns necessitated by their daily activities has been exciting as well as scientifically rewarding. The bulk of our understanding has come from the fields of paleontology, anthropology, epidemiology, and nutritional science.

Paleontology is the study of fossil remains. For example, the stature of Paleolithic humans can be estimated from the length of femora (thigh bones) according to a formula which relates total height to femoral length; it is not necessary to have all the bony components of a skeleton to make this determination. Such studies have shown that humans living in the eastern Mediterranean area 30,000 years ago were probably tall; males averaged 177.1 cm (5′ 9¾″) and females 166.5 cm (5′ 5½″), whereas in 1960 Americans averaged 174.2 cm (5′ 8½″) and 163.4 cm (5′ 4½″), respectively.

Skeletal height and pelvic depth both probably reflect nutritional factors, especially protein intake. With the advent of agriculture, animal protein intake decreased markedly so that average stature for both men and women ultimately declined by over 10 centimeters. The same phenomenon, a decrease in the animal protein content of the diet around the time that agriculture first appeared, is also documented by analysis of strontium/calcium ratios in bony remains. Strontium reaches the skeletons of living animals mainly through ingestion of plant foods so that herbivores have higher strontium levels in their bones than do carnivores. Studies of strontium/calcium ratios in the bones of humans who lived just before and during the changeover to agriculture confirm that the consumption of meat declined relative to that of vegetable foods around this period.

Skeletons also indicate muscularity; the prominence of muscular insertion sites and the area of articular surfaces both vary directly with the forces exerted by the muscles acting on them. Analyses of these features show that average preagricultural humans were apparently generally stronger than those who lived thereafter, including us today. Because of their hardness, teeth are very well represented in paleontological material. It is a telling comment about our current consumption of sugar (which approaches 125 lbs per person per year in the United States) that only about 2 percent of teeth from the Late Paleolithic period exhibit dental caries whereas some recent European populations have had more than 70 percent of their teeth so affected.

Anthropology is a broad discipline which includes the study of recent hunter-gatherers whose lives can be considered to mirror those of our remote ancestors in many ways. Of course, there are important differences: Such people have been increasingly forced from the most environmentally desirable areas into desert, arctic, or jungle habitats where the food quest must be far more difficult than it was for Paleolithic hunter-gatherers who exploited the most abundant and fruitful regions then available without competition from encroaching civilization. On the other hand, the technology of recent foragers is more advanced than that available to those living 25,000 years ago; an excellent example is the bow and arrow, perhaps developed no earlier than 10 to 15 thousand years ago. Nevertheless, study of recent hunter-gatherers does provide a kind of window into the Stone Age world; the nutrition, physical attributes, and health of individuals who have such parallel lives must be reasonably similar despite the millennia which separate them in time.

Anthropologists have studied over 50 hunter-gatherer societies sufficiently well to justify nutritional generalizations about them. When data from these groups are analyzed statistically, the average values all center around a subsistence pattern of 35 percent meat and 65 percent vegetable foods (by weight). There is, of course, considerable variation; arctic peoples may eat up to 90 percent animal products, whereas arid desert dwellers may obtain only 15 percent of their diet from such sources. Nevertheless, these data allow us to reasonably conclude that Paleolithic humans had a roughly similar range of subsistence patterns.

Epidemiology is the study of disease patterns. When a pathologic condition, such as lung cancer, is common in a specified population, for example, cigarette smokers, and uncommon in another specified group, such as nonsmokers, differences between the two groups may bear on the etiology of the disease condition under scrutiny. Information derived from various epidemiologic investigations can be used to help estimate what sorts of diseases might have afflicted Paleolithic humans and which ones must have been uncommon. For example, in today's world, people who consume a minimal amount of saturated fat tend to have little coronary heart disease and a relatively low incidence of cancer involving the breast, uterus, prostate, and colon. If we could be confident that the Stone Age diet contained little saturated fat we could rationally assume that individuals living then had a lower incidence of heart disease and cancers related to fat intake than do persons living in affluent, industrialized Western nations today. Similar arguments might be made concerning hypertension (as related to dietary sodium, potassium, and calcium) and, of course, lung cancer and emphysema (cigarettes). A tempting assumption is that, since illnesses of this sort tend to become manifest in older persons, Paleolithic humans (whose life expectancy was less than ours) would not have had the opportunity to develop them, no matter what their lifestyle. However, epidemiologists and pathologists have shown that young people in the Western world commonly have developing, asymptomatic forms of these illnesses, but hunter-gatherer youths do not. Furthermore, those members of technologically primitive cultures who survive to the age of 60 or more remain relatively free from these disorders, unlike their "civilized" counterparts.

Nutritional science furthers evaluation of Paleolithic life by providing analyses of the foods such people were likely to have eaten. An understanding of their overall nutrition is impossible without knowing that, although they ate more red meat than we do now, they nevertheless consumed much less saturated fat since wild game has less than a fifth the fat found in the domesticated animals currently bred and raised for meat production. Similarly, nutrition analyses of the wild, uncultivated fruits, vegetables, and nuts eaten by recent hunter-gatherers allow us to estimate the average nutritional values of the plant foods our ancestors ate. To this end we have been able to accumulate nutritional data characterizing 43 different wild animals ranging from kangaroos to wart hogs and 153 different wild vegetable foods—mainly roots, beans, nuts, tubers, and fruit but including items as diverse as truffles and seed pods. The search for this information has been challenging but entertaining; how else would one learn that bison meat contains only 40 mg of cholesterol per 100 grams of tissue or that the Australian green plum has the world's highest known vitamin C content (3150 mg per 100 grams)!

When information from these disparate scientific disciplines is correlated and coordinated, what is the picture that emerges? What was the diet of our ancestors; what are other important ways in which their lifestyle differs from ours; and do these differences have any relationship to the chronic illnesses from which we suffer, but from which recent hunter-gatherers seem immune?

To address the most straightforward, but certainly not unimportant, issues first, it is clear that our Stone Age ancestors were rarely if ever exposed to tobacco and alcohol. The manufacture of barley beer can be dated as early as 7000 years ago, but there is no convincing evidence for consumption of alcohol before this time, and recent technologically primitive groups have not been found to manufacture alcoholic beverages. Similarly, there is no indication that tobacco was available in Eurasia prior to the voyages of discovery only 500 years ago. But Late Paleolithic peoples were probably not altogether free from abusive substances; several recent hunter-gatherer groups have used some form of consciousness-altering drugs for ceremonial purposes and it seems likely that similar agents may have been available in the Late Stone Age although their use could hardly have been as prevalent as is currently the case.

The physical demands of life in the Late Paleolithic period insured that our ancestors, both men and women, were strong, fit, lean, and muscular. Their bones prove that they were robust—they resemble those of today's superior athletes. Furthermore, hunter-gatherers studied in the last 150 years have been trim and athletic in their appearance.

Modern nutritionists generally feel that items from four basic food groups—meat and fish; vegetables, nuts, and fruits; milk and milk products; and breads and cereals—are necessary for a balanced diet. But during the Paleolithic period older children and adults derived all their nutrients from the first two groups: wild game and vegetables, fruits, and nuts. Except for very young children, who were weaned much later than they are today, no one had any dairy foods at all and they apparently made comparatively little use of grain. Their only "refined" carbohydrate was honey, available only seasonally and obtained painfully. They seem to have eaten little seafood until fairly late in prehistory, though this assumption is questionable since the ancient sea level was much lower (because of water locked up in the extensive glaciers of that period), and the sites of Paleolithic seacoast dwellers are now under water.

After weaning, Paleolithic humans drank water, but the beverages we now consume generally deliver an appreciable caloric load as they quench our thirst. Mundane as it is, this example illustrates a pervasive pattern—caloric concentration. Since our meat is fattier, it contains more calories per unit weight (typically two to three times as many) than does wild game. Furthermore, the plant foods we eat are commonly refined and adulterated so that their basic caloric load is multiplied: french fries have more than twice and potato chips over five times the calories present in an equal weight of baked potato. Pumpkin pie has ten times the calories found in the same weight of pumpkin served alone.

The salt added to our foods as a seasoning and as a preservative insures that we now consume an average of six times the daily sodium intake of Paleolithic humans. In a similar vein, the process of refining carbohydrate foods provides us with quantities of sugar and white flour far in excess of what was available to our ancestors while reducing our complex carbohydrate (starch) and dietary fiber intake much below the levels they consumed. Not only do we eat twice the fat eaten by Stone Agers, its nature is different. Structural fat is a necessary constituent of cellular membranous structures; this type of fat is predominantly polyunsaturated in nature and was the major fat consumed by our remote ancestors. Conversely, depot or storage fat is the main type found in the adipose tissue stores of domesticated animals; this variety of fat is largely saturated and is very prominent in today's diets. Like game available now, the wild animals eaten 25,000 years ago had minimal depot fat; accordingly humans then ate considerably more polyunsaturated than saturated fat—but the reverse occurs in twentieth century affluent Western nations.

To summarize, these observations indicate that the Cro-Magnons and similar Late Paleolithic peoples consumed nearly three times the amount of protein we do, about a sixth of the sodium, more potassium, more calcium (which is very interesting in view of the prevalence of osteoporosis in today's society), and considerably more vitamin C (though not the amounts megavitamin enthusiasts would recommend). They ate about the same amount of carbohydrate that we do; however, it was predominantly in the form of starch and other complex carbohydrates, providing a good deal more dietary fiber than we have in our diet. For them refined carbohydrate and simple sugar, from honey and fruit, were available only seasonally and in limited amounts. They ate only half the fat we consume in twentieth century America and their fat was more polyunsaturated than saturated in nature.

Certain aspects of our ancestors' physical fitness bear further emphasis: Their "exercise program" was lifelong, it developed both endurance and strength, it applied to men and women alike, and the activities which comprised their "workouts" varied predictably with seasonal changes. Today's fitness enthusiasts might well ponder these Paleolithic training guidelines. Preagricultural humans were more like decathlon athletes than either marathoners or power lifters; our genes appear to have been programmed for the synergism which results when endurance and strength occur together. A lifelong program was unavoidable for them; for us it requires strategic planning. Really long-term training in just one exercise mode is almost impossible to maintain; overtraining, boredom, and burn-out tend to overcome even the most intense dedication. Paleolithic men and women were spared these phenomena because the activities of each season differed from those of the next. The Russians have perhaps unconsciously recreated these circumstances in a training approach they call "periodization." This system employs planned daily, weekly, and quarterly variation in the mode, volume, and intensity of exercise so that training remains fresh and invigorating, not dull and endlessly repetitive. Perhaps this recapitulation of our ancestral pattern partially explains the success their athletes have experienced in international competition.

What about the proposition we advanced at the beginning of this article: Do the diseases of civilization result from the mismatch between our genes and our current lifestyle? The evidence is strong that such a connection exists. In important respects the lifestyle of Paleolithic humans, that for which our genes have been selected, parallels recommendations made by the American Cancer Society, the American Heart Association, the American Diabetes Association and the Senate Select Committee on Nutrition. Furthermore, recent hunter-gatherers have been essentially free from the chronic illnesses which kill most Americans.

Anthropology, paleontology, medicine, epidemiology and nutrition can be likened to the facets of a prism, each providing a different view of the same subject. Our subject is the health and disease of persons living in affluent, industrialized Western society and when views provided by diverse scientific disciplines converge, the resulting implications acquire profound significance. There is nothing especially distinctive about human hunter-gatherers in biochemical and physiological terms. What they ate and how they lived fall well within the broad mammalian spectrum. During the past 10,000 years, however, humans have exceeded the bounds. Many of the lifestyle factors we now take for granted (particularly sedentary living, alcohol, tobacco and our high salt, high saturated fat, high refined carbohydrate diet) are unique in free-living vertebrate experience. They constitute a deviation so extreme that our bodies have responded by developing forms of illness not otherwise seen in nature. These are the diseases of civilization.

# 11

# The Tall and the Short of It

*Barry Bogin*

An important area of biological anthropology is the description and explanation of human biological diversity among people living today. When we look around, it is easy to see diversity in people's outward appearance (their phenotype) that results from differences in genetic inheritance (genotype) as well as their interaction with the environment, particularly during critical times in child growth and development. There was a time in the not-too-distant past when scientists thought that differences in groups' outward physical characteristics were completely inherited, fixed, and unchangeable. They also thought that such traits could be placed into biologically meaningful categories or races. Today it is clear that both of these ideas are wrong, even if they persist in people's folk biology.

Biological anthropologists do research on child growth and development—that is, measuring and explaining patterns of growth through the life cycle. Measurement of human biology—in stature, weight, fat folds, and so forth—is called anthropometry. In pediatrics, an individual baby's growth is plotted along a standardized growth curve; failure to grow is an indication that something is wrong. But is this to say that being short is a sign of unhealthiness? To what extent are anthropometric measurements a reflection of our genes, and to what extent do our body size and shape reflect environmental conditions? The most important environmental condition is nutrition—whether a child is getting enough food and the right kinds of food. If a child lives in poverty, his or her adult phenotype and overall health will be affected.

This topic was explored by the father of American anthropology, Franz Boas, who compared immigrant populations and their children raised in the United States during the 1920s. He documented a rapid increase in all anthropometric measurements, including stature and cranial measurement, for the U.S.-raised offspring, even though the genetic composition was identical. These people experienced a change in environment, particularly in child nutrition. Boas used this data to argue against the notion of fixed races based on phenotypic characteristics.

In this selection, Barry Bogin describes what is known about human plasticity—the change in phenotypic characteristics of a group over time. He raises hypotheses about why Americans used to be the tallest population in the world but are now behind the Dutch in height. These discoveries in biological anthropology have implications for public policy.

***As you read this selection, ask yourself the following questions:***

- Because biological anthropologists used aggregate data to talk about changes in average stature of a population, is it possible to extend these observations to the individual level?
- Is it correct to think of poverty as part of the environment? To what extent do humans create their own environment?
- Does access to food and social stimulation affect brain development? What does this mean in regard to the genetic potential and the actual achievements of children growing up in poverty?
- Why might Americans be one of the fattest populations of the world? What cultural factors might cause such biological changes?

***The following terms discussed in this selection are included in the Glossary at the back of the book:***

*adaptation*
*anthropometry*
*lactose intolerance*
*plasticity*
*stature*

As a biological anthropologist, I have just one word of advice for you: plasticity. *Plasticity* refers to the ability of many organisms, including humans, to alter themselves—their behavior or even their biology—in response to changes in the environment. We tend to think that our bodies get locked into their final form by our genes, but in fact we alter our bodies as the

Bogin, Barry. "The Tall and the Short of It." *Discover* Magazine (Feb. 1998):40–44. Reprinted with permission of the author.

conditions surrounding us shift, particularly as we grow during childhood. Plasticity is as much a product of evolution's fine-tuning as any particular gene, and it makes just as much evolutionary good sense. Rather than being able to adapt to a single environment, we can, thanks to plasticity, change our bodies to cope with a wide range of environments. Combined with the genes we inherit from our parents, plasticity accounts for what we are and what we can become.

Anthropologists began to think about human plasticity around the turn of the century, but the concept was first clearly defined in 1969 by Gabriel Lasker, a biological anthropologist at Wayne State University in Detroit. At that time scientists tended to consider only those adaptations that were built into the genetic makeup of a person and passed on automatically to the next generation. A classic example of this is the ability of adults in some human societies to drink milk. As children, we all produce an enzyme called lactase, which we need to break down the sugar lactose in our mother's milk. In many of us, however, the lactase gene slows down dramatically as we approach adolescence—probably as the result of another gene that regulates its activity. When that regulating gene turns down the production of lactase, we can no longer digest milk.

Lactose intolerance—which causes intestinal gas and diarrhea—affects between 70 percent and 90 percent of African Americans, Native Americans, Asians, and people who come from around the Mediterranean. But others, such as people of central and western European descent and the Fulani of West Africa, typically have no problem drinking milk as adults. That's because they are descended from societies with long histories of raising goats and cattle. Among these people there was a clear benefit to being able to drink milk, so natural selection gradually changed the regulation of their lactase gene, keeping it functioning throughout life.

That kind of adaptation takes many centuries to become established, but Lasker pointed out that there are two other kinds of adaptation in humans that need far less time to kick in. If people have to face a cold winter with little or no heat, for example, their metabolic rates rise over the course of a few weeks and they produce more body heat. When summer returns, the rates sink again.

Lasker's other mode of adaptation concerned the irreversible, lifelong modification of people as they develop—that is, their plasticity. Because we humans take so many years to grow to adulthood, and because we live in so many different environments, from forests to cities and from deserts to the Arctic, we are among the world's most variable species in our physical form and behavior. Indeed, we are one of the most plastic of all species.

One of the most obvious manifestations of human malleability is our great range of height, and it is a subject I've made a special study of for the last 25 years. Consider these statistics: in 1850 Americans were the tallest people in the world, with American men averaging 5′6″. Almost 150 years later, American men now average 5′8″, but we have fallen in the standings and are now only the third tallest people in the world. In first place are the Dutch. Back in 1850 they averaged only 5′4″—the shortest men in Europe—but today they are a towering 5′10″. (In these two groups, and just about everywhere else, women average about five inches less than men at all times.)

So what happened? Did all the short Dutch sail over to the United States? Did the Dutch back in Europe get an infusion of "tall genes"? Neither. In both America and the Netherlands life got better, but more so for the Dutch, and height increased as a result. We know this is true thanks in part to studies on how height is determined. It's the product of plasticity in our childhood and in our mothers' childhood as well. If a girl is undernourished and suffers poor health, the growth of her body, including her reproductive system, is usually reduced. With a shortage of raw materials, she can't build more cells to construct a bigger body; at the same time, she has to invest what materials she can get into repairing already existing cells and tissues from the damage caused by disease. Her shorter stature as an adult is the result of a compromise her body makes while growing up.

Such a woman can pass on her short stature to her child, but genes have nothing to do with it for either of them. If she becomes pregnant, her small reproductive system probably won't be able to supply a normal level of nutrients and oxygen to her fetus. This harsh environment reprograms the fetus to grow more slowly than it would if the woman was healthier, so she is more likely to give birth to a smaller baby. Low-birth-weight babies (weighing less than 5.5 pounds) tend to continue their prenatal program of slow growth through childhood. By the time they are teenagers, they are usually significantly shorter than people of normal birth weight. Some particularly striking evidence of this reprogramming comes from studies on monozygotic twins, which develop from a single fertilized egg cell and are therefore identical genetically. But in certain cases, monozygotic twins end up being nourished by unequal portions of the placenta. The twin with the smaller fraction of the placenta is often born with low birth weight, while the other one is normal. Follow-up studies show that this difference between the twins can last throughout their lives.

As such research suggests, we can use the average height of any group of people as a barometer of the health of their society. After the turn of the century both

principles with forensic anthropology. Indeed, focusing on empirical evidence in both the courts of history—where anthropological and archaeological theory provide frameworks for interpretation—and law—where evidence must be tightly linked to claims of guilt or innocence—can only strengthen the general standards of archaeology and anthropology in all realms.

## BALANCING ACT

The aftermath of the World Trade Center disaster was perhaps the most painful period in the history of New York City. To say that it was a "life-changing experience" now seems trite, but it was. Forensic anthropologists volunteering with DMORT conducted round-the-clock operations near the Office of the Chief Medical Examiner (OCME) to identify victims. This was a daunting task. There were extraordinary amounts of fragmented and commingled human remains.

It was also apparent that large amounts of fragmented human remains were scattered over wide areas of lower Manhattan beyond Ground Zero, and much of this was lost during the city cleanup. There was clearly a need for trained field teams of archaeologists to work in these areas to recover remains, personal effects, office documents, and other materials in a forensically controlled manner. This did not happen, however, until a trial recovery excavation a few months later under an invitation from the OCME demonstrated that such recoveries were possible. This volunteer team of field archaeologists, Providence Police, and other members of the Rhode Island community, known as Forensic Archaeology Recovery (FAR), continues to train regularly and to deploy as needed. Arguably, so much vital evidence was lost outside Ground Zero that the number of WTC victims identified so far from human remains stands at just under 60 percent. For archaeologists and forensic anthropologists, the World Trade Center was one of the first "wake-up" calls that there was a need to strengthen the field recovery remains as a first step in identifying victims.

A year after this trial effort, a terrible fire destroyed "The Station" nightclub in West Warwick, Rhode Island, killing 100 people and leaving over twice as many horribly burned or injured. Although small compared with the WTC, the aftermath was similar in its effects. Rhode Island is a small community, and many people who have lived here for a while had close ties with the fire victims. Once again, DMORT assisted the local authorities—in this case the State Medical Examiner's Office—with the result that all of the fire victims were identified within three days. This was my first deployment with DMORT, and as a learning experience it was like drinking from a fire hose. Then FAR was called to "The Station" site by the Rhode Island State Fire Marshal's Office and performed forensic recoveries there for the next 11 days, finally closing the site.

In this case, FAR's primary task was to recover personal effects and enter them in custody to go to the Medical Examiner's lab for eventual repatriation to the victims' families. Another equally important task, however, was to "clean up" the site. The Fire Marshal explained that after the police lines and fences come down after a major fire, people swarm over the site collecting everything they can find—including human remains. It may be hard to imagine, but it happens. We agreed that we would not let it happen in this case, and by the end of the operation nothing of that nature was left there for people to collect. This was a service to our community that we had never envisioned beforehand, but it demonstrated the value of controlled forensic archaeology at a disaster scene in a way that had major, positive effects within our community.

The experiences of major disasters in the scope of Sept. 11, "The Station" nightclub fire, and Hurricane Katrina have shown us that disaster anthropology is as much a humanitarian mission as it is an exercise of anthropologists' professional and academic skills. Those of us who participate in this work train like maniacs to prepare for the very thing we dread most, but when it happens we would not want to be anywhere else.

# PART II

# *Archaeology*

To be human is to have a cultural heritage. Although we are born into a social group, we must, through the processes of growing up, learn to become members of our society. In the context of the family, children learn not simply how to talk and how to "behave" but, more important, how to think and what to think. In other words, we learn the fundamental ideas, beliefs, and values of our society—assumptions about life and reality that are seldom questioned, at least by most people.

Anthropologists have studied and described the lifestyles and beliefs of hundreds of different societies throughout the modern world. The striking diversity of the cultures of humankind, each of which deserves to be understood in its own context, is one of the most important lessons of anthropology.

Anthropologists believe that despite this diversity, all cultures have some basic features in common. All cultures can be divided into three interdependent parts: (1) a material economy and technology; (2) a system of social organization; and (3) a system of beliefs and values. These components fit together; for example, the belief system may reinforce the social order and therefore help keep the economy running smoothly. A change in one cultural system, such as the economy, will result in changes in the other two systems. Culture is the primary mechanism by which humans adapt and survive in their environment. Cultural systems are always changing, and anthropologists are particularly interested in how and why cultures change. The major goal of the subfield of archaeology is the documentation and explanation of patterns of cultural change, or cultural evolution.

Every society has a unique cultural history—a story about how things got to be the way they are. However, written documents are available for only a tiny fraction of the time since the beginning of cultural history, and writing itself was used by only a minority of the world's cultures. Archaeology is a tool that allows us to overcome the temporal shallowness and the uneven cultural distribution of written historical documentation. Archaeology provides a key to understanding the chronologies of different prehistoric cultures; it is a scholarly method of uncovering and analyzing the material remains of people long dead. Archaeology is both a method and a body of knowledge about the prehistoric past. Of course, archaeology can also be applied to the historic past, not only to supplement the historic record but also to focus attention on the daily lives of people.

Most people have a general idea about what archaeologists do, but the popular caricature of the archaeologist as Indiana Jones is wrong. Indeed, archaeology may involve discovery, dirt, and even adventure, but most archaeological work requires careful and painstaking scholarship. When he or she digs, the archaeologist is not looking for valuable ancient artifacts as if they were pirate treasure. Artifacts taken out of context—that is, without knowing their relationship with other artifacts and nonartifactual remains at a particular depth and location—have little or no scholarly value. The isolated artifact is only a piece of a large and complex puzzle. The questions that the archaeologist asks are closely related to anthropological theory: How did cultures change and why did they change? The goal of the archaeologist is to establish a chronology of cultural change and to describe the lifeways of past societies. In doing this, the archaeologist preserves and interprets the cultural heritage—of ourselves and others—that was once buried in the ground.

The process of scientific archaeology has three parts: excavation, analysis, and interpretation. The methods must be very exact because the excavation of a particular place cannot be repeated. After locating an archaeological site, the modern archaeologist uses precise techniques to uncover, record, and preserve all possible information in a precise area. Excavation is followed by descriptive analysis of the artifacts in the laboratory; this analysis emphasizes the patterning of artifacts at different stratigraphic levels in the site. Sophisticated laboratory techniques developed in other sciences are now being applied to this archaeological analysis, such as reconstructing prehistoric ecological settings with pollen analysis or diagnosing a disease like schistosomiasis from an ancient burial.

The things archaeologists analyze are often the discarded "garbage" of prehistoric peoples. Artifacts might give clues to the economy and technology of a society or to its social organization or belief system. Most of the garbage, the material culture unearthed, is representative of the economic and technological spheres. The function of such artifacts is often better understood by drawing analogies to primitive societies studied by cultural anthropologists. Finally, the archaeologist interprets and explains what has been found and writes up these findings in the form of a report. Archaelogical analysis and interpretation are best when it comes to the economic system and least certain for artifacts as reflections of belief systems.

The methods developed for the study of prehistoric artifacts can be applied to our own society as well, with interesting results. In Selection 22, for example, Timothy Jones uses archaeological methods to investigate the problem of food loss.

Archaeology, like the other subdisciplines of anthropology, has both basic and applied dimensions. By establishing chronologies of cultural change in prehistoric societies, archaeologists add an important dimension of time depth to our understanding of the human story. For anthropology, this prehistoric information is critical for testing cultural evolutionary hypotheses about the patterns and direction of change. When we look at cultural history from this evolutionary standpoint, two "events" of the past seem particularly important: the domestication of plants and animals (that is, the beginning of farming) and the development of state societies characterized by urban centers and social stratification. These might be considered as two of the most important events in human history (see Selections 16 and 17).

The cultural evolutionary perspective shows a general pattern in cultural history, namely, the change from simple, small-scale organizations based on food foraging to large and complex ones based on agriculture and institutionalized inequality. When archaeologists examine a particular culture and how it changed over time, however, they often find that a traditional culture was clearly adapted to a particular local environment. Yet the archaeological record has many "cultural experiments" that failed—that is, cultures that flourished and then disappeared. These extinct societies and cultures, understood through the archaeological method, can be important lessons—warnings, really—for our contemporary world and our future.

One example would be the prehistoric southwestern United States, where the Anasazi culture reached a zenith in the fifteenth century; the monumental stone architecture of this culture was as impressive as the stone cathedrals of medieval Europe. Within a few years, however, magnificent cities were abandoned. Although many theories exist for this decline, most archaeologists believe that the Anasazi agricultural system, which depended on the concentrated use of irrigation systems, was poorly suited to the climate. The concentrated cultural system was not resistant to drought, and the civilization collapsed for lack of water.

The fact that these sophisticated cultures died out should make us pause and think about the directions of change in our own culture. The archaeological record contains other examples of how people have changed the face of the earth, often with unexpected negative consequences for the economy or the health of the people. We do not always recognize that our relationship with the environment is fragile and that ecological change is difficult to reverse. The economy and consumption patterns of contemporary American society have created a garbage crisis with few clear solutions.

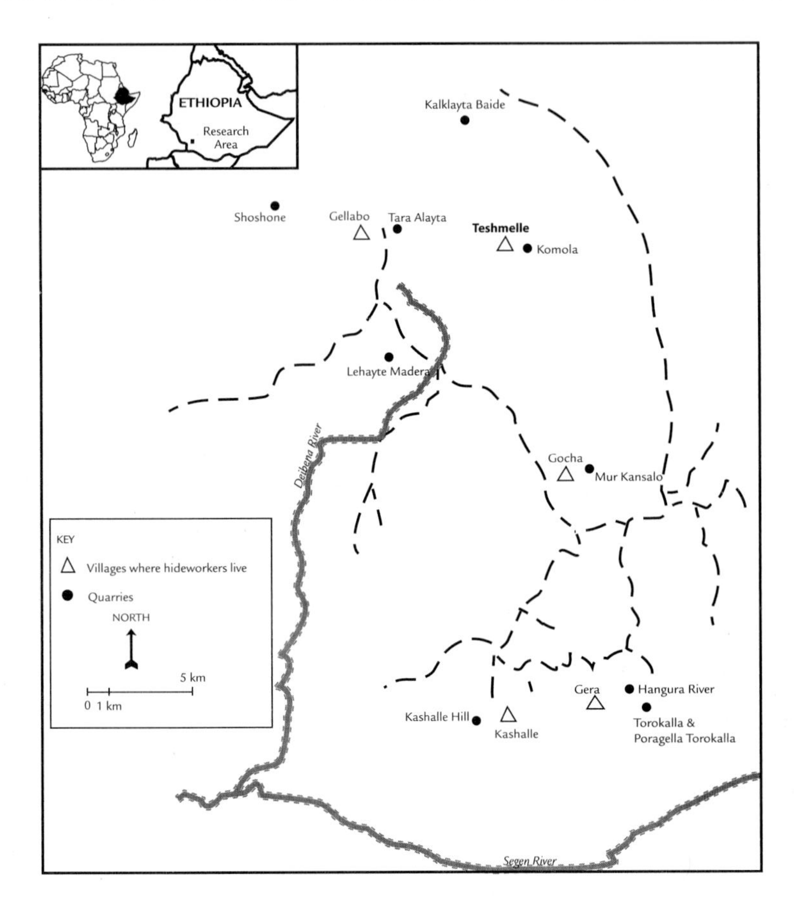


**FIGURE 1** Map of the Konso region locating hideworking villages and stone quarries.

I interviewed several Xauta women married to Ententa men, and most of these women, although living productive lifestyles, did not practice any craft until after their husbands' deaths. However, a union between an Ententa woman and a Xauta man is rarer, as many Konso consider it unproductive. Several Ententa men—including Marcos, a teacher who collects histories from Konso elders—said that when an Ententa woman marries a Xauta man people taunt her with a song.

**Kathy:** What happens if an Ententa marries a Xauta?

**Marcos:** If an Ententa woman marries a Xauta man, they sing a Xauta man will grind and smash you like a poisonous plant.

**K:** What is this poisonous plant?

**M:** It is a plant that is eaten only during famine period. Do you understand? The union is unfertile.

**K:** What about the man?

**M:** When a [Ententa] man marries a Xauta woman, they say he shook the bracelets; he has spoiled them and is no longer respected.

**K:** What bracelets?

**M:** The bracelets worn by the Poqualla [lineage heads who are political and ritual leaders and distribute land]

**K:** What do the bracelets mean?

**M:** They mean power. They mean the land. [conversation with author, [July 29, 2002]

Furthermore, in conversations with several Xauta, the use of the terms *grind (yokeda)* and *smash (kekebisa)* associated with a Xauta man reveals a deeper symbolic association between Xauta and gender roles. Most of the Xauta I interviewed repeatedly assigned separate gender tasks to men and women. They stated and I observed that for the most part men engage in hammering and penetrating activities exemplified in building houses, fences, and terraces and sowing fields. Furthermore, females commonly kneel *(glifefata)* to weed, harvest crops, collect water, grind *(yokeda)* grain, and smash *(kekebisa)* grain while cooking. Craftworks including potterymaking and ironworking require grinding, smashing and mixing, and cooking of clay and rock. Thus, the majority of Xauta men and women who create or reproduce the material world do so

through activities that many Konso consider feminine tasks.

Stone-tool technology used in hideworking also requires kneeling to grind and shape the stone into tools, to grind and scrape the hide, and to cook or heat treat the stone. As stated above, most Konso associate these skills and tasks with femininity, and within Konso society there are several lineages of Xauta women (instead of men) who are the primary knappers and hideworkers. Although many women told me they cook the stone to make it break more easily, several also mentioned that the Ententa called the cooked stone and the hideworkers *onayda*, which means worthless and unproductive. All 16 of the stone-using Xauta women I interviewed were upset by the use of the term *onayda* because they see their work as meaningful, even if others do not. In his earlier work, Hallpike (1972:143) suggested that, in Konso ideology, to cook earth (iron and stone) is unnatural and goes against the social order and against reproduction. In my interviews, several of the Ententa and many of the Xauta insisted that Ententa despise Xauta tasks because Ententa consider these tasks unclean, unnatural, and beneath them.

Xauta hideworkers *(Kollaya)* engage in feminine tasks to process wild (only in the past) and domesticated hides, producing a variety of feminine goods including skirts, hats, belts, bags, and bedding. These products—clothing worn for birth and harvest fertility ceremonies, bags that hold crops and children, and bedding and burial sheets—symbolize fertility and the human life cycle. Although the male Xauta Kollaya I interviewed scrape hides to produce bags, most of these men emphasized their past work in producing male goods such as saddles, shields, ritual belts, and hats, which did not require scraping, stone tools, or knapping. I met several Xauta men who worked hides and others who refused to learn, and each of these men resented or feared that Ententa would refer to him as *Sagkota*—an effeminate man.

The identification of individuals into categories of Xauta and Ententa has not remained stagnant through time, nor have Xauta craft-production tasks. Within the last decade, I witnessed a decline in the number of Xauta stone-using hideworkers from 33 in 1995 (Brandt and Weedman 1997) to only 19 (16 women and three men) in 2002. This decline is attributable to changes in government policy and economics. In the 1970s, the Marxist–Leninist government (referred to as the Derg, who ruled 1974–91) banned the production of indigenous leather clothing and increased access to factory produced goods such as clothing, blankets, rope and bags to replace hide products. An elderly hideworker lamented that the Derg government cut her income in half because they prohibited her from making clothing. Today only 30 percent of the practicing hideworkers are young or middle aged. Most stated that they use glass for hideworking instead of stone, and they have not learned how to make clothing or scrape wild animal hides because the current government prohibits the hunting of wild animals. In addition, economic reforms have led to a dramatically increased demand for exported leather (Hasen 1996), encouraging farmers to sell their hides through local merchants to industrial tanning shops in Addis Ababa for export. Today, the stimulation of the economy through neoliberal economic reforms and growing wealth and organization of Xauta through trade (PoXauta Fulto Association) provides incentives for Ententa to take up historically identified Xauta occupations (Ellison 2008, 2009). This would seem to exhibit a significant modification of previous Ententa-held ideologies concerning the demeaning nature of hideworking tasks. However, although some Ententa have begun to engage in merchant trade of hides, to my knowledge, no Ententa have begun to scrape hides or to knap stone. Some hideworkers express that the Ententa may want to learn crafts but still fear the stigma associated with craft production and, thus, are unlikely to pursue it.

**Kathy:** Why do Xauta scrape, smith, and make pots?
**Hideworker:** Before only Xauta do these things, Ententa do not like to do this work. The government made everyone equal and now everyone wants in their hearts to learn! Before the Derg came, the Ententa hated this work and they do not want to learn. If the Xauta do not make iron, they [Ententa] cannot farm, if Xauta do not make pots they cannot eat, and if Xauta do not scrape hides they do not sleep [they make bedding from hides].
**K:** What then would they do without the Xauta?
**H:** They would have to learn! [There is laughter.] [conversation with author, July 12, 2002]

Other Xauta hideworkers commented that, since the change in government, the Ententa have been envious of their craft and want to learn, and so, in their envy, they wish for Xauta scraping stones to break and hides to rip. Although changes in the social context seem to provide an avenue for expanding the transmission of knapping knowledge with the inclusion of Ententa in the PoXauta Fulto Association, hideworking with knapping remains a craft restricted to Xauta participation, and even among the Xauta, the number of skilled, knowledgeable artisans continues to decline.

## TRANSMISSION OF HIDE PRODUCTION AND LITHIC TECHNOLOGY

The 16 Xauta Kollaya stone-tool-using women I interviewed all selectively choose the individuals to whom they will teach the skills of hideworking and discourage

others, creating a community of practicing expert knappers through scaffolding (learning with the assistance of experienced individuals; Lave and Wenger 1991; Wenger 1998). All 19 women and men who knap today learned the craft from a female relative such as their mother, father's second wife, one of their grandmothers or aunts, or their husband's mother. Thus, there seems to be little historical depth to males using stone for hideworking. Furthermore, all 16 Xauta Kollaya women restrict the transfer of knowledge to their second or third daughter, as the eldest daughter does not usually have the time to learn hideworking because of other household obligations. For instance, on the first day that I observed Sokati, an elder and highly respected hideworker living in Gocha, scraping hides, her young granddaughter was grinding ochre and castor oil seeds to add to the hide for color and softening. Sokati disclosed that her granddaughter had a "special heart" and that she would teach her the trade. Across the Konso district, people admire Sokati's skill and many younger women claim that she taught them the craft; however, she is very particular concerning who she apprentices. I asked Sokati when she learned to shape the stones, and she responded:

> WhenIwas young, I did not want to scrape hides, it was hardwork, but my mother kept encouraging me. Finally when I married I realized the economic stability it could bring to my family. [conversations with author, June 15 and 19, 2001]

In a later interview, Sokati emphasized:

> It is important to teach hideworking to my children. I feel they should learn so that we can keep this history and not lose it. People will come and buy hides from them. It will keep the name of our family alive, so don't stop working the hides. [Belkin et al. 2006]

All 16 of the stone-using hideworking practitioners stated that they begin to encourage the assistance of selected six- to eight-year-old daughters, granddaughters, and nieces (see Table 1). They also begin to teach them the technical vocabulary associated with the actions and materials of hideworking. As an example, Sokati's granddaughter began the trade by discarding scraps of waste (lithic and hide), laying out a wet hide to dry before scraping, and softening a hide by stomping and rolling the hide with her feet.

Between the ages of 8 and 12 years old, selected Xauta Kollaya girls learn how to create mastic (from *Balanites aegiptica*, a tree resin used as adhesive) to secure stone scrapers into the single-socket haft (handle), to quarry stone, and to heat treat stone (see Table 1). The apprentices learn to use a metal-tipped tool to pry the stone tool loose from the mastic and to produce a new hole for inserting a tool in the mastic; this practice produces striations and scar damage on the stone tool that remain as visible indicators of hafting (Rots and Williamson 2004). I observed Turkana, a young hideworker living in Teshemelle, as she held a hafted scraper between her thumb and forefingers to show her young daughters the proper angle for hafting. Girls also start to accompany their mothers to the quarries to learn when, where, and how to procure the "right" type of stone. They observe the heat treatment of the raw material. Then they may practice kneeling on a cowhide, which is thick and more resistant to ripping, and scraping with a tool already made by an experienced practitioner.

When these same selected Xauta Kollaya girls are 14 to 16 years old, mothers, grandmothers, and aunts encourage them to observe and practice knapping for tool production (see Table 1). Practitioners usually examine the novices' scrapers and edge rejuvenation and may make their own alterations. Apprentices may scrape parts of hides, particularly cowhides, for the household, but they are not responsible for the entire hide-production sequence and do not have their own clients. Most women stated that they did not regularly begin to make their own scrapers until they were married, were living in their husbands' households, and recognized the importance of the income that hideworking provided. In their husbands' households, new hideworkers often discuss, practice, and receive assistance from their mothers-in-law or other female relatives of their husbands. Many hideworkers believe that an individual requires 10 to 15 years of practice before they produce good scrapers.

## KNOWLEDGE AND CONTROL OF RAW MATERIAL

All 19 (men and women) of the stone-using Xauta Kollaya refer to hide-processing stone as *paltita* (singular: *palta*), which they collect from hillsides and seasonal riverbeds eroding from the Burji Gneiss and Awata Gneiss formations (Fischer 2003). They mostly prefer chalcedony *(lingeto)* and distinguish among darker chert, flint, and jasper *(tema)* and lighter agate *(aahata)*, traveling up to 25 kilometers to acquire these precious resources (see Figure 1). Likay, an elderly female hideworker who lives in Gera and who has used stone for approximately the last 50 years to scrape hides, spoke to me about the names and types of stone she uses.

**Kathy:** Do you have a special name for this type of paltita? (I am pointing to a piece of chalcedony)
**Likay:** We call this paltita, lingeto [to kiss].
**K:** Why?
**L:** It is not easily broken like a kiss.

**TABLE 1 Summary of Hideworkers' Ages, Skills, and Technologies**

| Hideworkers' age in years | Materials used | Skills | Accomplished task |
|---|---|---|---|
| 6–8 | scraps of fat lithic debitage | knowledge of discard locations in village trash heap or gardens | discard |
| | enset leaves | wrap hide with leaves and bury for softening | softening hide |
| | castor oil beans (*ricinus communis*) ochre | identifying materials; learning location; collecting; grinding together trample into hide | softening hide |
| | wet hide | cut holes along edge insert pegs and lay on ground | drying hide |
| 8–12 | soapberry tree resin (*balanites aegiptica*), soot-juniper wood, side of pot or household post | learning location; learning identification; mix and grind into small balls; store mastic until use; heat mastic; remove old scraper with metal-tipped tool; replace tool; proper positioning of stone in haft | hafting stone |
| | stone | knowledge of location; selecting the right time of year for quarrying; selecting the right types of stone; reduce stone for transport | quarrying |
| | stone sometimes cotton, hair, wool, leaves, ceramics | which stone needs heat treating; burying stones under hearth; selecting insulator; selecting length of heating | heat treating stone |
| | hafted scraper, hide | learn proper scraping position; learn proper angle of scraper; learn correct amount of pressure on hide | scraping hide |
| 14–16 | hafted scraper | using the proper amount of force with iron percussor; assessing where and when the working edge of tool needs altering | reshapening tools |
| | raw stone material | identifying good striking platforms; strength and fine-tuned motor skills; angle to strike the raw material; size of tool for hafting creating a useful working edge on tool | knapping |

**K:** Why is it important that the paltita does not break easily? Don't you need it to break to use?
**L:** Some paltita like we find here [milky quartz] it falls into too many pieces when you break it. [conversation with author, July 16, 2002]

The stone-using hideworkers consistently find the highly valued tema paltita at Kalklayta, Baida, and aahata paltita at Komola, Teshmelle; both are near Duro. Duro is where the largest number of stone-using hideworkers live today (see Figure 1) and where the first Konso hideworkers lived. As I listened to hideworkers (112 stone and nonstone users) recount their genealogical histories, I learned that most of the hideworkers' female ancestors moved south from Duro, in accordance with their patrilocal postmarital-residence patterns. Several of the older stone-using hideworkers told me they either traveled to Duro and stayed with relatives while collecting raw material or met relatives at markets who brought the chalcedony to them.

In the late 1970s when leather working became a part-time craft, many hideworkers began to use more locally available quartz crystal and milky quartz and traveled only up to about eight kilometers to collect their raw materials (see Figure 1). Today, all 19 hideworkers use stone and one-third of them also use glass because of the decreased demand for hide products and the easy access to glass in the market. Currently, even local resources of usable stone are dwindling. Some hideworkers collect lithics from plowed archaeological sites, recycling them for present-day use. In Kashelle, the hideworkers use quartz crystal and have begun to use glass because people are now selling quartz crystal as souvenirs for tourists.

Despite the fact that most hideworking communities consist of affines related through marriage, most women from a single community travel together, enjoying one another's companionship, and sometimes stop at markets on their way to local quarry resources. When we went to the quarries, women often would compare, contrast, and comment on the raw material that each collected. The 16 stoneusing hideworkers select small pieces of raw material or reduce them to small pieces at the quarry (see Table 2). Although milky quartz and quartz crystal naturally break into small pieces, I saw large boulders of chert at Kalklayta. Many stone-using women search on the surface and use their iron-tipped digging sticks to mine the ground and search for materials. Kalle, an elder hideworker who lives in Gellabo near the most reliable sources of hideworking stone, stated that, in particular, she looks for natural flakes in preference to large pieces of raw

**TABLE 2 The Raw Material Collected During Ten Quarrying Events And The Associated Volume, Type Of Raw Material, And Average Number Of Produced Scrapers**

| Type of raw material | Average size in millimeters of raw material collected | Average volume of individual pieces of raw materials collected | Average number of scrapers produced |
|---|---|---|---|
| All raw material collected (N = 616) | 39% 10 millimeters or less<br>58% 10–70 millimeters<br>3% 70–120 millimeters | 196 cmm volume<br>sd = 279.2<br>range 4.8–1,448 | 4.863<br>sd = 5.46<br>range 0–22 |
| milky quartz (n = 19) | | 23.5 cmm volume<br>sd = 14.89<br>range 4–66 | 0.758<br>sd = 0.5<br>range 0–2 |
| quartz crystal (n = 10) | | 190.16 cmm volume<br>sd = 128.5<br>range 52.9–441.6 | 5.6<br>sd = 4.4<br>range 1–16 |
| chalcedony (n = 37) | | 287.67 cmm volume<br>sd = 336<br>range 6–1,461 | 6.7<br>sd = 6<br>range 0–22 |

material and prefers clear, smooth material that is not grainy. None of the 16 stone-using women form the raw material into intentional cores (a piece of raw material with scars reflecting the detachment of one or more flakes for tool production) at the quarry. Instead, they break up the raw material to ensure quality and size before transporting it back to their homes and work spaces. As they move across the landscape, most place the pieces in their skirts and tuck the edges of their skirts into their waistbands to keep the stones safe.

## SKILLED PRODUCTION AND MAINTENANCE OF STONE SCRAPERS

The majority of hideworkers using chalcedony and milky quartz begin production by heat treating the raw material to make it more brittle for reduction. The hideworker places the raw material on top of a broken piece of pottery with an insulator such as leaves, domesticated animal hair, wool, cotton, or additional pottery sherds in a pit under her hearth. There she leaves the stone for as little as 12 hours and up to three months. Once she "cooks" the stone, she then lets it cool for at least one day. Konso women knappers use different heat-treating methods based on the size, type, and quality of the raw material to increase the flakeability of the stone.

The women work stone in any shady place of their household compound. They usually knap alone, concentrating on their craft with the occasional exception of an apprenticing daughter or an older hideworker who advises the woman on the knapping process. I watched as all 16 used iron percussors (implements used for striking in stone-tool technology) to reduce the raw material with long, broad strokes and quick snaps of their wrists. I witnessed each woman reduce at least five pieces of raw material using a complex and skilled combination of direct percussion and bipolar techniques. In direct percussion, an individual directly strikes a stone that she holds in her hand with a percussor held in the other hand. Using the bipolar technique, a knapper uses a percussor to strike directly a stone that rests on an anvil (a flat stationary hard object, in this case often a stone).

Knappers select from a combination of direct percussion and bipolar technique based on the type of raw material, the size of the raw material, and on the knapping tradition used in the community in which the hideworker lives. For example, Tita, a middle-aged hideworker who lives in Kashelle, reduced a hexagonal quartz crystal (volume of 256 mm3), a natural pyramidal-shaped core, using only direct percussion in an alternating pattern. She also used direct percussion to shape the edges and reduce the dorsal thickness of the resulting 16 scrapers. All three individuals who reduced quartz crystal strictly used the direct-percussion technique in a radial or alternative-side style because they feared the impact on the anvil would shatter the stone.

Knappers using milky quartz and chalcedony often first used direct percussion and then implemented the bipolar technique. In addition, hideworkers intermittently used direct percussion for core trimming between uses of the bipolar technique. For instance, when Urmale, an elder hideworker who lives in Teshmelle, struck the raw chalcedony (volume of 269mm3) with her large iron percussor, it broke into four large preformed cores (raw material that a knapper has broken into pieces but that are not yet formal cores), flakes, and shatter. She switched to the bipolar technique to create core platforms and then reduced these cores producing six scrapers. Some hideworkers set the flatter side of a piece of raw material or preformed core on the anvil and struck the protruding surface creating more platforms. In other circumstances, they set the core platform on the anvil and struck the protruding surface creating small flakes and shatter. From the raw material, the women produced a variety of core types including multidirectional, single- and two-platform (sometimes opposed), and pyramidal-shaped cores. They usually trimmed the edges of the scrapers with direct percussion using a smaller iron percussor before hafting the scrapers.

However, some hideworkers chose to use the bipolar technique exclusively, especially when the raw material was less than 40 cubic millimeters in volume. Others employed the bipolar technique to grind off the edges of a flake to form a scraper or to grind the edges of the raw material (esp. milky quartz that tends in its raw form to be shaped like a small flake). When Likay firmly struck the small milky quartz (volume of 13.67 mm3), while it was resting on the anvil, only minute shatter fragments flew off the parent material. Likay rotated the flake on the anvil grinding the edges with the percussor until she had formed a single scraper.

Although there was little standardization in the production sequence, each woman exhibited a high degree of skill, producing, on average, five scrapers from relatively small pieces of raw material—with the exception of milky quartz (see Table 2). Each woman knapper, except those 65 and older, was able to produce between 10 and 22 scrapers from at least one of the five pieces of raw material. The only women who sometimes were unable to produce any scrapers from their raw material were those under the age of 20 or over 65. In addition, a study of five production events for each of the Konso Gellabo hideworkers suggested that there was a high degree of skill as indicated by the consistency in the size and weight of the flakes produced (Bridgeman 2003).

The Konso women I observed acquired knapping skill with practice and age, which was evident in the standardization of their unused and discarded scrapers. Conversely, there was a lack of standardization in scraper form with decreasing strength and elderhood. Konso women produced primarily unused informal scrapers (see Table 3). However, archaeologists would classify all of the discarded scrapers as formal end and side scrapers (see Table 4). Furthermore, in an earlier publication (Weedman 2005), I noted that, in rare Konso communities where female hideworkers are consanguine kin, women produced a specific scraper style. As a further measure of standardization in scraper morphology and skill of the knapper, I calculated the coefficient of variance (CV), which archaeologists (Bettinger and Eerkens 1997:CV 6–55) and ethnoarchaeologists (Weedman 2002:CV 10–27; White and Thomas 1972:CV 8–11) use to assess lithic standardization. The Konso knappers' CV range (11–30)

**TABLE 3 Informal Unused Scraper Types (n=471/680, 69 percent)**

| Informal tool types | Chalcedony | Milky quartz | Quartz crystal |
|---|---|---|---|
| modified flake | 32 | 4 | 7 |
| utilized flake | 6 | 2 | 2 |
| modified angular waste & core-trimming flake | 11 | 0 | 0 |
| cores | 4 | 0 | 0 |
| unmodified flake | 193 | 22 | 5 |
| unmodified flake fragment | 56 | 5 | 9 |
| unmodified angular waste | 104 | 2 | 1 |
| raw material | 5 | 1 | 0 |
| **Total** | **411** | **36** | **24** |

**TABLE 4 Formal Unused Scraper Types (n = 209/680, 31%) and Formal Discarded (n = 332) Scrapers**

| Formal scraper tool types | Unused chalcedony | Unused milky quartz | Unused quartz crystal | Discarded all raw material types |
|---|---|---|---|---|
| end | 51 | 8 | 40 | 194 |
| side | 19 | 2 | 3 | 109 |
| end and single side | 15 | 3 | 10 | 12 |
| end and double side | 9 | 1 | 7 | 5 |
| double end and double sided | 8 | 0 | 4 | 3 |
| limace | 1 | 0 | 0 | 0 |
| core | 4 | 0 | 1 | 1 |
| double side | 5 | 0 | 4 | 7 |
| double end | 1 | 0 | 6 | 0 |
| double end and single side | 2 | 0 | 2 | 0 |
| convergent | 0 | 0 | 0 | 1 |
| triangular | 2 | 0 | 0 | 0 |
| double end on ventral and dorsal | 1 | 0 | 0 | 0 |
| **Total** | **118 (56%)** | **14 (6.6%)** | **77 (37%)** | **332** |

indicated a high rate of standardization for both unused and discarded scrapers— with the exception of results for women under 20 or over 70 years of age (see Table 5). Importantly, women achieve lithic standardization through practice and increasing skill. Correspondingly, with loss of strength as a knapper grows older, standardization begins to wane.

Age and skill also are evident in the ability of knappers to maintain a sharp working edge on their stone scrapers. During use on the hides, Konso women reduce the length of their scrapers through edge rejuvenation, which requires skill and strength. As a result of sharpening the scraper by removing small flakes off the working edge, there is a considerable difference in the length of the scrapers (5.65 mm) between their unused and discarded phase. In my earlier studies of male knapping and skill (Weedman 2002), I noted that, compared to middle-aged knappers, younger and elderly individuals tended to break their scrapers more frequently while resharpening the edges of their tools because of their lack of skill or waning strength. In addition, younger and elder individuals often produced spurs (projections on the edge of the tool) not as a functional addition to the scraper (e.g., for puncturing or engraving) but, again, as a result of their lack of skill or strength.

**TABLE 5 Coefficient of Variance (CV) for Unused Scrapers and Discarded Scrapers**

| Hideworker's age (n = number of scrapers) | Mean length (mm) | SD | CV × 100 | Mean breadth (mm) | SD | CV × 100 |
|---|---|---|---|---|---|---|
| Unused | | | | | | |
| 75 (n = 44) | 19.05 | 4.78 | 25.09 | 16.99 | 5.04 | 29.6 |
| 72 (n = 50) | 19.44 | 5.5 | 28.29 | 14.35 | 4.32 | 30.10 |
| 16 (n = 42) | 19.44 | 4.3 | 22.12 | 13.93 | 4.29 | 30.79 |
| 65 (n = 30) | 16.01 | 2.31 | 14.43 | 14.28 | 3.1 | 21.7 |
| 62 (n = 33) | 22.5 | 3.16 | 14.04 | 15.87 | 2.9 | 18.27 |
| 48 (n = 97) | 17.25 | 3.7 | 21.45 | 11.28 | 2.4 | 20.18 |
| 35 (n = 95) | 17.7 | 3.21 | 18.14 | 13.78 | 3.2 | 23.22 |
| 32 (n = 42) | 19.44 | 3.7 | 19.03 | 13.62 | 2.66 | 19.53 |
| 27 (n = 35) | 19.29 | 3.17 | 16.43 | 14.67 | 3.56 | 24.26 |
| Discarded | | | | | | |
| 72 (n = 166) | 12.52 | 2.7 | 21.56 | 12.2 | 2.93 | 24.01 |
| 70 (n = 24) | 14.99 | 1.7 | 11.3 | 16.3 | 3.45 | 21.1 |
| 48 (n = 46) | 14.99 | 2.43 | 22 | 11.49 | 2.72 | 23.6 |
| 28 (n = 24) | 14.99 | 4.45 | 25.87 | 16.35 | 2.88 | 17.61 |
| 16 (n = 36) | 14.19 | 4.13 | 29.1 | 12.27 | 2.6 | 21.1 |

While I observed Konso knappers, I also noticed that women under 20 or over 70 years of age produced the largest proportion of scrapers with spurs (83 percent) and were responsible for all of the scrapers broken during use. Subsequently, when a spur was present on the scraper, practitioners urged novices to scrape thicker cattle hides that were more difficult to rip. However, there are no strong associations between Konso unused scraper morphologies and type of hide scraped (Behrend 2003). I also observed several of the novices and elderly hideworkers cut their fingers during production and edge rejuvenation, which resulted in collagen and blood residues identified through microscopic studies of these scraper edges (Rots and Williamson 2004). Thus, the ability to use and maintain a scraper without breaking it or creating spurs requires practice, skill, and strength.

## DISCUSSION

Diane Gifford-Gonzalez (1993) pointed out that when we reconstruct the past, we base it on our Western concepts of division of labor, ascribing women with the most labor intensive, dull, and unskilled tasks, which certainly extends to our descriptions of women's stone-tool assemblages. This review of women's lithic technology demonstrates how material culture (stone) and an individual's social position (Xauta), tasks (feminine), and experiences (age and skill) are transformed through learning and practice in a non-Western social context (Dietler and Herbich 1998; Dobres and Hoffman 1999; Gosselain 1998; Hodder 2003; Ingold 1993:436–439; Lechtman 1977; Pfaffenberger 1992; Weedman 2006). A majority of stone toolmakers among the Konso are women because most Konso people consider the associated tasks of cooking (heat treating), grinding (knapping and sharpening the edge), and kneeling (during cooking, knapping, and scraping) "feminine" activities. In other non-Western cultures, both male and female artisans are considered feminine because they transform materials (Sterner and David 1991), and in other cultures the art of hideworking is a feminine task because of its ideological association with rebirth or reviving the hide (Baillargeon 2005). Importantly, Konso stone-tool technology symbolically links fertility and women to lithic expertise, providing an alternative gender ideology to the "man-the-toolmaker" and "woman-the-gatherer" paradigm. Konso knappers reveal the growing recognition that gender tasks are fluid transformations across time and space (Jarvenpa and Brumbach 2006; Owen 2005). Viewing gender as symbolic and ambiguous does not destabilize archaeological reconstructions (Voss 2000); rather, it forces us to unearth a more nuanced understanding of the dynamic needs, desires, ideas, and practices of individuals buried in material culture.

Still, the enduring image of stone-tool enculturation is one of a prepubescent boy sitting adjacent to an experienced and skilled man, engaged in a time-consuming and sophisticated craft (Binford 1986; Crabtree 1982; Fischer 1990; Flenniken 1978; Gould 1980; Hayden 1979; Nelson 1977; Oakley 1949; Whittaker 1994; for critique, see Bamforth and Finlay 2008; Finlay 1997). Even well-intended articles acknowledging women as toolmakers unknowingly devalue female knapping technology by labeling it "expedient" and "unskilled" to distinguish it from men's technology (Bruhns and Stothert 1999; Casey 1998; Fischman 1992; Gero 1991; Kehoe 2005; Kohn and Mithen 1999; Sassaman 1992). Archaeologists commonly credit men with finely made tools such as projectile points (Whittaker 1994:294–298) and scrapers (Bordes 1961) because many researchers believe as Joanna Casey summarizes:

> men travel to hunt, but their tools have a life and mobility independent of the men to whom they belong. . . . they are lost . . . or break and are abandoned by their owners, are in a sense calling cards . . . exquisitely designed projectile points is the material expression of symbolic behavior for social or supernatural protection. [1998:99–100

In another attempt to include women in Stone Age technology, Kenneth Sassaman (1992) suggests that women's expedient technology may have contributed to the "degeneration" of lithic technology in the Ceramic periods in North America. His goal is to ensure that archaeologists consider the sexual division of labor as a source for technological change; however, in the process, he devalues women's technology. Linda Owen's (2005:38–39) criticisms of Marek Kohn and Steven Mithen (1999) highlight another instance of archaeologists associating women with less sophisticated and poorly made tools and crediting men with making finely made tools imbued with symbolic meaning and with creating new techniques.

> Males tend towards display, so conspicuously impractical handaxes were most likely made by males, whilst females would make less refined, more practical handaxes. . . . They [females] were now concerned about their relationships with their mates, not just the quality of their mates' genes, and their mate-choice criteria shifted accordingly; towards those males who were most reliable in the provision of resources. In response, males made their artefacts according to the demands of functional efficiency, developing varied toolkits as a result. Consequently, we see the development of Levallois technology for producing good-quality blanks, and the appearance of spears with stone points. [Kohn and Mithen 1999:523–524]

Konso female knappers demonstrate that women's lithic technology, like men's, is sophisticated and time consuming and takes place in a strict social context that provides selective apprenticeships. Knappers restrict the transmission of lithic technology within their endogamous-hereditary craft community of Xauta Kollaya (hideworkers). Transfer of hideworking and lithic technology usually involves explicit adult demonstration and explanation to young, "special," second or third daughters, who are not as encumbered with housework as first daughters, to enhance skill and performance. Novices generally begin knapping with the guidance of practitioners starting at age 14. Most Konso women demand 10 to 15 years of knapping practice and instruction before they deem a novice proficient. Prior to this benchmark, young women tend to (1) produce fewer useable scrapers from a piece of raw material, (2) produce less standardized scrapers (Ferguson 2008), (3) more frequently break their scrapers during use, and (4) primarily scrape thicker cow hides that are more difficult to rip because scraper-edge rejuvenation is poor and produces spurs (Weedman 2002). However, I did not observe novices producing larger tools (Stout 2002), cores that lack platform preparation (Fischer 1990; Pigeot 1990), or poor blades (Bodu et al. 1990). Elder knappers who have lost strength also more frequently break their scrapers and experience difficulties with edge rejuvenation. Importantly, women's technology and training parallels accounts of male knapping technology, which have been described as a time consuming and sophisticated skill that begins prior to puberty.

Like images of Stone Age life in The *Flintstones* (Hanna and Barbera 1960–66) cartoons, wherein women stay at home with the children and men work in the stone quarry, archaeologists continue to keep Stone Age women close to home where they use poor-quality local resources (Weedman 2005). But Konso women are not sadly stuck in the Stone Age. They have pride in their knapping skills and intentionally select, use, and prefer high quality stone raw materials to ensure the superiority of their hide products. In raw-material selection, stone-toolusing women reluctantly use local stone and spurn glass and iron resources in favor of long-distance resources. Konso women are not the only example of women who choose high-quality stone raw material or travel a long distance to acquire the material, as evidenced in worldwide ethnographic accounts (Allchin 1957:125; Beyries 2002; Dunn 1931:411; Gusinde 1931:353; Man 1883:380; Mason 1889:585; Nelson 1899:113; Roth 1899:151; Takase 2004; Webley 2005). Ethnographic evidence clearly illustrates that women are highly knowledgeable lithic practitioners who actively seek superior raw materials, thus dispelling myths that women are passive and careless in their selection of lithic resources.

In the film *2001: A Space Odyssey* (Kubrick and Clarke 1968), a prehuman form violently smashes a large stick against rocks that are sitting on a stone surface, recounting our first attempt to make stone tools. It is no wonder that we believe bipolar technology to be simplistic—after all, how hard can it be to bash rocks together? Early archaeologists reinforced this image of bipolar technology as simple and associated it with a lack of skill (Patterson 1979), lack of good-quality raw material (Binford and Quimby 1963; Bleed and Meier 1980), small raw-material size (de la Torre 2004; Flenniken 1981), and economizing and recycling resources (Goodyear 1993; Jeske 1992). Ethnographers have primarily described women as engaged in bipolar reduction (Albright 1984:57; Dunn 1931:41; Gorman 1995; Holmes 1919:316; Man 1883:380; Roth 1923:278–280; Sellers 1885:872; Sillitoe and Hardy 2003). Likely because of the prevalence of the bipolar technique and the reluctance to associate stone-tool technology with women, most archaeologists have not associated this technique with women— neither from the earliest Stone Age assemblages nor through each subsequent historic period across the world (de la Torre 2004; Johnson 1997; Schick and Toth 1993; Wadley 2005).

More recently, archaeologists have revealed the complex nature of identifying and practicing bipolar technology by renaming fabricators, wedges, *pièces esquillées* (scalared or irregular and overlapping flake scares on pieces of stone), and outils ´ecaill´es (scalar cores) as bipolar cores (Flenniken 1981; Hayden 1980; Shott 1989; White 1968) and through archaeological and experimental assemblage studies (Barham 1987; Berman et al. 1999; Kuijt et al. 1995; Mercader and Brookes 2001; Orton 2002). Konso women's lithic technology may look simple, but it supports growing evidence of the sophistication of bipolar reduction, as women tack between various bipolar and direct-percussion techniques and produce a good number of usable scrapers from small pieces of raw material. Jill Pruetz and Paco Bertolani (2007) recently suggested that when female primates have limited access to preferred resources, they compensate by developing new tool technologies, such as spears made by chimpanzees for hunting. They conclude that females may have developed the earliest tool technology. Similarly, early ethnographers associate women with bipolar technologies, and archaeologists believe knappers use bipolar technology to economize resources. Thus, because bipolar technology is among the earliest-known stone-tool technologies, I suggest that perhaps female hominids were the first to produce stone tools.

The idea of women as skilled toolmakers and perhaps the very first toolmakers is inspirational, but it is likely that future literature will either opt for gender neutrality on issues of flintknapping or continue to ignore the evidence. For instance, Brian Hayden (1992:35) stated that ethnographers recognize women worldwide as hideworkers and that the presence of hideworking tools then must indicate the presence of women. However, on the same page of his chapter in *Exploring Gender through Archaeology*, he noted that stone working, including hideworking stone technology, is the exclusive task of males. How are we to make sense of this? One of the longest-standing debates in archaeology concerns the variation present in Paleolithic hide scrapers (Andrefsky 1994; Bamforth 1986; Bisson 2001; Bordes 1961; Dibble 1987; Kuhn 1992; Meltzer 1981; Wobst 2000), yet no one has suggested that perhaps differences in sex and gender may account for the stone-scraper variability. The latter once again reflects the idea that archaeologists perceive women's technology as unskilled and expedient. In addition to the Konso, there are many ethnographic accounts indicating that women produce a variety of formal tool types including hidescrapers, arrowpoints, knives, and drills (Beyries 2002; Dunn 1931; Ewers 1930:10–13; Grey 1841:266; Hiller 1948; Holmes 1919:316; Lowie 1935:75–79; Mason 1889; Sellars 1885:872; Takase 2004; Turner 1894). Many Konso Xauta Kollaya women produce formal discarded end- and side-hide scrapers with a high degree of consistency and skill in overall size morphology that matches other studies of tool standardization as a measurement of skill (Bettinger and Eerkens 1997; Weedman 2002; White and Thomas 1972). I conclude that women can skillfully produce standardized formal tools, and archaeologists should consider sex and gender when analyzing Stone Age lithics.

In summary, Konso female stone-tool users are skilled knappers who develop their expertise through long-term practice and apprenticeship. They identify themselves with lithic technology in a socially embedded ideology that values their knapping skill as explicitly feminine. The small community of stone-using women has pride in their knapping skills and intentionally select, use, and prefer high-quality stone raw materials to ensure the quality of their hide products and in the process reject local stone and glass resources in favor of long-distance resources. Furthermore, women's bipolar lithic technology may look simple, but it is complex and sophisticated, requiring continual decision making and intensive learning and practice.

Thus, there is overwhelming evidence for women's sophisticated engagement with lithic technology to produce formal standardized tools. We must reevaluate our reconstructions of women's roles in the Stone Age. Ethnohistoric and ethnographic evidence strongly associates women with bipolar and stone hideworking technology. It is imperative that we reconsider the possibility that women are among—if not the first of—the earliest stone toolmakers, that women are responsible for Stone Age scraper tool kits, and that we cannot solely associate high-quality formal stone tools with men. In addition, the material visibility of an individual's role as novice apprentice, practitioner, and elder practitioner emphasizes that a finer-grained understanding of the individual and social dynamics is possible through studying lithic technology in the archaeological record.

## NOTE

***Acknowledgments.*** This project was generously funded by the National Science Foundation. For this, I am grateful to John Yellen, the program officer, and the proposal reviewers. I wish to thank *AA* editor, Tom Boellstorff, all *AA* anonymous reviewers, Thomas Hester, Jane Branham, and Mari Gillogly for their valuable detailed comments. I extend my deep gratitude to Ethiopia's Authority for Research and Conservation of Cultural Heritage; the Southern Nations, Nationalities, and Peoples Regional Government's Bureau of Culture and Information in Awasa, Arba Minch, and Konso; the National Museum of Ethiopia; and the Addis Ababa University Herbarium. In particular, I thank Jara Hailemarium, Yonis Bayene, Mamitu Yilma, Hasen Said, Menisay Girma, Sagoya Robia, Abebaw Ejigu, Denote Kusia Shinkara, Awoke Amayze, and Kuse Kelto. Many other people contributed greatly to the success of this project, and I thank them for their collegiality, scholarship, and written and cinematic works including Steven Brandt (Co-PI), John W. Arthur, Matt Behrend, Tara Belkin, Kara Bridgman, Harriet Clift, James Ellison, Erich Fischer, Birgitta Kimura, Rebecca Klein, Veerle Rots, Justin Shipley, and Bonny Williamson. Heartfelt thanks go toward many Konso people—but most especially to the hideworkers.

## REFERENCES CITED

Ainston, George 1929 Chipped Stone Tools of the Aboriginal Tribes East and North-East of Lake Eyre, South Australia. Papers and Proceedings of the Royal Society of Tasmania 1928:123–131.

Albright, Sylvia 1984 Tahltan Ethnoarchaeology. Vancouver: Department of Archaeology, Simon Fraser University.

Allchin, Bridget 1957 Australian Stone Industries, Past and Present. Journal of the Royal Anthropological Institute 87(1):115–136.

Andrefsky, William, Jr. 1994 Raw-Material Availability and the Organization of Technology.vAmerican Antiquity 59(1):21–35.

Arthur, Kathryn Weedman 2008 Stone-Tool Hide Production: The Gamo of Southwestern Ethiopia and Cross-Cultural Comparisons. Anthropozoologica 43(1):67–98.

Baillargeon, Morgan 2005 Hide Tanning: The Act of Reviving. *In* Gender and Hide Production. Lisa Frink and Kathryn Weedman, eds. Pp. 143– 52. Walnut Creek, CA: AltaMira.

Bamforth, Douglas 1986 A Comment on Functional Variability in an Assemblage of Endscrapers. Lithic Technology 15(2):61–64.

Bamforth, Douglas, and Nyree Finlay 2008 Introduction: Archaeological Approaches to Lithic Production Skill and Craft. Journal of Archaeological Method and Theory 15(1):1–27.

Barham, Lawrence 1987 The Bipolar Technique in Southern Africa:AReplication Experiment. South African Archaeological Bulletin 42(145):45–50.

Behrend, Matthew 2003 Stone Scraper Variation and Hide Type among the Konso of Southern Ethiopia. Paper presented at the Woman the Tool-Maker: Contemporary Flaked Stone Tool Production and Use among the Konso of Southern Ethiopia session; K. Weedman and S. Brandt, chairs; at the Annual Meeting of the Society for American Archaeology, Milwaukee, April 11.

Belkin, Tara, Steven Brandt, and Kathryn Weedman 2006 Woman the Toolmaker: Hideworking and Stone Tool Use in Konso, Ethiopia. Archaeological Methods and Practice. An Educational Film Series. 25 min. and 4 pp. Walnut Creek, CA: Left Coast.

Berman, Mary Jane, April Sievert, and Thomas Whyte 1999 Form and Function of Bipolar Lithic Artifacts from the Three Dog Site, San Salvador, Bahamas. Latin American Antiquity 10(4):415–432.

Bettinger, Robert, and Jelmer Eerkens 1997 Evolutionary Implications of Metrical Variation in Great Basin Projectile Points. *In* Rediscovering Darwin: Evolutionary Theory and Archaeological Exploration. C. Michael Barton and Geoffrey A. Clark, eds. Pp. 177–191. Arlington, VA: Papers of the American Anthropological Association.

Beyries, Sylvie 2002 Le Travail du Cuir chez les Tchouktches et les Athapaskans: Implications Ethno-Arch´eologiques [The leatherworking of the Tchouktches and Athapaskans: Ethnoarchaeological implications]. *In* Le travail du Cuir de la Prehistoire à nos Jours [Leatherworking of prehistory to the present]. Frédérique Audoin-Rouzeau and Sylvie Beyries, eds. Pp. 143–148. Antibes, France: ´Editions APDCA.

Binford, Lewis 1986 An Alyawara Day: Making Men's Knives and Beyond. American Antiquity 51(3):547–562.

Binford, Lewis, and George Quimby 1963 Indian Sites and Chipped Stone Materials in the Northern Lake Michigan Area. Fieldiana Anthropology 36:277–307.

Bird, C. F. M. 1993 Woman the Tool-Maker: Evidence for Women's Use and Manufacture of Flaked Stone Tools in Australia and New Guinea. *In* Women in Archaeology: A Feminist Critique. Hilary du Cros and Laura-jane Smith, eds. Pp. 22–30. Canberra: The Australian National University.

Bisson, Michael 2001 Interview with a Neanderthal: An Experimental Approach for Reconstructing Scraper Production Rules, and Their Implications for Imposed Form in Middle Paleolithic Tools. Cambridge Archaeological Journal 11(2):165–184.

Bleed, Peter, and Marlene Meier 1980 An Objective Test of the Effects of Heat Treatment of Flakeable Stone. American Antiquity 45(3):502–507.

Bodu, Pierre, Claudine Karlin, and Sylvie Ploux 1990 Who's Who? The Magdalenian Flintknappers of Pincevent, France. *In* The Big Puzzle: International Symposium on Refitting Stone Artefacts. Erwin Cziesla, Sabine Eickhoff, Nico Arts, and Doris Winter, eds. Pp. 143–163. Bonn: Holos.

Bordes, Francois 1961 Mousterian Cultures in France. Science 134(3482):803–810.

Brandt, Steven, and Kathryn Weedman 1997 The Ethnoarchaeology of Hide Working and Flaked Stone Tool Use in Southern Ethiopia. *In* Broader Perspective: Papers of the Twelfth International Conference of Ethiopian Studies. Katsuyoshi Fukui, Eisei Kurimoto, and Masayoshi Shigeta, eds. Pp. 351–361. Kyoto: Shokado Book Sellers.

Bridgeman, Kara 2003 Identifying the Individual: Debitage Studies of the Konso Hide Workers of Ethiopia. Paper presented at the Society of American Archaeology, Milwaukee, April 11.

Bruhns, Karen, and Karen Stothert 1999 Women in Ancient America. Norman: University of Oklahoma Press.

Casey, Joanna 1998 Just a Formality: The Presence of Fancy Projectile Points n a Basic Tool Assemblage. *In* Gender in African Prehistory. Susan Kent, ed. Pp. 83–104. Walnut Creek, CA: AltaMira.

Crabtree, Don 1982 An Introduction to Flintworking. Pocatello: Idaho Museum of Natural History.

de la Torre, Ignacio 2004 Omo Revisited: Evaluating the Technological Skills of Pliocene Hominids. Current Anthropology 45(4):439–465.

Dibble, Harold 1987 The Interpretation of Middle Paleolithic Scraper Morphology. American Antiquity 52(1): 109–117.

Dietler, Michael, and Ingrid Herbich 1998 Habitus, Techniques, Style: An Integrated Approach to Social Understanding of Material Culture and Boundaries. *In* The Archaeology of Social Boundaries. Miriam Stark, ed. Pp. 232–269. London: Smithsonian Institution Press.

Dobres, Marcia-Anne, and Christopher R. Hoffman 1999 Introduction: A Context for the Present and Future of Technology Studies. *In* The Social Dynamics of Technology. Marcia-Anne Dobres and Christopher R. Hoffman, eds. Pp. 1–22. Washington, DC: Smithsonian Institution Press.

Dunn, Edward 1931 The Bushman. London: Charles Griffin.

Elkin, Adolphus 1948 Pressure Flaking in the Northern Kimberley, Australia. Man 48(130):110–113.

Ellison, James 2008 "Everyone Can Do as He Wants": Economic Liberalization and Emergent Forms of Antipathy in Southern Ethiopia. American Ethnologist 33(4): 665–686.

2009 Governmentality and the Family: Neoliberal Choices and Emergent Kin Relations in Southern Ethiopia. American Anthropologist 11(1):81–92.

Ewers, John C. 1930 Blackfeet Crafts. Washington, DC: Department of the Interior Bureau of Indian Affairs.

Ferguson, James 2008 The When, Where, and How of Novices in Craft Production. Journal of Archaeological Method and Theory 15(1):51–67.

Finlay, Nyree 1997 Kid Knapping: The Missing Children in Lithic Analysis. *In* Invisible People and Processes: Writing Gender and Childhood into Archaeology. Jenny Moore and Eleanor Scott, eds. Pp. 202–212. London: Leicester University Press.

Fischer, Anders 1990 On Being a Pupil of a Flintknapper of 11,000 Years Ago. *In* The Big Puzzle: International Symposium on Refitting Stone Artefacts. Erwin Cziesla, Sabine Eickhoff, Nico Arts, and Doris Winter, eds. Pp. 143–163. Bonn: Holos.

Fischer, Erich 2003 Lithic Procurement Sites and Strategies among the Konso of Ethiopia. Paper presented at the Annual Meeting of the Society of American Archaeology, Milwaukee, April 11.

Fischman, Joshua 1992 Hard Evidence: By Re-Creating Stone Age Behavior, Researchers Are Learning That Neanderthals Were Nothing Like the People We Imagined. Discover (February):44–46.

Flenniken, J. Jeffrey 1978 Reevaluation of the Lindemeier Folsom: A Replication Experiment in Lithic Technology. American Antiquity 43(3):473–480.

1981 Replicative Systems Analysis:AModel Applied to the Quartz Artifacts from the Hoko River Site. Reports of Investigation, 59. Indianapolis: Indiana Historical Society.

Gallagher, James 1977 Ethnoarchaeological and Prehistoric Investigations in the Ethiopian Central Rift Valley. Ph.D. dissertation, Department of Anthropology, University of Michigan.

Gero, Joan 1991 Genderlithics: Women's Roles in Stone-Tool Production. *In* Engendering Archaeology: Women and Prehistory. Joan M. Gero and Margaret W. Conkey, eds. Pp. 163–193. Oxford: Blackwell.

Gifford-Gonzalez, Diane 1993 You Can Hide, But You Can't Run: Representation of Women's Work in Illustrations of Paleolithic Life. Visual Anthropology Review 9(1): 22–29.

Goodyear, Albert 1993 Tool Kit Entropy and Bipolar Reduction. North American Archaeologist 14(1):1–23.

Gorman, Alice 1995 Gender, Labour and Resources: The Female Knappers of the Andaman Islands. *In* Gender Archaeology: The Second Australian Women in Archaeology Conference. Jane Balme and Wendy Beck, eds. Pp. 87–91. Canberra: The Australian National University ANH Publications, RSPAS.

Gosselain, Oliver P. 1998 Social and Technical Identity in a Clay Crystal Ball. *In* The Archaeology of Social Boundaries. Miriam Stark, ed. Pp. 78–107. London: Smithsonian Institution Press.

Gould, Richard 1980 Living Archaeology. Cambridge: Cambridge University Press.

Grey, George 1841 Journals of Two Expedition of Discovery in North-West and Western Australia, During the Years 1837, 38, and 39, vol. 2. London: T. and W. Boone.

Gusinde, Martin 1931 The Fireland Indians, vol. 1: The Selk'nam, on the Life and Thought of a Hunting People of the Great Island of Tierra del Fuego. Berlin: Verlag.

Hallpike, Christopher 1972 The Konso of Ethiopia: A Study of the Values of a Cushitic People. Oxford: Claredon.

Harding, Sandra 1998 Is Science Multi-Cultural? Postcolonialisms, Feminisms, and Epistemologies. Bloomington: Indiana University Press.

Hasen, Abdulahi 1996 Livestock, Poultry and Beehives Population and Number of Holders by Size of Holding. Addis Ababa, Ethiopia: Office of Population and Housing Census Commission Central Statistical Authority.

Hayden, Brian 1979 Paleolithic Reflections: Lithic Technology and Ethnographic Excavation among Australian Aborigines. Atlantic Highlands, NJ: Humanities.

1980 Confusion in the Bipolar World. Lithic Technology 9:2–7.

1992 Observing Prehistoric Women. *In* Exploring Gender through Archaeology: Selected Papers from the 1991 Boone Conference. Cheryl Claassen, ed. Pp. 33–48. Madison, WI: Prehistory.

Hiller, W. R. 1948 Hidatsa Soft Tanning of Hides. Minnesota Archaeologists 14:4–11.

Hodder, Ian 2003 Archaeology beyond Dialogue. Salt Lake City: University of Utah Press.

Holmes, William H. 1919 Handbook of Aboriginal American Antiquities (Part I). Bulletin 60. Washington, DC: Washington Bureau of American Ethnology.

Ingold, Tim 1993 Technology, Language, Intelligence: A Reconsideration of Basic Concepts. *In* Tools, Language and Cognition in Human Evolution. Kathleen Gibson and Tim Ingold, eds. Pp. 449–472. Cambridge: Cambridge University Press.

Jarvenpa, Robert, and Hetty Jo Brumbach, eds. 2006 Circumpolar Lives and Livelihood: A Comparative Ethnoarchaeology of Gender and Subsistence. Lincoln: University of Nebraska Press.

Jeske, Robert 1992 The Archaeological Visibility of Bipolar Technology. Midcontinental Journal of Archaeology 15:131–160.

Johnson, Jay 1997 Stone Tools, Politics, and the Eighteenth-Century Chickasaw in Northeast Mississippi. American Antiquity 62(2):215–230.

Kehoe, Alice B. 2005 Expedient Angled-Tanged Endscrapers: Glimpsing Women's Work in the Archaeological Record. *In* Gender and Hide Production. Lisa Frink and Kathryn Weedman, eds. Pp. 133–142. Walnut Creek, CA: AltaMira.

Kohn, Marek, and Steven Mithen 1999 Handaxes: Products of Sexual Selection? Antiquity 73(281):518–526.

Kubrick, Stanley, and Arthur C. Clarke 1968 2001: A Space Odyssey. 141 min. Warner Studios. Santa Monica, CA.

Kuhn, Steven 1992 Blank Form and Reduction as Determinants of Mousterian Scraper Morphology. American Antiquity 57(1):115–128.

Kuijt, Ian, William C. Prentiss, and David L. Pokotylo 1995 Bipolar Reduction. Lithic Technology 20(2):116–127.

Latta, Forest 1949 Handbook of Yokuts Indians. Oildae, CA: Bear State.

Lave, Jean, and Etienne Wenger 1991 Situated Learning: Legitimate Peripheral Participation. Cambridge: Cambridge University Press.

Lechtman, Heather 1977 Style in Technology: Some Early Thoughts. *In* Material Culture: Styles, Organization, and Dynamics of Technology. Heather Lechtman and Robert Merrill, eds. Pp. 3–20. New York: West.

Lothrop, Samuel 1928 The Indians of Tierra del Fuego. New York: Museum of the American Indian Heye Foundation.

Lowie, Robert H. 1935 The Crow Indians. New York: Farrar and Rinehart.

MacCalman, H. Rona, and B. J. Grobbelaar 1965 Preliminary Report of Two Stone-Working Ova Tjimba Groups in the Northern Kaokoveld of S.W.Africa. Cimbebasia 13(1965):1–39.

Man, Edward Horace 1883 On Aboriginal Inhabitants of the Andaman Islands (Part 3), Journal of the Anthropological Institute of Britain and Ireland 12(1883): 327–434.

Mason, Otis 1889 Aboriginal Skin Dressing. Washington, DC: Smithsonian Institution Press.

Meltzer, David 1981 Study of Style and Function in a Class of Tools. Journal of Field Archaeology 8(3):313–326.

Mercader, Julio, and Alison S. Brookes 2001 Across Forest and Savannas: Later Stone Age Assemblages from Ituri and Semliki, Democratic Republic of Congo. Journal of Anthropological Research 57(2):197–217.

Moser, Stephanie 1993 Gender Stereotyping in Pictorial Reconstructions of Human Origins. *In* Women in Archaeology: A Feminist Critique. Hilary du Cros and Laurajane Smith, eds. Pp. 75–91. Canberra: The Australian National University Press.

Murdoch, John 1892 Ethnological Results of the Point Barrow Expedition. Washington, DC: Smithsonian Institution Press.

Nelson, Edward 1899 The Eskimo about Bering Strait. Washington, DC: Smithsonian Institution Press.

Nelson, Nels 1977[1916] Flintworking by Ishi. In Holmes Anniversary Volume: Anthropological Essays Presented to William Henry Holmes in Honor of His Seventieth Birthday, December 1, 1916. Pp. 397–402. New York: AMS Press.

Oakley, Kenneth P. 1949 Man the Tool-Maker. London: British Museum.

Orton, Jayson 2002 Patterns in Stone. South African Archaeological Bulletin 57(175):31–37.

Owen, Linda 2000 Lithic Functional Analysis as a Means of Studying Gender and Material Culture in Prehistory. *In* Gender and Material Culture in Archaeological Perspective. Moira Donald and Linda Hurcombe, eds. Pp. 185–205. London: MacMillan.

2005 Distorting the Past: Gender and the Division of Labor in the European Upper Paleolithic. Tubingen: Kerns Verlag.

Patterson, Leland W. 1979 Additional Comments on Bipolar Flaking. Flintknapper's Exchange 2:21–22.

Pfaffenberger, Brian 1992 Social Anthropology of Technology. Annual Review of Anthropology 21:491–516.

Pigeot, Nicole 1990 Technical and Social Actors: Flintknapping Specialists and Apprentices at Magdalenian Etiolles. Archaeological Review Cambridge 9(1):126–141.

Pruetz, Jill, and Paco Bertolani 2007 Savanna Chimpanzees, *Pan troglodytes versus*, Hunt with Tools. Current Biology 17:412–417.

Roth, H. Ling 1899 The Aborigines of Tasmania. Halifax: F. King and Sons.

Roth, Walter Edmond 1923 An Introductory Study of the Arts, Crafts, and Customs of the Guiana Indians. Thirty-Eighth Annual Report of the Bureau of American Ethnology (1916–1917):23–745.

Rots, Veerle, and Browynne Williamson 2004 Microwear and Residue Analyses in Perspective: The Contribution of Ethnoarchaeological Evidence. Journal of Archaeological Science 31(9):1287–1299.

Sassaman, Kenneth 1992 Gender and Technology at the Archaic-Woodland "Transition." *In* Exploring Gender through Archaeology: Selected Papers from the 1991 Boone Conference. Cheryl Claassen, ed. Pp. 71–79. Madison: Prehistory.

Schick, Kathy, and Nicholas Toth 1993 Making Silent Stones Speak: Human Evolution and the Dawn of Technology. New York: Simon and Schuster.

Sellers, George 1885 Observations on Stone-Chipping. Smithsonian Institute Annual Report (1885):871–891.

Shott, Michael 1989 Bipolar Industries: Ethnographic Evidence and Archaeological Implications. North American Archaeologist 10(1):1–24.

Sillitoe, Paul, and Karen Hardy 2003 Living Lithics: Ethnoarchaeology in Highland Papua New Guinea. Antiquity 77:555–566.

Soffer, Olga, James Adovasio, and David C. Hyland 2001 Perishable Technologies and Invisible People. *In* Enduring Records: The Environmental and Cultural Heritage of Wetlands. Barbara Purdy, ed. Pp. 233–245. Oxford: Oxbow.

Stepan, Nancy 1986 Race and Gender: The Role of Analogy in Science. ISIS 77(1):261–277.

Sterner, Judith, and Nicholas David 1991 Gender and Caste in the Mandara Highlands: Northeastern Nigeria and Northern Cameroon. Ethnology 30(4):355–369.

Stout, Dietrich 2002 Skill and Cognition in Stone Tool Production. Current Anthropology 43(5):693–722.

Takase, Katsunori 2004 Hide Processing of Oxen and Koryak: An Ethnoarchaeological Survey in Kamchatka Peninsula, Russia. Material Culture (Japan) 77:57–84.

Toth, Nicholas, John Desmond Clark, and Giancarlo Ligabue 1992 The Last Stone Ax Makers. Scientific American 267(1):88–93.

Turner, Lucien 1894 Ethnology of the Ungava District: Hudson Bay Territory. Eleventh Annual Report of the Bureau of Ethnology. Washington, DC: Smithsonian Institution Press.

Voss, Barbara 2000 Feminism, Queer Theories, and the Archaeological Study of Past Sexualities. World Archaeology 32(2):180–192.

Wadley, Lynn 1998 The Invisible Meat Providers: Women in the Stone Age. *In* Gender in African Prehistory. Susan Kent, ed. Pp. 39–68. Walnut Creek, CA: AltaMira.

2005 A Typological Study of the Final Middle Stone Age Stone Tools from Sibundu Cave, Kwazulu Natal. South African Archaeological Bulletin 60(182):51–63.

Watson, Elizabeth 1997 Ritual Leaders and Agricultural Resources in South-Western Ethiopia: "Poquallas," Land and Labour in Konso. *In* Broader Perspective: Papers of the Twelfth International Conference of Ethiopian Studies. Katsuyoshi Fukui, Eisei Kurimoto, and Masayoshi Shigeta, eds. Pp. 652–669. Kyoto: Shokado Book Sellers.

Webley, Lita 2005 Hideworking among Descendants of Khoekhoen Pastoralist in Northern Cape, South Africa. *In* Gender and Hide Production. Lisa Frink and Kathryn Weedman, eds. Pp. 153–174. Walnut Creek, CA: AltaMira.

Weedman, Kathryn 2002 On the Spur of the Moment: Effects of Age and Experience on Hafted Stone Scraper Morphology. American Antiquity 67(4):731–744.

2005 Gender and Stone Tools: An Ethnographic Study of the Konso andGamoHideworkers of Southern Ethiopia. *In* Gender and Hide Production. Lisa Frink and Kathryn Weedman, eds. Pp. 175–196. Walnut Creek, CA: AltaMira.

2006 An Ethnoarchaeological Study of Hafting and Stone Tools among the Gamo of Southern Ethiopia. Journal of Archaeological Method and Theory 13(3):188–237.

Wenger, Etienne 1998 Communities of Practice: Learning, Meaning, and Identity. Cambridge: Cambridge University Press.

White, J. Peter 1968 Fabricators, Outils Écaillés or Scalar Cores? Mankind 6(12):658–666.

White, J. Peter, and D. H. Thomas 1972 What Mean These Stones? Ethno-Taxonomic Models and Archaeological Interpretations in the New Guinea Highlands. *In* Models in Archaeology. David L. Clarke, ed. Pp. 275–308. London: Methuen.

Whittaker, John 1994 Flintknapping: Making and Understanding Stone Tools. Austin: University of Texas Press.

Wilson, D. E., and R. Meadows 1997 Evidence for Stone Tool Production in the Burial Population from Colha Operation 3017, A Late Classic Lithic Workshop in Northern Belize. Unpublished MS on file, Cohoal Project. (Courtesy of Thomas Hester, June 26, 2009).

Wobst, Hans Martin 2000 Agency in (Spite of ) Material Culture. *In* Agency in Archaeology. Marcia-Anne Dobres and John E. Robb, eds. Pp. 40–50. London: Routledge.

# 15

# The Secrets of Ancient Tiwanaku Are Benefiting Today's Bolivia

*Baird Straughan*

Archaeologists work to understand how prehistoric people lived and why their cultures changed. The artifacts they uncover and the site features they explore are often mysteries requiring interpretation. How is an archaeological discovery a clue about how prehistoric cultures worked? Archaeologists are most often motivated by genuine curiosity about the past. Many students of anthropology wonder if there is any practical usefulness that can come from archaeological curiosity and discovery. This case study is the result of an archaeological investigation that produced real practical solutions to current agricultural and socioeconomic problems in a poor country—Bolivia.

The archaeologists, Alan Kolata and Oswaldo Rivera, did not start their investigations with the goal of solving the problems of the local Aymara people. Rather, they wanted to understand an archaeological mystery—the expansion and eventual collapse of the prehistoric civilization of Tiwanaku, located 12,500 feet above sea level on the shores of Lake Titicaca. This civilization produced impressive monumental structures (like Dickson's Mounds described in Selection 16) for an urban area with a population as large as 50,000 people. Because this is an area with very poor agriculture today, the obvious question to the archaeologists was how this large population was fed. In answering this question, they "discovered" a very old solution that was practiced by the ancestors of the local Indians.

Serendipity can be a very important aspect of discovery. Over and over, there are cases in which researchers make important discoveries that were only marginally related to the topics that they intended to study. In the case of Tiwanaku, researchers discovered ways to apply knowledge to improve the human condition even when their purpose in doing the research was to advance basic knowledge. The archaeologists recognized the practical use of their discovery, and they worked with local farmers to demonstrate that practical use. Ultimately, they significantly improved agricultural production in the area, and they consequently decreased local malnutrition.

This selection describes fascinating archaeological research that involves important basic research into a pre-Inca civilization and a practical application of anthropological knowledge. Like the case of Easter Island, the civilization at Tiwanaku ultimately collapsed. If the archaeologists can determine why that happened, there may be practical payoffs as well.

***As you read this selection, ask yourself the following questions:***

- How might the archaeologists have known the meaning of the ridges and depressions on the boggy lands near Tiwanaku?
- Why did most of the local people not wish to try the new agricultural methods suggested by the archaeologists?
- What was the population of Tiwanaku in its heyday? Was much effort put into religious structures? Did it have a class system? How long did this city survive?
- How have the new farming methods affected nutritional levels?
- What forces might have brought this civilization to an end?

***The following terms discussed in this selection are included in the Glossary at the back of the book:***

*agrarian*
*arable land*
*carrying capacity*
*excavation*
*mound*

Straughan, Baird. "The Secrets of Ancient Tiwanaku Are Benefiting Today's Bolivia." *Smithsonian* Magazine 21, no. 11 (1991):38–43, 46–47. Reprinted with author's permission.

In 1987, Roberto Cruz didn't know his ancestors had built a civilization that lasted for nearly a thousand years. If you had told him their capital had been the nearby town of Tiwanaku, or that new research indicates they exercised control over a vast territory from Peru to Argentina, from the Pacific to the eastern slope of the Andes, he probably wouldn't have cared.

Cruz, an Aymara Indian living at 12,500 feet near the southern shores of Lake Titicaca in Bolivia, had enough trouble just surviving. His lands on the lake's floodplain, the Pampa Koani, were useless. Frosts there killed the crops, and boggy conditions rotted potatoes in the ground. His small fields on the hillside were exhausted, and he had no time to think about "the grandfathers," as he calls them.

That was before they reached out from the centuries and touched his life. They reached him through two outsiders whom Cruz met one day in 1987 walking across the pampa, over the strange pattern of parallel ridges and depressions that stretches for miles across the floodplain. He knew that they had been working for years among the ancient ruins nearby. But the two men told him some things he found hard to believe: that a thousand years ago his boggy lands had been fertile; that the ridges and depressions were the remains of a system of raised planting surfaces separated by canals; that if he redug the canals, the raised fields would produce again.

Cruz called together his neighbors. Could this be true? No, the Aymara concluded, the strangers probably just wanted to steal the land. No, they would continue farming the hillsides, where they had been as long as anybody could remember. The frosts were milder there. But Cruz was curious. He told the two they could redig the canals on his lowland fields.

His neighbors were incensed. They called him to a meeting, and when he wouldn't go willingly, they trapped him, gathered the villagers and castigated him. Outsiders were bad luck, digging up "virgin earth that had never seen the light of the sun." That disturbed the weather. It was why the region was suffering a severe drought. Thanks to Cruz, they said, the whole town would starve. They threatened banishment.

Cruz wouldn't back down. He planted a crop on the raised platforms between the canals and watched his potato plants grow taller than he'd ever seen. Then, just before harvest, came his worst fear—frost. That whole night the villagers stood watch in their fields, Cruz with them. By early morning 90 percent of the crop on the hillsides was lost. Cruz walked down toward his fields on the pampa, knowing he'd made a terrible mistake. He could feel the coldest air flowing downhill to gather on the floodplain, where it would kill everything. The community had been right. The strangers had tricked him.

But when Cruz arrived at his land he saw with surprise that a mist had formed over it, a low white cloud that covered his fields "like a blanket." It lasted until the first rays of the morning sun, then vanished. Cruz walked out onto the platforms and was amazed to find his plants virtually undamaged.

Shortly thereafter he took in a record harvest. Today the edge of the Pampa Koani near Cruz's home is lined with raised fields dug by his neighbors. Cruz is a respected member of the community again.

He still thinks back to that one particularly bitter frost, and how his crop was miraculously saved. In fact, he now knows that what he saw rising from his fields that freezing night was the genius of Tiwanaku, a powerful state built by some of the greatest hydrologists the world had ever known.

The altiplano gets a great deal of heat from the sun during the day, but at night that heat escapes from the soil. Because the canals, which make up about 30 percent of the surface area, retain heat, they remain at least tepid and create a large temperature gradient. Water begins to evaporate and produces a fine mist that covers the fields, creating an artificial microclimate. In addition to the fog blanket, water drawn up into the soil platform by capillary action conducts heat to the plants' root systems.

One of the outsiders Roberto Cruz met on the pampa in 1987 was Alan Kolata, who is a professor of archaeology and anthropology at the University of Chicago. He had come to Tiwanaku in 1978 through "a bit of serendipity," as he puts it. Given the opportunity to collaborate on a new archaeological project in Bolivia shortly after receiving his doctorate from Harvard, he flew to La Paz and was met by Oswaldo Rivera, a rising archaeologist from Bolivia's National Institute of Archaeology. Robert West, chairman of the board of Tesoro Petroleum Company of San Antonio, was setting up the Tiwanaku Archaeological Foundation to explore the ruins of the pre-Inca civilization on the altiplano bordering Lake Titicaca. Kolata and Rivera were to be in charge of it. "Dr. West has generously supported the project—and our work—with research funds ever since," Kolata says.

He began by surveying the Akapana Pyramid, Tiwanaku's most sacred temple. For the next four years the two archaeologists concentrated on excavation, finding fragments of Tiwanaku pottery and other artifacts among the ruins of the ancient city or on the nearby Pampa Koani.

A pattern of ridges and depressions on the floodplain intrigued them. They knew that similar

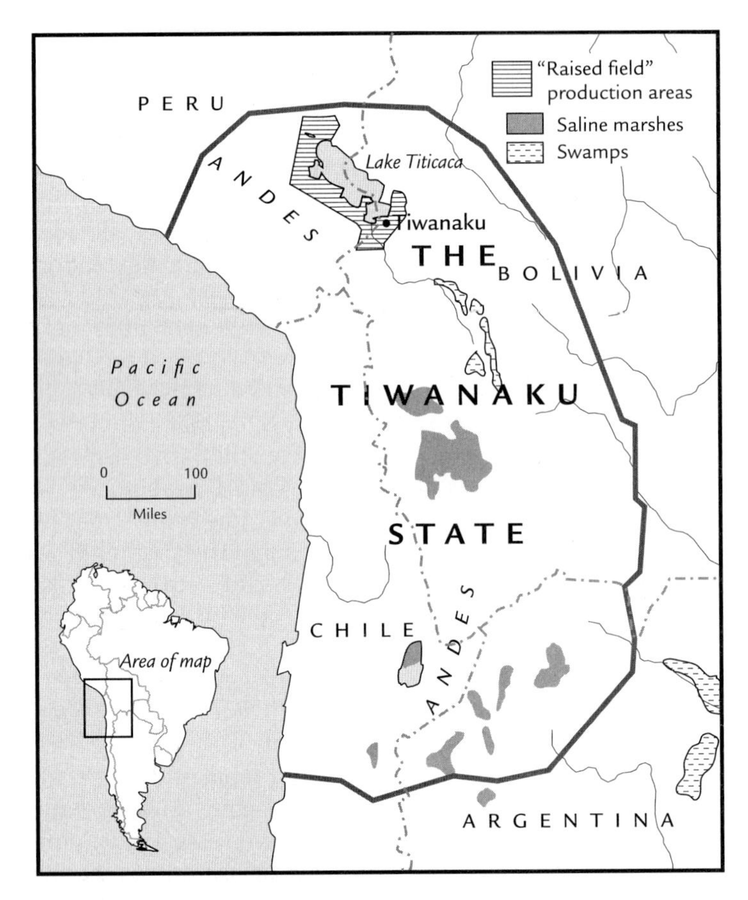


Tiwanaku map shows areas of historic raised fields; so far only a few of these have been reconstructed.
Straughan, Baird. "The Secrets of Ancient Tiwanaku Are Benefiting Today's Bolivia." Smithsonian Magazine 21 (1991), no. 11:38–43, 46–47. Reprinted with author's permission.

copography had been reconstructed into raised fields and irrigation canals in Maya and Aztec jungle areas of Central America. Could it be done here?

Soon after beginning their collaboration, Kolata and Rivera identified 40 square miles that were the remains of raised fields separated by interconnected irrigation canals linked to the Katari River. They were beginning to suspect that Tiwanaku had been a far larger civilization than had been thought, one that would have needed excess crop yields to sustain conquests, crafts, a complex social hierarchy. But Western agronomists consider the altiplano at best marginal land, beset as it is by frequent frosts and exhausted soils.

Could the ancient Tiwanakans have succeeded where modern mechanized agriculture has failed? Would these fields have produced enough to sustain such a civilization? Kolata and Rivera decided there was only one way to find out: rehabilitate a field and plant a crop. A similar project, led by a colleague, Clark Erickson of the University of Pennsylvania, was beginning across the lake in Peru.

In 1981, long before they met Cruz, they approached the community of Lacaya. Their presentation was well received. But as did the people of Cruz's village of Chokara several years later, the Lacayans soon blamed Kolata and Rivera for the severe drought. On one occasion campesinos stoned the two. "We were lucky to escape," Kolata recalls. It was not until 1987 that the reclamation project was back on track, first with Cruz and then at Lacaya. "We received major funding from the Inter-American Foundation. We put a lot of people to work and reintroduced the concept."

In April 1988, as Cruz was confounding his neighbors with his success, the first crop in the Lacaya fields yielded 90 metric tons of potatoes per hectare (about 2.5 acres); some were the size of grapefruit. It was seven times the average altiplano yield. There were also good crops of quinoa (a local grain), barley, oats, and vegetables such as lettuce and onions. Based on these yields, Kolata estimates that the Pampa Koani alone could have fed half a million people.

The new technique yielded another dividend: algae and aquatic plants began to grow, and with them, colonies of nitrogen-fixing bacteria. In several months a thick ooze formed at the bottom of the canals. When the harvest was in, the campesinos drained the canals and shoveled excellent organic fertilizer onto their fields.

There has been a complete turnabout in the reception the archaeologists receive. Kolata is now a welcome figure on the southern shores of Lake Titicaca. Clad in jeans and cowboy boots, his lanky 6-foot-2-inch frame towers above the Aymara, short people with broad torsos that house lungs big enough to cope with the thin air. Despite his appearance, he is completely at home among the campesinos in the fields or supervising the careful work of uncovering the secrets of the once glorious city called, according to legend, Taypi Kala, "The Stone in the Center."

A traveler who reached Tiwanaku, or Taypi Kala, at its height, around the seventh century A.D., would have come over the surrounding hills and been dazzled by the shining city, aglow with sunlight reflecting from gold-covered sculptural bas-reliefs on the walls of three major temples, all of them facing the rising sun.

A city of 50,000, it was situated on an ancient lake terrace that rose a few feet above a plain. Its ceremonial core, containing temples and the brightly painted palaces of the upper class, occupied almost a square mile, with the commoners sprinkled about the remaining three square miles. Of the major temples, the Akapana and Puma Punku were religious sites; Kolata believes the Kalasasaya to have been the seat of Tiwanaku's rulers. He also believes the state was basically a two-class society, an elite composed of the ruling class, its court and lesser nobility, with the rest being commoners. The discovery of bits of worked gold, obsidian and lapis lazuli in the royal sewer, and metalsmith's and lapidary's tools in the palace, indicates that the royal families may have been skilled craftsmen who fashioned the symbols of their own power.

The traveler might have been most likely to see the royalty on festival days. Sculpture and pottery show them emerging from their doorways, costumed as condors or pumas, or as highly stylized deities with enormous headdresses and capes. From the men's belts hung sacrificial knives and the trophy heads of their victims.

Human sacrifice was apparently a part of the celebrations. During these rituals, some archaeologists believe, the priests were under the influence of powerful hallucinogenic drugs, probably derivatives of cacti and other plants.

As in most ancient agrarian civilizations, the emperor-priest was responsible for propitiating the gods and assuring their blessing of the harvest. Guaranteeing an abundant crop isn't easy under the harsh conditions of the altiplano, but Tiwanaku's rulers apparently managed it for about 800 years. Clearly, they provided their subjects with a better diet than most Bolivians have today. The commoners subsisted on quinoa, potatoes, and fish. Royalty and the nobility dined on llama and corn, the latter a luxury probably imported from colonies or trading partners at lower altitudes. The upper class had regular access to coca leaves from the high valleys of the Amazon, possibly ocean fish from the Pacific coast of Chile, and peppers from southern Peru.

Gold-hungry Spaniards, who arrived in Tiwanaku in the sixteenth century, found the remains of a culture that had endured from around A.D. 200 to 1000. It had left no written records and was barely remembered by the peasant farmers, who believed that the gigantic stones of the ruins "existed before the sun shone in the heavens." Monuments had already suffered pillage for centuries, but nothing compared to that visited upon them by the conquistadores. Precious metal ornaments were stripped, statues defaced, tombs looted. The invaders rooted to the bottom of the Akapana, destroying a large part of it and heaping debris on the rest. Much of the stone they threw aside was later used to construct railroad bridges or buildings in nearby La Paz.

When American archaeologist E. George Squier came to the barren valley, inhabited by a few thousand impoverished farmers, in the 1860s, he described the Akapana as "a great rectangular mound of earth, originally terraced." Around it, partially buried, were the scattered remains of other large edifices.

Squier could see that the original temples had been stupendous constructions, made of blocks ranging up to 160 tons, probably transported from quarries across Lake Titicaca and then precision-fitted together. But he could find no evidence of the society that built them: no remains of domestic dwellings, no evidence of a substantial population base, no conceivable source of sustenance for a major civilization. He concluded, "Tiahuanuco may have been a sacred spot or shrine... but I can hardly believe that it was the seat of a dominion." Such reasoning was implicit in the work that followed.

It was a Bolivian archaeologist, Carlos Ponce, who in the 1950s began to provide evidence that Tiwanaku had been a great capital. Alan Kolata's painstaking work reinforces the premise that it was the center of a powerful state, and his conclusions are now receiving careful scrutiny.

David Browman, of Washington University in St. Louis, believes Tiwanaku was "the dominant member of a religious and trading federation." Browman goes on to say that the guerrilla activities of the terrorist group Sendero Luminoso are making it impossible to work in central and northern Peru, where many of his colleagues always believed the most important civilizations were located. "Now, there is a lot of research being done in southern Peru and Bolivia and northern Chile and Argentina, the areas that came under Tiwanaku's influence. There will be real changes in our vision of Tiwanaku quite soon."

Many of the new discoveries will come from Alan Kolata's excavations. Kolata, his colleagues and students work closely with crews of Aymara, whom they have trained in the precise discipline of excavating and recovering artifacts. The Aymara speak fondly of *"el Doctor,"* who not only pays their wages but also drinks beer with them and sponsors their soccer teams.

The work force, consisting of Aymara excavators and about a dozen graduate students from the United States and Bolivia, is doing broad horizontal excavation, going down level by level over large areas to diagram domestic life in Tiwanaku.

## RECOVERING TIWANAKU'S DAILY LIFE

Kolata belongs to the school of archaeology that finds the daily life of ancient peoples as fascinating as their monuments. Through advanced scientific techniques, he and his colleagues have been able to draw conclusions about Tiwanaku's social organization, and even about the diet of the average citizen. Graduate student Michael Marchbanks, back in his laboratory at the University of Wisconsin, is examining tiny samples of clay from the cooking pots and, through chemical tests, determining what foods the Tiwanakans ate. A team of limnologists is analyzing core sediment from Lake Titicaca, which contains layers of runoff from Tiwanaku's raised fields, to document past agricultural activity. Hydrologist Charles Ortloff is building computer models of Tiwanaku's water systems to see why they worked so well.

Kolata has not finished his interpretation of the results of all the combined research, to be published as a monograph by the Smithsonian Institution Press. But even the brief sketch he can give now is impressive.

On a walk around the temple complex, Kolata talks with respect of the Aymara, and with unreserved wonder at the achievements of their ancestors, "for instance, the drainage system of the Akapana." He points to the largest of Tiwanaku's structures, a 50-foot truncated pyramid with seven terraced levels, now emerging from the debris heaped upon it by the Spaniards. On the top, priests' residences surrounded a huge sunken court with a pool that collected tremendous amounts of water during the rainy season. The water flowed down inside the Akapana, gushed out onto the first terrace, flowed back into the temple, then out onto the next terrace and so on until it coursed from the bottom into a gigantic moat surrounding the ceremonial core. "The running water would have set up an acoustic effect, a roaring sound from within the structure," Kolata says. "It's pure virtuosity." And the moat would have made the ceremonial core a symbolic island, in obeisance to the sacred Island of the Sun in nearby Lake Titicaca.

The Akapana was designed to mimic the Quimsachata, a sacred mountain range with spouting and retreating torrents of rain and springwater, representing a life-giving cycle, flowing, evaporating, and falling again as rain.

Kolata seems particularly intrigued by the royal sewer of the central city. Channels beneath the palace floors merge into a massive rectangular conduit built of sandstone blocks a yard square, held together with copper clamps—a technique used in ancient Greece and Rome but heretofore unknown in the Americas. The sewer was buried nine feet deep in impermeable red clay. "It functioned for around 500 years," he explains. "It maintains a 3-percent grade all the way down to the river, a half-mile away."

Alan Kolata sets out over the ancient lake terrace on which the city was built. Underfoot, the ground is littered with pottery sherds, "virtually all from Tiwanaku." Here, the researchers are coming up with some of their biggest finds—the remains of Tiwanaku's domestic structures, precisely what Squier and other archaeologists thought were lacking. Kolata's excavations have uncovered the foundations of what were tightly spaced adobe houses, layer upon layer throughout generations. Most of last season's work was in these residential areas, but what is thought to be part of the city's external wall came to light, as well as the remains of what seems to have been a ceramics factory.

So massive an agricultural system as Tiwanaku's would have had to be organized on a regional scale and would have required the support of a powerful, centralized state. One evidence of the existence of such a state is the large mounds in the center of the fields. Ashlar architectural remains, decorated pottery and indications of a varied diet point to them as homes for local overseers who monitored field production. These mounds were connected to one another, to the villages and cities, and to smaller mounds by a network of causeways. The small mounds, mere bulges at the ends of raised fields, supported simple adobe huts that were seasonal homes for the *kamani,* or field guardians, who protected ripening crops from predators.

It had been necessary to divert the river about a mile to the north of the center of the pampa to open up the land for raised-field production. To control flooding, the river was secured by a huge berm, or levee. Kolata and his colleagues estimate that excavation, diversion, and construction were a gigantic public works project of at least one million man-days' labor.

## A LEGACY FROM "THE GRANDFATHERS"

Harvests such as those now being reaped on Tiwanaku's ancestral fields give hope for the future. About 1,200 campesinos are using raised fields. Oswaldo Rivera, who is now director of the National Institute of Archaeology, has requests for assistance from another 50 villages eager to apply the same principle. Some units of the Bolivian Army have begun a Plan Verde (Green Plan), teaching conscripts the raised-field technology. And the Bolivian government is looking for $40 million to spread the technique throughout the country. Large-scale development projects have a bad record in Bolivia, but if the government is successful in this one it would be in a better position to confront the country's burgeoning problems.

U.S. Ambassador Robert Gelbard, an enthusiastic supporter of and fundraiser for the project, urges that it be expanded as quickly as possible. "We are finding that nutritional levels have improved dramatically in these areas," he explains, "and not just because of the potato harvest. There are fish in the canals, the ducks lay eggs—protein levels have gone up considerably."

The potential benefits for Bolivia are tremendous. Chronic malnutrition afflicts nearly half of all Bolivian children, and the country must import food even though most of its citizens work in agriculture. Large numbers of farmers are abandoning their exhausted land on the altiplano and migrating to the Amazon basin, where they can grow coca or clear new farms in the rain forest by the slash-and-burn method.

Meanwhile, archaeological support is coming from another direction. The Getty Conservation Institute of Los Angeles is working with Bolivia's National Institute of Archaeology to devise plans for protection of ancient Tiwanaku's ruins from both environmental hazards and increased tourism.

Kolata ponders the most perplexing question still hanging over Tiwanaku: why it ended. "It was so good for so long, why did it collapse? We know that by A.D. 1000 the fields were no longer functional."

He has a possible answer. Ice cores from glaciers in southern Peru and sediment cores from Lake Titicaca indicate that sometime around the millennium the area suffered a severe drought lasting for decades. Rivers and underground springs watering the raised beds would have dried up, disrupting agricultural production. It is unlikely the Tiwanakans had enough provisions to withstand so prolonged a catastrophe. Starvation would have been widespread and most likely have led to the collapse of the government and its highly organized agricultural system. At present, this is just Kolata's hypothesis. But in the absence of historical records, paleoclimatological data may be the best evidence we have.

In any case, after A.D. 1000, Andean peoples moved to the hillsides, where they practiced the kind of terrace agriculture we associate with the later Inca civilization. The raised fields were abandoned and eventually forgotten. But luckily for the inhabitants of the Bolivian altiplano, Kolata and Rivera are now resurrecting them.

"The good thing about the system," according to Kolata, "is that it functions almost anywhere there's a secure source of water." As to the archaeologists' role, he says simply, "We're only giving back to the Aymara what their ancestors developed thousands of years ago."

# 16

# Disease and Death at Dr. Dickson's Mounds

*Alan H. Goodman and George J. Armelagos*

In a popular book, *The Third Wave,* Alvin Toffler identified three major "transformations" of global consequence. The first of these was the agricultural revolution, the second was the industrial revolution, and the third is the present-day technological revolution. The impacts of these events and processes are far-reaching and generally assumed to be quite positive. However, it is possible that there have been subtle, but exceedingly important, unintended consequences that have gone undetected. One of the best ways to raise awareness of these problems is to reexamine history. Of course, the agricultural revolution, which some anthropologists think may have been the most important event in human history, occurred during the prehistoric period. No written records were left, and it is therefore up to archaeologists to provide insights into the changes the agricultural revolution brought.

We do not need to go to the Near East, Asia, or Mesoamerica to study the transformation from hunting and gathering to agriculture. You can find it right in your own backyard. In this selection, Alan Goodman and George Armelagos examine the health consequences of the rise of agriculture. The paleopathological study of bones can be an important supplement to traditional archaeological description and analysis. Like the conclusions of Eaton and Konner on Paleolithic diet (Selection 10), cultural evolution does not always mean progress.

***As you read this selection, ask yourself the following questions:***

- What happened to the population density around Dickson's Mounds during the first fifty years of agriculture?
- What social changes seem to accompany the rise of agriculture?
- What three factors made possible the tracing of changing health patterns from preagricultural to postagricultural subsistence patterns?
- Did agriculture lead to a better diet and improved health conditions?
- Why did prehistoric people become farmers?

***The following terms discussed in this selection are included in the Glossary at the back of the book:***

*dental anthropology*
*Mississippian tradition*
*paleopathology*
*population pressure*
*sickle-cell anemia*

Clustered in west-central Illinois, atop a bluff near the confluence of the Illinois and Spoon rivers, are twelve to thirteen poorly defined earthen mounds. The mounds, which overlap each other to some extent, cover a crescent-shaped area of about an acre. Since at least the middle of the nineteenth century, local residents have known that prehistoric Native Americans built these mounds to bury their dead. But it was not until the late 1920s that Don Dickson, a chiropractor, undertook the first systematic excavation of the mounds located on farmland owned by his father. Barely into his thirties at the time, Dickson became so involved in the venture that he never returned to his chiropractic practice. Apparently, he was intrigued by the novel undertaking of unearthing skeletons and trying to diagnose the maladies of long-dead individuals. Later on, he became more concerned with the patterns of disease and death in this extinct group in order to understand how these people lived and why they often died at an early age.

The "Dickson Mounds" (the site also includes two early, unmounded burial grounds) quickly attracted the attention of professional anthropologists.

Goodman, Alan H. & George J. Armelagos. "Disease and Death at Dr. Dickson's Mounds" from *Natural History* (Sept. 1985):12–18; 

In the early 1930s, a team of University of Chicago archeologists exposed about 200 of the estimated 3,000 burials and identified a number of settlement sites in a 100-square-mile area. A second phase of excavation at Dickson began in the 1960s under the direction of Alan Harn, an archeologist working for the state of Illinois, whose crew excavated many of the local living sites and more than 800 additional burials. The archeological research revealed that these prehistoric people had taken part in an important transition, from hunting and gathering to an agricultural way of life.

About A.D. 950, hunter-gatherers lived along the Illinois River valley area near Dickson, subsisting on a wide range of local plants and animals, including grasses and seeds, fruits and berries, roots and tubers, vines, herbs, large and small mammals, migratory waterfowl and riverine birds, and fish. The moderate climate, copious water supply, and rich soil made this a bountiful and attractive area for hunter-gatherers. Groups occupied campsites that consisted of a few small structures, and the debris scattered around these sites suggests seasonal use. The population density was low, perhaps on the order of two to three persons per square mile. Then, about 1050, broken hoes and other agricultural tools, as well as maize, began to form part of village refuse, evidence of the introduction of maize agriculture. At the same time, the population grew. By 1200 the population density may have increased by a factor of ten, to about twenty-five persons per square mile. Living sites became larger and more permanent. The largest settlement in the area, Larson, was a residential and ceremonial center where some 1,000 inhabitants lived, many behind a palisaded wall.

Trade also flourished. Dickson became part of what archeologists call the Mississippian tradition, a network of maize-growing, mound-building societies that spread throughout most of the eastern United States. More and more, items used at the village sites or deposited as grave offerings were not of local origin. Some, such as marine shell necklaces, came from as far away as the Gulf of Mexico and Florida, one thousand miles to the south. Everyday objects such as spoons and jars were received from peoples of the eastern plains and the western prairies, while luxury items of ceremonial or decorative value arrived in trade from the south, probably coming upriver to Dickson through Cahokia, a Mississippian center some 110 miles away. Cahokia is a massive site that includes some 120 mounds within a six-square-mile area. As many as 30,000 persons lived at Cahokia and in the surrounding villages.

What we know about Dickson might have ended at this point, but continues because the skeletal remains that Harn excavated have been used to evaluate how the health of these prehistoric people fared following the adoption of agriculture and other changes in their life style. Interest in this issue stems from the writings of the eminent British archeologist V. Gordon Childe (1892–1957), who believed that the development of agriculture prompted the first great revolution in human technology, ushering in fundamental changes in economy, social organization, and ideology. Archeologists continue to debate the causes of agricultural revolutions. For example, some believe that in various regions of the world, increased population pressure, leading to food shortages and declining health, spurred the switch to agricultural food production. Others believe population increase was one of the consequences of agricultural revolutions. More important to us are the effects of an agricultural revolution on the health of people who lived at the time of such change.

Three circumstances have made it possible to test the effects agriculture had upon health at Dickson. First, Harn and those working with him valued the potential information to be gained from skeletons and therefore paid close attention to their excavation. Ultimately, the skeletal remains were sent to the University of Massachusetts at Amherst for analysis by George Armelagos and many of his graduate students (this is how we became involved). Second, the recovered remains include both individuals who lived before the development of maize agriculture (Late Woodland, or pre-Mississippian) and after (Mississippian). The two groups of individuals could be distinguished according to the mounds they were buried in, their placement within each mound, and their burial position (in earlier burials the bodies tend to be in a flexed or semiflexed position; in later burials they tend to be extended). The third enabling condition was provided by Janice Cohen, one of Armelagos's graduate students. Her analysis of highly heritable dental traits showed that although Dickson was in contact with persons from outside the central Illinois River valley area during the period of rapid cultural change, outside groups did not replace or significantly merge with the local groups. It is therefore possible to follow the health over time of a single population that, for all intents and purposes, was genetically stable.

As a doctoral student working under Armelagos in the early 1970s, John Lallo, now at Cleveland State University, set out to test whether health at Dickson improved, got worse, or remained the same with the advent of agriculture and its accompanying changes. Lallo argued that intensification of maize agriculture most likely resulted in a poorer diet. Although a common assumption is that the adoption of agriculture should have provided a prehistoric people with a better diet, there are good reasons to predict just the opposite. Heavy reliance on a single crop may lead to nutritional problems. Maize, for example, is deficient in lysine, an essential amino acid. Furthermore, agricultural societies that subsist on a few foodstuffs are more vulnerable to famines brought about by drought and other disasters. Finally, increased population density, a more sedentary life style, and greater trade, all of which are associated with agriculture, provide conditions for the spread and maintenance of infectious diseases.

The skeletons of individuals who lived before and after the introduction of maize agriculture were examined for a number of different health indicators, in order to provide a balanced picture of the pattern of stress, disease, and death that affected the Dickson population. The indicators that proved most sensitive to health differences were: bone lesions (scars) due to infection, nutritional deficiencies, trauma, and degenerative conditions; long bone growth; dental developmental defects; and age at death. To avoid unconscious bias, we and the other researchers involved measured these seven traits without knowing in advance which skeletons came from each of the two cultural periods.

Persistent bacterial infection leaves its mark on the outer, or periosteal, layer of bone. Tibias (shinbones) are the most frequently affected bones because they have relatively poor circulation and therefore tend to accumulate bacteria. Toxins produced by bacteria kill some of the bone cells; as new bone is produced, the periosteal bone becomes roughened and layered. Lallo and his co-workers found that following the introduction of agriculture there was a threefold increase in the percentage of individuals with such lesions. Eighty-four percent of the Mississippian tibias had these "periosteal reactions," as compared with only 26 percent of pre-Mississippian tibias. The lesions also tended to be more severe and to show up in younger individuals in the Mississippian population.

A second type of lesion, more easily seen in the thinner bones of the body (such as those of the skull), is a sign of anemia. In response to anemia, the body steps up its production of red blood cells, which are formed in the bone marrow. To accomplish this the marrow must expand at the expense of the outer layer of bone. In severe cases, this expansion may cause the outer layer of bone to disappear, exposing the porous, sievelike inner bone. This lesion, called porotic hyperostosis, can occur with any kind of anemia. In the Dickson Mounds populations, the lesions are not severe, are restricted to the eye sockets and crania, and occur mainly in children and young adult females. This pattern suggests anemia resulting from a nutritional deficiency, specifically an iron deficiency. (A hereditary anemia, such as sickle-cell anemia, would have been more severe in its manifestation and would have affected all ages and both sexes in the population.)

There is a significant increase in the frequency of porotic hyperostosis during the Mississippian period. Half the Mississippian infants and children had porotic hyperostosis, twice the rate found for pre-Mississippian infants and children. Individuals with both periosteal reactions and porotic hyperostosis tend to have suffered more severely from each condition. This may be evidence of a deadly synergism of malnutrition and infection, like that often reported among contemporary populations.

Traumatic lesions were measured by diagnosis of healed fractures of the long bones of the legs and arms. Adult males had the highest frequency of such fractures. Approximately one out of three Mississippian males had at least one fracture, twice the frequency of their predecessors. These fractures often occurred at the midshaft of the ulna and radius, the bones of the lower arm. Fractures at this location are called parry fractures because they are typically the result of efforts to ward off a blow.

The frequency of degenerative pathologies, including arthritic conditions found on joints and the contacting surfaces of the vertebral column, also increased through time. One or more degenerative conditions were diagnosed in 40 percent of pre-Mississippian adults but in more than 70 percent of Mississippian adults.

In addition to the studies of the changing pattern of disease and trauma, we, along with Lallo and Jerome Rose, now at the University of Arkansas, assessed differences in skeletal growth and developmental timing. Skeletal growth and development are susceptible to a wide variety of stressful conditions and therefore reflect overall health. We found that in comparison to pre-Mississippians of the same age, Mississippian children between the ages of five and ten had significantly shorter and narrower tibias and femurs (the major long bones of the legs). This difference may be explained by a decreased rate of growth before the age of five. The Mississippians apparently were able to catch up in growth after age ten, however, since adult Mississippians are only slightly smaller than pre-Mississippians.

A more detailed exploration of developmental changes came from studying defects in enamel, the hard white coating of the crowns of teeth. Ameloblasts, the enamel-forming cells, secrete enamel matrix in ringlike fashion, starting at the biting surface and ending at the bottom of the crown. A deficiency in enamel thickness, called a hypoplasia, may result if the individual suffers a systemic physiological stress during enamel formation. Since the timing of enamel secretion is well known and relatively stable, the position of such a lesion on a tooth corresponds to an individual's age at the time of stress.

We examined the permanent teeth—teeth that form between birth and age seven. For skeletons with nearly complete sets of permanent teeth, 55 percent of pre-Mississippians had hypoplasias, while among Mississippians the figure rose to 80 percent. In both groups, hypoplasias were most frequently laid down between the ages of one and one-half and four. However, the hypoplasias in the Mississippian group peak at age two and one-half, approximately one-half year earlier than the pre-Mississippian peak. The peak is also more pronounced. This pattern of defects may indicate both an earlier age at weaning and the use of cereal products as weanling foods.

The repeated occurrence of hypoplasias within individuals revealed an annual cycle of stress. Most likely there was a seasonal food shortage. This seems to have worsened in the period just before the population becomes completely "Mississippianized," suggesting that it provided a rationale for intensifying agriculture.

All the above six indicators point toward a decrease in health associated with cultural change at Dickson. However, they are not meaningful apart from an analysis of the pattern of death in these populations. Healthy-looking skeletons, for example, may be the remains of young individuals who died outright because their bodies were too weak to cope in the face of disease, injury, and other forms of stress. Conversely, skeletons that show wear and tear may be those of individuals who survived during stressful times and lived to a ripe old age.

At Dickson, however, the trend is unambiguous. Individuals whose skeletons showed more signs of stress and disease (for example, enamel hypoplasias) also lived shorter lives, on average, than individuals with fewer such indications. For the population as a whole, life expectancy at birth decreased from twenty-six years in the pre-Mississippian to nineteen years in the Mississippian. The contrast in mortality is especially pronounced during the infant and childhood years. For example, 22 percent of Mississippians died during their first year as compared to 13 percent of the pre-Mississippians. Even for those who passed through the dangerous early years of childhood, there is a differential life expectancy. At fifteen years of age, pre-Mississippians could expect to live for an average of twenty-three more years, while Mississippians could expect to live for only eighteen more years.

What caused this decline in health? A number of possibilities have been proposed. Lallo and others have emphasized the effect of agriculture on diet. Most of the health trends may be explained by a decline in diet quality. These include the trends in growth, development, mortality, and nutritional disease, all four of which have obvious links to nutrition. The same explanation may be offered for the increase in infectious diseases, since increased susceptibility may be due to poor nutrition. Furthermore, a population subject to considerable infectious disease would be likely to suffer from other conditions, including increased rates of anemia and mortality and decreased growth rates.

The link between diet and infectious disease is bolstered by an analysis of trace elements from tibial bone cores. Robert Gilbert found that the Mississippian bones contain less zinc, an element that is limited in maize. Building on this research, Wadia Bahou, now a physician in Ann Arbor, Michigan, showed that the skeletons with the lowest levels of zinc had the highest frequency of infectious lesions. This is strong evidence that a diet of maize was relied on to a point where health was affected.

The population increase associated with the changeover to agriculture probably also contributed to the decline in health. We do not believe that the population ever threatened to exceed the carrying capacity of the bountiful Dickson area (and there are no signs of the environmental degradation one would expect to find if resources were overexploited). However, increased population density and sedentariness, coupled with intensification of contact with outsiders, create opportunities for the spread of infectious disease. George Milner of the University of Kentucky, while still a graduate student at Northwestern University, argued this point in comparing Dickson with the Kane Mounds populations. Kane is located near Cahokia, the major center south of Dickson. Despite Kane's proximity to this large center, its population density was much lower than at Larson, the major agricultural village of the Dickson population. Of the two, Kane had the lower rate of infectious diseases.

While the "agricultural hypothesis," including the effects of population pressure, offers an explanation for much of the health data, it doesn't automatically account for the two remaining measures: degenerative and traumatic pathologies. Poor nutrition and infectious disease may make people more susceptible to degenerative disease. However, the arthritic conditions found in the Dickson skeletons, involving movable joints, were probably caused by strenuous physical activity. The link, then, is not with the consumption of an agricultural diet but, if anything, with the physically taxing work of agricultural production. An explanation for the increase in traumatic injuries is harder to imagine. Possibly, the increased population density caused social tension and strife to arise within communities, but why should this have happened?

A curious fact makes us think that explanations based only on agricultural intensification and population increase are missing an important contributing factor. Recent archeological research at Dickson suggests that hunting and gathering remained productive enterprises and were never completely abandoned. Many of the local Mississippian sites have a great concentration of animal bones and projectile points used for hunting. A balanced diet apparently was available. The health and trace element data, however, suggest that the Mississippian diet was deficient. There is a disparity between what was available and what was eaten.

At present our search for an explanation for this paradox centers on the relationship between Dickson and the Cahokia population. The builders of the Dickson Mounds received many items of symbolic worth from the Cahokia region, such as copper-covered ear spools and marine shell necklaces. Much of the health data would be explained if Dickson had been trading perishable foodstuffs for these luxury items. In particular, the diversion of meat or fish to Cahokia would explain the apparent discrepancy between diet and resources.

To have a food surplus to trade, individuals from the Dickson area may have intensified their agricultural production while continuing to hunt and gather. The increase in degenerative conditions could have resulted from such a heavy workload. The system may also have put social strain on the community, leading to internal strife. And the accumulation of wealth in terms of ceremonial or other luxury items may have necessitated protection from outside groups. This would explain why the Larson site was palisaded. Both internal and external strain may have led to the increase in traumatic pathologies.

To test the validity of this scenario, we are hoping to gather additional evidence, concentrating on an analysis of trade. The flow of perishable goods such as meat is hard to trace, but we can study the sets of animal bones found at Cahokia and at Dickson village and butchering sites. The distribution of animal bones at the archeological sites can then be compared with examples of bone distributions in areas where trading has been ethnographically recorded. Further evidence is provided by data such as Milner's, which showed that health at Kane—a community that shared in Cahokia's power—was better than at Dickson.

The trading of needed food for items of symbolic value, to the point where health is threatened, may not seem to make sense from an objective outsider's perspective. But it is a situation that has been observed in historic and modern times. An indigenous group learns that it can trade something it has access to (sugar cane, alpacas, turtles) for something it greatly admires but can only obtain from outside groups (metal products, radios, alcohol). The group's members do not perceive that the long-term health and economic results of such trade are usually unfavorable. Nor are all such arrangements a result of voluntary agreement. The pattern of health observed at Dickson is seen in most situations where there is a decline in access to, and control over, resources. For example, lower classes in stratified societies live shorter lives and suffer more from nearly all major diseases.

Agriculture is not invariably associated with declining health. A recent volume edited by Mark N. Cohen and George J. Armelagos, *Paleopathology and the Origins of Agriculture,* analyzed health changes in twenty-three regions of the world where agriculture developed. In many of these regions there was a clear, concurrent decline in health, while in others there was little or no change or slight improvements in health. Perhaps a decline is more likely to occur when agriculture is intensified in the hinterland of a political system. Groups living far away from the centers of trade and power are apt to be at a disadvantage. They may send the best fruits of their labors to market and receive little in return. And during times of economic hardship or political turmoil, they may be the ones to suffer the most, as resources are concentrated on maintaining the central parts of the system.

# 17

# Uncovering America's Pyramid Builders

*Karen Wright*

Travelers who pass through Collinsville, Illinoi, may know this Midwestern city as the "Horseradish Capital of the World" or as the home of a water tower in the shape of the world's largest ketchup bottle, but these superlatives are not what put this city on the list of United Nations World Heritage Sites. An earthen mound within city limits once served as the foundation of a 5,000 square foot temple bigger than any of the Egyptian pyramids at Giza. This mound, now known as Monks Mound, sat at the center of a thriving civilization that disappeared approximately 700 years ago.

The Cahokian civilization that built Monks Mound established their early city at the confluence of the Mississippi, Missouri, and Illinois rivers, creating an urban center that was a hub for regional trade. Many mysteries remain about Cohokia and its downfall, largely because this civilization did not use a written language and they used building materials that do not leave an enduring archaeological record. In this selection, Karen Wright presents conflicting interpretations about the size, nature, and collapse of what may have been the largest prehistoric settlement north of Mexico.

***As you read this selection, ask yourself the following questions:***

- How do the mounds of Cahokia and the civilization that built them compare with Pharaonic Egypt and the Great Pyramids of Giza?
- Why did migrants come to Cahokia in such great numbers?
- What factors may have contributed to the downfall of Cahokia?
- How and when were the Cahokian mounds re-discovered?
- How were Cahokia and Monks Mound named?

***The following terms discussed in this selection are included in the Glossary at the back of the book:***

*chiefdom*
*matriarchal*
*United Nations World Heritage Site*
*woodhenge*

When U.S. 40 reaches Collinsville, Illinois, the land is flat and open. Seedy storefronts line the highway: a pawnshop, a discount carpet warehouse, a taco joint, a bar. Only the Indian Mound Motel gives any hint that the road bisects something more than underdeveloped farmland. This is the Cahokia Mounds State Historic Site, a United Nations World Heritage Site on a par with the Great Wall of China, the Egyptian pyramids, and the Taj Mahal. The 4,000-acre complex preserves the remnants of the largest prehistoric settlement north of Mexico, a walled city that flourished on the floodplain of the Mississippi River 10 centuries ago. Covering an area more than five miles square, Cahokia dwarfs the ancient pueblos of New Mexico's Chaco Canyon and every other ruin left by the storied Anasazi of the American Southwest. Yet despite its size and importance, archaeologists still don't understand how this vast, lost culture began, how it ended, and what went on in between.

A thousand years ago, no one could have missed Cahokia—a complex, sophisticated society with an urban center, satellite villages, and as many as 50,000 people in all. Thatched-roof houses lined the central plazas. Merchants swapped copper, mica, and seashells from as far away as the Great Lakes and the Gulf of Mexico. Thousands of cooking fires burned night and day. And between A.D. 1000 and 1300, Cahokians built more than 120 earthen mounds as landmarks, tombs, and ceremonial platforms. The largest of these monuments, now called Monks Mound, still dominates the site. It is a flat-topped pyramid of dirt that covers more than 14 acres and once supported a 5,000-square-foot temple. Monks

Wright, Karen. "Uncovering America's Pyramid Builders." © 2004 Karen Wright. This article originally appeared in *Discover* magazine (Feb. 2004):50–55. Reprinted with permission of the author.

were black, one would not feel it so much, but their skins, except where tanned by exposure, are as white as ours" (Gibbons 1991:96). Two years later, the English satirical magazine *Punch* referred to the Irish as "A creature manifestly between the Gorilla and the Negro," and as late as 1885, British anthropologist John Beddoe referred to the Irish as "Africanoid" (Foster 1993:184; Young 1995:72). Not surprisingly, such attitudes were also expressed visually, and it was common during the eighteenth and nineteenth centuries for English artists to portray the Irish with apelike features (Curtis 1971). Racism thus became a common element of English-Irish interaction, as the English strove to establish the Irish as the Other, comparable to the many Others their country's explorers and colonists encountered around the globe (Doan 1997; Lebow 1976; Waters 1995).

When Irish immigrants began to flood the streets of America in the early-nineteenth century, it was not at all clear that they were members of the so-called White Race (Ignatiev 1995:41). Since Congress decreed in 1790 that only "whites" could be naturalized citizens, Irish immigrants found that they had to fight for the national privilege of being perceived as white. The American White Race was an invention, and since the days of the Puritans, the American power elite consciously worked to build a homogeneous Americanized state based on their perception of whiteness (Allen 1994; Carlson 1987). Before Emancipation, foremen and labor-gang bosses often used Irish laborers instead of slaves for the most dangerous jobs because the Irish, as poor freemen, were wholly expendable (Ignatiev 1995:109). As a people, the Irish did not move into the ranks of "white" America until they repudiated the rights of those deemed nonwhite. The stereotypic character of the evil Irish overseer on the southern slave plantation is a literary device intended to show this accommodation. Tara, mythic America's most famous plantation, was named for a venerated site in Ireland, and its owners had the time-honored Irish name of O'Hara (Mitchell 1936).

To summarize, the Irish in America had to struggle to attain the racial designation that put them in the nation's highest racial category. To accomplish this act of wholesale racial advance, they had to overcome years of discrimination to create a place for themselves in the American scheme of whiteness. Some Irish immigrants even climbed to the highest echelons of the American elite, with their names becoming synonymous with wealth, power, and the American Dream (Birmingham 1973; Greeley 1981). Nonetheless, the movement of the Irish into the ranks of White America has yet to interest American historical archaeologists. The Irish in America are still perceived monolithically as an ethnic group inhabiting the sphere of whiteness, and their place in White America is taken for granted.

## RACE IN THE FUTURE OF HISTORICAL ARCHAEOLOGY

If the present corpus of scholarship is any guide, the way in which Americans address issues of race and racism will undoubtedly be many and varied over the next several years. There is danger, of course, in the notion that the most serious discussions will be restricted to the realm of scholastic inquiry and will not reach a wider audience (Cole 1995). The problem of intellectual isolation is particularly acute for archaeology, since the only times the field is regularly mentioned outside the profession is when the popular media designates a new discovery as especially spectacular, or when pseudo-scientists have made some new outlandish claim.

The possible courses of action for the development of serious, concerted research in the historical archaeology of race are infinite, and we may well hope and expect that the approaches taken by archaeologists will be varied. I believe, however, that the examination of the material side of race and racism provides archaeologists with a rare opportunity to use their discipline's unique transdisciplinary insights and methods to promote greater understanding far beyond archaeology. In a nation like the United States—where the national ideology is wholly given over to capitalist accumulation and conspicuous consumption—the role of historical archaeologists may be easily expanded beyond the narrow halls of a few universities and the conference rooms of cultural resource management firms. At a time when political conservatives are using race in a wrongheaded and divisive manner—the effusive excitement over *The Bell Curve* (Herrnstein and Murray 1994) being one clear example—historical archaeologists are afforded the opportunity to show the historic origins and manifestations of racial categorization and the relationship of such pigeonholing to social and material inequality.

In an important essay, Jesse L. Jackson Jr. (1997) argues that it is not enough to talk about race in America without taking action on employment. To discuss one without the other is to engage in what Jackson calls "race entertainment." Racial justice is not synonymous with economic justice, but the two are clearly linked. As Jackson (1997:24) notes, "In a nation with the economic and technological ability to provide every American with a decent life, it is a scandal that there should be so much social misery."

Will race ever become an important subject in historical archaeology, or will historical archaeologists only engage in "race entertainment," forever examining race as if it were ethnicity? This question cannot be answered now, but to become true partners in the expanding anthropological discourse on race in America, historical archaeologists must seek to illustrate the effects of racism on African Americans and other peoples, developing at the same time a historical archaeology of whiteness. Baker (1978:113) inadvertently made this suggestion when he stated that to interpret the meaning of the ceramics at Lucy Foster's homesite, historical archaeologists must also conduct research on sites inhabited by poor whites. Most historical archaeologists now accept "whiteness as an unassailable fact of nature" rather than as a social construct (Epperson 1997:10). This tendency is adequately demonstrated by examining how historical archaeologists have examined, or not examined, the Irish in America.

Because the appellations of whiteness and nonwhiteness contain deep-seated notions of social inequality, studies of domination and resistance should constitute a major focus of research in historical archaeology (Paynter and McGuire 1991). Through this sustained research activity, historical archaeologists will be able to denaturalize the condition of whiteness, and to demonstrate the material dimensions of using whiteness as a source of racial domination even in cases, such as with the Irish, where racism may initially appear absent (Harrison 1995:63).

Recently, Robert Paynter (1997) proposed that historical archaeologists must understand the complexities inherent in examining social inequality in historic America. Three questions he posed as worthy of future study in historical archaeology are particularly relevant here:

> Under what conditions do stratified societies mark and hide social cleavages with material culture? How, during the age of capital, did wage labor, mass consumption, and white supremacy produce distinctive and shifting identities? And, how did local communities redefine identities among these global shifts in race, class, and gender relations? [Paynter 1997:11]

Providing answers to such questions as these will not only make historical archaeology more relevant to anthropological inquiry, it will also raise the profile and societal relevance of the field. Whether large numbers of historical archaeologists ever move to the examination of the material dimensions of racial categorization is simply a matter of what historical archaeologists wish their field to be.

## NOTE

*Acknowledgments.* I would like to thank Terry Epperson, Pedro Funari, and Paul Mullins for reading and providing their comments on this paper. My ideas about race and racism in historical archaeology have taken shape during discussions with these thoughtful scholars and with David Babson over the past few years. I would also like to thank Robert Paynter and the two anonymous reviewers for their thoughtful comments and suggestions. In addition, I wish to acknowledge the support and encouragement of Janice L. Orser. Needless to say, none of these individuals should be held in any way responsible for my statements and opinions.

## REFERENCES

Allen, Theodore W. 1994. The Invention of the White Race. London: Verso.

Babson, David W. 1987. The Tanner Road Settlement: The Archaeology of Racism on Limerick Plantation. Master's thesis, University of South Carolina, Columbia.

______. 1990. The Archaeology of Racism and Ethnicity on Southern Plantations. In *Historical Archaeology on Southern Plantations and Farms*, ed. Charles E. Orser Jr., Special issue. *Historical Archaeology* 24(4): 20–28.

Baker, Vernon G. 1978. Historical Archaeology at Black Lucy's Garden, Andover, Massachusetts: Ceramics from the Site of a Nineteenth Century Afro-American. Andover, MA: Phillips Academy.

______. 1980. Archaeological Visibility of Afro-American Culture: An Example from Black Lucy's Garden, Andover, Massachusetts. In *Archaeological Perspectives on Ethnicity in America: Afro-American and Asian American Culture History,* ed. Robert L. Schuyler, 29–37. Farmingdale, NY: Baywood.

Bartlett, Robert. 1993. The Making of Europe: Conquest, Colonization, and Cultural Change, 950–1350. Princeton, NJ: Princeton University Press.

Berkeley, George. 1871. The Works of George Berkeley, D. D. A. C. Fraser, ed. Oxford: Clarendon.

Birmingham, Stephen. 1973. *Real Lace: America's Irish Rich.* New York: Harper and Row.

Bullen, Adelaide K., and Ripley P. Bullen. 1945. Black Lucy's Garden. *Bulletin of the Massachusetts Archaeological Society* 6(2): 17–28.

Carlson, Robert A. 1987. *The Americanization Syndrome: A Quest for Conformity*. London: Croom Helm.

Childe, V. Gordon. 1926. *The Aryans: A Study of Indo-European Origins*. London: Kegan Paul.

Cole, Johnnetta B. 1995. Human Rights and the Rights of Anthropologists. *American Anthropologist* 97: 445–456.

Cook, Lauren J., Rebecca Yamin, and John P. McCarthy. 1996. Shopping as Meaningful Action: Toward a Redefinition of Consumption in Historical Archaeology. *Historical Archaeology 39*(4): 50–65.

Curtis, L. Perry, Jr. 1971. *Apes and Angels: The Irishman in Victorian Caricature*. Washington, DC: Smithsonian Institution Press.

Doan, James E. 1997. "An Island in the Virginian Sea": Native Americans and the Irish in English Discourse, 1585–1640. *New Hibernia Review* 1: 79–99.

Du Bois, W. E. B. 1961. *The Souls of Black Folk*. New York: Dodd and Mead.

Epperson, Terrence W. 1990a. "To Fix a Perpetual Brand": The Social Construction of Race in Virginia, 1675–1750. Ph.D. dissertation, Department of Anthropology, Temple University, Philadelphia.

______. 1990b. Race and the Disciplines of the Plantation. In *Historical Archaeology on Southern Plantations and Farms*, ed. Charles E. Orser Jr., *Historical Archaeology* 24(4): 29–36.

______. 1997. Whiteness in Early Virginia. *Race Traitor* 7: 9–20.

Fischer, Claude S., Michael Hout, Martín Sánchez Jankowski, Samuel R. Lucas, Ann Swidler, and Kim Voss. 1996. *Inequality by Design: Cracking the Bell Curve Myth*. Princeton, NJ: Princeton University Press.

Fitts, Robert K. 1996. The Landscapes of Northern Bondage. *Historical Archaeology* 30(2): 54–73.

Foster, Roy F. 1993. *Paddy and Mr. Punch: Connections in Irish and English History*. London: Allen Lane.

GAP (Group for the Advancement of Psychiatry). 1987. *Us and Them: The Psychology of Ethnonationalism*. New York: Brunner/Mazel.

Gibbons, Luke. 1991. Race against Time: Racial Discourse and Irish History. *Oxford Literary Review* 13: 95–113.

Greeley, Andrew M. 1981. *The Irish Americans: The Rise to Money and Power*. New York: Harper and Row.

Handsman, Russell G. 1985. Thinking about a Historical Archaeology of Alienation and Class Struggle. Paper presented at the annual meeting of the Society for Historical Archaeology, Boston, January.

Harrison, Faye V. 1995. The Persistent Power of "Race" in the Cultural and Political Economy of Racism. *Annual Review of Anthropology* 24: 47–74.

Hermstein. Richard J., and Charles Murray. 1994. *The Bell Curve: Intelligence and Class Structure in American Life*. New York: The Free Press.

Ignatiev, Noel. 1995. *How the Irish Became White*. New York: Routledge.

Jackson, Jesse L., Jr. 1997. Why Race Dialogue Stutters. *The Nation* 264(12): 22–24.

Kelly, Marsha C. S., and Roger E. Kelly. 1980. Approaches to Ethnic Identification in Historical Archaeology. In *Archaeological Perspectives on Ethnicity in America: Afro-American and Asian American Culture History*, ed. Robert L. Schuyler, 133–143. Farmingdale, NY: Baywood.

Lebow, Richard Ned. 1976. White Britain and Black Ireland: The Influence of Stereotypes on Colonical Policy. Philadelphia: Institute for the Study of Human Issues.

Leone, Mark P. 1995. A Historical Archaeology of Capitalism. *American Anthropologist* 97: 251–268.

McGuire, Randall H. 1982. The Study of Ethnicity in Historical Archaeology. *Journal of Anthropological Archaeology* 1: 159–178.

Mitchell, Margaret. 1936. *Gone with the Wind*. New York: Macmillan.

Mullins, Paul R. 1996. The Contradiction of Consumption: An Archaeology of African America and Consumer Culture, 1850–1930. Ph.D. dissertation, Department of Anthropology, University of Massachusetts, Amherst.

Oates, Joyce Carol. 1987. *On Boxing*. Garden City, NY: Dolphin Doubleday.

Orser, Charles E., Jr. 1988a. The Archaeological Analysis of Plantation Society: Replacing Status and Caste with Economics and Power. *American Antiquity* 53: 735–751.

______. 1988b. Toward a Theory of Power for Historical Archaeology: Plantations and Property. In *The Recovery of Meaning: Historical Archaeology in the Eastern United States*, eds. Mark P. Leone and Parker B. Potter Jr., 313–343. Washington, DC: Smithsonian Institution Press.

______. 1996. *A Historical Archaeology of the Modern World*. New York: Plenum.

Orser, Charles E., Jr., and Brian M. Fagan. 1995. *Historical Archaeology*. New York: HarperCollins.

Otto, John Solomon. 1980. Race and Class on Antebellum Plantations. In *Archaeological Perspectives on Ethnicity in America: Afro-American and Asian American Culture History*, ed. Robert L. Schuyler, 3–13. Farmingdale, NY: Baywood.

Paynter, Robert. 1997. Du Boisian Perspectives on Identities and Material Culture. *Anthropology Newsletter* 38(5): 11.

Paynter, Robert, and Randall H. McGuire. 1991. The Archaeology of Inequality: Material Culture, Domination, and Resistance. In *The Archaeology of Inequality*, eds. Randall H. McGuire and Robert Paynter, 1–27. Oxford: Blackwell.

Praetzellis, Adrian Charles. 1991. The Archaeology of a Victorian City: Sacramento, California. Ph.D. dissertation, Department of Anthropology, University of California, Berkeley.

Praetzellis, Adrian, Mary Praetzellis, and Marley Brown III. 1987. Artifacts as Symbols of Identity: An Example from Sacramento's Gold Rush Era Chinese Community. In *Living in Cities: Current Research in Urban Archaeology. Society for Historical Archaeology Special Publication Series,*

*No. 5*. ed. Edward Staski, 38–47. Tucson, AZ: Society for Historical Archaeology.

Rose, Peter I. 1974. *They and We: Racial and Ethnic Relations in the United States*. New York: Random House.

Shennan, Stephen. 1989. Introduction: Archaeological Approaches to Cultural Identity. In *Archaeological Approaches to Cultural Identity*, ed. Stephen Shennan, 1–32. London: Unwin Hyman.

Staski, Edward. 1990. Studies of Ethnicity in North American Historical Archaeology. *North American Archaeologist* 11: 121–145.

______. 1993. The Overseas Chinese in El Paso: Changing Goals, Changing Realities. In *Hidden Heritage: Historical Archaeology of the Overseas Chinese*, ed. Priscilla Wegars, 125–149. Amityville, NY: Baywood.

Thomas, Nicholas. 1991. *Entangled Objects: Exchange, Material Culture, and Colonialism in the Pacific*. Cambridge, MA: Harvard University Press.

Waters, Hazel. 1995. The Great Famine and the Rise of Anti-Irish Racism. *Race and Class* 37: 95–108.

Yamin, Rebecca. 1997. New York's Mythic Slums: Digging Lower Manhattan's Infamous Five Points. *Archaeology* 50(2): 44–53.

Young, Robert J. C. 1995. *Colonial Desire: Hybridity in Theory, Culture, and Race*. London: Routledge.

# 20

# Archaeology and *Vanua* Development in Fiji

*Andrew Crosby*

Most universities draw a sharp line between the sciences and the humanities. On one side of campus you have people who produce knowledge through the scientific method, and on the other are those who produce knowledge through more interpretive acts. Just like the universities in which Anthropology departments are housed, anthropologists also tend to demarcate qualitative from quantitative knowledge production. In fact, over the past two decades several notable anthropology departments actually splintered to create new but separate departments.

While four-field anthropology is a hybrid discipline with one foot in science and another in the humanities, it would be a mistake to assume that most anthropologists fit neatly into an empiricist versus interpretivist dyad. In one way or another, all anthropologists seek explanations for the unity and diversity of humankind, and most of us rely on qualitative and quantitative methods to seek answers to our research questions. Archaeologists, for example, rely on scientific techniques such as radiocarbon and potassium-argon dating to determine the age of their artifacts and fossilized human remains, but they also depend on less-scientific modes of knowledge production such as oral tradition and local histories.

While it may seem strange to non-anthropologists, traditional mythologies and creation stories of indigenous populations such as Australian aborigines contain hints and explanations that guide the scientific discovery and analysis of archaeological artifacts. In this chapter, archaeologist Andrew Crosby explains how his collaboration with non-scientific Fijian communities produces and integrates scientific knowledge with the values, priorities, and subjective points of view of local populations.

***As you read this selection, ask yourself the following questions:***

- What is the Waikatakata project, and why does the author describe it as a *vanua*-based archaeology project?
- What are some specific ways that Fijian communities contributed to and controlled the author's archaeological research?
- How has the relationship between Fijian chiefs and rural populations changed?
- How have tourism and development impacted the lives of ethnic Fijians?
- Why did the Waikatakata development project fail?

***The following terms discussed in this selection are included in the Glossary at the back of the book:***

*artifact*
*community archaeology*
*ecotourism*
*vanua*

## INTRODUCTION

There is an important divide between archaeology that attempts to incorporate or involve local communities into externally devised projects and those that are initiated by the communities themselves. On one side, the community may influence and participate in the timing, operation and goals of the project, and may benefit from it, but the project's *principal* objectives will be to generate publications that serve external interests. On the other side, there are usually no academic publications at all: the *point* of this sort of community archaeology is that it is entirely local, uncompromised by the interests of a broader academy. At their extremes, the two types of archaeology are of little relevance to each other, the two types of archaeologist seldom mix and there is a certain amount of name-calling that goes on between them. Nearer the center, however, post-colonial archaeology is less polemical and busies itself with genuine communication and accommodation of external and local community interests and attempts to

Crosby, Andrew. "Archaeology and *Vanua* Development in Fiji." *World Archaeology* 34 (October 2002):363–78, reprinted by permission of the publisher (Taylor & Francis Group, http://www.informaworld.com).

reach a quid pro quo—a mutually beneficial exchange of services and resources.

This paper is based on the author's experiences in Fiji over the period 1990–1994 conducting anthropological research into the construction of the modern chiefly system during the colonial period. Having previously conducted archaeological research in Fiji, I was frequently asked during my stay to advise and assist the Fiji Museum on projects ranging from field survey and excavation to fund-raising, which I was only too happy to do. And it is in this capacity—as an unpaid adviser to the Fiji Museum and participant in a number of community archaeological projects—that this paper is written. My anthropological research supports the proposition that a once fluid and balanced set of relationships between Fijian chiefs and commoners was transformed and then classified into a system of fixed class relationships. Despite this, the chiefly system is a famously beloved institution in Fiji and is a key ethnic marker that serves to define ethnic Fijians from the other main population groups: Fijian Indians, Europeans and Chinese. During the course of my parallel involvement in community archaeology projects, therefore, it surprised me to what degree Fijians in rural communities were disenchanted with their chiefs and were prepared to mobilize community development projects that directly challenged the chiefs' authority and provided local people with a measure of economic independence from them. Some years later I find it ironic that these projects have been considerably more effective in challenging the iniquitous chiefly system of Fiji than my self-consciously critical academic analysis. They have also raised more interesting questions. Perhaps I now understand what it means to be a post-colonial archaeologist.

## PROBLEMS

Fiji is a precarious economy for which the conservation of the natural and cultural heritage resource is an ill-afforded luxury. As with most "developing nations" the resources—forestry, agriculture and tourism—have been sold to the highest bidders, mostly overseas consortiums. Although this has provided the metropolitan government with the rental, licensing and tax revenues to square the balance sheet, there have been considerable costs to the environment and to the sense of self-determination and economic well-being of people in the rural communities. A series of quite specific problems emerged during the 1980s to bring some of these costs to near crisis point.

### Problem 1: Cultural Resource Management

Fiji is like most developing nations around the post-colonial world: the departing colonial administration bequeathed a toothless and ill-funded heritage management structure to an apathetic and nearly destitute beneficiary—one that was barely able to raise a mortgage for society's essential services, let alone the luxury of an archaeological past. In Fiji, the management of the archaeological resource was commended to the combined care of the Fiji Museum, the National Trust and the Department of Town and Country Planning, which, authorized and empowered by various Acts, have discharged their responsibilities with great dedication but negligible support.

Of primary significance is the Fiji Museum, which carries statutory responsibility for preserving and maintaining archaeological objects and monuments. Under the Preservation of Objects of Archaeological and Palaeontological Interest Act, 1978 the museum is authorized to declare sites to be national monuments and to acquire those monuments where appropriate. The museum, however, lacks the authority to prohibit the disturbance of archaeological sites that have not been declared monuments and cannot oblige the owner to enter into a preservation agreement. Severe funding restrictions ensure that compulsory purchases of monuments are unheard of and the legislation languishes untested and unused. Fiji has only one declared national archaeological monument—Wasavulu—which survives in a dilapidated and vandalized state (Watling and Chape 1992: 144). The museum instead focuses on maintaining a register of sites and on the custodial care of the portable components of heritage: objects, archives and oral histories. Where sites *have* been acquired, they are owned by the independently funded National Trust, which maintains them in consultation with the Fiji Museum. The number of properties, however, is few, the most significant being the archaeologically spectacular Sigatoka Sand Dunes (Marshall et al. 2000).

Of equal importance is the Department of Town and Country Planning, which is authorized by the Town Planning Act, 1946 to consider items and areas of historic interest in drawing up local planning schemes. Such schemes—such as at the old capital Levuka—*have* provided for the preservation of historic buildings of Fiji's post-European period (Watling and Chape 1992: 144; Takano 1996). But these are structures of colonialism, and it is therefore poignant that the inherited colonial legislation has been most effective in protecting its own architectural edifice. I am aware of only one or two occasions where the 1946 Act has been invoked to prevent the destruction of indigenous Fijian sites (Wood et al. 1998: 16–17).

The problem is only partially one of funding. By far the greatest destruction to the Fijian archaeological heritage is caused by the indifference, ignorance or commercial avarice of ethnic Fijians themselves. This occurs at a very small scale through repeated clearance, planting and occasional bulldozing of sites for crops by villagers and independent farmers. But it also occurs on a massive scale through the operations of commercial planters and foresters. The field officers of the Fiji Museum are well aware that the most effective course of action is not to enforce protection but to work with Fijians—especially villagers and farmers—to educate them about the very existence of the archaeology and of its value.

### Problem 2: Economic Inequality

There is a very uneven distribution of wealth among Fijians (Spate 1959; Burns et al. 1960; Fisk 1970). This is only partially due to the colonial creation of "Three Fijis", which for many decades has seen the ethnic Fijians as the majority landowners, subsistence farmers and political elite, the Fijian Indians as the predominant cash croppers, laborers, merchants and owners of small industry, and the ethnic Europeans and Chinese as the owners and managers of large manufacturing and service industries (Fisk 1970: 33–48; Knapman and Schiavo-Campo 1983). The land ownership system created by the Colonial Government and preserved at independence on 1970 recognizes communal land ownership by ethnic Fijians and it vests control of communal lands in local chiefs. Traditionally, chiefs would exercise their control for the benefit of the *mataqali and vanua* (landowning groups) (Ravuvu 1983, 1987, 1988). However, in the post-independence neo-colonial state the chiefs emerged as an elite class, dominating the House of Representatives and using their control over the vast majority of the land resources to form a hegemonic alliance with European capital (France 1969; Nayacakalou 1975; Durutalo 1985, 1986; Hau'ofa 1987: 10–11). Within the ethnic Fijian population, this resulted in the concentration of political power and economic wealth in the hands of chiefs generally and the chiefs of Eastern Fiji in particular.

The relevance for this paper is in several dimensions. Eighty-three percent of Fijian lands, and therefore 83 percent of the archaeological resource, lies in ethnic Fijian ownership. The usage of that land is steadily moving away from low-intensity subsistence use (Overton 1987, 1988). The chiefs have taken increasing amounts of communally owned lands—those nominally considered waste or excess to subsistence requirements—and leased them to yield a cash dividend: typically through forestry, farming or tourism. Few of the cash proceeds of those enterprises have found their way into the ethnic Fijian villages where the chiefs are also seldom to be found these days. The chiefs now form a new urban elite, whereas those Fijians remaining in the villages are forced to intensify their use of the remaining land for both subsistence and income. In the absence of the chiefs, the formal protocols surrounding land use are relaxing. In particular, much of the knowledge of the locations of ancestral sites has been forgotten or ignored and sites previously considered *tambu* (sacred) are now being cultivated, built upon and even bulldozed. The problem is one of outright apathy: the increasingly disenfranchised rural Fijians have little incentive to care for archaeological sites that take up valuable agricultural land, and the incentive to maintain the traditional "customs of respect" (Nation 1978) is diminishing with the migration of the chiefs to the towns.

### Problem 3: Diversification of Land Use

The Native Land Trust Board (NLTB) administers the 83 percent of all Fijian lands owned by ethnic Fijians (429,000 hectares). Approximately 65 percent of this land is leased for agricultural purposes—including commercial sugar and rice cultivation. The remainder is leased for a variety of purposes including tourism and forestry. The total rental pay out to ethnic Fijians in 1988 was very low, only F$6.5 million at the rate of just over F$15 per hectare. Of this, agricultural leases contributed approximately F$12 per hectare compared to F$20 per hectare for non-agricultural leases. The NLTB has come under increasing pressure to increase the rental returns on land (Volavola 1993), but, with the collapse of world sugar prices, cannot significantly increase the land rents paid by Indian sugar farmers. In an effort to stimulate income growth, land managers at the NLTB have been asked to meet income quotas and to diversify the uses for which land has been leased. This could perhaps be most easily achieved by increasing the area leased for forestry. However, environmental concerns over forestry and other environmentally damaging land uses have placed increasing scrutiny on the NLTB to allocate land leases to more environmentally sustainable uses.

The problem for the NLTB, then, is that it has come under simultaneous pressure to increase the returns from land leases and diversify its rentals away from low earners, such as sugar cultivation, and environmentally damaging operations, such as forestry. Apart from the damage caused to the natural and cultural heritage, the brunt of the forestry and other extractive operations has been felt by ethnic Fijians in the villages. Although forestry activities have typically been confined to relatively remote and steep areas unsuitable for arable or even subsistence agriculture (Watling and Chape 1992: 31), they have eroded the important resource available for traditional agro-forestry (Thaman 1994) and damaged the capacity of Fijians to manage production systems holistically (Clarke 1994). When questioned, many rural Fijians have expressed to me that they have met resistance and animosity when they have challenged the NLTB for issuing leases to forestry. As they explain it, the NLTB itself is made up of too many 'ratus' (chiefs), who indeed comprised 50 percent of the membership in 1988. Given that many of these chiefs are also principal shareholders, directors or beneficiaries of forestry enterprises, a clear conflict of interests exists (Durutalo 1985, 1986).

### Problem 4: Conservation of Native Forests

According to *The National State of the Environment Report* (Watling and Chape 1992: 54), Fiji has just under half of its total land area (1.83 million hectares) under forest. Of this, approximately 25 percent (237,000 hectares) comprises areas of native hardwoods exploited for timber production with a further 85,000 hectares of plantation forests managed by the Fiji Pine Commission and the Forestry Department. Between 1967 and 1992 an estimated 11–16 percent of the nation's forests were converted to non-forest use, with deforestation occurring at a rate of between 0.5 and 0.8 percent a year. This is particularly problematic for the Forestry Department, the government agency principally responsible for managing the forest resource. Although Fiji appears to be well forested, the resource is rapidly dwindling. In particular, there is a severe imbalance in the distribution of forest, with the drier parts of the larger islands and many smaller islands suffering the most severe deforestation.

The result has been something of a partitioning of the nation's forest resources and a separation of the forests away from the people, increasingly relegating the native hardwoods to inaccessible zones on steep lands and specially designated conservation areas. The effect is to increasingly remove agro-forestry—a traditionally important subsistence strategy—from everyday village life for ethnic Fijians (Thaman 1988, 1994; Thaman and Clarke 1983). Moreover, some within the Department of Forestry itself have expressed concern over the dividing off of forested areas from the traditionally holistic Fijian conceptualization of the *vanua* as a world in which the land, the people and the gods—the physical, cultural and spiritual spheres—are fully integrated (Ravuvu 1988: 6; Crosby 1994; personal communication Alivereti Bogiva 1992). The problem is the simultaneous contraction of the natural forest resource and its gradual removal from the everyday lives of ethnic Fijians. While the creation of forest conservation areas is beneficial in preserving native forest plant and animal species, there is great dissatisfaction that this has occurred at the expense of an important component of the traditional Fijian concept of community.

### Problem 5: Diversification of Tourism

The Fijian tourism industry is floundering. Second only to sugar as a revenue earner, tourism has been hit hard by political instability in Fiji and the recent world economic recession. More significantly, the market for selling "sun, sea and surf"—Fiji's traditional tourism marketing strategy—is a highly competitive one, with many other comparable holiday destinations offering weaker currencies and cheaper flights from North America and Europe. Fijian operators have recognized that the Fijian tourism industry needs to diversify to appeal to a wider range of holidaymakers, and to accentuate the cultural uniqueness of Fiji among the otherwise ubiquitous glossy beach brochures. This has been accomplished partially by modelling resort architecture on traditional Fijian building styles, by having displays of Fijian artifacts and textiles in hotel lobbies and by putting on cultural performances of Fijian dance groups and string bands. Since the early 1980s hotels and small independent tour operators have been increasingly guiding the more adventurous visitors out of the hotels to visit waterfalls and other natural beauty spots, to go on horseriding and walking treks and to visit Fijian villages.

Successful to a degree, the problem is that there has been little involvement of ethnic Fijians in this new venture, and little additional money has found its way into the pockets of Fijian villagers, who consider themselves the rightful custodians of Fijian culture and the environment. The problems are how to increase the overall tourism revenue through diversification and to distribute the benefits more evenly, particularly so that those who are the caretakers of Fijian culture past and present are more active stakeholders in its exploitation.

### Problem 6: Overseas Development Assistance

Overseas development agencies have consistently been criticized for failing to deploy their assistance in ways that are culturally appropriate, sustainable and targeted to the areas that most need stimulation. The domination of regional development ministries and departments by self-interested locals—frequently the chiefly elite—has exacerbated the problem and has led to the deployment of development funds in ways that have actually been damaging to local communities and their environments (Watters 1987). There have been many instances involving the implementation of rural development projects that have served only to increase the class domination of the urban elite, allowing them to exercise long-distance control over an increasingly disenfranchised rural labor force. Such projects, far from being culturally sensitive, have accelerated the break up of community as defined by the traditional *vanua* concept. The proceeds and benefits of the land have not been shared evenly, the physical environment has not been managed sustainably, and there has been a breakdown of the pathways of communication between members of the community. This has become increasingly embarrassing for overseas governments.

### Summary

The various problems outlined above, although disparate, demonstrate just some of the economic, political, social and environmental strands that weave together the context of Fijian heritage management. In essence, ethnic Fijians make much of their traditional concept of community: the *vanua*. It differentiates them ethnically from Fijian Indians, Europeans and others. In their view, it is what makes them *traditional*, it is what justifies their vast majority claim over the landholdings, it is the foundation of their political élite—their chiefs, it is what binds ethnic Fijians together into a social system and it is the source and repository of the historical knowledge and cultural understandings by which those social knots are tied. In reality, the *vanua* is somewhat different. The weave is nowhere near so tight, more an assemblage of threads from which any number of patterns can be woven, some exploitative and self-serving, others a determined effort by groups of villagers to develop a rural economy and preserve their local resources, both human and environmental.

## SOLUTIONS

Some ethnic Fijians recognize the heritage as a key resource, one that can be conserved, managed and sold to tourists in a way that would also re-awaken an interest in the past by villagers themselves—especially the youth. They hope that the preservation of archaeological sites for economic gain may also reinforce the historical knowledge of past social relationships and genealogical connections by which the *vanua* adheres as a community. During the 1990s several rural village communities, supported by sympathetic government agencies, initiated a momentum for community-led archaeology development projects.

### Waikatakata

As far as I am aware, Waikatakata is the first *vanua*-based archaeology development project in Fiji. It is situated near to the heart of Fiji's "Coral Coast", a string of resorts along the southwest coast of Viti Levu (Figure. 1). It includes an area of virgin native forest, hot springs, streams and waterfalls and is interspersed with several pre-European village and ceremonial *naga* sites—spectacular stone-walled enclosures in which initiation rituals are thought to have taken place. The archaeological sites were badly overgrown and dilapidated, threatened by logging and by guided horseback treks operated by private entrepreneurs.

The Department of Town and Country Planning initially proposed the project in 1986 with the following objectives:

- To widen the scope of visitor attractions within Fiji and, in particular, to develop an aspect of cultural tourism which to date has been largely neglected.
- To encourage greater participation of the local community in culturally oriented tourism development and to raise incomes through the creation of employment opportunities and visitor returns.
- To ensure, through controlled access and protective measures, that the archaeological (scientific), educational and cultural value of the sites is adequately preserved and in no way debased or impaired.
- To promote a general awareness and interest in Fiji's archaeological sites and monuments and an appreciation of the need to conserve/preserve this important aspect of Fiji's heritage.

Several similar projects were also proposed for the vicinity should the Waikatakata pilot scheme prove successful.

Initial progress was highly promising, with meetings by representatives of the Fiji Museum, the Department of Town and Country Planning, the NLTB, Forestry Department and other agencies with members of the local landowning communities. The proposal was for an integrated forest/tourism park, managed by the NLTB but operated by local villagers who would gain from employment in the park and a share of the tourism revenues. The local community would eventually take over management of the project. A trained archaeologist was appointed by the NLTB to complete a site survey, the archaeological sites were cleared of vegetation and partially rebuilt, and a plan was drawn up of walking/trekking routes, signage and shelters, with the prospect of building tourist accommodation in or adjacent to the park in the future. It seemed that Waikatakata would pave the way for a new kind of community-based archaeological development in which the archaeological and natural environments would be preserved to the benefit of the local ethnic Fijian community.

Too good to be true? Of course. To this day Waikatakata is again overgrown, undeveloped and threatened by logging. The Waikatakata project failed because it was imposed from afar by metropolitan bureaucrats. A cash cow was presented to the local community before any degree of consensus was achieved over vital questions such as who actually owned the land, how the proceeds should be divided, who should provide the labour and who should oversee and control the whole affair. It soon became clear that

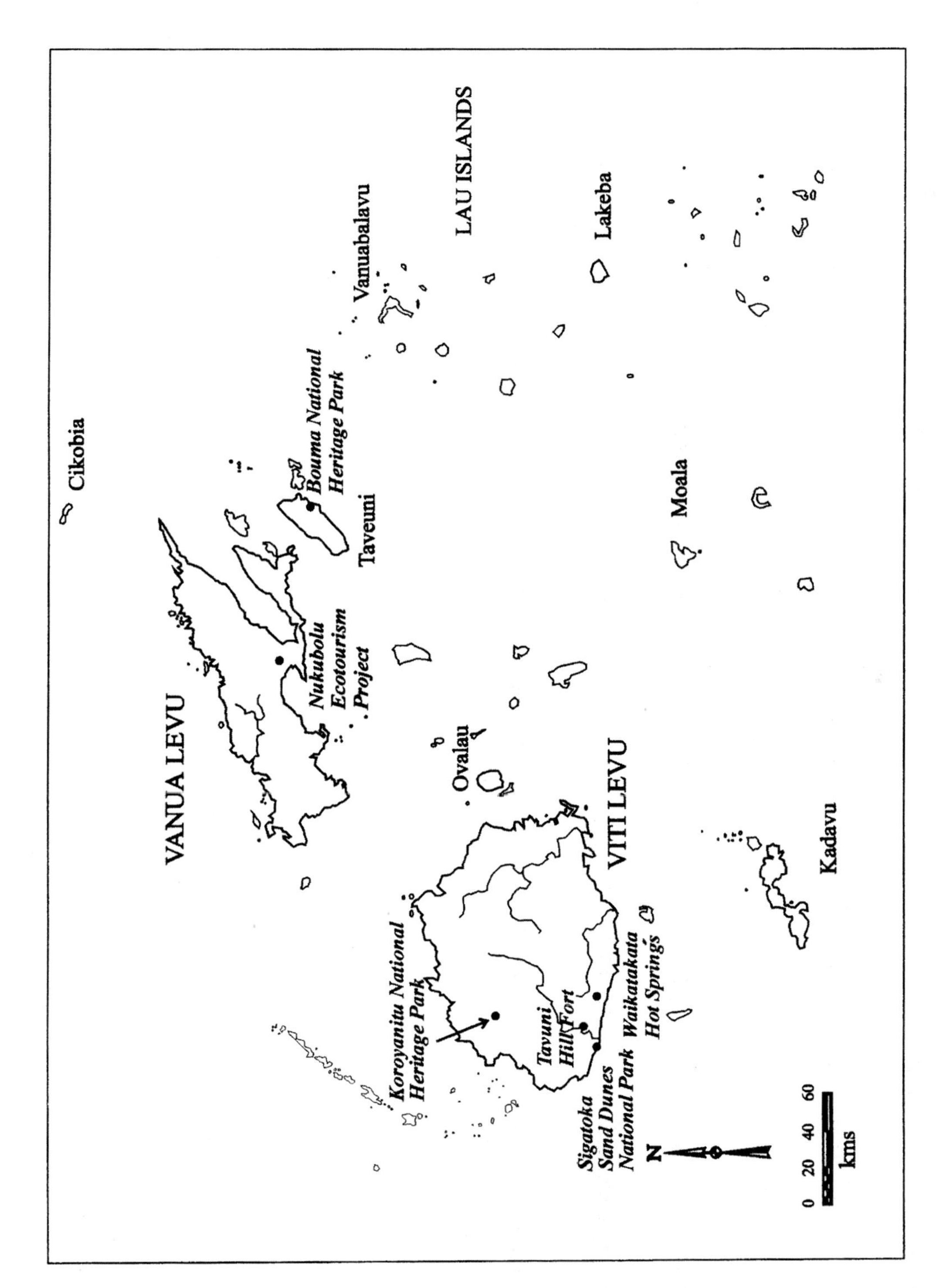


**FIGURE 1** Map of Fiji showing the archaeology and ecotourism projects discussed in the text.

those individuals who had wholeheartedly backed the initial proposals did not represent the wider group. The project stalled permanently through the classic Fijian strategy of passive resistance. Worse, acrimonious feuds erupted between villagers and the net result appears to have been to further split an already riven community.

### Bouma, Taveuni

Waikatakata, however, is a hearth from which several other more successful projects have risen. Paramount among these is a project located at Bouma at the northeastern end of Taveuni Island (Figures 1 and 2). The crucial difference with this project is that it proceeded from a request for assistance by the local landowning community itself. Bouma forms part of the Fijian chiefly confederacy of Cakaudrove, the paramount chief of which—Tui Cakau—resides on the other side of Taveuni at Somosomo. In 1988, when the project was initiated, the people of Bouma had been asked by Tui Cakau (who at that time was Ratu Sir Penaia Ganilau, President of Fiji) and his cousin at the Provincial Office to participate in a Korean forestry scheme. The Bouma people were attracted by the promised benefits of land rentals and employment, but felt bullied by the Somosomo chiefs and concerned about the unsustainability of forestry for future generations. They were aware of the Waikatakata project and requested the NLTB's assistance in initiating a similar programme of landowner-based tourism development.

Initially, the NLTB was approached by representatives of Nakorovou village to assist in establishing a forest park on their land. The area included the Tavoro falls, a series of spectacular waterfalls set within native forest. The Nakorovou villagers had obtained a modest and *ad hoc* income from guiding tourists to these falls for some time and now wished to develop the attraction. As stated, their aims were conserving and protecting their forest and cultural heritage resources while providing employment and incomegenerating opportunities. These aims were commensurate with the ideals of sustainability lying at the heart of ecotourism—conserving and preserving the resource in a way that provides some practical gain (Seroma 1995).

Their interests went further, however, and emphasized the development of the *vanua*, seeking to enhance their prosperity in spiritual and cultural dimensions as well (Ravuvu 1983: 76, 1988: 6; Crosby 1994). They were particularly concerned at the breakdown of traditional cultural values within the community. As they saw it, this was demonstrated by their own paramount chief's disregard for the natural resources of the forest, and by a widespread breakdown of social taboos marked by increased drunkenness and decreased co-operation within the village. They wanted a prosperity that also included social and spiritual harmony.

It became clear in preliminary discussions that *vanua* development should involve the cooperative effort of villagers communally sharing their skill and labor resources to create the forest park themselves under the leadership of their own village leaders. The process of creating the park would be developmentally beneficial in itself. What was required was outside support, advice and skill in implementing trails, visitor centres, conservation programmes and effective management practices. It also emerged that *vanua* development required preserving not just the natural heritage of the forest, but also the cultural heritage of *koro makawa*—the ancient settlements of the ancestors located in the forest. These sites had become damaged by gardening and neglect, and would have been destroyed by forestry, but they represented the historical foundations of the communities and are considered by some to be the spiritual abode of the ancestors themselves. The preservation of the old settlements and the remembrance of oral histories associated with those sites were seen as crucial to the rejuvenation of the spirituality of the *vanua*. Ever pragmatic, the Bouma people also saw the *koro makawa* as a further attraction for tourists.

Having learned from the divisiveness of Waikatakata, the NLTB insisted on the full participation of all four *yavusa* (landowning groups) that constitute the wider *vanua* of Bouma under the overall patronage of the *vanua* chief, the Vunisa of Bouma. To avoid future disputes, they recommended that each *yavusa* should control separate parts of the project, each of which could stand as a self-contained, independently managed concern (Figure. 2). Accordingly, a four-phase ecotourism project was devised covering 1,603 hectares of land extending from the coast to the island's mountainous central plateau and including Fiji's largest lake, Tagimoucia (Native Land Trust Board 1989, 1993). The bulk lies under tropical rainforest, some of which was already designated Forest Reserve. Phases 1-3 were designed to focus on three areas easily accessible from the coastal road and centred on attractions close to each of the main villages. Phase 1 would see the development of the Tavoro Falls based on Nakorovou. Phase 2 was a coastal walking trail and lodge based at Lavena. Phase 3 was an archaeological and forest trail based between Vidawa and Waitabu. Phase 4 was a longer-distance trail network accessible from all four villages. Each phase was to proceed at one-year intervals, to be overseen by a steering committee drawn principally from the NLTB, the Department

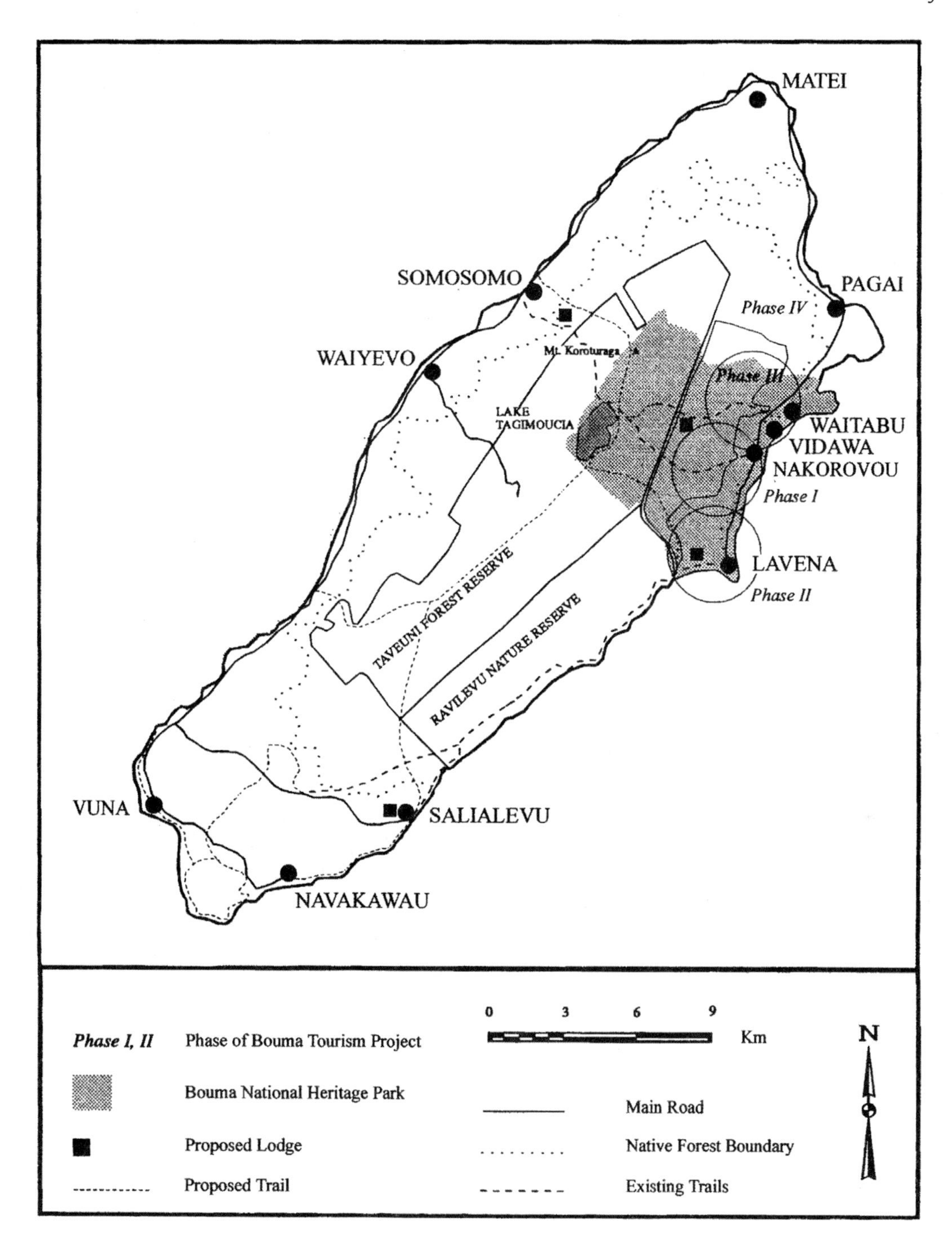


**FIGURE 2** Map of Taveuni showing the Bouma National Heritage Park and the four phases of the Bouma Tourism Project.

of Forestry, the Fiji Museum, the Ministry of Fijian Affairs and the Department of Tourism. The New Zealand Government funded the establishment of the first three phases. The villagers voluntarily supplied labor, and expertise was provided by the agencies forming the steering committee.

Phase 1 was opened in April 1991 and Phase 2 in June 1993. Both have since been operating as successful commercial ventures, charging tourists five Fiji dollars per visit. Phase 3, the Vidawa forest and heritage trail, was initiated with a formal management plan in 1991 (Wakelin 1991) and an archaeological survey in 1993 (Crosby and Marshall 1994). Oral histories were also recorded and a series of site plans and detailed recommendations were put forward, which culminated in a network of signposted walking trails linking two hill fortifications—Nasau and Navuga—with walks through native rainforest. All stages, from the archaeological survey to the construction of the trails and signs, were completed as a cooperative effort between outside experts and local villagers convened under the leadership of the village chiefs. After some delay, the Vidawa Forest Walk is now open for visitors and, for sixty Fiji dollars, visitors are guided on a full-day walk taking in the fortifications, bird watching and the Tavoro falls. On the way, visitors are informed about the basic principles of the Fijian *vanua* philosophy and about the traditional history of the Bouma people. Phase 4 is less formally structured but is now also completed and includes guided walks up to Lake Tagimoucia.

The project has not been without its problems. Proposed accommodation lodges were cancelled, partly due to fears over the intrusive effects of visitors staying near to the villages. And there have been disagreements over procedure and allocation of resources. By and large, however, the project has been successful and is promoted aggressively as the Bouma National Heritage Park by the Fiji Visitors Bureau and by independent tour operators. In its promotional literature, the Fiji Visitors Bureau proclaims: "The Park . . . wouldn't exist if it wasn't for the shared vision of four local villages, the Fiji and New Zealand Governments and other conservation organisations" (http://www.fijifvb.gov.fj/activity/listing/bouma.htm). The park is a major tourism resource that is being used to brand the whole tourism industry in Fiji as eco-friendly. Last but not least, the financial backers of the project—the New Zealand Government—are delighted to be able to demonstrate their investment in a rare commodity: a culturally appropriate and environmentally friendly overseas development project.

## Other Projects

The success of Bouma and the commitment of the Steering Committee have had immediate spin-offs elsewhere in Fiji. On the western side of Viti Levu, the Koroyanitu National Heritage Park (Figure. 1)—a more complex project involving 25,000 hectares of unlogged rainforest and fifty *mataqali* landowning groups—was initiated in 1993. This project, again, occurred at the request of the five villages that bounded the area, and began with ground and air-photo surveys of the forest and archaeological resources. The first stage of the project, the Abaca Village and Recreation Park, has been completed with the development of simple accommodation and a series of hiking trails taking in native forest, mountain walks and archaeological sites. As with Bouma, labor and expertise were all voluntarily provided as a cooperative effort between the landowning communities and government agencies.

A more explicitly archaeological project has also been completed at Tavuni Hill Fort near Sigatoka (Figure. 1), also initiated at the request of the local community: the four surrounding villages, each of which regard Tavuni as their ancestral settlement. Long abandoned and neglected, the hill-fort was first cleared using community labor and, following the advice of the Fiji Museum, parts of the site were repaired and a network of trails constructed to guide visitors around remnants of the fort's fifty-six structures. The Fiji Museum conducted oral historical research and prepared a guide to the site. Funding was received to construct signs, a car park and a combined visitor centre and museum. As with Bouma and Koroyanitu, the project has proved highly successful, is actively marketed and continues to provide the local community with income and employment.

Other projects are also being negotiated throughout Fiji, although not all have the degree of community agreement and leadership, the quality of physical or cultural attractions or the necessary tourism infrastructure to allow them to proceed at this time. Perhaps most advanced is the Nukubolu Ecotourism Project on *Vanua* Levu: a series of ring-ditch fortifications and hot-springs surrounded by rivers and rainforest (Figure. 1). The project is planned in three phases of trails and accommodation and is again being conducted as a community-led project.

## Summary

Community-led and community-operated ecotourism projects in Fiji appear to successfully resolve many of the problems outlined at the start of this paper. They take areas of natural and archaeological importance that would otherwise have been lost to forestry or neglect and develop them as tourism alternatives to sandy beach resorts. Crucially, control over the implementation and final operation of the projects has at all times remained with the local community, allowing a degree of resistance to bureaucratically imposed development and a buffer to the economic exploitation of the chiefs. The common denominators of the various projects are:

- They are initiated by local communities seeking alternative income and employment generating opportunities.
- They are based on the Fijian concept of the *vanua* and seek to integrate sustainable economic

development of the natural and cultural heritage with less tangible cultural benefits that include the development of community co-operation, the rejuvenation of a sense of history and the reassertion of 'traditional' Fijian values.

- They are expertly guided and assisted by a loose conglomerate of government and nongovernment agencies now formalized as the National Steering Committee. This is made up of representatives from all organizations involved in conservation, forestry and tourism, including the NLTB, the Departments of Forestry, Tourism, Lands, Fijian Affairs, Cooperatives and Economic Planning, the Environment Unit, the Development Bank, the National Trust of Fiji and the Fiji Museum.
- They are financially supported by government and overseas development assistance programmes that recognize the contribution to the national economy of sustainable and culturally appropriate development.

The benefits have extended beyond each individual project. The crucial involvement of the National Steering Committee has provided a forum for exchange and liaison between normally autonomous agencies that has effected a more integrated national conservation policy and has been to the great benefit of heritage conservation in particular.

## CONCLUSIONS

In Fiji, a series of apparently dislocated problems is being tackled jointly at grass roots level by community-led development projects aimed at sustainably promoting the natural and cultural heritage. Community archaeology has featured in all of these projects through the clearance, survey and repair of ancient sites and the collection and recording of oral historical information. This has usually been accomplished with the involvement and assistance of the Fiji Museum and visiting foreign archaeologists, but has in all cases led to a rejuvenation of local interest in the cultural heritage and the training of community members to manage the archaeological resource. Without exception, all projects have led to improvements in the economic fortunes of the villagers and to the condition of the archaeological sites concerned. In all cases, the projects have also empowered the communities to reclaim their local histories in ways that sometimes directly challenge the historical underpinnings of the Fijian chiefly élites.

There is nothing academic about these projects aside from the affiliations of the visiting archaeologists. Indeed, in some cases the archaeological interpretations that have ended up in the visitor guides and signs contravene orthodox academic understandings. Community archaeology in Fiji represents the claiming of the heritage resource by local Fijian communities to make of it what they will. But conventional academic archaeology is also the winner here. Apart from the conservation of the resource, the whole profile of archaeology has been raised in Fiji. The museum's funding and staffing levels have increased, the Fiji Government has taken cultural heritage much more seriously and the level of local debate about prehistory has risen to a level never previously attained.

In a post-colonial world this is the key message for archaeologists. For institutional and academic archaeologists the tendency has been to pay lip service to community-based archaeology—to entertain it, patronize it, exploit it in the name of appearing to be postcolonial, but to distance it from the "real" work of archaeology and to fear or ridicule the sometimes unorthodox or counter-hegemonic claims it may make. Perhaps, with a little more imagination, archaeologists will see that anything that raises the level of the debate and increases the involvement of people in the past will ultimately challenge and thereby enrich their own interpretations. Certainly for this archaeologist—laboring to understand the processes of state formation and the emergence of a political elite in Fijian history—it has been illustrative to be immersed in the present reality of political economy and the creative reinvention of tradition.

## ACKNOWLEDGEMENTS

The ideas put forward in this paper are the result of discussions with many people in Fiji more visionary and committed than myself. In particular I should like to thank Stefan Cabaniuk, Alivereti Bogiva and Sepeti Matararaba, whose single-minded zeal paved the way for the projects outlined above. More generally, I should like to thank everybody who participated on the projects for their kind assistance and hospitality, and the Fiji Museum, the Native Land Trust Board, the Department of Forestry and the New Zealand Government Nature Tourism Funding Programme for supporting community archaeology in Fiji. I am especially indebted to Yvonne Marshall who conducted much of the archaeology at Bouma and generously commented on an earlier draft of this paper.

*Department of Archaeology, University of Southampton, S017 1BJ, UK*

## REFERENCES


Bogiva, A. 1993. Personal communication, Department of Forestry Fiji, June.

Burns, Alan et al. 1960. *Report of the Commission of Enquiry into the Natural Resources and Population Trends of the Colony of Fiji*. London: The Crown Agents for Overseas Governments and Administration on behalf of the Fiji Government.

Clarke, W. C. 1994. Traditional land use and agriculture in the Pacific Islands. In *Science of Pacific Island Peoples*, Vol. II, *Land Use and Agriculture* (eds J. Morrison, P. Geraghty and L. Crowl). Suva: Institute of Pacific Studies, pp. 11–38.

Crosby, A. D. 1994. Fijian cosmology, *vanua*, development and ecology. In *Science of Pacific Island Peoples*, Vol. IV, *Education, Language, Patterns and Policy* (eds J. Morrison, P. Geraghty and L. Crowl). Suva: Institute of Pacific Studies, pp. 55–78.

Crosby, A. D. and Marshall, Y. M. 1994. Archaeological sites and development recommendations for Phase III, Bouma Environmental Tourism Project. Report prepared for The Native Lands Conservation and Preservation Projects Steering Committee, Suva.

Durutalo, S. 1985. Internal colonialism and unequal regional development: the case of Western Viti Levu, Fiji. MA thesis. Department of History and Politics, University of the South Pacific, Suva.

Durutalo, S. 1986. *The Paramountcy of Fijian Interest and the Politicization of Ethnicity*. South Pacific Forum Working Paper Number 6. Suva: University of the South Pacific Sociological Society.

Fisk, E. K. 1970. *The Political Economy of Independent Fiji*. Canberra: Australian National University Press.

France, P. 1969. *The Charter of the Land*. London: Oxford University Press.

Hau'ofa, E. 1987. The new South Pacific society: integration and independence. In *Class and Culture in the South Pacific* (eds A. Hooper, S. Britton, R. Crocombe, J. Huntsman and C. Macpherson). Auckland and Suva: University of Auckland and University of the South Pacific, pp. 1–12.

Knapman,B . and Schiavo-CampoS, . 1983. Growth and fluctuationso f Fiji's exports, 1875–1978. *Economic Development and Cultural Change*, 32: 97–119.

Marshall, Y. M., Crosby A. D., Matararaba, S. and Wood, S. 2000. *Sigatoka: The Shifting Sands of Fijian Prehistory*. University of Southampton Department of Archaeology Monograph Number 1. Oxford: Oxbow Books.

Nation, J. 1978. *Customs of Respect: The Traditional Basis of Fijian Communal Politics*. Canberra: Australian National University Development Studies Centre.

Native Land Trust Board 1989. A forest park and reserve proposal for Mataqali Naituku and the *Vanua* of Bouma, Taveuni. Plan prepared by the Native Land Trust Board, Suva.

Native Land Trust Board 1993. Taveuni environmental tourism project: concept plan. Plan prepared by the Native Land Trust Board, Suva.

Nayacakalou, R. R. 1975. *Leadership in Fiji*. Melbourne: Oxford University Press.

Overton, J. 1987. Fijian land: pressing problems, possible tenure solutions. *Singapore Journal of Tropical Geography*, 8:139-51.

Overton, J. 1988. A Fijian peasantry: galala and villagers. *Oceania*, 58: 193–211.

Ravuvu, A. 1983. *Vaka i Taukei: The Fijian Way of Life*. Suva: University of the South Pacific.

Ravuvu, A. 1987. *The Fijian Ethos*. Suva: Institute of Pacific Studies.

Ravuvu, A. 1988. *Development or Dependence: The Pattern of Change in a Fijian Village*. Suva: University of the South Pacific.

Seroma, L. 1995. Ecotourism: the Fijian experience. In *Beyond Timber: Social, Economic and Cultural Dimensions of Non-Wood Forest Products in Asia and the Pacific: Proceedings of a Regional Expert Consultation 28 November-2 December* (eds P. B. Durst and A. Bishop). Regional Office for Asia and the Pacific Publication 1995/13. Bangkok: Food and Agriculture Organization of the United Nations, Regional Office for Asia and the Pacific.

Spate, O. H. K. 1959. *The Fijian People: Economic Problems and Prospects*. Council Paper Number 13 of 1959. Suva: Government Press.

Takano, G. T. 1996. Learning from Levuka, Fiji-preservation in the first colonial capital. *CRM*, 19(3): 15–17.

Thaman, R. R. 1988. Fijian agroforestry: trees, people and sustainable polycultural development. In *Rural Fiji* (ed. J. Overton). Suva: Institute of Pacific Studies of the University of the South Pacific, pp. 31–58.

Thaman, R. R. 1994. Pacific Island agroforestry: an endangered science. In *Science of Pacific Island Peoples*, Vol. II, *Land Use and Agriculture* (eds J. Morrison, P. Geraghty and L. Crowl). Suva: Institute of Pacific Studies, pp. 191–222.

Thaman, R. R. and Clarke, W. C. 1983. Pacific Island agrosilviculture: systems for cultural and ecological stability. Paper presented to the Fifteenth Pacific Science Congress, Dunedin, 1–11 February.

Volavola, Ratu M. 1993. NLTB and landowner–in the same team, says general manager. *Vanua*, June: 1–4.

Wakelin, D. 1991. A management plan for Bouma Forest Park, Taveuni, Fiji Islands. Report prepared for the New Zealand Ministry of External Relations and Trade, Wellington.

Watling, D. and Chape, S. P. (eds) 1992. *Environment Fiji: The National State of the Environment Report*. Gland, Switzerland: IUCN-The World Conservation Union.

Watters, R. 1987. Mirab societies and bureaucratic elites. In *Class and Culture in the South Pacific* (eds A. Hooper, S. Britton, R. Crocombe, J. Huntsman and C. Macpherson). Auckland and Suva: University of Auckland and University of the South Pacific, pp. 32–55.

Wood, S., Marshall, Y. M. and Crosby, A. D. 1998. Mapping Sigatoka, Site VL 16/1: the 1992 field season and its implications. Report prepared for the Fiji Museum and the New Zealand High Commission, Suva. http://www.fijifvb.gov.fj/activity/listing/bouma.htm.

# 21

# Around the Mall & Beyond

*Michael Kernan*

Sometime, out of the clear blue—in the midst of doing something you have done a thousand times—an insight is born or a question is raised. Once, driving through a city neighborhood, I noticed all the windows covered with bars and suddenly realized that it was the bars on the windows and similar conditions on the streets that led me to think the neighborhood might be a dangerous place to be even though I had no idea of the local crime statistics. At the time, I happened to be researching and writing on the subject of urban crime prevention.

These kinds of moments happen occasionally when one is researching a phenomenon and totally entrenched in the subject. Sometimes this happens with undergraduate students, but usually they are engaged in so many courses and subjects that they are not totally immersed in a singular question or project that captivates their every waking hour.

Many anthropologists have said that anthropology is a mirror for humankind. As we study anthropology and other peoples, we come to see ourselves more clearly because we ask questions about why we do things differently than others do. Every discipline raises questions, though of a different type. Imagine a physicist or a chemist caught up in the workings of a pen; the physicist might ponder the role of friction or the chemist the viscosity of the ink inside. What of an engineer or historian?

So, what might an archaeologist think about if he or she had such an epiphany?

***As your read this selection, ask yourself the following questions:***

- What sorts of material items from your home or school might someday become artifacts of interest to archaeologists, and what sorts of things, if any, would they not be interested in?
- Do you agree that the National Historic Preservation Act is a useful public policy?
- Why would a mammoth bone be found in Maryland, of all places?
- In the study of a poor local community, what might archaeology offer that history does not?

***The following terms discussed in this selection are included in the Glossary at the back of the book:***

*artifacts*
*cultural resources*
*middens*
*shards*
*paleontologist*
*patent medicine*

Here I am, getting rid of my used-up Slim-Rite Wundertip felt pen and standing over the wastebasket ready to throw the thing in like a dart—when I stop in my tracks and tell myself, Wait a minute. Did I think this was nothing but a piece of trash? Jetsam from my frantic career? I am holding in my hands here a nugget of history.

Prior to the construction of the National Museum of the American Indian, just east of the National Air and Space Museum, a team of archaeologists excavated the site and unearthed a lot of trash. The National Historic Preservation Act requires that every federally funded building must first have its site vetted for possible impact on cultural resources, which means it has to be checked out for artifacts of bygone civilizations.

It is a useful policy. The practice of looking where we dig has had payoffs for the Smithsonian even when something other than early civilizations have been involved. A dozen years ago, at a construction site near Largo, Maryland, work was delayed for a few days when a giant bone pulled from the mud proved to be the rib of a mammoth. Plunging up to my knees in the mud, I reported the find for the *Washington Post*. And by the time Smithsonian paleontologists had examined

Kernan, Michael. "Around the Mall & Beyond." *Smithsonian* Magazine (Feb. 1995). 

the find, and the press reported it, we all knew a lot more about mammoths.

And I remember back in 1984 when a 29,000-year-old cyprus log was pulled from the hole that would become the underground complex of the Arthur M. Sackler Gallery and the National Museum of African Art. Once again we got a chance to learn a little something, that time about Washington at the beginning of the last ice age.

For years it was an open green space between the Air and Space Museum and the U.S. Botanical Garden. Now it is home to the Smithsonian Institution's 18th museum. But in the last half of the 19th century and as late as 1929, it was a residential neighborhood whose ambience is suggested by the name of a dirt roadway that ran behind the houses: Louse Alley.

It was not a high-rent district, and probably most residents were more or less transient. A Washington Gas Light Company tank loomed over the street, alongside the E. N. Gray & Co. Foundry and the Taylor and Low Stone Yard. Living in these narrow houses were immigrants from Europe and some African American families. There was no sign of the area's 17th-century inhabitants, the Conoy Indians, a rather sedate group of Algonquian farmers who apparently didn't want to settle on what was then marshland.

The search team dug as deep as eight feet through soil that had been brought in to fill the marshland when Tiber Creek (which ran roughly along today's Constitution Avenue) was drained and channelized in 1815, and they found "oyster shells, 400 pounds of oyster shells!" according to Donna Seifert, the project manager for John Milner Associates, urban archaeologists, planners and architects.

I don't know, maybe oysters were cheap in those days, but 400 pounds of oyster shells means a lot of oysters. It sounded to me as if someone must have had a grand party out there. "Oh no," Seifert says. "We looked on the map and found there had been an oyster house on the corner."

There were also many bucketfuls of crockery shards, blue pottery from Britain, kitchenware, antique beer bottles, medicine bottles, animal bones and a couple of dolls much the worse for wear. All these items have been taken to the Milner lab in Alexandria, Virginia, to be analyzed to determine, for example, what companies made the discarded dishes and bottles. A report is due this summer.

The archaeologists noticed that residents tended to pile up their refuse at the back of their yards, occasionally shoveling dirt on top. And since most of the houses had no running water or bathrooms, "we were hoping to find outhouses," Seifert says, "because a pit of any kind, a cistern or even a well, when it's abandoned, gets filled in relatively quickly with garbage. This makes still-life composed of the chaff of another time; objects were sifted from dirt using shaker screen with tripod. It is a sort of time capsule. But unfortunately the locals used only box privies, the kind with removable drawers for easy cleaning."

Too bad. Ah well. One problem with things that have been scattered about a yard and not neatly collected in a pit is that you often can't tell for sure whether they all really belong together in time and space.

I have seen an old photograph of Louse Alley, probably in connection with outraged articles about the neglected neighborhoods of Washington, showing rows of tumbledown wooden and brick buildings only a few blocks from the Capitol dome.

Back in the 19th century, Louse Alley couldn't have been any more charming than the rest of Washington as described by a French visitor in 1840: "the inhabitants all own cows and pigs, but no stables, and these animals wander about all day and all night through the city . . . the women milk their cows on the sidewalk and sprinkle the passers-by." There was no organized garbage pickup in the city until 1863, and even then, I suspect, Louse Alley may not have been the first neighborhood to have it.

But I am fascinated with the idea of winkling history out of trash, or more to the point, out of the things we take so utterly for granted that we never give them a thought. All we know of many of the very earliest cultures comes from what archaeologists have been able to deduce from the middens. Why shouldn't it work for modern cultures? It is precisely the things we don't pay any attention to, the everyday implements—the toothbrushes and spoons and bottle-tops, the givens—that often prove to be the clues to a particular society.

The mere discovery of a carefully laid out ancient grave in, say, Germany can produce a variety of insights and suggestions: a belief in an afterlife, for example. A bell-shaped, handleless drinking vessel may be found in the grave, causing the experts to slap their foreheads in amazement: the Beaker folk were here! Find enough beakers and a startling new picture of Bronze Age trade emerges, a network covering all of Western Europe. The smallest detail may contain the essence of our own time. A toothpick discarded today might give an archaeologist palpitations in the 22nd century.

What sorts of secrets the denizens of Louse Alley may have harbored, I have no idea. The original wood-frame houses were torn down in midcentury and replaced with brick row houses, and then the whole area was leveled in the 1930s. In World War II a temporary office building was erected there but removed about 25 years later. We do know that most of the people were short-term renters and that a few of the women who lived there at midcentury described themselves as prostitutes by profession, which was one of the entries listed on the census forms of the day. No big secret, obviously.

What clues will we get from these poor shards and bottles? It's astonishing how much a thinking person can make out of very little.

Take animal bones.

"If you look at the bones closely," says Theresa Singleton, from the anthropology department of the National Museum of Natural History, "and they are cut into short pieces, show slice marks or are extra brittle, then we might say they were boiled in a stew."

"Then you check out the ceramics," Singleton adds, "and if you see mostly bowls, you know those people ate soups or stews a good deal of the time."

Not many steak knives to be found on Louse Alley.

But how do we tell the African American poor from the Irish, German and French immigrants? "The hard part is figuring out whose trash we're looking at," says Donna Seifert.

"What you need is quantity. You need enough samples of consumer strategies to reach a conclusion. Now, medicine bottles can tell you something. At another site, to give you an example, we found that different ethnic groups tended to use different patent medicines," Singleton explains.

There is a certain amount of discussion, not to say controversy, among professionals over this sort of period research. It was only a generation ago that archaeologists began focusing on the debris of ordinary people from the 19th century. What does archaeology offer that's not in historical documents?

A lot, it seems to me, and if you think I don't see this Slim-Rite Wundertip felt pen in a new light, you haven't been listening. I mean, this is not just a pen, it is an artifact. Furthermore, the ink is, or was, violet, which I failed to notice when I bought it.

Who knows what they might make of it in the 22nd century?

# 22

# "Clean Your Plate. There Are People Starving in Africa!"

## *The Application of Archaeology and Ethnography to America's Food Loss Issues*

*Timothy W. Jones*

Excess food waste is a serious problem, particularly in the global context of widespread hunger, population growth, and dwindling environmental resources. As the author of this selection points out, millions of tons of edible food, worth more than $100 billion, are thrown out annually in the United States alone.

What causes this tremendous amount of waste? How do "normal" business practices, purchasing patterns, and eating habits contribute to this major problem? Moreover, how can a garbologist—an archaeologist specializing in the study of garbage—help explain the scope and nature of the problem or assist in finding solutions?

Understanding patterns of food use and food waste is no simple task. Researchers cannot obtain reliable information just by asking the people who grow, sell, or purchase and consume food. Many people simply do not know exactly how much food they waste, and others may be willing to answer questions but only offer the answers they think a researcher wants to hear. Moreover, food wastage, which the author of this selection calls "food loss," may be called by a different name, or it may be so ingrained in everyday business or household practices as to go unnoticed.

Although archaeology developed primarily as a means of studying the past, this article shows how its research methods can serve as important tools for understanding the problems of the present and, importantly, for developing solutions that can help bring about a better—and, in this case, a less wasteful—future.

***As you read this selection, ask yourself the following questions:***

- Why does America waste so much food?
- Why might behavioral data collected using interviews, questionnaires, or observation be inaccurate? How can archaeological research methods be used to gain a more accurate picture of what people actually do?
- Why might farmers choose to "walk by" a crop rather than harvest it?
- Why, according to this selection, is the commercial apple industry more efficient than most other forms of commercial agriculture?
- What is "shrinkage" in the retail food industry, and how might it be reduced?
- How did the author use archaeological methods to help understand the discrepancy between Americans' food purchasing behaviors and their food consumption patterns?

***The following terms discussed in this selection are included in the Glossary at the back of the book:***

*food loss*
*material culture*
*waste behavior*

Did your mother ever talk to you about starving people in Africa in an effort to get you to eat all of your food? If she did, it did not make much sense that the food could not be sent to starving people around the world. A recent study of food flows and losses in the American food system shows that food losses are having a negative economic, environmental, and social impact in the United States. The facts may encourage

Jones, Timothy W. "'Clean Your Plate. There Are People Starving in Africa!' The Application of Archaeology and Ethnography to America's Food Loss Issues." Reprinted with permission of the author.

you to tell your children, "Don't waste your food. It hurts the American economy and the environment!"

Over the past two decades, archaeologists have started to study problems and issues in contemporary societies by applying archaeological theory, method, and techniques. Archaeology is unique in the social sciences in that its subject matter is material culture and the human-constructed world. Contemporary archaeology provides a window to human behavior as expressed in the manufacture, use, discard, and recycling of materials and in the physical transformation of the natural landscape. Archaeology seeks explanations for social and cultural variability in the ways in which people interact with material culture. It complements those social sciences that focus on perception, attitude, and belief by providing an independent measure of individual and social action.

You might ask, "Why do we have to do archaeological studies in contemporary society? Why don't we just ask people what they do and measure material use in that way?" Considerable research has shown that information about behavior derived from the study of modern materials can provide different information from that derived from interviews, questionnaires, and observation (Binford 1977; Dobyns and Rathje 1985; Harrison and Ritenbaugh 1987; Hughes and Ho 1987; Johnstone 1986; Jones 1995; McGuire 1985; Rathje 1977, 1984, 1985a,b; Rathje et al. 1987). Further research has shown that archaeologically measured behavior is different from reported behavior—particularly repetitive everyday behavior such as food consumption. People also report far wider varieties and types of behavior than are actually measured archaeologically since their perceptions and realities are more likely to influence their reported behavior than their actual behavior (Jones et al. 1994; Jones 1995).

## FOOD LOSS

Food loss constitutes a significant portion of the solid waste stream, amounting to 12–15 percent of the waste that ends up in landfills (Environmental Protection Agency 2002, Rathje et al. 1992). The first studies on U.S. retail and service food loss estimated annual losses totalling nearly 80 billion pounds (Kantor et al. 1997), representing a loss of over $40 billion. Despite the significant implications of this degree of food loss, a comprehensive study had never been conducted. Instead, studies relied on compilations of existing information, much of which did not include empirical measures like those used in contemporary archaeology. To gain a better understanding of food loss, I conducted a study titled, "Food Loss from the Farm to the Landfill" for the United States Department of Agriculture (Jones 2003; Jones et al. 2002a, 2002b, 2003a, 2003b). The study collected food data from three separate sectors: (1) commercial farms (fresh vegetable, apple, and citrus), (2) retail food establishments (restaurants, fast foods, grocery, convenience stores), and (3) private households. Research methods include, first, quantifying food produced or purchased using receipts, accounting data, and interviews with management and workers; second, direct observation of food production, handling, and use; and third, measurements of the food deposited in refuse. The results provide surprising insights into sources of inefficiency in the American food system and the economic, environmental, and social effects of these efficiencies.

## FOOD LOSSES IN AMERICAN FARMING

If one looks across the nation's expansive fields of mechanized modern farms, it is difficult to imagine a more efficient food production system. But inefficiencies in farming and fresh-food processing keep more than 12 percent of America's agricultural bounty from reaching American tables. The cost to the farming and fresh-food-processing sector may be as much as $20 billion annually (Jones 2003).

Our study of farming food loss covered three core areas: the Salinas and inland valleys in California, the nation's primary center for growing and processing fresh vegetables; apple country in Washington and Oregon; and Florida's orange growing region. Each region experienced losses for different reasons.

The majority of the nation's fresh lettuce, cauliflower, broccoli, and carrots are grown in the Salinas Valley and some locations further inland. Most losses are due either to "walk-by's," when farmers decide not to harvest a crop, or to the production of "higher value" products, like salad mixes or broccoli crowns. A farmer's decision to walk by a ready crop is based on a whole host of factors, most focusing on profit. For instance, inconsistencies in predicting market prices often lead farmers to turn under marginally profitable crops rather than "take the risk" of a loss.

Prepared fresh vegetables offer convenience for consumers and higher profits for producers. But mechanized and rapid-hand preparation create more waste and make vegetables deteriorate more quickly. A head of lettuce will last for days in the refrigerator whereas a bag of lettuce is already on its way to becoming compost.

The focus on ever-higher profits comes out of the vegetable industry's gambling-style culture. By attempting to get the most money out of their crops, commercial growers keep playing in order to "hit" those years when prices soar and they bring in a "full house." They also complain about price fluctuations without much consideration for the ways in which their own practices accentuate those fluctuations.

The Florida orange industry has been besieged by cheap foreign frozen juice, catastrophic freezes and hurricanes, land-value pressures from the Florida housing boom, the dot-com crash, and soft consumer demand. During my fieldwork, I watched as one of the largest and most innovative orange processors and distributors declared bankruptcy, and I drank in local bars with industry employees who had been laid off for the first time in four generations. These difficult conditions have led to losses in the industry as high as 29 percent. Nearly half of these losses are due to a lack of interest in even harvesting the crops.

The apple orchards dotting the foothills of the Cascade Mountains, in contrast, represent an industry with a refreshing presentation of progress and innovation. Apple growers continue some very old and basic farming concepts. For them, it's all about respect for the land, a desire to feed fellow humans, a reverence for life and the life cycle, and the ability to make a decent living in a spectacular location. My interviews would often come to a halt as participants stopped to watch an eagle skirting the mountains or a deer nibbling fruit at the edge of an orchard. One participant commented, "I've seen those mountains every day for more than 80 years and every time I see them they take my breath away."

Losses in the Washington/Oregon apple industry appear high at about 12 percent. But apples are grown and harvested only seven or eight months of the year and stored the rest. For decades, the apple industry's goal has been to become a stable, sustainable, and profitable business in contrast to the race after short-term market fluctuations that characterizes much of today's farming.

To accomplish this degree of sustainability, growers work together to maximize orchard and harvest use and yields. In cooperation with one another, they determine the number of acres under cultivation based on demand, remove diseased and old trees, finance the development of higher-yielding varieties, and finance the development of more efficient storage mechanisms. They also cull apples that fail fresh standards to produce other products such as applesauce, apple juice, and sliced apples for canning and dehydration.

## FOOD LOSS IN THE RETAIL FOOD INDUSTRY

Food retailers work hard to satisfy the American demand for prepared and instant foods, yet many are unaware of the profits they lose through food loss. Each year, at least 35 million tons of edible food worth nearly $30 billion are thrown away from the nation's restaurants (both traditional and fast food), convenience stores, and supermarkets (Jones et al. 2002b, 2003c).

You can never stop all food loss. Fallible humans and the machines that transport, handle, and prepare food aren't perfect. But losses could potentially be cut in half, thereby adding nearly $15 billion in profits to retail food companies. Just how much food is lost and why varies by sector and even within sectors. Nearly every retail food sector in the study included at least one company that understood the importance of food loss. These firms provided an opportunity to evaluate just how efficient their sector could be. On average, losses at small mom-and-pop restaurants, convenience stores, and fast-food restaurants were about one-tenth the losses of their large, corporate brethren.

Losses were proportionally highest at convenience stores, where they amounted to about 25 percent. "Instant" food is one culprit. An important market niche for convenience stores is ready-to-eat sandwiches, hot dogs, pizza, fried chicken, and nachos. If not purchased within a limited time, such "instant foods" quickly end up in the garbage.

The other reason for such high loss is a lack of management and training. Store workers generally don't know how long they can safely leave prepared food out for sale, nor are they skilled at predicting potential demand. They often throw food out when it is still good and prepare more food than necessary before lunch, for special events, and at other peak demand periods.

One exception was a locally owned, four-store chain that made significant profits from lunch and special event rushes. Their employees were well paid and, at the time of the study, most had been with the company for more than a decade. Given their experience, they were consistently able to predict demand, often selling more than 500 sandwiches in less than two hours. The four or five sandwiches that weren't sold were consumed by the employees as a well-deserved lunch break.

Losses in fast-food establishments are two to three times higher than they calculate, at about 10 percent, on average. The miscalculation comes from faulty inventory practices and from what is called "shrinkage." Inventory information is only as good as the accuracy of the counts upon which they are based, and shrinkage is a measure of unaccounted inventory. Retail businesses often believe their shrinkage is due to theft. Based on what we observed in our study, however, much of that assumed theft is probably loss. There also are losses that are not measured in the inventory system. While our study cannot explain why the inventory system does not account for all food (since we did not have access to those systems), we are certain first, that food loss occurs, and second, that companies are not aware of the extent of the loss.

We were surprised to find loss rates as high as 20 percent to 40 percent in medium-sized fast-food restaurant chains (those with a few stores in one

Jones, T., A. Bockhorst, B. McKee, and A. Ndiaye. 2003b. *Percentage of food loss in the household, The USD A Food Loss Study.* Bureau of Applied Research in Anthropology, University of Arizona. Report to the Economic Research Service, United States Department of Agriculture.

Jones, T., S. Dahlen, K. Cisco, A. Bockhorst, and B. McKee. 2003c. *Commercial interview results and food loss percentages.* Bureau of Applied Research in Anthropology, University of Arizona. Report to the Economic Research Service, United States Department of Agriculture.

Jones, T., C. Steelink, and J. Sierka. 1994. An analysis of the causes of tooth decay in children in Tucson, Arizona. *Fluoride* 27(4).

Kantor, L., K. Lipton, A. Manchester, and V. Oliveira. 1997. Estimating and addressing America's food losses. *Food Review* 20: 3–11.

McGuire, R. 1985. Recycling. *American Behavioral Scientist* 28(1): 93–114.

Penny, G., L. Adair, and B. Popkin. 2003. The relationship of ethnicity, socioeconomic factors and overweight in U.S. adolescents. *Obesity Research* 11(1): 121–129.

Pool, R. 2001. *Fat: Fighting the Obesity Epidemic.* Oxford University Press.

Rathje, W. 1977. In praise of archaeology, Le Project du Garbage. In *Historic Archaeology and the Importance of Material Things,* ed. L. G. Ferguson, 36–42. Society for Historical Archaeology.

______. 1984. The garbage decade. *American Behavioral Scientist* 28(1): 9–29.

______. 1985a. Meat fat madness. *Livestock Industry Forum Proceedings, 1985,* pp. 14–15. Livestock Industry Institute, Kansas City.

______. 1985b. The NFCS syndromes: Building a theory of the difference between respondent reports and material realities. In *The NFCS Report/Refuse Study, Vol. I,* ed. S. Dobyns and W. L. Rathje, Appendix A, 28–44. A report to the Consumer Nutrition Division.

Rathje, W., and E. Ho. 1987. Meat fat madness: Conflicting patterns of meat fat consumption and their public health implications. *Journal of the American Dietetic Association* 87: 1357–1362.

Rathje, W., D. Wilson, and W. Hughes. 1987. *A characterization of hazardous household wastes in Marin County, California.* A report to the Association of Bay Area Governments. The Garbage Project, Bureau of Applied Research in Anthropology, Department of Anthropology, University of Arizona, Tucson.

Rathje, W., D. Wilson, W. Hughes, M. Tani, and T. Jones. 1992. The archaeology of contemporary landfills. *American Antiquity* 57(3): 437.

Ware, Caroline F. 1942. *The consumer goes to war: A guide to victory on the home front.* New York: Funk and Wagnalls Company.

Wilson, D., and W. Rathje. 1990. Modern middens. *Natural History* 90(5): 54–57.

Wilson, D., W. Rathje, and M. Tani. 1994. *Characterization and assessment of household hazardous wastes in municipal solid wastes.* Final report to the Water Quality Engineering Program, National Science Foundation, Washington, D.C.

# PART III

# *Linguistic Anthropology*

Language, whether spoken, written, or non-verbal, allows anthropologists to connect and better understand the human condition across time, space, and cultures. Early in the history of American Anthropology, anthropologists like John Wesley Powell and Franz Boas embraced linguistics as a critical subfield of the discipline. Powell collected and compared vocabularies from American Indian languages as part of an effort to racially classify North American Indian Nations. Because Boas did not believe that culture and language were biologically determined, he disagreed with Powell's approach. Instead, Boas trained his students to use linguistic anthropology to facilitate fieldwork; in his view, language was a window into culture. Regardless of their contrasting theoretical positions regarding the nature of language, Powell and Boas considered linguistics a critical component of anthropology. European anthropologists like Bronislaw Malinowski and E. E. Evans-Pritchard also valued language research as a component of cultural anthropology, but only in the U.S. academy did anthropologists incorporate linguistics as an actual subfield of anthropology.

At the dawn of the twentieth century, the transformation of Anthropology from an armchair pastime to a scientific, academic discipline coincided with the rapid extinction of cultural traditions and languages. When undocumented or poorly documented languages go extinct, humanity loses the specialized knowledge, histories, and worldviews embedded in these languages. In order to preserve and document "disappearing" cultures, early linguistic anthropologists focused primarily on documenting the vocabularies and grammars of endangered cultural traditions. Nevertheless, of an estimated 7,000 languages spoken in the world today, linguists predict that approximately half of these languages will become extinct in the twenty-first century. Contemporary anthropologists continue to document endangered languages, but the field of linguistic anthropology has grown considerably as researchers have developed new approaches to study language scientifically to explore what it means to be human.

Today, linguistic anthropologists typically divide their subfield into three specializations: Historical Linguistics, Descriptive Linguistics, and Sociocultural Linguistics. Historical linguistics includes research on extinct languages as well as the evolution and migration of languages. In Selection 23, Bhattacharjee explains how computer modeling helps linguists see the influence of children and migration on the evolution of language throughout the history of humankind. Because language is not confined to speech and the written word, descriptive linguistics also studies the development of specialized sign languages to learn about the evolution of language (Selection 25).

Linguistic anthropologists who specialize in descriptive linguistics specialize in unraveling a language. Many anthropologists study descriptive linguistics so they can quickly learn an unwritten or lesser-known language in the field. Descriptive linguistics researchers study words (morphology), sentences (syntax), and meaning (semantics), as well as the physical qualities (phonetics) and structure (phonology) of speech. Sociocultural linguists, on the other hand, examine the relationship between language and sociocultural systems. For example, a focus on speech behavior and miscommunication between males and females (Selection 28), can tell an anthropological fieldworker a great deal about a society in which he or she studies and their cultural values.

In sum, linguistic anthropology is a multidisciplinary and scientific study of human language. Linguists apply their skills as teachers and researchers in universities, but you will also find them working in government agencies, professional consulting firms, the corporate setting, and more recently in the high-tech sector (to design and improve Internet search engines, speech recognition, computer language modeling, the development of artificial intelligence, and computer mediated communication). Ultimately, the linguistic anthropologist uses her or his unique methodological toolkit to do what cultural anthropologists, biological anthropologists, and archaeologists do; they develop and test hypotheses to examine the complex diversity and universals of the human experience across time and space.

# 23

# From Heofonum to Heavens

*Yudhijit Bhattacharjee*

New Technology is one of the many ways new words enter our daily vocabulary. Before 2001 the terms "iPod" and "podcast" did not exist, but now these are ubiquitous words used every day on college campuses throughout the United States. New words like "podcast" and "email" may seem like benign additions to our language, but not everyone is ambivalent to this technology-inspired linguistic evolution.

In 2008, for example, linguists from the Ministry of Culture in France banned the word "podcast" along with over 500 other words like "wi-fi" and "supermodel." Because these non-French words have crept into daily French vocabularies, the Ministry of Culture seeks to prevent these linguistic intrusions by offering alternative terms such as "courriel" instead of "email." Linguistic nationalism and transformation is not unique to France; it was not long ago that the U.S. Congress legislated that french fries in the Capitol Hill cafeteria would be called "freedom fries."

Languages evolve to fit the needs and lives of the people who use them. In this selection, Bhattacharjee explains how computer modeling helps linguists see the influence of children and migration on linguistic transformation throughout the history of humankind.

***As you read this selection, ask yourself the following questions:***

- Why do anthropologists study the evolution of words and grammar?
- Why do languages change, and why do linguists view language change as a paradox?
- What role do children play in linguistic evolution?
- How do non-native speakers transform a language?
- How does population growth impact the evolution of a language?

***The following terms discussed in this selection are included in the Glossary at the back of the book:***

| | |
|---|---|
| *creole* | *sociolinguistics* |
| *computational linguistics* | *verb-second structure* |

If a modern-day priest were to chance upon an eleventh century manuscript of *The Lord's Prayer* in English, he would need the Lord's help to decipher its meaning. Much of the text would be gobbledygook to him, apart from a few words that might have a recognizable ring, such as heofonum (heavens) and yfele (evil). And even after a word-for-word translation, the priest would be left with the puzzling grammatical structure of sentences like "Our daily bread give us today."

Although researchers generally think of languages as having evolved slowly over many millennia, language change occurring over time spans of a few centuries has confounded scholars since medieval times. After trying to read a 600-year-old document, the first known printer of English works, William Caxton, lamented in 1490, "And certainly it was written in such a way that it was more like German than English. I could not recover it or make it understandable" (translated from Old English).

The comparative analysis of such texts is the closest that researchers can get to tracing the evolutionary path of a language. By studying the evolution of words and grammar over the past 1200 years of recorded history, linguists hope to understand the general principles underlying the development of languages. "Since we can assume that language and language change have operated in the same way for the past 50,000 years, modern language change can offer insights into earlier changes that led to the diversification of languages,"

Bhattacharjee, Yudhijit. "From Heofonum to Heavens." *Science* 303, no. 5662 (27 Feb. 2004):1326–1328. Reprinted with permission from AAAS.

and new adult learners converged on an SVO grammar after two generations. That matches empirical studies showing that many features of Hawaiian Creole, including an SVO word order, did not stabilize until the second generation of learners.

Salikoko Mufwene, a sociolinguist at the University of Chicago, says that a detailed picture of mechanisms of language change could emerge if computational researchers succeed in modeling very specific contexts. For instance, he says, modeling spoken exchanges on a homestead of eight Europeans and two African slaves could help illuminate the linguistic evolution of the larger community. "The two Africans in this example are likely to be so well immersed that after a few months they would be speaking a second language variety of the European language. Say one of the Africans is a woman and bears a child with one of the white colonists. The child is likely to speak like the father because the father's language happens to be dominant at the homestead. Growing up, this child will serve as a model for children of new slaves," explains Mufwene. "Nonnative speakers will exert only a marginal influence on the emergent language of the community," in this case the native European variety.

But if the population increases significantly through a large influx of new slaves, he says, the dynamics of interaction change, and more adult nonnative speakers of the European language serve as models. Children now have a greater likelihood of acquiring some of the features spoken by adult nonnatives and transmitting them to future learners; over time, a new variety of the European language will emerge.

Detailed modeling along these lines, Mufwene says, could unveil the significance of factors that researchers may have missed, such as the pattern of population growth and the pace of demographic shifts. "Even without real-world number crunching," he says, "the exercise would suggest what questions we should be asking and what kinds of evidence we should be looking for."

## REFERENCES

Niyogi, P. 2006. *The Computational Nature of Language Learning and Evolution.* MIT Press.

# 24

# "To Give up on Words"

## *Silence in Western Apache Culture*

*Keith H. Basso*

Can you imagine working on a four-person cattle crew for several days without being introduced to or speaking with one of the other members, whom you did not know? For the Apache, this is a normal occurrence; they do not feel obligated to introduce strangers to one another. Instead, the Apache believe that when the time is right, the strangers will begin speaking to one another.

Would you find it uncomfortable to go on a date and sit in silence for an hour because you had only recently met your companion? What would you think if after returning home from several months' absence your parents and relatives didn't speak to you for several days? Although these situations seem unusual to us, they are considered appropriate among the Apache. Although it seems natural to us that when people first meet introductions are in order and that when friends and relatives reunite greetings and catching up will immediately follow, this is not the case for all cultures.

In this selection Keith Basso shows how, among the Apache, certain situations call for silence rather than communication and how silence makes sense within its cultural context.

***As you read this selection, ask yourself the following questions:***

- What are some of the ways silence is used in European American communication, and how are they different from those in Apache culture?
- How are the meaning and function of silence affected by the social and cultural context?
- What is the critical factor in an Apache's decision to speak or keep silent?
- How do Apaches interact upon meeting a stranger, courting, welcoming children home, "getting cussed out," and being with people who are sad?
- Despite the variety of situations in which Apaches are silent, what is the underlying determinant?

***The following terms discussed in this selection are included in the Glossary at the back of the book:***

| | |
|---|---|
| *hypothesis* | *socialization* |
| *informant* | *sociolinguistics* |
| *kinship* | *status* |

*It is not the case that a man who is silent says nothing.*

—Anonymous

### I[1]

Anyone who has read about American Indians has probably encountered statements which impute to them a strong predilection for keeping silent or, as one writer has put it, "a fierce reluctance to speak except when absolutely necessary." In the popular literature, where this characterization is particularly widespread, it is commonly portrayed as the outgrowth of such dubious causes as "instinctive dignity," "an impoverished language," or, perhaps worst of all, the Indians' "lack of personal warmth." Although statements of this sort are plainly erroneous and dangerously misleading, it is noteworthy that professional anthropologists have made few attempts to correct them. Traditionally, ethnographers and linguists have paid little attention to cultural interpretations given to silence or, equally important, to the types of social contexts in which it regularly occurs.

This study investigates certain aspects of silence in the culture of the Western Apache of east-central Arizona. After considering some of the theoretical issues involved, I will briefly describe a number of situations—recurrent in Western Apache society—in which one or

Basso, Keith H. "'To Give up on Words': Silence in Western Apache Culture." *Southwestern Journal of Anthropology* 26, no. 3 (Autumn 1970):213–230. Reprinted with permission of the Journal of Anthropological Research and the author.

more of the participants typically refrain from speech for lengthy periods of time.[2] This is accompanied by a discussion of how such acts of silence are interpreted and why they are encouraged and deemed appropriate. I conclude by advancing an hypothesis that accounts for the reasons that the Western Apache refrain from speaking when they do, and I suggest that, with proper testing, this hypothesis may be shown to have relevance to silence behavior in other cultures.

## II

A basic finding of sociolinguistics is that, although both language and language usage are structured, it is the latter which responds most sensitively to extra-linguistic influences (Hymes 1962, 1964; Ervin-Tripp 1964, 1967; Gumperz 1964; Slobin 1967). Accordingly, a number of recent studies have addressed themselves to the problem of how factors in the social environment of speech events delimit the range and condition the selection of message forms (cf. Brown and Gilman 1960; Conklin 1959; Ervin-Tripp 1964, 1967; Frake 1964; Friedrich 1966; Gumperz 1961, 1964; Martin 1964). These studies may be viewed as taking the now familiar position that verbal communication is fundamentally a decision-making process in which, initially, a speaker, having elected to speak, selects from among a repertoire of available codes that which is most appropriately suited to the situation at hand. Once a code has been selected, the speaker picks a suitable channel of transmission and then, finally, makes a choice from a set of referentially equivalent expressions within the code. The intelligibility of the expression he chooses will, of course, be subject to grammatical constraints. But its acceptability will not. Rules for the selection of linguistic alternates operate on features of the social environment and are commensurate with rules governing the conduct of face-to-face interaction. As such, they are properly conceptualized as lying outside the structure of language itself.

It follows from this that for a stranger to communicate appropriately with the members of an unfamiliar society it is not enough that he learn to formulate messages intelligibly. Something else is needed: a knowledge of what kinds of codes, channels, and expressions to use in what kinds of situations and to what kinds of people—as Hymes (1964) has termed it, an "ethnography of communication."

There is considerable evidence to suggest that extra-linguistic factors influence not only the use of speech but its actual occurrence as well. In our own culture, for example, remarks such as "Don't you know when to keep quiet?" "Don't talk until you're introduced," and "Remember now, no talking in church" all point to the fact that an individual's decision to speak may be directly contingent upon the character of his surroundings. Few of us would maintain that "silence is golden" for all people at all times. But we feel that silence is a virtue for some people some of the time, and we encourage children on the road to cultural competence to act accordingly.

Although the form of silence is always the same, the function of a specific act of silence—that is, its interpretation by and effect upon other people—will vary according to the social context in which it occurs. For example, if I choose to keep silent in the chambers of a Justice of the Supreme Court, my action is likely to be interpreted as a sign of politeness or respect. On the other hand, if I refrain from speaking to an established friend or colleague, I am apt to be accused of rudeness or harboring a grudge. In one instance, my behavior is judged by others to be "correct" or "fitting;" in the other, it is criticized as being "out of line."

The point, I think, is fairly obvious. For a stranger entering an alien society, a knowledge of when *not* to speak may be as basic to the production of culturally acceptable behavior as a knowledge of what to say. It stands to reason, then, that an adequate ethnography of communication should not confine itself exclusively to the analysis of choice within verbal repertoires. It should also, as Hymes (1962, 1964) has suggested, specify those conditions under which the members of the society regularly decide to refrain from verbal behavior altogether.

## III

The research on which this paper is based was conducted over a period of sixteen months during the years (1964–1969) in the Western Apache settlement of Cibecue, which is located near the center of the Fort Apache Indian Reservation in east-central Arizona. Cibecue's 800 residents participate in an unstable economy that combines subsistence agriculture, cattle-raising, sporadic wage-earning, and government subsidies in the form of welfare checks and social security benefits. Unemployment is a serious problem, and substandard living conditions are widespread.

Although Reservation life has precipitated far-reaching changes in the composition and geographical distribution of Western Apache social groups, consanguineal kinship—real and imputed—remains the single most powerful force in the establishment and regulation of interpersonal relationships (Kaut 1957; Basso 1970). The focus of domestic activity is the individual "camp," or *gową́ą*. This term labels both the occupants and the location of a single dwelling or, as is more apt to be the case, several dwellings built within a few feet of each other. The majority of *gową́ą* in Cibecue are occupied by nuclear families. The next largest residential unit is the *gotáá* (camp cluster), which is a group of spatially localized *gowąą*, each having at least one adult member who is related by ties of matrilineal kinship to persons living in all the others. An intricate system of exogamous clans serves to extend kinship relationships beyond the *gowąą* and *gottáá* and facilitates concerted action in projects, most notably the presentation of ceremonials, requiring large amounts of manpower. Despite the presence in Cibecue of a variety of Anglo missionaries and a dwindling number of medicine men, diagnostic and curing rituals, as well as the girls' puberty ceremonial, continue to be performed with regularity (Basso 1966, 1970). Witchcraft persists in undiluted form (Basso 1969).

## IV

Of the many broad categories of events, or scenes, that comprise the daily round of Western Apache life, I shall deal here only with those that are coterminous with what Goffman (1961, 1964) has termed "focused gatherings" or "encounters." The concept *situation,* in keeping with established usage, will refer inclusively to the location of such a gathering, its physical setting, its point in time, the standing behavior patterns that accompany it, and the social attributes of the persons involved (Hymes 1962, 1964; Ervin-Tripp 1964, 1967).

In what follows, however, I will be mainly concerned with the roles and statuses of participants. The reason for this is that the critical factor in the Apache's decision to speak or keep silent seems always to be the nature of his relationships to other people. To be sure, other features of the situation are significant, but apparently only to the extent that they influence the perception of status and role.[3] What this implies, of course, is that roles and statuses are not fixed attributes. Although they may be depicted as such in a static model (and often with good reason), they are appraised and acted upon in particular social contexts and, as a result, subject to redefinition and variation.[4] With this in mind, let us now turn our attention to the Western Apache and the types of situations in which, as one of my informants put it, "it is right to give up on words."

## V

1. "Meeting strangers" *(nda dòhwáá iłtsééda).* The term, *nda,* labels categories at two levels of contrast. At the most general level, it designates any person—Apache or non-Apache—who, prior to an initial meeting, has never been seen and therefore cannot be identified. In addition, the term is used to refer to Apaches who, though previously seen and known by some external criteria such as clan affiliation or personal name, have never been engaged in face-to-face interaction. The latter category, which is more restricted than the first, typically includes individuals who live on the adjacent San Carlos Reservation, in Fort Apache settlements geographically removed from Cibecue, and those who fall into the category *kii dòhandáágo* (non-kinsmen). In all cases, "strangers" are separated by social distance. And in all cases it is considered appropriate, when encountering them for the first time, to refrain from speaking.

The type of situation described as "meeting strangers" *(nda dòhwáá iłtsééda)* can take place in any number of different physical settings. However, it occurs most frequently in the context of events such as fairs and rodeos, which, owing to the large number of people in attendance, offer unusual opportunities for chance encounters. In large gatherings, the lack of verbal communication between strangers is apt to go unnoticed, but in smaller groups it becomes quite conspicuous. The following incident, involving two strangers who found themselves part of a four-man round-up crew, serves as a good example. My informant, who was also a member of the crew, recalled the following episode:

> One time, I was with A, B, and X down at Gleason Flat, working cattle. That man, X, was from East Fork [a community nearly 40 miles from Cibecue] where B's wife was from. But he didn't know A, never knew him before, I guess. First day, I worked with X. At night, when we camped, we talked with B, but X and A didn't say anything to each other. Same way, second day. Same way, third. Then, at night on fourth day, we were sitting by the fire. Still, X and A didn't talk. Then A said, "Well, I know there is a stranger to me here, but I've been watching him and I know he is all right." After that, X and A talked a lot. . . . Those two men didn't know each other, so they took it easy at first.

As this incident suggests, the Western Apache do not feel compelled to "introduce" persons who are unknown to each other. Eventually, it is assumed, strangers will begin to speak. However, this is a decision that is properly left to the individuals involved, and no attempt is made to hasten it. Outside help in the form of introductions or other verbal routines is viewed as presumptuous and unnecessary.

Strangers who are quick to launch into conversation are frequently eyed with undisguised suspicion. A typical reaction to such individuals is that they "want something," that is, their willingness to violate convention is attributed to some urgent need which is likely to result in requests for money, labor, or transportation. Another common reaction to talkative strangers is that they are drunk.

If the stranger is an Anglo, it is usually assumed that he "wants to teach us something" (i.e., give orders or instructions) or that he "wants to make friends in a hurry." The latter response is especially revealing, since Western Apaches are extremely reluctant to be hurried into friendships—with Anglos or each other. Their verbal reticence with strangers is directly related

about this, my informants volunteered three types of explanations. The first is that persons "who are sad" are so burdened with "intense grief" (*dółgozóóda*) that speaking requires of them an unusual amount of physical effort. It is courteous and considerate, therefore, not to attempt to engage them in conversation.

A second native explanation is that in situations of this sort verbal communication is basically unnecessary. Everyone is familiar with what has happened, and talking about it, even for the purpose of conveying solace and sympathy, would only reinforce and augment the sadness felt by those who were close to the deceased. Again, for reasons of courtesy, this is something to be avoided.

The third explanation is rooted in the belief that "intense grief," like intense rage, produces changes in the personality of the individual who experiences it. As evidence for this, the Western Apache cite numerous instances in which the emotional strain of dealing with death, coupled with an overwhelming sense of irrevocable personal loss, has caused persons who were formerly mild and even-tempered to become abusive, hostile, and physically violent.

> That old woman, X, who lives across Cibecue Creek, one time her first husband died. After that she cried all the time, for a long time. Then, I guess she got mean because everyone said she drank a lot and got into fights. Even with her close relatives, she did like that for a long time. She was too sad for her husband. That's what made her like that; it made her lose her mind.
>
> My father was like that when his wife died. He just stayed home all the time and wouldn't go anywhere. He didn't talk to any of his relatives or children. He just said, "I'm hungry. Cook for me." That's all. He stayed that way for a long time. His mind was not with us. He was still with his wife.
>
> My uncle died in 1911. His wife sure went crazy right after that. Two days after they buried the body, we went over there and stayed with those people who had been left alone. My aunt got mad at us. She said, "Why do you come back over here? You can't bring my husband back. I can take care of myself and those others in my camp, so why don't you go home." She sure was mad that time, too sad for someone who died. She didn't know what she was saying because in about one week she came to our camp and said, "My relatives, I'm all right now. When you came to help me, I had too much sadness and my mind was no good. I said bad words to you. But now I am all right and I know what I am doing."

As these statements indicate, the Western Apache assume that a person suffering from "intense grief" is likely to be disturbed and unstable. Even though he may appear outwardly composed, they say, there is always the possibility that he is emotionally upset and therefore unusually prone to volatile outbursts. Apaches acknowledge that such an individual might welcome conversation in the context of "being with people who are sad," but, on the other hand, they fear it might prove incendiary. Under these conditions, which resemble those in Situation No. 4, it is considered both expedient and appropriate to keep silent.

6. "Being with someone for whom they sing" (*ndeb`dúd`stááha bigąą́*). The last type of situation to be described is restricted to a small number of physical locations and is more directly influenced by temporal factors than any of the situations we have discussed so far. "Being with someone for whom they sing" takes place only in the context of "curing ceremonials" (*gòǰitáł*). These events begin early at night and come to a close shortly before dawn the following day. In the late fall and throughout the winter, curing ceremonials are held inside the patient's wickiup or house. In the spring and summer, they are located outside, at some open place near the patient's camp or at specially designated dance grounds where group rituals of all kinds are regularly performed.

Prior to the start of a curing ceremonial, all persons in attendance may feel free to talk with the patient; indeed, because he is so much a focus of concern, it is expected that friends and relatives will seek him out to offer encouragement and support. Conversation breaks off, however, when the patient is informed that the ceremonial is about to begin, and it ceases entirely when the presiding medicine man commences to chant. From this point on, until the completion of the final chant next morning, it is inappropriate for anyone except the medicine man (and, if he has them, his aides) to speak to the patient.[6]

In order to appreciate the explanation Apaches give for this prescription, we must briefly discuss the concept of "supernatural power" (*diyí*) and describe some of the effects it is believed to have on persons at whom it is directed. Elsewhere (Basso 1969:30) I have defined "power" as follows:

> The term *diyí* refers to one or all of a set of abstract and invisible forces which are said to derive from certain classes of animals, plants, minerals, meteorological phenomena, and mythological figures within the Western Apache universe. Any of the various powers may be acquired by man and, if properly handled, used for a variety of purposes.

A power that has been antagonized by disrespectful behavior towards its source may retaliate by causing the offender to become sick. "Power-caused illnesses" (*kásitį kiyí bił*) are properly treated with curing ceremonials in which one or more medicine men, using chants and various items of ritual paraphernalia, attempt to neutralize the sickness-causing power with powers of their own.

Roughly two-thirds of my informants assert that a medicine man's power actually enters the body of the patient; others maintain that it simply closes in and envelops him. In any case, all agree that the patient is brought into intimate contact with a potent supernatural force which elevates him to a condition labeled *gòdiyò'* (sacred, holy).

The term *gòdiyò'* may also be translated as "potentially harmful" and, in this sense, is regularly used to describe classes of objects (including all sources of power) that are associated with taboos. In keeping with the semantics of *gòdiyò'*, the Western Apache explain that, besides making patients holy, power makes them potentially harmful. And it is this transformation, they explain, that is basically responsible for the cessation of verbal communication during curing ceremonials. Said one informant:

> When they start singing for someone like that, he sort of goes away with what the medicine man is working with (i.e., power). Sometimes people they sing for don't know you, even after it (the curing ceremonial) is over. They get holy, and you shouldn't try to talk to them when they are like that . . . it's best to leave them alone.

Another informant made similar comments:

> When they sing for someone, what happens is like this: that man they sing for doesn't know why he is sick or which way to go. So the medicine man has to show him and work on him. That is when he gets holy, and that makes him go off somewhere in his mind, so you should stay away from him.

Because Apaches undergoing ceremonial treatment are perceived as having been changed by power into something different from their normal selves, they are regarded with caution and apprehension. Their newly acquired status places them in close proximity to the supernatural and, as such, carries with it a very real element of danger and uncertainty. These conditions combine to make "being with someone for whom they sing" a situation in which speech is considered disrespectful and, if not exactly harmful, at least potentially hazardous.

## VI

Although the types of situations described above differ from one another in obvious ways, I will argue in what follows that the underlying determinants of silence are in each case basically the same. Specifically, I will attempt to defend the hypothesis that keeping silent in Western Apache culture is associated with social situations in which participants perceive their relationships *vis-à-vis* one another to be ambiguous and/or unpredictable.

Let us begin with the observation that, in all the situations we have described, *silence is defined as appropriate with respect to a specific individual or individuals.* In other words, the use of speech is not directly curtailed by the setting of a situation nor by the physical activities that accompany it but, rather, by the perceived social and psychological attributes of at least one focal participant.

It may also be observed that, in each type of situation, *the status of the focal participant is marked by ambiguity*—either because he is unfamiliar to other participants in the situation or because, owing to some recent event, a status he formerly held has been changed or is in a process of transition.

Thus, in Situation No. 1, persons who earlier considered themselves "strangers" move towards some other relationship, perhaps "friend" (*š̀dikéé*), perhaps "enemy" (*š̀kédnd˝*). In Situation No. 2, young people who have relatively limited exposure to one another attempt to adjust to the new and intimate status of "sweetheart." These two situations are similar in that the focal participants have little or no prior knowledge of each other. Their social identities are not as yet clearly defined, and their expectations, lacking the foundation of previous experience, are poorly developed.

Situation No. 3 is somewhat different. Although the participants—parents and their children—are well known to each other, their relationship has been seriously interrupted by the latter's prolonged absence from home. This, combined with the possibility that recent experiences at school have altered the children's attitudes, introduces a definite element of unfamiliarity and doubt. Situation No. 3 is not characterized by the absence of role expectations but by the participants' perception that those already in existence may be outmoded and in need of revision.

Status ambiguity is present in Situation No. 4 because a focal participant is enraged and, as a result, considered "crazy." Until he returns to a more rational condition, others in the situation have no way of predicting how he will behave. Situation No. 5 is similar in that the personality of a focal participant is seen to have undergone a marked shift which makes his actions more difficult to anticipate. In both situations, the status of focal participants is uncertain because of real or imagined changes in their psychological makeup.

In Situation No. 6, a focal participant is ritually transformed from an essentially neutral state to one which is contextually defined as "potentially harmful." Ambiguity and apprehension accompany this transition, and, as in Situations No. 4 and 5, established patterns of interaction must be waived until the focal participant reverts to a less threatening condition.

This discussion points up a third feature characteristic of all situations: *the ambiguous status of focal participants is accompanied either by the absence or suspension of established role expectations.* In every instance, nonfocal participants (i.e., those who refrain from speech) are either uncertain of how the focal participant will behave towards them or, conversely, how they should behave towards him. Stated in the simplest way possible, their roles become blurred with the result that established expectations—if they exist—lose their relevance as guidelines for social action and must be temporarily discarded or abruptly modified.

We are now in a position to expand upon our initial hypothesis and make it more explicit.

1. In Western Apache culture, the absence of verbal communication is associated with social situations in which the status of local participants is ambiguous.
2. Under these conditions, fixed role expectations lose their applicability and the illusion of predictability in social interaction is lost.
3. To sum up and reiterate: keeping silent among the Western Apache is a response to uncertainty and unpredictability in social relations.

## VII

The question remains to what extent the foregoing hypothesis helps to account for silence behavior in other cultures. Unfortunately, it is impossible at the present time to provide anything approaching a conclusive answer. Standard ethnographies contain very little information about the circumstances under which verbal communication is discouraged, and it is only within the past few years that problems of this sort have engaged the attention of sociolinguists. The result is that adequate cross-cultural data are almost completely lacking.

As a first step towards the elimination of this deficiency, an attempt is now being made to investigate the occurrence and interpretation of silence in other Indian societies of the American Southwest. Our findings at this early stage, though neither fully representative nor sufficiently comprehensive, are extremely suggestive. By way of illustration, I quote below from portions of a preliminary report prepared by Priscilla Mowrer (1970), herself a Navajo, who inquired into the situational features of Navajo silence behavior in the vicinity of Tuba City on the Navajo Reservation in east-central Arizona.

> I. *Silence and Courting:* Navajo youngsters of opposite sexes just getting to know one another say nothing, except to sit close together and maybe hold hands. . . . In public, they may try not to let on that they are interested in each other, but in private it is another matter. If the girl is at a gathering where the boy is also present, she may go off by herself. Falling in step, the boy will generally follow. They may just walk around or find some place to sit down. But, at first, they will not say anything to each other.
>
> II. *Silence and Long Absent Relatives:* When a male or female relative returns home after being gone for six months or more, he (or she) is first greeted with a handshake. If the returnee is male, the female greeter may embrace him and cry—the male, meanwhile, will remain dry-eyed and silent.
>
> III. *Silence and Anger:* The Navajo tend to remain silent when being shouted at by a drunk or angered individual because that particular individual is considered temporarily insane. To speak to such an individual, the Navajo believe, just tends to make the situation worse. . . . People remain silent because they believe that the individual is not himself, that he may have been witched, and is not responsible for the change in his behavior.
>
> IV. *Silent Mourning:* Navajos speak very little when mourning the death of a relative. . . . The Navajo mourn and cry together in pairs. Men will embrace one another and cry together. Women, however, will hold one another's hands and cry together.
>
> V. *Silence and the Ceremonial Patient:* The Navajo consider it wrong to talk to a person being sung over. The only people who talk to the patient are the medicine man and a female relative (or male relative if the patient is male) who is in charge of food preparation. The only time the patient speaks openly is when the medicine man asks her (or him) to pray along with him.

These observations suggest that striking similarities may exist between the types of social contexts in which Navajos and Western Apaches refrain from speech. If this impression is confirmed by further research, it will lend obvious cross-cultural support to the hypothesis advanced above. But regardless of the final outcome, the situational determinants of silence seem eminently deserving of further study. For as we become better informed about the types of contextual variables that mitigate against the use of verbal codes, we should also learn more about those variables that encourage and promote them.

## NOTES

1. At different times during the period extending from 1964–1969 the research on which this paper is based was supported by U. S. P. H. S. Grant MH-12691-01, a grant from the American Philosophical Society, and funds from the Doris Duke Oral History Project at the Arizona State Museum. I am pleased to acknowledge this support. I would also like to express my gratitude to the following scholars for commenting upon an earlier draft: Y. R. Chao, Harold C. Conklin, Roy G. D'Andrade, Charles O. Frake, Paul Friedrich, John Gumperz, Kenneth Hale, Harry Hoijer, Dell Hymes, Stanley Newman, David M.

Schneider, Joel Sherzer, and Paul Turner. Although the final version gained much from their criticisms and suggestions, responsibility for its present form and content rests solely with the author. A preliminary version of this paper was presented to the Annual Meeting of the American Anthropological Association in New Orleans, Louisiana, November 1969. A modified version of this paper is scheduled to appear in *Studies in Apachean Culture and Ethnology* (ed. by Keith H. Basso and Morris Opler), Tucson: University of Arizona Press, 1970.

2. The situations described in this paper are not the only ones in which the Western Apache refrain from speech. There is a second set—not considered here because my data are incomplete—in which silence appears to occur as a gesture of respect, usually to persons in positions of authority. A third set, very poorly understood, involves ritual specialists who claim they must keep silent at certain points during the preparation of ceremonial paraphernalia.
3. Recent work in the sociology of interaction, most notably by Goffman (1963) and Garfinkel (1967), has led to the suggestion that social relationships are everywhere the major determinants of verbal behavior. In this case, as Gumperz (1967) makes clear, it becomes methodologically unsound to treat the various components of communicative events as independent variables. Gumperz (1967) has presented a hierarchical model, sensitive to dependency, in which components are seen as stages in the communication process. Each stage serves as the input for the next. The basic stage, i.e., the initial input, is "social identities or statuses." For further details see Slobin 1967:131–134.
4. I would like to stress that the emphasis placed on social relations is fully in keeping with the Western Apache interpretation of their own behavior. When my informants were asked to explain why they or someone else was silent on a particular occasion, they invariably did so in terms of *who* was present at the time.
5. Among the Western Apache, rules of exogamy discourage courtships between members of the same clan (*kii àł hánigo*) and so-called "related" clans (*kii*), with the result that sweethearts are almost always "non-matrilineal kinsmen" (*dòhwàk˘da*). Compared to "matrilineal kinsmen" (*kii*), such individuals have fewer opportunities during childhood to establish close personal relationships and thus, when courtship begins, have relatively little knowledge of each other. It is not surprising, therefore, that their behavior is similar to that accorded strangers.
6. I have witnessed over 75 curing ceremonials since 1961 and have seen this rule violated only six times. On four occasions, drunks were at fault. In the other two cases, the patient fell asleep and had to be awakened.

## REFERENCES


Basso, Keith H. 1966. *The Gift of Changing Woman.* Bureau of American Ethnology, Bulletin 196.

______. 1969. *Western Apache Witchcraft.* Anthropological Papers of the University of Arizona, no. 15.

______. 1970. *The Cibecue Apache.* New York: Holt, Rinehart and Winston, Inc.

Brown, R. W., and Albert Gilman. 1960. The Pronouns of Power and Solidarity. In *Style and Language,* ed. T. Sebeok, 253–276. Cambridge: The Technology Press of Massachusetts Institute of Technology.

Conklin, Harold C. 1959. Linguistic Play in Its Cultural Context. *Language* 35: 631–636.

Ervin-Tripp, Susan. 1964. An Analysis of the Interaction of Language, Topic and Listener. In *The Ethnography of Communication,* ed. J. J. Gumperz and D. Hymes, 86–102. *American Anthropologist,* Special Publication, vol. 66, no. 6, part 2.

______. 1967. *Sociolinguistics.* Language-Behavior Research Laboratory, Working Paper no. 3. Berkeley: University of California.

Frake, Charles O. 1964. How to Ask for a Drink in Subanun. In *The Ethnography of Communication,* ed. J. J. Gumperz and D. Hymes, 127–132. *American Anthropologist,* Special Publication, vol. 66, no. 6, part 2.

Friedrich, P. 1966. Structural Implications of Russia Pronominal Usage. In *Sociolinguistics,* ed. W. Bright, 214–253. The Hague: Mouton.

Garfinkel, H. 1967. *Studies in Ethnomethodology.* Englewood Cliffs, N.J.: Prentice-Hall, Inc.

Goffman, E. 1961. *Encounters: Two Studies in the Sociology of Interaction.* Indianapolis: The Bobbs-Merrill Co., Inc.

______. 1963. *Behavior in Public Places.* Glencoe, Ill.: Free Press.

______. 1964. The Neglected Situation. In *The Ethnography of Communication,* ed. J. J. Gumperz and D. Hymes, 133–136. *American Anthropologist,* Special Publication, vol. 66, no. 6, part 2.

Gumperz, John J. 1961. Speech Variation and the Study of Indian Civilization. *American Anthropologist* 63: 976–988.

______. 1964. Linguistic and Social Interaction in Two Communities. In *The Ethnography of Communication,* ed. J. J. Gumperz and D. Hymes, 137–153. *American Anthropologist,* Special Publication, vol. 66, no. 6, part 2.

______. 1967. The Social Setting of Linguistic Behavior. In *A Field Manual for Cross-Cultural Study of the Acquisition of Communicative Competence (Second Draft),* ed. D. I. Slobin, 129–134. Berkeley: University of California.

Hymes, Dell. 1962. The Ethnography of Speaking. In *Anthropology and Human Behavior,* ed. T. Gladwin and W. C. Sturtevant, 13–53. Washington, D. C.: The Anthropological Society of Washington.

______. 1964. Introduction: Toward Ethnographies of Communication. In *The Ethnography of Communication,* ed, J. J. Gumperz and D. Hymes, 1–34. *American Anthropologist,* Special Publication, vol. 66, no. 6, part 2.

Kaut, Charles R. 1957. *The Western Apache Clan System: Its Origins and Development.* University of New Mexico Publications in Anthropology, no. 9.

Martin, Samuel. 1964. Speech Levels in Japan and Korea. In *Language in Culture and Society,* ed. D. Hymes, 407–415. New York: Harper & Row.

Mowrer, Priscilla. 1970. Notes on Navajo Silence Behavior. MS, University of Arizona.

Slobin, Dan I. (ed.). 1967. *A Field Manual for Cross-Cultural Study of the Acquisition of Communicative Competence (Second Draft).* Berkeley: University of California.

# 25

# Village of the Deaf

## *In a Bedouin Town, a Language Is Born*

*Margalit Fox*

Sign language, like any language, differs from place to place. In 1924 when athletes from Belgium, Czechoslovakia, France, Great Britain, Holland, and Poland gathered at the first World Games for the Deaf, they had to develop a new language to communicate with each other. Their impromptu system of hand signs became the foundation of a global sign language called International Sign.

Despite the existence of International Sign, deaf people and others throughout the world have developed unique sign languages to fit the uniqueness of their lived experiences. In recent years, for example, deaf and non-deaf poets have adapted sign languages to share their worldviews in ways that words and speech alone cannot. Pioneering sign language poets like Clayton Valli have helped the hearing world understand that signing, like speech, has rhymes, rhythm, and meter.

Humans communicate to connect and understand each other. This desire to connect is no different in the deaf community, even in remote locations where deaf people may not have opportunities to learn established sign languages. This selection describes the evolution of Al-Sayyid Bedouin Sign Language, a language created in a remote Israeli village where an inherited form of deafness has created an incidence of deafness approximately forty times that of the general population. Linguistic anthropologists "discovered" this island of the deaf in the late 1990s and have collaborated with the local population to learn more about the evolution of language.

***As you read this selection, ask yourself the following questions:***

- In what ways is Al-Sayyid an "island of the deaf?"
- What is the difference between first and second generation users of Al-Sayyid Bedouin Sign Language?
- How do Al-Sayyid Bedouin Sign Language, American Sign Language, and British Sign Language differ?
- In what ways is Al-Sayyid an "island of the deaf?"
- How does Bedouin Sign Language grammar differ from the verb-second grammar discussed in Bhattarcharjee's chapter "From Heofonum to Heavens?"

***The following terms discussed in this selection are included in the Glossary at the back of the book:***

| | |
|---|---|
| *Babel* | *homesigns* |
| *Bedouin* | *language instinct* |

On this summer evening, the house is alive with people. In the main room, the owner of the house, a stocky man in a plaid shirt, has set a long plastic banquet table on the earthen floor, with a dozen plastic patio chairs around it. Children materialize with platters of nuts, sunflower seeds, and miniature fruit. At the head of the table, the owner is joined by a group of men in their thirties and forties. Down one side of the table is a row of boys, from toddlers to teenagers. At the foot of the table sits a knot of six visitors: four linguistics scholars, a video camera operator, and me.

The man and his family are Bedouins, and the house is at the edge of their village, Al-Sayyid. Though they live in the desert, the Bedouins of Al-Sayyid are not nomads. Their people have inhabited this village, tucked into an obscure corner of what is now Israel, miles from the nearest town, for nearly 200 years. They are rooted, even middle class. Men and boys are

Fox, Margalit. "Village of the Deaf: In a Bedouin Town, a Language Is Born." *Discover* Magazine (July 2007):66–69 from *Talking Hands: What Sign Language Reveals About the Mind* by Fox. (Simon & Schuster, 2007). Reprinted with permission of the author.

bareheaded and dressed in Western clothing, mostly T-shirts and jeans. They own automobiles, computers, and VCRs. But there is something even more remarkable about the Al-Sayyid Bedouins—an unusual language, never documented until now.

The house is a Babel tonight. Around the table, six languages are flowing. There are snatches of English, mostly for my benefit. There is Hebrew: two of the linguists are from an Israeli university, and many men in Al-Sayyid speak Hebrew as well. There is a great deal of Arabic, the language of the home for Bedouins throughout the Middle East. But in the illuminated room, it is the other languages that catch the eye. They are signed languages, the languages of the deaf. As night engulfs the desert and the cameraman's lights throw up huge, signing shadows, it looks as though language itself has become animate, as conversations play out in silhouette on the whitewashed walls.

There are three signed languages going. There is American Sign Language, used by one of the visitors, a deaf linguist from California. There is Israeli Sign Language (ISL), the language of the deaf in that country, whose structure the two Israeli scholars have devoted years to analyzing. And there is a third language, the one the linguists have journeyed here to see: Al-Sayyid Bedouin Sign Language (ABSL), which is spoken in this village and nowhere else in the world.

In Al-Sayyid, the four linguists have encountered a veritable island of the deaf. In this isolated traditional community, where marriage to outsiders is rare, a form of inherited deafness has been passed down from one generation to the next for the last 70 years. Of the 3,500 residents of the village today, nearly 150 are deaf, an incidence forty times that of the general population. As a result, an indigenous signed language has sprung up, evolving among the deaf villagers as a means of communication. But what is so striking about the sign language of Al-Sayyid is that many hearing villagers can also speak it. It permeates every aspect of community life, used between parents and children, husbands and wives, from sibling to sibling and neighbor to neighbor.

The team plans to observe the language, to record it, and to produce an illustrated dictionary, the first-ever documentary record of the villagers' signed communication system. But the linguists are after something even larger. Because Al-Sayyid Bedouin Sign Language has arisen entirely on its own, it offers a living demonstration of the "language instinct," man's inborn capacity to create language from thin air. If the linguists can decode this language—if they can isolate the formal elements that make Al-Sayyid Bedouin Sign Language a language—they will be in possession of compelling new evidence in the search for the ingredients essential to all language. And in so doing, they will have helped illuminate one of the most fundamental aspects of what it means to be human.

When Wendy Sandler, a linguist at the University of Haifa, first heard about Al-Sayyid in the late 1990s, she knew at once that she had to investigate. Over the next few years, she and Irit Meir, a colleague at Haifa, made cautious forays into Al-Sayyid, setting in motion the diplomacy that is a critical part of linguistic fieldwork: explaining their intentions, hosting a day of activities at the village school, over time earning the trust of a number of the villagers.

Their work has a sense of urgency. Although the sign language of Al-Sayyid arose in a linguistic vacuum, the social realities of modern life, even in a remote desert community, make it impossible for it to remain that way. Over the years, many of Al-Sayyid's deaf children have been bused to special classes for the deaf in nearby towns, where they are taught all day in spoken language—Hebrew or Arabic—accompanied by signs from Israeli Sign Language, a language utterly different from their own. In just one generation, when the older Bedouin signers die, the unique signed language of the village, at least in its present form, may be significantly altered.

Omar, the owner of the home in which we gathered for the first recording session, greeted us in Hebrew. Although he is hearing, Omar has deaf siblings and knows the village sign language. Carol Padden, a linguist from the University of California, San Diego, who is deaf, starts to sign to him, using gestures international enough that they can be readily understood. Omar replies expansively in Al-Sayyid Bedouin Sign: the seeds of a simple contact pidgin have been sown. When signers of different languages come together, communication is achieved partly through the use of the most transparent gestures possible, partly through a shared understanding of the particular devices that signed languages use to convey meaning. (Just such a contact language, called International Sign Pidgin, has developed over the years at places like sign-linguistics meetings, where deaf people from many countries converge.)

The sign language of a particular country is rarely contingent on the spoken language that surrounds it. American and British Sign Languages are mutually unintelligible. A deaf American will have an easier time understanding a deaf Frenchman: ASL is historically descended from French Sign Language. Even the manual alphabet used by deaf signers can differ from one country to another. The letters of the American manual alphabet are signed using one hand; those of the British manual alphabet are made with two hands.

In her lab's mission statement, Wendy sums up how studying sign languages can illuminate how the mind works: "It usually comes as a surprise to the layman to learn that nobody sat down and invented the sign languages of the deaf. These languages arise spontaneously, wherever deaf people have an opportunity to congregate. That shows that they are the natural product of the human brain, just like spoken languages. But because these languages exist in a different physical modality, researchers believe that they offer a unique window into the kind of mental system that all human language belongs to."

Linguists have long believed that the ideal language to analyze would be one in its infancy. They even dream of the following experiment: simply grab a couple of babies, lock them in a room for a few years and record the utterances they produce. The scenario came to be known as the Forbidden Experiment.

It's been tried. The historian Herodotus, writing in the fifth century B.C., told of the Egyptian pharaoh Psammetichus, who, in an attempt to discover what the oldest civilization was, took two infants from their mothers and dispatched them to an isolated hut under the care of a mute shepherd. Eventually, one of the babies uttered the word *bekos*, which turned out to be the Phrygian word for "bread," bringing the experiment to a happy conclusion.

But near the end of the twentieth century, linguists began to realize that their sought-after virgin language existed in the sign language of the deaf. Signed languages spring from the same mental machinery that spoken languages do, but they are linguistic saplings.

The conditions that create an Al-Sayyid—a place where hundreds of people are habitual signers—are extremely particular. First, you need a gene for a form of inherited deafness. Second, you need huge families to pass the gene along, yielding an unusually large deaf population in a short span of time. Of Al-Sayyid's 3,500 residents, about one in 25 is deaf—4 percent of the population. For deafness, a rate of 4 percent is a staggering figure: in the United States, the incidence of deafness in the general population is about one in 1,000. The presence of so many deaf signers in their midst also encourages widespread signing among the hearing. This helps keep the indigenous signed language alive for the village as a whole.

Wendy and her colleagues aren't claiming that Al-Sayyid Bedouin Sign Language (ABSL) mirrors the evolutionary development of language in *Homo sapiens*. Rather, as Wendy explained, "we're able to see, given the fully developed human brain, what happens when it has to make a language out of nothing."

The first deaf children were born in Al-Sayyid 70 years ago, about ten of them in a single generation. By the time of our visit, only one member of the first deaf generation was still alive, an elderly woman too infirm to be interviewed. Today, the 150 or so deaf people of Al-Sayyid include the second generation, men and women in their thirties and forties; and the third generation, their children.

When they were small, the first-generation signers had developed systems of gestures, called homesigns, to communicate with their families. With so many homesigners in close proximity, a functional pidgin could develop quickly. And in just one generation, the children of these signers, like children of pidgin speakers everywhere, took their parents' signed pidgin and gave it grammar, spontaneously transforming it into the signed language of Al-Sayyid.

Over time, the language developed complexity. "People can talk about things that are not in the here-and-now," says Wendy. "They can talk about the traditional folklore of the tribe and say, 'People used to do it this way and now they don't,' They're able to transmit a lot of information—and things that are quite abstract." For example, "A signer told us about the traditional method of making babies immune to scorpion bites. It takes a high degree of sophistication about their culture, and it also takes a high degree of abstraction to be able to convey it."

Another villager, Anwar, is a particularly fine signer. On the linguists' previous visit, they recorded him telling a story nearly half an hour long, of how he was lost in Egypt for several years as a child. When Anwar was about eight, he somehow found his way onto a bus bound for Egypt. Because he couldn't communicate with anyone, he had no idea where he was supposed to be going, or where to get off. He left the bus somewhere in Egypt, where he knew no one. He was taken in by a local family and lived with them for three years. One day, someone from Al-Sayyid passed through and heard the story of the mysterious deaf boy. He recognized Anwar and brought him home. Anwar recounted this for the linguists entirely in the village sign language.

In all human languages, the task of showing who did what to whom is one of the principal functions of grammar. Many languages do this through verb agreement. But as a young, relatively bare language, ABSL displayed little of the elaborate verb agreement—made by altering the path of a verb's movement through space—that is the hallmark of established sign languages. Yet in the sentences they signed every day, the people of Al-Sayyid conveyed, clearly and without ambiguity, who did what to whom. Identifying the way in which they did so was the team's first important discovery.

In most spoken languages, there is a trade-off between verb agreement and rigid word order when it comes to expressing who did what to whom. And rigid word order the sign language of Al-Sayyid had with a vengeance. The-second-generation signers of ABSL, the team discovered, routinely rely on word order to encode the who-did-what-to-whom of discourse. As the linguists wrote in their first major paper on the village, "In the space of one generation from its inception, systematic grammatical structure has emerged in the language."

As the team analyzed sentence after sentence of ABSL, they saw signers use the same word order again and again: subject-object-verb, or SOV. In some sentences, subject or object might be absent (as in MONEY COLLECT, "I saved money," which has no overt subject). But in almost all of them, the verb appeared at the very end of the sentence or clause.

It was noteworthy that this very young language already had word order of any kind, especially given that ABSL, like any signed language, could just as easily do without it. This was truly astonishing: the emerging language of Al-Sayyid makes vigorous use of word order even though it doesn't have to.

As long as the grant money holds out, and as long as the people of Al-Sayyid will have them, the linguists will come back to the village at least twice a year. It is too soon to tell whether the village sign language in the pure, isolated form will endure much beyond this generation. The signing of the deaf children, Al-Sayyid's third generation, is already permeated with ISL. Most parents in Al-Sayyid believe that for their deaf children to make their way in Israeli society, they will need to know the national signed language, and no one disputes their point. "We don't know how the language will change, and for us, that's where the drama is," Wendy wrote me in an e-mail message a few years after our trip. "And that's why we have to keep studying it very carefully across the generations."

# 26

# Shifting Norms of Linguistic and Cultural Respect: Hybrid Sociolinguistic Zulu Identities

*Stephanie Inge Rudwick*

Imagine you just arrived in Kwazulu-Natal as a Peace Corps volunteer. You arrive in your host village, where you are immediately expected to greet the elders. As you nervously walk toward their receiving line, your thoughts jump back to your college anthropology class. You are trying to remember what your professor said about establishing positive relationships in a new study community. All you can remember is something about respecting the elders, but that advice seems rather obvious as the distinguished old man seated in front of you reaches out his hand to welcome you.

Determined to err on the side of caution, you do everything you can to demonstrate your utmost respect. Your grandmother always taught you to look at people straight in the eyes when you speak, and to never sit down in front of an elder or boss until you are told to take a seat. So you look down into the eyes of that first elder, and you share a firm handshake and a smile. You remain standing as you wait for permission to take a seat, and then you see what you've feared all along. The eyes of that first elder tell you that you must have committed a serious offense. In an instant, a kind youngster grabs your hand and guides you to sit down. After redirecting your gaze away from the elders, your new best friend whispers some terrific advice: "In our village we show respect for elders by avoiding direct eye contact during conversation, and when we talk with elders we always sit down; it's impolite to make them look up to see you."

The idea of respecting your elders is not complicated, but translating that relatively universal idea into practice is another matter. In this selection, linguist Stephanie Inge Rudwick describes the cultural variability of showing respect with a compelling field study that compares the linguistic and social norms of respect among isi-Zulu speakers in urban KwaZulu-Natal.

***As you read this selection, consider the following questions:***

- What is the difference between *hlonipha* and *isi-Hlonipho*?
- Why do some urban isi-Zulu speaking women disregard some, but not all traditional *hlonipha* behaviors?
- How does ku*hlonipha* (act of showing respect) reinforce traditional Zulu values in terms of age, status and gender? *Hlonipha*
- How do the changing linguistic and social norms of "respect" among urban isi-Zulu speakers compare to the way you were taught to interact with elders?

***The following terms discussed in this selection are included in the Glossary at the back of the book:***

*code-switching*
*linguistic hybridity*
*linguistic register*
*sociolinguistics*
*speech event*

## 1. INTRODUCTION

Lack of respect, though less aggressive than an outright insult, can take an equally wounding form. No insult is offered another person, but neither is recognition extended; he or she is not *seen*—as a full being whose presence matters (Sennett 2003: 3).

Rudwick, Stephanie Inge. "Shifting Norms of Linguistic and Cultural Respect: Hybrid Sociolinguistic Zulu Identities." *Nordic Journal of African Studies* 17 (2008):152–174. Reprinted by permission of the publisher.

One of the most prolific social thinkers of our time, Richard Sennett, wonders why respect should be in short supply while it costs nothing and provides people with a sense of dignity and pride. Admittedly, Sennett's work has focused mainly on "western" and U.S. American models of thinking while norms of respect and the understanding of what precisely constitutes respectful social or linguistic behaviour varies greatly from one culture to another. Many traditional African societies prescribe great significance to respectful behavior towards males and elders. This is because many social practices and cultural customs in these societies are based on strict patriarchy and seniority principles. Sociolinguistic scholars, such as Mills (2003, 2004), for instance, have rightly argued that respect and politeness is fundamentally based on particular approaches to class, race and gender and warns that what is considered "respectful", "polite" and "courteous" is often mistakenly associated with the behavior of one particular class, more often than not that of the white middle class. This, of course, raises questions as regards the relevance and applicability of models of politeness, such as the influential, albeit dated, model by Brown and Levinson (1978) to work on Africa.[1]

What I would like to argue here, however, is that Sennett's analysis of disrespected people[2] and what happens, if they as individuals are not felt accounted for as full and recognizable human beings, is universally relevant. In brief, an individual who feels disrespected may experience the complete loss of self-confidence and self-worth. Although the mechanism underlying the kind of disrespectful, unequal social power dynamic Sennett describes has primarily socio-economic foundations, the results of feeling disrespected may well occur due to a particular cultural set-up as well. It has long been acknowledged that "just as groups of people can be oppressed economically and politically, they can also be oppressed and humiliated culturally" and "that the concern for social justice needs to include not just economic but also cultural rights" (Parekh, 2000: 6).

One could argue that a certain standard of respect is laid down in the nuclear family while more general principles of respectful social and linguistic behavior are acquired in the immediate environment, the larger society and in private and public interaction. Hence, the understanding of what constitutes respectful behavior is embedded in one's culture, but also significantly in one's personal upbringing and socialization. There are doubtlessly many social and linguistic behavioral respect patterns which are culturally acquired and may trigger misunderstandings in intercultural encounters.[3] The concerns of this paper are, however, not inter-cultural dynamics but intra-cultural ones. I discuss how contrastive and conflictual patterns of respect emerge within one reasonably homogenous ethno- and sociolinguistic group, i.e. young (below the age of 30) Zulu people in urban KwaZulu-Natal (KZN).

There has been a recent debate in the South African media about the notion of the term "coconut". A possible definition of "coconut" is an urban "Eurocentric" African person who speaks what is perceived as an excessive amount of English with a "white" accent.[4] While there are a number of criteria used in assigning people "coconut"-status[5], the issue of language does seems to feature prominently in boundary constructions among isiZulu-speakers in South Africa. Considering that the vast socio-economic and political change in South Africa has resulted in increasingly complex and diverging identity formation patterns, norms of respects within particular ethnic, social, linguistic, cultural or religious communities also diverge and vary. Individuals may be perceived to be rude or to be acting disrespectful by members of their own "in-group" which could be based on ethnicity, linguistic background, religion or any other sociocultural affiliation. Furthermore, *age* is an important social variable when it comes to perceptions of "respect". In any society the older generation often has a different understanding of what constitutes respectful behavior then the young generation. Norms of respect are by no means static and bound; they are both fluid and fluctuating and, perhaps even more importantly, context-dependent. More over, in some instances, idiosyncratic differences in social respect patterns may transcend cultural or generational ones.[6]

This article emerges as part of a research project based on an empirical investigation of the contemporary linguistic and social norms of *hlonipha* [respect] among isiZulu-speakers in KwaZulu-Natal in rural-urban comparison but focuses only on the data collected among young (below the age of 30) urban participants. After providing some socio-historical background information on Zulu people in South Africa in general, I outline some of the traditional norms of respect significant for this ethnic group and distinguish between *hlonipha* as a cultural and social custom and *isiHlonipho* as a linguistic register. The following section discusses the theoretical approach of this paper and explains why cultural theories that are based on transgression concepts are particularly valuable in urban, post-apartheid South Africa. The research methodology, data analysis and discussion are presented in the next section which constitutes the backbone of the argument presented here. Many urban isiZulu-speakers critically evaluate traditionalist notions of *hlonipha*, revise them according to their needs and consequently construct hybrid cultural and sociolinguistic identities which take into account a variety of different reference points as regards respectful social and linguistic behavior. This article concurs with the argument of Pavlenko and Blackledge (2003: 27) that "individuals are agentive beings who are constantly in search of new social and linguistic resources, which allow them to resist identities that position them in undesirable ways; produce new identities; and assign alternative meanings to the links between identities and linguistic varieties".

## 2. BRIEF BACKGROUND TO ISIZULU-SPEAKERS

IsiZulu-speakers make up about 22 percent of the South African population (Census, 2001[7]) and the vast majority resides in the province KwaZulu-Natal where this research was conducted. Literally translated *hlonipha* means "respect" in isiZulu. Social *hlonipha* actions are fundamental to traditional Zulu life and what is considered "proper" behavior within the community. Among traditional Zulu people *ukuhlonipha* [to respect] as a social custom, reinforces a complex value system which is based on the social variables age, status and gender. *Hlonipha* actions entail conventions regulating and controlling posture, gesture, dress code and other behavioral patterns, but also align with status based on privileges of material nature. The most detailed study on Zulu *hlonipha* is arguably that by Raum (1973) who argues that one needs to distinguish two poles of sociological significance in *hlonipha* interactions, the *inferior status agent* and the *superior referent* (ibid.).

Higher status, seniority, and frequently also the male gender automatically qualify one as the referent of *hlonipha* actions. Furthermore, the significance of *amadlozi* [ancestors] is omnipresent in the execution of respectful behavior as it is in particular the ancestors and their names which need to be respected. The way in which names are given respect is by avoidance. *IsiHlonipho*[8], also termed the "language of respect" is essentially based on verbal taboo and has been researched most extensively among Xhosa women[9]. The linguistic aspect of *hlonipha*, termed *isiHlonipho* in the literature, manifests itself in its most "proper" sense, in the avoidance of the usage of syllables occurring in the names of relatives of older and/or superior status and in reference to the names of ancestors. The "deep" variety of *isiHlonipho* comprises of a large corpus of lexical items which are synonyms for the expressions which carry syllables that need to be avoided. Finlayson (1978) documented what she termed an *isiHlonipho* core vocabulary. The "soft" variety of *isiHlonipho* can be understood as the simple avoidance of the names of individuals and ancestors who need to be respected through the usage of common *isiHlonipho* terms, based on neologisms, lexical borrowings, or circumlocutions.

## 3. TRANSGRESSION AND CULTURAL HYBRIDITY

The anthropological approach to "culture" long ago moved from the understanding of "culture" as a certain kind of monolithic construct which could be meaningful described in terms of stable constituents to the insight that "culture" is inherently versatile, flexible, context-dependent and variably understood. Alexander (2002) suggests in the South African context that "culture" should be approached as something which is essentially in motion implying that what "culture" is to a group of people today may be different from how "culture" is understood by individuals in this group tomorrow. So-called "cultural groups" are not homogenous and individuals who perceive themselves as belonging to the same cultural group may have very different perceptions of what exactly it is that constitutes their "culture". Furthermore, these perceptions may vary from one situation to another and are situational and highly context-dependent (Ferdman and Horenczyk, 2000).

Although it may be commonly acknowledged that culture gives meaning to people's lives, many individuals and groups find it difficult to respect other peoples' cultural customs and their practical manifestations. Parekh (2000: 176) aptly points out that full respect for a culture entails not only "respect for a community's right to its culture" but also "for the content and character of that culture". It is the latter aspect which is what creates great challenges for individuals and entire groups in South Africa. The former contention is based on the idea that human beings have a fundamental right to choose how they want to live and how they construct and communicate their sense of self and their identities in a way that "every community has as good a right to its culture as any other, and there is no basis for inequality" (ibid.). The latter dimension of the concept concerning the content and character of culture is more problematic as, to mention only two examples, feminists find it impossible to tolerate patriarchy and traditionalists detest modern and revised approaches to their traditions.

Despite some opposing views[10], most scholars working on theories of multiculturalism[11] argue that embeddedness in language and culture is a constitutive factor of people's identity. Kymlicka (2007), in particular, stresses the inherent human need for a cultural and linguistic context of choice which gives meaning to people's lives and allows for a sense of freedom. While De Schutter (2007: 46) acknowledges the importance of Kymlicka's emphasis on cultural freedom, he justifiably rejects the scholar's monolithic approach to language and culture.[12] This criticism echoes well in the context of contemporary South Africa, as specifically in urban areas of the country individuals derive their linguistic and cultural embeddedness not only from one single monolithic source but from many different contexts. In an increasingly urbanized and globalized world, the notions of culture and identity become highly complex and multifaceted. Most individuals have more than just a single cultural reference point adopting hybrid cultural identities. Urban spaces in South Africa are no exception to this development as will be seen below.

Cultural Hybridity as understood by Homi Bhabha (1994, 1999) involves human beings as the creators, not the bearers of culture. Due to the individuality and the innovativeness of each human being it also follows that any particular culture cannot be concretely described in terms of its specific contents and constituents.[13] Clearly, there is not just one single point of reference for the construction of sociolinguistic or socio-cultural identities. This is particularly true with regard to individuals challenged to create identities in radically multilingual and multicultural spaces such as those that typify much of South Africa. Even in KZN, a province characterized by considerable homogeneity in terms of its black ethno-linguistic landscape, there are multiple and differing reference points for people as will be seen below.[14] Recent research in the KwaZulu-Natal township Umlazi suggests that the Zulu-speaking township youths negotiate their identities in various patterns, some more local, others more national (Rudwick 2004). These findings demonstrate that strong identification with Zulu ethnicity and simultaneous embracing of western norms and values, including the English language, are by no means contradictory for an individual. Total language-shift from isiZulu to English, however, is widely seen as betrayal of language, culture and tradition and gives rise to tensions in the Zulu community. Generally, these empirical findings provide further evidence that there is an increasing diversification of patterns which construct identities within what are traditionally regarded as homogenous groups (Tierney, 2007). From this perspective it needs to be stressed that a monolithic approach to culture and identity is deeply antiquated and requires rethinking. More specifically, these findings also account for the diversity amongst cultural customs of respect. Individuals may adopt certain respect patterns from groups outside their own cultural "in-group". It is on these grounds, that many young educated isiZulu-speakers have started to question and scrutinize respect patterns in their own traditional communities.

The notion of "de-linking, de-constructing of culture, place and identity" (Frello, 2006) derives from Hall's (1990, 1997) conceptualization of hybridity as "displacement" rather than as mere "blending" and "mixture" which is particularly useful for the purpose of this study. It draws on an approach to cultural identity as something "that belongs to the future as much as to the past" (1990: 225). In this sense, cultural identities, albeit inspired by history, transform constantly and are context-dependent. The hybrid individual (and this paper provides a platform for documenting the voices of such individuals), is capable of critically interrogating dominant and hegemonic formations by integrating "otherness" within the dominant center (Frello, 2006). Displaced categories are not conceptualized as "culturally different" but as "excluded" in the culture. This kind of approach allows the researcher to focus on the very complex struggles over power, identity and legitimate speech positions which are involved in isiZulu-speakers' critical engagement with *hlonipha* as a custom and speech form.

## 4. THE STUDY

While the larger project, from which this paper emerges, is based on an urban-rural comparison, this paper focuses exclusively on the sociolinguistic data elicited from young (30 years and younger) urban Zulu participants in the *eThekwini* (Durban city) region in KZN. I chose a multi-methods paradigm comprised of questionnaires (50 participants), interviews (18 participants) and participant observation in private homes. Participants were given the choice of filling in the questionnaires or being interviewed in English and/or isiZulu. The questionnaire[15] included a table with 47 lexical items based on what has been identified as core *hlonipha* vocabulary by Finlayson (1978). Participants were asked to fill in the appropriate *hlonipha* item for each isiZulu stimulus. The design of the interviews was based on a narrative approach (Mayring, 1996: 55) and yielded information on a variety of linguistic and social topics around the custom of *hlonipha*. Participant observation in different households has proven very valuable in complementing the interviews and in order to present a holistic and authentic picture of the sociolinguistic dynamics at work here. Speech situations and speech events were explored and language choices of individuals were systematically observed and contextualized. While it may be suggested that the "best" and most "valuable" data is linked to recorded speech, it must be stressed that it is engagement with and knowledge about the socio-cultural world in which speech occurs that ultimately leads sociolinguists to their findings (Johnstone, 2000: 84).

## 5. QUESTIONNAIRES

The questionnaires were distributed among 50 participants (equal distribution of males and females: 25/25) under the age of 30 residing in the *eThekwini* region. The majority were university students, about 10 participants were employed in various professions and a few were unemployed. While the questionnaires primarily aimed to elicit the lexical knowledge of an *isiHlonipho* core vocabulary (consisting of 47 lexical items) it also included a number of open-ended questions and tasks, two of which are particularly relevant for this paper. The first required the participants to rate the significance and value of *ukuhlonipha* [lit. translated as "showing respect"] as a social custom, the second required the same in reference to *isiHlonipho* [the language of respect] as a linguistic custom. An adapted Likert scale from 1–10 (1 = very important, 10 = not important) gave insight into the significance participants prescribed *ukuhlonipha* as a social custom and *isiHlonipho* as a linguistic variety. The analysis of the questionnaires suggests that the vast majority of participants rated the social value of *hlonipha* much more highly than the linguistic aspects of the custom. 82 percent of the participants gave *hlonipha* as a social custom a rating between 1–3–, on the scale and hence identified it as "very important", while only 34 percent rated *isiHlonipho* as "very important" (1–3).

The low rating of the linguistic aspect is, however, not surprising as very few participants (8 percent) were able to identify more than half (at least 24 out of 47) of the *isiHlonipho* lexical items on the table in the questionnaire, showing that the knowledge of the core vocabulary is rather poor in the investigated urban group.[16] This suggests that the linguistic aspect of the *hlonipha* custom is not central and not particularly significant in the life experiences of the questionnaire participants. In contrast, the social behavior codex inherent in the custom [*ukuhlonipha*] continues to be valued although it should be noted that perceptions of what exactly characterizes *ukuhlonipha* may vary from one participant to the next. While the questionnaires do provide a first insight into the contrast between the social and linguistic embeddedness of participants' constructions of identities regarding *hlonipha*, they do not provide detailed information regarding subjective notions of what kind of *ukuhlonipha,* or respectful behavior was meant.

Regarding the lexical analysis, it is noteworthy that the urban participants, on average, only knew roughly 32 percent of the lexical items provided in the table.[17] While some individuals were able to fill in more than half of the table, others only knew 3 or 4 words. In a few questionnaires the participant identified lexical item as isiHlonipo terms derived from the English language, for example *umeleko* [milk], *izindishi* [dishes] and *isipuni* [spoon]. Although the questionnaire was designed in a way that there was additional space for elaboration and further comments only few participants used the opportunity to give explanations for their responses. The lengthy one to two hour interviews with individual participants provided a much more accurate picture of the reasoning behind certain perceptions and attitudes. For this paper, I chose three themes that emerged from the interviews in order to portray how young urban Zulu people construct hybrid identities which mediate between tradition and modernity on the issue of *hlonipha*.

## 6. SELECTION OF SIGNIFICANT COMPONENTS IN HLONIPHA

What emerged from all interviews was a profound sense of the general significance of "social respect" [*ukuhlonipha*] among the young Zulu participants. While this consensus is noteworthy it only indicates participants' general agreement on the importance of the social custom not necessarily a unified and consensual understanding of the exact rules and facets of *ukuhlonipha* per se. Some interviewees juxtaposed the social with the linguistic aspects of *hlonipha* and highlighted, in line with the questionnaire ratings, *isiHlonipho* "proper" as marginally or only partially important. What this means for an isiZulu-speaker, is that the names of ancestors and living people that need to be respected would have to be avoided but the syllables that occur in these names could be pronounced without showing disrespect. The extract below exemplifies this:

> Respect is the most important thing, *ukuhlonipha* makes you who you are, also in the way you are and how you speak. I will teach my child a part of it, because in our days it is not necessary to use the specific words . . . (Nqobile, 24, Umlazi).

This young female student emphasizes the existential significance of *ukuhlonipha* as a social behavior of respect for her as a Zulu woman. For her, it is a matter of identity, of how you present yourself to the world, also on a linguistic level, but not primarily. What the quote above confirms is that the part of *hlonipha* which is still being passed on by urban Zulu people does not necessarily include the knowledge of specific *hlonipha* lexical items such as those in the core vocabulary table.

Respect for seniority is still rated very high among the interviewees. The same individual [quoted above] refers to the paramount importance of respect for older people at a later point in the interview. Another female interviewee explains that although friends respect each other, the respect one shows towards your relatives, in particular those that are older or of higher status, is substantially more profound and significant. Kinship and status relations, for instance, trump the variable age and fundamentally govern who is the agent and

who was that?" he'd ask. "Your boss?" "No, my boss is Susan. This was my friend." Often he'd still be in the previous story. But whenever she told them about her work, it was her mother who would get lost as soon as she mentioned a second step: "That was your tech report?" "No, I handed my tech report in last month. This was a special project."

Frances's mother and father, like many other men and women, had honed their listening and remembering skills in different areas. Their experience talking to other men and other women gave them practice in following different kinds of talk.

Knowing whether and how we are likely to report events later influences whether and how we pay attention when they happen. As women listen to and take part in conversations, knowing they may talk about them later makes them more likely to pay attention to exactly what is said and how. Since most men aren't in the habit of making such reports, they are less likely to pay much attention at the time. On the other hand, many women aren't in the habit of paying attention to scientific explanations and facts because they don't expect to have to perform in public by reciting them—just as those who aren't in the habit of entertaining others by telling jokes "can't" remember jokes they've heard, even though they listened carefully enough to enjoy them.

So women's conversations with their women friends keep them in training for talking about their relationships with men, but many men come to such conversations with no training at all—and an uncomfortable sense that this really isn't their event.

## "WHAT DO YOU MEAN, MY DEAR?"

Most of us place enormous emphasis on the importance of a primary relationship. We regard the ability to maintain such relationships as a sign of mental health—our contemporary metaphor for being a good person.

Yet our expectations of such relationships are nearly—maybe in fact—impossible. When primary relationships are between women and men, male–female differences contribute to the impossibility. We expect partners to be both romantic interests and best friends. Though women and men may have fairly similar expectations for romantic interests, obscuring their differences when relationships begin, they have very different ideas about how to be friends, and these are the differences that mount over time.

In conversations between friends who are not lovers, small misunderstandings can be passed over or diffused by breaks in contact. But in the context of a primary relationship, differences can't be ignored, and the pressure cooker of continued contact keeps both people stewing in the juice of accumulated minor misunderstandings. And stylistic differences are sure to cause misunderstandings—not, ironically, in matters such as sharing values and interests or understanding each other's philosophies of life. These large and significant yet palpable issues can be talked about and agreed on. It is far harder to achieve congruence—and much more surprising and troubling that it is hard—in the simple day-to-day matters of the automatic rhythms and nuances of talk. Nothing in our backgrounds or in the media (the present-day counterpart of religion or grandparents' teaching) prepares us for this failure. If two people share so much in terms of point of view and basic values, how can they continually get into fights about insignificant matters?

If you find yourself in such a situation and you don't know about differences in conversational style, you assume something's wrong with your partner or you, or you for having chosen your partner. At best, if you are forward-thinking and generous-minded, you may absolve individuals and blame the relationship. But if you know about differences in conversational style, you can accept that there are differences in habits and assumptions about how to have conversation, show interest, be considerate, and so on. You may not always correctly interpret your partner's intentions, but you will know that if you get a negative impression, it may not be what was intended and neither are your responses unfounded. If he says he really is interested even though he doesn't seem to be, maybe you should believe what he says and not what you sense.

Sometimes explaining assumptions can help. If a man starts to tell a woman what to do to solve her problem, she may say, "Thanks for the advice but I really don't want to be told what to do. I just want you to listen and say you understand." A man might want to explain, "If I challenge you, it's not to prove you wrong; it's just my way of paying attention to what you're telling me." Both may try either or both to modify their ways of talking and to try to accept what the other does. The important thing is to know that what seem like bad intentions may really be good intentions expressed in a different conversational style. We have to give up our conviction that, as Robin Lakoff put it, "Love means never having to say "What do you mean?""

# PART IV

# *Cultural Anthropology*

Cultural anthropology is concerned with the description and analysis of people's lives and traditions. In the past, cultural anthropologists almost always did research in far-off "exotic" societies, but today we have expanded our research interests to include our own society. Cultural anthropology can add much to both the basic and the applied scientific understanding of human behaviors and beliefs. The study and interpretation of other societies—of their traditions, history, and view of the world—is inherently interesting and important because it documents the diversity of human lifestyles. The anthropological approach to understanding other societies also has practical value for addressing contemporary human problems and needs.

The concept of *culture* is central to anthropology. It refers to the patterns of economy, social organization, and belief that are learned and shared by members of a social group. Culture is traditional knowledge that is passed down from one generation to the next. Although generally stable over time, culture is flexible and fluid, changing through borrowing or invention. The influential American anthropologist Franz Boas championed the concept of culture for understanding human diversity; culture, Boas argued, is distinct from biological race or language. Anthropologists believe that all cultural lifestyles have intrinsic value and validity. Other societies deserve to be studied and understood without being prejudged using our own narrow (and sometimes intolerant) beliefs and values. This universal tendency to prejudge based on the supposed superiority of one's own group, called *ethnocentrism,* is something everyone should avoid.

Culture is the crowning achievement of human evolution. To understand ourselves is to appreciate cultural diversity. Dependence on culture as our primary mechanism of survival sets humans apart from other members of the animal kingdom. This dependence is responsible for the tremendous evolutionary success of our species, which has grown in population (sometimes to the point of overpopulation) and can inhabit nearly every niche on the planet.

The paradox of culture is that as we humans learn to accept our own cultural beliefs and values, we unconsciously learn to reject those of other peoples. At birth, we are capable of absorbing any culture and language. We are predisposed to cultural learning, but we are not programmed to adopt a particular culture. As we grow, our parents, our schools, and our society teach us what is right and wrong, good and evil, acceptable and unacceptable. At the subconscious level, we learn the symbolic meanings of behavior and through them interpret the meanings of actions. Beliefs, values, and symbols must be understood within the context of a particular culture. This is the principle of *cultural relativity.* At the same time, culture supplies us with the cognitive models or tools—software programs, if you will—that allow us to perceive or construct a particular version of reality. Culture permeates our thinking and our expectations; this is the principle of *cultural construction.*

The anthropological approach to the study of human behavior and belief has two essential characteristics: a holistic approach and a comparative framework. A *holistic approach* means that anthropologists see a particular part of culture—for example, politics, the economy, or religion—in relation to the larger social system. Individuals are viewed not in isolation but as part of an intricate web of social relationships. Although an anthropological study may have a particular focus, the holistic approach means that the broader cultural context is always considered important because the different parts of a cultural system are interrelated. When, for example, the economy or the technology changes, other aspects of the culture will change as well.

A *comparative framework* means that explanations or generalizations are achieved through cross-cultural research. Questions about humanity cannot be based on information from a single society or a single type of society—such as the industrial societies of the United States and Europe. Such a limited framework is simply too narrow for understanding the big picture that basic anthropological research seeks. By studying others, we can better understand ourselves. If other cultures are a mirror in which we see ourselves, then anthropology is a mirror for humankind.

The broad generalizations about culture and society that we have been talking about are based on detailed knowledge of the world's cultures. To gain this knowledge, anthropologists go to the people. Often accompanied by spouses and children, we pack our bags and travel to far-off lands—to the highlands of New Guinea, the frozen arctic, the savannas of Africa, or the jungles of South America. Increasingly, anthropologists are bringing their research methods and comparative, holistic perspective into the cities and suburbs of America, the American schoolroom, and the corporate jungle. This research adventure has become the hallmark of cultural anthropology.

The research methods used by the cultural anthropologist are distinctive because they depend, to a large extent, on the firsthand experiences and interpretations of the field researcher. Cultural anthropologists conduct research in natural settings rather than in laboratories or over the telephone. This method for studying another society is often called *participant observation, ethnography,* or *qualitative methods.* The goal of describing, understanding, and explaining another culture is a large task. It is most often accomplished by living in the society for an extended period, by talking with people, and, as much as possible, by experiencing their lives.

The fieldwork experience usually involves a kind of culture shock in which the researcher questions his or her own assumptions about the world. In this way, fieldwork is often a rewarding period of personal growth. In their work, anthropologists expect to find that other people's behavior, even when it seems bizarre when seen from the outside, makes sense when viewed from the people's own point of view. That is why anthropological research often means letting people speak for themselves. While doing research, the anthropologist often thinks of herself or himself as a child—as being ignorant or uninformed and needing to be taught by the people being studied. This approach often involves in-depth interviewing with a few key informants and then interpreting (and writing about) that other culture for the researcher's own society. The ethnographic method, pioneered and developed in anthropology, is now being used in a range of applied areas, including marketing, management research, and school evaluation.

The applications of cultural anthropology are diverse. Internationally, anthropologists are involved in programs of technical assistance and economic aid to Third World nations. These programs address needs in such areas as agriculture and rural development; health, nutrition, and family planning; education; housing and community organizing; transportation and communication; and energy. Anthropologists do many of the same things domestically as well. They evaluate public education, study agricultural extension programs, administer projects, analyze policy (such as U.S. refugee resettlement programs), and research crime and crime prevention, for example.

In the private sector, cultural anthropologists can add a fresh perspective to market research (see Selection 43). Moreover they analyze office and industrial organization and culture and create language and cultural training workshops for businesspeople and others who are going overseas. These workshops reduce the likelihood of cross-cultural misunderstanding and the problems of culture shock for the employee and his or her family.

Applied anthropological work can be divided into three categories. In the first group, applied research and basic research look very much alike, except that the goal of applied research is more directly linked with a particular problem or need. For example, in Selection 45, Aaron Podolefsky studies the causes of the re-emergence of tribal warfare in New Guinea. Such a study provides planners and policymakers with important insights for understanding the problem. This knowledge can then be used in the design and implementation of programs that may help bring an end to warfare in the region.

In the second category, anthropologists may work as researchers for a government agency, a corporation, or an interest group on a specific task defined by the client.

In the third category, anthropologists work as consultants to business and industry or to government agencies that need in-depth cultural knowledge to solve or prevent a problem. Anthropologists often act as cultural brokers, mediating and translating between groups who are miscommunicating not because of their words but because of cultural meanings.

A great deal of anthropological work remains to be done, although this seems to be a well-kept secret. People have a far easier time focusing on the individual as the level of analysis. When divorce, drug abuse, or suicide affects small numbers of people, we may look to the individual and to psychology for answers. When divorce rates climb to 50 percent of all marriages and the suicide rate increases tenfold, however, we must look beyond the individual to forces that affect society at large. Because we are so immersed in our own culture, we have difficulty seeing it as a powerful force that guides—even controls—our behavior.

# 29

# Body Ritual among the Nacirema

*Horace Miner*

Generations of anthropologists have traveled the globe, reaching to the far corners of the five continents to discover and describe the many ways of humankind. Anthropologists have gathered a diverse collection of exotic customs, from the mundane to the bizarre. Understanding and appreciating other societies requires us to be culturally relative. But people tend to judge others by their own cultural values in a way that is *ethnocentric.* This is because people take their cultural beliefs and behaviors for granted; they seem so natural that they are seldom questioned. Among the most interesting social customs on record are the rituals of the Nacirema. By viewing Nacirema behaviors as *rituals,* we gain insight into their culture and into the meaning of the concept of *culture.* We also gain insight into the problem of ethnocentrism.

Ritual is a cultural phenomenon. Ritual can be found in all societies. It can be defined as a set of acts that follow a sequence established by tradition.

Throughout the world, ritual reflects the fundamental cultural beliefs and values of a society by giving order to important activities and particular life crises like death and birth. Every day, however, mundane rituals are performed unconsciously. In fact, most Nacirema people do these things without being aware of their underlying symbolic meanings. Pay particular attention to the quotation at the end of the selection.

***As you read this selection, ask yourself the following questions:***

- How do the Nacirema feel about the human body?
- Do you think that the charms and magical potions used by the Nacirema really work?
- Can you list those aspects of social life in which magic plays an important role?
- What is your opinion of the importance of body ritual, and if you went to live among the Nacirema, would you tell them of your opinion?
- Viewed from the perspective of living among the Nacirema, their behaviors sometimes appear bizarre. Do you think the Nacirema themselves feel this way?

***The following terms discussed in this selection are included in the Glossary at the back of the book:***

*clan*
*culture*
*ethnocentrism*
*ritual*

The anthropologist has become so familiar with the diversity of ways in which different peoples behave in similar situations that he is not apt to be surprised by even the most exotic customs. In fact, if all of the logically possible combinations of behavior have not been found somewhere in the world, he is apt to suspect that they must be present in some yet undescribed tribe. This point has, in fact, been expressed with respect to clan organization by Murdock (1949:71). In this light, the magical beliefs and practices of the Nacirema present such unusual aspects that it seems desirable to describe them as an example of the extremes to which human behavior can go.

Professor Linton first brought the ritual of the Nacirema to the attention of anthropologists twenty years ago (1936:326), but the culture of this people is still very poorly understood. They are a North American group living in the territory between the Canadian Cree, the Yaqui and Tarahumare of Mexico, and the Carib and Arawak of the Antilles. Little is known of their origin, although tradition states that they came from the east. According to Nacirema mythology, their nation was originated by a culture hero, Notgnihsaw, who is otherwise known for two great feats of strength—the throwing of a piece of wampum across the river Pa-To-Mac and the chopping down of a cherry tree in which the Spirit of Truth resided.

Miner, Horace. "Body Ritual among the Nacirema." *American Anthropologist* 58 (1956):503–507. www.anthrosource.net

Nacirema culture is characterized by a highly developed market economy which has evolved in a rich natural habitat. While much of the people's time is devoted to economic pursuits, a large part of the fruits of these labors and a considerable portion of the day are spent in ritual activity. The focus of this activity is the human body, the appearance and health of which loom as a dominant concern in the ethos of the people. While such a concern is certainly not unusual, its ceremonial aspects and associated philosophy are unique.

The fundamental belief underlying the whole system appears to be that the human body is ugly and that its natural tendency is to debility and disease. Incarcerated in such a body, man's only hope is to avert these characteristics through the use of the powerful influences of ritual and ceremony. Every household has one or more shrines devoted to this purpose. The more powerful individuals in the society have several shrines in their houses and, in fact, the opulence of a house is often referred to in terms of the number of such ritual centers it possesses. Most houses are of wattle and daub construction, but the shrine rooms of the more wealthy are walled with stone. Poorer families imitate the rich by applying pottery plaques to their shrine walls.

While each family has at least one such shrine, the rituals associated with it are not family ceremonies but are private and secret. The rites are normally only discussed with children, and then only during the period when they are being initiated into these mysteries. I was able, however, to establish sufficient rapport with the natives to examine these shrines and to have the rituals described to me.

The focal point of the shrine is a box or chest which is built into the wall. In this chest are kept the many charms and magical potions without which no native believes he could live. These preparations are secured from a variety of specialized practitioners. The most powerful of these are the medicine men, whose assistance must be rewarded with substantial gifts. However, the medicine men do not provide the curative potions for their clients, but decide what the ingredients should be and then write them down in an ancient and secret language. This writing is understood only by the medicine men and by the herbalists who, for another gift, provide the required charm.

The author of this article used the term *man* to refer to humanity in general. This term is not used by modern anthropologists because, to many people, it reflects an unconscious sexist bias in language and rhetoric. At the time that this article was written, however, the generalized *man* was a common convention in writing. In the interest of historical accuracy we have not changed the wording in this article, but students should be aware that nonsexist terms (*humans, people, Homo sapiens,* and so on) are preferred.—The Editors.

The charm is not disposed of after it has served its purpose, but is placed in the charm-box of the household shrine. As these magical materials are specific for certain ills, and the real or imagined maladies of the people are many, the charm-box is usually full to overflowing. The magical packets are so numerous that people forget what their purposes were and fear to use them again. While the natives are very vague on this point, we can only assume that the idea in retaining all the old magical materials is that their presence in the charm-box, before which the body rituals are conducted, will in some way protect the worshipper.

Beneath the charm-box is a small font. Each day every member of the family, in succession, enters the shrine room, bows his head before the charm-box, mingles different sorts of holy water in the font, and proceeds with a brief rite of ablution. The holy waters are secured from the Water Temple of the community, where the priests conduct elaborate ceremonies to make the liquid ritually pure.

In the hierarchy of magical practitioners, and below the medicine men in prestige, are specialists whose designation is best translated "holy-mouth-men." The Nacirema have an almost pathological horror of and fascination with the mouth, the condition of which is believed to have a supernatural influence on all social relationships. Were it not for the rituals of the mouth, they believe that their teeth would fall out, their gums bleed, their jaws shrink, their friends desert them, and their lovers reject them. They also believe that a strong relationship exists between oral and moral characteristics. For example, there is a ritual ablution of the mouth for children which is supposed to improve their moral fiber.

The daily body ritual performed by everyone includes a mouth-rite. Despite the fact that these people are so punctilious about care of the mouth, this rite involves a practice which strikes the uninitiated stranger as revolting. It was reported to me that the ritual consists of inserting a small bundle of hog hairs into the mouth, along with certain magical powders, and then moving the bundle in a highly formalized series of gestures.

In addition to the private mouth-rite, the people seek out a holy-mouth-man once or twice a year. These practitioners have an impressive set of paraphernalia, consisting of a variety of augers, awls, probes, and prods. The use of these objects in the exorcism of the evils of the mouth involves almost unbelievable ritual torture of the client. The holy-mouth-man opens the client's mouth, and using the above mentioned tools, enlarges any holes which decay may have created in the teeth. Magical materials are put into these holes. If there are no naturally occurring holes in the teeth, large sections of one or more teeth are gouged out so that the supernatural substance can be applied. In the client's view, the purpose of these ministrations is to arrest decay and to draw friends. The extremely sacred and traditional character of the rite is evident in the fact that the natives return to the holy-mouth-men year after year, despite the fact that their teeth continue to decay.

It is to be hoped that, when a thorough study of the Nacirema is made, there will be careful inquiry into the personality structure of these people. One has to but watch the gleam in the eye of a holy-mouth-man as he jabs an awl into an exposed nerve, to suspect that a certain amount of sadism is involved. If this can be established, a very interesting pattern emerges, for most of the population shows definite masochistic tendencies. It was to these that Professor Linton referred in discussing a distinctive part of the daily body ritual which is performed only by men. This part of the rite involves scraping and lacerating the surface of the face with a sharp instrument. Special women's rites are performed only four times during each lunar month, but what they lack in frequency is made up in barbarity. As part of this ceremony, women bake their heads in small ovens for about an hour. The theoretically interesting point is that what seems to be a preponderantly masochistic people have developed sadistic specialists.

The medicine men have an imposing temple, or *latipso,* in every community of any size. The more elaborate ceremonies required to treat very sick patients can only be performed at this temple. These ceremonies involve not only the thaumaturge but a permanent group of vestal maidens who move sedately about the temple chambers in distinctive costume and headdress.

The *latipso* ceremonies are so harsh that it is phenomenal that a fair proportion of the really sick natives who enter the temple ever recover. Small children whose indoctrination is still incomplete have been known to resist attempts to take them to the temple because "that is where you go to die." Despite this fact, sick adults are not only willing but eager to undergo the protracted ritual purification, if they can afford to do so. No matter how ill the supplicant or how grave the emergency, the guardians of many temples will not admit a client if he cannot give a rich gift to the custodian. Even after one has gained admission and survived the ceremonies, the guardians will not permit the neophyte to leave until he makes still another gift.

The supplicant entering the temple is first stripped of all his or her clothes. In everyday life the Nacirema avoids exposure of his body and its natural functions. Bathing and excretory acts are performed only in the secrecy of the household shrine, where they are ritualized as part of the body-rites. Psychological shock results from the fact that body secrecy is suddenly lost upon entry into the *latipso.* A man, whose own wife has never seen him in an excretory act, suddenly finds himself naked and assisted by a vestal maiden while he performs his natural functions into a sacred vessel. This sort of ceremonial treatment is necessitated by the fact that the excreta are used by a diviner to ascertain the course and nature of the client's sickness. Female clients, on the other hand, find their naked bodies are subjected to the scrutiny, manipulation and prodding of the medicine men.

Few supplicants in the temple are well enough to do anything but lie on their hard beds. The daily ceremonies, like the rites of the holy-mouth-men, involve discomfort and torture. With ritual precision, the vestals awaken their miserable charges each dawn and roll them about on their beds of pain while performing ablutions, in the formal movements of which the maidens are highly trained. At other times they insert magic wands in the supplicant's mouth or force him to eat substances which are supposed to be healing. From time to time the medicine men come to their clients and jab magically treated needles into their flesh. The fact that these temple ceremonies may not cure, and may even kill the neophyte, in no way decreases the people's faith in the medicine men.

There remains one other kind of practitioner, known as a "listener." This witch-doctor has the power to exorcise the devils that lodge in the heads of people who have been bewitched. The Nacirema believe that parents bewitch their own children. Mothers are particularly suspected of putting a curse on children while teaching them the secret body rituals. The counter-magic of the witch-doctor is unusual in its lack of ritual. The patient simply tells the "listener" all his troubles and fears, beginning with the earliest difficulties he can remember. The memory displayed by the Nacirema in these exorcism sessions is truly remarkable. It is not uncommon for the patient to bemoan the rejection he felt upon being weaned as a babe, and a few individuals even see their troubles going back to the traumatic effects of their own birth.

In conclusion, mention must be made of certain practices which have their base in native esthetics but which depend upon the pervasive aversion to the natural body and its functions. There are ritual fasts to make fat people thin and ceremonial feasts to make thin people fat. Still other rites are used to make women's breasts larger if they are small, and smaller if they are large. General dissatisfaction with breast shape is symbolized in the fact that the ideal form is virtually outside the range of human variation. A few women afflicted with almost inhuman hypermammary development are so idolized that they make a handsome living by simply going from village to village and permitting the natives to stare at them for a fee.

Reference has already been made to the fact that excretory functions are ritualized, routinized, and relegated to secrecy. Natural reproductive functions are similarly distorted. Intercourse is taboo as a topic and scheduled as an act. Efforts are made to avoid pregnancy by the use of magical materials or by limiting intercourse to certain phases of the moon. Conception is actually very infrequent. When pregnant, women dress so as to hide their condition. Parturition takes place in secret, without friends or relatives to assist, and the majority of women do not nurse their infants.

Our review of the ritual life of the Nacirema has certainly shown them to be a magic-ridden people. It is hard to understand how they have managed to exist so long under the burdens which they have imposed upon themselves. But even such exotic customs as these take on real meaning when they are viewed with the insight provided by Malinowski when he wrote (1948:70):

> Looking from far and above, from our high places of safety in the developed civilization, it is easy to see all the crudity and irrelevance of magic. But without its power and guidance early man could not have mastered his practical difficulties as he has done, nor could man have advanced to the higher stages of civilization.

## REFERENCES

Linton, Ralph. 1936. *The Study of Man.* New York: D. Appleton-Century Co.

Malinowski, Bronislaw. 1948. *Magic, Science, and Religion.* Glencoe, IL: The Free Press.

Murdock, George P. 1949. *Social Structure.* New York: The Macmillan Co.

Polonius hide behind a cloth that hung against the wall of Hamlet's mother's sleeping hut. Hamlet started to scold his mother for what she had done."

There was a shocked murmur from everyone. A man should never scold his mother.

"She called out in fear, and Polonius moved behind the cloth. Shouting, 'A rat!' Hamlet took his machete and slashed through the cloth." I paused for dramatic effect. "He had killed Polonius!"

The old men looked at each other in supreme disgust. "That Polonius truly was a fool and a man who knew nothing! What child would not know enough to shout, 'It's me!'" With a pang, I remembered that these people are ardent hunters, always armed with bow, arrow, and machete; at the first rustle in the grass an arrow is aimed and ready, and the hunter shouts "Game!" If no human voice answers immediately, the arrow speeds on its way. Like a good hunter Hamlet had shouted, "A rat!"

I rushed in to save Polonius's reputation. "Polonius did speak. Hamlet heard him. But he thought it was the chief and wished to kill him to avenge his father. He had meant to kill him earlier that evening . . ." I broke down, unable to describe to these pagans, who had no belief in individual afterlife, the difference between dying at one's prayers and dying "unhousell'd, disappointed, unaneled."

This time I had shocked my audience seriously. "For a man to raise his hand against his father's brother and the one who has become his father—that is a terrible thing. The elders ought to let such a man be bewitched."

I nibbled at my kola nut in some perplexity, then pointed out that after all the man had killed Hamlet's father.

"No," pronounced the old man, speaking less to me than to the young men sitting behind the elders. "If your father's brother has killed your father, you must appeal to your father's age mates; *they* may avenge him. No man may use violence against his senior relatives." Another thought struck him. "But if his father's brother had indeed been wicked enough to bewitch Hamlet and make him mad that would be a good story indeed, for it would be his fault that Hamlet, being mad, no longer had any sense and thus was ready to kill his father's brother."

There was a murmur of applause. *Hamlet* was again a good story to them, but it no longer seemed quite the same story to me. As I thought over the coming complications of plot and motive, I lost courage and decided to skim over dangerous ground quickly.

"The great chief," I went on, "was not sorry that Hamlet had killed Polonius. It gave him a reason to send Hamlet away, with his two treacherous age mates, with letters to a chief of a far country, saying that Hamlet should be killed. But Hamlet changed the writing on their papers, so that the chief killed his age mates instead." I encountered a reproachful glare from one of the men whom I had told undetectable forgery was not merely immoral but beyond human skill. I looked the other way.

"Before Hamlet could return, Laertes came back for his father's funeral. The great chief told him Hamlet had killed Polonius. Laertes swore to kill Hamlet because of this, and because his sister Ophelia, hearing her father had been killed by the man she loved, went mad and drowned in the river."

"Have you already forgotten what we told you?" The old man was reproachful. "One cannot take vengeance on a madman; Hamlet killed Polonius in his madness. As for the girl, she not only went mad, she was drowned. Only witches can make people drown. Water itself can't hurt anything. It is merely something one drinks and bathes in."

I began to get cross. "If you don't like the story, I'll stop."

The old man made soothing noises and himself poured me some more beer. "You tell the story well, and we are listening. But it is clear the elders of your country have never told you what the story really means. No, don't interrupt! We believe you when you say your marriage customs are different, or your clothes and weapons. But people are the same everywhere; therefore, there are always witches and it is we, the elders, who know how witches work. We told you it was the great chief who wished to kill Hamlet, and now your own words have proved us right. Who were Ophelia's male relatives?"

"There were only her father and her brother." Hamlet was clearly out of my hands.

"There must have been many more; this also you must ask of your elders when you get back to your country. From what you tell us, since Polonius was dead, it must have been Laertes who killed Ophelia, although I do not see the reason for it."

We had emptied one pot of beer, and the old men argued the point with slightly tipsy interest. Finally one of them demanded of me, "What did the servant of Polonius say on his return?"

With difficulty I recollected Reynaldo and his mission. "I don't think he did return before Polonius was killed."

"Listen," said the elder, "and I will tell you how it was and how your story will go, then you may tell me if I am right. Polonius knew his son would get into trouble, and so he did. He had many fines to pay for fighting, and debts from gambling. But he had only two ways of getting money quickly. One was to marry off his sister at once, but it is difficult to find a man who will marry a woman desired by the son of a chief. For if the chief's heir commits adultery with your wife, what can you do? Only a fool calls a case against a man who will someday be his judge. Therefore Laertes had to take the second way: he killed his sister by witchcraft, drowning her so he could secretly sell her body to the witches."

I raised an objection. "They found her body and buried it. Indeed Laertes jumped into the grave to see his sister once more—so, you see, the body was truly there. Hamlet, who had just come back, jumped in after him."

"What did I tell you?" The elder appealed to the others. "Laertes was up to no good with his sister's body. Hamlet prevented him, because the chief's heir, like a chief, does not wish any other man to grow rich and powerful. Laertes would be angry, because he would have killed his sister without benefit to himself. In our country he would try to kill Hamlet for that reason. Is this not what happened?"

"More or less," I admitted. "When the great chief found Hamlet was still alive, he encouraged Laertes to try to kill Hamlet and arranged a fight with machetes between them. In the fight both the young men were wounded to death. Hamlet's mother drank the poisoned beer that the chief meant for Hamlet in case he won the fight. When he saw his mother die of poison, Hamlet, dying, managed to kill his father's brother with his machete."

"You see, I was right!" exclaimed the elder.

"That was a very good story," added the old man, "and you told it with very few mistakes. There was just one more error, at the very end. The poison Hamlet's mother drank was obviously meant for the survivor of the fight, whichever it was. If Laertes had won, the great chief would have poisoned him, for no one would know that he arranged Hamlet's death. Then, too, he need not fear Laertes' witchcraft; it takes a strong heart to kill one's only sister by witchcraft.

"Sometime," concluded the old man, gathering his ragged toga about him, "you must tell us some more stories of your country. We, who are elders, will instruct you in their true meaning, so that when you return to your own land your elders will see that you have not been sitting in the bush, but among those who know things and who have taught you wisdom."

# 31

# Eating Christmas in the Kalahari

*Richard Borshay Lee*

An *economy* is a social system for the production, exchange, and consumption of goods and services. Using this definition, anthropologists believe that all human societies have economies and that economic systems can work without money and markets.

People in food-foraging societies, like the !Kung San described in this selection, have received much attention by anthropologists. To a large degree, this is because they represent (at least by analogy) the original lifestyle of our ancestors. A major discovery of research on food foragers is that their life is not "nasty, brutish, and short." In fact, the food forager's diet might be an ideal one for people living in industrialized societies.

In the hunter-gatherer economy, anthropologists have discovered that the exchange of goods is based on rules of gift giving or reciprocity. In this selection, Richard Lee tells of his surprise at the !Kung San's lack of appreciation of a Christmas gift. As we have already seen, a group's customs and rules about appropriate social behavior can reflect important cultural values. When people act in unexpected ways, anthropologists see this as an opportunity to better understand their culture and world view. That is the case in this selection.

All people give gifts to each other, but there are rules and obligations about those gifts. In our own society, there are rules about the polite way to receive a present. We are supposed to act appreciative (even if we hate the gift) because the gift is less important than the social relationship at stake. The !Kung break those rules, but in the process, Richard Lee discovers that there are important cultural messages behind their "impoliteness."

***As you read this selection, ask yourself the following questions:***

- Why did Richard Lee feel obligated to give a valuable gift to the !Kung at Christmas? Why did they think he was a miser?
- Why did the !Kung people's insults about the impending gift bother the anthropologist so much? Were the people treating him in a special way?
- What does Lee mean by saying, "There are no totally generous acts?" Do you agree?
- What are some cultural rules about gift giving in our own society?

***The following terms discussed in this selection are included in the Glossary at the back of the book:***

*cultural values*
*economy*
*egalitarian society*
*hunter-gatherers*
*reciprocal gift*

The !Kung Bushmen's knowledge of Christmas is thirdhand. The London Missionary Society brought the holiday to the southern Tswana tribes in the early nineteenth century. Later, native catechists spread the idea far and wide among the Bantu-speaking pastoralists, even in the remotest corners of the Kalahari Desert. The Bushmen's idea of the Christmas story, stripped to its essentials, is "praise the birth of white man's god-chief:" what keeps their interest in the holiday high is the Tswana-Herero custom of slaughtering an ox for his Bushmen neighbors as an annual goodwill gesture. Since the 1930s, part of the Bushmen's annual round of activities has included a December congregation at the cattle posts for trading, marriage brokering, and several days of trance dance feasting at which the local Tswana headman is host.

As a social anthropologist working with !Kung Bushmen, I found that the Christmas ox custom suited my purposes. I had come to the Kalahari to study the hunting and gathering subsistence economy of the !Kung, and to accomplish this it was essential not to provide them with food, share my own food, or interfere in any way with their food-gathering activities. While liberal handouts of tobacco and medical supplies

---

Lee, Richard Borshay. "Eating Christmas in the Kalahari" from *Natural History* (Dec. 1969):14–22, 60–64; 

were appreciated, they were scarcely adequate to erase the glaring disparity in wealth between the anthropologist, who maintained a two-month inventory of canned goods, and the Bushmen, who rarely had a day's supply of food on hand. My approach, while paying off in terms of data, left me open to frequent accusations of stinginess and hardheartedness. By their lights, I was a miser.

The Christmas ox was to be my way of saying thank you for the cooperation of the past year; and since it was to be our last Christmas in the field, I determined to slaughter the largest, meatiest ox that money could buy, insuring that the feast and trance dance would be a success.

Through December I kept my eyes open at the wells as the cattle were brought down for watering. Several animals were offered, but none had quite the grossness that I had in mind. Then, ten days before the holiday, a Herero friend led an ox of astonishing size and mass up to our camp. It was solid black, stood five feet high at the shoulder, had a five-foot span of horns, and must have weighed 1,200 pounds on the hoof. Food consumption calculations are my specialty, and I quickly figured that bones and viscera aside, there was enough meat—at least four pounds—for every man, woman, and child of the 150 Bushmen in the vicinity of /ai/ai who were expected at the feast.

Having found the right animal at last, I paid the Herero £20 ($56) and asked him to keep the beast with his herd until Christmas day. The next morning word spread among the people that the big solid black one was the ox chosen by /ontah (my Bushman name; it means, roughly, "whitey") for the Christmas feast. That afternoon I received the first delegation. Ben!a, an outspoken sixty-year-old mother of five, came to the point slowly.

"Where were you planning to eat Christmas?"

"Right here at /ai/ai," I replied.

"Alone or with others?"

"I expect to invite all the people to eat Christmas with me."

"Eat what?"

"I have purchased Yehave's black ox, and I am going to slaughter and cook it."

"That's what we were told at the well but refused to believe it until we heard it from yourself."

"Well, it's the black one," I replied expansively, although wondering what she was driving at.

"Oh, no!" Ben!a groaned, turning to her group. "They were right." Turning back to me she asked, "Do you expect us to eat that bag of bones?"

"Bag of bones! It's the biggest ox at /ai/ai."

"Big, yes, but old. And thin. Everybody knows there's no meat on that old ox. What did you expect to eat off of it, the horns?"

Everybody chuckled at Ben!a's one-liner as they walked away, but all I could manage was a weak grin.

That evening it was the turn of the young men. They came to sit at our evening fire. /gaugo, about my age, spoke to me man-to-man.

"/ontah, you have always been square with us," he lied. "What has happened to change your heart? That sack of guts and bones of Yehave's will hardly feed one camp, let alone all the Bushmen around /ai/ai." And he proceeded to enumerate the seven camps in the /ai/ai vicinity, family by family. "Perhaps you have forgotten that we are not few, but many. Or are you too blind to tell the difference between a proper cow and an old wreck? That ox is thin to the point of death."

"Look, you guys," I retorted, "that is a beautiful animal, and I'm sure you will eat it with pleasure at Christmas."

"Of course we will eat it: it's food. But it won't fill us up to the point where we will have enough strength to dance. We will eat and go home to bed with stomachs rumbling."

That night as we turned in, I asked my wife, Nancy, "What did you think of the black ox?"

"It looked enormous to me. Why?"

"Well, about eight different people have told me I got gypped; that the ox is nothing but bones."

"What's the angle?" Nancy asked. "Did they have a better one to sell?"

"No, they just said that it was going to be a grim Christmas because there won't be enough meat to go around. Maybe I'll get an independent judge to look at the beast in the morning."

Bright and early, Halingisi, a Tswana cattle owner, appeared at our camp. But before I could ask him to give me his opinion on Yehave's black ox, he gave me the eye signal that indicated a confidential chat. We left the camp and sat down.

"/ontah, I'm surprised at you; you've lived here for three years and still haven't learned anything about cattle."

"But what else can a person do but choose the biggest, strongest animal one can find?" I retorted.

"Look, just because an animal is big doesn't mean that it has plenty of meat on it. The black one was a beauty when it was younger, but now it is thin to the point of death."

"Well I've already bought it. What can I do at this stage?"

"Bought it already? I thought you were just considering it. Well, you'll have to kill it and serve it, I suppose. But don't expect much of a dance to follow."

My spirits dropped rapidly. I could believe that Ben!a and /gaugo just might be putting me on about the black ox, but Halingisi seemed to be an impartial critic. I went around that day feeling as though I had bought a lemon of a used car.

In the afternoon it was Tomazo's turn. Tomazo is a fine hunter, a top trance performer . . . and one of my most reliable informants. He approached the subject of the Christmas cow as part of my continuing Bushman education.

"My friend, the way it is with us Bushmen," he began, "is that we love meat. And even more than that, we love fat. When we hunt we always search for the fat ones, the ones dripping with layers of white fat: fat that turns into a clear, thick oil in the cooking pot, fat that slides down your gullet, fills your stomach and gives you a roaring diarrhea," he rhapsodized.

"So, feeling as we do," he continued, "it gives us pain to be served such a scrawny thing as Yehave's black ox. It is big, yes, and no doubt its giant bones are good for soup, but fat is what we really crave and so we will eat Christmas this year with a heavy heart."

The prospect of a gloomy Christmas now had me worried, so I asked Tomazo what I could do about it.

"Look for a fat one, a young one . . . smaller, but fat. Fat enough to make us *//gom* (evacuate the bowels), then we will be happy."

My suspicions were aroused when Tomazo said that he happened to know a young, fat, barren cow that the owner was willing to part with. Was Tomazo working on commission, I wondered? But I dispelled this unworthy thought when we approached the Herero owner of the cow in question and found that he had decided not to sell.

The scrawny wreck of a Christmas ox now became the talk of the /ai/ai water hole and was the first news told to the outlying groups as they began to come in from the bush for the feast. What finally convinced me that real trouble might be brewing was the visit from u!au, an old conservative with a reputation for fierceness. His nickname meant spear and referred to an incident thirty years ago in which he had speared a man to death. He had an intense manner; fixing me with his eyes, he said in clipped tones:

"I have only just heard about the black ox today, or else I would have come earlier. /ontah, do you honestly think you can serve meat like that to people and avoid a fight?" He paused, letting the implications sink in. "I don't mean fight you, /ontah; you are a white man. I mean a fight between Bushmen. There are many fierce ones here, and with such a small quantity of meat to distribute, how can you give everybody a fair share? Someone is sure to accuse another of taking too much or hogging all the choice pieces. Then you will see what happens when some go hungry while others eat."

The possibility of at least a serious argument struck me as all too real. I had witnessed the tension that surrounds the distribution of meat from a kudu or gemsbok kill, and had documented many arguments that sprang up from a real or imagined slight in meat distribution. The owners of a kill may spend up to two hours arranging and rearranging the piles of meat under the gaze of a circle of recipients before handing them out. And I knew that the Christmas feast at /ai/ai would be bringing together groups that had feuded in the past.

Convinced now of the gravity of the situation, I went in earnest to search for a second cow; but all my inquiries failed to turn one up.

The Christmas feast was evidently going to be a disaster, and the incessant complaints about the meagerness of the ox had already taken the fun out of it for me. Moreover, I was getting bored with the wisecracks, and after losing my temper a few times, I resolved to serve the beast anyway. If the meat fell short, the hell with it. In the Bushmen idiom, I announced to all who would listen:

"I am a poor man and blind. If I have chosen one that is too old and too thin, we will eat it anyway and see if there is enough meat there to quiet the rumbling of our stomachs."

On hearing this speech, Ben!a offered me a rare word of comfort. "It's thin," she said philosophically, "but the bones will make a good soup."

At dawn Christmas morning, instinct told me to turn over the butchering and cooking to a friend and take off with Nancy to spend Christmas alone in the bush. But curiosity kept me from retreating. I wanted to see what such a scrawny ox looked like on butchering, and if there was going to be a fight, I wanted to catch every word of it. Anthropologists are incurable that way.

The great beast was driven up to our dancing ground, and a shot in the forehead dropped it in its tracks. Then, freshly cut branches were heaped around the fallen carcass to receive the meat. Ten men volunteered to help with the cutting. I asked /gaugo to make the breast bone cut. This cut, which begins the butchering process for most large game, offers easy access for removal of the viscera. But it allows the hunter to spot-check the amount of fat on an animal. A fat game animal carries a white layer up to an inch thick on the chest, while in a thin one, the knife will quickly cut to the bone. All eyes fixed on his hand as /gaugo, dwarfed by the great carcass, knelt to the breast. The first cut opened a pool of solid white in the black skin. The second and third cut widened and deepened the creamy white. Still no bone. It was pure fat; it must have been two inches thick.

"Hey /gau," I burst out, "that ox is loaded with fat. What's this about the ox being too thin to bother eating? Are you out of your mind?"

"Fat?" /gau shot back. "You call that fat? This wreck is thin, sick, dead!" And he broke out laughing. So did everyone else. They rolled on the ground, paralyzed with laughter. Everybody laughed except me; I was thinking.

I ran back to the tent and burst in just as Nancy was getting up. "Hey, the black ox. It's fat as hell! They were kidding about it being too thin to eat. It was a joke or something. A put-on. Everyone is really delighted with it."

"Some joke," my wife replied. "It was so funny that you were ready to pack up and leave /ai/ai."

If it had indeed been a joke, it had been an extraordinarily convincing one, and tinged, I thought, with more than a touch of malice as many jokes are. Nevertheless, that it was a joke lifted my spirits considerably, and I returned to the butchering site where the shape of the ox was rapidly disappearing under the axes and knives of the butchers. The atmosphere had become festive. Grinning broadly, their arms covered with blood well past the elbow, men packed chunks of meat into the big cast-iron cooking pots, fifty pounds to the load, and muttered and chuckled all the while about the thinness and worthlessness of the animal and /ontah's poor judgment.

We danced and ate that ox two days and two nights; we cooked and distributed fourteen potfuls of meat and no one went home hungry and no fights broke out.

But the "joke" stayed in my mind. I had a growing feeling that something important had happened in my relationship with the Bushmen and that the clue lay in the meaning of the joke. Several days later, when most of the people had dispersed back to the bush camps, I raised the question with Hakekgose, a Tswana man who had grown up among the !Kung, married a !Kung girl, and who probably knows the culture better than any other non-Bushman.

"With us whites," I began, "Christmas is supposed to be the day of friendship and brotherly love. What I can't figure out is why the Bushmen went to such lengths to criticize and belittle the ox I had bought for the feast. The animal was perfectly good and their jokes and wisecracks practically ruined the holiday for me."

"So it really did bother you," said Hakekgose. "Well, that's the way they always talk. When I take my rifle and go hunting with them, if I miss, they laugh at me for the rest of the day. But even if I hit and bring one down, it's no better. To them, the kill is always too small or too old or too thin; and as we sit down on the kill site to cook and eat the liver, they keep grumbling, even with their mouths full of meat. They say things like, 'Oh, this is awful! What a worthless animal! Whatever made me think that this Tswana rascal could hunt!'"

"Is this the way outsiders are treated?" I asked.

"No, it is their custom; they talk that way to each other too. Go and ask them."

/gaugo had been one of the most enthusiastic in making me feel bad about the merit of the Christmas ox. I sought him out first.

"Why did you tell me the black ox was worthless, when you could see that it was loaded with fat and meat?"

"It is our way," he said smiling. "We always like to fool people about that. Say there is a Bushman who has been hunting. He must not come home and announce like a braggart, 'I have killed a big one in the bush!' He must first sit down in silence until I or someone else comes up to his fire and asks, 'What did you see today?' He replies quietly, 'Ah, I'm no good for hunting. I saw nothing at all (pause) just a little tiny one.' Then I smile to myself," /gaugo continued, "because I know he has killed something big.

"In the morning we make up a party of four or five people to cut up and carry the meat back to the camp. When we arrive at the kill we examine it and cry out, 'You mean to say you have dragged us all the way out here in order to make us cart home your pile of bones? Oh, if I had known it was this thin I wouldn't have come.' Another one pipes up, 'People, to think I gave up a nice day in the shade for this. At home we may be hungry but at least we have nice cool water to drink.' If the horns are big, someone says, 'Did you think that somehow you were going to boil down the horns for soup?'

"To all this you must respond in kind. 'I agree,' you say, 'this one is not worth the effort; let's just cook the liver for strength and leave the rest for the hyenas. It is not too late to hunt today and even a duiker or steenbok would be better than this mess.'

"Then you set to work nevertheless; butcher the animal, carry the meat back to the camp and everyone eats," /gaugo concluded.

Things were beginning to make sense. Next, I went to Tomazo. He corroborated /gaugo's story of the obligatory insults over a kill and added a few details of his own.

"But," I asked, "why insult a man after he has gone to all that trouble to track and kill an animal and when he is going to share the meat with you so that your children will have something to eat?"

"Arrogance," was his cryptic answer.

"Arrogance?"

"Yes, when a young man kills much meat he comes to think of himself as a chief or a big man, and he thinks of the rest of us as his servants or inferiors. We can't accept this. We refuse one who boasts, for someday his pride will make him kill somebody. So we always speak of his meat as worthless. This way we cool his heart and make him gentle."

"But why didn't you tell me this before?" I asked Tomazo with some heat.

"Because you never asked me," said Tomazo, echoing the refrain that has come to haunt every field ethnographer.

The pieces now fell into place. I had known for a long time that in situations of social conflict with Bushmen I held all the cards. I was the only source of tobacco in a thousand square miles, and I was not incapable of cutting an individual off for noncooperation. Though my boycott never lasted longer than a few days, it was an indication of my strength. People resented my presence at the water hole, yet simultaneously dreaded my leaving. In short I was a perfect target for the charge of arrogance and for the Bushman tactic of enforcing humility.

I had been taught an object lesson by the Bushmen; it had come from an unexpected corner and had hurt me in a vulnerable area. For the big black ox was to be the one totally generous, unstinting act of my year at /ai/ai and I was quite unprepared for the reaction I received.

As I read it, their message was this: There are no totally generous acts. All "acts" have an element of calculation. One black ox slaughtered at Christmas does not wipe out a year of careful manipulation of gifts given to serve your own ends. After all, to kill an animal and share the meat with people is really no more than the Bushmen do for each other every day and with far less fanfare.

In the end, I had to admire how the Bushmen had played out the farce—collectively straight-faced to the end. Curiously, the episode reminded me of the *Good Soldier Schweik* and his marvelous encounters with authority. Like Schweik, the Bushmen had retained a thoroughgoing skepticism of good intentions. Was it this independence of spirit, I wondered, that had kept them culturally viable in the face of generations of contact with more powerful societies, both black and white? The thought that the Bushmen were alive and well in the Kalahari was strangely comforting. Perhaps, armed with that independence and with their superb knowledge of their environment, they might yet survive the future.

# 32

# Our Babies, Ourselves

*Meredith F. Small*

Nature or nurture? Genes or environment? A perennial question in anthropology is the relative importance of innate human biology or particular cultural and early-childhood influences in people's social and psychological development. Cross-cultural variation in thought and behavior patterns is the hallmark of human diversity. Most anthropologists believe that there is individual variation within cultural variation. That is, members of a society share ideas of appropriate behavior, including the ways to raise children, and those shared ideas supercede individual variation. The influence of culture on personality development has been a theme in cultural anthropology since the days of Margaret Mead. These questions require us to study child-raising practices in a cross-cultural perspective.

This selection describes how parenting behaviors vary across societies. The way in which we interact with our own babies and children influences the adults they become. Sometimes we use the computer analogy of biology being the hardware (the brain) and culture as the software (the models with which we think and pattern our behavior) to think about nature and nurture. That analogy misses the fact that as babies learn they are physically shaping their neural pathways. With this in mind, the study of parenting and child development is even more important. In this regard, so-called traditional societies might have a lot to teach us. People may be reticent to learn from others ("If it was good enough for us . . .") or to change behaviors, like extended breast-feeding.

***As you read this selection, ask yourself the following questions:***

- Why do Americans put babies in their own cribs, or feed them on schedules, or "let them cry it out?" What underlying cultural values might parents be trying to teach?
- How might high infant mortality risk affect parents' behaviors?
- How much stimulation for infants is appropriate? Why did the Dutch mother put her baby down for a nap right after the bath?
- Who is best to take care of a baby? How do people decide that?
- Why do anthropologists report that babies in traditional societies like the !Kung do not cry as much?

***The following terms discussed in this selection are included in the Glossary at the back of the book:***

| | |
|---|---|
| *adaptation* | *socialization* |
| *ethnopediatrics* | *weaning* |

During one of his many trips to Gusiiland in southwestern Kenya, anthropologist Robert LeVine tried an experiment: he showed a group of Gusii mothers a videotape of middle-class American women tending their babies. The Gusii mothers were appalled. Why does that mother ignore the cries of her unhappy baby during a simple diaper change? And how come that grandmother does nothing to soothe the screaming baby in her lap? These American women, the Gusii concluded, are clearly incompetent mothers. In response, the same charge might be leveled at the Gusii by American mothers. What mother hands over her tiny infant to a six-year-old sister and expects the older child to provide adequate care? And why don't those Gusii women spend more time talking to their babies, so that they will grow up smart?

Both culture—the traditional way of doing things in a particular society—and individual experience guide parents in their tasks. When a father chooses to pick up his newborn and not let it cry, when a mother decides to bottle-feed on a schedule rather than breast-feed on

Small, M.F., R.A. LeVine, S. Harkness, C.M. Super, E.Z. Tronick, R.G. Barr, K.A. Dettwyler, & J.J. McKenna. "Our Babies, Ourselves" from *Natural History* (Oct. 1997):42–51; copyright © Natural History Magazine, Inc. 1997. Reprinted with permission.

## GUSII SURVIVAL SKILLS

*By Robert A. LeVine*

Farming peoples of subSaharan Africa have long faced the grim reality that many babies fail to survive, often succumbing to gastrointestinal diseases, malaria, or other infections. In the 1970s, when I lived among the Gusii in a small town in southwestern Kenya, infant mortality in that nation was on the decline but was still high—about eighty deaths per thousand live births during the first year, compared with about ten in the United States at that time and six to eight in Western Europe.

The Gusii grew corn, millet, and cash crops such as coffee and tea. Women handled the more routine tasks of cultivation, food processing, and trading, while men were supervisors or entrepreneurs. Many men worked at jobs outside the village, in urban centers or on plantations. The society was polygamous, with perhaps 10 percent of the men having two or more wives. A woman was expected to give birth every two years, from marriage to menopause, and the average married woman bore about ten live children—one of the highest fertility rates in the world.

Nursing mothers slept alone with a new infant for fifteen months to insure its health. For the first three to six months, the Gusii mothers were especially vigilant for signs of ill health or slow growth, and they were quick to nurture unusually small or sick infants by feeding and holding them more often. Mothers whose newborns were deemed particularly at risk—including twins and those born prematurely—entered a ritual seclusion for several weeks, staying with their infants in a hut with a constant fire.

Mothers kept infants from crying in the early months by holding them constantly and being quick to comfort them. After three to six months—if the baby was growing normally—mothers began to entrust the baby to the care of other children (usually six to twelve years old) in order to pursue tasks that helped support the family. Fathers did not take care of infants, for this was not a traditional male activity.

Because they were so worried about their children's survival, Gusii parents did not explicitly strive to foster cognitive, social, and emotional development. These needs were not neglected, however, because from birth Gusii babies entered an active and responsive interpersonal environment, first with their mothers and young caregivers, and later as part of a group of children.

demand, when a couple bring the newborn into their bed at night, they are prompted by what they believe to be the best methods of caregiving.

For decades, anthropologists have been recording how children are raised in different societies. At first, the major goals were to describe parental roles and understand how child-rearing practices and rituals helped to generate adult personality. In the 1950s, for example, John and Beatrice Whiting, and their colleagues at Harvard, Yale, and Cornell Universities, launched a major comparative study of childhood, looking at six varied communities in different regions: Okinawa, the Philippines, northern India, Kenya, Mexico, and New England. They showed that communal expectations play a major role in setting parenting styles, which in turn play a part in shaping children to become accepted adults.

More recent work by anthropologists and child-development researchers has shown that parents readily accept their society's prevailing ideology on how babies should be treated, usually because it makes sense in their environmental or social circumstances. In the United States, for example, where individualism is valued, parents do not hold babies as much as in other cultures, and they place them in rooms of their own to sleep. Pediatricians and parents alike often say this fosters independence and self-reliance. Japanese parents, in contrast, believe that individuals should be well integrated into society, and so they "indulge" their babies. Japanese infants are held more often, not left to cry, and sleep with their parents. Efe parents in Congo believe even more in a communal life, and their infants are regularly nursed, held, and comforted by any number of group members, not just parents. Whether such practices help form the anticipated adult personality traits remains to be shown, however.

Recently, a group of anthropologists, child-development experts, and pediatricians have taken the cross-cultural approach in a new direction by investigating how differing parenting styles affect infant health and growth. Instead of emphasizing the development of adult personality, these researchers, who call themselves ethnopediatricians, focus on the child as an organism. Ethnopediatricians see the human infant as a product of evolution, geared to enter a particular environment of care. What an infant actually gets is a compromise, as parents are pulled by their offspring's needs and pushed by social and personal expectations.

Compared with offspring of many other mammals, primate infants are dependent and vulnerable. Baby monkeys and apes stay close to the mother's body, clinging to her stomach or riding on her back, and nursing at will. They are protected in this way for many months, until they develop enough motor and cognitive skills to move about. Human infants are at the extreme: virtually helpless as newborns, they need

## AN INFANT'S THREE Rs

*By Sara Harkness and Charles M. Super*

You are an American visitor spending a morning in a pleasant middle-class Dutch home to observe the normal routine of a mother and her six-month-old baby. The mother made sure you got there by 8:30 to witness the morning bath, an opportunity for playful interaction with the baby. The baby was then dressed in cozy warm clothes, her hair brushed and styled with a tiny curlicue atop her head. The mother gave her the midmorning bottle, then sang to her and played patty-cake for a few minutes before placing her in the playpen to entertain herself with a mobile while the mother attended to other things nearby. Now, about half an hour later, the baby is beginning to get fussy.

The mother watches her for a minute, then offers a toy and turns away. The baby again begins to fuss. "Seems bored and in need of attention," you think. But the mother looks at the baby sympathetically and in a soothing voice says, "Oh, are you tired?" Without further ado she picks up the baby, carries her upstairs, tucks her into her crib, and pulls down the shades. To your surprise, the baby fusses for only a few more moments, then is quiet. The mother returns looking serene. "She needs plenty of sleep in order to grow," she explains. "When she doesn't have her nap or go to bed on time, we can always tell the difference—she's not so happy and playful."

Different patterns in infant sleep can be found in Western societies that seem quite similar to those of the United States. We discovered the "three Rs" of Dutch child rearing—*rust* (rest), *regelmaat* (regularity), and *reinheid* (cleanliness)—while doing research on a sample of sixty families with infants or young children in a middle-class community near Leiden and Amsterdam, the sort of community typical of Dutch life styles in all but the big cities nowadays. At six months, the Dutch babies were sleeping more than a comparison group of American babies—a total of fifteen hours per day compared with thirteen hours for the Americans. While awake at home, the Dutch babies were more often left to play quietly in their playpens or infant seats. A daily ride in the baby carriage provided time for the baby to look around at the passing scene or to doze peacefully. If the mother needed to go out for a while without the baby, she could leave it alone in bed for a short period or time her outing with the baby's nap time and ask a neighbor to monitor with a "baby phone."

To understand how Dutch families manage to establish such a restful routine by the time their babies are six months old, we made a second research visit to the same community. We found that by two weeks of age, the Dutch babies were already sleeping more than same-age American babies. In fact, a dilemma for some Dutch parents was whether to wake the baby after eight hours, as instructed by the local health care providers, or let them sleep longer. The main method for establishing and maintaining this pattern was to create a calm, regular, and restful environment for the infant throughout the day.

Far from worrying about "adequate stimulation," these mothers were conscientious about avoiding overstimulation in the form of late family outings, disruptions in the regularity of eating and sleeping, or too many things to look at or listen to. Few parents were troubled by their babies' nighttime sleep routines. Babies's feeding schedules were structured following the guidelines of the local baby clinic (a national service). If a baby continued to wake up at night when feeding was no longer considered necessary, the mother (or father) would most commonly give it a pacifier and a little back rub to help it get back to sleep. Only in rare instances did parents find themselves forced to choose between letting the baby scream and allowing too much night waking.

Many aspects of Dutch society support the three Rs throughout infancy and childhood—for example, shopping is close to home, and families usually have neighbors and relatives nearby who are available to help out with child care. The small scale of neighborhoods and a network of bicycle paths provide local play sites and a safe way for children to get around easily on their own (no "soccer moms" are needed for daily transportation!). Work sites for both fathers and mothers are also generally close to home, and there are many flexible or part-time job arrangements.

National policies for health and other social benefits insure universal coverage regardless of one's employment status, and the principle of the "family wage" has prevailed in labor relations so that mothers of infants and young children rarely work more than part-time, if at all. In many ways, the three Rs of Dutch child rearing are just one aspect of a calm and unhurried life style for the whole family.

twelve months just to learn to walk and years of social learning before they can function on their own.

Dependence during infancy is the price we pay for being hominids, members of the group of upright-walking primates that includes humans and their extinct relatives. Four million years ago, when our ancestors became bipedal, the hominid pelvis underwent a necessary renovation. At first, this new pelvic architecture presented no problem during birth because the early hominids, known as australopithecines, still had rather small brains, one-third the present size. But starting about 1.5 million years ago, human brain size ballooned. Hominid babies now had to twist and bend to pass through the birth canal, and more important, birth had to be triggered before the skull grew too big.

## DOCTOR'S ORDERS

*By Edward Z. Tronick*

In Boston, a pediatric resident is experiencing a vague sense of disquiet as she interviews a Puerto Rican mother who has brought her baby in for a checkup. When she is at work, the mother explains, the two older children, ages six and nine, take care of the two younger ones, a two-year-old and the three-month-old baby. Warning bells go off for the resident: young children cannot possibly be sensitive to the needs of babies and toddlers. And yet the baby is thriving; he is well over the ninetieth percentile in weight and height and is full of smiles.

The resident questions the mother in detail: How is the baby fed? Is the apartment safe for a two-year-old? The responses are all reassuring, but the resident nonetheless launches into a lecture on the importance of the mother to normal infant development. The mother falls silent, and the resident is now convinced that something is seriously wrong. And something is—the resident's model of child care.

The resident subscribes to what I call the "continuous care and contact" model of parenting, which demands a high level of contact, frequent feeding, and constant supervision, with almost all care provided by the mother. According to this model, a mother should also enhance cognitive development with play and verbal engagement. The pediatric resident is comfortable with this formula—she is not even conscious of it—because she was raised this way and treats her own child in the same manner. But at the Child Development Unit of Children's Hospital in Boston, which I direct, I want residents to abandon the idea that there is only one way to raise a child. Not to do so may interfere with patient care.

Many models of parenting are valid. Among Efe foragers of Congo's Ituri Forest, for example, a newborn is routinely cared for by several people. Babies are even nursed by many women. But few individuals ever play with the infant; as far as the Efe are concerned, the baby's job is to sleep.

In Peru, the Quechua swaddle their infants in a pouch of blankets that the mother, or a child caretaker, carries on her back. Inside the pouch, the infant cannot move, and its eyes are covered. Quechua babies are nursed in a perfunctory fashion, with three or four hours between feedings.

As I explain to novice pediatricians, such practices do not fit the continuous care and contact model; yet these babies grow up just fine. But my residents see these cultures as exotic, not relevant to the industrialized world. And so I follow up with examples closer to home: Dutch parents who leave an infant alone in order to go shopping, sometimes pinning the child's shirt to the bed to keep the baby on its back; or Japanese mothers who periodically wake a sleeping infant to teach the child who is in charge. The questions soon follow. "How could a mother leave her infant alone?" "Why would a parent ever want to wake up a sleeping baby?"

The data from cross-cultural studies indicate that child-care practices vary, and that these styles aim to make the child into a culturally appropriate adult. The Efe make future Efe. The resident makes future residents. A doctor who has a vague sense that something is wrong with how someone cares for a baby may first need to explore his or her own assumptions, the hidden "shoulds" that are based solely on tradition. Of course, pediatric residents must make sure children are cared for responsibly. I know I have helped residents broaden their views when their lectures on good mothering are replaced by such comments as "What a gorgeous baby! I can't imagine how you manage both work and three others at home!"

As a result, the human infant is born neurologically unfinished and unable to coordinate muscle movement. Natural selection has compensated for this by favoring a close adult–infant tie that lasts years and goes beyond meeting the needs of food and shelter. In a sense, the human baby is not isolated but is part of a physiologically and emotionally entwined dyad of infant and caregiver. The adult might be male or female, a birth or adoptive parent, as long as at least one person is attuned to the infant's needs.

The signs of this interrelationship are many. Through conditioning, a mother's breast milk often begins to flow at the sound of her own infant's cries, even before the nipple is stimulated. New mothers also easily recognize the cries (and smells) of their infants over those of other babies. For their part, newborns recognize their own mother's voice and prefer it over others. One experiment showed that a baby's heart rate quickly synchronizes with Mom's or Dad's, but not with that of a friendly stranger. Babies are also predisposed to be socially engaged with caregivers. From birth, infants move their bodies in synchrony with adult speech; they are hardwired to absorb the cadence of speech and the general nature of language. Babies quickly recognize the arrangement of a human face—two eyes, a nose, and a mouth in the right place—over other more Picasso-like rearrangements. And mothers and infants will position themselves face-to-face when they lie down to sleep.

Babies and mothers seem to follow a typical pattern of play, a coordinated waltz that moves from attention to inattention and back again. This innate

## THE CRYING GAME

*By Ronald G. Barr*

All normal human infants cry, although they vary a great deal in how much. A mysterious and still unexplained phenomenon is that crying tends to increase in the first few weeks of life, peaks in the second or third month, and then decreases. Some babies in the United States cry so much during the peak period—often in excess of three hours a day—and seem so difficult to soothe that parents come to doubt their nurturing skills or to begin to fear that their offspring is suffering from a painful disease. Some mothers discontinue nursing and switch to bottle-feeding because they believe their breast milk is insufficiently nutritious and that their infants are always hungry. In extreme cases, the crying may provoke physical abuse, sometimes even precipitating the infant's death.

A look at another culture, the !Kung San hunter-gatherers of southern Africa, provides us with an opportunity to see whether caregiving strategies have any effect on infant crying. Both the !Kung San and Western infants escalate their crying during the early weeks of life, with a similar peak at two or three months. A comparison of Dutch, American, and !Kung San infants shows that the number of individual crying episodes are virtually identical. What differs is their length: !Kung San infants cry about half as long as Western babies. This implies that caregiving can influence only some aspects of crying, such as duration.

What is particularly striking about child-rearing among the !Kung San is that infants are in constant contact with a caregiver; they are carried or held most of the time, are usually in an upright position, and are breast-fed about four times an hour for one to two minutes at a time. Furthermore, the mother almost always responds to the smallest cry or fret within ten seconds.

I believe that crying was adaptive for our ancestors. As seen in the contemporary !Kung San, crying probably elicited a quick response, and thus consisted of frequent but relatively short episodes. This pattern helped keep an adult close by to provide adequate nutrition as well as protection from predators. I have also argued that crying helped an infant forge a strong attachment with the mother and—because new pregnancies are delayed by the prolongation of frequent nursing—secure more of her caregiving resources.

In the United States, where the threat of predation has receded and adequate nutrition is usually available even without breast-feeding, crying may be less adaptive. In any case, caregiving in the United States may be viewed as a cultural experiment in which the infant is relatively more separated—and separable—from the mother, both in terms of frequency of contact and actual distance.

The Western strategy is advantageous when the mother's employment outside of the home and away from the baby is necessary to sustain family resources. But the trade-off seems to be an increase in the length of crying bouts.

social connection was tested experimentally by Jeffrey Cohn and Edward Tronick in a series of three-minute laboratory experiments at the University of Massachusetts, in which they asked mothers to act depressed and not respond to baby's cues. When faced with a suddenly unresponsive mother, a baby repeatedly reaches out and flaps around, trying to catch her eye. When this tactic does not work, the baby gives up, turning away and going limp. And when the mother begins to respond again, it takes thirty seconds for the baby to reengage.

Given that human infants arrive in a state of dependency, ethnopediatricians have sought to define the care required to meet their physical, cognitive, and emotional needs. They assume there must be ways to treat babies that have proved adaptive over time and are therefore likely to be most appropriate. Surveys of parenting in different societies reveal broad patterns. In almost all cultures, infants sleep with their parents in the same room and most often in the same bed. At all other times, infants are usually carried. Caregivers also usually respond quickly to infant cries; mothers most often by offering the breast. Since most hunter-gatherer groups also follow this overall style, this is probably the ancestral pattern. If there is an exception to these generalizations, it is the industrialized West.

Nuances of caretaking, however, do vary with particular social situations. !Kung San mothers of Botswana usually carry their infants on gathering expeditions, while the forest-living Ache of Paraguay, also hunters and gatherers, usually leave infants in camp while they gather. Gusii mothers working in garden plots leave their babies in the care of older children, while working mothers in the West may turn to unrelated adults. Such choices have physiological or behavioral consequences for the infant. As parents navigate between infant needs and the constraints of making a life, they may face a series of trade-offs that set the caregiver–infant dyad at odds. The areas of greatest controversy are breast-feeding, crying, and sleep—the major preoccupations of babies and their parents.

Strapped to their mothers' sides or backs in traditional fashion, human infants have quick access to the breast. Easy access makes sense because of the nature of human milk. Compared with that of other mammals,

## WHEN TO WEAN

*By Katherine A. Dettwyler*

Breast-feeding in humans is a biological process grounded in our mammalian ancestry. It is also an activity modified by social and cultural constraints, including a mother's everyday work schedule and a variety of beliefs about personal autonomy, the proper relationship between mother and child (or between mother and father), and infant health and nutrition. The same may be said of the termination of breast-feeding, or weaning.

In the United States, children are commonly bottle-fed from birth or weaned within a few months. But in some societies, children as old as four or five years may still be nursed. The American Academy of Pediatrics currently advises breast-feeding for a minimum of one year (this may be revised upward), and the World Health Organization recommends two years or more. Amid conflicting advice, many wonder how long breast-feeding should last to provide an infant with optimal nutrition and health.

Nonhuman primates and other mammals give us some clues as to what the "natural" age of weaning would be if humans were less bound by cultural norms. Compared with most other orders of placental mammals, primates (including humans) have longer life spans and spend more time at each life stage, such as gestation, infant dependency, and puberty. Within the primate order itself, the trend in longevity increases from smaller-bodied, smaller-brained, often solitary prosimians through the larger-bodied, larger-brained, and usually social apes and humans. Gestation, for instance, is eighteen weeks in lemurs, twenty-four weeks in macaques, thirty-three weeks in chimpanzees, and thirty-eight weeks in humans.

Studies of nonhuman primates offer a number of different means of estimating the natural time for human weaning. First, large-bodied primates wean their offspring some months after the young have quadrupled their birth weight. In modern humans, this weight milestone is passed at about two and a half to three years of age. Second, like many other mammals, primate offspring tend to be weaned when they have attained about one third of their adult human weight; humans reach this level between four and seven years of age. Third, in all species studied so far, primates also wean their offspring at the time the first permanent molars erupt; this occurs at five and a half to six years in modern humans. Fourth, in chimpanzees and gorillas, breast-feeding usually lasts about six times the duration of gestation. On this basis, a human breast-feeding would be projected to continue for four and a half years.

Taken together, these and other projections suggest that somewhat more than two and a half years is the natural minimum age of weaning for humans and seven years the maximum age, well into childhood. The high end of this range, six to seven years, closely matches both the completion of human brain growth and the maturation of the child's immune system.

In many non-Western cultures, children are routinely nursed for three to five years. Incidentally, this practice inhibits ovulation in the mother, providing a natural mechanism of family planning. Even in the United States, a significant number of children are breast-fed beyond three years of age. While not all women are able or willing to nurse each of their children for many years, those who do should be encouraged and supported. Health care professionals, family, friends, and nosy neighbors should be reassured that "extended" breast-feeding, for as long as seven years, appears physiologically normal and natural.

Substantial evidence is already available to suggest that curtailing the duration of breast-feeding far below two and a half years—when the human child has evolved to expect more—can be deleterious. Every study that includes the duration of breast-feeding as a variable shows that, on average, the longer a baby is nursed, the better its health and cognitive development. For example, breast-fed children have fewer allergies, fewer ear infections, and less diarrhea, and their risk for sudden infant death syndrome (a rare but devastating occurrence) is lower. Breast-fed children also have higher cognitive test scores and lower incidence of attention deficit hyperactivity disorder.

In many cases, specific biochemical constituents of breast milk have been identified that either protect directly against disease or help the child's body develop its own defense system. For example, in the case of many viral diseases, the baby brings the virus to the mother, and her gut-wall cells manufacture specific antibodies against the virus, which then travel to the mammary glands and go back to the baby. The docosahexanoic acid in breast milk may be responsible for improved cognitive and attention functions. And the infant's exposure to the hormones and cholesterol in the milk appears to condition the body, reducing the risk of heart disease and breast cancer in later years. These and other discoveries show that breast-feeding serves functions for which no simple substitute is available.

primate milk is relatively low in fat and protein but high in carbohydrates. Such milk is biologically suitable if the infant can nurse on a frequent basis. Most Western babies are fed in a somewhat different way. At least half are bottle-fed from birth, while others are weaned from breast to bottle after only a few months. And most—whether nursed or bottle-fed—are fed at scheduled times, waiting hours between feedings. Long intervals in nursing disrupt the manufacture of breast milk, making it still lower in fat and thus less

## BEDTIME STORY

*By James J. McKenna*

For as far back as you care to go, mothers have followed the protective and convenient practice of sleeping with their infants. Even now, for the vast majority of people across the globe, "cosleeping" and nighttime breast-feeding remain inseparable practices. Only in the past 200 years, and mostly in Western industrialized societies, have parents considered it normal and biologically appropriate for a mother and infant to sleep apart.

In the sleep laboratory at the University of California's Irvine School of Medicine, my colleagues and I observed mother–infant pairs as they slept both apart and together over three consecutive nights. Using a polygraph, we recorded the mother's and infant's heart rates, brain waves (EEGs), breathing, body temperature, and episodes of nursing. Infrared video photography simultaneously monitored their behavior.

We found that bed-sharing infants face their mothers for most of the night and that both mother and infant are highly responsive to each other's movements, wake more frequently, and spend more time in lighter stages of sleep than they do while sleeping alone. Bed-sharing infants nurse almost twice as often, and three times as long per bout, than they do while sleeping alone. But they rarely cry. Mothers who routinely sleep with their infants get at least as much sleep as mothers who sleep without them.

In addition to providing more nighttime nourishment and greater protection, sleeping with the mother supplies the infant with a steady stream of sensations of the mother's presence, including touch, smell, movement, and warmth. These stimuli can perhaps even compensate for the human infant's extreme neurological immaturity at birth.

Cosleeping might also turn out to give some babies protection from sudden infant death syndrome (SIDS), a heartbreaking and enigmatic killer. Cosleeping infants nurse more often, sleep more lightly, and have practice responding to maternal arousals. Arousal deficiencies are suspected in some SIDS deaths, and long periods in deep sleep may exacerbate this problem. Perhaps the physiological changes induced by cosleeping, especially when combined with nighttime breast-feeding, can benefit some infants by helping them sleep more lightly. At the same time, cosleeping makes it easier for a mother to detect and respond to an infant in crisis. Rethinking another sleeping practice has already shown a dramatic effect: In the United States, SIDS rates fell at least 30 percent after 1992, when the American Academy of Pediatrics recommended placing sleeping babies on their backs, rather than face down.

The effect of cosleeping on SIDS remains to be proved, so it would be premature to recommend it as the best arrangement for all families. The possible hazards of cosleeping must also be assessed. Is the environment otherwise safe, with appropriate bedding materials? Do the parents smoke? Do they use drugs or alcohol? (These appear to be the main factors in those rare cases in which a mother inadvertently smothers her child.) Since cosleeping was the ancestral condition, the future for our infants may well entail a borrowing back from ancient ways.

---

satisfying the next time the nipple is offered. And so crying over food and even the struggles of weaning result from the infant's unfulfilled expectations.

Sleep is also a major issue for new parents. In the West, babies are encouraged to sleep all through the night as soon as possible. And when infants do not do so, they merit the label "sleep problem" from both parents and pediatricians. But infants seem predisposed to sleep rather lightly, waking many times during the night. And while sleeping close to an adult allows infants to nurse more often and may have other beneficial effects, Westerners usually expect babies to sleep alone. This practice has roots in ecclesiastical laws enacted to protect against the smothering of infants by "lying over"—often a thinly disguised cover for infanticide—which was a concern in Europe beginning in the Middle Ages. Solitary sleep is reinforced by the rather recent notion of parental privacy. Western parents are also often convinced that solitary sleep will mold strong character.

Infant care is shaped by traditions, fads, science, and folk wisdom. Cross-cultural and evolutionary studies provide a useful perspective for parents and pediatricians as they sift through the alternatives. Where these insights fail to guide us, however, important clues are provided by the floppy but interactive babies themselves. Grinning when we talk to them, crying in distress when left alone, sleeping best when close at heart, they teach us that growth is a cooperative venture.

when a previous child has died in infancy. Manuel Lizarralde claims the strategy makes perfect sense, given the Barí belief that the best way to cure a sick child is for the father to blow tobacco smoke over the child's body. "It is easy to imagine a bereaved mother thinking to herself that if she had only provided a secondary father and so more smoke for her dead child, she might have saved him—and vowing to provide that benefit for her next child."

Beckerman says extra fathers may have always been insurance for uncertain times: "Because the Barí were once hunted as if they were game animals—by other Indians, conquistadors, oilmen, farmers, and ranchers—the odds of a woman being widowed when she still had young children were one in three, according to data we gathered about the years 1930 to 1960. The men as well as the women knew this. None of these guys can go down the street to Mutual of Omaha and buy a life insurance policy. By allowing his wife to take a lover, the husband is doing all he can to ensure the survival of his children."

Barí women are also freer to do as they wish because men need their labor—having a wife is an economic necessity because women do the manioc farming, harvesting, and cooking, while men hunt and fish. "The sexual division of labor is such that you can't make it without a member of the opposite sex," says Beckerman. Initially, the researchers worried that jealousy on the part of husbands would make Barí women reticent about discussing multiple sexual partners. "In our first interviews, we would wait until the husband was out of the house," says Beckerman. "But one day we interviewed an old couple who were enjoying thinking about their lives; they were lying in their hammocks, side by side, and it was obvious he wasn't going anywhere. So we went down the list of her children and asked about other fathers. She said no, no, no for each child, and then the husband interrupted when we got to one and said, 'That's not true, don't you remember, there was that guy . . .' And the husband was grinning."

Not all women take lovers. Manuel Lizarralde has discovered through interviews that one-third of 122 women were faithful to their husbands during their pregnancies. "These women say they don't need it, or no one asked, or they have enough support from family and don't require another father for their child," Lizarralde says. "Some even admit that their husbands were not that happy about the idea." Or it may be a sign of changing times. Based on his most recent visits to the Barí, Lizarralde thinks that under the influence of Western values, the number of people who engage in multiple fatherhood may be decreasing. But his father, who has worked with the Barí for more than 40 years, disagrees. He says the practice is as frequent but that the Barí discuss it less openly than before, knowing that Westerners object to their views. After all, it took the anthropologists 20 years to hear about other fathers, and today the Barí are probably being even more discreet because they know Westerners disapprove of their beliefs.

"What this information adds up to," Beckerman says, "is that the Barí may be doing somewhat less fooling around within marriage these days but that most of them still believe that a child can have multiple fathers."

More important, the Barí idea that biological paternity can be shared is not just the quirky custom of one tribe; anthropologists have found that this idea is common across South America. The same belief is shared by indigenous groups in New Guinea and India, suggesting that multiple paternity has been part of human behavior for a long time, undermining all previous descriptions of how human mating behavior evolved.

Since the 1960s, when anthropologists began to construct scenarios of early human mating, they had always assumed that the model family started with a mom and dad bonded for life to raise the kids, a model that fit well with acceptable Western behavior. In 1981 in an article titled "The Origin of Man," C. Owen Lovejoy, an anthropologist at Kent State University, outlined the standard story of human evolution as it was used in the field—and is still presented in textbooks today: Human infants with their big brains and long periods of growth and learning have always been dependent on adults, a dependence that separates the humans from the apes. Mothers alone couldn't possibly find enough food for these dependent young, so women have always needed to find a mate who would stick close to home and bring in supplies for the family. Unfortunately for women, as evolutionary psychologists suggest, men are compelled by their biology to mate with as many partners as possible to pass along their genes. However, each of these men might be manipulated into staying with one woman who offered him sex and a promise of fidelity. The man, under those conditions, would be assured of paternity, and he might just stay around and make sure his kids survived.

This scenario presents humans as naturally monogamous, forming nuclear families as an evolutionary necessity. The only problem is that around the world families don't always operate this way. In fact, as the Barí and other cultures show, there are all sorts of ways to run a successful household.

The Na of Yunnan Province in China, for example, have a female-centric society in which husbands are not part of the picture. Women grow up and continue to live with their mothers, sisters, and brothers; they never marry or move away from the family compound. As a result, sisters and brothers rather than married pairs are the economic unit that farms and fishes together. Male lovers in this system are simply visitors. They have no place or power in the household, and children are brought up by their mothers and by the mothers' brothers. A father is identified only if there is a resemblance between him and the child, and even so, the father has no responsibilities toward the child. Often women have sex with so many partners that the biological father is unknown. "I have not found any term that would cover the notion of father in the Na language," writes Chinese anthropologist Cai Hua in his book *A Society Without Fathers or Husbands: The Na of China*. In this case, women have complete control over their children, property, and sexuality.

Across lowland South America, family systems vary because cultures put their beliefs into practice in different ways. Among some native people, such as the Canela, Mehinaku, and Araweté, women control their sex lives and their fertility, and most children have several fathers. Barí women are also sexually liberated from an early age. "Once she has completed her puberty ritual, a Barí girl can have sex with anyone she wants as long as she doesn't violate the incest taboo," Beckerman explains. "It's nobody's business, not even Mom's and Dad's business." Women can also turn down prospective husbands.

In other cultures in South America, life is not so free for females, although members of these cultures also believe that babies can have more than one father. The Curripaco of Amazonia, for instance, acknowledge multiple fatherhood as a biological possibility and yet frown on women having affairs. Paul Valentine, a senior lecturer in anthropology at the University of East London who has studied the Curripaco for more than 20 years, says, "Curripaco women are in a difficult situation. The wives come into the village from different areas, and it's a very patrilineal system." If her husband dies, a widow is allowed to turn only to his brothers or to clan members on his side of the family for a new husband.

The relative power of women and men over their sex lives has important consequences. "In certain social and economic systems, women are free to make mate choices," says Valentine. In these cultures women are often the foundation of society, while men have less power in the community. Sisters tend to stay in the same household as their mothers. The women, in other words, have power to make choices. "At the other extreme, somehow, it's the men who try to maximize their evolutionary success at the expense of the women," says Valentine.

Men and women often have a conflict of interest when it comes to mating, marriage, and who should invest most in children, and the winners have sometimes been the men, sometimes the women. As Beckerman wryly puts it, "Anyone who believes that in a human mating relationship the man's reproductive interests always carry the day has obviously never been married."

The Barí and others show that human systems are, in fact, very flexible, ready to accommodate any sort of mating system or type of family. "I think that human beings are capable of making life extremely complicated. That's our way of doing business," says Ian Tattersall, a paleoanthropologist and curator in the division of anthropology at the American Museum of Natural History in New York City. Indeed, such flexibility suggests there's no reason to assume that the nuclear family is the natural, ideal, or even most evolutionarily successful system of human grouping. As Beckerman says, "One of the things this research shows is that human beings are just as clever and creative in assembling their kin relations as they are putting together space shuttles or symphonies."

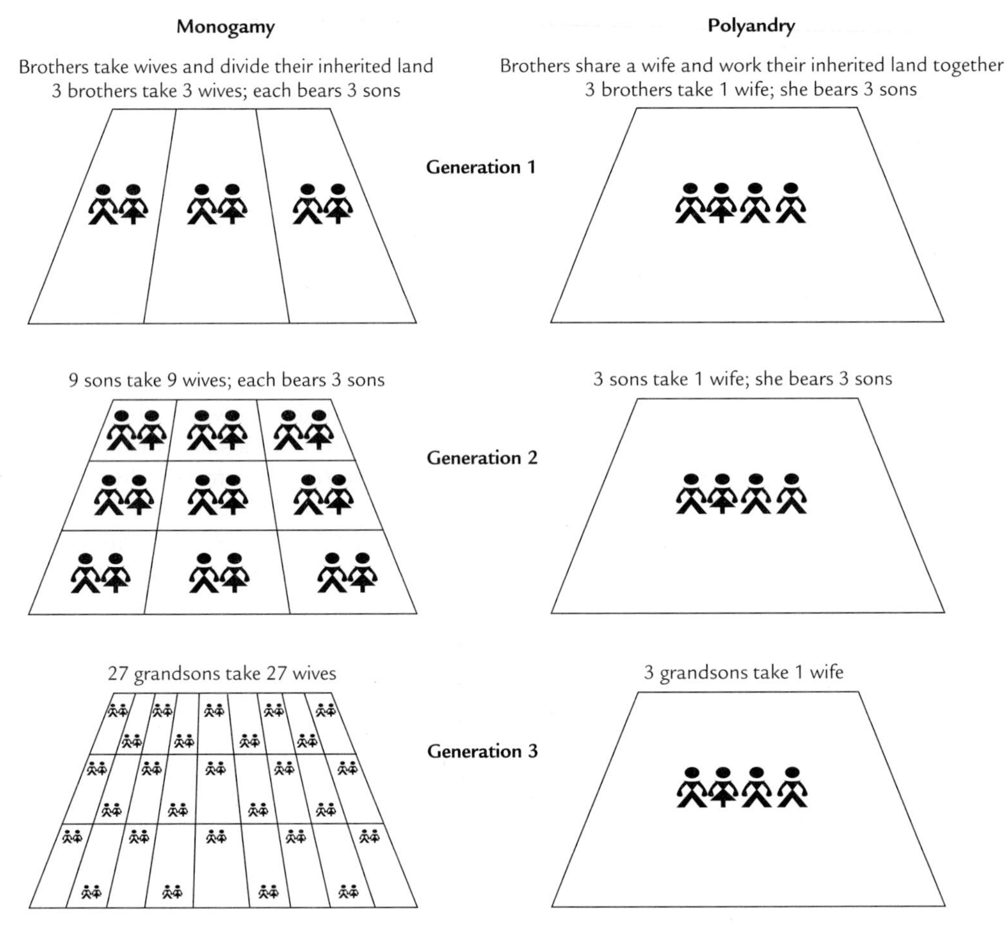


Goldstein, Melvyn C. "When Brothers Share a Wife" from *Natural History* (March 1987):39-48. Illustration reprinted with permission of Joe LeMonnier.

senior. Sometimes such a bride finds the youngest husband immature and adolescent and does not treat him with equal affection; alternatively, she may find his youth attractive and lavish special attention on him. Apart from this consideration, when a younger male like Dorje grows up, he may consider his wife "ancient" and prefer the company of a woman his own age or younger. Consequently, although men and women do not find the idea of sharing a bride or a bridegroom repulsive, individual likes and dislikes can cause familial discord.

Two reasons have commonly been offered for the perpetuation of fraternal polyandry in Tibet: that Tibetans practice female infanticide and therefore have to marry polyandrously, owing to a shortage of females; and that Tibet, lying at extremely high altitudes, is so barren and bleak that Tibetans would starve without resort to this mechanism. A Jesuit who lived in Tibet in the eighteenth century articulated this second view: "One reason for this most odious custom is the sterility of the soil, and the small amount of land that can be cultivated owing to the lack of water. The crops may suffice if the brothers all live together, but if they form separate families they would be reduced to beggary."

Both explanations are wrong, however. Not only has there never been institutionalized female infanticide in Tibet, but Tibetan society gives females considerable rights, including inheriting the family estate in the absence of brothers. In such cases, the woman takes a bridegroom who comes to live in her family and adopts her family's name and identity. Moreover, there is no demographic evidence of a shortage of females. In Limi, for example, there were (in 1974) sixty females and fifty-three males in the fifteen- to thirty-five-year age category, and many adult females were unmarried.

The second reason is also incorrect. The climate in Tibet is extremely harsh, and ecological factors do play a major role perpetuating polyandry, but polyandry is not a means of preventing starvation. It is characteristic, not of the poorest segments of the society, but rather of the peasant landowning families.

In the old society, the landless poor could not realistically aspire to prosperity, but they did not fear starvation. There was a persistent labor shortage throughout Tibet, and very poor families with little or no land and few animals could subsist through agricultural labor, tenant farming, craft occupations such as carpentry, or by working as servants. Although the per person family income could increase somewhat if brothers married polyandrously and pooled their wages, in the absence of inheritable land, the advantage of fraternal polyandry was not generally sufficient to prevent them from setting up their own households. A more skilled or energetic younger brother could do as well or better alone, since he would completely control his income and would not have to share it with his siblings. Consequently, while there was and is some polyandry among the poor, it is much less frequent and more prone to result in divorce and family fission.

An alternative reason for the persistence of fraternal polyandry is that it reduces population growth (and thereby reduces the pressure on resources) by relegating some females to lifetime spinsterhood. Fraternal polyandrous marriages in Limi (in 1974) averaged 2.35 men per woman, and not surprisingly, 31 percent of the females of child-bearing age (twenty to forty-nine) were unmarried. These spinsters either continued to live at home, set up their own households, or worked as servants for other families. They could also become Buddhist nuns. Being unmarried is not synonymous with exclusion from the reproductive pool. Discreet extramarital relationships are tolerated, and actually half of the adult unmarried women in Limi had one or more children. They raised these children as single mothers, working for wages or weaving cloth and blankets for sale. As a group, however, the unmarried women had far fewer offspring than the married women, averaging only 0.7 children per woman, compared with 3.3 for married women, whether polyandrous, monogamous, or polygynous. While polyandry helps regulate population, this function of polyandry is not consciously perceived by Tibetans and is not the reason they consistently choose it.

If neither a shortage of females nor the fear of starvation perpetuates fraternal polyandry, what motivates brothers, particularly younger brothers, to opt for this system of marriage? From the perspective of the younger brother in a landholding family, the main incentive is the attainment or maintenance of the good life. With polyandry, he can expect a more secure and higher standard of living, with access not only to his family's land and animals, but also to its inherited collection of clothes, jewelry, rugs, saddles, and horses. In addition, he will experience less work pressure and much greater security because all responsibility does not fall on one "father." For Tibetan brothers, the question is whether to trade off the greater personal freedom inherent in monogamy for the real or potential economic security, affluence, and social prestige associated with life in a larger, labor-rich polyandrous family.

A brother thinking of separating from his polyandrous marriage and taking his own wife would face various disadvantages. Although in the majority of Tibetan regions all brothers theoretically have rights to their family's estate, in reality Tibetans are reluctant to divide their land into small fragments. Generally, a younger brother who insists on leaving the family will receive only a small plot of land, if that. Because of its power and wealth, the rest of the family usually can block any attempt of the younger brother to increase his share of land through litigation. Moreover, a younger brother may not even get a house and cannot expect to receive much above the minimum in terms of movable possessions, such as furniture, pots, and pans. Thus, a brother contemplating going it on his own must plan on achieving economic security and the good life not through inheritance but through his own work.

The obvious solution for younger brothers—creating new fields from virgin land—is generally not a feasible option. Most Tibetan populations live at high altitudes (above 12,000 feet), where arable land is extremely scarce. For example, in Dorje's village, agriculture ranges only from about 12,900 feet, the lowest point in the area, to 13,300 feet. Above that altitude, early frost and snow destroy the staple barley crop. Furthermore, because of the low rainfall caused by the Himalayan rain shadow, many areas in Tibet and northern Nepal that are within appropriate altitude range for agriculture have no reliable sources of irrigation. In the end, although there is plenty of unused land in such areas, most of it is either too high or too arid.

Even where unused land capable of being farmed exists, clearing the land and building the substantial terraces necessary for irrigation constitute a great undertaking. Each plot has to be completely dug out to a depth of two to two and a half feet so that the large rocks and boulders can be removed. At best, a man might be able to bring a few new fields under cultivation in the first years after separating from his brothers, but he could not expect to acquire substantial amounts of arable land this way.

In addition, because of the limited farmland, the Tibetan subsistence economy characteristically includes a strong emphasis on animal husbandry. Tibetan farmers regularly maintain cattle, yaks, goats, and sheep, grazing them in the areas too high for agriculture. These herds produce wool, milk, cheese, butter, meat, and skins. To obtain these resources, however, shepherds must accompany the animals on a daily basis. When first setting up a monogamous household, a younger brother like Dorje would find it difficult to both farm and manage animals.

In traditional Tibetan society, there was an even more critical factor that operated to perpetuate fraternal polyandry—a form of hereditary servitude somewhat analogous to serfdom in Europe. Peasants were tied to large estates held by aristocrats, monasteries, and the Lhasa government. They were allowed the use of some farmland to produce their own subsistence but were required to provide taxes in kind and corvée (free labor) to their lords. The corvée was a substantial hardship, since a peasant household was in many cases required to furnish the lord with one laborer daily for most of the year and more on specific occasions such as the harvest. This enforced labor, along with the lack of new land and the ecological pressure to pursue both agriculture and animal husbandry, made polyandrous families particularly beneficial. The polyandrous family allowed an internal division of adult labor, maximizing economic advantage. For example, while the wife worked the family fields, one brother could perform the lord's corvée, another could look after the animals, and a third could engage in trade.

Although social scientists often discount other people's explanations of why they do things, in the case of Tibetan fraternal polyandry, such explanations are very close to the truth. The custom, however, is very sensitive to changes in its political and economic milieu and, not surprisingly, is in decline in most Tibetan areas. Made less important by the elimination of the traditional serf-based economy, it is disparaged by the dominant non-Tibetan leaders of India, China, and Nepal. New opportunities for economic and social mobility in these countries, such as the tourist trade and government employment, are also eroding the rationale for polyandry, and so it may vanish within the next generation.

# 35

# How Families Work

## *Love, Labor and Mediated Oppositions in American Domestic Ritual*

*Mark Auslander*

All human groups engage in rituals that involve both action and meaning. Rituals are often sacred, but they can also be secular. Anthropologists have long noted that rituals are organized group actions or ceremonies that have a set sequence, ritual objects, and historical continuity. Many rituals mark the passage of time in either the social life cycle (i.e., rites of passage) or the annual calendar. Rituals are part of cultural "tradition" through which people create meaning through the use of symbols.

Humans use religion and ritual to help them "make sense" of the mysteries, challenges, and paradoxes of their lives. Anthropological research about cultural rituals requires the interpretation of such symbols and symbolic acts so that we can better understand their deeper meaning and social functions. However, the participants themselves seldom engage in such symbolic interpretation because "this is the way we have always done things." Local people sometimes find the anthropologist's symbolic interpretation problematic.

In this selection, Mark Auslander interprets the domestic rituals of middle-class American society as a way to mediate between two opposing parts of life—work and family. In our socioeconomic system, work involves productivity, whereas family involves kinship and emotions like love. These two worlds are in structural opposition because they imply different ideas about the purpose of life. He argues that these two worlds are ritually mediated through economic consumption and reciprocal gift-giving. In a sense, the American nuclear family is designed to self-destruct and regenerate from generation to generation. Family rituals, even if they are relatively recent historical inventions, evoke feelings of nostalgia and tradition even when one family is ending and another beginning. Auslander begins his analysis in the classic anthropological tradition of cross-cultural comparison. He uses an interpretation of a ritual of the Ngoni, an African people, as a lens for understanding American domestic rituals like Halloween, Thanksgiving, Christmas, and especially the "White Wedding." As a member of American society, you might have some problems with the anthropological interpretation of your own domestic rituals, but that may be because it is so difficult to see our own culture from within.

***As you read this selection, ask yourself the following questions:***

- Why do many Americans spend so much money on weddings? On Christmas?
- What does the author intend with the double meaning of the title?
- How and why are the rituals of the American "holiday season" focused on children?
- How does the Ngoni mugeniso ritual help ease tensions between the two opposing kinship groups in a patrilineal society? Why are cows important?
- What might be people's reaction to possible "mistakes" in a ritual like a wedding?
- What is more important—love or work? If you were an anthropologist from Mars, how would you know?

***The following terms discussed in this section are included in the Glossary in the back of the book:***

*cultural mediation*
*kinship*
*ritual*
*rites of passage*
*social reproduction*

## INTRODUCTION

Sigmund Freud, dark prophet of the bourgeois psyche, once famously defined sanity as the capacity to "love and work." Yet balancing and integrating

Auslander, Mark. "How Families Work: Love, Labor and Mediated Oppositions in American Domestic Ritual." Reprinted by permission of the author.

these fundamental imperatives, paired enterprises that Freud suggestively termed the "parents of human civilization," has not proved easy for middle-class families from Freud's time onwards. The relentless pursuit of getting and spending in the outer world has long threatened to overwhelm the domestic domain, even if the home fires are in principle exempted from the frigid logic of the marketplace. Home may be where the heart is, but declarations of love are deeply embedded in the symbolic media of material consumption and the workplace-whether one chooses to say it with flowers and diamonds or by developing intricate activity schedules for children. For all of its troubling and troubled aspects, modern work has come in many respects to be thought of as the measure of all things, the preeminent source of self-worth and fulfillment. Work promises an escape from the complex, fraught psychic terrain of the family so long ago excavated by Freud and his disciples, while leaving many with the sense that in the pursuit of work they have betrayed key obligations to loved ones.

My title, "how families work," evokes these intertwined paradoxes of middle-class domestic life. In most societies for most of human history, the reproduction of the family within larger social frameworks has been a directly economic enterprise, since the family was usually a primary productive unit. The work of kinship in most other societies has been profoundly continuous with other forms of work, the processes through which persons transform natural elements into cultural products and through which they exchange abstract signs of their labor and productive capacity—in the form of shells, cattle, women, money or other valued media. In contrast, since the mid 19th century the western bourgeois family has been formally defined as the social unit most directly opposed to the domain of work and commerce. The family has long been idealized as a haven in a heartless world, a secure enclave that protects its members from the predations of wage labor and financial calculation, a clearly-bounded zone within which unconditional love and sentiment reign supreme. "Family time" has in principle long been contrasted with its antithesis, "work time."

Nonetheless, the middle-class family has since its inception been intimately enmeshed within the cultural logics and practical necessities of capitalist labor regimes. In normative terms, "making a living" has usually implied supporting a family. Middle-class wage levels have, in principle at least, been tied to the cultural ideal of home ownership and reproducing a subsequent generation at least at the same socioeconomic level as its antecedents. Since the high Victorian era the family and home life have been expected to restore and replenish exhausted wage earners, readying them for productive re-engagement in the business world. Middle-class families have been structured, in conjunction with the middle and upper tiers of the educational system, to reproduce a set of dispositions and orientations in each new generation, so as to meet the emerging labor requirements of the managerial and professional markets. Consumer spending for Christmas and other family holidays has for generations been understood as a bedrock of the national economy. In many respects, then, although the site of the "family" is usually formally contrasted with sites of "work," our families are "at work" continuously, laboring to support externally oriented economic productivity while constituting the home as a uniquely privileged site of "love," in both romantic and non-romantic senses of the term.

For over a century, ritual has proven an especially apt medium for dramatizing, and to some extent redressing, this fundamental tension between love and labor in middle-class households. Rituals of the family have also served to mediate, with varying degrees of success, a set of related, pervasive oppositions in modern American kinship and society, including those between the (natal) family of orientation and the (affinal) family of procreation, between immediate and extended families, between autonomy and dependence, between the claims of self and community, between nature and culture, and between life and death, as well as across the complex boundaries of generation, class, race and gender. Ritual practices ranging from Christmas and Halloween to family reunions and funerals simultaneously help constitute and crosscut these fundamental categorical distinctions (Herve, 1977; Bradd, 2003).

The enormous, fraught burdens placed on middle-class "family time" and on the domestic rituals staged within it may be conceived in terms of the contradictory overall social organization of temporality and labor in modern society. Modern conceptions of personhood are fundamentally tied to economically productive labor: the question "what do you do?" is the single most salient inquiry for middle-class Americans about an interlocutor's status and identity. Yet in the chaos of the marketplace, persons continuously risk being rendered anonymous, their labor time commoditized, their contributions rendered abstract or invisible, their projects absorbed without a trace. As businesses go under, jobs are lost and economies shift, familiar guideposts, through which persons might have kept track of their life progress, may swiftly vanish. The bourgeois family system is expected, in a compensatory fashion, to provide an enduring architecture of temporal continuity, telling its members where they have come from and where they are going. The family is, in effect, charged with maintaining coherent temporal scaffolds for making sense of relations between past, present and future, and most directly, with providing its members with reassuring visions of a viable future.

Yet in contrast to earlier bourgeois dynastic families, of the type memorialized by Thomas Mann in his novel *Buddenbrooks*, modern American middle-class nuclear families are structured to self-destruct each generation (Thomas, 1994). As Bradd Shore argues our children are trained, often in subtle ways, to detach themselves from their natal families and homes, even during moments when the values of family continuity and stability appear to be most manifestly celebrated (Bradd, 2003). In family rituals and everyday domestic scenarios, our children are socialized into achieving multiple futures, which are not always mutually consistent. They are told, in effect, that "the family" is as eternal as the Christmas tree or menorah, yet are conditioned to seek ultimate fulfillment by becoming parents themselves and presiding over an independent household of their own. Simultaneously, they learn that real self-definition depends upon economic productivity in the workplace and that adult citizenship is achieved through autonomous commodity consumption, governed by the prevailing fashions of the market.

Not surprisingly, these ambiguous ritual messages yield decidedly ambiguous consequences for family members. At times, those participating in domestic rituals derive a reassuring sense of coordinated wholeness and fulfillment, experiencing lineal continuity that coherently stretches back through the generations to time immemorial. Yet at other times, participation in these rites can provoke profound crises of faith, foregrounding failed attempts to balance love and work, deep anxiety over the validity and sincerity of family relations, and nagging doubts over market-governed definitions of worldly success.

Since the early 1970s, as the overt economic mobilization of American middle-class families has dramatically intensified, the double-edged potentials of family rituals to heal or harm have arguably increased. As both parents are increasingly engaged in (or at least looking for) full time employment, and as time available for sentimental expressions seems to be more and more compressed, time-limited ritual occasions have been correspondingly idealized and elaborated. Ironically, as work increasingly invades the home, family rituals are often researched, planned and pursued with work-like intensity, in the apparent hope of restoring the categorical distinctions between work and family, and between labor and love that have long been eroded in practice. In a society that often expresses skepticism over the value of "mere" ritual, the stakes for family ritual—and for the "family time" that these rituals epitomize—may be higher than ever before.

## WHAT IS RITUAL AND HOW DOES IT WORK?

Anthropologists have studied ritual since the discipline's inception, and many would regard the study of "ritual" as one of the few, distinctive features of anthropological inquiry left (Erving, 1967). Yet there is little consensus as to the definition, organization, consequences or ultimate efficacy of ritual action. Most would agree that ritual is a highly structured and prescribed form of action, in which actors tend to deny the ultimate authorship of their acts, ascribing their motive force to an external authority (be it the gods, the ancestors, law, or tradition) and in which participants understand themselves to be in a context significantly different from ordinary life. The internal structure of ritual is often characterized by intensive repetition, reversibility, severe restrictions on improvisation and accessibility, strict regulation of bodily comportment and emotional expression, marked distinctions in the time and place of performance, secrecy or elaborate control over perception (as in masking or the use of esoteric or archaic language and other restricted codes), the use of highly meaningful words and objects, and the simultaneous deployment of multiple (and usually multisensory) channels of communication and expression, often including music and dance. Yet many activities that would be generally recognized as "ritual" do not exhibit many of these characteristics, and some actions sharing many of these qualities would not necessarily be classified as "ritual" in the strictest sense.

Perhaps because of the multiple frames and meanings embedded in ritual practice, scholarly discussion of the topic is invariably marked by dispute, hedging and qualifying. Rituals often uphold the established sociocultural order and status quo, tending to socialize persons into taken-for-granted commonplace assumptions about the world (Fustel, 1980; Emile, 1915; Claude, 1966; Pierre, 1977; Maurice, 1989). Yet ritual arenas are especially well suited to the ambiguous dramatization of paradox and may challenge, subvert or resist dominant sensibilities and structures of authority (Victor, 1969; Carlo, 1986; Stuart, 1993; David, 1985; Pater, 1986; Jean, 1985). Ritual is often associated with intensive faith, yet ritual performance, notes Rappaport is not necessarily coincident with belief in any manifest sense of the term (Roy, 1999).

(Consider Niels Bohr's reputed response to a student shocked that he hung a luck-bringing horseshoe in his laboratory: "Of course I don't believe in the horseshoe, but I understand that my lack of belief has no negative impact upon its efficacy!") Ritual tends to integrate practitioners into wider social collectivities, yet there are extensively documented private (non-shared) rituals and ritual activities may dramatize the radical separation of a person or persons from the larger social field (Keith, 1969; Dick, 1979). Ritual generally proceeds by imposing radical separations between persons, objects and categories but tends to establish intimate conjoining or unions between that which had been rendered distinct (Claude, 1966; Valerio, 1985; Nancy, 1992). Ritual is usually thought of as solemn, yet is sometimes playful, hilarious or uproarious (Huizinga, 1949; Mikhail, 1968; Clifford, 1973; Keith, 1979). Although in principle conventional and scripted, ritual acts are at times strikingly original, imaginative, and improvisational (Barbara, 1978). Preparation for successful ritual performance often demands intensive concentration, purposeful discipline and conscious reflection upon the rite, yet performances may enable experiential states of altered consciousness in which normal distinctions between act and actor or subject and object are transcended: "the dance dances the dancer (Bradd, 1996)."

## SOCIAL REPRODUCTION, SOCIAL TIME AND RITUAL MEDIATION: AN AFRICAN EXAMPLE

The extraordinary mutability and diverse potentials of ritual frameworks perhaps help account for the fact that in human societies the world over, rituals mark and help organize significant moments in the developmental cycles of domestic groups and their changing relationships with higher-level social institutions. Social reproduction, never an easy process, is usually predicated on the social repression and regulation of sexuality and other libidinal drives, the exchange of marriage partners between discrete groups, the transfer of rights, property and obligations between generations, and the controlled, phased waxing and waning of relations between close kin. Amidst the inevitable conflicts that result over resources, power and loyalties, actors are often torn in multiple directions. Young and old can easily be overwhelmed by the divergent pressures of the immediate moment. Ritual provides highly evocative mechanisms for bringing underlying conundrums into the open in a structured fashion and rendering them, for the most part, manageable and negotiable (Mark, 2002). Ritual dramas, which themselves proceed through highly structured temporal sequences, offer persons and groups meaningful guideposts for understanding larger passages of social time, and for apprehending normally inchoate continuities in collective experience. By the same token, rituals of social reproduction at times offer social actors particularly effective platforms upon which to pursue short-term and long-term political strategies within their families and in the wider community.

An extended example drawn from my fieldwork in south-central Africa may help to clarify how ritual action dramatizes and modulates the contradictory processes entailed in the enterprise of reproducing society. The Ngoni of eastern Zambia hold a special ceremony known as the mugeniso, around the time that the first-born son of a marriage union is able to walk. In principle, following the rite, strict prohibitions on the new husband eating in the presence of his wife's parents will be relaxed. In accounting for the ceremony, Ngoni informants explain that the first few years of marriage are nearly always tense. The bride, in a prolonged probationary state, is watched carefully by her husband's kin for signs of laziness, disobedience or disloyalty. She may often return to her mother and father's compound, bearing complaints of ill treatment, and her brothers may be tempted to take revenge on their brother-in-law and his agnates. Cattle or monetary bridewealth transactions, which ought to flow at a regular rate from the husband's people to the bride's people, are often stalled, and mutual recriminations and traditional court proceedings between affines (in-laws) are not unusual. The purpose of the mugeniso, it is usually said, is to "heal" or "cool" the burning animosity between the comparatively new affines and to celebrate their common bond, the first male child of the conjugal union.

In the initial phase of the mugeniso ceremony, the husband and wife's families dramatize these underlying tensions by playing at combat over a head cattle. On the morning of the rite, the husband, wife and child, accompanied by members of the husband's patrilineage (a classification often extended to his entire village) should journey to the bride's natal home bringing a bovine, usually an ox, as a gift to the bride's father. In precolonial days, I was told, the members of the military age regiment, to which the husband had belonged before marriage, would escort the procession. Once they come to the edge of the host village, the approaching party brandishes spears, knobkerries and shields and repeatedly hurls themselves towards the wife's natal relatives, who have danced out to greet them, shouting taunts and insults. The wife's people, in turn, stage mock charges upon the "foreigners, attempting to seize the ox and the boy from them.

This physically enacted opposition is to some extent undercut by the choice of *ngoma* war songs performed by the two parties as they dance, including the song allegedly sung in the 19th century by the Ngoni's traditional enemy, the Bemba, as the Ngoni legions approached, "Tipasile Mkhondo." There is a good deal of exaggerated leaping, laughter, and playful mock dueling as performers sing the words of the song, "Prepare the spears/the spears/we are all going to die/the Ngoni are coming." In time, the host group "captures" the ox, and moments later the two groups merge into one another, singing songs of war victory as they dance together towards the compound of the wife's father. The young boy will usually be invited to dance with his matrilaterals at the head of the procession and his mother's female relatives will loudly ululate their praises as the child enters the compound.

After the maternal grandparents and their kin have formally welcomed the young family and their relations, the young boy is entitled to enter his maternal grandfather's cattle byre and select a single beast for slaughter. In most cases that I have observed or heard about, the boy seems to understand that regardless of his grandfather's protestations and his subtle (or not so subtle) hints to select a modest beast, the child is really expected to pick the plumpest and most desirable animal. Many times, I've heard Ngoni men rapturously and uproariously recount, "Oh, the old man cried, he just cried, when he saw the beast the boy had chosen. It was his favorite animal, but he had no choice. So he just cried!"

After the beast has been slaughtered and the meal prepared, the husband and his family are invited to enter the house of the wife's parents and to eat with them. The husband is scrupulous to avoid establishing direct eye contact with his father-in-law or mother-in-law, and will be very careful not to sit or crouch near the wall of his in-laws' sleeping quarters. In practice, sons-in-law tend not to eat much at this event, but the groundwork is laid for future commensality and collaboration. Both sides of the family take great delight if the first-born boy eats his food with zest. In several cases, I heard the maternal grandfather tell his grandson, only partly in jest, that he was going to keep him in the compound for good, since his father and his agnates were clearly incapable of paying all the promised bridewealth. The exchanges of food, speeches, teasing and laughter usually have the desired effect. "After the mugeniso," I was often told, "the families will be so much easier with each other."

The mugeniso rite thus effectively dramatizes and to some extent defuses a set of underlying tensions between affines through a series of ambiguous enactments. It begins with a tussle over one of the bridewealth cattle, a persistent source of argumentation between the two families. Appropriately, this struggle quickly merges into a struggle over the young boy, the product of the union that has been legalized through bridewealth cattle; in capturing the ox, his matrilaterals in a sense seem to be capturing their sister's child. At one level, the opposition between the two parties is deflected through the singing of a song about the common enemy of the Ngoni, the Bemba, whom they allegedly vanquished. Yet there is a semi-serious edge to this song, as well, which alludes to the Bemba's status, in Ngoni's eyes, as "food of the spear" (chakudya chamkhondo); it is never clear after all, in relations among affines, just whom is going to "eat" (or subsume) whom. Similarly, the practice of having the young boy lead the procession once it has been unified once it has been unified can be interpreted in multiple ways. It is sometimes explained as showing the underlying unity among the extended family, which has an equal interest in the new offspring. Yet the husband's people usually tend to state that boy is a warrior "conquering" the village of his mother, while the wife's people assert he is "coming back to his real home."

Overlapping, ambiguous interpretive frames are especially evident in the byre episode, which calls forth a complex mixture of seriousness and hilarity. The scenario of the little boy annihilating his grandfather's favorite beast is a miniature rite of reversal, calling to mind a standard bone of contention between younger and older men. Juniors are forever pleading with their elders to slaughter or sell their cattle, yet men of the senior generation are invariably reluctant to do this, for cattle are the foundation of a patriarch's wealth, prestige and influence. Young men complain endlessly of their older male relatives "love only cattle, not their children" Hence the delight taken in seeing a small boy imperiously and successfully demand a beast from a senior man, especially from a man with whom the boy's own father would be loath to quarrel. At the same time, the incident anticipates the eventual passage of generational succession, when the boy will ultimately inherit the patrimony of the ascendant generation and become the master of its herds.

In principle, this episode teaches the boy the lesson that he may always go to his matrilaterals for aid, for they love him unconditionally, in contrast to his agnates who may resent him as a potential competitor for the common resources of the patrilineage. Yet, there is unquestionably an aggressive edge to the pressure on the boy to pick the finest animal, a choice that invariably pleases his agnates, who are thus reassured that the boy has the makings of a virile, assertive male who will not be overly under the spell of his matrilaterals, whom, they suspect, seek to spoil and "soften" the youth.

Ngoni regard it as particularly hilarious (yet also deeply propitious) if the boy picks one of the cattle that had been given as bridewealth for his mother by his father's people. Significantly, his agnates and matrilaterals tend to differ over just what the joke is. The boy "knows his own beasts," the agnates joke, and is "taking his own back." In contrast, matrilaterals proclaim with a smile, "he feels free since he knows he is in his real home now!" Picking one of the bridewealth cattle raises a delightful paradox: the boy is annihilating one of the media through which the legitimacy of his own birth was established and through which he has legally been made a member of his father's patriline. Interestingly, the demonstrable (and I believe sincere) anguish of the maternal grandfather over the loss of a valued bovine is seen as a good omen by both sides of the family. As one agnate of the boy told me, "When the grandfather cries so hard, that means he and the boy will always be good friends!" A maternal uncle of the boy agreed, laughing, "Oh, he will be a wild one, that one!"

Only once the child has symbolically triumphed over his mother's father may relations of avoidance between affines be relaxed. This victory and subsequent transformation of relations are only possible because of the ambiguous status of the child during the rite; he "belongs" to both his father's people and his mother's people. (If the child unambiguously represented his father's patrilineage at this moment, the assault on the matrilaterals' livestock would presumably seem too aggressive.)

Two further points should be emphasized. First of all, the ritual management of the marriage bond in this instance demands the participation of three generations: the tense relationship between adjacent generations (of the father-in-law and his son-in-law) is successfully manipulated by shifting the focus of attention to relations between alternate generations (of the maternal grandfather and his daughter's son). In effect, solidarity between generations one and three helps to secure the reconciliation of affines, especially between generations one and two.

Secondly, note that these generational reconfigurations are effected through the medium of cattle, the overarching embodiment of social and economic value in Ngoni society. Cattle here operate as the pivotal switch point between the social levels of descent and kinship, between the agnatic principle of patrilineal organization and the interpersonal ties of complementary filiation. In regular bridewealth transactions, cattle mark the boundaries of distinct descent groups, dividing the donating family of the husband from the receiving family of the wife. In the mugeniso rite, performed once the marriage has proven its solidity, these former lines of contrast are blurred; in seizing his maternal grandfather's cow, the little boy (the fruit of the marriage union) operates as a bridge between the two families, establishing a new intimacy that is exemplified by their subsequent act of eating together. Although cattle are the enduring source of aggressive conflict among affines, the seized cow in this instance establishes the enduring "love" between the child and his matrilaterals, who welcome the youth to his "real home." Through the selection and slaughter of the second head of cattle, chosen by the daughter's son of the host, this cross-generational affection is partially transferred to the relationship between the host father-in-law and his guest son-in-law. Up until this moment, in effect, father-in-law and son-in-law have only been linked through the daughter/wife, a highly fraught link suffused with sexual anxiety. (Indeed, many Ngoni insist that it would be akin to incest for affines to eat together before the mugeniso.) Now, the assured presence of a healthy young grandson/son, a common heir, more securely links the two men. Appropriately, all parties celebrate their transformed relationship by safely consuming together the flesh of a slaughtered beast that embodies the salutary three-way relationship between father-in-law, son-in-law and grandson.

## HOW DOES RITUAL MEDIATION WORK IN NORTH AMERICA? THE CASE OF THE WEDDING PARTY

At first consideration, the elaborate ritual logic of the Ngoni mugeniso—defusing affinal tension through a highly valued economic medium that is manipulated to dramatize positive cross-generational solidarity—would seem worlds apart from modern American family rituals. Yet the above analysis casts some light on the internal symbolic mechanisms through which structural oppositions are mediated in middle-class North America. Consider, as an illustrative example, the functions of the wedding party in the standard American neotraditional "white wedding" ceremony, which emerged in the late 19th and early 20th centuries (John, 1996; Martin, 1990).

Over the course of the wedding ceremony, the bride and groom must be visibly separated from their natal families (and especially from their parents) and established as a discrete couple capable of eventually being a family of their own. At the same time, enduring bonds of filial love between parent and child must be emphasized and preserved. This phased attenuation is partly accomplished through the performance of generational solidarity among the couple's peers, in the form of the costumed wedding party, who are visibly contrasted with the couple's parents and families of origin seated in the audience. The process somewhat resembles the much more elaborate functions of age-grades or age-sets in some small-scale, age-ranked societies, in which induction into a male or female cohorts is a necessary precondition to marriage and promotion to full social adulthood and in which age-mates actively assist in the marriage process. (Recall that in the mugeniso the Ngoni husband is escorted by his former age regiment.) The American wedding party is typically composed of a group of male peers of the groom and a group of female peers of the bride. At the start of many wedding ceremonies, a series of paired bridesmaids and groomsmen often walk down the aisle, in a ritual foreshadowing of the eventual conjugal pairing of the actual bride and groom. Upon reaching the altar each couple of the wedding party will separate and retire to their respective sides of the altar, forming a line of women on the left and a line of men on the right (in some weddings, this division conforms to the distinction between bride's party and groom's party in the seated audience.)

The wedding party, flanking the altar in a gender divided fashion, thus tangibly paves the way for the bridal couple. This line of peers, which may include the couple's siblings, friends, and a few young cousins (or children of the bride or groom from previous marriages or relationships), stands facing the seated audience, which normally includes the couple's parents and other members of ascendant generations. Standing, among other things, signifies the virility and endurance of the youthful wedding party, who function as representatives of the rising generation on the cusp of social maturity. Appropriately, the wedding party is made up of paired cohorts of male and female peers who may be younger than the couple but who are (in most cases) structurally contrasted with the parents' generation. This twinned peer group in effect frames, and helps to create, the charged ritual space of transformation which will moments later be occupied by the couple. The transition to the adult state of marriage is thus accomplished through the simultaneous performance of generational solidarity and opposition. As they stand before the assembled, the couple is established as structurally like the youthful members of the standing wedding party, and structurally unlike their seated parents and natal families, to whom the bride and groom have turned their backs.

From the late Victorian period onwards the potent generational solidarity of the youthful wedding party, which helps in effect to break bonds between the new spouses and their parents, has been predicated on a manifest gender hierarchy. The groom should from the start of the ceremony stand by his best man and the other male members of the wedding party near the altar at the right front of the church or hall, waiting for his bride. She should enter, escorted by her father or another male who "gives her away" and process down the aisle, in full sight of the assembled, who stand in respect as she does so. She is to be met by the groom, who takes her from her guardian and with her faces the altar and the officiant. This procession enacts the classic principles in European kinship of patriarchy and virilocality; the bride is moved out of her father's family into her husband's domain, and is presented as an elaborate, decorated "gift." The walk down the aisle may also enact the European principle of mild hypergamy; the woman is, in principle, lifted up in status through marriage, as she is absorbed into the relatively superior estate of her husband's family.

The maid of honor and bridesmaids receiving the bride are thus in a significant sense differentiated from the best man and groomsmen standing by the groom, in more ways than gender per se. The line of males of the junior, rising generation, of which the groom is a part, constitutes the key fulcrum of ritual action, the base to which the mobile bride is delivered by a male figure of the senior generation. The line of young women bridesmaids offer protective solidarity to their peer, the bride, but inasmuch as they are "maids" they are destined to follow her lead as eventual brides, escorted in their turn to the altar by their own fathers. This motif is explicitly dramatized when the bride's train is held by girl bridesmaids who follow behind her, a vignette that is invariably viewed as adorable and poignant, for it anticipates the little girls' eventual journey down the aisle as brides themselves. (In contrast, little boys who are junior groomsmen would rarely process down the aisle behind the bride, but are rather expected to stand in the line of males at the front of the church by the altar.) The groom and his best man, in contrast, do not walk down the aisle but appear from another entrance to take up their place at the altar. The groom, in receiving his bride, steps forward from the community of his young male peers, while the bride, in effect, is brought forward to stand near her female peers, although she never precisely stands with them.

In this respect, the work of male generational solidarity is to constitute the fixed social base from which the groom emerges, as an exemplary embodiment of society's ascendant generation. (The groom in most cases is dressed in the same attire as his groomsmen, while her bridesmaids should never emulate the bride's attire.) In contrast to the male wedding party's solid public stability, the primary ritual work of female generational solidarity undertaken by the

and in that sense may signal enduring anxiety over the capacity of the "the real world" or marketplace to provide ultimate meaning in life. Individual and family trajectories are both interlaced and juxtaposed in class reunions and homecoming games, which are often characterized by intermingled nostalgic elegies for lost innocence, celebrations of material success and family vitality, and anxiety over failed opportunities (Sherry, 1993).

As suggested above, these multi-track, contradictory processes culminate in the modern wedding. On the hand, the rite simultaneously celebrates the free, coequal autonomous selfhoods of the individual persons being married, recognizes the gradual ascension of an entire younger generation, and honors the couple's parents (and often their grandparents). At the same time, it subtly re-instantiates principles of patriarchy, attenuates the couple's relationships with their natal families, asserts that the couple is "one flesh," directs them to procreate, and disciplines the parties into the rigors of married life and bourgeois convention. It is striking that these diverse objectives, implicating so many different persons and overlapping relationships, are all dramatized and mediated through obsessive ritual attention to a single person, the bride herself. Dressed in white, she visually dominates the entire proceeding, and becomes, during the central phase of the rite, a veritable vessel of the eternal and the sacred. (The wedding rite might in this respect be regarded as a curious resurfacing of the ancient cult of the goddess, or a sanitized Protestant rendition of the medieval cult of the virgin.) The blessings of life itself seem to flow from her as marches down the aisle, greeted by an appropriately reverential sighs.

Various objects associated with the bride carry traces of the numinous qualities that temporarily inhabit her; like ritual paraphernalia in other societies these objects are characterized by what Turner terms the "polyvocality" of ritual symbols, the capacity of a given object or act to evoke different meanings or associations at various levels of experience (Victor, 1967). Initially, her elaborate white dress connotes virginity, purity, aristocratic bearing, demureness and sacredness. Yet later in the ceremony, when her veil is drawn back for the dramatic kiss, her attire takes on more erotic and procreative associations, anticipating her "deflowering" on the wedding night and her hoped-for fertility. (These associations are dramatically accentuated by the increasingly popular practice, at some receptions, of the groom crawling beneath the bride's billowing skirts, to the raucous cheers of onlookers, to retrieve her garter belt.) Similarly, the bouquet she carries down the aisle initially has extensive associations with her hoped-for fertility (a single flower, after all, would usually seem as inappropriate as a single handful of rice). Yet when the bride tosses the bouquet a different set of meanings comes to the fore: she is not discarding hopes of fertility but is rather, as noted above, shedding her liminal state as wife-to-be. She thus dramatizes her new married state through a playful (but ultimately serious) contrast with her unmarried former peers.

At one level, the white wedding cake, the same color as the bride's dress, evokes the sweetness and pleasure of conjugal unity (on the anticipated marital bed), as emphasized in the (quasi-erotic) moment when the bride and groom feed one another, as well as the resplendent and unique status of the couple, as often signified by small dolls of the couple atop the wedding cake. The cake may also be said to signify the collective investment of the assembled guests in the future procreative generativity of the couple and the hoped-for fecundity of the bride's body. After the couple has exchanged bites, all the guests are expected to eat a piece of the cake, in effect sealing through a shared act of commensality their united witnessing of the marriage and their common hopes for fruits of the union. The cake's associations with fecundity are further emphasized by its large, rotund shape (anticipating the bride's pregnant body) and by the practice of saving a piece to be consumed one year after the wedding, the idealized moment when a newborn baby is expected. In turn, the many handfuls of white rice thrown by the wedding party's members simultaneously re-emphasize their collective commitment to recognizing the marriage and evoke the union's hoped-for fecundity; appropriately, this action both marks the formal end of the rite and signals the commencement of a new liminal period, the honeymoon, during which the couple is traditionally supposed to initiate the sexual union that will lead to conception and birth.

In short, the bride's body and its symbolic extensions function as polyvalent symbolic media through which all members of the wedding are brought into close relationship with one another and with the mythic narrative of conception, fertility and the regeneration of life. The wedding is thus a supreme bourgeois ritual, producing a tangible, optimistic vision of a viable future, centered on the symbolic "birth" of a new nuclear family.

At the other end of the spectrum, the American funeral rite also centers on a single body, that of the corpse, in order to orchestrate another set of complex social and temporal relationships. The dead person may be thought of as moving from initial separation (through special treatment, including embalming), into the ambiguous liminal status of funeral corpse, to a final state of integration into the domain of the dead (signified through burial or cremation). This close attention to the dead body not only manages the deceased's social transition out of the living world, but separates the mourners as a collective social unit out of ordinary life, placing them into an ambiguous interstitial space and time. They wear special somber clothes, adopt a solemn demeanor, and may even be expected to view or kiss the corpse, before the coffin lid is closed and the service begins. At the rite's conclusion, they are collectively reintegrated into ordinary life, often through actions, such as food and lively conversation at a reception, that emphasize the renewal of life.

The ultimate consequence of the funeral's double tripartite structure is an achieved marked separation between the categories of life and death, Paradoxically, this ritual distance enables subsequent moments of communion between the living and the dead, as in visits to the cemetery, which are often tied to key moments in the annual calendar, such as Christmas, Memorial Day, or Mother's Day (Richard, 1979; Lloyd, 1959; John, 1996).

## THE ANNUAL RITUAL CYCLE: INTEGRATIVE AND DISPERSIVE TENDENCIES IN THE "HOLIDAY SEASON"

Rites of passage thus primarily concentrate upon individual life stage transitions, while simultaneously evoking collective transformations in family and kinship configurations. Conversely, calendrical family rites tend to foreground the collective institutional existence of the family, while secondarily highlighting personal life course journeys through successive family spheres.

To some extent, our major calendrical rites can be conceived as compensatory retreats from the external domains of commerce, getting and spending. Anthropologist Gwen Neville suggests that the modern family reunion (a North American practice developed after the Civil War) is an inverted kind of Protestant pilgrimage (Gwen, 1987; Gwen, 2003). The medieval Catholic pilgrim typically set off from a rural kinship-based setting and moved across a sacral landscape into the wider world toward a distant site, often marked by holy relics, through which he or she might come into intimate contact with the divine. In contrast, as Weber argued, the modern Protestant subject moves through a disenchanted landscape, sensing divine election only through disciplined work and persistent self-actualization in the marketplace. Hence, Neville, maintains, the modern longing, epitomized by the family reunion, to return periodically to the bonds of kinship within a nostalgic agrarian setting, such as the "old home place" or a state park (Bradd, 2003; Mark, 2003). This insight may be extended to other modern calendrical ceremonies, which are also grounded in an imagined agrarian past, including the harvest festival (Thanksgiving and Halloween), the midwinter rite of sun return (Christmas, Kwanza and Hanukah) and spring fertility festivals (Easter and Passover). In contrast to earlier public festivals, however, the celebration of these rites has been privatized since the mid-nineteenth century, more and more confined to the interiors of nuclear family households. During the past century and a half, these rites have been increasingly homogenized, as regional variations have been leveled (although some distinguishing ethnic markers are often reinserted). These annual holidays thus function as apparent refuges from the wider world of work, enclaved from the rationalized calculations of the economy. Yet, paradoxically, the rites also celebrate the integration of the family into the larger nation and economy.

To appreciate the multiple dimensions of calendrical rites, let us briefly concentrate on the annual "holiday season," stretching from Halloween through Christmas. This two month period—centered on the image of pure child surrounded by a loving family—is characterized by mounting mass commodity consumption, during which all Americans are surrounded by the sights and sounds of marketing, from blinking lights, to storefront displays to Christmas carols. Building on Warner, Bellah approaches Thanksgiving as an integrative rite, binding discrete families into the national "civic religion" of shared sacrifice and imputed grace (Warner, 1970). The turkey might in this light be conceived of as symbolizing both the solidarity of the family (hence the common prohibition on cutting the turkey before all members and branches of the family have assembled at the table!) and the unity of the nation. In partaking of a piece of the turkey (partly consecrated by a common prayer or murmured words of thanks) family members are thus more intimately bound to one another and to their fellow citizens—symbolically integrated into what Benedict Anderson terms the "imagined community" of the nation (Benedict, 1983). In some families, this integration is hierarchically ordered; all "children," including unmarried persons of any age, are confined to the "children's table."

Although commentators have for generations dutifully denounced the "commercialization" of Christmas as contrary to the day' spiritual and religious principles, it is manifestly a festival of mass commodity consumption, arguably the most important context through which the domestic domain is integrated into the broader public sphere (Schmidt, 1995). Preparatory mini-pilgrimages to department store or shopping mall Santas are de rigeur in many families (Waits, 1993; Golby, 1986). A Christmas morning featuring only homemade toys would hardly count as Christmas; enormous emphasis is placed on obtaining fashionable and expensive industrially manufactured gifts, especially those celebrated in the mass media. The common myth that Santa Claus, and not the parents, miraculously places the gifts under the Christmas tree could be interpreted as poetically evoking the nearly magical status of the commodity at the symbolic heart of the American family system. The gifts, after all, really do come from somewhere else (if not the North Pole) and through interacting with the outer world of the marketplace the parents have translated mere money into expressions of love, the foundation of the family unit. As Nancy Munn perceptively notes, the polyvalent symbol of the wrapped Christmas present effectively conflates two kinds of parental love (Nancy, 1973). The outer colored wrapping evokes nurturing affection, classically associated with maternal love and aesthetics, while the material value of the store-bought gift within the wrapping evokes the parents' monetary contributions, classically associated with the wage-earning working father. Significantly, on Christmas morning, all these gifts, evoking the multiple relationships (parent-parent, parent-child, sibling-sibling) that constitute the nuclear family unit, are assembled around a singular ritual object, the Christmas tree. There should be only one tree per family, topped by one single star, but the tree itself should have been previously decorated through the collaborative work of the entire family, using objects that often evoke previous Christmas celebrations and key persons and events in family history. The idealized tableau of Christmas morning—children and parents delightedly opening gifts under the tree—is an exemplary model of the American family system, in which close relatives are bound together as a single unit by exchanging tokens of love derived from the wider market-driven culture.

The Christmas tree, while sometimes spoken of as a sign of family continuity, is also a potent sign of rupture between successive nuclear families. Once a new couple has established their own household, they are likely to have a tree of their own, and are considerably less likely to receive presents under their parents' trees in their natal households. Each newly established Christmas tree embodies the virtual sanctification of the new bourgeois home and nuclear family. Santa Claus, significantly, is believed to deposit his gifts at the symbolic core of domestic space, descending the chimney and entering the "living room" through the fireplace/hearth, an eminently maternal site.

These symbolic complexes may be read as striking evidence of the enduring resonance of premodern and pre-Christian symbolism in modern American culture. Levi-Strauss proposes that Father Christmas carries traces of a pagan quasi-shamanic figure, the King of Saturnalia, who embodies the seasonal cycles of death and the regeneration of life (Claude, 1995). By giving gifts to children—who for the three months following Halloween incarnate the spirits of the Dead—adults propitiate Death and enhance the vitality of the human world. Hence, parents tenderly struggle to maintain children's faith in Santa Claus for as long as possible. "Is it not that, deep within us," asks Levi-Strauss, "there is a small desire to believe in boundless generosity, kindness without ulterior motives, a brief interlude during which all fear, envy and bitterness are suspended? No doubt we cannot fully share the illusion, but sharing with others at least gives us a chance to warm our hearts by the flame that burns in young souls (Claude)." In a similar vein, ethnographer Cindy Dell Clark observes that Christmas is not so much for children as it is a "a holiday in which other members of the culture socially situate themselves vis-à-vis children (Cindy, 1995)." In the wedding rite, as we have seen, the assembled take pleasure in the eventual prospect of the bride's fertility and the birth of children; in turn, on December 25th all are expected to rejoice in the realization of this promise, reveling in dramas of childish energy and vitality.

Pagan symbolism also runs through the rite that inaugurates the holiday season, Halloween, the night during which the souls of the dead were classically thought to roam the earth. Like Christmas, Halloween also centers on children, but with a different set of emphases. Disguised as ghosts, goblins and other supernatural beings, children would seem to function as temporary vessels of the dead traveling from house to house. The requirement that adults give gifts to these masked beings, on penalty of destructive mischief, could be read as an attempt to propitiate the forces of death, at precisely the moment in the northern hemisphere that the darkest and coldest season of the year descends. In this regard, illuminated jack-o-lanterns made of grimacing, carved pumpkins and placed on threshold sites such as porches might be interpreted as polyvalent (and prophylactic) talismans, simultaneously simulating feared goblins and guarding the home against intrusions by the dark spirits of the night.

Perhaps because of this underlying symbolism of inversion, death and disorder, Halloween celebrates the emergence of children's autonomy and individuation over their normative, vertical integration into the social collectivity. In spite (or perhaps because of) parental and mass media anxiety over child abduction and rumors of poisoned candy, children avidly campaign for trick-or-treating, a practice that dates only to the 1930s (Elizabeth, 2000). Costumed trick-or-treating could be interpreted as a kind of "deep play" a symbolic rehearsal of adolescence and adulthood, as children try on new roles and identities (in the form of masks and costumes, often associated with miraculous powers) and venture out into the wider world, especially into the normally prohibited domains of other households—precisely the kind of sites they will come to know once they leave the nest of their parents' homes. In contrast to the integrative communion meals of Thanksgiving, Christmas, Passover or Easter, Halloween is centered on a kind of anti-meal, candy, which is not consumed in a collective context. As in classic carnival or saturnalia the world is "turned upside down" during Halloween (Mikhail, 1968). Children shout out commands to adults, venture out into the darkness, violate social conventions of decorum, flirt with the grotesque by over-eating and hanging toilet paper, and actively seek out frightening experiences. In temporarily taking control of instruments of secrecy, children may be tentatively exploring more pervasive mysteries and secrets of the adult social world. Each year, the complex dance of collaboration and conflict between parents and children over the precise nature of Halloween activities dramatizes in microcosm parents and children's deeper ambivalence over the maturation process: how much dependence or independence is desirable and tolerable?

Like the other family rituals we have considered, Halloween ambiguously dramatizes both the centrifugal and centripetal tendencies in American kinship. On the one hand, the rite exemplifies the child's growing horizontal integration into a socializing peer group, within which solidarity will be increasingly established (especially in adolescence) through carefully calibrated exercises in common risk-taking. On the other hand, Halloween also occasions intimate collaboration and solidarity between parents and children. The whole family often works together on elaborate scary decorations in the front yard, parents help dress the children in costume, and adults increasingly escort their children through the neighborhood on trick-or-treat ventures.

Taken as a whole, then, the entire holiday season may be regarded as a ritual drama evoking and "solving" the forces of dissolution and dispersal that threaten the American kinship system in a society that has radically separated the family from economic production, and which, in so doing, periodically preempts tri-generational households. The season begins on Halloween night, as children make ambiguous, experimental forays out to other households, testing the limits of parental forbearance and anxiety. Grandparents are often not present at Halloween, but the disturbing specters of more distant antecedents, in the form of the dead unleashed from the graveyard, are sensed and must be placated through ritual play. In turn, on Thanksgiving, at least three living generations should ideally be present to engage in joyous commensality. Significantly, Norman Rockwell's now mythic "Freedom from Want" World War II poster prominently displays loving grandparents at the top of the table, and places happy, expectant grandchildren at the table's base, evoking the affective solidarity between generations one and three. Finally, at Christmas, the ritual focus shifts from alternate generations (who may have traveled to be together) to the adjacent generations inhabiting a single nuclear family household. The white-haired Santa Claus makes a purported appearance as a substitute grandfather, but he is not, appropriately, to be seen by the children. In playing at being the grandfatherly Santa Claus, the parents, in effect, transfer the affective solidarity of alternate generations into the compressed nuclear home, reconciling proximate generations at the end of yet another year of inevitable parent-child negotiation and conflict. (One week later, on New Year's Eve, parents are rewarded with a night that is in principle for adults only, marking the final conclusion of the holiday season.)

## CONCLUSION: FROM CONTRADICTION TO PARADOX

Rather like the Ngoni mugeniso ceremony, modern middle-class American family rituals poetically encapsulate and work upon a set of pervasive conundrums at the heart of our kinship and economic system, revolving around problematic generational sequencing and ambiguous signs of abstracted exchange value. When these rituals "succeed," the radical formal divides between love and work, between family of origin and family of procreation, and between dependence and autonomy are, in effect, translated from the level of overt contradiction to a more inchoate level of paradoxical coexistence. In the context of a well-performed wedding, for instance, the costumed bride functions as a composite symbolic paradigm that simultaneously evokes separation and union, filial piety and conjugal eroticism, youth and maturity, poignant loss and the joyous regeneration of life. She is in one respect pure and authentic, an oasis of aesthetic perfection unsullied by the crude logic of the market. She is another respect the embodiment of financial solidity and the fruits of hard work, a tangible celebration of the wealth of her parents or of the marital couple itself. She makes her advent in the rite as a child, being passed away from the hand of her father; she disappears from view at its conclusion as a wife clutching her new husband's hand, showered by rice that evokes the new child she will, in principle, bring forth.

In a comparable fashion, Christmas promises to collapse everyday distinctions between emotion and economy, affection and rationality, juniors and seniors. On the one hand, Christmas is the annual culmination of the cult of domesticity, promising a tableau of unconditional love equally available to rich and poor alike. On the other hand, Christmas celebrates the cornucopia of commodity consumption, and is the apotheosis of every dream and fantasy the market has to offer. It celebrates the transcendental self, rewarded through gifts and the pleasures of unbridled acquisition, yet locates that self within a coherent familial framework, under the encompassing sign of the Christmas tree. Each Christmas evokes the benevolent presence of grandfatherly figures, even it subtly moves the actual incumbents of generations one off stage, towards the mythical, invisible domain of Mr. and Mrs. Claus at the North Pole. Successive Christmases provide temporal benchmarks as persons move through the life cycle, from their natal family to new nuclear family units, allowing for periodic reflections on the shape of one's life and for what Shore terms "identity-updating (Bradd, 2006)."

Our greatest mythic narrative of Christmas, Charles Dickens' *A Christmas Carol*, directly addresses both the intertwining of the market and the holiday and the complex intersections of personal biography and intergenerational temporal sequencing. Scrooge, the embodiment of soulless capitalist rationality, demands that Bob Cratchet work on Christmas Day, then fires him on this day, of all days. He is punished by successive visitations (significantly, brought to him by the dead themselves) of the spirits of Christmas Past, Present and Yet to Come. In his visions of the past, he re-experiences the pain of love lost and friendship betrayed. In the present, he sees the immediate consequences of his action. In the future, he glimpses the possible legacies of his selfishness, in his own unlamented death and in the preventable death of Cratchet's young son, Tiny Tim. Finally, embracing the spirit of Christmas through joyous commodity consumption and distribution, Scrooge saves Tiny Tim and, in so doing, remakes the future and saves himself. He thereby grasps the basic paradox of Christmas and of the sentimental domestic cult: in giving unstintingly to the junior generation that will in time replace both the middle and senior generations, elders actively secure their own vitality and achieve symbolic immortality. Appropriately, it falls to the youngest child, Tiny Tim, to pronounce the closing words of salvation over the elderly Scrooge and the extended family of Christmas revelers: "God bless us, everyone."

As *A Christmas Carol* reminds us, although family rites produce powerful visions of the past, present and future, they do not, in themselves, determine whether or not the future will be bleak or joyous, alienating or transcendent. As most of us have learned, family rituals can trigger moments of devastating isolation, or afford exquisite glimpses of the sublime. Ritual provides microcosmic, condensed models of the contradictory texture of lived experience, yet these models are not fixed templates, but are only the potential building blocks out of which we may, under certain conditions, come to know ourselves, our antecedents and our descendants more deeply. In creatively manipulating these building blocks, we may improvise more effective and meaningful relations with love ones.

Here, then, lies the greatest paradox of our family rituals: in subordinating ourselves to preexistent structures that we neither fully understand nor control, we are afforded the possibility of discovering novel aspects of ourselves and our relations with others, living and dead. Such visions may be as fleeting as a bride's tossed bouquet, a Christmas gift's wrapping, the menorah's flickering flame, or a tossed clod of earth. Yet it is out of such glimpses that we may fabricate meaningful trajectories of self and collectivity. In our ritual performances, enigmatic dramas of the insolvable puzzles of our common world, we pursue the enduring double task of reconciling our love with our work, our predecessors with our posterity.

## REFERENCES

Herve Varenne, *Americans Together, Structured Diversity in a Midwestern Town* (New York Teachers' College Press, 1977); Bradd Shore, *Family Time: Studying Myth and Ritual in Working Families* (Emory Center for Myth and Ritual in American Life, Working Paper 028-03, 2003).

Thomas Mann, *Buddenbrooks: The Decline of a Family*. Trans., John E. Wood (New York: Random House, 1994). In a sense, Mann's novel prophesies the emergence of the modern nuclear family.

Bradd Shore, *Family Time: Studying Myth and Ritual in Working Families* (Emory Center for Myth and Ritual in American Life, Working Paper 028-03, 2003).

Sociologists working in the tradition of Erving Goffman tend to use the term "ritual" in a rather broader sense, to refer to any patterned, repeated behavior. See Erving Goffman, *Interaction Rituals* (Garden City, NY: Anchor Books. 1967).

N.D. Fustel de Coulanges, *The ancient city* (Baltimore: Johns Hopkins University Press. 1980 [1864]); Emile Durkheim, *The Elementary Forms of the Religious Life* (New York: Basic Book, 1915); Claude Levi-Strauss, *Structural anthropology*, Volume I (New York: Basic Books. 1966); Pierre Bourdieu, *Outline of a theory of practice*. Translated by Richard Nice. (Cambridge and New York: Cambridge University Press. 1977); Maurice Bloch, *Ritual, history and power: Selected papers in anthropology* (London: Atlantic Highlands, NJ: Athlone Press, 1989).

Victor Turner, *The ritual process: Structure and anti structure* (Chicago: University of Chicago Press, 1969); Carlo Ginzburg, *The night battles; Witchcraft and agrarian cults in the 16th and 17th Centuries*. Trans. J. & A. Tedeschi (New York: Penguin Books. 1986); Stuart Hall, & T. Jefferson (Eds.), *Resistance through rituals: Youth subcultures in post-war Britain* (London: Routledge, 1993); David Lan, *Guns and rain: Guerrillas and spirit mediums in Zimbabwe* (Berkeley: University of California Press, 1985); Pater Stallybrass and Albon White, *The Politics and Poetics of Transgression* (London. Methuen. 1986); Jean Comaroff, *Body of power, spirit of resistance: The culture and history of a South African people* (Chicago: University of Chicago Press, 1985).

Roy Rappaport, *Ritual and Religion in the making of humanity* (Cambridge, UK: Cambridge University Press, 1999).

Keith Burridge, *New heaven, new earth: A study of millenarian activities* (New York: Schocken Books, 1969); Dick Hebdige, *Subculture: The meaning of style* (London: Methuen, 1979).

Claude Levi-Strauss, *Structural anthropology*. Volume I (New York: Basic Books, 1966); Valerio Valeri, *Kingship and Sacrifice: Ritual and Society in Ancient Hawaii* (Chicago: University of Chicago Press, 1985); Nancy Jay, *Throughout your generations forever: Sacrifice, religion and paternity* (Chicago: University of Chicago Press, 1992).

J. Huizinga, Homo Ludens: *A study of the play element of culture* (London, Routledge & K. Paul, 1949); Mikhail Bakhtin, *Rabelais and his world*. Translated by Helene Iswolsky (Cambridge, MA: M.I.T. Press, 1968); Clifford Geertz, *The interpretation of cultures* (New York: Basic Books, 1973); Keith Basso, *Portraits of the "the Whiteman": Linguistic play and cultural symbols among the western Apache* (Cambridge and New York: Cambridge University Press, 1979).

Barbara Babcock (ed.) *The reversible world: Symbolic inversion in art and society* (Ithaca, NY: Cornell University Press, 1978).

Bradd Shore. *Culture in mind: Cognition, culture and the problem of meaning* (New York: Oxford University Press, 1996) p. 50.

For an overview of American middle-class ritual, see Mark Auslander, "Rituals of the Family" *Sloan Work Family Encyclopedia*. 2002, http://wfnetwork.bc.edu/encyclopedia_entry.php?id=253.

John Gillis, *A world of their own making; Myth, ritual and the quest for family values* (New York: Basic Books, 1996). For an illuminating discussion of French bourgeois rituals of the 19th century, see A. Martin-Fugier, *Bourgeois rituals*. In M. Perot (Ed.), *A history of private life*, Volume 4 (Cambridge, MA: Harvard University Press. 1990), pp. 261–337.

Arnold van Gennep, *The Rites of Passage* (London: Routledge, 2004); Victor Turner, Betwixt and Between; The Liminal Period in Rites de Passage. In Victor Turner, *The forest of symbols. Aspects of Ndembu ritual* (Ithaca, NY: Cornell University Press, 1967).

Yaya Ren, personal communication.

R.E. Davis-Floyd, *Birth as an American rite of passage* (Berkeley: University of California Press, 1992).

Felicity H Paxton, *America at the Prom: Ritual and regeneration* (Ph.D. Dissertation. University of Pennsylvania, 2000).

Sherry Ortner, Ethnography among the Newark: The class of '58 of Weequakic high school. *Michigan Quarterly Review*, 32, 1993, pp. 411–429.

Victor Turner, *The forest of symbols. Aspects of Ndembu ritual* (Ithaca, NY: Cornell University Press, 1967).

Richard Huntington and Peter Metcalfe, *Celebrations of death: The anthropology of mortuary ritual* (Cambridge: Cambridge University Press, 1979); Lloyd Warner, *The living and the dead: A study of the symbolic life of Americans* (New Haven: Yale University Press, 1959); John Gillis, *A world of their own making; Myth, ritual and the quest for family values.* (New York: Basic Books, 1996).

Gwen Neville Kennedy, *Kinship and Pilgrimage: Rituals of Reunion in American Protestant Culture* (New York: Oxford University Press, 1987); see also, Gwen Kennedy Neville, *Kinship and Pilgrimage: Rituals of Reunion in American Protestant Culture* (Working Paper 023-03, Emory Center for Myth and Ritual in American Life, 2003).

This argument is developed in reference to Protestant camp meetings by Bradd Shore, in his *Spiritual Work, Memory Work: Revival and Recollection at Salem Camp Meeting* (Center for Myth and Ritual in American Life, Working Paper 024-03, 2003). For a discussion of American family reunions, with particular attention to African American reunions, see Mark Auslander, *Something we need to get back to: Mythologies of Origin and Rituals of Solidarity in African American Working Families* (Working Paper, Emory Center for Myth and Ritual in American Life, 2003).

Warner, op cit; R. Bellah, *Civil religion in America*. In Bellah, *Beyond belief: Essays on religion in a post-traditional word* (New York: Harper and Row, 1970), pp. 168–187.

Benedict Anderson. *Imagined communities: Reflections on the origins and spread of nationalism* (London: Verso. 1983).

L.E. Schmidt, *Consumer rites: The buying and selling of American holidays* (Princeton NJ: Princeton University Press, 1995).

W.B. Waits, *The modern Christmas in America* (New York: New York University Press, 1993); J.M. Golby & A.M. Purdue, *The making of modern Christmas* (Athens, GA: University of Georgia Press. 1986).

of cross-sex reincarnation. Among the Ingalik, an Athapaskan group of the Alaskan interior, both male and female berdaches have been reported, and male berdaches often had shamanic powers.

Russian explorers, traders, and missionaries were well aware of gender diversity among Alaskan natives. The explorer Lisiansky reported that a Russian priest almost married an Aleut chief to a berdache before being informed that the "bride" was male. Among the Chugach and Koniag, Pacific Eskimo (Yup'ik) groups, such individuals were believed to be "two persons in one." Despite Russian attempts to suppress the role, third gender individuals were esteemed and encouraged by their families, who considered them lucky. Many were shamans. Early observers reported that some feminine boys were raised as girls from childhood by families lacking a daughter.

In the vast subarctic region, alternative genders have been reported for the Athapaskan-speaking Kaska and among the widely dispersed Cree and Ojibway. The linguistic relationship between terms for male berdaches in Algonkian-speaking groups (including the Fox and Illinois) is evident.

*Northwest Coast and Columbia Plateau.* Among the Northwest Coast Haisla, berdaches were reportedly "fairly common." A supernatural berdache was portrayed in masked dances by the neighboring Bella Coola. Among the Eyak, however, berdaches did not have supernatural power and their status was low. Alternative male genders have been widely reported for the Columbia Plateau region but with few details. Among the Flathead of western Montana and the Klamath of southern Oregon, berdaches were often shamans. The career of one Klamath *tw!ĭnnă'ĕk*, known as Muksamse'lapli, or White Cindy, has been briefly described by Spier and by McCleod.

*West and Southwest.* Male and female alternative genders have been documented throughout the Great Basin, California, Colorado River, and Southwest culture areas. They are consistently described as doing the work of the other sex, less consistently as cross-dressing. As elsewhere, they formed relationships with non-berdache members of their own sex. Among some groups (Shoshone, Ute, Kitanemuk, Pima-Papago), families held a kind of initiation rite to confirm male berdache identity. The child was placed in a circle of brush with a bow and a basket (men's and women's objects, respectively). The brush was set on fire, and whichever object the boy picked up as he ran away served to identify his gender preference. The choice of the basket signified male berdache status. Among the Shoshone, who acquired horses and adopted a Plains-oriented lifestyle, male berdaches joined war parties.

In California, third/fourth gender individuals often had ceremonial roles relating to death and burial. Among the Yokuts and Tubatulabal, and possibly the Chumash, male berdaches served as undertakers, handling and burying the deceased and conducting mourning rites. Berdaches also participated in mourning rites among the Monache (Mono), Pomo, Miwok, Achumawi, Atsugewi, and Shasta. Among the Wappo, Mattole, Hupa, Chilula, Tolowa, Maidu, Achumawi, Shasta, and Modoc, male berdaches, and less often female berdaches, were sometimes shamans. One of the last chiefs of the Kawaiisu was a third gender male.

Alternative roles for males (but apparently not females) existed among the Pueblo communities of Isleta, San Felipe, San Juan, Santa Ana, Santo Domingo, Tesuque, Acoma, Laguna, Zuni, and Hopi. Among the western Pueblos, man-woman kachinas, or gods, were portrayed in masked dances and ceremonies. The Zuni *lhamana* We'wha was a religious specialist who regularly participated in ceremonies. Other Pueblo berdaches are described primarily in terms of their specialization in pottery and other pursuits of women.

Alternative gender roles also existed among the Papago and Pima of the Southwest and northern Mexico. Like Plains berdaches, Papago *wiik'ovat* taunted the scalps brought home by warriors, and they were visited for sexual liaisons by men to whom they gave obscene nicknames. A fire test was employed to confirm their identity.

# 37

# Tricking and Tripping

## *Fieldwork on Prostitution in the Era of AIDS*

*Claire E. Sterk*

Students often think of anthropological fieldwork as requiring travel to exotic tropical locations, but that is not necessarily the case. This reading is based on fieldwork in the United States—on the streets in New York City as well as Atlanta. Claire Sterk is an anthropologist who works in a school of public health and is primarily interested in issues of women's health, particularly as it relates to sexual behavior. In this selection, an introduction to a book by the same title, she describes the basic fieldwork methods she used to study these women and their communities. Like most cultural anthropologists, Sterk's primary goal was to describe "the life" of prostitution from the women's own point of view. To do this, she had to be patient, brave, sympathetic, trustworthy, curious, and non-judgmental. You will notice these characteristics in this selection; for example, Sterk begins her book with a poem written by one of her informants. Fieldwork is a slow process, because it takes time to win people's confidence and to learn their language and way of seeing the world. In this regard, there are probably few differences between the work of a qualitative sociologist and that of a cultural anthropologist (although anthropologists would not use the term "deviant" to describe another society or a segment of their own society).

Throughout the world, HIV/AIDS is fast becoming a disease found particularly in poor women. Sex workers or prostitutes have often been blamed for AIDS, and they have been further stigmatized because of their profession. In reality, however, entry into prostitution is not a career choice; rather, these women and girls are themselves most often victims of circumstances such as violence and poverty. Public health officials want to know why sex workers do not always protect their health by making men wear condoms. To answer such questions, we must know more about the daily life of these women. The way to do that, the cultural anthropologist would say, is to ask and to listen.

***As you read this selection, ask yourself the following questions:***

- What happens when Sterk says, "I'm sorry for you" to one of her informants? Why?
- Why do you think fieldwork might be a difficult job?
- Do you think that the fact that Sterk grew up in Amsterdam, where prostitution is legal, affected her research?
- Which of the six themes of this work, described at the end of the article, do you think is most important?

***The following terms discussed in this selection are included in the Glossary at the back of the book:***

*demography*
*fieldwork*
*key respondent*
*sample*
*stroll*

*Prostitution is a way of life. IT IS THE LIFE.*
*We make money for pimps who promise us*
*love and more,*
*but if we don't produce, they shove us out the door.*
*We turn tricks who have sex-for-pay.*
*They don't care how many times we serve every day.*

*The Life is rough. The Life is tough.*
*We are put down, beaten up, and left for dead.*
*It hurts body and soul and messes with*
*a person's head.*
*Many of us get high. Don't you understand it is*
*a way of getting by?*

*The Life is rough. The Life is tough.*
*We are easy to blame because we are lame.*

—Piper, 1987[1]

Sterk, Claire E. "Tricking and Tripping: Fieldwork on Prostitution in the Era of AIDS." Reprinted with permission of author.

One night in March of 1987 business was slow. I was hanging out on a stroll with a group of street prostitutes. After a few hours in a nearby diner/coffee shop, we were kicked out. The waitress felt bad, but she needed our table for some new customers. Four of us decided to sit in my car until the rain stopped. While three of us chatted about life, Piper wrote this poem. As soon as she read it to us, the conversation shifted to more serious topics—pimps, customers, cops, the many hassles of being a prostitute, to name a few. We decided that if I ever finished a book about prostitution, the book would start with her poem.

This book is about the women who work in the lower echelons of the prostitution world. They worked in the streets and other public settings as well as crack houses. Some of these women viewed themselves primarily as prostitutes, and a number of them used drugs to cope with the pressures of the life. Others identified themselves more as drug users, and their main reason for having sex for money or other goods was to support their own drug use and often the habit of their male partner. A small group of women interviewed for this book had left prostitution, and most of them were still struggling to integrate their past experiences as prostitutes in their current lives.

The stories told by the women who participated in this project revealed how pimps, customers, and others such as police officers and social and health service providers treated them as "fallen" women. However, their accounts also showed their strengths and the many strategies they developed to challenge these others. Circumstances, including their drug use, often forced them to sell sex, but they all resisted the notion that they might be selling themselves. Because they engaged in an illegal profession, these women had little status: their working conditions were poor, and their work was physically and mentally exhausting. Nevertheless, many women described the ways in which they gained a sense of control over their lives. For instance, they learned how to manipulate pimps, how to control the types of services and length of time bought by their customers, and how to select customers. While none of these schemes explicitly enhanced their working conditions, they did make the women feel stronger and better about themselves.

In this book, I present prostitution from the point of view of the women themselves. To understand their current lives, it was necessary to learn how they got started in the life, the various processes involved in their continued prostitution careers, the link between prostitution and drug use, the women's interactions with their pimps and customers, and the impact of the AIDS epidemic and increasing violence on their experiences. I also examined the implications for women. Although my goal was to present the women's thoughts, feelings, and actions in their own words, the final text is a sociological monograph compiled by me as the researcher. Some women are quoted more than others because I developed a closer relationship with them, because they were more able to verbalize and capture their circumstances, or simply because they were more outspoken.

## THE SAMPLE

The data for this book are qualitative. The research was conducted during the last ten years in the New York City and Atlanta metropolitan areas. One main data source was participant observation on streets, in hotels and other settings known for prostitution activity, and in drug-use settings, especially those that allowed sex-for-drug exchanges. Another data source was in-depth, life-history interviews with 180 women ranging in age from 18 to 59 years, with an average age of 34. One in two women was African American and one in three white; the remaining women were Latina. Three in four had completed high school, and among them almost two-thirds had one or more years of additional educational training. Thirty women had graduated from college.

Forty women worked as street prostitutes and did not use drugs. On average, they had been prostitutes for 11 years. Forty women began using drugs an average of three years after they began working as prostitutes, and the average time they had worked as prostitutes was nine years. Forty women used drugs an average of five years before they became prostitutes, and on the average they had worked as prostitutes for eight years. Another forty women began smoking crack and exchanging sex for crack almost simultaneously, with an average of four years in the life. Twenty women who were interviewed were ex-prostitutes.

## COMMENTS ON METHODOLOGY

When I tell people about my research, the most frequent question I am asked is how I gained access to the women rather than what I learned from the research. For many, prostitution is an unusual topic of conversation, and many people have expressed surprise that I, as a woman, conducted the research. During my research some customers indeed thought I was a working woman, a fact that almost always amuses those who hear about my work. However, few people want to hear stories about the women's struggles and sadness. Sometimes they ask questions about the reasons why women become prostitutes. Most of the time, they are surprised when I tell them that the prostitutes as well as their customers represent all layers of society. Before presenting the findings, it seems important to discuss the research process, including gaining access to the women, developing relationships, interviewing, and then leaving the field.[2]

## LOCATING PROSTITUTES AND GAINING ENTREE

One of the first challenges I faced was to identify locations where street prostitution took place. Many of these women worked on strolls, streets where prostitution activity is concentrated, or in hotels known for prostitution activity. Others, such as the crack prostitutes, worked in less public settings such as a crack house that might be someone's apartment.

I often learned of well-known public places from professional experts, such as law enforcement officials and health care providers at emergency rooms and sexually transmitted disease clinics. I gained other insights from lay experts, including taxi drivers, bartenders, and community representatives such as members of neighborhood associations. The contacts universally mentioned some strolls as the places where many women worked, where the local police focused attention, or where residents had organized protests against prostitution in their neighborhoods.

As I began visiting various locales, I continued to learn about new settings. In one sense, I was developing ethnographic maps of street prostitution. After several visits to a specific area, I also was able to expand these maps by adding information about the general atmosphere on the stroll, general characteristics of the various people present, the ways in which the women and customers connected, and the overall flow of action. In addition, my visits allowed the regular actors to notice me.

I soon learned that being an unknown woman in an area known for prostitution may cause many people to notice you, even stare at you, but it fails to yield many verbal interactions. Most of the time when I tried to make eye contact with one of the women, she quickly averted her eyes. Pimps, on the other hand, would stare at me straight on and I ended up being the one to look away. Customers would stop, blow their horn, or wave me over, frequently yelling obscenities when I ignored them. I realized that gaining entrée into the prostitution world was not going to be as easy as I imagined it. Although I lacked such training in any of my qualitative methods classes, I decided to move slowly and not force any interaction. The most I said during the initial weeks in a new area was limited to "how are you" or "hi." This strategy paid off during my first visits to one of the strolls in Brooklyn, New York. After several appearances, one of the women walked up to me and sarcastically asked if I was looking for something. She caught me off guard, and all the answers I had practiced did not seem to make sense. I mumbled something about just wanting to walk around. She did not like my answer, but she did like my accent. We ended up talking about the latter and she was especially excited when I told her I came from Amsterdam. One of her friends had gone to Europe with her boyfriend, who was in the military. She understood from her that prostitution and drugs were legal in the Netherlands. While explaining to her that some of her friend's impressions were incorrect, I was able to show off some of my knowledge about prostitution. I mentioned that I was interested in prostitution and wanted to write a book about it.

Despite the fascination with my background and intentions, the prostitute immediately put me through a Streetwalker 101 test, and apparently I passed. She told me to make sure to come back. By the time I left, I not only had my first conversation but also my first connection to the scene. Variations of this entry process occurred on the other strolls. The main lesson I learned in these early efforts was the importance of having some knowledge of the lives of the people I wanted to study, while at the same time refraining from presenting myself as an expert.

Qualitative researchers often refer to their initial connections as gatekeepers and key respondents. Throughout my fieldwork I learned that some key respondents are important in providing initial access, but they become less central as the research evolves. For example, one of the women who introduced me to her lover, who was also her pimp, was arrested and disappeared for months. Another entered drug treatment soon after she facilitated my access. Other key respondents provided access to only a segment of the players on a scene. For example, if a woman worked for a pimp, [she] was unlikely . . . to introduce me to women working for another pimp. On one stroll my initial contact was with a pimp whom nobody liked. By associating with him, I almost lost the opportunity to meet other pimps. Some key respondents were less connected than promised—for example, some of the women who worked the street to support their drug habit. Often their connections were more frequently with drug users and less so with prostitutes.

Key respondents tend to be individuals central to the local scene, such as, in this case, pimps and the more senior prostitutes. Their function as gatekeepers often is to protect the scene and to screen outsiders. Many times I had to prove that I was not an undercover police officer or a woman with ambitions to become a streetwalker. While I thought I had gained entrée, I quickly learned that many insiders subsequently wondered about my motives and approached me with suspicion and distrust.

Another lesson involved the need to proceed cautiously with self-nominated key respondents. For example, one of the women presented herself as knowing everyone on the stroll. While she did know everyone, she was not a central figure. On the contrary, the other prostitutes viewed her as a failed streetwalker whose drug use caused her to act unprofessionally. By associating with me, she hoped to regain some of her status. For me, however, it meant limited access to the other women because I affiliated myself with a woman who was marginal to the scene. On another occasion, my main key respondent was a man who claimed to own three crack houses in the neighborhood. However, he had a negative reputation, and people accused him of cheating on others. My initial alliance with him delayed, and almost blocked, my access to others in the neighborhood. He intentionally tried to keep me from others on the scene, not because he would gain something from that transaction but because it made him feel powerful. When I told him I was going to hang out with some of the other people, he threatened me until one of the other dealers stepped in and told him to stay away. The two of them argued back and forth, and finally I was free to go. Fortunately, the dealer who had spoken up for me was much more central and positively associated with the local scene. Finally, I am unsure if I would have had success in gaining entrance to the scene had I not been a woman.

## DEVELOPING RELATIONSHIPS AND TRUST

The processes involved in developing relationships in research situations amplify those involved in developing relationships in general. Both parties need to get to know each other, become aware and accepting of each other's roles, and engage in a reciprocal relationship. Being supportive and providing practical assistance were the most visible and direct ways for me as the researcher to develop a relationship. Throughout the years, I have given countless rides, provided child care on numerous occasions, bought groceries, and listened for hours to stories that were unrelated to my initial research questions. Gradually, my role allowed me to become part of these women's lives and to build rapport with many of them.

Over time, many women also realized that I was uninterested in being a prostitute and that I genuinely was interested in learning as much as possible about their lives. Many felt flattered that someone wanted to learn from them and that they had knowledge to offer. Allowing women to tell their stories and engaging in a dialogue with them probably were the single most important techniques that allowed me to develop relationships with them. Had I only wanted to focus on the questions I had in mind, developing such relationships might have been more difficult.

At times, I was able to get to know a woman only after her pimp endorsed our contact. One of my scariest experiences occurred before I knew to work through the pimps, and one such man had some of his friends follow me on my way home one night. I will never know what plans they had in mind for me because I fortunately was able to escape with only a few bruises. Over a year later, the woman acknowledged that her pimp had gotten upset and told her he was going to teach me a lesson.

On other occasions, I first needed to be screened by owners and managers of crack houses before the research could continue. Interestingly, screenings always were done by a man even if the person who vouched for me was a man himself. While the women also were cautious, the ways in which they checked me out tended to be much more subtle. For example, one of them would tell me a story, indicating that it was a secret about another person on the stroll. Although I failed to realize this at the time, my field notes revealed that frequently after such a conversation, others would ask me questions about related topics. One woman later acknowledged that putting out such stories was a test to see if I would keep information confidential.

Learning more about the women and gaining a better understanding of their lives also raised many ethical questions. No textbook told me how to handle situations in which a pimp abused a woman, a customer forced a woman to engage in unwanted sex acts, a customer requested unprotected sex from a woman who knew she was HIV infected, or a boyfriend had unrealistic expectations regarding a woman's earnings to support his drug habit. I failed to know the proper response when asked to engage in illegal activities such as holding drugs or money a woman had stolen from a customer. In general, my response was to explain that I was there as a researcher. During those occasions when pressures became too severe, I decided to leave a scene. For example, I never returned to certain crack houses because pimps there continued to ask me to consider working for them.

Over time, I was fortunate to develop relationships with people who "watched my back." One pimp in particular intervened if he perceived other pimps, customers, or passersby harassing me. He also was the one who gave me my street name: Whitie (indicating my racial background) or Ms. Whitie for those who disrespected me. While this was my first street name, I subsequently had others. Being given a street name was a symbolic gesture of acceptance. Gradually, I developed an identity that allowed me to be both an insider and an outsider. While hanging out on the strolls and other gathering places, including crack houses, I had to deal with some of the same uncomfortable conditions as the prostitutes, such as cold or warm weather, lack of access to a rest room, refusals from owners for me to patronize a restaurant, and of course, harassment by customers and the police.

I participated in many informal conversations. Unless pushed to do so, I seldom divulged my opinions. I was more open with my feelings about situations and showed empathy. I learned quickly that providing an opinion can backfire. I agreed that one of the women was struggling a lot and stated that I felt sorry for her. While I meant to indicate my genuine concern for her, she heard that I felt sorry for her because she was a failure. When she finally, after several weeks, talked with me again, I was able to explain to her that I was not judging her, but rather felt concerned for her. She remained cynical and many times asked me for favors to make up for my mistake. It took me months before I felt comfortable telling her that I felt I had done enough and that it was time to let go. However, if she was not ready, she needed to know that I would no longer go along. This was one of many occasions when I learned that although I wanted to facilitate my work as a researcher, that I wanted people to like and trust me, I also needed to set boundaries.

Rainy and slow nights often provided good opportunities for me to participate in conversations with groups of women. Popular topics included how to work safely, what to do about condom use, how to make more money. I often served as a health educator and a supplier of condoms, gels, vaginal douches, and other feminine products. Many women were very worried about the AIDS epidemic. However, they also were worried about how to use a condom when a customer refused to do so. They worried particularly about condom use when they needed money badly and, consequently, did not want to propose that the customer use one for fear of rejection. While some women became experts at "making" their customers use a condom—for example, by hiding it in their mouth prior to beginning oral sex—others would carry condoms to please me but never pull one out. If a woman was HIV positive and I knew she failed to use a condom, I faced the ethical dilemma of challenging her or staying out of it.

Developing trusting relationships with crack prostitutes was more difficult. Crack houses were not the right environment for informal conversations. Typically, the atmosphere was tense and everyone was suspicious of each other. The best times to talk with these women were when we bought groceries together, when I helped them clean their homes, or when we shared a meal. Often the women were very different when they were not high than they were when they were high or craving crack. In my conversations with them, I learned that while I might have observed their actions the night before, they themselves might not remember them. Once I realized this, I would be very careful to omit any detail unless I knew that the woman herself did remember the event.

## IN-DEPTH INTERVIEWS

All interviews were conducted in a private setting, including women's residences, my car or my office, a restaurant of the women's choice, or any other setting the women selected. I did not begin conducting official interviews until I developed relationships with the women. Acquiring written informed consent prior to the interview was problematic. It made me feel awkward. Here I was asking the women to sign a form after they had begun to trust me. However, often I felt more upset about this technicality than the women themselves. As soon as they realized that the form was something the university required, they seemed to understand. Often they laughed about the official statements, and some asked if I was sure the form was to protect them and not the school.[3] None of the women refused to sign the consent form, although some refused to sign it right away and asked to be interviewed later.

In some instances the consent procedures caused the women to expect a formal interview. Some of them were disappointed when they saw I only had a few structured questions about demographic characteristics, followed by a long list of open-ended questions. When this disappointment occurred, I reminded the women that I wanted to learn from them and that the best way to do so was by engaging in a dialogue rather than interrogating them. Only by letting the women identify their salient issues and the topics they wanted to address was I able to gain an insider's perspective. By being a careful listener and probing for additional information and explanation, I as the interviewer, together with the women, was able to uncover the complexities of their lives. In addition, the nature of the interview allowed me to ask questions about contradictions in a woman's story. For example, sometimes a woman would say that she always used a condom. However, later on in the conversation she would indicate that if she needed drugs she would never use one. By asking her to elaborate on this, I was able to begin developing insights into condom use by type of partner, type of sex acts, and social context.

privacy. The use of pseudonyms is suggested by guidelines to protect the privacy of study participants (American Anthropological Association; American Sociological Association).

2. For more information about qualitative research methods, see, for example, Patricia Adler and Peter Adler, *Membership Roles in Field Research* (Newbury Park: Sage, 1987); Michael Agar, *The Professional Stranger* (New York: Academic Press, 1980) and *Speaking of Ethnography* (Beverly Hills: Sage, 1986); Howard Becker and Blanche Geer, "Participant Observation and Interviewing: A Comparison," *Human Organization* 16 (1957): 28–32; Norman Denzin, *Sociological Methods: A Sourcebook* (Chicago: Aldine, 1970); Barney Glaser and Anselm Strauss, *The Discovery of Grounded Theory: Strategies for Qualitative Research* (Chicago: Aldine, 1967); Y. Lincoln and E. Guba, *Naturalistic Inquiry* (Beverly Hills: Sage, 1985); John Lofland, "Analytic Ethnography: Features, Failings, and Futures," *Journal of Contemporary Ethnography* 24 (1996): 30–67; and James Spradley, *The Ethnographic Interview* (New York: Holt, Rinehart and Winston, 1979) and *Participant Observation* (New York: Holt, Rinehart and Winston, 1980).

3. For a more extensive discussion of informed consent procedures and related ethical issues, see Bruce L. Berg, *Qualitative Research Methods for the Social Sciences,* 3rd edition, Chapter 3: "Ethical Issues" (Boston: Allyn and Bacon, 1998).

# 38

# Law, Custom, and Crimes against Women

## *The Problem of Dowry Death in India*

*John van Willigen and V. C. Channa*

Anthropologists find many societies with unusual customs, beliefs, and behaviors. Usually they discover, after careful study and reflection, that these perform some useful function within the society, as discussed in Goldstein's *When Brothers Share a Wife.* But is this always the case? Must we assume that simply because a custom exists it is healthy for the members of society? We think not, and the Christians who were fed to lions and the Aztec slaves who were sacrificed to a bloodthirsty god would most likely agree.

Times change; hunters and gatherers plant crops, tribal people rush headlong into peasantry, and small-scale farmers become urban wage earners. Traditions that helped maintain a healthy society in one context may become dysfunctional in another. For better or worse, traditions and beliefs run deep and are almost impossible to unlearn. It is the nature of culture to resist change.

As you will read, the practice of dousing a bride with kerosene and creating a human torch certainly indicates that the payment of dowry is a traditional practice gone awry. That said, what can be done? Laws, even those that carry serious penalties, are light ammunition against the armor of strongly held cultural beliefs. Governments will solve such problems only through public policy based on in-depth cultural understanding.

***As you read this selection, ask yourself the following questions:***

- What do you think the authors mean when they suggest that dowry death presents a problem for ethnologists because of ethnological theory's functional cast?
- Why does the institution of dowry make college education problematic for some young women?
- What are the present-day approaches to solving the dowry death problem?
- How can women's access to production roles and property, delocalization of social control, and economic transformation affect the problem of dowry death?
- Dowry-related violence in India is related to the economic value of women. What might be said about the relationship between the economic position and the social status of women in America?

***The following terms discussed in this selection are included in the Glossary at the back of the book:***

*caste*
*cultural materialism*
*demography*
*dowry*
*ethnology*
*peasants*
*sex roles*

*A 25-year-old woman was allegedly burnt to death by her husband and mother-in-law at their East Delhi home yesterday. The housewife, Mrs. Sunita, stated before her death at the Jaya Prakash Narayana Hospital that members of her husband's family had been harassing her for bringing inadequate dowry.*

*The woman told the Shahdara subdivisional magistrate that during a quarrel over dowry at their Pratap Park house yesterday, her husband gripped her from behind while the mother-in-law poured kerosene over her clothes.*

*Her clothes were then set ablaze. The police have registered a case against the victim's husband, Suraj Prakash, and his mother.*

—*Times of India,* February 19, 1988

van Willigen, John & Channa, V.C. "Law, Custom, and Crimes against Women: The Problem of Dowry Death in India." Reproduced by permission of the Society for Applied Anthropology (SfAA) from *Human Organization* 50, no. 4 (1991):369–377.

This routinely reported news story describes what in India is termed a "bride-burning" or "dowry death." Such incidents are frequently reported in the newspapers of Delhi and other Indian cities. In addition, there are cases in which the evidence may be ambiguous, so that deaths of women by fire may be recorded as kitchen accidents, suicides, or murders. Dowry violence takes a characteristic form. Following marriage and the requisite giving of dowry, the family of the groom makes additional demands for the payment of more cash or the provision of more goods. These demands are expressed in unremitting harassment of the bride, who is living in the household of her husband's parents, culminating in the murder of the woman by members of her husband's family or by her suicide. The woman is typically burned to death with kerosene, a fuel used in pressurized cook stoves, hence the use of the term "bride-burning" in public discourse.

Dowry death statistics appear frequently in the press and parliamentary debates. Parliamentary sources report the following figures for married women 16 to 30 years of age in Delhi: 452 deaths by burning for 1985; 478 for 1986 and 300 for the first six months of 1987 (Bhatia 1988). There were 1,319 cases reported nationally in 1986 (*Times of India,* January 10, 1988). Police records do not match hospital records for third degree burn cases among younger married women; far more violence occurs than the crime reports indicate (Kumari 1988).

There is other violence against women related both directly and indirectly to the institution of dowry. For example, there are unmarried women who commit suicide so as to relieve their families of the burden of providing a dowry. A recent case that received national attention in the Indian press involved the triple suicide of three sisters in the industrial city of Kanpur. A photograph was widely published showing the three young women hanging from ceiling fans by their scarves. Their father, who earned about 4,000 Rs. [rupees] per month, was not able to negotiate marriage for his oldest daughter. The grooms were requesting approximately 100,000 Rs. Also linked to the dowry problem is selective female abortion made possible by amniocentesis. This issue was brought to national attention with a startling statistic reported out of a seminar held in Delhi in 1985. Of 3,000 abortions carried out after sex determination through amniocentesis, only one involved a male fetus. As a result of these developments, the government of the state of Maharashtra banned sex determination tests except those carried out in government hospitals.

The phenomenon of dowry death presents a difficult problem for the ethnologist. Ethnological theory, with its residual functionalist cast, still does not deal effectively with the social costs of institutions of what might be arguably referred to as custom gone bad, resulting in a culturally constituted violence syndrome.

This essay examines dowry and its violent aspects, and some of the public solutions developed to deal with it in India. Our work consists of a meta-analysis of some available literature. We critique the legal mechanisms established to regulate the cultural institution of dowry and the resultant social evils engendered by the institution, and argue that policies directed against these social evils need to be constructed in terms of an underlying cause rather than of the problem itself. We consider cause, an aspect of the problem infrequently discussed in public debate. As Saini asserts, "legal academicians have shown absolutely no interest in the causal roots of dowry as practiced in contemporary India" (1983:143).

## THE INSTITUTION

Since ancient times, the marriage of Hindus has required the transfer of property from the family of the bride to the family of the groom. Dowry or *daan dehej* is thought by some to be sanctioned by such religious texts as the *Manusmriti.* Seen in this way, dowry is a religious obligation of the father of a woman and a matter of *dharma* (religious duty) whereby authority over a woman is transferred from her father to her husband. This transfer takes different forms in different communities in modern India (Tambiah 1973). In public discussion, the term "dowry" covers a wide range of traditional payments and expenses, some presented to the groom's family and others to be retained by the bride. Customs have changed through time. The financial burdens of gifts and the dowry payments per se are exacerbated by the many expenses associated with the marriage celebration itself, but dowry payment is especially problematic because of its open-ended nature. As Tambiah notes, "marriage payments in India usually comprise an elaborate series of payments back and forth between the marrying families" and "this series extends over a long period of time and persists after marriage" (1973:92). Contemporary cases such as the death of Mrs. Sunita, often revolve around such continued demands.

A daughter's marriage takes a long time to prepare and involves the development of an adaptive strategy on the part of her family. An important part of the strategy is the preparation for making dowry payments; family consumption may be curtailed so as to allow accumulation of money for dowry. Seeing to marriage arrangements may be an important aspect of retirement planning. The dowries that the family receives on behalf of their sons may be "rolled over" to deal with the daughter's requirements. Families attempt to cultivate in both their sons and daughters attributes that will make them more attractive in marriage negotiations. Many things besides dowry are considered in negotiations: "non-economic" factors have demonstrable effect on the expectations for dowry and the family's strategy concerning the dowry process.

Education is a variable to be considered in the negotiation process. Education of young women is somewhat problematic because suitable husbands for such women must also be college educated. The parents of such young men demand more dowry for their sons. A consideration in sending a young woman to college will therefore be her parents' capacity to dower her adequately so as to obtain an appropriate groom. In any case, education is secondary to a man's earning power and the reputation of a woman's family. Education is, however, important in the early stages of negotiation because of the need to coordinate the level of the education of the men and women. Education qualifications are also less ambiguously defined than other dimensions of family reputation. Physical attractiveness is a consideration, but it is thought somewhat unseemly to emphasize this aspect of the decision.

Advertisements in newspapers are used for establishing marriage proposals (Aluwalia 1969; Niehoff 1959; Weibe and Ramu 1971), but contacts are more typically established through kin and other networks. Some marriages may be best termed "self-arranged," and are usually called "love marriages." In these cases, young men and women may develop a relationship independent of their families and then ask that negotiations be carried out on their behalf by family representatives.

Analysis of matrimonial advertisements shows some of the attributes considered to be important. Listed in such advertisements are education, age, income and occupation, physical attributes, *gotra* (a kind of unilineal descent group) membership, family background, place of residence, personality features, consideration of dowry, time and type of marriage, and language.

Consideration of dowry and other expenditures are brought out early in the negotiations and can serve as a stumbling block. Dowry negotiations can go on for some time. The last stage is the actual "seeing of the groom" and the "seeing of the bride," both rather fleeting encounters whose position at the end of the process indicates their relative lack of importance.

Marriage is a process by which two families mutually evaluate each other. The outcome of the negotiations is an expression of the relative worth of the two persons, a man and a woman, and, by extension, the worth of their respective families. This estimation of worth is expressed in marriage expenditures, of which dowry is but a part. There are three possible types of expenditures: cash gifts, gifts of household goods, and expenditures on the wedding celebration itself. The cash gift component of the dowry goes to the groom's father and comes to be part of his common household fund. The household goods are for use by the groom's household, although they may be used to establish a separate household for the newlyweds. When separate accommodations are not set up, the groom's family may insist that the goods do not duplicate things they already have.

Dates for marriages are set through consideration of horoscopes; horoscopy is done by professional astrologers *(pandits)*. This practice leads to a concentration of marriage dates and consequent high demand for marriage goods and services at certain times of the year. During marriage seasons, the cost of jewelry, furniture, clothes, musicians' services, and other marriage related expenditures goes up, presumably because of the concentration of the demand caused by the astrologers.

The expenditures required of the woman's family for the wedding in general and the dowry in particular are frequently massive. Paul reports, for a middle-class Delhi neighborhood, that most dowries were over 50,000 Rs. (1986). Srinivas comments that dowries over 200,000 Rs. are not uncommon (1984).[1]

## ETHNOLOGICAL THEORIES ABOUT DOWRY

Dowry had traditionally been discussed by ethnologists in the context of the functionalist paradigm, and much theorizing about dowry appears to be concerned with explaining the "contribution" that the institution makes to social adaptation. The early theoretician Westermarck interpreted dowry as a social marker of the legitimacy of spouse and offspring, and as a mechanism for defining women's social roles and property rights in the new household (Westermarck 1921:428). Murdock suggests that dowry may confirm the contract of marriage (1949). Dowry is interpreted by Friedl as a means to adjust a woman to her affinal home as it rearranges social relationships including the social separation of the man from his parents (1967). Dowry payments are public expressions of the new relationship between the two families, and of the social status of the bride and groom.

Dowry is seen in the social science literature as a kind of antemortem or anticipated inheritance by which a widow is assured of support, and provision for her offspring (Friedl 1967; Goody 1973, 1976). It transfers money to where the women will be and where they will reproduce; as a result, resources are also placed where the children will benefit, given the practice of patrilineal inheritance of immovable, economically valuable property like farm land.

In India, dowry is also seen as an expression of the symbolic order of society. According to Dumont, dowry expresses the hierarchal relations of marriage in India and lower status of the bride (Dumont 1957). The amount of dowry given is an expression of prestige. The capacity to buy prestige through dowry increases the potential for social mobility (Goody 1973). Dowry is a kind of delayed consumption used to demonstrate or improve social rank (Epstein 1960).

There is a significant discontinuity between discussions of dowry in the ethnological theory and in public discourse. Certainly the dowry problem does appear in the writing of contemporary ethnologists, but it is simply lamented and left largely uninterpreted and unexplained.

## THE EXTANT SOLUTIONS TO THE PROBLEM

The Dowry Prohibition Act of 1961, as amended in 1984 and 1986, is the primary legal means for regulating the dowry process and controlling its excesses. The laws against dowry are tough. Dowry demand offenses are "cognizable" (require no warrant) and nonbailable, and the burden of proof is on the accused. There are, in fact, convictions under the law.

The act defines dowry as "any property of valuable security given or agreed to be given either directly or indirectly—(a) by one party to a marriage to the other party to a marriage; or (b) by parents of either party to a marriage or by any other person, to either party to the marriage or to any other person" (Government of India 1986:1). The act makes it illegal to give or take dowry, "If any person after the commencement of this act, gives or takes or abets the giving or taking of dowry, he shall be punishable with imprisonment for a term which shall not be less than five years; and with fine which shall not be less than fifteen thousand rupees or the amount of the value of such dowry whichever is more" (Government of India 1986:1). While this section unambiguously prohibits dowry, the third section allows wedding presents to be freely given. Thus the law does not apply to "presents which are given at the time of marriage to the bride (without demand having been made in that behalf)" (Government of India 1986:1). Identical provisions apply to the groom. Furthermore, all such presents must be listed on a document before the consummation of the marriage. The list is to contain a brief description and estimation of the value of the gifts, name of presenting person, and the relationship that person has with the bride and groom. This regulation also provides "that where such presents are made by or on the behalf of the bride or any other person related to the bride, such presents are of a customary nature and the value thereof is not excessive having regard to the financial status of the person by whom, or on whose behalf, such presents are given" (Government of India 1986:2). Amendments made in 1984 make it illegal for a person to demand dowry with the same penalty as under the earlier "giving and taking" provision. It was also declared illegal to advertise for dowry, such an offense being defined as not bailable, with the burden of proof on the accused person.

This legislation was coupled with some changes in the Indian Penal Code that legally established the concept of "dowry death." That is, "where the death of a woman is caused by any burns or bodily injury or occurs otherwise than under normal circumstances within seven years of her marriage and it is shown that soon before her death she was subjected to cruelty or harassment by her husband or any relative of her husband for, or in connection with, any demand for dowry, such death shall be called 'dowry death,' and such husband or relative shall be deemed to have caused her death" (Government of India 1987:4). The Indian Evidence Act of 1871 was changed so as to allow for the presumption of guilt under the circumstances outlined above. Changes in the code allowed for special investigation and reporting procedures of deaths by apparent suicide of women within seven years of marriage if requested by a relative. There were also newly defined special provisions for autopsies.

To this point, however, these legal mechanisms have proved ineffective. According to Sivaramayya, the "act has signally failed in its operation" (1984:66). Menon refers to the "near total failure" of the law (1988:12). A similar viewpoint is expressed by Srinivas, who wrote, "The Dowry Prohibition Act of 1961 has been unanimously declared to be an utterly ineffective law" (1984:29).

In addition to the legal attack on dowry abuses, numerous public groups engage in public education campaigns. In urban settings, the most noteworthy of these groups are specialized research units such as the Special Cell for Women of the Tata Institute of Social Sciences (Bombay), and the Center for Social Research (New Delhi). Also involved in the effort are private voluntary organizations such as the Crimes Against Women Cell, Karmika, and Sukh Shanti.

These groups issue public education advertising on various feminist issues. The anti-dowry advertisement of the Federation of Indian Chambers of Commerce and Industry Ladies Organization exemplifies the thrust of these campaigns. In the following advertisement, which was frequently run in the winter of 1988 in newspapers such as the *Times of India*, a photograph of a doll dressed in traditional Indian bridal attire was shown in flames.

> Every time a young bride dies because of dowry demands, we are all responsible for her death. Because we allow it to happen. Each year in Delhi hospitals alone, over 300 brides die of third degree burns. And many more deaths go unreported. Most of the guilty get away. And we just shrug helplessly and say, "what can we do?" We can do a lot.
>
> Help create social condemnation of dowry. Refuse to take or give dowry. Protest when you meet people who condone the practice. Reach out and help the girl being harassed for it. Act now.
>
> Let's fight it together.
>
> As parents, bring up educated, self-reliant daughters. Make sure they marry only after 18. Oppose dowry; refuse to even discuss it. If your daughter is harassed after marriage stand by her.
>
> As young men and women, refuse marriage proposals where dowry is being considered. As friends and neighbors, ostracize families who give or take dowry. Reach out to help victims of dowry harassment.
>
> As legislators and jurists, frame stronger laws. Ensure speedy hearings, impose severe punishments. As associations, give help and advice. Take up the challenge of changing laws and attitudes of society. Let us all resolve to fight the evil. If we fight together we can win.
>
> SAY NO TO DOWRY.

Also engaged in anti-dowry work are peasant political action groups such as Bharatiya Kisan Union (BKU). BKU consists of farmers from western Uttar Pradesh whose political program is focused more generally on agricultural issues. The group sponsored a massive 25-day demonstration at Meerut, Uttar Pradesh, in 1988. The leadership used the demonstration to announce a social reform program, most of it dealing with marriage issues. According to news service reports, "The code of social reforms includes fixing the maximum number of persons in a marriage party at 11, no feasts relating to marriage, and no dowry except 10 grams of gold and 30 grams of silver" (*Times of India*, February 11, 1988). Buses plying rural roads in western Uttar Pradesh are reported to have been painted with the slogan "The bride is the dowry." Private campaigns against dowry occur in the countryside as well as among the urban elites, although it is likely that the underlying motivations are quite different.

## POLICY ANALYSIS

Our argument is based on the assumption that social problems are best dealt with by policies directed at the correction of causative factors, rather than at the amelioration of symptoms. While current legal remedies directly confront dowry violence, the linkage between cause and the problematic behavior is not made. Here we develop an argument consisting of three components: women's access to production roles and property; delocalization of social control; and economic transformation of society. The pattern of distribution of aspects of the institution of dowry and its attendant problems is important to this analysis. Although dowry practices and the related crimes against women are distributed throughout Indian society, the distribution is patterned in terms of geography, caste rank, socioeconomic rank, urban/rural residence, and employment status of the women. In some places and among some people there are demonstrably more violence, more intensity of dowry practices, and more commitment to dowry itself. Much of the distributional data are problematic in one way or another. The most frequent problem is that the studies are not based on national samples. Furthermore, the interpretation of results is often colored by reformist agendas. There is a tendency to deemphasize differences in frequency from one segment of the population to another so as to build support of dowry death as a general social reform issue. Nevertheless, while the data available for these distributions are of inconsistent quality, they are interpretable in terms of our problem.

### Women's Access to Production Roles and Property

Dowry violence is most frequent in north India. Some say that it is an especially severe problem in the Hindi Belt (i.e., Uttar Pradesh, Haryana, Punjab, Delhi, Bihar) (Government of India 1974:75). It is a lesser, albeit increasing problem in the south. There is also a north/south difference in the marriage institution itself. To simplify somewhat, in the north hypergamy is sought after in marriage alliances, in which case brides seek grooms from higher rank descent groups within their caste group (Srinivas 1984). In the south, marriages are more typically isogamous.

The literature comparing north and south India indicates important contrasts at both the ecological and the institutional levels. Based on conceptions developed by Boserup (1970) in a cross-cultural comparative framework on the relationship between the farming system and occupational role of women, Miller (1981) composed a model for explaining the significant north-south differences in the juvenile sex ratio [the ratio of males to females ten years of age and below]. The farming systems of the north are based on "dry-field plow cultivation," whereas in the south the farming systems are dominated by "swidden and wet-rice cultivation" (Miller 1981:28). These two systems make different labor demands. In the wet rice or swidden systems of the south, women are very important sources of labor. In the north, women's involvement in agricultural production is limited. According to Miller, women in the north are excluded from property holding and receive instead a "dowry of movables." In the south, where women are included in the production activities, they may receive "rights to land" (Miller 1981:28). In the north, women are high-cost items of social overhead, while in the south, women contribute labor and are more highly valued. In the north there is a "high cost of raising several daughters" while in the south there is "little liability in raising several daughters." There is thus "discrimination against daughters" and an "intense preference for sons" in the north, and "appreciation for daughters" and "moderate preference for sons" in the south. Miller thus explains the unbalanced-toward-males juvenile sex ratios of the north and the balanced sex ratios of the south (Miller 1981:27–28). The lower economic value of women in the north is expressed in differential treatment of children by sex. Females get less food, less care, and less attention, and therefore they have a higher death rate. In general the Boserup and Miller economic argument is consistent with Engels's thesis about the relationship between the subordination of women and property (Engels 1884; Hirschon 1984:1).

Miller extended her analysis of juvenile sex ratios to include marriage costs (including dowry), female labor participation, and property owning, and found that property owning was associated with high marriage costs and low female labor force participation, both of which were associated with high juvenile sex ratios. That is, the death rate of females is higher when marriage costs are high and women are kept from remunerative employment. Both of these patterns are associated with the "propertied" segment of the population (Miller 1981:156–159). Her data are derived from the secondary analysis of ethnographic accounts. The literature concerning the distribution of dowry practices and dowry death is consistent with these results.

Miller's analysis shows a general pattern of treatment of females in India. Their access to support in various forms is related to their contribution to production (Miller 1981). This analysis does not explain the problem of dowry violence, but it does demonstrate a fundamental pattern within which dowry violence can be interpreted.

The distribution of dowry varies by caste. In her study of dowry violence victims in Delhi, Kumari found that members of the lower ranking castes report less "dowry harassment" than do those in higher ranking castes (Kumari 1988:31). These results are consistent with Miller's argument since the pattern of exclusion of women from economic production roles varies by caste. Women of lower castes are less subject to restrictions concerning employment outside the realm of reproduction within the household. These women are often poor and uneducated, and are subject to other types of restrictions.

In the framework of caste, dowry practices of higher caste groups are emulated by lower caste groups. This process is known as "Sanskritization" and it may relate to the widely held view that dowry harassment is increasing in lower ranking castes. Sanskritization is the process by which lower ranked caste groups attempt to raise their rank through the emulation of higher rank castes. The emulation involves discarding certain behaviors (such as eating meat or paying bride price) and adopting alternatives (Srinivas 1969). Attitudinal research shows that people of the lower socio-economic strata have a greater commitment to dowry than do those of higher strata (Hooja 1969; Khanna and Verghese 1978; Paul 1986). Although the lower and middle classes are committed to dowry, the associated violence, including higher death rates, is more typically a middle class problem (Kumari 1988).

Employment status of women has an effect on dowry. In her survey of dowry problems in a south Delhi neighborhood, Paul (1986) found that the amount of dowry was less for employed middle class women than it was for the unemployed. This pattern is also suggested by Verghese (1980) and van der Veen (1972:40), but disputed by others (Murickan 1975). This link is also manifested among tribal people undergoing urbanization. Tribal people, ranked more toward the low end of the social hierarchy, typically make use of bride price (i.e., a payment to the bride's family) rather than dowry (Karve 1953). As these groups become more integrated into national life, they will shift to dowry practices to emulate high castes while their women participate less in gainful employment (Luthra 1983). Croll finds a similar relationship in her analysis of post-revolutionary China. She says, "it is the increased value attributed to women's labor which is largely responsible for the decline in the dowry" (1984:58).

Both Kumari (1988) and Srinivas (1984) developed arguments based on non-economic factors. Kumari in effect indicated that if dowry could be explained in economic terms, marriage would be simply a calculation of the value of a woman: if the value were high, bride price would be paid, and if the value were low, dowry transactions would occur. This formulation was presented as a refutation of Madan's dowry-as-compensation argument (Kumari 1988). We agree that reducing this practice to purely economic terms is an absurdity. The argument is not purely economic, but it is certainly consistent with a cultural materialist perspective (Harris 1979) in which symbolic values are

Furthermore, property that is allowed to remain in the name of the deceased for any length of time, as is frequently the case in India, should revert to the state. As it stands, property may remain in the name of a deceased ancestor, while his descendants divide it informally among themselves.

The establishment of a gender-neutral inheritance law represents a significant shift in public policy. We argue that there is a link between pro-male property laws and violence toward women. While we assert this position, we also need to recognize that the property laws give coherence and stability to an essential Indian institution, the joint family. The Mitakshara principle of male inheritance rights is both a reflection and a cause of family solidarity. Modifying this principle in an attempt to reduce violence toward women could have a deleterious effect on family coherence. In addition, the fundamental nature of these institutions makes it inconceivable that there would be substantial resistance to these changes. Yet if one considers this issue in historic terms, it is apparent that during the twentieth century, legal change is in the direction of gender neutrality, a process that started with the Hindu Law of Inheritance (Amendment) Act (1929) and the Hindu Succession Act (1956), and continues through judicial decisions to the present (Diwan 1988:384). As Diwan notes in reference to the changes brought by the Hindu Succession Act of 1956, "the Mitakshara bias towards preference of males over females and of agnates over cognates has been considerably whittled down" (1988:358). Such change is not easy. The changes brought with the Hindu Succession Act in 1956 were achieved only after overcoming "stiff resistance from the traditionalists" (Government of India 1974:135). The same report states, "The hold of tradition, however, was so strong that even while introducing sweeping changes, the legislators compromised and retained in some respects the inferior position of women" (Government of India 1974:135). It must be remembered that the texts that are the foundations of contemporary law include legislation (such as the Hindu Succession Act itself), case law, and religious texts, so that the constitutional question is also a question for religious interpretation, despite the constitutional commitment to secularism.

We are advocating further steps toward gender neutrality of the inheritance laws so that women and men will receive an equal share under intestate succession, and have an equal chance to be testamentary heirs. The law should thus be gender-neutral while still permitting a range of decisions allowing property to stay in a male line if the holder of the property so chooses. The required social adjustment could be largely achieved through the decisions of a family, backed by the power of the state. Families could express their preferences, but the state would not serve to protect the economic interests of males. The process could involve the concept of birthright as well as succession at death. We do not choose to engage those arguments, but do point out that the rapid aging of the Indian population may suggest that a full abrogation of the Mitakshara principle of birthright would be the best social policy because doing so would give older people somewhat greater control over their property in an economy virtually devoid of public investment in social services for older people (Bose and Gangrade 1988, Sharma and Dak 1987).

There are precedents for such policy at the state level. In Andhra Pradesh, the Hindu Succession Act was amended to provide for a female's birthright interest in the Mitakshara property. In Kerala, the Mitakshara property concept was legally abrogated altogether. Other gender asymmetries in the laws of India need to be attacked. The overall goal of policy should be to increase the economic value of women.

Ethnological theory directs our attention to social recognition of marriage and property transfer as functionally important features of the institution. The state can provide a means of socially recognizing marriage through registration and licensure. The law expresses no explicit preference for traditional marriage ritual, and it is possible to have a civil marriage under the provisions of the Special Marriage Act (1954) through registration with a magistrate. Nevertheless, this system coexists parallel with the traditional system of marriage, which is beyond the reach of state control. Other marriages may be registered under this act if the persons involved so choose, and if a ceremony has been carried out. These special marriages are an alternative to an unregistered marriage.

We conclude that a useful mechanism for state control of dowry problems is the establishment of universal marriage registration, which does not exist at the present time. Marriage registration is also called for by the first Round Table on Social Audit of Implementation of Dowry Legislation (Bhatia 1988), which may serve to provide some monitoring of dowry abuses and perhaps to manifest the state's interest in an effective marriage institution. It would be naive to assume that such a policy would be widely honored, but as it is, low-income persons do not get married because they do not have the resources for marriage under the traditional non-state controlled regime. There are numerous reform groups that organize mass marriage ceremonies of village people so as to help them escape the burden of marriage expenditures. The point is that compliance is a large problem even under current circumstances.

In conclusion, we feel that the causes of the dowry problems are a product of the low economic value of women, loss of effective social control of abuse through

delocalization, and pressures caused by economic transformation. The traditional family, caste group, and community controls which have been reduced in effectiveness should be replaced by state functions. The foundation of state control is universal marriage registration and licensure. The impact of the economic value of women on the problem is indicated by the transition from bride price to dowry among tribal people. It is also associated with a reduction in the extent of gainful employment and lower dowry amounts demonstrated for employed women. A broad program to increase the economic value of women would be the most useful means of dealing with the problem of dowry. Further restrictions on dowry without providing for a radically different property right for females is probably not in the interests of Indian women, since dowry represents ante-mortem inheritance. This underlying paradox may explain the commitment to dowry revealed in attitudinal research with Indian women, even though it is also an important feminist issue. The alternatives include the abolishment of the legal basis for the joint family as a corporate unit as has been done in Kerala, or the legal redefinition of the joint family as economically duolineal, as has occurred in Andhra Pradesh.

## NOTE

1. For purposes of comparison, a mid-career Indian academic might be paid 60,000 Rs. per year.

## REFERENCES


Aluwalia, H. 1969. Matrimonial Advertisements in Panjab. *Indian Journal of Social Work* 30:55–65.

Bhatia, S. C. 1988. Social Audit of Dowry Legislation. Delhi: Legal Literacy Project.

Bose, A. B., and K. D. Gangrade. 1988. *The Aging in India, Problems and Potentialities.* New Delhi: Abhinav.

Boserup, Ester. 1970. *Women's Role in Economic Development.* New York: St. Martin's Press.

Chandrachud, Y. V. 1984. Foreword. In *Inequalities and the Law.* B. Sivaramayya, ed. Pp. iv–vi. Lucknow: Eastern Book Company.

Croll, Elisabeth. 1984. The Exchange of Women and Property: Marriage in Post-revolutionary China. In *Women and Property—Women as Property,* ed. Renee Hirschon, 44–61. London/New York: Croom Helm/St. Martin's Press.

Diwan, Paras. 1988. *Modern Hindu Law, Codified and Uncodified.* Allahabad: Allahabad Law Agency.

Dumont, Louis. 1957. *Hierarchy and Marriage Alliance in South Indian Kinship.* London: Royal Anthropological Institute.

Engels, Fredrich. 1884. *The Origin of Family, Private Property and the State.* New York: International.

Epstein, T. Scarlett. 1960. Peasant Marriage in South India. *Man in India* 40: 192–232.

Friedl, Ernestine. 1967. *Vasilika, A Village in Modern Greece.* New York: Holt, Rinehart and Winston.

Goody, Jack. 1973. Bridewealth and Dowry in Africa and Eurasia. In *Bridewealth and Dowry,* eds. Jack Goody and S. J. Tambiah, 1–58. Cambridge: Cambridge University Press.

______. 1976. *Production and Reproduction, A Comparative Study of the Domestic Domain.* Cambridge: Cambridge University Press.

Government of India. 1974. *Towards Equality: Report of the Committee on the Status of Women.* New Delhi: Government of India, Ministry of Education and Social Welfare.

______. 1985. The Hindu Succession Act. New Delhi: Government of India.

______. 1986. The Dowry Prohibition Act, 1961 (Act No. 28 of 1961) and Connected Legislation (as on 15th January, 1986). New Delhi: Government of India.

______. 1987. *India 1986, A Reference Manual.* Delhi: Ministry of Information and Broadcasting.

Harris, Marvin. 1979. *Cultural Materialism: The Struggle for a Science of Culture.* New York: Random House.

Hirschon, Renee. 1984. Introduction: Property, Power and Gender Relations. In *Women and Property—Women as Property,* ed. Renee Hirschon, 1–22. London/New York: Croom Helm/St. Martin's Press.

Hooja, S. L. 1969. *Dowry System in India.* New Delhi: Asia Press.

Karve, Irawati. 1953. *Kinship Organization in India.* Bombay: Asia Publishing.

Khanna, G., and M. Verghese. 1978. *Indian Women Today.* New Delhi: Vikas Publishing House.

Kumari, Ranjana. 1988. Practice and Problems of Dowry: A Study of Dowry Victims in Delhi. In *Social Audit of Dowry Legislation,* ed. S. C. Bhatia, 27–37. Delhi: Legal Literacy Project.

Luthra, A. 1983. Dowry Among the Urban Poor, Perception and Practice. *Social Action* 33: 207.

Mathew, Anna. 1987. Attitudes Toward Dowry. *Indian Journal of Social Work* 48: 95–102.

Menon, N. R. Madhava. 1988. The Dowry Prohibition Act: Does the Law Provide the Solution or Itself Constitute the Problem? In *Social Audit of Dowry Legislation,* ed. S. C. Bhatia, 11–26. Delhi: Legal Literacy Project.

Miller, Barbara D. 1981. *The Endangered Sex, Neglect of Female Children in Rural North India.* Ithaca, NY: Cornell University Press.

Murdock, George P. 1949. *Social Structure.* New York: Macmillan.

Murickan, J. 1975. Women in Kerala: Changing Socio-economic Status and Self Image. In *Women in Contemporary India,* ed. A. de Souza, 73–95. Delhi: Manohar.

Niehoff, Arthur H. 1959. A Study of Matrimonial Advertisements in North India. *Eastern Anthropologist* 12: 37–50.

Paul, Madan C. 1986. *Dowry and the Position of Women in India. A Study of Delhi Metropolis.* New Delhi: Inter India Publishers.

Saini, Debi. 1983. Dowry Prohibition Law, Social Change and Challenges in India. *Indian Journal of Social Work* 44(2): 143–147.

Sharma, M. L., and T. Dak. 1987. *Aging in India, Challenge for the Society.* Delhi: Ajanta Publications.

Sharma, Ursula. 1984. Dowry in North India: Its Consequences for Women. In *Women and Property—Women as Property,* ed. Renee Hirschon, 62–74. London/New York: Croom Helm/St. Martin's Press.

Sivaramayya, B. 1984. *Inequalities and the Law.* Lucknow: Eastern Book Company.

Srinivas, M. N. 1969. *Social Change in Modern India.* Berkeley, CA: University of California Press.

______. 1984. *Some Reflections on Dowry.* Delhi: Oxford University Press.

Tambiah, S. J. 1973. Dowry and Bridewealth and the Property Rights of Women in South Asia. In *Bridewealth and Dowry,* eds. Jack Goody and S. J. Tambiah, 59–169. Cambridge: Cambridge University Press.

van der Veen, Klaus W. 1972. *I Give Thee My Daughter—A Study of Marriage and Hierarchy Among the Anavil Brahmins of South Gujarat.* Assen: Van Gorcum.

Verghese, Jamila. 1980. *Her Gold and Her Body.* New Delhi: Vikas Publishing House.

Weibe, P. O., and G. N. Ramu. 1971. A Content Analysis of Matrimonial Advertisements. *Man in India* 51: 119–120.

Westermarck, Edward. 1921. *The History of Human Marriage.* London: MacMillan and Co.

# 39

# Culture and the Evolution of Obesity

*Peter J. Brown*

As a people, Americans rank as one of the fattest societies in history. This epidemiological fact remains despite the tremendous amount of money, effort, and worry that Americans put into diet, exercise, and the quest for the perfect body. For some people, particularly young women, the quest to be thin can become such an obsession that they develop life-threatening eating disorders, like anorexia nervosa. But in other cultures, young women may go to great lengths to try to gain weight to look attractive. There are no universal standards of physical beauty; in fact, there is considerable cross-cultural variation. Culture defines normality.

How do conditions like obesity come to be expressed? Biologists usually say that it is a combination of genes and environment. There is good evidence that genes predispose people toward conditions, but there is seldom evidence that the chain of causation is entirely genetic. A complete explanation must be both biological and cultural. In other words, if a condition like obesity is caused by an interaction of genetic and cultural/behavioral predispositions, then both the genes and culture must be the product of evolutionary processes.

In this selection, Peter Brown provides a cross-cultural and evolutionary analysis of how both biological and cultural factors in obesity evolved. This analysis explains the sociological distribution of obesity today. It also emphasizes that peripheral body fat (characteristic of women) is a small health hazard compared to abdominal fat (characteristic of men).

Dietary patterns are obviously shaped by culture. But human tendencies to value meat, fatty foods, and sweets must be understood in the context of our evolutionary past.

***As you read this selection, ask yourself the following questions:***

- Have you ever noticed that there are gender differences in the locality of fat storage in the body? Why would this be the case?
- Why are fat people ridiculed and discriminated against in the United States? Are these social reactions worse for men or for women?
- What does the author mean when he says that in a rich society, slenderness can be an individual symbol of conspicuous consumption?
- Given the difference in health risk between peripheral body fat and central body fat, why might weight not be the best way to measure one's risk?
- Why do humans like foods that are "bad" for them?

***The following terms discussed in this selection are included in the Glossary at the back of the book:***

| | |
|---|---|
| *adipose tissue* | *gender dimorphism* |
| *cultural ideals* | *ideal body images* |
| *culture* | *obesity* |
| *epidemiology* | *sexual dimorphism* |
| *food scarcity* | |

The etiology or cause of obesity can be understood in the context of human cultural and genetic evolution. The cause of human obesity and overweight involves the interaction of genetic traits with culturally patterned behaviors and beliefs. Both these genes and culture traits, remarkably common in human societies, are evolutionary products of similar processes of selection related to past food scarcities. This idea is not new: The notion of "thrifty phenotypes rendered detrimental by progress" was introduced more than a quarter-century ago. In recent years, the evidence for the existence of genes that enable individuals to use food energy efficiently and store energy reserves in the form of fat has been increasingly impressive; those individuals with "fat phenotypes" are likely to develop adult obesity (Stunkard et al. 1986, 1990).

Brown, Peter J. "Culture and the Evolution of Obesity." *Human Nature* 2 (1991):31–57. 

It is important to recognize that these "thrifty" genes are, at least in the human context, necessary but not sufficient factors in the causation of obesity. In actuality, the new discoveries in the genetics of obesity highlight our ignorance about the role of nongenetic or cultural factors, which are usually subsumed in the term *environment* in the medical literature. The purpose of this paper is to examine why and how cultures have evolved behaviors and beliefs that appear to predispose individuals to develop obesity. I believe that an anthropological model of culture has significant advantages over the commonly used undifferentiated concept of "environment" for generating hypotheses about behavioral causes of obesity. This cultural approach is particularly useful for improving our understanding of the social epidemiological distribution of obesity.

It is valuable to raise an obvious question at the outset: Why do people find it very difficult to reduce their intake of dietary fat and sugar even when the medical benefits of this behavioral change are well known to them? The answer is not obvious, since neither the physiological nor the cultural attraction of these foods is well understood. The proximate mechanisms for this attraction are linked to brain physiology and biochemistry (Wurtman and Wurtman 1987). The ultimate answers are linked to our evolutionary heritage. Human predispositions to obesity are found in both genetic and cultural traits that may have been adaptive in the context of past food scarcities but are maladaptive today in the context of affluence and constant food surpluses.

## THE PROBLEMS OF OBESITY AND OVERWEIGHT

Throughout most of human history, obesity was neither a common health problem nor even a realistic possibility for most people. Today, particularly in affluent societies like the United States, obesity is very common, affecting about 12 percent of adult men and women; overweight is even more common, affecting an additional 20 to 50 percent of adult Americans depending on the definitions used (Bray 1987). Not only are overweight and obesity relatively common conditions in our society, they are also extremely complex and intractable. Obesity is a serious public health problem because of its causal connection to major causes of morbidity and mortality from chronic diseases, including cardiovascular disease, type 2 diabetes mellitus (NIDDM), and hypertension. On the individual level, obesity and overweight bring with them an enormous amount of personal psychological pain. The fact that the obese are subjected to significant social and economic discrimination is well documented.

Fat is extraordinarily difficult to shed because the body guards its fat stores. The evidence concerning the effectiveness over a 5-year period of diet therapies indicates that nearly all of the weight that is lost through diets is eventually regained. The remarkable failure of diet therapies has made some researchers rethink their commonsensical theory of obesity as being caused by overeating; the clinical evidence of the past 40 years simply does not support this simplistic notion.

Even in the absence of scientific data about the effectiveness of diet therapy, the diet and weight-loss industry in the United States is remarkably successful in its ability to capture the hope and money of people who perceive themselves to be overweight. This industry thrives because of a complex of cultural beliefs about the ideal body and sexual attractiveness rather than medical advice and the prevention of chronic diseases per se. The American cultural concern about weight loss and the positive valuation of slenderness for women of the middle and upper classes are difficult to overemphasize. Chernin (1981) has referred to this cultural theme as an "obsession" and the "tyranny of slenderness." In this light, it is impossible to claim that obesity is purely a medical issue.

## OBESITY AND HUNGER

It is important to remember that for most citizens of the world today, as it has been in the past, the possibility of obesity is remote whereas the possibility of hunger is close to home. There is a palpable irony in the fact of an epidemic of obesity in a world characterized by hunger. For example, in the United States an estimated 20 million people are hungry because they are on a "serious diet;" generally these people are of the middle and upper classes, and most are women. At the same time in the same rich nation, another estimated 20 million Americans are hungry and poorly nourished largely because they lack sufficient money; generally these people are elderly, homeless, or rural inhabitants. This sad symmetry in the estimates of voluntary and involuntary hunger in the United States is a valuable starting point for a discussion of the etiology of obesity. From an evolutionary standpoint, past food shortages have acted as powerful agents of natural selection, shaping both human genetics and behavior.

A theory of the etiology of obesity must not only account for the influences of genes and learned behaviors but also explain its social distribution. Before the problem of causation is addressed, it is worthwhile to examine the nature of human obesity.

## CHANGING DEFINITIONS OF OBESITY

The most basic scientific issues regarding obesity are, in fact, controversial. The definitions of obesity and overweight have been the subject of substantial medical debate, in part because they must be based on inferred definitions of normality or "ideal" body proportions. Although obesity refers to excessive adiposity (fat deposits), the most common measurement is not of fat tissue at all but an indirect inference based on measures of stature and total body weight (Bray 1987).

The social history of height and weight standards in the United States is interesting. Until recently, the task of defining both obesity and ideal weights has been the domain of the life-insurance industry. The most well-known table of desirable weights was developed by the Metropolitan Life Insurance Company using correlation statistics between height/weight and mortality among insurance applicants. Ideal weights were based on data from 25-year-old insurance applicants, despite the nonrepresentative nature of the "sample" pool and the fact that in most human populations, individuals increase in weight until around age 50. Obesity was defined as 120 percent of the Ideal Body Weight (IBW), and overweight was defined as 110 percent IBW. Individual life-insurance applicants outside the recommended weight range were required to pay a surcharge on insurance premiums. In 1959, the concept of "frame size" was introduced, although the resulting categories were never given operational definitions using anthropometric measures.

Definitions of obesity have changed throughout history. From 1943 to 1980, definitions of "ideal weights" for women of a particular height were consistently lowered, while those for men remained approximately the same. In 1983, a major debate on the definition of obesity began when Metropolitan Life revised its tables upward, based on new actuarial studies of mortality. Many organizations and experts in the diet industry, including experts in medical fields, rejected these new standards.

In the current medical literature, weight and height tables have been replaced by the Body Mass Index (BMI), defined as body weight (in kilograms) divided by the square of body height (in meters). BMI ($W/H^2$) is strongly correlated with total body fat, and a value greater than 30 is generally considered obese. Current recommendations include slight increases in BMI with age (Bray 1987). Nevertheless, there continues to be little agreement on precise definitions of either overweight or obesity.

An important added dimension to the questions of definition of obesity involves the distribution of fat around the body trunk or on the limbs. Central or trunk body fat distribution is closely correlated with serious chronic diseases, such as cardiovascular disease, whereas peripheral body fat in the hips and limbs does not carry similar medical risks. Because of this clinically important distinction, measures of fat distribution like waist to hips ratio (WHR), wherein lower WHR values indicate lower risk of chronic disease consequences, will be a valuable addition to future definitions of obesity.

## FOUR FACTS ABOUT THE SOCIAL DISTRIBUTION OF OBESITY

Humans are among the fattest of all mammals, and the primary function of our fat is to serve as an energy reserve. The nonrandom social distribution of adiposity within and between human populations may provide a key to understanding obesity. Four facts about this social distribution are particularly cogent for an evolutionary reconstruction: (1) the gender difference in the total percent and site distribution of body fat, as well as the prevalence of obesity; (2) the concentration of obesity in certain ethnic groups; (3) the increase in obesity associated with economic modernization; and (4) the powerful and complex relationship between social class and obesity. Any useful theory concerning the etiology of obesity must account for these social epidemiological patterns.

### Sexual Dimorphism

Humans show only mild sexual dimorphism in variables like stature. Males are only 5 to 9 percent taller than females. The sample of adults from Tecumseh, Michigan, seen in Figure 1 are typical. Men are larger than women in height and total body mass, but women have more subcutaneous fat as measured by skinfold thicknesses in 16 of 17 sites (the exception is the suprailiac region—so-called "love handles"). The greatest degree of sexual dimorphism is found in the site of distribution of fat tissue; women have much more peripheral fat in the legs and hips (Kissebah et al. 1989). This difference is epidemiologically important because the greater proportion of peripheral fat in females may be associated with reduced morbidity compared to males with identical BMI values.

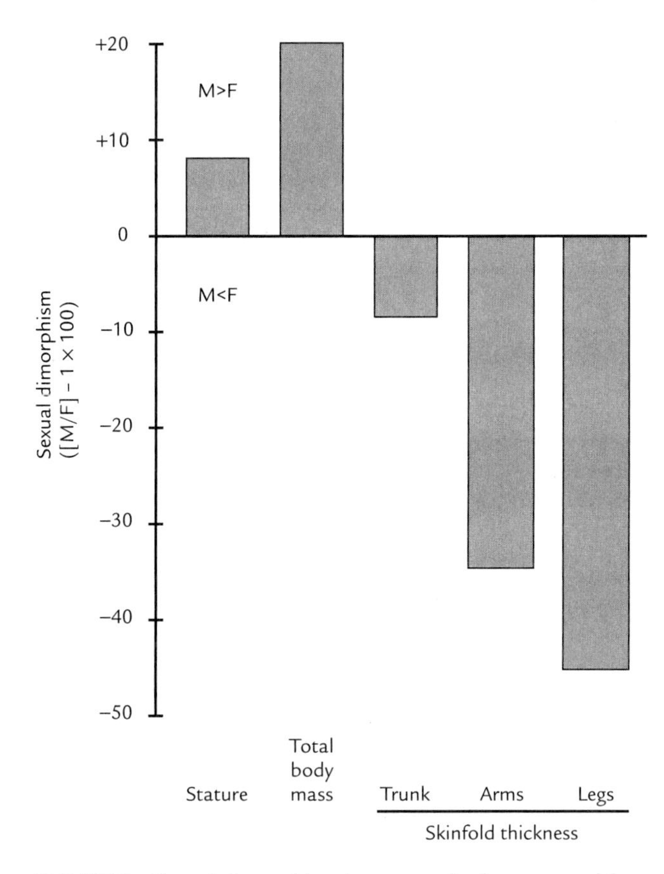


**FIGURE 1** Sexual dimorphism in stature, body mass, and fat measures among white Americans aged 20 to 70 in Techumseh, Michigan. Sexual dimorphism is calculated by comparing male and female means; positive figures refer to greater male measures. Skinfold thicknesses are means of four sites on the trunk or five sites on the arms and legs; the mean dimorphism for all 17 fat measures is -19 percent. From Brown, P.J., & M. Konner. "An Anthropological Perspective on Obesity." *Annals of the New York Academy of Sciences* 499 (1987):29–46. Copyright © 1987 by The New York Academy of Sciences. Reprinted by permission of John Wiley & Sons, Inc.

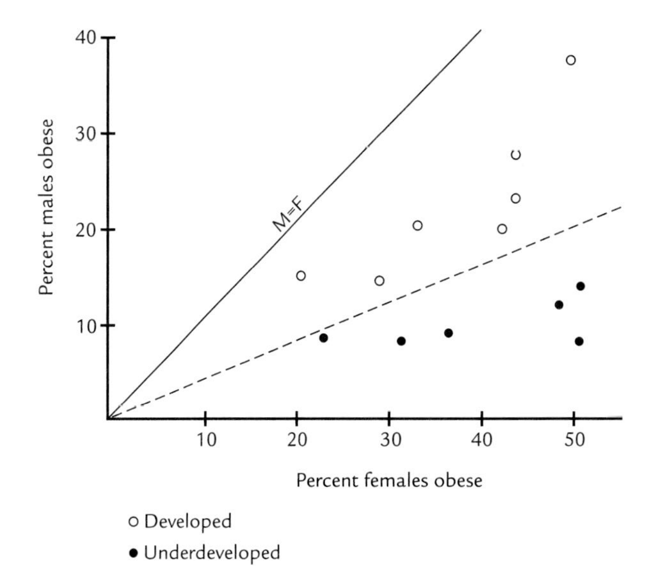


**FIGURE 2** Gender differences in prevalences of obesity in 14 populations by general industrial development. Operational definitions of obesity differ between studies. See Brown and Konner (1987) for references. The unbroken line demarcates equal male-female obesity prevalences. The broken line indicates an apparent distinction in gender proportions of obesity in developed and underdeveloped countries. From Brown, P.J., & M. Konner. "An Anthropological Perspective on Obesity." *Annals of the New York Academy of Sciences* 499 (1987):29–46. Copyright © 1987 by The New York Academy of Sciences. Reprinted by permission of John Wiley & Sons, Inc.

Sex differences are also seen in the prevalence of obesity. Despite methodological differences in the categorization of obesity, data from the 14 population surveys shown in Figure 2 indicate that in all of the studies, females have a higher prevalence of obesity than males. A greater risk of obesity for females appears to be a basic fact of human biology.

## Economic Modernization

The social distribution of obesity varies among societies, depending on their degree of economic modernization. Studies of traditional hunting and gathering populations report *no obesity*. In contrast, numerous studies of traditional societies undergoing the process of economic modernization demonstrate rapid increases in the prevalence of obesity. Trowell and Burkitt's (1981) 15 case studies of epidemiological change in modernizing societies conclude that obesity is the first of the "diseases of civilization" to appear. The rapidity with which obesity becomes a common health problem in the context of modernization underscores the critical role of cultural behaviors in the causation of obesity, since there has been insufficient time for changes in gene frequencies.

Figure 2 also suggests that variations in the male-female ratio of obesity prevalence are related to economic modernization. In less industrially developed societies female obesity is much more common than male obesity, but in more affluent societies the ratio is nearly equivalent. Recent World Health Organization data on global obesity also support this observation (Gurney and Gorstein 1988).

Cultural changes with modernization include the seemingly invariable pattern of diet in industrial countries—decreased fiber intake and increased consumption of fat and sugar. Modernization is also associated with decreased energy expenditures related to work, recreation, or daily activities. From the perspective of the populations undergoing economic modernization, increasing average weight might be seen as a good thing rather than a health problem.

### Ethnicity

The idea that particular populations have high rates of a genotype that predisposes individuals to obesity and related diseases is not new but is now supported by a convincing body of adoption and twin data (Stunkard et al. 1986, 1990) and by studies of particular obesity-prone populations like the Pima Indians (Ravussin et al. 1988). In the United States, ethnic groups with elevated rates of obesity include African Americans (particularly in the rural South), Mexican Americans, Puerto Ricans, Gypsies, and Pacific Islanders (Centers for Disease Control 1989).

The fact that certain ethnic groups have high rates of obesity is not easy to interpret because of the entanglement of the effects of genetic heredity, social class, and cultural beliefs. The association of obesity with ethnicity is not evidence for the exclusive role of genetic transmission, since social factors like endogamy (marriage within the group) or group isolation are critical for defining the population structure—that is, the social system through which genes are passed from generation to generation.

### Social Class

Social class (socioeconomic status) can be a powerful predictor of the prevalence of obesity in both modernizing and affluent societies, although the direction of the association varies with the type of society. In developing countries, there is a strong and consistent *positive association* between social class and obesity for men, women, and children; correspondingly, there is an inverse correlation between social class and protein-calorie malnutrition. In heterogeneous and affluent societies, like the United States, there is a strong *inverse correlation* of social class and obesity for females. The association between obesity and social class among women in affluent societies is not constant through the life cycle. Economically advantaged girls are initially fatter than their low-income counterparts, but the pattern is reversed beginning at puberty. For females, social class remains the strongest social epidemiological predictor of obesity.

## OBESITY AND HUMAN EVOLUTION

Human biology and behavior can be understood in the context of two distinct processes of evolution. Biological evolution involves changes through time in the frequency of particular genes, primarily because of the action of natural selection on individuals. Cultural evolution involves historical changes in the configurations of cultural systems, that is, the learned patterns of behavior and belief characteristics of social groups. Cultural evolution includes the striking and rapid transformation of human lifestyles from small food-foraging societies to large and economically complex states in a span of less than 5,000 years.

### The Context of Food Scarcities

Food shortages have been very common in human prehistory and history; in fact, they could be considered a virtually inevitable fact of life for most people. As such, they have been a powerful evolutionary force.

A cross-cultural ethnographic survey of 118 nonindustrial societies (with hunting and gathering, pastoral, horticultural, and agricultural economies) found some form of food shortages for *all* of the societies in the sample (Whiting 1958). Shortages occur annually or even more frequently in roughly half of the societies, and every 2 to 3 years in an additional 24 percent. The shortages are "severe" (i.e., including starvation deaths) in 29 percent of the societies sampled. Seasonal availability of food results in a seasonal cycle of weight loss and weight gain in both hunting and gathering and agricultural societies, although the fluctuation is substantially greater among agriculturalists.

### Scarcity and Cultural Evolution

A hunting and gathering economy was characteristic of all human societies for more than 95 percent of our history, yet it is represented by only a handful of societies today. In general, food foragers enjoy high-quality diets, maintain high levels of physical fitness, suffer the risk of periodic food shortages, and are generally healthier than many contemporary populations that rely on agriculture. Without romanticizing these societies, the evidence is persuasive enough to suggest a "paleolithic prescription" of diet and exercise for the prevention of chronic diseases (Eaton et al. 1988). This recommendation refers to the quality of preindustrial diets and not to their dependability or quantity.

Approximately 12,000 years ago, some human groups shifted from a food-foraging economy to one of food production. This economic transformation allowed the evolution of urban civilizations. Many archaeologists believe that people were "forced" to adopt the new agricultural economy because of ecological pressures from population growth and food scarcities or because of military coercion. The archaeological record clearly shows that agriculture was associated with nutritional stress, poor health, and diminished stature (Cohen and Armelagos 1984). The beginning of agriculture is also linked to the emergence of social stratification, a system of inequality that improved the Darwinian fitness of the ruling class relative to that of the lower classes. Social inequality, particularly differential access to strategic resources, plays a critical role in the distribution of obesity in most societies.

Certain ecological zones appear to be prone to severe food shortages. For example, archaeological analysis of tree rings from the southwestern United States shows that the prehistoric past was characterized by frequent and severe droughts. The impressive agricultural societies of the prehistoric Southwest had expanded during an extended period of uncharacteristically good weather and could not be maintained when the lower and more characteristic rainfall patterns resumed. Ecological conditions leading to severe scarcity may have acted as strong forces of selection for "thrifty" genotypes.

### Scarcity and Genetic Evolution

Since food shortages were ubiquitous for humans under natural conditions, selection favored individuals who could effectively store calories in times of surplus. For most societies, these fat stores would be called on at least every 2 or 3 years. Malnutrition increases infectious disease mortality, as well as decreasing birth weights and rates of child growth. The evolutionary scenario is this: Females with greater energy reserves in fat would have a selective advantage over their lean counterparts in terms of withstanding the stress of food shortages, not only for themselves but also for their fetuses or nursing children. Humans have evolved the ability to "save up" food energy for inevitable food shortages through the synthesis and storage of fat.

Selection has favored the production of peripheral body fat in females, whose reproductive fitness is influenced by the nutritional demands of pregnancy and lactation. This peripheral fat is usually mobilized after being primed with estrogen during the late stages of pregnancy and during lactation. In addition, a minimal level of fatness increases female reproductive success because of its association with regular cycling and early menarche (Frisch 1987).

In this evolutionary context the usual range of human metabolic variation must have produced many individuals with a predisposition to become obese; yet they would, in all likelihood, never have had the opportunity to do so. Furthermore, in this context there could be little or no natural selection against this tendency. Selection could not provide for the eventuality of continuous surplus simply because it had never existed before.

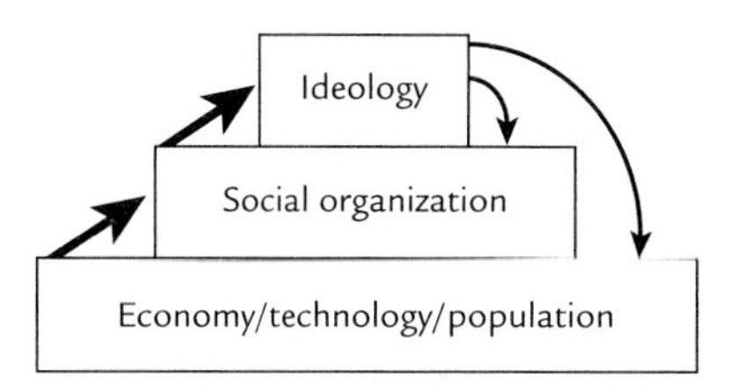


**FIGURE 3** A materialist model of culture. From Brown, Peter J. "Culture and the Evolution of Obesity." *Human Nature* 2 (1991):31–57. Copyright © 1991 by Walter de Gruyter, Inc., New York. With kind permission from Springer Science+Business Media.

## CULTURE AND ADAPTATIONS TO FOOD SCARCITY

Food scarcities have shaped not only our genes but also, and perhaps more important, human cultures. Because the concept of culture is rarely considered in medical research on obesity, and because I am suggesting that this concept has advantages over the more common and undifferentiated term *environment*, it is necessary to review some basic aspects of this anthropological term. *Culture* refers to the learned patterns of behavior and belief characteristic of a social group. As such, culture encompasses *Homo sapiens'* primary mechanism of evolutionary adaptation, which has distinct advantages of greater speed and flexibility than genetic evolution.

Cultural behaviors and beliefs are usually learned in childhood and they are often deeply held and seldom questioned by adults, who pass this "obvious" knowledge and habits to their offspring. In this regard, cultural beliefs and values are largely unconscious factors in the motivation of individual behaviors. Cultural beliefs define "what is normal" and therefore constrain the choices of behaviors available to an individual.

One useful way of thinking about culture in relation to obesity is a cultural materialist model as seen in Figure 3. This model divides culture into three layers. The material foundation of a cultural system is the economic mode of production, which includes the technology and the population size that the productive economy allows and requires. Population size is maintained by the social system, sometimes called the mode of reproduction. Contingent on the first layer is the system of social organization, which includes kinship patterns, marriage and family practices, politics, and status differentiation. Contingent on the social structure is the ideology or belief system, including ideas, beliefs, and values, both secular and sacred. Most anthropologists believe that the ideology is an extremely important part of culture, in part because it rationalizes and reinforces the economy and social structure. Ideology enables people to make sense of their world and to share their common world view through symbols. As such, ideology includes sacred concepts from religion as well as secular concepts (with symbolic components) like health or sexual attractiveness.

A culture is an integrated system: A change in one part causes changes in the other layers. The materialist model indicates that the direction of causal change is from the bottom layer upward (the solid arrows in Figure 3). An economic change, like the invention of agriculture or the Industrial Revolution, has drastic implications for population size, social organization, and associated beliefs. On the other hand, most people within a society tend to explain things from the top down. Of course, people can hold contradictory beliefs and values that are not necessarily linked to their actual behavior.

## CULTURAL PREDISPOSITIONS TO OBESITY

Obesity is related to culture in all three levels of the materialist model.

### Productive Economy and Food Scarcity

Humans have evolved a wide variety of cultural mechanisms to avoid or minimize the effects of food scarcities. The most important adaptation to scarcity is the evolution of systems of food production and storage. As noted previously, the primary weakness of preindustrial systems of food production is a vulnerability to food shortages. The universality of food shortages discussed above is largely because of the technological limitations in food production and storage.

On the other hand, the energy-intensive (and energy-inefficient) system of agriculture in industrialized societies produces large surpluses of food. These agricultural surpluses are seldom used to eliminate hunger; rather they are used to transform and process foods in particular ways—often to add calories, fat, or salt. For example, we feed "extra" grain to beef cattle to increase the proportion of fat in their meat; consumers say that this overfeeding makes the meat "juicy." Similarly, potatoes are transformed into french fries and potato chips. From a nutritional standpoint the original vegetable is actually reduced to a vehicle for fat and salt. Endemic hunger exists even in the most affluent societies, where it is caused not by poor production but by inequitable distribution.

Technological changes associated with cultural evolution almost exclusively reduce the energy requirements of human labor. In general, cultural evolution has meant the harnessing of greater amounts of energy through technology (one aspect of the mode of production). To prevent obesity, people in developed societies must burn energy through daily workouts rather than daily work.

### Reproduction and Energy Expenditure

The concept of the *mode of reproduction* is also related to predispositions to obesity. Pregnancy and lactation represent serious and continuing energy demands on women in societies that have not undergone the demographic transition. Industrial and nonindustrial societies differ in terms of the historical changes from high to low fertility and the reduction of mortality attributable to infectious disease. Higher numbers of pregnancies and longer periods of breast-feeding place high energy demands on women, especially if they cannot supplement their diet during these critical periods. As a result, women suffer greater risk of protein-energy malnutrition. Conversely, with fewer pregnancies and the reduction of breast-feeding, women in industrial societies have less opportunity to mobilize peripheral fat stores and suffer greater risk of obesity. In contemporary societies like the United States, mothers in lower social classes tend to have more children and to feed their infants with bottled formula rather than breast milk. Use of infant formulas allows women to retain their fat stores. These different social patterns in reproduction may play a role in the inverse association of obesity and social class for females.

### Social Structure and Obesity

Characteristics of social organization may function as predispositions to obesity. In highly stratified and culturally heterogeneous societies, the distribution of obesity is associated with ethnicity and social class. Marriage patterns typically illustrate ethnic or social class endogamy, that is, marriage within the group. In the United States, members of ethnic minorities choose marriage partners from the same group at extremely high rates. This social practice may concentrate the genetic predispositions to conditions like obesity in particular subpopulations. Similarly, data suggest a pattern of "assortative mating" by social class as well as body type (particularly stature), which may be related to the genetic etiology of obesity. Genetic admixture with Native American groups of the Southwest has been suggested as a cause of elevated rates of type 2 diabetes mellitus and obesity among Mexican Americans (Gardner et al. 1984).

The pervasive and complex relationship between obesity and social class, or socioeconomic status (SES), is important. SES is related to particular behavior patterns that cause obesity. This statement underemphasizes the fact that these learned behaviors are *characteristic* of particular social groups or classes. In other words, the cultural patterns of social class groups are primary, not the individual behaviors themselves.

From a cross-cultural perspective, the general association between obesity and social position is positive: The groups with greater access to economic resources have higher rates of obesity. This pattern is logical and expected because socially dominant groups with better access to strategic resources should have better nutrition, better health, and consequently greater reproductive success.

As discussed earlier, the remarkable and important exception is women in industrial societies, who exhibit a strong *inverse* correlation between obesity and social class. The challenge for researchers is to explain why and how upper-class women in industrial societies remain thin. For many women the ideal of thinness requires considerable effort, restrained eating, and often resources invested in exercise. The social origins of the ideal of thinness in American women are associated with historical changes in women's economic roles, marriage patterns, and family size.

Low-income people in industrial societies might be considered well off by worldwide standards, and this access to resources is reflected in obesity prevalences. Yet in the context of perceived relative deprivation and economic stability, many people in societies like the United States live in stressful conditions—just one paycheck away from hunger. In terms of life priorities, economic security may be a higher and more immediate objective than more elusive goals like an "ideal body" or even long-term health. Amid the daily stresses of poverty, food may be the most common avenue of pleasure and psychological relief. Ethnographic studies of low-income urban black communities in the United States show a social emphasis on food sharing as a tool for marking family ties and demonstrating community cohesiveness.

### Cultural Beliefs as Predispositions to Obesity

The third and possibly most important level of the model of culture shown in Figure 3 encompasses cultural symbols, beliefs, and values. Aspects of ideology relevant to the etiology of obesity include the symbolic meaning of fatness, ideal body types, and perceived risks of food shortages.

Fatness is symbolically linked to psychological dimensions, such as self-worth and sexuality, in many societies of the world, but the nature of that symbolic association is not constant. In mainstream U.S. culture, obesity is socially stigmatized, but for most cultures of the world, fatness is viewed as a welcome sign of health and prosperity. Given the rarity of obesity in preindustrial societies, it is not surprising that they lack ethnomedical terms for obesity. Much more attention is placed on "thinness" as a symptom of starvation, like among the !Kung San (Lee 1979), or in contemporary Africa as a sign of AIDS (sometimes called "the slim disease"). In the context of the AIDS epidemic, plumpness is indeed a marker of health.

Perhaps it is large body size, rather than obesity per se, that is admired as a symbol of health, prestige, prosperity, or maternity in agricultural societies. The Tiv of Nigeria, for example, distinguish between a very positive category, "too big" *(kehe),* and an unpleasant condition "to grow fat" *(ahon)* (Bohannan and Bohannan 1969). The first is a compliment because it is a sign of prosperity; the second is a rare and undesirable condition.

For women, fatness may also be a symbol of maternity and nurturance. In traditional societies in which women attain status only through motherhood, this symbolic association increases the cultural acceptability of fatness. A fat woman, symbolically, is well taken care of, and in turn she takes good care of her children. Fellahin Arabs in Egypt describe the proper woman as fat because she has more room to bear the child, lactates abundantly, and gives warmth to her children. The cultural ideal of thinness in industrial societies, in contrast, is found where motherhood is not the sole or even primary means of status attainment for woman. The idea that fat babies and children are healthy children is very widespread. Food can be treated as a symbol of love and nurturance; in some cultures it may be impolite for a guest to refuse food that has been offered, but it is taboo to refuse food from one's mother.

In the industrialized United States, ethnic variation in culturally accepted definitions of obesity is significant. Some Mexican Americans have coined a new term, *gordura mala* (bad fatness), because the original term *gordura* continues to have positive cultural connotations (Ritenbaugh 1982). For this group cultural identity has a stronger and independent effect on risk of obesity than socioeconomic status. An ethnographic study of the cultural meanings of weight in a Puerto Rican community in Philadelphia (Massara 1989) documents the positive associations and lack of social stigma of obesity. Additional quantitative evidence suggests significant differences in ideal body preferences between this ethnic community and mainstream American culture. Positive evaluations of fatness may also occur among lower-class African Americans and Mexican Americans. These ethnic groups are heterogeneous, however, and upwardly mobile ethnics tend to resemble mainstream American culture in their attitudes about obesity and ideal body shape.

In a low-income housing project in Atlanta, Georgia, a sociological interviewer was asked by a group of obese black women, "Don't you know how hard it is to keep this weight *on*?" Their views of the advantages of a large body included being given respect and reduced chances of being bothered by young "toughs" in the neighborhood. For these women, fatness was part of their positive self-identity, and if a friend lost weight she was thought to look sickly. Among lower-income groups, the perceived risk of a food shortage—not for the society as a whole but for the immediate family—may be very important, especially if lack of food was personally experienced in the past. The perception of the risk of future "bad times" and insufficient food is the reality upon which people act.

## FATNESS AND CROSS-CULTURAL STANDARDS OF BEAUTY IN WOMEN

Culturally defined standards of beauty vary between societies. In a classic example, Malcom (1925) describes the custom of "fattening huts" for elite Efik pubescent girls in traditional Nigeria. A girl spent up to 2 years in seclusion and at the end of this rite of passage possessed symbols of womanhood and marriage-ability—a three-tiered hairstyle, clitoridectomy, and fatness. Fatness was a primary criterion of beauty as it was defined by the elites, who alone had the economic resources to participate in this custom. Similarly, fatter brides demand significantly higher bridewealth payments among the Kipsigis of Kenya (Borgerhoff Mulder 1988).

Among the Havasupai of the American Southwest, if a girl is thin at puberty, a fat woman "stands" (places her foot) on the girl's back so she will become attractively plump. In this society, fat legs and, to a lesser extent, arms are considered essential to beauty. The Tarahumara of northern Mexico consider fat legs a fundamental aspect of the ideal feminine body; an attractive woman is called a "beautiful thigh." Among the Amhara of Ethiopia in northern East Africa, thin hips are called "dog hips" in a typical insult (Messing 1957).

It is difficult to know how widespread among the world's cultures is the association of plumpness and beauty. A preliminary indication can be found through a cross-cultural survey based on data from the Human Relations Area Files (a cross-indexed compilation of ethnographic information on more than 300 of the most thoroughly studied societies). The results of this survey are summarized in Table 1. Although conclusions made from these data are weak because of the small number and possibly nonrepresentative nature of the cases, as well as the fact that most ethnographies are difficult to code on this variable, some preliminary generalizations are possible. Cultural standards of beauty do not refer to physical extremes. No society on record has an ideal of extreme obesity. On the other hand, the desirability of "plumpness" or being "filled out" is found in 81 percent of the societies for which this variable can be coded. This standard, which probably includes the clinical categories of overweight and mild obesity, apparently refers to the desirability of fat deposits, particularly on the hips and legs.

**TABLE 1 Cross-Cultural Standards of Female Beauty**

| | Number of Societies | Percent of Societies |
|---|---|---|
| Overall body | | |
| Extreme obesity | 0 | 0 |
| Plump/moderately fat | 31 | 81 |
| Thin/abhorrence of fat | 7 | 19 |
| Breasts | | |
| Large or long | 9 | 50 |
| Small/abhorrence of large | 9 | 50 |
| Hips and Legs | | |
| Large or fat | 9 | 90 |
| Slender | 1 | 10 |
| Stature | | |
| Tall | 3 | 30 |
| Moderate | 6 | 60 |
| Small | 1 | 10 |

*Source:* From Brown, P.J., & M. Konner. "An Anthropological Perspective on Obesity." *Annals of the New York Academy of Sciences* 499 (1987):29–46. 

Although cross-cultural variation is evident in standards of beauty, this variation falls within a certain range. American ideals of thinness occur in a setting in which it is easy to become fat, and preference for plumpness occurs in settings in which it is easy to remain lean. In context, both standards require the investment of individual effort and economic resources; furthermore, each in its context involves a display of wealth. Cultural beliefs about attractive body shape in mainstream American culture place pressure on females to lose weight and are involved in the etiology of anorexia and bulimia.

## IDEAL BODY-TYPE, SIZE, AND SYMBOLIC POWER IN MEN

The ethnographic record concerning body preferences for males is extremely weak, yet preliminary research suggests a universal preference for a muscular physique and for tall or moderately tall stature. In general, members of all human societies appear to admire large body size as an attribute of attractiveness in men, because it symbolizes health, economic success, political power, and social status. "Big men," political leaders in tribal New Guinea, are described by their constituents in terms of their size and physical well-being: He is a man "whose skin swells with 'grease' [fat] underneath" (Strahern 1971). The spiritual power (*mana*) and noble breeding of a Polynesian chief is expected to be seen in his large size. In American society vestiges of a similar idea remain; for example, a "fat cat" is a wealthy and powerful man who can "throw his weight around." The political metaphor of weight and power in American society has been explored by social historians. Most male college students in the U.S., in contrast with women, want to gain weight because it is equivalent to gaining muscle mass and physical power in a process called "bulking up."

## CONCLUSIONS

Two sets of conclusions can be drawn from this discussion of culture and its relationship to obesity—one practical and one theoretical. First, recognition of cultural variation in beliefs and behaviors related to obesity needs to be incorporated into health programs aimed at reducing the prevalence of obesity. The second conclusion regards the need for more research on the role of culture, as it interacts with genes, on the etiology of obesity.

### The Importance of Culture in Health Interventions

Existing cultural beliefs must be taken into account in the design and implementation of health promotion projects. In an obesity prevention campaign in a Zulu community outside of Durban, one health education poster depicted an obese woman and an overloaded truck with a flat tire, with a caption "Both carry too much weight." Another poster showed a slender woman easily sweeping under a table next to an obese woman who was using the table for support; it had the caption "Who do you prefer to look like?" The intended message of these posters was misinterpreted by the community because of a cultural connection between obesity and social status. The woman in the first poster was perceived to be rich and happy, since she was not only fat but had a truck overflowing with her possessions. The second poster was perceived as a scene of an affluent mistress directing her underfed servant.

Health interventions must be culturally acceptable, and we cannot assume that people place the highest priority on their health. The idea of reducing *risk factors* for chronic diseases that may develop later may not be an effective strategy for populations who do not feel empowered or who live in a fundamentally risky world.

### Implications for the Etiology of Obesity

The frequency of past food shortages, the social distribution of obesity, and the cultural meanings of fatness, when taken together, suggest a biocultural hypothesis of the evolution of obesity. Both genetic and cultural predispositions to obesity may be products of the same evolutionary pressures, involving two related processes: first, genetic traits that cause fatness were selected because they improved chances of survival in the face of food scarcities, particularly for pregnant and nursing women; second, in the context of unequal access to food, fatness may have been socially selected because it is a cultural symbol of social prestige and an index of general health. Under Western conditions of abundance, our biological tendency to regulate body weight at levels above our ideal cannot be easily controlled even with a reversal of the widespread cultural ideal of plumpness.

This evolutionary model is obviously congruent with the current etiological theory about obesity, which combines genetic predispositions with "environmental" causes. Recent research both in epidemiology and human laboratory research demonstrates without a doubt the central role of genetic heredity in the etiology of obesity. Similar genetic evidence exists for variables like the distribution of fat on the body and basal metabolic rates. To an anthropologist, these important studies are welcome and expected.

The recent advances in understanding the genetic bases of obesity remind us, however, of our ignorance about the precise role of the "environment." One problem is that "environment" has been poorly defined and treated as if it were idiosyncratic for every individual or family. Another problem is that "environment" is essentially treated as a residual category—one that cannot be explained by genetic heredity. This paper has attempted to show how the anthropological concept of culture may be useful in conceptualization of the different components of the "environment" and the generation of hypotheses for future research in behavioral medicine.

The most convincing demonstrations of a strong genetic component for obesity have been in populations with relatively high levels of cultural homogeneity. In social contexts like Denmark, Iowa, or among Pima Indians, the influence of culture—including learned behaviors and beliefs—is minimized by the sample selected for study in order to emphasize the importance of genotypical variation. Essentially, cultural variation has been treated as if it were "noise." An essential goal in future research must be the identification of specific cultural factors—whether economic, social, or ideological—that predispose people to obesity.

From the standpoint of the prevention of obesity, it is critical to stress that genetic predisposition is not destiny. Genetic predispositions to obesity have apparently been maintained in populations throughout most of our species' history, yet it has rarely been expressed phenotypically. Culture is adaptive because it can be changed. Habitual patterns of behavior—of an individual or an entire society—can be changed to reduce morbidity and mortality linked to obesity and overweight. These changes must include social and political efforts to reduce the risk of hunger and food scarcity, even in affluent societies.

## REFERENCES

Bohannan, P., and L. Bohannan. 1969. *A Source Notebook on Tiv Religion.* New Haven, CT: Human Relations Area Files.

Borgerhoff Mulder, M. 1988. Kipsigis Bridewealth Payments. In *Human Reproductive Behavior,* eds. L. Betzig, M. Borgerhoff Mulder, and P. Turke, 65–82. Cambridge: Cambridge University Press.

Bray, G. A. 1987. Overweight Is Risking Fate: Definition, Classification, Prevalence and Risks. In *Human Obesity,* eds. R. J. Wurtman and J. J. Wurtman, *Annals of the New York Academy of Sciences* 499: 14–28.

Brown, P. J., and M. Konner. 1987. An Anthropological Perspective on Obesity. In *Human Obesity,* eds. R. J. Wurtman and J. J. Wurtman, *Annals of the New York Academy of Sciences* 499: 29–46.

Centers for Disease Control. 1989. Prevalence of Overweight—Behavioral Risk Factor Surveillance System, 1987. *Morbidity and Mortality Weekly Report* 38: 421–423.

Chernin, K. 1981. *The Obsession: Reflections on the Tyranny of Slenderness.* New York: Harper & Row.

Cohen, M. N., and G. J. Armelagos, eds. 1984. *Paleopathology at the Origins of Agriculture.* New York: Academic Press.

Eaton, S. B., M. Shostak, and M. Konner. 1988. *The Paleolithic Prescription.* New York: Harper & Row.

Frisch, R. E. 1987. Body Fat, Menarche, Fitness and Fertility. *Human Reproduction* 2: 521–533.

Gardner, L. I., M. P. Stern, S. M. Haffner, S. P. Gaskill, H. Hazuda, and J. H. Relethford. 1984. Prevalence of Diabetes in Mexican Americans. *Diabetes* 33: 86–92.

Gurney, M., and J. Gorstein. 1988. The Global Prevalence of Obesity—An Initial Overview of Available Data. *World Health Statistics Quarterly* 41: 251–254.

Kissebah, A. H., D. S. Freedman, and A. N. Peiris. 1989. Health Risks of Obesity. *Medical Clinics of North America* 73: 11–138.

Lee, R. B. 1979. *The !Kung San: Men, Women, and Work in a Foraging Society.* Cambridge, MA: Harvard University Press.

Malcom, L. W. G. 1925. Note on the Seclusion of Girls Among the Efik at Old Calabar. *Man* 25: 113–114.

Massara, E. B. 1989. *Que Gordita! A Study of Weight Among Women in a Puerto Rican Community.* New York: AMS Press.

Messing, S. D. 1957. *The Highland Plateau Amhara of Ethiopia.* Ph.D. dissertation, Department of Anthropology, University of Pennsylvania, Philadelphia.

Ravussin, E., S. Lillioja, and W. C. Knowler, et al. 1988. Reduced Rate of Energy Expenditure as a Risk Factor for Body-Weight Gain. *New England Journal of Medicine* 318: 467–472.

Ritenbaugh, C. 1982. Obesity as a Culture-Bound Syndrome. *Culture, Medicine and Psychiatry* 6: 347–361.

Strahern, A. 1971. *The Rope of Moka.* New York: Cambridge University Press.

Stunkard, A. J., T. I. A. Sorenson, C. Hanis, T. W. Teasdale, R. Chakaborty, W. J. Schull, and F. Schulsinger. 1986. An Adoption Study of Obesity. *New England Journal of Medicine* 314: 193–198.

Stunkard, A. J., J. R. Harris, N. L. Pedersen, and G. McClearn. 1990. The Body-Mass Index of Twins Who Have Been Reared Apart. *New England Journal of Medicine* 322: 1483–1487.

Trowell, H. C., and D. P. Burkitt. 1981. *Western Diseases: Their Emergence and Prevention.* Cambridge, MA: Harvard University Press.

Whiting, M. G. 1958. *A Cross-Cultural Nutrition Survey.* Doctoral Dissertation, Harvard School of Public Health, Cambridge.

Wurtman, R. J., and J. J. Wurtman, eds. 1987. Human Obesity. *Annals of the New York Academy of Sciences* 499.

# 40

# Pocahontas Goes to the Clinic

## *Popular Culture as Lingua Franca in a Cultural Borderland*

*Cheryl Mattingly*

Technical competence may be a critical component of medical practice, but it alone cannot heal. In U.S. hospitals and clinics, medical technology and practice depend on the ability of patients and physicians to trust, communicate, and understand each other. In urban hospitals, patients, doctors, and other medical personnel may share similar goals, but they may not share the same languages and ethnicities. Linguistic and ethnic diversity have transformed the medical clinic into a cultural borderland, which now more than ever demands anthropological perspectives.

Sickle-cell patients in the U.S. often experience the negative effects of medical treatment undermined by a lack of sociocultural understanding. Sickle-cell anemia is a serious condition in which red blood cells can become stiff, sticky, and sickle-shaped; clumps of sickle cells can block blood flow and lead to chronic pain, infection, and organ failure. This medical condition affects African Americas, Hispanic Americans, as well as populations from Africa, South America, Central America, India, Saudi Arabia, and Caribbean and Mediterranean countries. Because sickle-cell anemia impacts African Americans and Hispanic Americans, the legacies of racial and ethnic divisions in the United States often creep into the treatment of sickle-cell patients. For example, the chronic pain associated with sickle-cell anemia leads some clinicians to inappropriately label African American teenage boys with sickle-cell as "med-seeking" patients.

Establishing effective communication and understanding between patients and caregivers is complicated by ethnic divisions, differences in language, and racial/ethnic stereotyping. Nonetheless, creative clinicians find ways to bridge the cultural borderlands of the medical clinic. In this selection, Cheryl Mattingly examines how global icons like Disney characters and Spider Man help patients and doctors create trust and communicative contexts for healing.

***As you read this selection, ask yourself the following questions:***

- How is the medical clinic a "borderland?" What is a borderland?
- What is a healing drama and how do they apply to medical practice?
- How do cultural misunderstandings influence medical care?
- How does culture in the hybrid environment of a borderland differ from culture in a more homogeneous context?
- How is the practice of culture a practice of othering?
- In what ways can race and class impact the quality and efficacy of medical treatment?

***The following terms discussed in this selection are included in the Glossary at the back of the book:***

| | |
|---|---|
| *indigenized* | *othering* |
| *lingua franca* | *sickle-cell anemia* |

The first time I met Pocahontas in a hospital was in the mid-1990s. Of course, as a U.S. citizen, I had known her since childhood. But I had forgotten all about her until she appeared, quite unexpectedly, in hospitals in Chicago and Los Angeles where I was carrying out

Mattingly, Cheryl. "Pocahontas Goes to the Clinic: Popular Culture as Lingua Franca in a Cultural Borderland." Reproduced by permission of the American Anthropological Association from *American Anthropologist*, Volume 108, Issue 3, pp. 494–501, September 2006. Not for sale or further reproduction.

research. She looked very different than I remembered. Older, and less, well, historical. She had been dusted off, Disneyfied, transformed into a gorgeous teenage beauty with a head of the most magnificent black hair and a body as enviably proportioned as Barbie. She could sing too. And it was Disney who sent her to the clinic. For not only was she a larger-than-life figure in a popular animated movie, she was packaged into craft sets, costumes, dolls, and an array of other cultural artifacts that began to find their way into all sorts of children's places—including children's hospitals. She traveled internationally as well. I saw her once, resplendently arrayed, hair flowing, on a large poster board in a duty free shop at the Copenhagen airport. Internet chat rooms carried on worldwide conversations about her adventures. Pocahontas had gone global.

This apparently frivolous example of the circulation of global goods has special and, indeed, profound significance in the context of health care, as I have gradually come to realize. Drawing from ethnographic research carried out over the past nine years among African American families who have children with severe illnesses and disabilities, I examine how children's popular culture, exported by such mass media empires as Disney, operates in the fraught borderland that constitutes the urban clinic. Children's films and television programs provide characters and plights that are creatively localized in health care encounters. A child's beloved character can offer a kind of narrative shadow, a cultural resource that children, families, and health care professionals readily turn to in the ongoing task of creating socially shared meaning, especially the sort of meaning that has to do with trying to positively shape a child's future.

Stories, it has long been noted, tend to provoke the imagination. They spur us to consider life in the subjunctive mode (Bruner 1986, 2002), in terms of a "what if" universe of possibilities. Thus, it is not surprising that anthropologists have looked at the way stories created by global media inspire new imaginative constructions of lives and worlds. The study of media has been intimately connected to the reinvention of culture as a contested space, a point of particular relevance to this article. Media is often treated as a force for constructing a distinctive identity—for creating boundaries and marking distinctions—but here I explore it as a vehicle for creating commonalities. Its role as mediator between the worlds of family and clinic takes on special importance in clinical encounters marked by differences in race and social class. Children's popular culture offers resources for building bridges among groups who perceive themselves as Other but who are compelled to collaborate because of the need to tend to a sick or disabled child. A Disneyfied Pocahontas is only one of the mass-marketed figures that plays an important role in the clinic, especially in creating" common ground" between the world of the hospital and home, and among the various key actors who care for severely ill or disabled children. Global icons like these can function as a lingua franca, offering a language of publicly available symbols on which families, health professionals, and children can draw to signal a common heritage or to create shared imaginative space across racial, class, and sufferer–healer divides. Why is a trade language so necessary in the U.S. urban hospital?

## WHEN CULTURE IS A BORDERLAND: THE URBAN CLINIC

Urban hospitals constitute an example of what is arguably the most visible site in anthropology these days—the border zone, which James Clifford describes as a place of "hybrid cosmopolitan experiences" (1997:25). Border zones have emerged as part of the refiguration of culture, a shift from the discipline's traditional task of elucidating "the crystalline patterns of a whole culture" to a focus on "the blurred zones in between" (Rosaldo 1989:209). Anthropologists have been moving from the heartlands to the borders for quite some time. This has meant a shift away from studying isolated communities in favor of geographic areas—such as urban centers or national border zones, which are characterized by ethnic pluralism and a fast changing cultural scene. It has also meant paying special attention to sites of heightened commerce among actors who are culturally diverse. A focus on border zones is part of a fertile rethinking of traditional concepts of culture by anthropologists and culture theorists.

In a borderland, culture emerges more vividly as a space of encounter than of enclosure. For many, culture has come to designate a noisy, pluralistic, contested, ever-changing public sphere, rather than a substance, common property, or a shared commitment to a way of life. This perspective emphasizes connections—including media-created connections—that are often political and often unexpected among these diverse communities and commodities.[1] Viewed in this way, culture is not to be found in a group's shared set of beliefs and values so much as in its practices of drawing contrasts and boundaries with other groups as well as challenging those contrasts. This sort of cultural world is characterized by politically charged, difference-making exchanges among actors.

The clinical world has often been recognized as contested terrain. The urban hospital is a place in which misreadings and conflicts routinely arise. The United States is growing rapidly more ethnically diverse, and this means that health care increasingly involves providing treatment for diverse populations. Urban health care in the United States is characterized by a dizzying array of languages, nationalities, racial identifications, social classes, and religions.[2] It has been well documented that ethnic diversity is accompanied by unequal access to health care. Racism also plays a key role in adverse health outcomes. African Americans continue to be one of the least well-served minority groups, a recognition that has provoked examination of the connections between race and health.[3]

A great deal of the work in medical anthropology has explored transactions within biomedical encounters marked by cultural confusions and misunderstandings—border talk, in fact. But the figure of clinic as border zone takes on a decidedly less familiar cast when situated within the recent debates about culture, place, and space that have arisen among scholars far removed from anything clinical—those who have been delivering, or responding to, challenges concerning the location of culture in the face of a globalizing and decolonizing world. This work offers an intriguing vantage point for examining the border activities of health care practices. In this discursive context, the familiar figure of the misunderstood patient emerges as startlingly emblematic, an exemplary citizen of that new nation, the land of the culturally in-between. If the practice of culture is, in part, the practice of Othering, of identifying cultural (and racial) difference in a thousand subtle and unconscious ways, this is of special importance in clinical encounters. Failures of communication are magnified to intense proportions in situations characterized by both perceptions of difference and high stakes. Cultural identities constructed by race, class, gender, and other potentially stigmatizing markers take on profound meaning here. What might, in another context, be a small slight or a confusing conversation, can, under these heightened circumstances, take on enormous importance. To feel neglected by one's doctor when one's child is seriously ill is not the same as being ignored by the grocery clerk.

The primary research that informs this article is a longitudinal ethnography that began in Los Angeles in January 1997 and is still ongoing. It has been carried out by an interdisciplinary team of anthropologists and occupational therapists. We initially recruited 30 African American families from the Los Angeles area whose children (ages from birth to eight) were being treated in several clinical sites. Most, although not all families, were low income. Eighteen of those initially recruited have continued to participate. Others joined subsequently as some families left the study for various reasons (e.g., moving out of state). All families now participating have been part of the project for at least three years.

This continuity of families has allowed us to come to know the ebbs and flows of chronic illness and to witness what that means in the never-ending process of negotiating health care with shifting casts of health professionals and changing bureaucratic processes. The research has involved accompanying families to clinical visits, observing and sometimes videotaping those encounters, and separately interviewing participants about what they perceived happened in the encounters. We have also observed and videotaped children and families at home and in the community, especially at key family events. This kind of longitudinal design has revealed a great deal about clinical encounters as events in family lives and about multiple perspectives between families and clinicians as these develop and change over time.

In this article, I provide examples and quotations from clinicians and family members that exemplify some themes that have arisen repeatedly in our data and are important to the arguments I make here. The data I cite come not only from my own interviews and observations but also from research conducted by other members of the research team.[4]

Not surprisingly, a key issue for families concerns whether or not they can trust their clinicians. The most minute nuances and gestures of health professionals (esp. doctors) are routinely scrutinized, becoming a subject of storytelling and puzzling. What are they trying to tell me? parents wonder. What are they hiding? Do they treat me this way because I'm black? A man without a job? A single mother? Do they think I'm a "ghetto mom?" Do they think I'm abusing my child? Are they experimenting on my child? Are they ignoring me because I'm on Medicaid? Do they think I'm not strong enough, bright enough, educated enough, to hear the truth? These are the sorts of questions asked by families in our research, and they are asked again and again. If cultures are spaces in which cultural differences are constructed and Othering is an everyday occurrence, this is profoundly consequential when a child's health or life is on the line.

## THE HAZARDS OF BORDER CROSSING

If health encounters operate in a "border zone," all the key actors—especially minority patients and families—are attempting to cross borders. When children have chronic medical conditions, successful treatment demands cooperation and alliance building among children, family members, and professionals.[5] This can be a daunting task for all involved, especially when clients have had a difficult time receiving decent health care, as is the case with many of the families in this study. When stigmatizing class and racial categorizations arise, or are suspected of arising, tensions intensify. Mistrust on all sides tends to run high. Othering tactics practiced by clinicians are often subtle and largely unconscious, becoming most visible when patients, including parenting kin, are perceived as noncompliant. Explicit racial designations are rarely used, but there is a common taxonomy of "difficult clients" that is often attached to low-income minorities, a language so polite that its stigmatizing influences are largely undetected by clinicians. In our research with children, negative labels are often affixed to the parents rather than the children themselves. In addition to obvious negative markers—such as the "abusive, noncompliant, or neglectful parent"—there is a language of compassion that can also serve to create difference: the "overwhelmed parent," the "too many things going on at home parent," the "doesn't really understand the clinical picture" parent, or the "still in denial" parent.

One of the most insidious features of these categories is that when people have been placed in one of them, their capabilities and strengths are hidden from view. This problem is exacerbated by the fact that health care encounters are based on expert models of service delivery: Clients have problems, professionals have problem-solving expertise. This too, can make it difficult for professionals to see the need to identify their clients' strong points or to learn from them. In addition to the problematic categories that abound in informal health care discourse, professionals also learn narrative strategies that can effectively disguise the abilities of clients. They operate with a common set of narrative scripts or work to construct stories that "make sense" of problematic or difficult clients in a way that leaves little room for the client to emerge as an agent, to influence the framing of the problem or the path of treatment (Mattingly 1998b). Although these problematic features of health care are by no means peculiar to minority populations, they are certainly intensified for minorities in which racial designations are likely to influence the clinical encounter.

One place this has emerged with startling clarity in our study is with children suffering from sickle-cell disease. The sickle-cell clinic has been the place where race is most openly discussed by clinical staff as well as parents. One mother in our study remarked that children with this disease are "not being treated with dignity and respect" in many hospitals, a lack of respect that includes parents as well. Because of some humiliating experiences at the hospital in which her child had been a patient for years, she transferred her daughter to another hospital, even though they lacked the same level of expertise in treating sickle-cell disease. She put it this way: "I'm not a radical. I'm not a feminist. . . . I just think you should be treated a certain way, and I should be treated like the person next to me who maybe is a different skin color."

Several clinicians in our study concurred. One physician who has treated sickle-cell patients for 25 years (and who happens to be white) angrily noted the dismissive way clinical staff tend to view sickle cell, a dismissiveness that also extended to the clinicians who treat such children:

> I'll tell you I don't even listen to them, the attendings. They say, "Ah well, we have a chemotherapy patient coming in so we need to send your sickle patient off the floor because this patient's more important." You know? And I won't tell you what I'd like to say to them. . . . There's very much the attitude that well, this is something that anybody can take care of and it's just like pneumonia. And they don't really believe that there's anything in particular, that special expertise, that's going to help you take care of these kids. And you find out real quick that that's not true.

A vivid illustration of problematic, race-based categorizing is the "med-seeking" label regularly attached to those with sickle-cell disease who go into a pain crisis. Adolescent African American boys, in particular, are often refused crucial pain medication or are seen as crazy, violent, or drug seeking when in a pain crisis. The physician quoted above told the following story in an interview:

> Try being a 17-year-old black male with severe pain going into an emergency room and asking for narcotics and see how far you get. . . . Some of the best advice that I ever heard was from an adult with sickle cell, this is from family day that we had a few years ago. And this adult said, "What you need to do is when you're totally fine, you're not in the middle of a crisis, go to the emergency room and ask to meet the head of the emergency room and sit down for five minutes with him and say, "Hi, my name is blank, remember me? I was an extremist the other night and I'm just on my way to my law firm today, but you know, but on the way to the business I own or the job I have doing X, Y, Z, I wanted to stop in and let you know that I don't always go around in my undershirt and underwear screaming, asking for narcotics."

An African American social worker we also interviewed in this same clinic echoed this: "As soon as the house staff hears there's a sickle-cell patient, something goes up that says, 'I've got a kid here that's drug-seeking, you know, manipulating,' without actually doing any assessment of the child."

The difficulty of not being heard or of being subjected to racially based Othering, although especially articulated with sickle-cell disease, pervades clinical encounters. How do families, children, and clinicians attempt to cross a clinical border zone heightened by racial wariness and mistrust? They cultivate border-crossing skills: They learn to "read the minds" of professional Others, and in light of those readings, to devise strategies to present themselves as worthy of care. Border crossing can be very tricky business because African American clients routinely must be noncompliant to get the care they or their children need. Learning to read the culture of a clinic and of an individual health professional means learning how to execute the right kind of noncompliance that will lead to getting care rather than being turned away or, worse, reported to the social worker as a "problem parent." One mother explained how she has learned to "shuffle through and play this politicking thing"—that is, to appear compliant even in situations in which she knows more about her child's disease than the professional and may privately disregard what the clinician tells her to do. In situations in which she felt she must fight directly, even when she was proved medically correct, she was then faced with yet more "shuffling" and "playing" the "politicking thing" to reestablish good relationships with estranged clinicians. In other words, she had to apologize and act grateful even when she was right to challenge professionals:

> A lot of times you, as parents, you kind of specialize in a disease. You know a lot more than the doctor knows and it's scary when you have doctors that say, "Oh, I'm Dr. So and So" and . . . then they say something off the wall and you know that they are completely wrong. And how do you deal with a doctor and his ego? And so that's part of the game that I've mentioned before. You have to know how to shuffle through and play this politicking thing when you shouldn't have to do that.

## CHILDREN'S POPULAR CULTURE AS LINGUA FRANCA

It is within this charged and wary context that the power of children's popular culture needs to be understood. If failed encounters produce and reinforce narratives of the stigmatized Other, successful ones counter these powerful narratives by producing ones in which clinicians and patients come to share, if sometimes fleetingly, a narrative of mutuality and belonging.[6] So, for instance, when an oncologist stops an examination to ask a parent about his or her Thanksgiving and to recount a story about problematic in-laws at the dinner, the oncologist speaks, in an important way, to a shared world of values and practices. The ability of professionals to recognize, acknowledge, and build on commonalities that cross lines of race, class, and culture is as important as recognizing the existence of race-based stereotyping or cultural difference.

Common worlds are routinely created in clinic interactions, drawing on cultural resources that are familiar to all the parties. For clinicians who have sustained relationships with clients, the ability of the actors to call on the small things—a joke remembered, a movie just seen, a disastrous Thanksgiving dinner—can be extremely powerful in forging bonds across formidable social divides. The importance of doing this has been noted repeatedly in the African American community with whom we have been involved. When things go very well in a clinical interaction, as they sometimes do, an important ingredient is that patients, clinicians, and even family caregivers are able to "read" one another well enough to create a shared narrative. That is, they are able to participate as actors in an unfolding story they help construct, one for which they have real commitment and one that embodies or suggests healing possibilities. This is what I have elsewhere called a "healing drama" (Mattingly 1998a, 2000; Mattingly and Lawlor 2001). Healing dramas need not depend on the possibility of curing; in fact, they can embrace death. But they do depend on moments in which shared experiences are created between professionals and clients. Such moments can draw members together even when they come from diverse social positions.

As it turns out, popular culture as offered up by mass media plays a critical role in facilitating the construction of these shared narratives. Global popular culture is often drawn on by families and health professionals to develop a shared story of hope. By *shared*, of course, I do not mean that health professionals and clients come to see or experience things in the same way, but that, at minimum, there is sufficient consensus to agree about treatment options and other practical matters and there is a sense that everyone is working in the best interest of the child. At times, though, there is a kind of collective imagining that goes far beyond this minimal level. Stories from children's popular culture are woven into clinic life and into interactions with home health professionals. They become part of stories acted out or referred to, especially during rehabilitation therapies that try to incorporate treatment into some form of child play. Rehabilitation therapists and aides mention that to treat children, they find that they need to watch the same movies that children are seeing simply to be able to understand them in therapy. Children repeat phrases or initiate actions in therapy that imitate their favorite film stories.

It is no surprise that characters from Disney films turn up with such regularity in pediatric hospitals and find their way into all kinds of clinical sessions. Disney has been the primary exporter of children's popular culture for decades, a matter that has long provoked critiques from, for example, critical social theorists of the well-known Frankfurt School.[7] The power of mass media to shape cultural identities has also been a topic of central concern within contemporary culture theory. Stuart Hall, for example, has argued that mass media is a primary vehicle for ideological production, a means through which groups construct images of their lives (Hall 1997). Mass media might be colonizing but ethnographic studies of the actual practices of cultural production and reception help to complicate the picture of media as ideology machine. Such studies reveal the way that the global is made "local" in specific contexts and show that the meaning of a media text is not given by the text itself but by the processes through which it is taken up and consumed by particular interpretive communities (Abu-Lughod 1991; Metcalf 2001; Rapp and Ginsburg 2001). Reception theories in media studies have been at pains to argue that meaning is a complex and local practice of negotiation between the world of the text and the world of the audience. It is a historically particular and local invention (see Spitulnik 1993 for a review of this literature). In other words, the audience does not merely consume, it "poaches," as Michel de Certeau (1984) puts it, helping to construct meaning through its practices of consumption.

## CONSUMING POPULAR CULTURE: CHILDREN AND FAMILIES

Children's popular culture (esp. Disney) is everywhere in the lives of this African American community. Disney and other popular culture products have a fundamental role in the ongoing (playful) practice of these children as they imagine themselves in various scenes, playing various parts. In these playful constructions of possible selves, characters gleaned from Disney (as well as other media) stories provide easily adapted cultural material. Children often try out characters borrowed from scenes in movies or television shows, inviting adults to play their appropriate part in the scenarios they set in motion. The cultural space of Disneyland itself profoundly feeds the imagination of children, shaping a sense of life possibilities even if they are only possibilities that can be played with. For example, one critically ill four-year-old declared, in a fit of wishful thinking, "My daddy's gonna take me to Disneyland with—with Michael Jackson."[8]

When young children identify with certain characters in movies and television programs, it is not simply that they like those characters. Rather, they become those characters, at least for moments at a time, and they do so with particular delight when they can find others who will cooperate. Identifications with a particular character are social achievements, for it takes not only the child but the support of those around her for this identity to become "real." It requires cooperative efforts if these characters are to be incorporated in the scenes of everyday life. Identity play may be initiated or actively discouraged by parents or other adults. When a three-year-old boy declared that he was one of the "Powerpuff Girls," his mother laughingly told us how she dissuaded him from this identification; he received no social support for seeing himself as a girl. This identity work is far from passive; it is actively carried out through a variety of efforts, often orchestrated by parents, in which the ongoing connection of their child with a popular character is ensured. Parents tell other important adults—including clinicians—about their child's favorite movie characters, thus widening the net of those who participate in the co-construction of a child as fantasy figure. They take their children to Disneyland or even far away Orlando's Walt Disney World to meet "their" special character. They dress children up as these characters for special occasions like birthdays and Halloween. They buy the dolls, coloring books, underwear, lunch boxes, tee shirts, stickers, pillow cases, curtains, and other merchandise that import the character into everyday life. They organize elaborate children's birthday parties to which dozens of people (including many adults) are invited and at which they recreate scenes from the movie in which their child's favorite character stars.

It is striking how consistently a child (or parent) chooses a character similar to the child in gender, racial or ethnic identity, or even disability. Even more intriguing, the kinds of adventures these characters face have their parallels in key events in a child's life. The happy endings that characterize children's movies and television programs offer hopeful visions of a child's future in "real life." Fascinatingly, this match may result from a striking mismatch, where a superhero possesses exactly the qualities that a child conspicuously lacks but longs for. Movie plots and life plots have a curious symmetry, although most often a symmetry by which a character's extraordinary or magical abilities provide a wishful identification for a child.

## CONSUMING CHILDREN'S POPULAR CULTURE: THE CLINICAL COMMUNITY

Pediatric clinicians routinely draw on popular culture to connect with children. This is most apparent and most elaborate in rehabilitation therapies in which clinicians struggle to get children to cooperate with what can be painful or difficult exercises. Especially in acute hospital settings, there is a certain desperation in calling on this trade language. Often there is little time to get to know children who must be asked to participate in activities that are likely to frighten or pain them. Over the years, we have interviewed a number of physical and occupational therapists about their use of Disney and other mass media narratives in clinical work. I include some of the comments they have made in our interviews about how and why children's popular culture figures so pervasively in health care encounters. One occupational therapist mentioned that she always looks at children's shoes to see what character or movie they like. Another therapist said,

> It's not like you have a couple of sessions to develop rapport. You're seeing them just that one time and the parents say, "There's this issue and you absolutely have to get this assessment done right now." And the doctor wants to know what you think right then. And you have to develop a rapport very quickly. And that's when you just grab whatever you can that you can just kind of key into them with.

Certain favorite characters are woven into therapy sessions. Many come from Disney films because, as an occupational therapist noted dryly, "They have a pretty big corner on the market." When there is time to listen, a physical therapist pointed out, it is possible to "let them [the children] lead you," which is the very best way to work. A physical and occupational therapist at a pediatric burn unit reflected on the importance of these characters for the children they treated. The therapist noted, mimicking the children, "Different kids, especially at different ages, tend to attach to different things. Like the girls, like we had so many little girl patients that were really into, like, Snow White."

This attachment is used by clinicians as a "motivator" during therapy sessions. A physical therapist offered this example:

> I think we use it as a motivator if they indicate to us that that's something they really like to do. Like my one little girl, Anita, who loves, loves Snow White. I mean it was something. So we would call her Snow White and we would say . . . let's have you walk like a Princess Snow White and we'll go over and see if we can drop little things for the little seven dwarfs.

Children's popular culture can provide a "key" into the world of a child's imagination, a world in which the clinician can become an ally rather than an enemy, and one in which a child can do things impossible in ordinary life. To illustrate, I offer the following example. One occupational therapist told a story about how she came to incorporate "Spiderman" into her sessions with a child suffering severe sensory motor problems. This eight-year-old boy was so afraid of heights he slept with his mattress on the floor and refused to play on swings, slides, or monkey bars on the playground. As a result, he spent many lonely hours at school recess and home while his friends and schoolmates played together. During their first clinic session, she found him extremely shy, remembering that "when Manny first entered the clinic, he had his face buried into his mother's side and he would not turn around or make eye contact with me." After several false starts that yielded only silence, the therapist noticed he was wearing a "Spiderman" shirt and shoes. She decided "it was worth a try" to see if Spiderman could draw him out. When she produced a Spiderman coloring book, "a smile began to creep over his face." Coloring the Spiderman book together began their many Spiderman adventures. As Manny colored, he told her of Spiderman's great feats and enemies, and out of this, as she put it, "a pact had been formed for future therapy sessions" for in all subsequent sessions "Spiderman played a prominent role." Manny donned a special Spiderman vest for therapy time. There was one session the therapist described in some detail because she saw it as a turning point in her work with the boy. For this session, she used a rope hammock swing (a typical piece of therapy equipment for children with sensory motor difficulties), which she announced was a spider's web. (The Spiderman's web, in fact.) After much coaxing, Manny eventually climbed into the web with her, although he was so frightened that his teeth chattered. To distract him, she sang the Spiderman Song, which she also recited for me. This song includes such telling lines as

> Can he swing from a thread?
> Take a look overhead.
> Hey there, there goes the Spiderman!

Manny gradually calmed as he heard the song, which allowed the therapist to begin a game of throwing beanbags at various Spiderman "enemies" (beanie babies she had set up in different spots around the therapy room). She took on the voices of these hapless enemies as Manny bashed them with beanbags. He became so enthusiastic that, in an unprecedented moment, he insisted they swing higher and higher so that even while he was in a "tornado" he could "fight against evil." This therapist was convinced that Manny's capacity to become Spiderman in these therapy episodes was critical to her success with him, as evidenced by his willingness to take on such terrifying challenges as swinging high above ground.

Notably popular icons are extremely versatile cultural resources. The same character can take on different meanings for different children. Whereas for Manny, it is Spiderman's brave capacities to, for example, "swing from a thread" that are salient, for another child facing a different sort of disabling condition, other features become central. For example, Spiderman also became a favorite cultural icon for a boy in our study forced to wear medical masks to treat a severe burn injury to his face. In this case, Spiderman's identity as a "masked hero" is emphasized; in Manny's case, it is his skill at gravity defying leaps through space.

## CONCLUSION

Popular culture provides a common language for adults and children, a set of public symbols that they can draw on to try to connect with one another. Even comparative strangers, like health professionals, can readily draw on them to connect to a child they do not know and who is, likely as not, afraid of them.

Globally circulated and mass-produced texts are made meaningful in local ways and offer powerful cultural resources that serve local ends. Popular culture offers characters and plots that are remade, "indigenized" as Arjun Appadurai (1991, 1996) says, to fit specific needs and circumstances. As the Spiderman examples illustrate, the meaning of a popular media text does not reside in the text-in-itself and can never be reduced to mere "consumption;" it always involves situated constructions that do practical work for particular actors.

Popular-culture stories and heroes provide potent vehicles for overcoming the dreary, frightening, or embattled relations between clinicians and patients and do so in a way that supports hope. When clinicians draw on these loved characters in their interactions with children, they may be connecting with children and parenting kin in a far more powerful way than they sometimes realize. When clinicians speak to families only in the medicalized language of statistical probabilities, especially if prognoses are poor, mistrust is easily heightened. It is not that clients want to be lied to or have medical information withheld. But they are also concerned that clinicians support a subjunctive reading of their child's chances and that they make every effort, even for, as parents sometimes say, "a little black kid" (Mattingly 2004). How can families come to trust that professionals have not "given up" on their children, despite the fact that they have severe disabilities and are African American? In the racial climate of the United States, this is not a question that can be asked and answered directly. Clues must be indirect. It is here that, in its own oblique and playful way, the lingua franca of children's popular culture—when exemplified by, for example, a joking exchange between a nurse and mother about how quickly Spiderman recovered from surgery (the very same surgery a child has just undergone)— suggests possibilities that go far beyond the ostensible topic. In a wary place like the urban clinic, when people are struggling to connect across all kinds of barriers, a Pocahontas or a Spiderman, one might say, travels well.

## ACKNOWLEDGMENTS

I would like to thank members (past and present) of the research team: Erica Angert, Nancy Bagatell, Jeanine Blanchard, Jeannie Gaines, Lanita Jacobs-Huey, Teresa Kuan, Stephanie Mielke, Ann Neville-Jan, Melissa Park, Carolyn Rouse, Katy Sanders, and Kim Wilkinson. Particular, heartfelt thanks goes to my long-time research partner, Mary Lawlor. Thanks also to the Narrative Study Group for comments on drafts of this article: Linda Garro, Elinor Ochs, Janet Hoskins, Marjorie Goodwin, Gelya Frank, Nancy Lutkehaus, and again, Mary Lawlor. I gratefully acknowledge support by Maternal and Child Health Bureau (MCJ #060745) and National Center for Medical Rehabilitation Research, National Institute of Child Health and Human Development, National Institutes of Health (1RO1HD38878, 2RO1HD38878).

## NOTES

1. A number of scholars have explored how mass media produces connections and even diasporic communities in ways that further complicate any simple use of the term *culture* (Abu-Lughod 1991; Appadurai 1991; Diouf 2000; Erlmann 1996; Mbembe 1992; Metcalf 2001; Pollock et al. 2000; Price 1999; Schein 2002).
2. See Good et al. 2002, Cooper-Patrick et al. 1999, and Doescher et al. 2000.
3. In a careful review of research findings on health disparities, an Institute of Medicine Committee reported that minorities are less likely than whites to receive needed services, including clinically necessary procedures. These disparities exist in a number of disease areas, including cancer, cardiovascular disease, HIV/AIDS, diabetes, and mental illness, and are found across a range of procedures, including routine treatments for common health problems. [Institute of Medicine 2002:2; see also Good et al. 2002]

   Although health disparities for all minorities as compared to whites have been consistently documented, African Americans are routinely subjected to the greatest racial stereotyping and to the least access to health services (Bailey 1991; James 1994; Whitehead 1997). Some research indicates this is regardless of social class, education, economic status, or type of health care coverage (Dressler 1993; Good et al. 2002). Other research challenges this in claiming that social class plays a larger role than race, per se, in quality of health care (e.g., Lareau 2002). In any case, it is clear that when race and class are confounded, as they are for most of the families we have been following, receiving good health care services is an ongoing challenge. For further discussion of the connection between race and health, see also Barbee 1993; Jackson 1993; Porter 1994; and Wailoo 2001.

4. For the sake of simplicity and to help protect confidentiality of informants, throughout the article, when quoting participants, I refer to the research team collectively, as in "we interviewed" or "we observed," rather than identifying particular researchers.
5. General concern to improve the capacity of clinicians to communicate with minority clients has spurned a vast, cross-disciplinary literature on "cultural competence" (Brach and Fraser 2000; Guarnaccia and Rodriguez 1996; Lopez 1997; Pierce and Pierce 1996) and on "culturally compatible interventions" (Takeuchi et al. 1995).
6. This point was brought home with force in the way the African American families in our study talked about the meaning of September 11th. They underscored not only the concern to be designated as different from Euro-Americans but also the need to be recognized as sharing a common national culture and heritage (Mattingly et al. 2002).
7. See Henry Giroux's (1999) critique of the Disney empire for a fascinating, and more recent, exposition along these lines.
8. As Giroux states, Disney is hardly a monolithic empire. Rather, he explains,

   The Disney culture offers potentially subversive moments and pleasures in a rage of contradictory and complex experiences. In fact, any approach to studying Disney must address the issue of why so many kids and adults love Disney and experience its theme parks, plays, and travel opportunities as a counterlogic that allows them to venture beyond the present while laying claim to unrealized dreams and hopes. [1999:5]

## REFERENCES


Abu-Lughod, Lila. 1991. Writing against Culture. In *Recapturing Anthropology: Working in the Present*, ed. Richard Fox, 137–162. Santa Fe: School of American Research Press.

Appadurai, Arjun. 1991. Global Ethnoscapes: Notes and Queries for a Transnational Anthropology. In *Recapturing Anthropology: Working in the Present*, ed. Richard Fox, 191–210. Santa Fe: School of American Research Press.

______.1996. *Modernity at Large: Cultural Dimensions of Globalization.* Minneapolis: University of Minnesota Press.

Bailey, Eric. 1991. Hypertension: An Analysis of Detroit African-American Health Care Treatment Patterns. *Human Organization* 50(3): 287–296.

Barbee, Evelyn. 1993. Racism in U.S. Nursing. *Medical Anthropology Quarterly* 7(4): 346–362.

Brach, C., and I. Fraser. 2000. Can Cultural Competency Reduce Racial and Ethnic Health Disparities? A Review and Conceptual Model. *Medical Care Research and Review* 57 (Suppl. 1): 181–217.

Bruner, Jerome. 1986. *Actual Minds, Possible Worlds.* Cambridge, MA: Harvard University Press.

______.2002 *Making Stories: Law, Literature, Life.* New York: Farrar, Straus, and Giroux.

Clifford, James. 1997. *Routes: Travel and Translation in the Twentieth Century.* Cambridge, MA: Harvard University Press.

Cooper-Patrick, L., J. Gallo, J. Gonzales, H. Vu, N. Powe, C. Nelson, and D. Ford. 1999. Race, Gender, and Partnership in the Patient-Physician Relationship. *Journal of the American Medical Association* 282(6): 583–589.

de Certeau, Michel. 1984. *The Practice of Everyday Life.* S. Rendall, trans. Berkeley: University of California Press.

Diouf, Mamadou. 2000. *The Senegalese Murid Trade Diaspora and the Making of a Vernacular Cosmopolitanism.* S. Rendall, trans. Public Culture 12: 679–702.

Doescher, M., B. Saver, P. Franks, and K. Fiscella. 2000. Racial and Ethnic Disparities in Perceptions of Physician Style and Trust. *Archives of Family Medicine* 9(10): 1156–1163.

Dressler, William. 1993. Health in the African American Community: Accounting for Health Disparities. *Medical Anthropology Quarterly* 7(4): 325–345.

Erlmann, Veit. 1996. The Aesthetics of the Global Imagination: Reflections on World Music in the 1990s. *Public Culture* 8: 467–487.

Giroux, Henry. 1999. *The Mouse That Roared: Disney and the End of Innocence.* Lanham, MD: Rowman and Littlefield.

Good, Mary-Jo DelVecchio, C. James, Byron Good, and A. Becker. 2002. The Culture of Medicine and Racial, Ethnic, and Class Disparities in Healthcare. Pp. 594–625. *Report by the Institute of Medicine on Unequal Treatment.* Washington, DC: National Academy Press.

Guarnaccia, P., and O. Rodriguez. 1996. Concepts of Culture and Their Role in the Development of Culturally Competent Mental Health Services. *Hispanic Journal of Behavioral Sciences* 18: 419–443.

Hall, Stuart. 1997. *Representation: Cultural Representations and Signifying Practices.* London: Sage.

Institute of Medicine. 2002. *Unequal Treatment: What Healthcare Providers Need to Know about Racial and Ethnic Disparities in Healthcare.* Washington, DC: National Academy Press.

Jackson, Eileen. 1993. Whiting-Out Difference: Why U.S. Nursing Research Fails Black Families. *Medical Anthropology Quarterly* 7(4): 363–385.

James, Sherman. 1994. John Henryism and the Health of African Americans. *Culture, Medicine and Psychiatry* 18: 163–182.

Lareau, Annette. 2002. Invisible Inequality: Social Class and Childrearing in Black Families and White Families. *American Sociological Review* 67: 747–776.

Lopez, Steven. 1997. Cultural Competence in Psychotherapy: A Guide for Clinicians and Their Supervisors. In *Handbook of Psychotherapy Supervision*, ed. C. E. Watkins Jr., 570–588. New York: John Wiley and Sons.

Mattingly, Cheryl. 1998a. *Healing Dramas and Clinical Plots: The Narrative Structure of Experience.* Cambridge: Cambridge University Press.

______.1998b. In Search of the Good: Narrative Reasoning in Clinical Practice. *Medical Anthropology Quarterly* 12(3): 273–297.

______.2000. Emergent Narratives. In *Narrative and the Cultural Construction of Illness and Healing*, eds. Cheryl Mattingly, and Linda Garro, 181–211. Berkeley: University of California Press.

______.2004. Performance Narratives in Clinical Practice. In *Narrative Research in Health and Illness*, eds. B. Hurwitz, T. Greenhalgh, and V. Skultans, 73–94. London: Blackwell Publishing.

Mattingly, Cheryl, and Mary Lawlor. 2001. The Fragility of Healing. *Ethos* 29(1): 30–57.

Mattingly, Cheryl, Mary Lawlor, and Lanita Jacobs-Huey. 2002. Narrating September 11: Race, Gender, and the Play of Cultural Identities. *American Anthropologist* 104(3): 743–753.

Mbembe, Achille. 1992. The Banality of Power and the Aesthetics of Vulgarity in the Postcolony. *Public Culture* 4: 1–30.

Metcalf, Peter. 2001. Global "Disjunctive" and the "Sites" of Anthropology. *Cultural Anthropology* 16(2): 165–182.

Pierce, Robert, and Lois Pierce. 1996. Moving toward Cultural Competence in the Child Welfare System. *Children Youth Services Review* 18(8): 713–731.

Pollock, Sheldon, Homi Bhabha, Carol Breckenridge, and Dipesh Chakrabarty. 2000. Cosmopolitanisms. *Public Culture* 12: 577–589.

Porter, Cornelia. 1994. Stirring the Pot of Differences: Racism and Health. *Medical Anthropology Quarterly* 8(1): 102–106.

Price, Monroe. 1999. Satellite Broadcasting as Trade Routes in the Sky. *Public Culture* 11: 69–85.

Rapp, Rayna, and Faye Ginsburg. 2001. Enabling Disability: Rewriting Kinship, Reimagining Citizenship. *Public Culture* 13(3): 533–556.

Rosaldo, Renato. 1989. *Culture and Truth: The Remaking of Social Analysis.* Boston, MA: Beacon.

Schein, Louisa. 2002. Mapping Hmong Media in Diasporic Space. In *Media Worlds: Anthropology on New Terrain*, eds. Faye Ginsburg, Lila Abu-Lughod, and Brian Larkin, 229–244. Berkeley: University of California Press.

Spitulnik, Debra. 1993. Anthropology and the Mass Media. *Annual Review of Anthropology* 22: 293–315.

Takeuchi, D., S. Sue, and M. Yeh. 1995. Return Rates and Outcomes from Ethnicity-Specific Mental Health Programs in Los Angeles. *American Journal of Public Health* 85: 638–643.

Wailoo, Keith. 2001. *Dying in the City of the Blues: Sickle Cell Anemia and the Politics of Race and Health.* Chapel Hill: North Carolina University Press.

Whitehead, Tony. 1997. Urban Low-Income African American Men, HIV/AIDS, and Gender Identity. *Medical Anthropology Quarterly* 11(4): 411–417.

# 41

# Culture, Poverty, and HIV Transmission

## *The Case of Rural Haiti*

*Paul Farmer*

AIDS is currently the deadliest infectious disease in the world, killing more than 3 million people every year. While antiretroviral drugs have lengthened the lives of many people infected with HIV, these drugs are expensive, and millions of people who need them still cannot afford them. Without medications, counseling, and support, people living with HIV are likely to infect others, and then die.

In the history of this epidemic, anthropologists have played an important role in describing and helping to explain how behavioral practices are related to the transmission of the HIV virus. So, too, have anthropologists helped demonstrate how poverty and other inequalities affect people's likelihood of contracting AIDS in the first place.

In this selection, we learn about the circumstances under which three Haitians developed AIDS, and how circumstances such as poverty and gender inequality put them at dramatically increased risk of infection. Much of the public discourse about AIDS reflects moral judgments about people's lifestyles and places blame for the disease on the sufferers. This selection shows how circumstances beyond individuals' control can place them at risk of infection. Paul Farmer, the author of this selection, is both a physician and an anthropologist, and he has been one of the most prominent and vocal advocates for people whose social and political circumstances place them at increased risk of HIV and other infectious diseases. Students interested in learning more about the work of Paul Farmer might be interested in reading his biography, *Mountains Beyond Mountains,* by Tracy Kidder.

While the biomedical challenge of AIDS is great, the challenge of coping with the human dimensions of AIDS is enormous, requiring resources, compassion, and cross-cultural understanding. Anthropologists have made, and continue to make, important contributions to the efforts of doctors, hospitals, nongovernment organizations, and other people and institutions to cope with the human dimensions of this devastating virus.

***As you read this selection, ask yourself the following questions:***

- How does poverty affect one's risk of becoming infected with HIV?
- What cultural and political factors influence the distribution of AIDS in Haiti?
- How can HIV infection be seen as *not* the result of bad personal decisions?
- What are some practical suggestions for reducing the human suffering caused by AIDS?
- What does Farmer mean when he says that there is "an AIDS of the North, and an AIDS of the South?"

***The following terms discussed in this selection are included in the Glossary at the back of the book:***

| | |
|---|---|
| *AIDS* | *seropositive* |
| *epidemic* | *seroprevalence* |
| *HIV* | *SIDA* |
| *medical anthropology* | *transmission* |

Haiti, a country of well over seven million inhabitants, is generally considered to be a substantially rural nation,[1] yet few studies of HIV transmission have been conducted in rural parts of the country.

Early reports by Pape and Johnson, based on small studies conducted in 1986–87, noted that the

Farmer, Paul. "Culture, Poverty, and HIV Transmission: The Case of Rural Haiti." From *Infections and Inequalities: The Modern Plagues* by Paul Farmer, pp. 129–149. 

seroprevalence rate for HIV averaged 3 percent "in rural areas."[2] The seroprevalence in 97 mothers of children hospitalized with dehydration was 3 percent; of 245 unscreened rural blood donors, 4 percent had antibodies to HIV. In an area even more distant from urban centers, only 1 percent of 191 adults who came for immunizations were seropositive. Unfortunately, we know little about the individuals bled for these studies. Just how rural were they? What was the nature of their ties to Port-au-Prince and other high-prevalence cities? How did the seropositive individuals come to be at risk for HIV? How did they differ from seronegative controls? How rapidly was HIV making inroads into the rural population? What, in short, are the dynamics of HIV transmission in rural Haiti?

To understand the rural Haitian AIDS epidemic, we must move beyond the concept of "risk groups" to consider the interplay between human agency and the powerful forces that constrain it, focusing especially on those activities that promote or retard the spread of HIV. In Haiti, the most powerful of these forces have been inequality, deepening poverty, and political dislocations, which have together conspired to hasten the spread of HIV. This chapter details research on HIV transmission in a rural area of Haiti—and also recounts some of the ways such large-scale social forces become manifest in the lives of particular individuals.

## AIDS IN A HAITIAN VILLAGE

The setting for the research described here is the Péligre basin of Haiti's Central Plateau, home to several hundred thousand mostly rural people. Although all parts of Haiti are poor, the Péligre basin region and its villages may be especially so.

Before 1956, the village of Kay was situated in a deep and fertile valley in this area, near the banks of the Rivière Artibonite. For generations, the villagers farmed the broad and gently sloping banks of the river, selling rice, bananas, millet, corn, and sugarcane in regional markets. Harvests were, by all reports, bountiful; life then is now recalled as idyllic. With the construction of Haiti's largest hydroelectric dam in 1956, however, thousands of families living in this region were flooded out. The displaced persons were largely peasant farmers, and they received little or no compensation for their lost land.

The hilltop village of Do Kay was founded by refugees from the rising water. The flooding of the valley forced most villagers up into the hills on either side of the new reservoir. Kay became divided into "Do" (those who settled on the stony backs of the hills) and "Ba" (those who remained down near the new waterline). By all standard measures, both parts of Kay are now very poor; its older inhabitants often blame their poverty on the massive buttress dam a few miles away and note bitterly that it brought them neither electricity nor water.

Though initially a dusty squatter settlement of fewer than two hundred persons, Do Kay has grown rapidly in the past decade and now counts about two thousand inhabitants. In spite of the hostile conditions, most families continue to rely to some extent on small-scale agriculture. But many villagers are involved in a series of development projects designed to improve the health of the area's inhabitants. Since 1984, for example, a series of outreach initiatives have complemented the work of our growing team of clinicians, based in Do Kay at the Clinique Bon Sauveur. The most significant efforts were undertaken under the aegis of Proje Veye Sante, the "health surveillance project." Proje Veye Sante, conducted in large part by village-based community health workers from about thirty nearby communities, provides preventive and primary care to close to fifty thousand rural people.

Through Proje Veye Sante, AIDS surveillance began well before the epidemic was manifest in the region. It is thus possible to date the index, or first, case of AIDS to 1986, when a young schoolteacher, Manno Surpris, fell ill with recurrent superficial fungal infections, chronic diarrhea, and pulmonary tuberculosis. Seropositive for HIV, he died a year later.

Although Manno Surpris was from another part of the Central Plateau, it was not long before we began to diagnose the syndrome among natives of Do Kay. The sections that follow offer brief case histories of the first three villagers known to have died of AIDS. None had a history of transfusion with blood or blood products; none had a history of homosexual contact or other "risk factors" as designated by the CDC. They did, however, share two important, if poorly understood, risk factors: poverty and inequality.

### Anita

Anita Joseph was born in approximately 1966 to a family that had lost its land to the Péligre dam. One of six children, she briefly attended school until her mother, weakened by the malnutrition then rampant in the Kay area, died of tuberculosis. Anita was then thirteen. Her father became depressed and abusive, and she resolved to run away: "I'd had it with his yelling. . . . When I saw how poor I was, and how hungry, and saw that it would never get any better, I had to go to the city. Back then I was so skinny—I was saving my life, I thought, by getting out of here."

Anita left for Port-au-Prince with less than $3 and no clear plan of action. She worked briefly as a *restavèk,* or live-in maid, for $10 a month but lost this position when her employer was herself fired from a factory job.

Cast into the street, Anita eventually found a relative who took her in. The kinswoman, who lived in a notorious slum north of the capital, introduced her to Vincent, a young man who worked unloading luggage at the airport. Anita was not yet fifteen when she entered her first and only sexual union. "What could I do, really?" she sighed as she recounted the story much later. "He had a good job. My aunt thought I should go with him."

Vincent, who had at least one other sexual partner at the time, became ill less than two years after they began sharing a room. The young man, whom Anita cared for throughout his illness, died after repeated infections, including tuberculosis. Not long after his death, Anita herself fell ill with tuberculosis.

Upon returning to Do Kay in 1987, she quickly responded to antituberculous therapy. When she relapsed some months later, we performed an HIV test, which revealed the true cause of her immunosuppression. Following a slow but ineluctable decline, Anita died in February 1988.

### Dieudonné

Dieudonné Gracia, born in Do Kay in 1963, was also the child of two "water refugees." One of seven children, he attended primary school in his home village and, briefly, secondary school in a nearby town. It was there, at the age of nineteen, that he had his first sexual contact. Dieudonné remarked that his girlfriend had had "two, maybe three partners" before they met; he was sure that one of her partners had been a truck driver from a city in central Haiti.

When a series of setbacks further immiserated his family, Dieudonné was forced to drop out of secondary school and also to drop his relationship with the young woman. He returned to Do Kay to work with his father, a carpenter. In 1983, however, the young man decided to "try my luck in Port-au-Prince." Through a friend from Do Kay, Dieudonné found a position as a domestic for a well-to-do family in a suburb of the capital.

While in the city, Dieudonné's sexual experience broadened considerably. He had five partners in little more than two years, all of them close to his own age. Asked about the brevity of these liaisons, Dieudonné favored an economic explanation: "A couple of them let go of me because they saw that I couldn't do anything for them. They saw that I couldn't give them anything for any children."

In 1985, Dieudonné became ill and was dismissed from his job in Port-au-Prince. He returned to Do Kay and began seeing his former lover again. She soon became pregnant and moved to Do Kay as the young man's *plase,* a term designating a partner in a more or less stable conjugal union.[3]

During this interlude, Dieudonné was seen at the Do Kay clinic for a number of problems that suggested immunodeficiency: herpes zoster and genital herpes, recurrent diarrhea, and weight loss. In the months following the birth of their baby, the young mother fell ill with a febrile illness, thought by her physician to be malaria, and quickly succumbed. Less than a year later, Dieudonné, much reduced by chronic diarrhea, was diagnosed with tuberculosis. Although he initially responded to antituberculous agents, Dieudonné died of AIDS in October 1988.

### Acéphie

Acéphie Joseph was born in 1965 on a small knoll protruding into the reservoir that had drowned her parents' land. Acéphie attended primary school somewhat irregularly; by the age of nineteen, she had not yet graduated and decided that it was time to help generate income for her family, which was sinking deeper and deeper into poverty. Hunger was a near-daily occurrence for the Joseph family; the times were as bad as those right after the flooding of the valley. Acéphie began to help her mother, a market woman, by carrying produce to a local market on Friday mornings.

It was there that she met a soldier, formerly stationed in Port-au-Prince, who began to make overtures to the striking young woman from Do Kay. Although the soldier had a wife and children and was known to have more than one regular partner, Acéphie did not spurn him. "What would you have me do? I could tell that the old people were uncomfortable, worried—but they didn't say no. They didn't tell me to stay away from him. I wish they had, but how could they have known? . . . I looked around and saw how poor we all were, how the old people were finished. . . . It was a way out, that's how I saw it."

Within a short time, the soldier fell ill and was diagnosed in the Do Kay clinic with AIDS. A few months after he and Acéphie parted, he was dead.

Shaken, Acéphie went to a nearby town and began a course in what she euphemistically termed a "cooking school," which prepared poor girls for work as servants. In 1987, twenty-two years old, Acéphie went to Port-au-Prince, where she found a $30-per-month job as a housekeeper for a middle-class Haitian woman who worked for the U.S. embassy. She began to see a man, also from the Kay region, who chauffeured a small bus between the Central Plateau and Port-au-Prince.

Acéphie worked in the city until late in 1989, when she discovered that she was pregnant. This displeased both her partner and her employer. Sans job and sans boyfriend, Acéphie returned to Do Kay in her third trimester.

Following the birth of her daughter, Acéphie was sapped by repeated opportunistic infections, each one caught in time by the staff of the clinic in Do Kay. Throughout 1991, however, she continued to lose weight; by January 1992, she weighed less than ninety pounds, and her intermittent fevers did not respond to broad-spectrum antibiotics.

Acéphie died in April 1992. Her daughter, the first "AIDS orphan" in Do Kay, is now in the care of Acéphie's mother. The child is also infected. A few months after Acéphie's death, her father hanged himself.

Sadly, however, this is not simply the story of Acéphie and her family. The soldier's wife, who is much thinner than last year, has already had a case of herpes zoster. Two of her children are also HIV-positive. This woman, who is well known to the clinic staff, is no longer a widow; once again, she is the partner of a military man. Her late husband had at least two other partners, both of them poor peasant women, in the Central Plateau. One is HIV-positive and has two sickly children. The father of Acéphie's child, apparently in good health, is still plying the roads from Mirebalais to Port-au-Prince. His serostatus is unknown.

## Individual Experience in Context

When compared to age-matched North Americans with AIDS, Anita, Dieudonné, and Acéphie have sparse sexual histories: Anita had only one partner; Dieudonné had six; Acéphie had two. Although a case-control study by Pape and Johnson suggested that HIV-infected urban men, at least, had larger numbers of partners than our patients did,[4] research conducted in Anita's neighborhood in Port-au-Prince suggests that her case is not as unique as it would seem:

> The high seropositivity rate (8%) found in pregnant women 14 to 19 years of age suggests that women [in Cité Soleil] appear to acquire HIV infection soon after becoming sexually active. Moreover, this age group is the only one in which a higher seropositivity rate is not associated with a greater number of sexual partners. Women with only one sexual partner in the year prior to pregnancy actually have a slightly higher prevalence rate (although not significantly so) than the others. This suggests that they were infected by their first and only partner.[5]

**TABLE 1 Case-Control Study of AIDS in Rural Haitian Women**

| Patient Characteristics | Patients with AIDS (N = 25) | Control Group (N = 25) |
|---|---|---|
| Average number of sexual partners | 2.7 | 2.4 |
| Sexual partner of a truck driver | 12 | 2 |
| Sexual partner of a soldier | 9 | 0 |
| Sexual partner of a peasant only | 0 | 23 |
| Ever lived in Port-au-Prince | 20 | 4 |
| Worked as a servant | 18 | 1 |
| Average number of years of formal schooling | 4.5 | 4.0 |
| Ever received a blood transfusion | 0 | 2 |
| Ever used illicit drugs | 0 | 0 |
| Ever received more than ten intramuscular injections | 17 | 19 |

The stories of Anita, Dieudonné, and Acéphie are ones that reveal the push-and-pull forces of contemporary Haiti. In all three cases, the declining fortunes of the rural poor pushed young adults to try their chances in the city. Once there, all three became entangled in unions that the women, at least, characterized as attempts to emerge from poverty. Each worked as a domestic, but none managed to fulfill the expectation of saving and sending home desperately needed cash. What they brought home, instead, was AIDS.

How representative are these case histories? Over the past several years, the medical staff of the Clinique Bon Sauveur has diagnosed dozens more cases of AIDS and other forms of HIV infection in women who arrive at the clinic with a broad range of complaints. In fact, the majority of our patients have been women—a pattern rarely described in the AIDS literature. With surprisingly few exceptions, those so diagnosed shared a number of risk factors, as our modest case-control study suggests.

We conducted this study by interviewing the first twenty-five women we diagnosed with symptomatic HIV infection who were residents of Do Kay or its two neighboring villages. Their responses to questions posed during a series of open-ended interviews were compared with those of twenty-five age-matched, seronegative controls. In both groups, ages ranged from 16 to 44, with a mean age of about 27 years. Table 1 presents our findings.

None of these fifty women had a history of prostitution, and none had used illicit drugs. Only two, both members of the control group, had received blood transfusions. None of the women in either group had

had more than five sexual partners in the course of their lives; in fact, seven of the afflicted women had had only one. Although women in the study group had on average more sexual partners than the controls, the difference is not striking. Similarly, we found no clear difference between the two groups in the number of intramuscular injections they had received or their years of education.

The chief risk factors in this small cohort seem to involve not number of partners but rather the professions of these partners. Fully nineteen of the women with HIV disease had histories of sexual contact with soldiers or truck drivers. Three of these women reported having only two sexual partners: one a soldier, one a truck driver. Of the women diagnosed with AIDS, none had a history of sexual contact exclusively with peasants (although one had as sole partner a construction worker from Do Kay). Among the control group, only two women had a regular partner who was a truck driver; none reported contact with soldiers, and most had had sexual relations only with peasants from the region. Histories of extended residence in Port-au-Prince and work as a domestic were also strongly associated with a diagnosis of HIV disease.

How can we make sense of these surprising results? In the sociographically "flat" region around the dam—after all, most area residents share a single socioeconomic status, poverty—conjugal unions with nonpeasants (salaried soldiers and truck drivers who are paid on a daily basis) reflect women's quest for some measure of economic security. In the setting of a worsening economic crisis, the gap between the hungry peasant class and the relatively well-off soldiers and truck drivers became the salient local inequality. In this manner, truck drivers and soldiers have served as a "bridge" from the city to the rural population.

Truck drivers and soldiers will soon no longer be necessary components of the rural epidemic. Once introduced into a sexually active population, HIV will work its way to those with no history of residence in the city, no history of contact with soldiers or truck drivers, no history of work as a domestic. But these risk factors—all of which reflect a desperate attempt to escape rural poverty—are emblematic of the lot of the rural Haitian poor, and perhaps especially of poor women.

## HIV in a Haitian Village

Extended residence in Port-au-Prince, work as a servant, and sexual contact with nonpeasants—although these risk factors were far different from those described for North Americans with AIDS, they characterized the majority of our male and female patients afflicted with AIDS. The majority of the residents of the area served by Proje Veye Sante shared none of these attributes, however. Did this suggest that few would prove to be infected with HIV? Although a good deal of ethnographic research into the nature of AIDS had already been conducted in the region, no research had addressed the question of HIV prevalence among asymptomatic adults.

Troubled by this lacuna, the staff of the clinic and of Proje Veye Sante established the Groupe d'étude du SIDA dans la Classe Paysanne.[6] GESCAP has a mandate to research the mechanisms by which poverty puts young adults, and especially young women, at risk of HIV infection.[7] With community approval, GESCAP is attempting to illuminate case histories with serologic surveys, an expanded case-control study, and cluster studies (such as those that revealed how a single HIV-positive soldier came to infect at least eleven natives of the region, one of whom was Acéphie).

After considerable discussion, the members of GESCAP decided to undertake a study of all asymptomatic adults living in Do Kay. The study was to include all members of the community who might plausibly be sexually active (fifteen years and older) and who were free of any suggestion of immunodeficiency; patients with active tuberculosis were excluded from this study. Anyone who was the regular sexual partner of a person with known HIV infection was also excluded.

Of the first one hundred villagers enrolling in the program, ninety-nine were seronegative for HIV.[8] The one young woman with HIV infection, Alourdes, had a history of extended residence in Port-au-Prince and also in 1985 of regular sexual contact with a salaried employee of the national electric company. This man, who had several sexual partners during his tenure in central Haiti, was rumored to have died of AIDS. In 1986, Alourdes had been the partner of a young man from her home village, a construction worker. He later developed tuberculosis, initially attributed to respiratory contact with his wife, who had pulmonary tuberculosis. Both were later found to be infected with HIV; neither had ever had sexual contact outside the Do Kay area. The discovery of HIV infection in Alourdes, who was known to have risk factors as defined in the case-control study, helped to identify the routes of exposure of the couple who had HIV-related tuberculosis.

Such discrete studies do not, however, fully define the nature of the large-scale social forces at work. The discussion in the following sections summarizes the factors that seem to be most significant in the ultimate rate of progression of HIV in rural Haiti. Perhaps an examination of these forces can serve to inform understandings of the dynamics of HIV transmission in other parts of Latin America and also in areas of Asia and Africa where prevalence rates in rural regions are currently low. It is a cautionary tale that argues for aggressive preventive measures:

> If a disaster is to be prevented in rural Haiti, vigorous and effective prevention campaigns must be initiated at once. And although such efforts must begin, the prospects of stopping the steady march of HIV are slim. AIDS is far more likely to join a host of other sexually transmitted diseases—including gonorrhea, syphilis, genital herpes, chlamydia, hepatitis B, lymphogranuloma venereum, and even cervical cancer—that have already become entrenched among the poor.[9]

Only massive and coordinated efforts may yet avert the ongoing disaster that has befallen urban Haiti, Puerto Rico, inner-city North America, Thailand, Brazil, and many nations in sub-Saharan Africa.

## THE DYNAMICS OF HIV TRANSMISSION IN RURAL HAITI

Wherever HIV infection is a sexually transmitted disease, social forces necessarily determine its distribution. Cultural, political, and economic factors, while each inevitably important, cannot be of equal significance in all settings. In rural Haiti, we can identify a number of differentially weighted, synergistic forces that promote HIV transmission.

### Population Pressures

Haiti, which covers 27,700 square kilometers, is one of the most crowded societies in the hemisphere. In 1980, only 8,000 square kilometers were under cultivation, giving an effective population density of 626 persons per square kilometer. Unfortunately, Haiti's topsoil is now prey to runaway forces that further compound the overcrowding: "The land suffers from deforestation, soil erosion, and exhaustion; the country is periodically ravaged by hurricanes which cause enormous damage."[10] As the land becomes increasingly exhausted, more and more peasants abandon agriculture for the lure of wage-labor in cities and towns.

Indeed, one of the most striking recent demographic changes has been the rapid growth of Port-au-Prince. More than 20 percent of the Haitian population now lives in the capital, a city of over 1.5 million. Although this concentration is not impressive by Caribbean standards (more than 30 percent of Puerto Ricans live in San Juan), the rate of growth in Port-au-Prince has been striking: "The urban population was 12.2 percent of the total in 1950, 20.4 percent in 1971 and an estimated 27.5 percent in 1980."[11] Haitian demographers estimate that by the year 2000 urban dwellers will constitute 37 percent of the total population.

As is the case with so many Third World countries, internal migration has played the most significant role in the growth of the capital. Locher estimates that "between 1950 and 1971 rural-urban migration accounted for 59 percent of Haitian urban growth, while natural population increase accounted for only 8 percent."[12] Neptune-Anglade has observed that the growth of Port-au-Prince is substantially the result of a "feminine rural exodus," leaving the city approximately 60 percent female.[13] Younger women of rural origin—women like Anita and Acéphie—are most commonly employed as servants.[14] Migrants of both sexes maintain strong ties with their regions of origin. In these respects, the three index cases of AIDS from Do Kay are illustrative of the trends documented by demographers and others who speak of Port-au-Prince as "a city of peasants."

### Economic Pressures

Rural Haiti, always poor, has become palpably poorer in recent decades. A per capita annual income of $315 in 1983 masked the fact that income hovered around $100 in the countryside; in the late 1990s the average annual per capita income is down to around $175.[15] Accompanying the population growth and a loss of arable land to erosion and alkalinization has been an inevitable growth in landlessness. All of these factors have inevitably had a devastating effect on agricultural production. For example, Girault typifies the decade preceding 1984 as marked chiefly "by the slow-down of agricultural production and by a decrease in productivity."[16]

This decline has been further compounded by striking rural-urban disparities in every imaginable type of goods and service. In 1984, Girault was able to complain that "Port-au-Prince with 17–18 percent of the national population consumes as much as 30 percent of all the food produced in the country and a larger share of imported food."[17] Government statistics reveal that the "Port-au-Prince agglomeration" consumed 93 percent of all electricity produced in the country in 1979. As Trouillot notes, the city "houses 20 percent of the national population, but consumes 80 percent of all State expenditures."[18]

In short, current economic conditions push people out of the countryside and into the city or, often enough, out of the country altogether. The Haitian people have long since left behind a peasant standard of living (which did not necessarily mean an exceptionally low one). Whereas Haiti was once a nation with an extremely high percentage of landholders, late-twentieth-century Haiti is increasingly a country of unemployed and landless paupers. When the Population Crisis Committee published its "international index of human suffering" in 1992, based on a variety of measures of human welfare, Haiti had the dubious distinction of heading the list of all countries in this hemisphere. Of the 141 countries studied, only three were deemed to have living conditions worse than those in Haiti—and all three of these countries were at the time being consumed by civil war.[19]

### Patterns of Sexual Union

In the numerous studies of conjugal unions in rural Haiti, most have underlined the classic division between couples who are *marye* (joined by civil or religious marriage) and those who are *plase* (joined in a conjugal union that incurs significant and enduring obligations to both partners). *Plasaj* (from French, *plaçage*) has generally been the most common form of conjugal union in rural Haiti, outnumbering marriages by two or three to one.

Early studies usually considered *plasaj* to be polygamous, with one man having more than one *plase* partner. This is often no longer the case, as Moral suggested over three decades ago: "It is 'plaçage honnête'—that is, monogamy—that best characterizes matrimonial status in today's rural society."[20] The reason for this shift toward monogamy, he believed, was the same one that leads many rural people to avoid marriage in the first place: formal unions are costly. "If the considerable growth of *plaçage* is to be explained in part by economic factors," continued Moral, "the form that *plaçage* now takes is greatly influenced by the poverty spreading throughout the countryside."

Allman's review suggests that contemporary sexual unions are considerably more complex than the bipolar model just described. In a survey in which women who had sexual relations with the same partner for a minimum of three months were considered to be "in union," interviews revealed an emic typology with five major categories: three of these—*rinmin, fiyanse,* and *viv avèk*—did not usually involve cohabitation and engendered only slight economic support; two others—*plase* and *marye*—were deemed much stronger unions, generally involving cohabitation as well as economic support.[21]

In addition, a number of other sexual practices have often been loosely termed "prostitution," in Haiti a largely urban phenomenon and much understudied.[22] It is clear, however, that unemployed women from rural areas may become involved in occasional and often clandestine sex work (variously described by terms such as *ti degaje, woulman*) when other options are exhausted. There are few avenues of escape for those caught in the web of urban migration, greater than 60 percent unemployment, and extreme poverty.[23]

How are these forms of sexual union related to the dynamics of HIV transmission? To those working in rural clinics, *plasaj* is often implicated in the spread or persistence of sexually transmitted diseases such as gonorrhea and chlamydial disease. Treatment of one or two members of a network is of course inadequate, as even women who have but one sexual partner are indirectly in regular sexual contact with any other *plase* partners of their mate. Regarding HIV, polygamous *plasaj* may be considered a preexisting sociocultural institution that serves to speed the spread of HIV and that constitutes a risk in and of itself, particularly for monogamous women. Women throughout the world bear similar risks—which are compounded wherever gender inequality erodes women's power over condom use.

The unremitting immiseration of Haiti has clearly undermined stable patterns of union such as marriage and *plasaj* by creating economic pressures to which women with dependents are particularly vulnerable. In the wake of these pressures, new patterns have emerged: "serial monogamy" might describe the monogamous but weak unions that lead to one child but last little longer than a year or two. After such unions have dissolved, the woman finds herself with a new dependent and even more in need of a reliable partner.

Equally dangerous, as we have seen, is the quest for a union with a financially "secure" partner. In rural Haiti, men of this description once included a substantial fraction of all peasant landholders. In recent decades, however, financial security has become elusive for all but a handful of truck drivers, representatives of the state (such as soldiers and petty officials), and landholders (*grandòn*). As noted, truck drivers and soldiers are clearly groups with above average rates of HIV infection.

### Gender Inequality

"The ability of young women to protect themselves from [HIV] infection becomes a direct function of power relations between men and women."[24] Gender inequality has weakened women's ability to negotiate safe sexual encounters, and this sapping of agency is especially amplified by poverty. The Haitian economy counts a higher proportion of economically active women—most of them traders—than any other developing society, with the exception of Lesotho.[25] It is not surprising, then, that the *machismo* that has so marked other Latin American societies is less pronounced in Haiti.[26] (Even the head of the Duvaliers' dreaded paramilitary force was a woman.) But gender inequality is certainly a force in political, economic, and domestic life.

It would be difficult to argue with Neptune-Anglade when she states that, in all regards, rural women "endure a discrimination and a pauperization that is worse than that affecting [rural] men."[27]

Preliminary ethnographic research in the Do Kay area suggests that many rural women do not wield sufficient authority to demand that *plase* partners (or husbands) use condoms. A growing literature documents similar patterns throughout the developing world and in the inner cities of the United States.[28] These considerations lead us to agree with those calling for preventive efforts that are "women-centered." "In societies where the female has a weaker hand," Desvarieux and Pape argue, "effective methods of prevention have a better chance of working if the woman does not have to rely on either the consent or the willingness of her partner."[29]

## Other "Cultural" Considerations

Practices such as the widespread and unregulated use of syringes by "folk" practitioners unschooled in aseptic techniques received a fair amount of attention as possible sources of HIV transmission. But far more frequently invoked were "voodoo practices," which played a peculiarly central role in early speculations about the nature of the AIDS epidemic. These speculations, which sparked waves of anti-Haitian sentiment, had the added disadvantage of being incorrect; none of these leads, when investigated, panned out. In urban Haiti, GHESKIO did not even consider these hypotheses worthy of serious investigation.

In our small-scale but in-depth study of AIDS in the Central Plateau, we did not find any strong implication of nonsexual transmission of HIV.[30] Similarly, the Collaborative Study Group of AIDS in Haitian-Americans initiated the first and (so far) only controlled study of risk factors for AIDS among Haitians living in the United States. Compiling data from several North American research centers, the investigators reached the following conclusion: "Folklore rituals have been suggested as potential risk factors for [HIV] transmission in Haiti. Our data do not support this hypothesis."[31] Such hypotheses reflect less an accurate reading of existing data and more a series of North American folk theories about Haitians.[32]

There have been few ethnographic studies of Haitian understandings of AIDS, and most of these have been conducted in Montreal, New York, or Miami. To my knowledge, the only such study conducted in rural Haiti demonstrated that such understandings were in fact changing, at first quite rapidly. Over time, however, a stable illness representation of *sida*—as AIDS is termed—seemed to evolve.[33]

In the Do Kay region, serial interviews with the same group of villagers permitted us to delineate a complex model of illness causation, one linked fairly closely to understandings of tuberculosis. Villagers often, but not always, cited sorcery in discussions about *sida*, which nonetheless came to be seen as a fatal illness that could be transmitted by sexual contact. Local understandings of *sida* did not seem to affect disease distribution, but certainly they may hamper preventive efforts if not taken into account when designing interventions. Far more disabling, however, has been the nation's political situation.

## Political Disruption

It is unfortunate indeed that HIV arrived in Haiti shortly before a period of massive and prolonged social upheaval. Political unrest has clearly undermined preventive efforts and may have helped, through other mechanisms, to spread HIV. Although many commentators observed that political struggles served to divert the public's interest away from AIDS, this was not the case in the Do Kay region. In fact, periods of increased strife were associated with increased public discourse about the new sickness.

But the same political disruptions that may have stimulated commentary about AIDS also served to paralyze coordinated efforts to prevent HIV transmission. For example, although the Haitian Ministry of Health has identified AIDS prevention as one of its top priorities, the office charged with coordinating preventive efforts has been hamstrung by six coups d'état, which have led, inevitably, to personnel changes—and to more significant disruptions. At the time GESCAP was founded, in 1991, *there had been no comprehensive effort to prevent HIV transmission in rural Haiti*. Even in Port-au-Prince, what has been accomplished thus far has often been marred by messages that are either culturally inappropriate or designed for a small fraction of the population (for example, Haitians who are francophone, literate, and television-owning). These messages are especially unsuccessful in rural areas, where even well-funded "social marketing" schemes have had little cultural currency.

A sense of hopefulness, rare in Haiti, returned to the public health community in 1991, when the country's first democratic elections brought to office a social-justice government headed by a progressive priest. A new Ministry of Health promised to make AIDS, tuberculosis, and other infectious pathogens its top priority. But in September of that year, a violent military coup brought a swift end to Haiti's democratic experiment. The impact on the population's health was incalculable.[34]

Political upheaval did not simply hobble coordinated responses to the AIDS epidemic. It has had far more direct effects. One of the most epidemiologically significant events of recent years may prove to be the coup d'état of September 1991. As noted earlier, surveys of asymptomatic adults living in Cité Soleil revealed seroprevalence rates of approximately 10 percent, whereas surveys of asymptomatic rural people were likely to find rates an order of magnitude lower. Following the coup, the army targeted urban slums for brutal repression. A number of journalists and health care professionals estimated that fully half of the adult residents of Cité Soleil fled to rural areas following the army's lethal incursions. It takes little imagination to see that such flux substantially changes the equations describing the dynamics of HIV transmission in rural areas sheltering the refugees.[35] Similar patterns have been noted elsewhere, particularly in sub-Saharan Africa:

> Women living in areas plagued by civil unrest or war may be in a situation of higher risk. In many countries, relatively high percentages of male military and police personnel are infected and their unprotected (voluntary or forced) sexual encounters with local women provide an avenue for transmission. Patterns of female infection have been correlated with the movements of members of the military in parts of Central and Eastern Africa.[36]

## Concurrent Disease

The progression of HIV disease depends on host variables such as age, sex, and nutritional status; viral load, $CD_4$-cell number and function; and concurrent disease. Concurrent illness can alter this progression in at least three ways: first, any serious illness, including opportunistic infections (most notably, tuberculosis), may hasten the progression of HIV disease; second, various diseases can heighten an individual's "net state of immunosuppression," rendering him or her increasingly vulnerable to infection; and, third, certain infections seem to increase the risk of *acquiring* HIV—the point considered here.

Sexually transmitted diseases have been cited as AIDS co-factors in a number of studies, especially those conducted in tropical and subtropical regions.[37] Researchers view STDs as particularly important in the heterosexual spread of HIV, as the virus is less efficiently transmitted from women to men than vice versa. Thus vaginal and cervical diseases—even those as ostensibly minor as trichomoniasis—may increase the risk of HIV transmission through "microwounds" and even through mere inflammation (as certain lymphocytes are, after all, the target cells of HIV).[38]

Although researchers are now collecting important data about STDs in Port-au-Prince,[39] few studies have focused on rural areas.[40] But there is no evidence to suggest that villagers are more sexually active than their urban counterparts; there is even less evidence to suggest that rural Haitians are more sexually active than age-matched controls from North America. What is evident is that a majority of STDs go untreated—which certainly implies that sores, other lesions, and inflammation will persist far longer in rural Haiti than in most areas of the world.

Other diseases—including leprosy, yaws, endemic syphilis, and various viruses—have been suggested as possible co-factors in "tropical" AIDS, but their roles have not been clarified. It seems safe to add, however, that serious co-infections do enhance the net state of immuno-suppression. Similarly, malnutrition clearly hastens the advent of advanced, symptomatic disease among the HIV-infected, although this dynamic may lessen the risk of transmission: the Haitian variant of "slim disease" is now popularly associated with AIDS, and visible cachexia is likely to drive away potential sexual partners.[41]

## Access to Medical Services

Finally, in seeking to understand the Haitian AIDS epidemic, it is necessary to underline the contribution, or lack thereof, of a nonfunctioning public health system. Medical care in Haiti is something of an obstacle course, one that places innumerable barriers before poor people seeking care. Failure to have an STD treated leads to persistence of important cofactors for HIV infection; failure to treat active tuberculosis causes rapid progression of HIV disease and death—to say nothing of its impact on HIV-negative individuals, for HIV-infected patients with tuberculosis have been shown to be efficient transmitters of tuberculosis.[42] Contaminated blood transfusions alternate with no transfusions at all. Condoms are often not available even to those who want them. The cost of pharmaceuticals, always prohibitive, has skyrocketed in recent years. Antivirals are in essence unavailable to most Haitians: in February 1990, "local radio stations announced . . . that for the first time, the drug AZT is available in Haiti. It might as well have been on Mars. A bottle of 100 capsules costs $343—more than most Haitians make in a year."[43] Since that time, it has become possible to find newer, highly active antiretroviral agents in Haiti—but for a prince's ransom.

## AIDS, ANALYSIS, ACCOUNTABILITY

Identifying and weighting the various social forces that shape the HIV epidemic is a perennial problem, but one too rarely addressed by medical anthropology, which is often asked to elucidate the "cultural component" of particular subepidemics. By combining social analysis with ethnographically informed epidemiology, however, we can identify the most significant of these forces. The factors listed here are differentially weighted, of course, but each demonstrably plays a role in determining HIV transmission in rural Haiti:

1. Deepening poverty
2. Gender inequality
3. Political upheaval
4. Traditional patterns of sexual union
5. Emerging patterns of sexual union
6. Prevalence of and lack of access to treatment for STDs
7. Lack of timely response by public health authorities
8. Lack of culturally appropriate prevention tools

Many of these factors are a far cry from the ones that anthropologists were exhorted to explore—for example, ritual scarification, animal sacrifice, sexual behavior in "exotic subcultures"—during the first decade of AIDS. But the forces underpinning the spread of HIV to rural Haiti are as economic and political as they are cultural, and poverty and inequality seem to underlie all of them. Although many working elsewhere would agree that poverty and social inequalities are the strongest enhancers of risk for exposure to HIV, international conferences on AIDS have repeatedly neglected this subject. Of the hundreds of epidemiology-track posters presented in 1992 in Amsterdam, for example, only three used "poverty" as a keyword; two of these were socioculturally naïve and did not seem to involve the collaboration of anthropologists.

What were anthropologists doing in the early years of AIDS? The mid to late 1980s saw the formation of task forces and research groups as well as an increasing number of AIDS-related sessions at our professional meetings. The central themes of many of the early sessions focused on the "special understanding of sexuality" that was, suggested certain speakers, the province of anthropologists. The scenario most commonly evoked was one in which ethnographers, steeped in local lore after years of participant-observation, afforded epidemiologists and public health authorities detailed information about sexual behavior, childbearing, and beliefs about blood and blood contact. This knowledge transfer was deemed indispensable to determining which "behaviors" put individuals and communities at risk for HIV infection.

Fifteen years into the AIDS pandemic, after at least a decade of social science studies of AIDS, we must ask, How substantial were these claims? How many secret, AIDS-related "behaviors" have we unearthed in the course of our ethnography? Anthropologists deeply involved in AIDS prevention now know that many such claims were immodest. Everywhere, it seems, HIV spreads from host to host through a relatively restricted set of mechanisms. We've also learned that preventive efforts, even the most culturally appropriate ones, are least effective in precisely those settings in which they are most urgently needed. Africa, long a favored proving ground for anthropology, offers the most obvious and humbling example. Haiti offers another.

In the interest of enhancing the efficacy of interventions, it's important to pause and take stock of the situation. How might anthropology best contribute to efforts to prevent HIV transmission or to alleviate AIDS-related suffering? One major contribution would be to help show where the pandemic is going, which leads us back to analytic challenges such as these:

> Identifying and differentially weighting the major factors promoting or retarding HIV transmission
>
> Linking the sexual choices made by individual actors to the various shifting conditions that restrict choice, especially among the poor
>
> Understanding the contribution of the culturally specific—not only local sexualities but also kinship structures and shifting representations of disease—without losing sight of the large-scale economic forces shaping the AIDS pandemic
>
> Investigating the precise mechanisms by which such forces as racism, gender inequality, poverty, war, migration, colonial heritage, coups d'état, and even structural-adjustment programs become embodied as increased risk

Anthropology, the most radically contextualizing of the social sciences, is well suited to meeting these analytic challenges, but we will not succeed by merely "filling in the cultural blanks" left by epidemiologists, physicians, scientists, and policy makers. Nor will we succeed without a new vigilance toward the analytic traps that have hobbled our understanding of the AIDS pandemic.[44]

First, we often find widespread, if sectarian, ascription to behaviorist, cognitivist, or culturalist reductionism. Just as many physicians regard social considerations as outside the realm of the central, so too have psychologists tended to reify individual psychology, while economists have reified the economic. Anthropologists writing of AIDS have of course tended to reify culture. We must avoid confusing our own desire for personal efficacy with sound analytic purchase on an ever-growing pandemic: HIV cares little for our theoretical stances or our disciplinary training. AIDS demands broad biosocial approaches. Jean Benoist and Alice Desclaux put it well:

> The conditions limiting or promoting transmission, illness representations, therapeutic itineraries, and health care practices—none of these subjects are captured by disciplinary approaches. They evade even the distinction between biology and social sciences, so tightly are biological realities tied to behaviors and representations, revealing links that have not yet been fully explored.[45]

Second, much anthropologic analysis focuses overmuch (or exclusively) on local factors and local actors, which risks exaggerating the agency of the poor and marginalized. Constraints on the agency of individual actors should be brought into stark relief so that prevention efforts do not come to grief, as they have to date. To explore the relation between personal agency and supraindividual structures—once the central problematic of social theory—we need to link our ethnography to systemic analyses that are informed by history, political economy, and a critical epidemiology. It is not possible to explain the strikingly patterned distribution of HIV by referring exclusively to attitude, cognition, or affect. Fine-grained psychological portraits and rich ethnography are never more than part of the AIDS story.

Third, the myths and mystifications that surround AIDS and slow AIDS research often serve powerful interests. If, in Haiti and in parts of Africa, economic policies (for example, structural-adjustment programs) and political upheaval are somehow related to HIV transmission, who benefits when attention is focused largely or solely on "unruly sexuality" or alleged "promiscuity?" The lasting influence of myths and immodest claims has helped to mask the effects of social inequalities on the distribution of HIV and on AIDS outcomes.

The recent advent of more effective antiviral therapy could have an enormous impact on what it means to have AIDS at the close of the twentieth century—if you don't happen to live in Africa or Haiti or Harlem. Protease inhibitors and other drugs raise the possibility of transforming AIDS into a chronic condition to be managed over decades, but they also remind us that there are two emerging syndromes: an AIDS of the North, and an AIDS of the South.

Perhaps this does not sound much like an anthropologist speaking. Why talk of latitude (North/South) and class (rich/poor) before speaking of culture? One answer to this question is that, for many of us, the view that AIDS is a culturally constructed phenomenon is not open to debate. AIDS, like sexuality, is inevitably embedded in local social context; representations and responses must necessarily vary along cultural lines. The contribution of cultural factors to the lived experience of AIDS is and will remain enormous. Indeed, the true and vast variation of HIV lies not, as we had been led to believe, in its modes of spread, nor is it found in the mechanisms by which the virus saps the host. The variation of HIV lies, rather, in its highly patterned distribution, in its variable clinical course among the infected, and in the ways in which we respond, socially, to a deadly pathogen.

## NOTES

1. In their consideration of unequal exchange and the urban informal sector, Portes and Walton (1982, p. 74) designate Haiti as the most rural of all Latin American nations: in 1950, the nation was described as 88 percent rural; in 1960, 85 percent; in 1970, 81 percent.
2. Pape and Johnson 1988.
3. See Allman 1980 and Vieux 1989 for extended discussions of *plasaj*.
4. See Pape and Johnson 1988.
5. Desvarieux and Pape 1991, p. 275.
6. GESCAP (whose name is translated as "Study Group on AIDS in the Peasant Class") was founded with the generous support of the World AIDS Foundation.
7. Given that the staff of the clinic and of Proje Veye Sante are accountable to the communities served rather than to funding organizations or to research institutions, and given the poverty and non-HIV-related sickness in the region, it is not surprising that research as such is not seen as a high priority. In order to meet our obligations to the community, all serologic studies became part of a *dossier préventif.* This instrument included a series of laboratory examinations (such as hematocrit and RPR), a chest radiograph, and a physical examination. Any abrnormal findings were to be pursued aggressively; free dental care was also offered as part of the program. This proposal was presented to members of the community in four different public meetings, engendering considerable enthusiasm for the undertaking.

8. One additional young woman, the regular sexual partner of a truck driver, was also found to be seropositive. She died suddenly during the course of the study, however, less than a week after a negative physical examination. Although the cause of death is unclear—she had explosive, watery diarrhea and presented in shock—she is not considered in this cohort.
9. Farmer 1992, p. 262.
10. Feilden, Allman, Montague, and Rohde 1981, p. 6.
11. Ibid., p. 4.
12. Locher 1984, p. 329.
13. Neptune-Anglade 1986, p. 150.
14. "Note that, in the cities, the [economically] active 10–14-year-old girls are essentially all domestics. . . . These 'restaveks' find themselves at the very bottom of the social hierarchy" (ibid., p. 209). My translation.
15. See Farmer 1988b for a review of data concerning the Haitian economy. In a personal communication on 18 September 1998, a desk officer at the US State Department's Haiti desk offered an annual per capita income estimate of $175 (not adjusted for Purchasing Power Parity); she cited internal IMF memos from April 1998 as her source.
16. Girault 1984, p. 177.
17. Ibid., p. 178. For a critical perspective on more recent "food security" issues, see Woodson 1997.
18. Trouillot 1986, p. 201. My translation.
19. Population Crisis Committee 1992.
20. Moral 1961, p. 173. My translation.
21. Allman 1980.
22. But see Laguerre 1982.
23. This is a cursory discussion of a very complex—and changing—subject. For a more complete discussion of sexual unions in Haiti, see Lowenthal 1984, Murray 1976, Neptune-Anglade 1986, Sylvain-Comhaire 1974, and Vieux 1989.
24. United Nations Development Program 1992, p. 6.
25. See Mintz 1964, Neptune-Anglade 1986, and Nicholls 1985.
26. See Murray 1976.
27. Neptune-Anglade 1986, p. 155. My translation.
28. Maria de Bruyn offers a helpful review of these issues as they affect women in developing countries. She writes: "Even if they dare suggest avoiding risky sexual acts or using condoms, they often encounter male refusal, are accused of adultery or promiscuity (the desire to use condoms being interpreted as evidence of extramarital affairs), are suspected of already being infected with HIV or are said to accuse their partners of infidelity" (1992, p. 256). The mechanisms by which gender inequality conspires with poverty to enhance women's risk for HIV are the subject of Farmer, Connors, and Simmons 1996.
29. Desvarieux and Pape 1991, p. 277.
30. Farmer 1992.
31. Collaborative Study Group of AIDS in Haitian-Americans 1987, p. 638.
32. On American "folk models" of Haitians, see Lawless 1992 and, as related to AIDS, Farmer 1992.
33. The word "*sida*" is derived from the French acronym SIDA, for *syndrome immunodéficience acquise*. The French acronym is commonly rendered as S.I.D.A., SIDA, or Sida; *sida* is the Creole orthography. I have adopted the latter here in order to reflect the substantial difference between the terms as used in different national and cultural settings.
34. See Farmer 1996a for a more complete discussion of "Haiti's lost years."
35. Farmer 1996a examines the effects of the 1991 coup d'état on rates of HIV diagnosis in the Kay region.
36. de Bruyn 1992, p. 253.
37. See, for example, Laga, Manoka, Kivuvu, et al. 1993.
38. Poor, young women may be especially at risk of genital trauma: "Non-consensual, hurried or frequent intercourse may inhibit mucus production and the relaxation of vaginal musculature, both of which would increase the likelihood of genital trauma. A lack of control over the circumstances in which the intercourse occurs may increase the frequency of intercourse and lower the age at which sexual activity begins. A lack of access to acceptable health services may leave infections and lesions untreated. Malnutrition not only inhibits the production of mucus but also slows the healing process and depresses the immune system" (United Nations Development Program 1992, pp. 3–4).
39. For example, see Liautaud et al. 1992; Deschamps, Pape, Williams-Russo, Madhavan, Ho, and Johnson, 1993; and Behets, Desormeaux, Joseph, et al. 1995.
40. We do know that in one study of one hundred women presenting to our women's health clinic in 1991 fully 25 percent had trichomoniasis. GESCAP thanks Dr. Anna Contomitros for conducting this study, which included Pap smears. See also Fitzgerald 1996.
41. Data from GHESKIO (e.g., Deschamps et al. 1992) suggest, however, that those ill with HIV disease continue to have sex.
42. DiPerri, Cade, Castelli, et al. 1993.
43. Lief 1990, p. 36.
44. For a review of recent anthropological writings on AIDS, see Farmer 1997b.
45. Benoist and Desclaux 1995, p. 363. My translation.

## REFERENCES

Allman, J. 1980. "Sexual Unions in Rural Haiti." *International Journal of Sociology of the Family* 10: 15–39.

Behets, F. M. T., J. Desormeaux, D. Joseph, et al. 1995. "Control of Sexually Transmitted Diseases in Haiti: Results and Implications of a Baseline Study Among

Pregnant Women Living in Cité Soleil Shantytowns." *Journal of Infectious Diseases* 172(3): 764–771.

Benoist, J., and A. Desclaux, eds. 1995. *Sida et Anthropologie: Bilan et Perspectives.* Paris: Karthala.

Collaborative Study Group of AIDS in Haitian-Americans. 1987. "Risk Factors for AIDS Among Haitians Residing in the United States: Evidence of Heterosexual Transmission." *Journal of the American Medical Association* 257(5): 635–639.

de Bruyn, M. 1992. "Women and AIDS in Developing Countries." *Social Science and Medicine* 34(3): 249–262.

Deschamps, M. M., et al. 1992. "HIV Seroconversion Related to Heterosexual Activity in Discordant Haitian Couples." Poster presented at the Eighth International Conference on AIDS/Third STD World Congress, 19–24 July, Amsterdam. Abstract C1087.

Deschamps, M. M., J. W. Pape, P. Williams-Russo, S. Madhavan, J. Ho, and W. Johnson. 1993. "A Prospective Study of HIV-Seropositive Asymptomatic Women of Childbearing Age in a Developing Country." *Journal of Acquired Immune Deficiency Syndromes* 6(5): 446–451.

Desvarieux, M., and J. W. Pape. 1991. "HIV and AIDS in Haiti: Recent Developments." *AIDS Care* 3(3): 271–279.

DiPerri, G., G. P. Cade, F. Castelli, et al. 1993. "Transmission of HIV-Associated Tuberculosis to Health Care Workers." *Infection Control and Hospital Epidemiology* 14: 67–72.

______. 1988b. "Blood, Sweat, and Baseballs: Haiti in the West Atlantic System." *Dialectical Anthropology* 13: 83–99.

______. 1992. *AIDS and Accusation: Haiti and the Geography of Blame.* Berkeley: University of California Press.

______. 1996a. "Haiti's Lost Years: Lessons for the Americas." *Current Issues in Public Health* 2: 143–151.

______. 1997b. "Ethnography, Social Analysis, and the Prevention of Sexually Transmitted HIV Infections Among Poor Women in Haiti." In *The Anthropology of Infectious Disease,* ed. M. Inhorn and P. Brown, 413–438. New York: Gordon and Breach.

Farmer, Paul, Margaret Connors, Janie Simmons, eds. 1996. *Women, Poverty, and AIDS. Sex, Drugs and Structural Violence.* Monroe, ME: Common Courage Press.

Farmer, Paul. 1992. *AIDS and Accusation: Haiti and the Geography of Blame.* Berkeley: University of California Press.

Farmer, Paul. 1996. On Suffering and Structural Violence: A View From Below. *Daedalus,* 125(1): 261-283.

Feilden, R., J. Allman, J. Montague, and J. Rohde. 1981. *Health, Population, and Nutrition in Haiti: A Report Prepared for the World Bank.* Boston: Management Sciences for Health.

Fitzgerald, D. 1996. *Final Report HAS: Project 2005.* Boston: Management Sciences for Health.

Girault, C. 1984. "Commerce in the Haitian Economy." In *Haiti—Today and Tomorrow: An Interdisciplinary Study,* ed. C. Foster and A. Valdman, 173–179. Lanham, Md.: University Press of America.

Laga, M., A. Manoka, M. Kivuvu, et al. 1993. "Non-Ulcerative Sexually Transmitted Diseases as Risk Factors for HIV-1 Transmission in Women: Results from a Cohort Study." *AIDS* 7 (1): 95–102.

Laguerre, M. 1982. *Urban Life in the Caribbean.* Cambridge, Mass.: Schenkman.

Lawless, R. 1992. *Haiti's Bad Press.* Rochester, Vt.: Schenkman Books.

Liautaud, B., et al. 1992. "Preliminary Data on STDs in Haiti." Poster presented at the Eighth *International Conference on AIDS/Third STD World Congress,* 19–24 July, Amsterdam. Abstract C4302.

Lief, L. 1990. "Where Democracy Isn't About to Break Out." *U.S. News and World Report,* 12 February, pp. 34–36.

Locher, U. 1984. "Migration in Haiti." In *Haiti—Today and Tomorrow: An Interdisciplinary Study,* ed. C. Foster and A. Valdman, 325–336. Lanham, Md.: University Press of America.

Lowenthal, I. 1984. "Labor, Sexuality, and the Conjugal Contract in Rural Haiti." In *Haiti—Today and Tomorrow: An Interdisciplinary Study,* ed. C. Foster and A. Valdman, 15–33. Lanham, Md.: University Press of America.

Mintz, S. W. 1964. "The Employment of Capital by Market Women in Haiti." In *Capital, Saving, and Credit in Peasant Societies,* ed. R. Firth and B. Yamey, 56–78. Chicago: Aldine.

Moral, P. 1961. *Le Paysan Haïtien.* Port-au-Prince: Les Éditions Fardins.

Murray, G. 1976. "Women in Perdition: Ritual Fertility Control in Haiti." In *Culture, Natality, and Family Planning,* ed. by J. Marshall and S. Polgar, 59–78. Chapel Hill: Carolina Population Center, University of North Carolina.

Neptune-Anglade, M. 1986. *"L'Autre Moitié du Développement: A Propos du Travail des Femmes en Haïti."* Pétion-Ville, Haïti: Éditions des Alizés.

Nicholls, D. 1985. *Haiti in Caribbean Context: Ethnicity, Economy, and Revolt.* New York.

Pape, J. W., and W. Johnson. 1988. "Epidemiology of AIDS in the Caribbean." *Baillière's Clinical Tropical Medicine and Communicable Diseases* 3(1): 31–42.

Portes, A., and J. Walton. 1982. *Labor, Class, and the International System.* New York: Academic Press.

Sylvain-Comhaire, Suzanne. 1974. "La paysanne de Kenscoff." In *La Femme de Couleur en Amerique Latine,* ed. Roger Bastide. Paris: Anthropus.

Trouillot, M. R. 1986. *Les Racines Historiques de l'État Duvaliérien.* Port-au-Prince: Imprimerie Henri Deschamps.

United Nations Development Program. 1992. *Young Women: Silence, Susceptibility, and the HIV Epidemic.* New York: UNDP.

Vieux, S. 1989. *Le Plaçage: Droit Coutumier et Famille en Haïti.* Paris: Éditions Publisud.

Woodson, D. 1997. "Lamanjay, Food Security, Sécurité Alimentaire." *Culture and Agriculture* 19(3): 108–122.

# 42

# Circumcision, Pluralism, and Dilemmas of Cultural Relativism

*Corinne A. Kratz*

One of the things about studying anthropology is that we encounter cultural ideas and practices that are very alien to our own. Encountering the "other" can be a challenge in two ways. On an intellectual level, it can be a challenge to understand vastly different cultures and customs—why do people do/believe that? How does it fit within the wider context of their lives? The second of these challenges can be on a personal level, because the beliefs and practices of others might offend our own notions of morality and propriety. Studying and living in other cultures sometimes brings up our own ugly ethnocentrism.

At the same time, it is fair to ask, Are there limits to cultural relativism? Looking cross-culturally, anthropologists can identify some universal (or at least extremely common) elements in cultural codes about proper personal conduct. All societies follow the ethnocentric line of thought that *their own traditions* are correct and right, but at the same time there are gigantic areas of controversy. In a complex society, the laws that are recognized and enforced often reflect the interests of the dominant social group.

The topic of this selection, female circumcision, really bothers some students; they can hardly believe that such cultural practices exist in the twenty-first century. In Africa, female circumcision has been a controversial topic for nearly a century, and there have been repeated international efforts to "eradicate" the custom, as if it were a disease. But this is not simply a medical issue, and to oversimplify the complex issue misses the point.

It is important to recognize that the single term *FGM (female genital modification* or *mutilation)* refers to a wide variety of surgeries with different levels of invasiveness. It is also important to remember that the symbolic and ritual meanings of this practice also vary among cultures. Finally, as students of anthropology, we need to recognize that there are at least two different views of what is at stake here, and, as in many other arenas of public controversy, there is real value to a sympathetic understanding of both sides.

This selection has two parts. The first provides a description of female circumcision in Africa—reporting the "facts" almost as it might be reported in a reference book. The second part discusses the author's strategies for *teaching* about the female circumcision controversy in the college classroom context. This controversy is both local and global—it involves traditional cultures, immigrants, and international nongovernmental organizations (NGOs). Understanding the different dimensions of the argument is an important educational goal; hopefully, it will also challenge you to come to your own well-informed opinion.

***As you read this selection, ask yourself the following questions:***

- For the women in the societies that practice it, FGM is related to beliefs about aesthetics of the body. Can you think of traditions in your own culture that transform or modify the body for purposes of beauty or identity? (Try relating this to Miner's description of body ritual among the Nacirema in Selection 29.)
- What are the potential health complications of female circumcision? What are the possible social complications of not being circumcised?
- What are the human rights issues involved? Is this a question that local societies should debate themselves, or is international intervention necessary?
- Why does this tradition persist even when it is made against the law? Why would loving parents have this done to their daughters?
- Is the analogy to male circumcision in the West appropriate?

***The following terms discussed in this selection are included in the Glossary at the back of the book:***

*clitorectomy*
*FGM*
*human rights*
*infibulation*
*neocolonial*
*sunna circumcision*

Kratz, Corinne A. "Circumcision, Pluralism, and Dilemmas of Cultural Relativism." Reprinted with permission of the author.

Differences of social and cultural practice have been a source of both puzzlement and edification around the world and throughout human history, interpreted and treated in vastly different ways in different circumstances.[1] They have been perennial resources through which people form their own identities, defining themselves through contrasts with other cultures. Distinctions in dress, cuisine, language, music, and ritual are particularly common as such markers of identity and difference. When ethnic or religious groups and minorities are reviled, differences in cultural practice have been used to help justify derogatory attitudes and discrimination. In other settings, cultural difference and diversity have been celebrated through various forms of multiculturalism.

With such remarkable diversity in the world, however, situations inevitably arise where incompatible social and cultural values, practices, and aesthetics produce conflict or controversy. How should they be dealt with? Cultural relativism would suggest that each set of practices and understandings is valid within its own circumstances and way of life. Yet plural societies combine and blend different beliefs and practices within the same social settings. Further, certain practices seem to challenge the nonjudgmental tolerance that cultural relativism implies (Shweder 2002) and raise serious questions about how to define human rights and who should define them. To many Americans, for instance, religious practices of discipline and self-mortification might seem extreme when they include self-flagellation, or political martyrdom might be taken as a sign of fanaticism. To people in other parts of the world, on the other hand, certain American economic practices might seem exploitative and certain modes of American dress might be seen as indecent or immoral.

Anthropologists seek to understand cultural production, i.e., how cultural meanings and social worlds continually take shape and change through daily interaction, communication, and exchange, through interpretations of personal and community histories and negotiations of political economic differences. They seek to understand the range of experience, meanings, and values produced by the world's diverse societies and cultures, examining how people perceive and make sense of lives and circumstances as different as those of African pastoralists caught in a long civil war, Chinese women working in a silk factory, men in an urban homeless shelter in the United States, contemporary Australians maintaining complex ritual traditions and fighting for land and mining claims, or radical political activists in Europe (Hutchinson 1996; Rofel 1999; Desjarlais 1997; Dussart 2000; Holmes 2000). In doing so, anthropologists may move beyond simple relativism to develop knowledge and judgments based on pluralism. Philosopher and social theorist Isaiah Berlin describes the distinction between relativism and pluralism (1991:10–11):

> "I prefer coffee, you prefer champagne. We have different tastes. There is no more to be said." That is relativism. . . . [Pluralism is] the conception that there are many different ends that men [sic] may seek and still be fully rational, fully men [sic], capable of understanding each other and sympathising and deriving light from each other, as we derive it from reading Plato or the novels of medieval Japan—worlds, outlooks, very remote from our own.
>
> Members of one culture can, by the force of imaginative insight, understand . . . the values, the ideals, the forms of life of another culture or society, even those remote in time or space. They may find these values unacceptable, but if they open their minds sufficiently they can grasp how one might be a full human being, with whom one could communicate, and at the same time live in the light of values widely different from one's own, but which nevertheless one can see to be values, ends of life, by the realisation of which men [sic] could be fulfilled.

Anthropological research may not be able to resolve conflicts and controversies that emerge from social and cultural difference, but the knowledge produced can provide the foundation of understanding needed for engagement and debate grounded in pluralism. It can help to identify the basic value contradictions and issues at stake as well as the different positions and interests in play. It is also important to pay attention to such controversies and debates themselves as cultural phenomena, analyzing their rhetorics, weighing competing arguments, and placing them within their own social and historical contexts. These analytical skills are important in understanding debates concerning issues of social justice, abortion rights, defining human rights, or controversial practices such as *sati* in India, and they are critical to effective political action related to any of these issues.

This essay considers a widespread cultural practice that has many different forms and meanings throughout the world and a long history of sparking debate and controversy at different times and places: forms of genital modification commonly called circumcision. Vehement debates have swirled around male and female circumcision alike, but the essay focuses particularly on practices of female genital modification because they currently receive the greatest attention and are at the center of recent contention. After outlining the varied practices of female genital modification and some of the meanings associated with them, the essay will turn to controversies and debates about these cultural practices.

## THE VARIED PRACTICES AND MEANINGS OF FEMALE GENITAL MODIFICATION

*Female circumcision* is a term commonly used to refer to surgical operations performed in over thirty African, Middle Eastern, and Southeast Asian countries, by immigrants from those communities living elsewhere, and for roughly a century (about 1850 to 1950) by physicians in Europe and the United States. As this geographic and historical span suggests, the operations are embedded in a wide range of cultural and historical contexts and can be quite different in definition, meaning, and effect. All involve surgical modification of female genitals in some way, though this ranges from relatively minor marking for symbolic purposes to the most radical operation, infibulation.[2]

The general term *female circumcision* includes at least three clinically distinct kinds of surgery. Clitoridectomy removes all or part of the clitoris and the hood, or prepuce, covering it.[3] The second type, excision, includes clitoridectomy but also removes some or all of the labia minora; all or part of the labia majora might also be cut. The most extreme form of circumcision, infibulation, goes beyond excision.[4] After removing the labia, the sides of the vulva are joined so that scar tissue forms over the vaginal opening, leaving a small gap for urination and menstruation. Infibulated women often require surgical opening to allow first intercourse and birthing; in many cases women are reinfibulated after each childbirth. In addition to these three well-recognized types of female circumcision, a fourth is sometimes included. The mildest form, this involves a symbolic pricking or slight nicking of the clitoris or prepuce. Excision and infibulation are the most widely practiced types of female genital modification. In Africa, infibulation is common primarily in the Horn of Africa (Somalia, Sudan, Djibouti, Ethiopia).

Whether and how circumcision practices affect women's sexuality is much debated. It is important to distinguish sexual desire, sexual activity, and sexual pleasure when considering this question. Sexual desire and sexual activity may not diminish with female genital operations. Evidence about sexual feeling and pleasure is variable, difficult to define or measure, and hard to come by.[5] Euro-American opponents of the practices assert that circumcised women feel no sexual pleasure, but a number of African women disagree with these assertions. Studies suggest that the effect varies widely with type of operation, with prior sexual experience, and other circumstances as well. Some African activists also suggest that the stress on sexual pleasure in anticircumcision campaigns reflects a recent, primarily Western concept of sexuality.[6]

The operations have also been said to carry a number of health risks. While the range of possible health problems is well known, there has been little epidemiological research to determine how widespread each problem might be in different areas. Immediate risks include infection, shock, excessive bleeding, and urinary retention, risks that are related to hygienic conditions and care during and after the operations. Longer term health problems are most common with infibulation but can be associated with excision as well. Most of these problems are related to heavy scarring and to covering over of vaginal and urinary openings after infibulation: keloid scars, vulvar cysts, retention of urine or menses, painful menstruation, difficulty urinating, and chronic pelvic infections. Clinical studies on the relation between these health problems and genital modification are contradictory, however, and a recent study in Gambia found that many negative consequences commonly cited for the operations were not significantly more common in women who had been cut (Morison et al. 2001).[7]

In many places where female circumcision is practiced, the physical operation is but one moment in an elaborate ceremony that contains many other events. For Okiek people in Kenya, for instance, initiation into adulthood includes circumcision for boys and excision for girls, but the full initiation process continues for several months and includes much more as well: moral teaching, family and community engagement, the negotiation of new social relationships, and important cultural meanings and values. While the operations are a central initiation trial and create a permanent physical mark of adulthood, initiation cannot be reduced to circumcision or excision alone. In many other societies, initiation does not involve circumcision at all.

In every case the purposes and meanings of female genital modification are related to specific cultural understandings of identity, personhood, morality, adulthood, gender, bodily aesthetics, and other important issues. In the Sudan, for instance, it is seen as enhancing a woman's purity, cleanliness, and beauty. For the Kikuyu people of Kenya, circumcision was the foundation of moral self-mastery for women and men alike, performed as part of initiation into adulthood. The age of those circumcised varies widely according to these cultural understandings. In much of Mali and the Sudan, for instance, girls are circumcised at six to eight years, while various communities in Kenya and Sierra Leone perform the operation in the early teens. Yoruba people in Nigeria often circumcise their children at just a few days old, much like male circumcision in the United States and Europe. Circumcision and excision are not connected with initiation for the Yoruba people, but they do relate the operations to moral concepts associated with shame and fertility. Circumcision is not regularly performed after puberty in Africa, where the operation is usually seen as related to a person's social and moral development.[8] The history of female circumcision in Europe and the United States contrasts with most of the world with regard to circumcision age. For roughly a century beginning in the 1850s, clitoridectomy was prescribed for adult women in Europe and the United States as medical treatment for insomnia, sterility, and masturbation (which was defined as an ailment at that time).

Many societies practice male but not female circumcision, but the reverse is rare. Where both are practiced, they can only be understood fully when considered together, in relation to one another. In many societies, cultural meanings and patterns link the two and equate them. A single word refers to both operations in many African languages, and this correspondence is often central to the way their practitioners understand them. The English translation, "female circumcision," maintains this parallel between male and female genital operations, though anticircumcision activists have criticized the term for being misleading (as discussed below).

## DEBATES AND CONTROVERSIES ABOUT CIRCUMCISION

Both male and female genital operations have engendered long histories of debate and opposition; these have often involved cross-cultural disagreements about the meaning and worth of the practices. The value of Jewish male circumcision, for instance, was debated in Rome during the first century A.D., and male circumcision has become a topic of heated opposition in the United States again today. The most widespread and vociferous opposition currently centers on female genital modification, but these practices have been the subject of international political controversies and abolition campaigns since at least the 1910s.[9] Contemporary campaigns continue the tradition and rhetoric of colonial and missionary opposition and also build on decades of Africa-based activism. Health consequences have consistently been part of the debate, particularly in relation to infibulation, but the issues have also been defined at times in terms of colonialism, neocolonialism, feminism, sexuality, and human rights.

Controversies can be confusing. Heated arguments based on strong convictions are rarely presented in ways that make clear the different assumptions, perspectives, and interests fueling contention. When controversies cross cultural and national boundaries, they can be very complicated indeed. To begin to understand circumcision debates, it is important to first identify the grounds of controversy: Who is involved, what is it about, and what is at issue. Circumcision controversies concern a wide variety of actors and cross a number of social and legal arenas, from family and household relations to international tribunals. This renders it impossible to characterize the debates in simple terms. It is inaccurate and misleading to describe them merely as contests of women versus men or Africans versus outsiders.

To understand today's debates, it is helpful to think about them in relation to several contexts. Most central are the sociocultural contexts of the varied practices at issue and the history and contexts of the current controversies themselves. An effective way to highlight the issues and perspectives involved is to consider these contexts comparatively, to relate different situations and practices, or to explore similarities and differences between several controversies (e.g., debates about male and female genital operations, debates that occur at different historical periods, or debates that might concern different practices but are presented in similar ways (such as *sati* in India[10]). Examining cultural practices in context also means identifying the different actors, perspectives, and meanings involved (see below). It is important to recognize that trying to understand unfamiliar practices does not necessarily mean supporting them. However, to oppose or help alter practices that some might consider problematic, it is essential to work *with* the people involved, as equal peers. Such understanding is critical to effective engagement.

One of the best-documented historical examples of circumcision controversy took place in central Kenya during the colonial era. Colonial missionaries and administrators there made judgments about which local customs violated Christian behavior and sought to discourage them. Campaigns to abolish female circumcision in central Kenya were among these efforts. When the Church of Scotland Mission and segments of the Church Missionary Society tried to prohibit the practice in the 1910s and 1920s, Kikuyu female circumcision became connected with the anticolonial movement and defense of cultural tradition (Murray 1974, 1976). Jomo Kenyatta, later president of Kenya, was a prominent opponent of colonial attempts to alter Kikuyu custom. These local protests against abolishing female circumcision provided an impetus for starting independent schools and churches in central Kenya.

Arenas encompassed in this debate, then, included British politics (with pressure from feminist parliamentarians and anticolonial activists), rivalries between Christian denominations with missions in Kenya, the colonial administration in Kenya, and local Kenyan communities. In addition to anticolonial movements and defense of cultural tradition, the debate also became connected with relations of authority between men and women and between women of different generations, and even the introduction of maternity clinics.[11] Since 1979, the Kenyan government has conducted several anticircumcision campaigns that were tinged with Christian and colonial overtones, banning female circumcision in 1982, but with little effect. In 1996, a national organization proposed an alternative initiation ceremony as a substitute. Like Kenya, each country has its own such history of circumcision debates and policies.

To place contemporary controversies in context, we should also consider their own history and the different arenas where debates occur. The debates have been related to feminist movements in various times and places, to colonial administration and missionary campaigns, to Islamic religious movements, and a number of other issues. Arenas of debate shift as different parties become involved. Several decades after the Kenyan controversy, in the late 1950s, international efforts to have the World Health Organization (WHO) address female circumcision were not effective. Later, in the 1970s, a number of publicizing efforts and publications converged to galvanize international attention. These included articles in African publications in the mid-1970s, a press conference held in Switzerland before the WHO assembly in 1977, and publications by Fran Hosken (1979) and Mary Daly (1990) in the United States. The Inter-African Committee on Traditional Practices affecting the Health of Women and Children was formed in Geneva in 1977. A 1979 WHO seminar in Khartoum helped to begin regular discussion of female genital operations by international bodies and at regular conferences. The resurgence of anticircumcision activity in the 1970s was also buoyed by the United Nations Decade of Women (1975–1985).

Since the early 1990s, international debates about female genital modification have again become increasingly heated and highly politicized. Greater media coverage in the 1990s and publicity over legal cases concerning African immigrants in France and the United States brought the debates to a wider public than previously.[12] In the United States, involvement by such well-known figures as novelist Alice Walker also helped to publicize and polarize the debate. A number of African scholars and activists based in the United States (such as Seble Dawit, Salem Mekuria, and Micere Mugo) have been highly critical of the way Walker and others have represented female circumcision in Africa.[13] They argue that Walker and others are engaged in neocolonial depictions that demonize African practitioners, distort the social meanings and contexts involved, portray African women only as victims, ignore decades of activism in Africa, and isolate female circumcision from other issues of women's health, economic status, and education.

Both practices of female genital modification and the arenas of debate have shifted over the years as other circumstances changed and different constituencies became involved. Public health education about the potential risks of the operations has increased in most countries where they are practiced. Similarly, an increasing number of female genital modifications are being performed either by specialists who have received some hygienic training or in health clinics and hospitals. As noted above, alternative rituals have also been proposed in some countries, though it is not clear whether they will be widely adopted. Shifts in practice also include adoption of genital modification by noncircumcising communities (Leonard 1999) and modification of long-standing rituals toward what I call "circumcision by pronouncement" or "performative circumcision," i.e., substituting a verbal formula for actual cutting (Abusharaf 1999:7; Hernlund 1999). There are intense debates among African activists about whether a medicalized, minor form of female genital modification should be promoted as an interim substitute for more severe operations (Obiora 1997; Shell-Duncan 2001). African immigrant communities in Europe and the United States often continue traditional practices in new ways in their new homes. Their preservation of the practices has brought all these debates to the fore in those countries as immigrant communities and their children have grown in recent decades. Sweden, Switzerland, the United Kingdom, and several other European countries passed laws restricting the operations in the 1980s and early 1990s. The United States followed suit in 1997.

## CONTEXTS FOR UNDERSTANDING THE DEBATES AND ISSUES

These examples illustrate how many different parties and perspectives can become involved in these controversies. In tracing the shape of today's debates, it is useful to distinguish the following three interacting arenas. The social, cultural, and historical contexts of debates about female and male genital operations can be examined for each:

1. *Home countries* are countries in Africa, the Middle East, and Southeast Asia where circumcising practices have traditional standing. There may be a variety of traditions and practices that include genital modification within each home country and a number of different positions within each community, if the practices are debated.
2. The *United States* and *Europe* are the second arena to consider. These countries also have a history of genital operations for both boys and girls. The histories are related to changing understandings of health, class, ethnicity, gender, and sexuality.

In the U.K., for instance, male circumcision had become a middle-class fashion by the 1920s (Lonsdale 1992:388). In Nazi Germany, it was taken as a mark of Jewish identity. In the United States today, white men are more likely to be circumcised than African Americans or Hispanics; higher education levels are also related to higher circumcision rates (Laumann et al. 1997:1053–1054). Clitoridectomy was a recognized medical treatment for women in these countries for decades, as noted above. Concern about female genital operations within these countries is now related particularly to immigrants from home countries.

3. The third arena is that of *international campaigns.* Though obviously related to the other two, it is useful to consider how international campaigns differ from debates within the other arenas, how international bodies and action groups establish their legitimacy to intervene in other countries, and how the international arena redefines issues central to particular communities and nations.[14]

In addition to identifying the complex social geographies and range of actors involved, it is equally important to pay attention to the ways that language and rhetoric shape the presentation of issues and convey particular values and judgments. For instance, the growing intensity of the debates became encapsulated in the very terms used for female genital operations between the 1970s and 1990s, illustrating the political divisions and rhetorics involved. *Female circumcision* was the most common term for decades, the English phrase ordinarily used in the debates about British colonial attempts to outlaw female genital operations in Kenya in the 1920s–30s. In the 1970s, anticircumcision activists increasingly criticized the term *female circumcision,* claiming that it condoned a brutal custom by creating what they considered false similarities between male and female circumcision.[15] A more partisan alternative was coined and eventually popularized: *female genital mutilation.*[16] The new term did not attempt impartial description, but condemned the practices through a label that defined them all as intentional mistreatment and disfigurement. Promotion of the new "mutilation" term was part of an escalating anticircumcision campaign that used more sensationalism and gory images.[17] As this term became more common, it was shortened to an acronym, "FGM." Others reject this term as misrepresenting the intentions of African families, criminalizing parents and relatives, and judging them through Euroamerican cultural values.

The increasingly heated and polarized nature of the debate thus became embedded in its very terms. Attempting to find an appropriate phrase, *New York Times* reporter Celia Duggers used the term *genital cutting* in her late 1996 articles, a term she adopted from demographic and health surveys.[18] A number of other alternative terms also came into use in the mid-1990s, seeking more neutral ground: genital surgery, genital operations, genital modification, and body modification. This last term acknowledges broad similarities among such practices as male and female genital surgeries, genital/body piercing, and other cosmetic surgery. Female circumcision, genital cutting, and FGM remain the most common terms in English, though the acronym FGM has now also been redefined as "female genital *modification*" in efforts to use less polarizing, descriptive language.

Whatever terms are used, the topic at the center of controversy is a generalized category defined and shaped by that very debate. The category is created by extracting and combining fragments from many different cultural practices found in dozens of countries, a variety of practice described above. The fragments all concern genital modification but may share little else. Taken out of their social and cultural contexts, they combine to form a new, abstract category (e.g., "female circumcision"). Scientific, medical language is an important tool in this process. The clinical emphasis makes the general category seem like an objective and universal way to talk about women's bodies, but it also narrows the range of information defined as relevant to the debate. For instance, the physically different operations described above are combined and treated as the same thing, though they vary considerably in extent and effects. The rest of the ceremonies in which the physical operations may be embedded are often ignored.

The terms used in circumcision controversies convey different impressions of the people involved as well. A number of African women and others have objected to the word *mutilation,* for instance, because it misrepresents parents and families. It suggests that they intend harm to their children, likening to child abuse what they themselves might see as a cultural triumph, "carried out for the noblest of reasons, the best of intentions, and in good faith" (Iweriebor 1996). Accounts often demonize women who perform the operations as well. In recent French legal cases, for instance, they were portrayed as avaricious and predatory and received the harshest rulings.

A prominent example concerns the way African or "Third World" women in general are represented as a single, unified group, as seen across a range of sources: news media, informational publicity material produced by action groups, scholarly writing, or novels.[19] This stereotyped concept of "African women" is usually formed by homogenizing divergent circumstances;

it assumes women to be a pre-existent, coherent group with shared interests and desires. This requires removing the concept of "woman" from any specific cultural context and isolating it from related notions that help form understandings of gender. How are differences based on nationality, class, ethnicity, religion, education, or age accommodated in this generalized figure and how might these variations affect the debates? The "average" Third World woman that emerges is set in contrast to elite women, though the contrast is often implicit. Elite women are presented as self-conscious, active, choice-making agents. They are not exclusively Western, but also include women born in the Third World who have joined the campaign against female genital modification. Yet African activists consistently protest that their work is rarely recognized when controversies are described. The rhetoric and structure of these controversies might be examined further by looking at how different kinds of men are portrayed, or by considering parallel cases in contemporary campaigns against male genital operations, abortion, or welfare.[20]

These different portrayals of Third World women and other actors in circumcision controversies are often bound up with notions of "progress" and other values as they have been defined in Euroamerican contexts. But conflicting values are the very crux of controversy. Diverse social and political positions inform the perspectives of those involved, but they are also grounded in different cultural frameworks, competing definitions of the practices at issue, and what seem to be irreconcilable values. In seeking to understand circumcision debates, it can be helpful to identify the various positions on each issue, along with the priorities and cultural values associated with each. Issues at stake would include the following:

***Human Rights*** Circumcision debates presented in human rights terms often emphasize the integrity and inviolability of the human body, sometimes using analogies with torture and child abuse. As noted above, this falsely attributes evil intent to parents and relatives. "Human rights" as a concept is itself under considerable debate. Should social and economic rights be included? Whose values will be enshrined as universal when there are fundamental disagreements (An-Na`im 1992; An-Na`im and Deng 1990)? How might the language of human rights accommodate the diverse people, practices, and circumstances involved?

***Self-Determination*** The human rights approach does not fit easily with another common way that circumcision debates are framed, in terms of self-determination.[21] However, self-determination can be defined in relation to individuals, families, or communities, each with rather different implications. Upholding family autonomy, community values, or religious freedom would seem to support continuing traditional practices understood as central to personal and community identity. Does this include male and female initiation ceremonies? How does individual self-determination apply in the intricate contexts of family and community relations? How do questions of self-determination apply to children of different ages?

***Health Issues and Sexuality*** These were discussed earlier in this essay. Both have been central to debates about female genital modification. Questions of sexuality have also figured in opponents' efforts to explain the operations. They commonly assert that male desire to control female sexuality is the origin and reason for all such practices. This universal conspiracy theory, however, does not correspond to what is known about circumcising practices. There is no evidence or discussion of when or how this might have happened in so many places, how this explanation would account for the variety of circumcising practices, why women also staunchly defend them, or how the theory relates to explanations offered by practitioners.[22]

Yet even when the issues and stances in circumcision controversies are delineated, the fact remains that the debates involve fundamentally different perceptions and lived understandings of aesthetics, morality, society, and personhood that come together with questions of authority, class, power, gender, and history.[23] There are no simple, single answers to the issues they raise. They pinpoint a nexus whose very opaqueness of understanding illustrates recalcitrant problems and issues of cultural translation. In this respect, recent circumcision controversies draw attention to the limits and dilemmas of cultural relativism and moral judgments. How are such judgments, choices, and even laws to be made in plural societies (which ultimately means all societies)? Can incommensurable values be accommodated? As Sir Isaiah Berlin noted, "A certain humility in these matters is very necessary" (1991:18).

## CULTURAL AND MORAL VALUES: DILEMMAS OF RELATIVISM

Many people would agree that cultural difference and diversity should be recognized, respected, and accommodated. Cultural relativism has fairly wide currency in the United States as a general way to approach cultural difference, though it coexists with popular notions of cultural evolution and civilizational hierarchy. The relativist view that each society's practices and values are valid and understandable in the particular context of their lives may be easiest to hold, however, when applied to distant people or to practices that seem strange but harmless. What happens when people with incompatible practices and values live closely together, when culturally justified practices seem to be physically harmful, or when an overarching national legal system must deal with radically different values? Does cultural relativism imply moral relativism as well?

The controversies over genital operations present such dilemmas and flashpoints. Usually associated with ceremonial performances, the songs, dances, costumes, and other beliefs that give meaning to the ceremonies are readily accepted as part of "tradition," as markers of particular forms of ethnic or religious identity. Scarification or tattooing might also be recognized and appreciated as part of a different aesthetic or religion, so what is different about genital operations? Why are they seen as an exception that raises this moral dilemma? What other practices pose similar dilemmas?

In the last decade, legal cases dealing with African immigrants in the United States and Europe have raised these issues in particularly clear and urgent ways. Examining these cases—particularly court procedure and sections of testimony—provides a way to again consider the different actors and interests involved, this time in situations even closer to home (Kratz 2002). Among the many questions that these cases raise are the following:

- Legislation is written in general terms, intended as applicable to the broadest range of cases. However, laws are interpreted through individual cases and precedents. Should a case about, for instance, Somali immigrants (who practice infibulation for young girls) serve as precedent for families from Sierra Leone (where initiated individuals are older, the operation is less severe, and family relations are quite different)?
- Whose legal rights should be protected and when? Parents' rights to raise their children in accordance with their beliefs and traditions? What if parents disagree? The rights of the girls affected? What if they *choose* to undergo the operation? What if they are minors legally?
- When female genital operations are outlawed, who is legally responsible and liable for prosecution? At different times and places, the accused have included fathers, mothers, initiates, and surgeons. What constructions of actors, intentions, and meanings are involved in each of these scenarios?
- When court proceedings involve immigrants, how are issues of adequate translation and adequate legal representation handled? These were important problems in the way French cases in the 1990s were handled.
- Are judges, juries, lawyers, and those concerned with civil liberties informed about the communities and cultural values involved? For instance, a lawyer in one case argued that the girls affected would have psychological problems when they realized they were not like other women, but the "other women" assumed in this statement were not women of the immigrant community. In fact, most women in their own ethnic community had had the operation, making the argument one that would more appropriately support the operation (cf. Matias 1996:4).
- How do gendered differences in immigrant experiences influence knowledge about relevant laws and services and the ways people participate in legal proceedings?

These questions raise some of the difficult practical implications of general issues of cultural translation and the moral dilemmas involved. They provide another way to ground the circumcision debates in specific questions and situations. Such groundings provide useful ways to understand and engage with controversies that are puzzling and sometimes troubling in their passions and complexities.

## NOTES

1. This paper includes portions of Kratz (1999a) and (1999b) that have been combined, revised, and updated for inclusion here.
2. Wide variation in female genital modification can be found on the African continent alone, where it is practiced across a band of the continent that includes parts of Mauritania, Senegal, Gambia, Guinea-Bissau, Sierra Leone, Liberia, Mali, Burkina Faso, Côte d'Ivoire, Ghana, Togo, Benin, Niger, Nigeria, Chad, Cameroon, Central African Republic, Democratic Republic of the Congo (formerly Zaire), Sudan, Egypt, Eritrea, Ethiopia, Djibouti, Somalia, Kenya, Tanzania, and Uganda. The percentage of women circumcised in each country varies considerably (e.g., 5–10 percent in Uganda, 25–30 percent in Ghana, 80 percent in the Sudan), as does the kind of operation practiced, its cultural and personal significance, and its history. Female circumcision is not practiced at all in some communities within this broad area, but it is commonplace in others. Regional, ethnic, and religious variation in practice is considerable. Christians, Muslims, and followers of traditional religions all might practice forms of female circumcision. Communities have adopted, abandoned, and modified the practices in various ways over the centuries, in keeping with the complex histories of political and religious influence and interaction among societies on the African continent.
3. This is sometimes called *sunna circumcision*, though *sunna circumcision* might also refer to preputial cutting alone. The name *sunna* relates the practice to Islamic traditions, though most Muslim scholars and theologians deny Koranic justification for female circumcision.

Schwartzman's (1989) study on meetings in a mental health organization. Her definition of a meeting is a useful starting point. For Schwartzman (1989:7) a meeting is:

> A communicative event involving three or more people who agree to assemble for a purpose ostensibly related to the functioning of an organization or group, for example, to exchange ideas or opinions, to solve a problem, to make a decision, or negotiate an agreement, to develop policy and procedures, to formalize recommendations. . .a meeting is characterized by talk that is episodic in nature.

Because advertising creative meetings occur in a designated place, the agency's or client's conference room, for a discrete period of time, normally 60 to 90 minutes, they can be viewed analytically as frames (Goffman 1974; Moeran 2005:43–57). Moeran's (2005:63–79) discussion of frames in a business context is useful for seeing creative meetings not only as a frame within agency life, but also as the key frame for interpreting and understanding agency/client relationships.

## THE MEETING PARTICIPANTS

In creative meetings, agency attendees include account managers and the "creatives," or executives directly responsible for creating the advertising. Larger agencies might also include account planners (Malefyt 2003). Client participants are the marketing management employees of the manufacturing company that has hired the agency.

Advertising agency account managers represent the agency to the client, communicate client needs to the agency, and help ensure that agency departments get the work done on strategy, on time, and on budget. They are relationship managers, problem solvers, and communicators. They are more similar to the client than any other agency staffer. As one client said, they "dress and speak like us; they are more like us (than creative people)." Creatives are organized into copy writer–art director teams that develop the advertising ideas. A creative director, with experience in writing or art direction, supervises creative teams. In creative meetings, the creative director is the selling partner of the account team but argues from a creative rather than a business perspective, which is the function of account managers. Creatives are conceptual, imaginative people who invent, design, and produce "the work." They differ temperamentally and stylistically from their MBA-trained clients. Client marketing managers conceive and execute the marketing plan for a brand. Their responsibilities include managing product development, quality control, product distribution to retailers, sales tracking, consumer promotions such as coupons, and developing advertising. In advertising creative meetings, clients are the gatekeepers for creative work and they must be convinced that the work merits exposure to consumers.

Advertising creative meetings involve the interaction of client and agency teams as two entities, as well as the interaction of members within teams. Hirschman (1989) speaks to both dimensions when, citing Turow (1984:21), she characterizes clients as patrons of the agency (Hirschman 1989:42–43) and then describes the roles of several participants in the creative development process. Miller, remarking on the tension between account managers and creatives in Trinidad, notes that creatives are "artists" and account managers are responsible for clients' "commercial concern" (Miller 1997:188). Even within creative teams, Young (2000) found that copy writers and art directors have different feelings about creative development. Across agency and client lines, within agencies, and, to a lesser extent, within client teams, contrasting responsibilities and attitudes have a major impact on the conduct and outcome of creative meetings.

## GOALS: MUTUAL AND OTHERWISE

Agency and client personnel enter creative meetings to reach agreement on the work and advance the most promising creative ideas to the next step in the development process. Clients hope to manage a smooth process within specified time and production cost parameters. They also strive to showcase their professional skills to management. Clients are acutely aware that their comments during creative meetings are heard not only by the agency but also by their superiors, and clients believe that "looking smart" to both the agency and their superiors is critical. As one client said, "If you say what your boss agrees with and he says he agrees, the agency (as well as your boss) thinks you are smart." Agency personnel share the desire to move the process forward seamlessly. They know that the better the clients appear to their own management, the more loyal these clients will be to the agency. Agency staff enter the meeting with a strong desire to sell specific creative work that makes the agency team, and specific individuals within the agency team, look insightful and inventive.

The agency also has an agency-building agenda; imaginative creative work can help win new business. Additionally, creative work is often "pushed" by individuals who want to build their personal "reel" for future jobs. Most importantly, agencies must leave

## STATUS AND ROLE

When senior agency executives select flanker positions to the far left or right of the center of the conference table they do so to stress their separateness from other agency staff and to occupy a perch from which to offer commentary during the creative meeting. Their distance from the fray carries other symbolism; it is a vantage point from which they can make the "big picture" statements that demonstrate a mastery of the full business context of the creative work. Seating is also important for agency managers to assess and respond to client reactions, which is why they place themselves within the direct sight line of senior clients.

The sequence and content of client commentary reflect the status and role of the speaker (see Schwartzman 1989:291–293 on social position and speaking sequences in meetings). The lower the status, the earlier one speaks and the more circumspect the comments. Higher-status clients offer their thoughts after lower level managers, giving them the dual advantage of having heard what their colleagues said and additional time to reflect on the creative work.

## RULES OF ENGAGEMENT

The agency team is a kind of secret society (Goffman 1959:104) with unwritten rules of engagement in the presence of those outside the society (Meerwarth, Briody, and Devadatta 2005). Internally, as Hirschman (1989:51) observes, "conflict, mutual distrust and power struggles are inherent in the advertising process, but the agency must show a 'united front' to the client" (Kover and Goldberg 1995:55). One of the more egregious sins occurs when an agency representative deviates from the previously agreed upon agency position during a creative meeting. When this agreement is violated, the consequences can be severe. Reprimands of subordinates who diverge from the agency's recommendation are common; cautionary tales tell of employees who transgressed being fired on the return airplane flight after a client meeting. Clients are under less pressure to express a uniform point of view, but most client cultures encourage consensus, and clients know that moving creative work forward requires agreement on the direction they provide to the agency.

## READING THE ROOM

Just before a creative meeting, a well-known advertising executive was asked by one of his agency associates what he recommended. His reply: "Read the room." His meaning: assess client reactions as ideas are presented and adjust the agency recommendation to match the ideas that the client will accept. During creative meetings, agency executives do not watch their colleagues present; they watch their clients. They scan faces for confusion, comprehension, and delight. They study eyes and body language. They pay attention to how many notes clients are taking and they watch for client reactions to specific graphics and copy. When the agency summarizes the body of work, when clients comment, when the agency responds and the client counters, agency executives read the room.

Reading the room helps the agency control creative meetings. When a client is perceived as unreceptive to an agency recommendation, an agency executive formulates a defense that shows cognizance of the client's discomfort: "The idea in this board is totally new in this category. It will startle the consumer and it will cut through the clutter of competitive advertising. This approach may make us a bit uncomfortable but it is precisely the kind of advertising the brand needs right now." If the executive senses that the favored board is being judged extremely poorly and even a strong argument will not persuade the client, the executive will cast a glance at colleagues and soften the agency recommendation: "The idea in this board is totally new in this category. It will startle the consumer and it will cut through the clutter of competitive advertising. But, because it is so cutting edge, we should test it among consumers to see if we have gone too far."

One agency creative director described how he visualizes a conference room swaying as arguments veer side to side. He prepares his arguments and chooses a position based on where the room "lands." He may agree or disagree with the prevailing client point of view, but he will choose his statements carefully to ensure that the meeting does not become contentious. The process of reading the room is like comprehending the difference between a wink and a blink (Geertz 1973:6–7). It requires contextual understanding: knowing the psychology of the participants, the strength of the creative work, the corporate cultures, and the relationships of the meeting attendees. The power and accuracy of an individual manager's intuition, of knowing by seeing and listening, is critical.

## DEFENDING THE WORK

Clients may criticize creative work because they believe it is off strategy, it fails their checklist of acceptable advertising, or it is inconsistent with "what we know works." A major issue for creative personnel is how to best protect the integrity of their idea when clients feel, as an associate creative director said, that "challenging their beliefs is like challenging their religion." Kover and Goldberg (1995:56–59) describe several strategies that copywriters use to argue for their work, all of which are also applied by art directors and account managers. These tactics include: 1) selling with passion; 2) a frontal attack, which is effective when clients seek highly creative work; 3) creating work that is likely to sell, a risky proposition, as noted earlier; 4) offering the appearance of acceptance, then doing what they wish, which may be effective with small revisions but is not viable when the issue is whether an idea should even be produced; and 5) the "aleatory game," which entails hoping for the best outcome. Experienced agency account managers lower rising temperatures in creative meetings by intervening with phases such as, "That's a good thought. We'll consider that." Agency colleagues and clients depend upon account managers to control meetings; account managers know that an adroit defense of creative work and the ability to defuse difficult situations is a measure of their value.

Although clients often claim they want breakthrough advertising, most clients are nervous that "edgy" creative work will violate the character of their brand, unless the brand character is, by definition, "edgy." Moreover, many creatives feel that clients often "don't get it" when particularly inventive executions are presented, a reaction that Schudson (1984:81) terms "aesthetic insensitivity." Clients' lack of understanding of a creative idea is demonstrated by the common client practice of expressing a wish that selected copy or graphics used in one storyboard also be used in other storyboards. Similarly, when a client feels that an execution has too much humor, the client may ask the agency to "dial it back." As one creative said, "When they change the board, they pull out the one thread that holds it together." Clients' desire for a recitation of a brand's features, attributes, and benefits can snuff out a creative idea. As a creative director said, "The idea gets whittled away by the client's checklist." Clients believe that they own the creative work. When they want changes, the agency should, after discussion, agree to make them. Creatives feel that they, as the inventors of the idea, own it (Hirschman 1989; Kover and Goldberg 1995; Young 2000), which adds tension to creative meetings. As Kover (1995:604) writes, "Copywriters have a 'reputation' in the folklore of the advertising business. They are charged with defending their work and its integrity against any charge, no matter how small." Kover's explanation for this behavior is that "Copywriters do not merely present advertising, they present *themselves*." (Kover 1995:604, emphasis in original). He notes that copy writers speak about their work as if it is "a piece carved from their private being" (ibid.) and Kover and Goldberg (1995:53) remark on the "resentment" that creatives feel when clients alter their work.

How aggressively creatives and account managers defend creative work is contingent upon agency and client cultures. Many clients see challenges to their criticisms as evidence of agency conviction, and they respond positively, as long as the defense is respectful and cordial. Seeing an agency "roll over" when a storyboard is criticized suggests that the agency has little heart for the work, and the client may wonder why the agency presented it. When the agency fights too long and hard, clients become annoyed. Clients also know when agency executives claim, "I agree with everything you have said," they are about to disagree and prolong a discussion. In such situations, clients anticipate that after the meeting they will have a conversation with a senior account manager who will "fix it." If the account manager cannot deliver what the client wants, then that manager risks replacement by one who will. When the choice is between fighting the good fight for the creative work and protecting the agency–client relationship, the latter is the necessary course. Agency executives understand that advertising may be at the intersection of commerce and art, but commerce is the main drag, and clients control the road.

## AGREEMENTS

Agreements are the actions that will be taken to revise, test, or produce creative work after a meeting. The word agreement has an egalitarian and conciliatory connotation; it also implies that the client and agency concur on what needs to be done. However, to *agree* does not always mean to be *in agreement*. The recitation of agreements in creative meetings is, in fact, a recitation of client directives. The word agreement fuels the illusion that the client and agency are peers and it smoothes over disagreements that may have occurred during the meetings, but there is no mistake that the clients are in charge.

## IMPRESSION MANAGEMENT AND IMPRESSING MANAGEMENT

Presentations by agencies in creative meetings are performances according to Goffman's definition: "all the activity of a given participant on a given occasion which serves to influence in any way the other participants" (Goffman 1959:15) and are "social dramas" (Turner 1974, 1986). As a creative director said, "The spotlight is on you. You have the chance to convince someone that something you have created is worth the world seeing." A central tenet of Goffman's analysis, impression management, is evident throughout creative meetings. Agencies attempt to impress clients with an understanding of the client's business, their devotion to the brand, and their passion for the creative work. An expression of passion can persuade clients that creative work is worthy of acceptance. As a creative director phrased it, "Passion can be contagious." Meeting participants also aim to impress management. Junior clients want to demonstrate to bosses that they are managing the creative development process effectively and, since they know their judgments are being judged, that they bring their share of insights to the meeting. When creative work is received poorly and no progress is made, a midlevel client can "die inside because it makes my life worse. The process is stalled and I'll get slammed." Junior agency personnel want to impress senior staff as well, and all of the agency presenters must impress their clients.

## RITES OF PASSAGE

Creative meetings are a rite of passage as classically defined by Van Gennep (1960; Moeran 1996:94). Creative work is separated from its development while in storyboard form; selected ideas are transformed during the meeting by suggested revisions and then returned to the development process for consumer assessment or airing. Creative meetings are the liminal period (Van Gennep 1960:21), "betwixt and between" (Turner 1964; Malefyt 2003:145; Sherry 2005:72–74), during which the transformation occurs. The successful transition of a storyboard from preclient exposure to initiation as a "client approved board" is hailed with as much jubilation as other rites of passage throughout the world. Meeting participants are transformed as well. It is not only the storyboard that is evaluated in creative meetings, it is also the people who created or contributed to the work. Extending the argument from Geertz (1973) that cocks symbolize men and Kover (1995) that storyboards represent copy writers, all of the agency and client personnel who display their imagination, intellect, experience, and professionalism in a creative meeting are as exposed and judged as the advertising ideas. In this sense, approval or disapproval of a body of work and the achievement of goals in creative meetings is not just business. It is personal.

## CONCLUSION

Creative meetings are, as Schwartzman notes of all meetings, "sense makers" that help participants "define, represent, and also reproduce social entities and relationships" (Schwartzman 1989:39) and they function as "social and cultural validators" that enhance a sense of community and identity within an organization (Schwartzman 1989:41). Moeran observed this phenomenon in a Japanese advertising agency when he noted that meetings are "frames in which participants made sense of their organization and their actions taken therein" (Moeran 2005:14). Sense-making modes in creative meetings include the comprehension of verbal codes that mollify tense situations, the reading of verbal and nonverbal behavior, the understanding of the subtle machinations surrounding the client–agency balance of power, and the craft of negotiation. Miller (1990), writing about an agency in Trinidad, agrees with Moeran, writing about an agency in Japan, that presentations "define and maintain the advertising community as a whole" (Moeran 1993:88). Schwartzman contends that meetings are organization life "writ small" (Schwartzman 1989:39). Similarly, creative meetings contain the essence of client–agency relationships: conflicting objectives, displays of status, opportunities to show supreme insight, to control without appearing controlling, to demonstrate passion without being combative, to persuade without browbeating, and to accept without embracing. Agencies work hard to preserve creative integrity, but preservation of the client–agency relationship is paramount, for without the relationship, there is no creative presentation.

Despite the conflicts in creative meetings, the confluence of professional and personal objectives makes these meetings a powerful mechanism of action in the advertising industry. They function because they provide a venue for commercial ideas to be challenged and often made stronger, and for participants to achieve goals that secure their positions and advance their careers. In creative development, the agency's desire for art shaped by the demands of commerce meets the clients' need for commerce clothed in seductive art. During creative meetings, the often dazzling fusion of business goals and creativity, and of divergent organizational, attitudinal, and temperamental styles, converge. Some advertising agency executives say, "It's all about the work." Others view their business cynically, as the management of client–agency relationships. Both are correct. The work of the agency is the creative product and the creative meeting itself.

## REFERENCES


Ante, Spencer E. 2006. The Science of Desire. *BusinessWeek,* June 6: 99–106.

Della Femina, Jerry. 1970. *From Those Wonderful Folks Who Gave You Pearl Harbor: Front-line Dispatches from the Advertising War,* ed. Charles Sopkin. New York: Simon and Schuster.

Denny, Rita. 1999. Consuming Values: *The Culture of Clients,* Researchers and Consumers. In *The Race for Innovation,* 375–384. Amsterdam: ESOMAR.

Geertz, Clifford. 1973. *The Interpretation of Cultures.* New York: Basic Books.

Goffman, Erving. 1959. *The Presentation of Self in Everyday Life.* New York: Doubleday.

______. 1974. *Frame Analysis.* Cambridge, Mass.: Harvard University Press.

Henry, Jules. 1963. *Culture Against Man.* New York: Random House.

Hirschman, Elizabeth C. 1989. Role-Based Models of Advertising Creative and Production. *Journal of Advertising* 18(4): 42–53.

Inglessis, Maria Garcia. 2006. For Marketers or Scholars? *Quirk's Marketing Research Review,* December: 58–62.

Johnson, Steve. 2006. The Rational and Emotional "Tells" to Get the Most from Agency Presentations. *Product Management Today.* January: 26–27.

Kemper, Steven. 2003. How Advertising Makes its Object. In *Advertising Cultures,* eds. Timothy Dewaal Malefyt and Brian Moeran, 35–54. Oxford and New York: Berg.

Kover, Arthur J. 1995. Copywriters' Implicit Theories of Communications: An Exploration. *Journal of Consumer Research* 21: 596–611.

Kover, Arthur J. and Stephen M. Goldberg. 1995. The Games Copywriters Play: Conflict, Quasi-Control, a New Proposal. *Journal of Advertising Research,* July/August: 52–62.

Lasch, Christopher. 1979. *The Culture of Narcissism.* New York: W. W. Norton & Company.

Louis J. C. 1985. It's Anthropological: Research Takes a "Cultural" Bent. *Advertising Age,* January 14: 3:31.

Malefyt, Timothy Dewaal. 2003. Models, Metaphors and Client Relations: The Negotiated Meanings of Advertising. In *Advertising Cultures,* eds. Timothy Dewaal Malefyt and Brian Moeran, 139–163. New York: Berg.

Malefyt, Timothy Dewaal, and Brian Moeran, eds. 2003. *Advertising Cultures.* New York: Berg.

Mazzarella, William T.S. 2003. *Shoveling Smoke: Advertising and Globalization in Contemporary India.* Durham, N.C.: Duke University Press.

Meerwarth, Tracy L., Elizabeth K. Briody, and Devadatta M. Kulkarni. 2005. Discovering the Rules: Folk Knowledge for Improving GM Partnerships. *Human Organization.* 64: 286–302.

Michell, Paul C. N., and Nicholas H. Sanders. 1995. Loyalty in Agency–Client Relations: The Impact of the Organizational Context. *Journal of Advertising Research,* March/April: 9–14.

Miller, Annetta. 1990. You Are What You Buy. *Newsweek,* June 4: 59.

Miller, Daniel. 1997. *Capitalism: An Ethnographic Approach.* New York: Berg.

______. 2003. Advertising, Production and Consumption as Cultural Economy. In *Advertising Cultures,* eds. Timothy Dewaal Malefyt and Brian Moeran, 75–89. Oxford and New York: Berg.

Moeran, Brian. 1993. A Tournament of Value: Strategies of Presentation in Japanese Advertising. *Ethnos* 54: 73–93.

______. 1996. *A Japanese Advertising Agency.* Honolulu: University of Hawaii Press.

______. 2005. *The Business of Ethnography: Strategic Exchanges, People and Organizations.* New York: Berg.

Monari, Gina-Louise. 2005. Anthropology: Not Just for Academia. *MedAdNews,* August: 1, 28.

Murphy, Richard McGill. 2005. Getting to Know You. *Fortune Small Business,* June: 41–46.

Reinharz, Shulamit. 1988. *On Becoming a Social Scientist.* Piscataway, N.J: Transaction Books.

Sanders, Elizabeth. 2002. How "Applied Ethnography" Can Improve Your NPD Research Process. *PDMA Visions* 26(2): 8–11.

Schudson, Michael. 1984. Advertising, *The Uneasy Persuasion.* New York: Basic Books.

Schwartzman, Helen. 1989. *The Meeting.* New York: Plenum Press.

Sherry, John. 1987. Advertising as a Cultural System. In *Marketing and Semiotics: New Directions in the Study of Signs for Salc,* ed. Jean Umiker-Sebeok, 441–461. Berlin: Mouton de Gruyter.

______. 2003. Foreword: A Word from Our Sponsor—Anthropology. In *Advertising Cultures,* eds. Timothy Dewaal Malefyt and Brian Moeran, xi–xiii. New York: Berg.

______. 2005. We Might Never Be Post-Sacred: A Tribute to Russell Belk on the Occasion of His Acceptance of the Converse Award. In 16th Paul D. Converse Symposium, eds. Abbie Griffin and Cele C. Otnes, 67–77. Chicago: American Marketing Association.

Steel, Jon. 1998. *Truth, Lies, and Advertising.* New York: John Wiley & Sons.

TNS Media Intelligence, February 2006. (Industry Report)

Turner, Victor W. 1964. *Betwixt and Between: The Liminal Period in Rites de Passage.* The Proceedings of the American Ethnological Society, Symposium on New Approaches to the Study of Religion. Pp. 4–20. Washington, D.C.: U.S. Government Printing Office.

______. 1974. *Dramas, Fields and Metaphors.* Ithaca, N.Y.: Cornell University Press.

______. 1986. *The Anthropology of Performance.* New York: PAJ Publications.

Turow, Joseph. 1984. *Media Industries: The Production of News and Entertainment.* New York: Longman.

Underhill, Paco. 2000. *Why We Buy.* New York: Touchstone.

Van Gennep, Arnold. 1960. *The Rites of Passage.* Chicago: University of Chicago Press.

Wasserman, Todd. 2003. Watch and Learn. *Adweek,* November 3: 21–22.

Wellner, Alison Stein. 2002. Watch Me Now. *American Demographics,* October: S1–S5.

Young, Charles E. 2000. Creative Differences Between Copy Writers and Art Directors. *Journal of Advertising Research,* May/June: 19–26.

# 44

# Just Another Job?

## *The Commodification of Domestic Labor*

*Bridget Anderson*

For most women, working is a necessity, not an option. There are reasons to celebrate the fact that women have become active participants in the workforce alongside their male counterparts. But this socioeconomic transformation has also created a "double shift" for many women, who work a full day and then return home to the additional unpaid jobs with home, household, and family each night.

Many families try to alleviate this "double shift" by "outsourcing" domestic work to a paid worker. This outsourcing is what the author of this selection means by the "commodification of domestic labor." In other words, domestic labor can be bought and sold like other services or goods. Although domestic labor is an increasingly important commodity in societies throughout western Europe, the United States, and other world regions, it is generally poorly paid. Employers look for potential employees who are willing to work for the lowest wages and, quite frequently, the individuals they hire are migrants from poor, faraway countries.

While the wages middle-income Western families pay their domestic workers may be low by local standards, they are often very high in comparison to wages available in poor countries. As a result, millions of people from countries as diverse as the Philippines, Sri Lanka, Ghana, Nigeria, Columbia, and El Salvador have left their homes and families in order to take their chance of working abroad as a domestic worker. Even educated people with professional experience—among them journalists, teachers, bankers, nurses, and others—are prepared to take on the risks of transnational migration since the benefits are perceived as being so high.

This selection illustrates the difficulties of being a transnational migrant in domestic work. It can be very challenging to work within the intimate space of another person's, or another family's, home—especially within a foreign culture. At the same time is it difficult to live far away from family and friends, including, quite often, one's own children. Relationships between employers and employees are frequently marked by asymmetries of race, nationality, language, class, and citizenship, since many transnational domestic workers have migrated on an undocumented or "illegal" basis. As this selection illustrates, these asymmetries leave transnational domestic workers vulnerable to various forms of discrimination, exploitation, and abuse. Globalization is not just about manufacturing being done in China or call centers in India; globalization hits close to home.

***As you read this selection, ask yourself the following questions:***

- What is the "commodification of domestic labor?" What factors have contributed to the rise in demand for domestic workers in western Europe?
- Why are so many domestic workers in western Europe transnational migrants from Southeast Asia, West Africa, or eastern Europe?
- From the perspective of the domestic workers the author interviewed, what are the advantages of live-in as opposed to live-out domestic work? What are the disadvantages?
- How do racial stereotypes and other forms of prejudice contribute to the mistreatment of some domestic workers?
- Some employers describe their domestic employees as "one of the family." How might this way of characterizing their employment relationship actually contribute to the exploitation and abuse of the migrant women they employ?

***The following terms discussed in this selection are included in the Glossary at the back of the book:***

*commodification*
*domestic labor*
*maternalism*

Anderson, Bridget. "Just Another Job? The Commodification of Domestic Labor." Reprinted with permission of the author.

Paid domestic work looks in many ways like just another undesirable job. The hours are long, the pay is low, and the tasks are often regarded as demeaning. The same could be said of hamburger flipping or garbage collection. But there is much to distinguish the culture of domestic labor from other kinds of low-wage work. Significantly, domestic work is deeply embedded in status relationships, some of them overt, but others less so. And these relationships are all the more complex because they fall along multiple axes. They are relationships among women, but often women of different races or nationalities—certainly of different classes. They take place in a space that can be intimate, loving, and private but that can also be a form of social plumage, demonstrating to visitors the home owner's comfort and leisure. And the worker, often a migrant without legal protection or proper papers, may depend on the employer for more than her paycheck, just as the employer depends on the worker for more than her elbow grease.

The demand for domestic workers has been steadily rising in Europe, and although one can point to many economic and demographic forces that may have contributed to this trend—the retrenchment of the welfare state, the rise in the ratio of older to younger people, the feminization of the workforce, the rise in divorce, and the decline of the extended family—they leave a good deal unexplained. For instance, many domestic workers are employed by women who do not work outside their homes. Moreover, many paid domestic workers are cleaners rather than carers. While a working couple might need someone to look after their children or elderly relatives, no one *has* to employ a cleaner in the same way. Ironed clothes, dust-gathering ornaments, polished floors, and clean windows are not necessities; but such markers affirm a household's status by displaying its access to financial and human resources.

The migrant domestic workers I interviewed, many of them through a British support organization called Kalayaan, seemed to spend much of their time servicing lifestyles that their employers would have found difficult and even undesirable to sustain had they undertaken their upkeep themselves. Said Aida, a Filipina live-in in Paris:

> Every day I clean for my madam one pair of riding shoes, two pairs of walking shoes, house shoes. That is every day, just for one person. . . . Plus the children: that's one pair of rubbers and one pair of everyday school shoes. . . . Fourteen pairs of shoes every day. My time is already finished. . . . You will be wondering why she has so many bathrobes, one silk and two cotton. I say, Why does madam have so many bathrobes? Every day you have to hang them up. Every day you have to press the back because it is crumpled.

Siryani, a Sri Lankan live-in in Athens, recounted, "They have a very big house, and white carpet everywhere. They have three dogs. I hate those dogs with long, long hair. Even one hair will show on the white carpet."

When a cleaner is not enabling her employers to enjoy an extravagant lifestyle or an impractically appointed home (would Siryani's employers have had both white carpet and dogs if they'd had to clean their own home?), she allows her middle-class, female employer to devote "quality" time to her children and husband. In effect, employing a cleaner enables middle-class women to take on the feminine role of moral and spiritual support to the family, while freeing her of the feminine role of servicer, doer of dirty work. The employment of a paid domestic worker thereby facilitates status reproduction, not only by maintaining status objects but also by allowing the worker to serve as a foil to the lady of the house. Simply by hiring a domestic worker, the employer lowers the status of the work that employee does. After all, the employer has better or more lucrative things to do with her time.

Many middle-class, heterosexual couples in the United Kingdom employ a cleaner once they have children, thereby averting gender and generational conflict over domestic work.[1] But there is no total amount of domestic work that can be divided fairly between equal partners or delegated to someone who is paid to do it. When one does not have to do the work oneself, standards change. Eliska, a Czech au pair in the United Kingdom recounted, "Her teenage daughter changes her clothes five, six times a day and leaves them on the floor. I have to pick them up, wash them, iron them, put them away. I cannot tell her, Tasha, you cannot change your clothes so many times. And my employer does not notice."

Economic explanations, then, fail to fully account for the popularity of domestic workers in middle- to upper-class European households, because they fail to consider the status implications of hiring such workers. Similarly, the prevalence of migrant labor in this sector cannot be attributed only to avoidance of tax and national insurance, for there is a supply of cheap, nonmigrant female laborers willing to work off the books. Despite the relatively high wages of Polish workers in Berlin, they still account for a significant proportion of domestic workers. Filipina workers are the most popular in Athens, and they are also the most expensive.

Significantly, migrant workers are more willing than local ones to live with their employers. Live-in workers may be considerably less expensive than live-out workers, in some cases because their board and lodging are set against their wages, but especially because employers get more labor and greater flexibility for their money. Whatever hours a live-in nanny and housekeeper is supposed to work, there is virtually no time when she can comfortably refuse to "help" her employer with a household task. Domestic workers and au pairs commonly complain of having to be available at both ends of the day, early in the morning for children and late at night for entertaining guests. It is a question not simply of long hours but of permanent availability. Said Teresa, a Filipina domestic in Athens:

> You're working the minute you open your eyes until the minute you close your eyes. You keep your strength and your body going so that you will finish your work. . . . You keep waiting on your employers until they go to sleep because, although you finish your work, for example you finish ironing everything, putting the children or the elder person to bed, even if you put them to bed at ten o'clock, there are still other members of the family. So you keep on observing, "Oh, can I sleep or maybe they will call me to give them food or to give them a yogurt." . . . And even if you are sleeping you sometimes feel that you are still on duty.

A 1998 survey of thirty-nine Kalayaan members found that although the workers were well organized and belonged to a trade union, only 18 percent worked eight hours or less a day. Nearly 30 percent averaged more than twelve hours a day.

Although the long hours, low pay, and lack of privacy render live-in domestic work extremely unpopular among the population in general, migrants, particularly new arrivals, can find it advantageous: problems of accommodations and employment are solved in one, and the worker can both minimize expenses and acclimatize herself to a new language and culture. Moreover, housing is more than a place to live: it is shelter from the police, and many new arrivals are undocumented and terrified of deportation. Employers appreciate live-in migrants because, unlike local domestic workers, migrants cannot leave their employers to go tend to their own sick children or other family obligations. Undocumented workers in particular have extremely limited access to their own families or, really, to any life outside the employing home.

Such women, however, isolated in private households, without papers or legal protection, are strikingly vulnerable to abuse. Their work can be singularly degrading: cleaning cats' anuses, flushing employers' toilets, scrubbing the floor with a toothbrush three times a day, or standing by the door in the same position for hours at a time. One worker told a researcher of a particularly degrading experience: "We were three Filipinas, she brought us into the room where her guests were, she made us kneel down and slapped each one of us across the face."[2] Sadly, these are not isolated instances. Kalayaan keeps annual figures detailing the kinds of difficulties faced by the workers they register. In 1996–1997, 84 percent reported psychological abuse, 34 percent physical abuse, and 10 percent sexual abuse. Additionally, 54 percent were locked in, 55 percent did not have their own beds, and 38 percent were not fed regularly.

Racial stereotypes play a role both in the abuse of domestic workers and in the selection of migrant workers over local citizens in the first place. Certainly, such stereotypes help manufacture a sense of difference between the female employer and her domestic worker: "other" women are presumed suited to such service work, and these others are so alien that some employers actually fear that the migrants' bodies will contaminate their homes. Workers are typically required to wash their clothes separately from those of the family, and they are given their own cutlery and plates. Said Rose, a Ghanaian domestic worker in Athens, of her employer's family, "The daughter wouldn't even accept water from my hand, simply because I am black." Irene, a Filipina I interviewed in Athens, recounted the following story: "I heard children playing house. One child said, 'I am a Daddy.' The other child said, 'I am a Mummy,' and then, 'She is a Filipina.' So what does the child mean? Even the child knows or is already learning that if you are a Filipina, you are a servant inside the house."

Agencies and employers tend to express preferences for specific nationalities of domestic workers, and these preferences often reflect racial hierarchies that rank women by precise shades of skin color. One volunteer from Caritas, the international Catholic social service and relief agency, in Athens told me, "The Ethiopians are very sweet. They are not like the African Africans, who are ugly." Said a worker at an agency in Barcelona, "Moroccans are difficult to place. . . . Their religion is very different, they observe Ramadan. . . . They are very different, though like Peruvians they are brought up to be servile. . . . Filipinas are easiest to place." And according to a community volunteer in Paris, "You know the black people are used to being under the sun, and the people in France think they are very lazy, they are not going very quick, and you know, another breed, but they are very good with children, very maternal."

Some hierarchies are based on particular national or personal prejudices. Greek employers and agencies tend to frown upon Albanians and Ukrainians. In Paris, many employers evince a preference for Haitians, who are generally darker-skinned than the expressly shunned Moroccans and Algerians. Stereotypes differ across European states, but also across households: one household might display an "eccentric" liking for Congolese, for example, on the basis of household myths of an almost folkloric character. A "bad" experience with a domestic worker might lead a family to generalize about her entire nationality. Consider the comments of this Athens employer:

> I have a problem with women from Ethiopia: they are lazy, and they have no sense of duty, though they are good-hearted. . . . I have a lot of experience. I have had ten girls from Ethiopia. They like to be well-dressed—hair, nails; for that they are good. . . . Then the Albanians—that was terrible. They are liars, always telling lies. And telephone maniacs because they have never had telephones. And they had no knowledge of electrical appliances. For seven months I had that girl. . . . Then I had one from Bulgaria. The Bulgarians are more civilized, more sincere, more concerned about work. But they are very unhappy.

Of course, not all employers are racist or abusive. Some women hire migrants in the hope of helping them. Certainly, migrant workers need the money. Why not match the needs of hard-pressed working mothers, on the one hand, with those of desperate migrants on the other?

Many of the domestic workers I met said that traveling abroad had enabled them to make important contributions to their families back home. But most of the more than four thousand workers at Kalayaan had never intended to come to Britain. Some had migrated first to the Middle East, from where they accompanied their employers to London on business trips or holidays; others had taken jobs in their countries of origin and traveled with their employers to the United Kingdom. While domestic workers who had papers felt that their work brought benefits to their families, others, especially those still undocumented, found the price too high. Said Nora, a Filipina working in London, "My life is worse than before. I'm on this dark road with no way out, that's how I feel. . . . All I want to do is go back home, even though we're very poor. But then, what kind of life will my daughter have?"

Hidden costs become apparent to many workers when they return home. They often feel ill at ease in their home countries, where things have changed in their absence, and where they may feel that they no longer belong. When their families meet them at the airport, these women commonly do not recognize their own kin. They talk of the embarrassment of having sex with husbands who have become virtual strangers, and of reuniting with children who doubt their mothers' love. Often a woman's relatives will have died or moved away. It is thus scarcely surprising that such women are very ambivalent when asked whether they would recommend migration to their daughters. Most migrants would prefer that their daughters did not have to make the choice between hunger and moving abroad.

So is employing a migrant domestic worker an act of sisterhood toward a woman in need or of complicity with abusive power structures? Employers often make contact with Kalayaan after they have seen a television program or read an article exposing the situation of migrant domestic workers in London. They want to help, they explain, and to offer board and lodging in return for "help around the house." A place in a British home is proffered as a kind of charity, and the woman's labor power is a little extra on the side. But even under the best of circumstances, the employer has power over the worker, and this power is greatly increased when the worker is an undocumented migrant. How the employer chooses to exercise that power is up to her.

As Judith Rollins has noted, a kind of "maternalism" sometimes marks these relationships, wherein friendliness between the women works to confirm the employer's sense of her own kindness and of the worker's childlike inferiority.[3] Through kindness, pity, and charity, the employer asserts her power. Nina, an employer in Athens, had hired dozens of migrant domestic workers to care for her very disabled mother over the years, because, she said, "This is the Greek way to help foreigners." She claimed to offer exceptional working conditions (though the wages she told me were extremely low) and a loving household. But her employees, she lamented, have turned out to be gold diggers:

> There is no feeling for what I offer. I'll give you an example of the last woman from Bulgaria. . . . I had a bright idea: "She needs to see her friends." Because I was tired of all the turnover, I gave her Sunday off. . . . Now, every morning, including Sundays, the girl wakes, helps grandmother to the toilet and changes her Pamper. . . . Then she goes, but she must be back before seven P.M. . . . Then after all I do for her, the girl says every Sunday she would like to be back at midnight, and not to do any work—that is, not to change the Pamper in the morning.

This worker was being denied twelve consecutive hours off in a week—an arrangement that would still have placed her hours well above the European legal maximum.

Some employers express their maternalism through gifts, giving their domestic workers mostly unwanted, cast-off household goods. Said Maggie, a Zairean working in Athens, "You need the money to feed your children, and in place of pay they give you old clothes. 'I give you this, I give you this.' They give you things, but me, I need the money. Why? I am a human being."

All of these exercises of power, whether through direct abuse, through the insistence that a worker perform degrading tasks, or through acts of maternalism, expose the relationship between worker and employer as something other than a straightforward contractual one. But that is not the only relationship in the domestic workplace that is fraught with ambiguity and complexity. When we hire someone to care for children or the elderly, we cannot pay simply for the physical labor of care, leaving the emotional labor to those who are genetically linked to those cared for. Magnolia, a Dominican nanny in Barcelona, noted, "Sometimes when they say to me that I should give her lots of love, I feel like saying, well, for my family I give love free, and I'm not discriminating, but if it's a job you'll have to pay me."

Indeed many parents hire nannies rather than sending their children to day care precisely because they want their children to develop personal, emotional relationships with the people who care for them. But can the emotional labor of care really be bought? The worker may carry out the physical work of care, entering into a sort of intimacy with the children, but her caring engenders no mutual obligations, no entry into a community, and no real human relationship—just money. A worker may care for a child over many years, spending many more hours with that child than the child's natural mother does, but should the employer decide to terminate the relationship, the worker will have no further right to see the child. As far as the employer is concerned, money expresses the full extent of her obligation to the worker. To the worker, this view is deeply problematic; indeed, it denies the worker's humanity and the very depth of her feelings. Juliette, a nanny from Côte d'Ivoire working in Parma, recalled, "I cared for a baby for his first year. . . . The child loves you as a mother, but the mother was jealous and I was sent away. I was so depressed then, seriously depressed. All I wanted was to go back and see him. . . . I will never care for a baby again. It hurts too much."

The idea that the worker can be considered "part of the family" allows some employers to negotiate these difficulties. Interestingly, this language even appears in U.K. immigration legislation with reference to au pairs. But the analogy does not withstand scrutiny. A relative who contracts a long-term illness is not expelled from the family; domestic workers usually are, even if they are given a nice severance package. And although being a part of the family does not entitle the worker to unconditional love or support, it does entitle the employer to encroach on the worker's off-duty hours for "favors." In fact, many employers will invoke either a contractual or a family relationship under different circumstances, depending on what is most convenient. Writes Miranda Miles:

> The disadvantages of being "one of the family" far outweighed the advantages. Wages tended to be lower and erratically paid on the premise that the maid would "understand" their financial situation. Incorporating a domestic worker into the family circle is usually, although not always, a sure way of depressing wages and possibly hiding even the most discreet forms of exploitation involved in the employer-employee relationship.[4]

These are vexed questions, for while informality clearly leaves workers open to exploitation—excessive hours, for instance, or low pay—workers also value having personal relationships with their employers, particularly because domestic work can be highly isolating. In some cases, a woman will decide to work for low wages precisely because she feels that a particular family is "nice" or an employer "treats me as part of the family." Professionalizing employment relations and rendering them more anonymous may therefore introduce new difficulties. Labor is a social, not simply an economic process.

This is not to say that labor contracts for domestic work are not important. We should welcome the emergence of domestic labor into the realm of recognized and productive work. Professionalization is a means of giving respect to domestic workers as workers, as well as of managing the personal relationships that develop from care work.

Certainly, it is possible to argue for the social significance of care work. Changing an elderly person's incontinence pads is surely as important and as deserving of social respect and status as the work of a stockbroker. But the work of cleaners and housekeepers sometimes occupies a more problematic space. Cleaning can be part and parcel of caring, and tidying up for a disabled person, for instance, can be construed as socially valuable. But many cleaners, like those described at the start of this essay, do work that simply expresses the employer's status, leisure, and power. Can such race-, class-, and gender-based divisions be resolved through contracts? Undocumented migrants, for example, cannot draw boundaries or refuse work they find demeaning. They simply do not have the power. The most effective way to protect them is to make sure that they have basic employment rights, as well as access to the means to implement those rights. For migrants, these rights begin with work permits.

Because both the workers and the employers in this sector tend to be women, it is tempting to draw on notions of sisterhood in order to reform the relationships between employers and employees. But the power relations among these women are very complex, to the point where even acts of kindness work to reproduce an employer's status and self-image, and they do not always, in the end, benefit the worker. This does not mean that employers should not respect their domestic workers but, rather, that they should also be aware that the very act of employing a domestic worker weaves them into a status relationship. Real sisterhood, then, should take concerned women beyond their own homes: it means campaigning and organizing around issues of migration and domestic labor, having as an important first demand that domestic work be treated, in the best sense, like just another job.

## NOTES

1. Nicky Gregson and Michelle Lowe, *Servicing the Middle Classes: Class, Gender and Waged Domestic Labour in Contemporary Britain* (London: Routledge, 1994).
2. Margaret Healy, "Exploring the Slavery of Domestic Work in Private Households," unpublished M.A. thesis, University of Westminster, 1994.
3. Judith Rollins, *Between Women: Domestic Workers and Their Employers* (Philadelphia: Temple University Press, 1985).
4. Miranda Miles, Working in the City: The Case of Migrant Women in Swaziland's Domestic Service Sector. In *Gender, Migration and Domestic Service,* ed. Janet Momsen. London: Routledge, 1999.

# 45

# Contemporary Warfare in the New Guinea Highlands

*Aaron Podolefsky*

Within political units—whether tribes or nations—there are well-established mechanisms for handling conflict nonviolently. Anthropologists have described a wide range of conflict resolution mechanisms within societies. Between politically autonomous groups, however, few mechanisms exist. Consequently, uncontained conflict may expand into armed aggression—warfare. In both primitive and modern forms, warfare always causes death, destruction, and human suffering. It is certainly one of the major problems confronting humankind.

New Guinea highlanders can tell you why they go to war—to avenge ghosts or to exact revenge for the killing of one of their own. As we have seen in previous selections, people do not seem to comprehend the complex interrelationship among the various parts of their own social system. Throughout the world, anthropologists find that people do not fathom the causes of their own social behavior. If they did, finding solutions would certainly be a far simpler matter.

The leaders of Papua New Guinea see intertribal fighting as a major social problem with severe economic consequences. Although fighting itself may be age-old, the reemergence of warfare in this area in the 1970s appears to have a new set of causes. In this selection, Aaron Podolefsky shows how the introduction of Western goods may have inadvertently resulted in changes in economic arrangements, marriage patterns, and, ultimately, warfare.

***As you read this selection, ask yourself the following questions:***

- What is the theoretical orientation (research strategy) of this paper?
- When did tribal fighting reemerge as a national problem in New Guinea?
- How did intertribal marriage constrain the expansion of minor conflict into warfare?
- How has the rate of intertribal marriage changed? Why did it change?
- How are the introduction of Western goods, trade, marriage, and warfare interrelated?

***The following terms discussed in this selection are included in the Glossary at the back of the book:***

*affinal kin*
*aggression*
*agnates*
*blood relatives*
*cross-cutting ties*
*cultural materialism*
*hypothesis*
*lineage*
*multiplex relationships*
*pacification*
*tribe*

After decades of pacification and relative peace, intergroup warfare reemerged in the Papua New Guinea highlands during the late 1960s and early 1970s, only a few years before national independence in 1975. Death and destruction, martial law, and delay in highlands development schemes have been the outcome.

Most explanations of the resurgence either posit new causes (such as psychological insecurity surrounding political independence from Australian rule or disappointment at the slow speed of development) or attribute the increased fighting to relaxation of government controls which suppressed fighting since the pacification process began. None of the explanations thus far advanced has looked at changes in the structure or infrastructure of highlands societies themselves which could account for behavioral changes in the management of conflict.

Podolefsky, Aaron. "Contemporary Warfare in the New Guinea Highlands." *Ethnology: An International Journal of Cultural and Social Anthropology* 23 (1984):73–87. Reprinted by permission of Ethnology.

This paper employs a cultural materialist strategy in which the efficacy of explanatory models are ranked: infrastructure, structure, and superstructure.[1] From a macrosociological perspective, infrastructural changes unintentionally induced during the colonial era resulted in changes in the structural relations between groups. These changes reduced existing (albeit weak) indigenous mechanisms constraining conflict. Traditionally, groups maintained differential access to resources such as stone used for axes and salt. Axe heads and salt were produced in local areas and traded for valuables available elsewhere. I argue that the introduction and distribution of items such as salt and steel axes reduced the necessity for trade, thereby altering the need for intertribal marriage as well as reducing extratribal contacts of a type which facilitated marriage between persons of different tribes. The reduction of intertribal marriage, over time, resulted in a decay of the web of affinal and nonagnatic kin ties which had provided linkages between otherwise autonomous tribal political units. Thus, the resurgence of tribal fighting is, in part, a result of the reduction of constraints which might otherwise have facilitated the containment of conflict rather than its expansion into warfare. This view sees warfare as one possible end result of a process of conflict management.

An advantage of this strategy is that it suggests a testable hypothesis which runs counter to conventional wisdom and informed opinion that the rate of intertribal marriage would increase after pacification. Some researchers believed that once tribal fighting ended men would be able to wander farther afield and develop relationships with single teenage girls over a wide area. Pacification, then, might reasonably be expected to result in an increase in intertribal marriage. An increase or lack of change in the rate of intergroup marriage since contact would invalidate the explanation. The hypothesis will be tested on data collected in the Gumine District, Simbu (formerly Chimbu) Province, Papua New Guinea.

## BACKGROUND

Warfare in traditional highlands societies has been regarded as chronic, incessant, or endemic, and is said to have been accepted as a part of social living in most areas. Indeed, the pattern of warfare was one of the most continuous and violent on record.

However, hostilities were neither random nor did highlanders live in a perpetual state of conflict with all surrounding groups. Some neighboring groups maintained relations of permanent hostility and had little to do with one another. In contrast, most neighboring tribes intermarried and attended one another's ceremonies.

Pacification was an early goal of the colonial administration. By the end of the 1930s fighting was rare in the vicinity of Simbu province government stations. By 1940 Australian authority was accepted and attacks on strangers and tribal fighting had nearly ended, although the entire highlands was not pacified until the 1960s. This period also witnessed the introduction of Western goods such as salt and the steel axe.

Change came quickly to New Guinea. Sterling writes in 1943: "Headhunters and cannibals a generation ago, most of the natives of British New Guinea have now become so accustomed to the ways of the whites that they have been trained as workers and even to assist in administering the white man's law."

From the end of World War II through the 1970s, educational and business opportunities expanded, local government and village courts were introduced, and national self-government was attained in 1975. Highlanders came to expect that development would lead to material gains.[2]

Tribal warfare began to reemerge as a significant national problem in about 1970, five years before independence. By 1973 the government had become concerned that the situation might deteriorate to a point that they could no longer effectively administer parts of the highlands. In 1972, according to a government report, 28 incidents involving 50 or more persons were reported in the Western Highlands District. A decade later, Bill Wormsley (1982) reports 60 fights per year in the Enga Province (the figures are of course not directly comparable). Although the level of fighting declined in Enga during 1980 due to the declaration of a state of emergency, it increased again in 1981 and 1982. Martial law has also been declared in the Simbu Province. Deaths lead to payback killing and to demands for compensation payments. Inflated demands for "excess" compensation further compound the problem.

Of the five major theories of warfare outlined by Koch in 1974 (biological evolution, psychological theories, cultural evolution, ecological adaptation, and social-structure analysis), scholars have used only psychological theories and social-structural analysis to explain the recent emergence of tribal warfare.

Some researchers favor explanations which combine the traditional cultural heritage of violence with issues in development. Others seem to argue that the problem lies in the Enga's perception that the government, especially the courts, has become weaker and that this had led to the breakdown in law and order. Rob Gordon notes, however, that the police force in Enga has increased from 72 in 1970 to 300 in 1981, and that the average sentence for riotous behavior has grown from 3 months in 1970 to 9.6 months in 1978–9 with no apparent deterrent effect. Kiaps (field officers), Gordon suggests, have in fact lost power for several reasons. Most interesting from the perspective of the present analysis involves the kiaps' loss of control over access to goods. He (1983:209) states that "The importance that the Enga attach to trade-goods should not be underestimated." An old Engan is quoted as saying "The first Kiaps gave beads, salt, steel axes—everyone wanted it so they all followed the Kiap and stopped fighting. We stopped fighting because we did not want to lose the source of these things." I would add that once they "followed the kiaps" for these goods, previous important trade relations no longer needed to be kept up. In a 1980 study, Gordon also acknowledges problems created by intergroup suspicion, generational conflict exacerbated by education, and decline in men's houses and clan meetings. Similarly, Paula Brown (1982a) believes that pacification was a temporary effect in which fighting was suppressed. The Simbu do not see the government as holding power.

Explanations also combine development problems with psychologically oriented theories. Contemporary violence is sometimes thought to be a protest rising out of psychological strain created by the drastic social change of an imposed economic and political system. In a 1973 paper Bill Standish describes the period leading up to independence as one of stress, tension, and insecurity. He argues that the fighting is an expression of primordial attachments in the face of political insecurity surrounding national independence from Australian colonial rule. Paula Brown (1982a, 1982b) suggests that during the colonial period expectations for the future included security, wealth, and the improvement of life. "Disappointment that these goals have not been realized is expressed in disorder." She suggests that what is needed is a political movement rather than the imposition of Western institutions and suppression of fighting.

The present paper cannot and does not formally refute any of these explanations. Indeed, some make a great deal of sense and fill in part of a very complex picture. However, it is difficult to evaluate the validity of these explanations since very little data are presented. For example, Standish (1973) presents no evidence to assess whether, in fact, the level of stress has changed over time (precontact, postcontact, or independence era), or whether stress is associated with fighting or even with differential levels of awareness about independence, the latter likely expressing itself geographically around centers of population and development.

## ETHNOGRAPHIC BACKGROUND—THE MUL COMMUNITY

Mul lies approximately 3 miles east of the Gumine District Headquarters and 32 miles south of Kundiawa, the capital of the Simbu province. The Gumine patrol post was established in 1954. During the early 1960s a dirt road was constructed linking Gumine to the capital and within a few years the road was extended through Mul. Lying at an elevation of about 5,500 feet, Mul is the central portion of a larger tribal territory which extends steeply from the southern edge of the Marigl Gorge to elevations of 8,000 to 9,000 feet.

The area is densely populated. Land is either cultivated or fallow in grass or scrub regrowth. Individually owned trees are scattered and there are a yearly increasing number of coffee trees. With 295 persons per square mile on cultivatable land, this density is high compared with other highland groups (see Brown and Podolefsky 1976).

The people of Mul are Simbus. Social relations and cultural patterns follow in most important respects those extensively documented by Paula Brown in numerous publications. I will describe here only those dimensions of organization most directly relevant to the resurgence of tribal fighting.

Mul residents trace kinship through males, and their social groupings are patrilineal. Hierarchical segments link themselves as father/son, while parallel segments are seen as brothers. Individuals, however, are less concerned with this overall construct and tend to interact in terms of group composition and alignments. The likelihood of an individual conflict escalating into warfare is directly related to the structural distance between conflicting parties.

The largest political group to unite in warfare is the tribe, a group of several thousand individuals. Tribes are segmented into clans whose members see themselves as a unified group. Generally, individually owned plots of land tend to cluster and people can point out rough boundaries between adjacent clans. Plots of land belonging to members of a particular subclan tend to cluster within the clan area. The subclan section (or one-blood group) is the first to mobilize for warfare. The potential for expansion of such conflicts depends to a large degree on whether the relative position of the groups in the segmentary system lends itself to opposing alignments at the higher levels of segmentation and upon the past relations between the groups.

Unlike subclan sections in most highlands societies there is no restriction upon fighting between sections of the subclan. Within the subclan section, however, there are moral restrictions on internal fighting. If comembers become extremely angry they may attack with fists, clubs, or staffs, but not with axes, arrows, or spears. These restrictions are related to the notion that members of the subclan have "one-blood," and that this common blood should not be shed.

Segmentary principles operate in situations of cooperation as well as conflict. Members of a subclan section may enclose garden plots within a single fence and cooperate in the construction of men's houses. Brown (1970:99–103) similarly notes that in the central Simbu transactions between clans and tribes are competitive while those within the clan are reciprocal. Generally speaking, in terms of proximity of land holdings and residence, cooperation in gardening and house construction and the willingness to unite in common defense and ceremonial exchange, the solidarity of a social group is inversely related to the position in the segmentary hierarchy.

Cross-cutting these segmentary principles are a variety of interpersonal ties (e.g., affinal and other non-agnatic relations, exchange ties, and personal friendships) which affect behavior in conflict situations. It is these ephemeral or transitory linkages which provide the avenues through which structurally autonomous tribal groups interact.

## MARRIAGE AND WARFARE

Marriage and warfare are linked in the minds of New Guinea highlanders. Early writers report indigenous notions that highlanders marry their enemies. The Siane say, "They are our affinal relatives; with them we fight" (Salisbury 1962:25). Enga informants report, "We marry those whom we fight" (Meggitt 1958:278). In an extensive study of Enga warfare, Meggitt (1977:42) supports these assertions by reporting quite strong correlations between rates of intergroup marriage and killing.

While there is little doubt that there is a strong association between marriage and warfare, it is not clear at all that they are causally related in any direct fashion, i.e., warfare causing marriage or marriage causing warfare. It is highly unlikely that warfare causes marriage. Researchers have noted the difficulty in arranging marriages between hostile groups. It is similarly unlikely that marriage causes warfare (although exceptions can certainly be pointed out). While disputes may arise between bride and groom or their families, the relations are generally highly valued and long term. The association between marriage and warfare can be reduced to two separate relationships. First, highlanders most frequently marry their neighbors. Second, highlanders most frequently go to war with their neighbors. This is because in the highlands, where travel is restricted and relations are multiplex, neighbors are the parties most likely to be involved in a dispute. Thus propinquity is causally related to both marriage and warfare; the positive correlation between marriage and warfare is spurious. Indeed, the essence of the argument made here is that if other variables could be "controlled" the association between warfare and marriage would in fact be negative.

The notion that there is no direct (as opposed to inverse) causal relationship between warfare and marriage is critical. Warfare results from precipitating disputes in the absence of sufficiently powerful third party mechanisms and other constraints which control the dispute. One dimension of constraint stems from marriage links.

In her paper "Enemies and Affines," Paula Brown (1964) carefully describes the relevant social relations among the central Simbu. During wedding ceremonies speeches proclaim that the groups of the bride and groom (consisting of subclansmen, some clansmen, kin, and affines) should remain on friendly terms and exchange visits and food. The marriage creates individual ties and obligations outside the clan which, while not institutionalized, are not wholly voluntary. At various stages in the life cycle payments are obligatory. Given the widely documented emphasis on transaction in highlands social relations, it is important to note that whenever a formal food presentation occurs between clans, the donors and recipients are related to one another through marriage. Extratribal relatives play an important role in conflict situations.

> The prevailing hostility between neighboring tribes gives extratribal relatives a special complex role. Men try not to injure their close kin and affines in any conflict between their agnatic group and the group of their relatives, but they may not attempt to prevent or stop hostilities. In any dealings between neighboring tribes, men with connections in both take a leading part; their political sphere of action encompasses both. When intermediaries and peacemakers are required these men are active (Brown 1964:348).

Thus, in Central Simbu, affines played some role in attempting to prevent warfare and were important in restoring peace. No amount of oral history data will tell us how many wars did not occur due to efforts made through these channels. Nor can such data tell us how many wars were shorter or less intense than they would have been had there been fewer cross-cutting ties. The importance of cross-cutting ties is recognized among the densely populated Enga.

> Even while or after two men or groups fight over an issue, others may intervene to urge negotiation and compromise. . . . Whether, however, noncombatants initiate some kind of conciliation or simply stand by and watch the fighting spread depends on a complex set of conditions . . . relevant factors . . . include, for instance, the importance traditionally ascribed to the object in contention (is it a pig or a sweet potato garden?), the number of antagonists, the kinship, affinal, or exchange connections among some or all of them, and between them and interested noncombatants (Meggitt 1977:12).

Moreover, the frequency of intergroup marriage is related to the expansion or containment of a dispute. That is, the more intermarriage the greater the chance that disputes will be handled without violence or that the violence can be contained.

**TABLE 1 Marriage Ties by Time Period**

| | Before Contact | | After Contact | |
|---|---|---|---|---|
| | N | % | N | % |
| Between tribes | 85 | 75% | 30 | 40% |
| Within tribes | 29 | 25% | 44 | 60% |
| Total | 114 | 100% | 74 | 100% |

chi squared = 21.86 1 df
p < 0.001 (one tail)
phi = .341

From Podolefsky, Aaron. "Contemporary Warfare in the New Guinea Highlands." *Ethnology: An International Journal of Cultural and Social Anthropology* 23 (1984):73–87. Reprinted by permission of Ethnology.

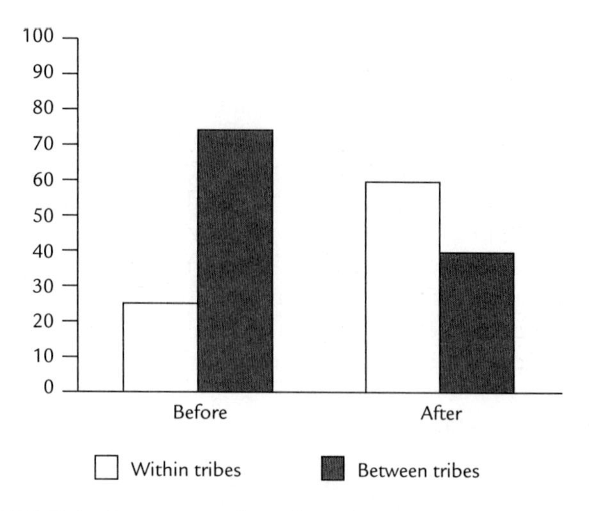


**FIGURE 1** Percentage of Marriage Ties. From Podolefsky, Aaron. "Contemporary Warfare in the New Guinea Highlands." *Ethnology: An International Journal of Cultural and Social Anthropology* 23 (1984):73–87. Reprinted by permission of Ethnology.

> Especially within the tribe, the supporters of each party include men with affines on the other side, most of whom are on good terms with their in-laws and have no wish to offend them. In such cases some men stay out of the fight while others, while participating, avoid meeting their affines in combat. This may serve to confine interclan conflict. Between tribes, similar serious disputes can more easily lead to fighting because fewer men have close ties which restrain them from supporting their fellow tribesmen (Brown 1964:352).

In sum, while there is an apparent correlation between marriage and warfare, marriage, in fact, establishes a social relationship which acts primarily as a constraint upon the expansion of a dispute. Second, as Meggitt suggests, it is not merely the marriage ties between the two groups, but also between them and their allies, i.e., the web of affinal relations. Third, the frequency of marriage, or density of the web, is related to efficacy of conflict management processes.

## CHANGING PATTERN OF INTERTRIBAL MARRIAGE

A null hypothesis that the proportion of intertribal marriages has gone up or remained the same can be rejected ($p < 0.001$) on the basis of the data shown in Table 1. Thus, we tend to believe, based upon these data, that there has in fact been an overall decline in intertribal marriage.

The data reveal a statistically significant change in the marriage pattern in the anticipated direction. Figure 1 describes the proportion of marriage ties within and between tribes, before and after Western influence. Comparing the intertribal (between) and intratribal (within) marriage rates in the precontact sample (labeled before), we see that intertribal marriage was nearly three times as frequent as intratribal marriage. Of the 114 marriage ties recorded in the precontact sample, 85 (75 percent) were between members of different tribes while only 29 (25 percent) were within the tribe. This allowed for a dense network of affinal ties between autonomous political groups. In the recent postcontact period (labeled after), in contrast, the number of intertribal marriages drops below the number of intratribal marriages. Of the 74 marriage ties in the postcontact sample, only 30 (40 percent) were between persons of different tribes while 44 (60 percent) were within the tribe. The intertribal marriage rate in the recent period is nearly half that of the precontact period.

The argument presented in this paper is that the dramatic reduction of intertribal marriage rates had significant implications for the structure of relations between politically autonomous tribal groups.

### A Secondary Analysis

Sometimes it is possible to replicate one's findings by performing a secondary analysis on data collected by other researchers.

In 1964, Paula Brown published data on the marriage of some men in the Naregu tribe who live in the central Simbu near the capital of Kundiawa. Data for two clans are divided into previous generations (prior to 1930) and present generation. Brown's categories for marriage ties may be collapsed to match those used above.

What should we expect, a priori? Since Brown did not arrange the data to address this particular question, we expect some differences. Her temporal dichotomy is previous and present generation rather than before and after contact. Europeans did not reach this area

**TABLE 2 Marriages of Some Men in the Naregu Tribe**

| | *Pre-1930 (Before)* | | *Post-1930 (After)* | |
|---|---|---|---|---|
| | N | % | N | % |
| Between tribes | 154 | 60% | 130 | 47% |
| Within tribes | 102 | 40% | 144 | 53% |
| Total | 256 | 100% | 274 | 100% |

chi squared = 8.597 1 df
$p < 0.005$ (one tail)
phi = .1272

From Podolefsky, Aaron. "Contemporary Warfare in the New Guinea Highlands." *Ethnology: An International Journal of Cultural and Social Anthropology* 23 (1984):73–87. Reprinted by permission of Ethnology.

until the mid-1930s and Brown's data are dichotomized at 1930. This means that precontact marriages are included in the present generation sample. Neither do Brown's data allow for a decade of transition. Based upon these differences in the data sets, we would expect the difference between the previous and present samples to be less extreme than the difference between the before and after sample in the Mul data (i.e., we expect a lower measure of association).

The data in Table 2 reveal a statistically significant change in the marriage pattern, although the association is lower (as we expected it would be) than in Mul. The between-tribe marriage rate (in the sample) dropped from 60 percent to 47 percent. This change was sufficient to draw Brown's attention. While the analysis fits our predictions, we cannot be certain that the change in marriage pattern observed by Paula Brown in central Simbu represents the same process occurring in Mul nearly twenty years later. Nevertheless, the analysis is intriguing. I think Brown was observing the initial stages of a process of change initiated by a reduction in the necessity for trade.[3]

## TRADE AND MARRIAGE

Given the conventional wisdom that pacification would lead to greater intertribal contact and, therefore, an increase in the rate of intertribal marriage, it remains to be explained why the proportion of intertribal marriages decreased. In other words, what forces or situations affected the marriage pattern?

Interviews with young men of marriageable age and some of the oldest men in the community elicited two different perspectives. (Unfortunately, it was not possible for me, being a male, to maintain serious conversation with women on this topic.) Young men typically explained that they do not find wives from other areas because they are "tired;" they just do not have any desire to travel the long distances to visit women of other areas when there are women close at hand. This emic explanation is not particularly satisfactory from an anthropological perspective.

While the older men could not explain why the distribution of marriages in their younger days differed from that of more recent years, they were able to describe the ways young men and women met prospective spouses from other tribes prior to the coming of Europeans scarcely twenty years earlier. The old men reported that when they were young trade was very important. Salt, stone axes, bird of paradise feathers, shells of different kinds, pandanus oil, carpul fur, and the like were traded between tribes during trading expeditions. Figure 2 maps the trade network as described by the older residents of Mul.

When they were young, the old men reported, they would dress in their finest decorations and travel to the places described in Figure 2. The women at these places, they said, would see them arrayed in all their finery and want to marry them. Of course, the situation may not have been quite this straightforward.

These reports drew my attention to the link between intertribal marriage and trade for scarce necessary and luxury resources. What would be the effect of the introduction of European goods upon trade? And, could this affect marriage patterns?

According to the old men, pigs from Mul were traded south to the lower elevation, less densely populated areas in return for bird of paradise feathers and carpul fur (see Figure 2). Some of the fur and feathers were traded for cowrie shells with people from Sina. Cowries, in turn, were traded to the Gomgales for kina shells. Carpul fur and pandanus oil were traded to the east for salt. Finally, some of the fur and feathers obtained from the south and the salt obtained from the east were traded to the northeast for stone axes and small shells, which had in turn been brought in from even further off.

Enter the ubiquitous steel axe; exit the stone axe. No one in Mul today would use a stone axe. Indeed, it was difficult to find someone who recalled how to attach the stone to a handle. The effect was that the primary reason for trade between the peoples of Mul and Era (i.e., the need for stone axes) was eliminated and the Muls' need for fur, feathers, and salt was reduced (what may have begun to increase was a need for cash). Similarly, salt increasingly became more readily available. Nowadays it can be purchased at the store on the government station or in small trade stores which stock, for example, three bags of salt, two packs of cigarettes, a bit of rice, and two or three tins

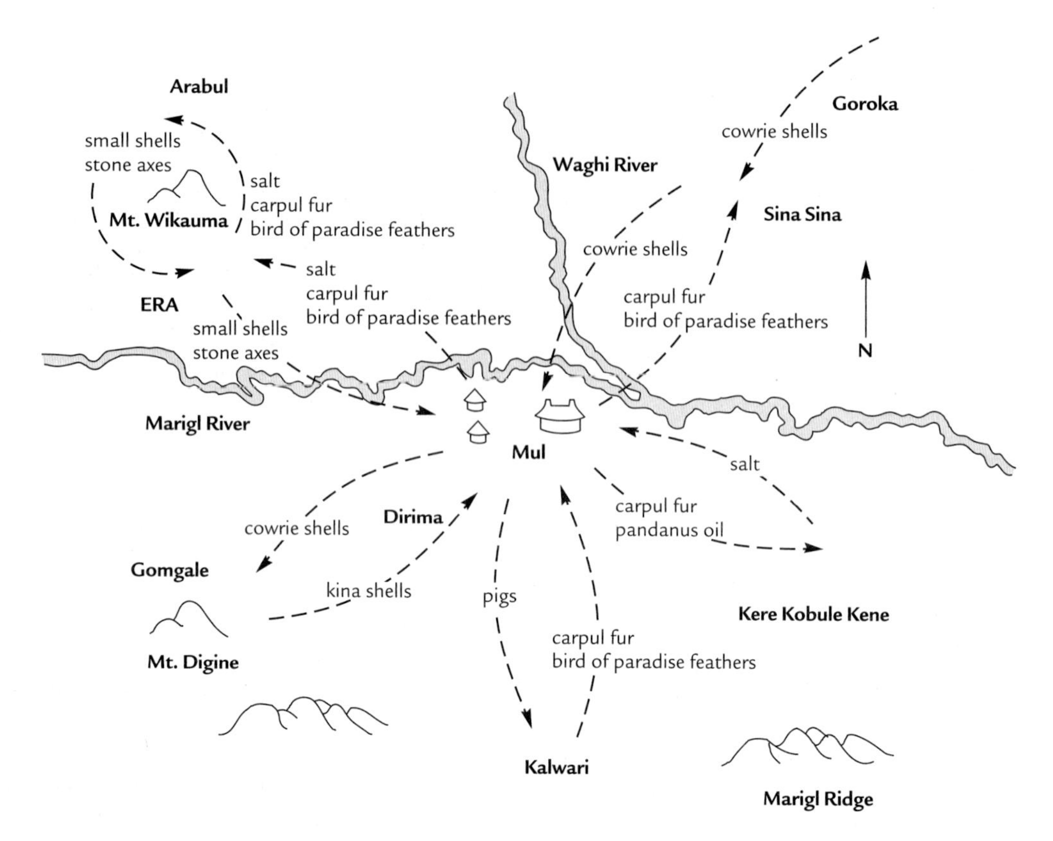


**FIGURE 2** Traditional Exchange Network

From Podolefsky, Aaron. "Contemporary Warfare in the New Guinea Highlands." *Ethnology: An International Journal of Cultural and Social Anthropology* 23 (1984):73–87. Reprinted by permission of Ethnology.

of mackerel. The availability of salt locally eliminates the need to trade for it and further reduces the need for fur. Thus, two of the five trade routes shown on Figure 2 become totally unnecessary and the usefulness of trade items from a third is reduced.

The elimination of the need to trade for necessary scarce resources allowed some trade relations to atrophy. I use the term *atrophy* since the process was probably one of gradual disuse of trade networks rather than a catastrophic change. The remaining trade relations were reliant upon the need for luxury items such as shells and feathers. Scholars who have done long-term research in New Guinea have described the highlanders' declining interest in these decorative items.

With the introduction of Western goods and the reduction of trade, both the need and the opportunity for intermarriage declined. Intertribal marriage was functional in that it facilitated intergroup economic transactions. While there are a range of rights and obligations as well as affective ties which make marriage into neighboring groups preferable, more distant marriages have recognized importance. This same point was made by Roy Rappaport in his study of the Tsembaga Maring:

> While unions between men and women of a single local group are generally preferred, the Tsembaga recognize certain advantages in marriage to members of other local groups . . . unions with groups north of the Sambai River and south of the Bismarks strengthen trading relationships. Bird-of-paradise plumes and shell ornaments are still obtained from these groups and until the 1950s stone axes from the Jimi Valley were traded for salt manufactured in the Simbai Valley (1969:121).

An early paper on the Siani linked trade and marriage directly by focusing on the exchange of nonutilitarian valuables which occurred at marriage and at the rites of passage for children of the marriage (Salisbury 1956). Valuables were traded in from the coast about 70 miles to the northeast. Trading took the form of ceremonial gift exchange between affines. At the same time, Salisbury reports a statistically significant trend for Siane men to obtain wives from the south and west while their sisters marry into groups from the north and east (the direction from which valuables come).

Even more interesting for the present purpose is Salisbury's report on the effect of the introduction of European wealth goods. The European settlements nearest the Siane were in Goroka and Asaroka, 30 miles to the east and north. Groups nearest these (who were already closer than the Siane to coastal wealth) quickly became wealthy in shells, cloth, and other European goods. Salisbury reports that, as a result of this increased wealth, the movement of women in that direction became more pronounced. He also notes that "Neither the wealth difference nor the movement of women is recognized in Siane idealogy."

Thus, Salisbury clearly links marriage patterns to the need to obtain wealth not locally available, although no mention is made of utilitarian goods. While the initial response to "wealthy neighbors" is to increase "wife giving," it is easy to see that once wealth is more evenly (and locally) distributed this reason for marrying out will no longer be of major consequence.

Particularly in the many areas of the highlands where marriages were arranged by families with minimal, if any, consultation with the bride or groom, consideration of trade relations was likely to play a role in the selection of a spouse. Families had an interest in the establishment or maintenance of trade relations.

At the same time that the function of intertribal marriage for maintaining the economic system in terms of access to necessary resources was eliminated, the decline in trade itself reduced the opportunity to make marriage arrangements between non-adjacent groups. Generally speaking, opportunity for marriage is not random but may be structured by factors such as class, caste, religious affiliation, sorority membership, or political borders. Changes in this structure of opportunity may lead to observable changes in marriage patterns. In other words, a change in the visiting (or trading) pattern between autonomous political groups could affect the structure of opportunity. The importance of opportunity remains whether the individuals are free to choose their own mates or whether such choices are made for them.

In central Simbu elders choose a person's spouse for them and, although they can refuse, the bride and groom usually accept even though they may never have met. Brown (1969) reports that some groups do not intermarry because of the lack of opportunity to make arrangements.

Administrative policy and mission influence may have speeded the process. In some areas, such as South Fore or Manga, Australian patrol officers insisted (or at least strongly urged) that brides consent and that women have a right to choose a spouse. Nowadays in central Simbu more marriages are being initiated by the couples themselves. Choice in a mate is likely to further increase the importance of the structure of opportunity.

In sum, the argument here is that the replacement, by Western goods, of resources secured through trade reduced the economic need (function) for intergroup marriage and the opportunity to arrange such marriages. The effects of these changes were not felt immediately because of the extant relations between groups. Over time fewer and fewer intertribal marriages were arranged to replace those of the passing generation. The net effect was a gradual decay of the web of affinal and non-agnatic ties which cut across tribal boundaries.

## CONCLUSION

Gordon (1980) has insightfully pointed out that there is very little sense in talking about or planning development if people live in fear of renewed tribal fighting. Moreover, he notes that this is a testing time for anthropologists "who find that their explanatory models are somewhat inadequate." Indeed, few of the explanations begin from a particular theoretical position nor even a unified conceptual model; there is little discussion of the mechanisms by which suggested "causes" result in the behavior being explained; and, little evidence is presented to test the explanations.

In this paper, I have employed a particular theoretic strategy, namely, cultural materialism, in which the efficacy of explanatory models are ranked: infrastructure, structure, and superstructure.

Prior to contact with the outside world, stone axe heads and salt were produced in local areas where these resources were available. Redistribution was accomplished through trade. One of the functions of intertribal marriage was the facilitation of trade between autonomous political groups. With the early introduction of Western goods, particularly steel axes and salt, local production was discontinued and marriage was no longer necessary to maintain these trade relations. As trade was discontinued, so declined the opportunity to make marriage arrangements between non-adjacent groups. Of course, existing marriage ties facilitated continued contact between groups, but probably less frequently, and there was no pragmatic reason for young people to marry others from distant areas. Particularly in the case of women, where such a marriage necessitated a move far from her natal family, there were distinct disadvantages. Thus, as older people died and fewer marriages were arranged between groups, the web of affinal and non-agnatic kin ties decayed. Intertribal marriages provided a linkage through which groups could communicate, and a mechanism and reason for containing conflict. With the decline in intergroup marriage over time, the likelihood of a dispute expanding into full-scale warfare increased.

This explanation began with infrastructural conditions (production) and showed how they were causally related to structural changes (trade relations) which in turn caused further structural changes (the web of kin ties), finally leading to changes in conflict behaviors. I have tried to explain each of the stages in this temporal process, i.e., the relationship between trade and marriage and the relationship between marriage and warfare.

Scientific hypotheses and models can be tested by examining predictions which can be deduced from them. The model which I have outlined predicts the unlikely occurrence that, with pacification and the ability to wander further afield without the threat of life and limb, intertribal marriage actually declined rather than rose as was thought would be the case. The hypothesis was tested on genealogical data collected in this research site as well as on data published earlier from a different area of the Simbu province. This is but a single case study and there is no statistical reason to extend the findings to other areas of the highlands. However, the inability to falsify the hypothesis in this case lends support to the general efficacy of the explanation.

## NOTES

1. Financial support from the National Science Foundation (Grant No. BNS76-218 37) is gratefully acknowledged.
2. For a more extensive discussion of this period with special reference to the resurgence of fighting, see Brown 1982a and 1982b.
3. Paula Brown reports (pers. comm.) that recently many Simbu women are marrying outside the Simbu to men they had met in the district or on visits. She notes that there are, now, advantages for older men having a daughter married to a prestigious outsider. Naregu men who migrate probably also marry outsiders.

   Such marriages further the process described here since, although they are extra-tribal, they do not link neighboring potential enemy groups.

## REFERENCES

Brown, P. 1964. Enemies and Affines. *Ethnology* 3: 335–356.

______. 1969. Marriage in Chimbu. In *Pigs, Pearlshells and Women,* eds. R. M. Glasse and M. Meggitt, 77–95. Englewood Cliffs, NJ: Prentice-Hall.

______. 1970. Chimbu Transactions. *Man* 5: 99–117.

______. 1982a. Conflict in the New Guinea Highlands. *Journal of Conflict Resolution* 26: 525–546.

______. 1982b. Chimbu Disorder: Tribal Fighting in Newly Independent Papua New Guinea. *Pacific Viewpoint* 22: 1–21.

Brown, P. and A. M. Podolefsky. 1976. Population Density, Agricultural Intensity, Land Tenure, and Group Size in the New Guinea Highlands. *Ethnology* 15: 211–238.

Gordon, R. 1980. Rituals of Governance and the Breakdown of Law and Order in Papua New Guinea. Paper presented at the annual meeting of the American Anthropological Association. Washington, D.C.

______. 1983. The Decline of the Kiapdom and the Resurgence of "Tribal Fighting" in Enga. *Oceania* 53: 205–223.

Howlett, D., et al. 1976. *Chimbu: Issues in Development.* Development Studies Centre Monograph No. 4 Canberra.

Koch, K. 1974. *The Anthropology of Warfare.* Addison-Wesley Module in Anthropology No. 52.

Meggitt, M. 1958. The Enga of the New Guinea Highlands. *Oceania* 28: 253–330.

______. 1977. *Blood Is Their Argument: Warfare Among the Mae Enga Tribesmen of the New Guinea Highlands.* Palo Alto, CA: Mayfield.

Rappaport, R. 1969. Marriage Among the Maring. In R. M. Glasse and M. Meggitt (eds.), *Pigs, Pearlshells and Women,* 117–137. Englewood Cliffs, NJ: Prentice-Hall.

Salisbury, R. F. 1956. Asymmetrical Marriage Systems. *American Anthropologist* 58: 639–655.

______. 1962. *From Stone to Steel.* London: Cambridge University Press.

Standish, B. 1973. The Highlands. *New Guinea* 8: 4–30.

Wormsley, W. 1982. Tribal Fighting, Law and Order, and Socioeconomic Development in Enga, Papua New Guinea. Paper presented at the meeting of the American Anthropological Association. Washington, D.C.

# 46

# The Kpelle Moot

*James L. Gibbs, Jr.*

Some scholars argue that law, like marriage, is a major institution found in all societies, although in widely divergent forms. Others argue that law exists only where some individual or group possesses the authority to impose punishments. Debates about what is and what isn't law aside, conflict exists in all societies. Further, all societies have culturally defined mechanisms by which people attempt to settle their differences.

Conflict-management procedures must be geared to meet the needs of particular social systems. In the urban centers of Western society, people live in faceless anonymity. Relations between people can be characterized as single interest. For example, generally a person's landlord is neither kin nor neighbor. The landlord-tenant relationship is not complicated by any other social bonds. A person who has a car accident is unlikely to have run into a friend or a relative. Our legal system, with its narrow focus on the grievance itself, fits our social system of one-dimensional relationships.

In small-scale social systems, people are often involved with one another on multiple levels. A landlord may also be a neighbor and a relative. In such settings, people are born, grow up, grow old, and die in the same community. Because their social relationships are long-term and highly valued, people in such communities need to resolve disputes in a way that maintains good relations.

Today in the United States, government agencies and grassroots organizations are establishing programs—Neighborhood Justice Centers or Dispute Resolution Centers—based on models of consensus and conciliation. According to the *Citizen's Dispute Resolution Handbook,* the potential of local-level conflict resolution was originally recognized in the work of an anthropologist who had described these processes in Africa.

***As you read this selection, ask yourself the following questions:***

- How are formal courtroom hearings different from moots?
- In what kinds of cases is the formal court effective and in what kinds is it ineffective?
- How is a mediator different from a judge?
- What is the function of the blessing at the beginning of the moot?
- In contrast to the official court, how does the procedure used during the moot facilitate harmony and reconciliation?
- Why does the author consider the moot therapeutic?

***The following terms discussed in this selection are included in the Glossary at the back of the book:***

*clan*
*culture area*
*extended family*
*mediator*
*moot*
*multiplex relationship*
*palaver*
*patrilineal*
*single-interest relationship*
*social control*

Africa as a major culture area has been characterized by many writers as being marked by a high development of law and legal procedures.[1] In the past few years research on African law has produced a series of highly competent monographs such as those on law among the Tiv, the Barotse, and the Nuer.[2] These and related shorter studies have focused primarily on formal processes for the settlement of disputes, such as those which take place in a courtroom, or those which are, in some other way, set apart from simpler measures of social control. However, many African societies have informal, quasi-legal, dispute-settlement procedures, supplemental to formal ones, which have not been as well studied, or—in most cases—adequately analyzed.

Gibbs, Jr., James. L. "The Kpelle Moot." *Africa,* 33 (1963), no. 1. Reprinted with permission of the author.

In this paper I present a description and analysis of one such institution for the informal settlement of disputes, as it is found among the Kpelle of Liberia; it is the moot, the *bɛrɛi mu meni saa* or "house palaver." Hearings in the Kpelle moot contrast with those in a court in that they differ in tone and effectiveness. The genius of the moot lies in the fact that it is based on a covert application of the principles of psychoanalytic theory which underlie psychotherapy.

The Kpelle are a Mande-speaking, patrilineal group of some 175,000 rice cultivators who live in Central Liberia and the adjoining regions of Guinea. This paper is based on data gathered in a field study which I carried out in 1957 and 1958 among the Liberian Kpelle of Panta Chiefdom in north-east Central Province.

Strong corporate patrilineages are absent among the Kpelle. The most important kinship group is the virilocal polygynous family which sometimes becomes an extended family, almost always of the patrilineal variety. Several of these families form the core of a residential group, known as a village quarter, more technically, a clan-barrio.[3] This is headed by a quarter elder who is related to most of the household heads by real or putative patrilineal ties.

Kpelle political organization is centralized although there is no single king or paramount chief, but a series of chiefs of the same level of authority, each of whom is superordinate over district chiefs and town chiefs. Some political functions are also vested in the tribal fraternity, the Poro, which still functions vigorously. The form of political organization found in the area can thus best be termed the polycephalous associational state.

The structure of the Kpelle court system parallels that of the political organization. In Liberia the highest court of a tribal authority and the highest tribal court chartered by the Government is that of a paramount chief. A district chief's court is also an official court. Disputes may be settled in these official courts or in unofficial courts, such as those of town chiefs or quarter elders. In addition to this, grievances are settled informally in moots, and sometimes by associational groupings such as church councils or cooperative work groups.

In my field research I studied both the formal and informal methods of dispute settlement. The method used was to collect case material in as complete a form as possible. Accordingly, immediately after a hearing, my interpreter and I would prepare verbatim transcripts of each case that we heard. These transcripts were supplemented with accounts—obtained from respondents—of past cases or cases which I did not hear litigated. Transcripts from each type of hearing were analysed phrase by phrase in terms of a frame of reference derived from jurisprudence and ethno-law. The results of the analysis indicate two things: first, that courtroom hearings and moots are quite different in their procedures and tone, and secondly, why they show this contrast.

Kpelle courtroom hearings are basically coercive and arbitrary in tone. In another paper[4] I have shown that this is partly the result of the intrusion of the authoritarian values of the Poro into the courtroom. As a result, the court is limited in the manner in which it can handle some types of disputes. The court is particularly effective in settling cases such as assault, possession of illegal charms, or theft where the litigants are not linked in a relationship which must continue after the trial. However, most of the cases brought before a Kpelle court are cases involving disputed rights over women, including matrimonial matters which are usually cast in the form of suits for divorce. The court is particularly inept at settling these numerous matrimonial disputes because its harsh tone tends to drive spouses farther apart rather than to reconcile them. The moot, in contrast, is more effective in handling such cases. The following analysis indicates the reasons for this.[5]

The Kpelle *bɛrɛi mu meni saa,* or "house palaver," is an informal airing of a dispute which takes place before an assembled group which includes kinsmen of the litigants and neighbors from the quarter where the case is being heard. It is a completely ad hoc group, varying greatly in composition from case to case. The matter to be settled is usually a domestic problem: alleged mistreatment or neglect by a spouse, an attempt to collect money paid to a kinsman for a job which was not completed, or a quarrel among brothers over the inheritance of their father's wives.

In the procedural description which follows I shall use illustrative data from the Case of the Ousted Wife:

> Wama Nya, the complainant, had one wife, Yua. His older brother died and he inherited the widow, Yokpo, who moved into his house. The two women were classificatory sisters. After Yokpo moved in, there was strife in the household. The husband accused her of staying out late at night, of harvesting rice without his knowledge, and of denying him food. He also accused Yokpo of having lovers and admitted having had a physical struggle with her, after which he took a basin of water and "washed his hands of her."
>
> Yokpo countered by denying the allegations about having lovers, saying that she was accused falsely, although she had in the past confessed the name of one lover. She further complained that Wama Nya had assaulted her and, in the act, had committed the indignity of removing her headtie, and had expelled her from the house after the ritual hand-washing. Finally, she alleged that she had been thus cast out of the house at the instigation of the other wife who, she asserted, had great influence over their husband.

> Kɔlɔ Waa, the Town Chief and quarter elder, and the brother of Yokpo, was the mediator of the moot, which decided that the husband was mainly at fault, although Yua and Yokpo's children were also in the wrong. Those at fault had to apologize to Yokpo and bring gifts of apology as well as local rum[6] for the disputants and participants in the moot.

The moot is most often held on a Sunday—a day of rest for Christians and non-Christians alike—at the home of the complainant, the person who calls the moot. The mediator will have been selected by the complainant. He is a kinsman who also holds an office such as town chief or quarter elder, and therefore has some skill in dispute settlement. It is said that he is chosen to preside by virtue of his kin tie, rather than because of his office.

The proceedings begin with the pronouncing of blessings by one of the oldest men of the group. In the Case of the Ousted Wife, Gbenai Zua, the elder who pronounced the blessings, took a rice-stirrer in his hand and, striding back and forth, said:

> This man has called us to fix the matter between him and his wife. May ɣala (the supreme, creator deity) change his heart and let his household be in good condition. May ɣala bless the family and make them fruitful. May He bless them so they can have food this year. May He bless the children and the rest of the family so they may always be healthy. May He bless them to have good luck. When Wama Nya takes a gun and goes in the bush, may he kill big animals. May ɣala bless us to enjoy the meat. May He bless us to enjoy life and always have luck. May ɣala bless all those who come to discuss this matter.

The man who pronounces the blessings always carries a stick or a whisk (*kpung*) which he waves for effect as he paces up and down chanting his injunctions. Participation of spectators is demanded, for the blessings are chanted by the elder (*kpung namu* or "*kpung* owner") as a series of imperatives, some of which he repeats. Each phrase is responded to by the spectators who answer in unison with a formal response, either *e ka ti* (so be it), or a low, drawn-out *eeee*. The *kpung namu* delivers his blessings faster and faster, building up a rhythmic interaction pattern with the other participants. The effect is to unite those attending in common action before the hearing begins. The blessing focuses attention on the concern with maintaining harmony and the well-being of the group as a whole.

Everyone attending the moot wears their next-to-best clothes or, if it is not Sunday, everyday clothes. Elders, litigants, and spectators sit in mixed fashion, pressed closely upon each other, often overflowing onto a veranda. This is in contrast to the vertical spatial separation between litigants and adjudicators in the courtroom. The mediator, even though he is a chief, does not wear his robes. He and the oldest men will be given chairs as they would on any other occasion.

The complainant speaks first and may be interrupted by the mediator or anyone else present. After he has been thoroughly quizzed, the accused will answer and will also be questioned by those present. The two parties will question each other directly and question others in the room also. Both the testimony and the questioning are lively and uninhibited. Where there are witnesses to some of the actions described by the parties, they may also speak and be questioned. Although the proceedings are spirited, they remain orderly. The mediator may fine anyone who speaks out of turn by requiring them to bring some rum for the group to drink.

The mediator and others present will point out the various faults committed by both the parties. After everyone has been heard, the mediator expresses the consensus of the group. For example, in the Case of the Ousted Wife, he said to Yua: "The words you used towards your sister were not good, so come and beg her pardon."

The person held to be mainly at fault will then formally apologize to the other person. This apology takes the form of the giving of token gifts to the wronged person by the guilty party. These may be an item of clothing, a few coins, clean hulled rice, or a combination of all three. It is also customary for the winning party in accepting the gifts of apology to give, in return, a smaller token such as a twenty-five cent piece[7] to show his "white heart" or good will. The losing party is also lightly "fined;" he must present rum or beer to the mediator and the others who heard the case. This is consumed by all in attendance. The old man then pronounces blessings again and offers thanks for the restoration of harmony within the group, and asks that all continue to act with good grace and unity.

An initial analysis of the procedural steps of the moot isolates the descriptive attributes of the moot and shows that they contrast with those of the courtroom hearing. While the airing of grievances is incomplete in courtroom hearings, it is more complete in the moot. This fuller airing of the issues results, in many marital cases, in a more harmonious solution. Several specific features of the house palaver facilitate this wider airing of grievances. First, the hearing takes place soon after a breach has occurred, before the grievances have hardened. There is no delay until the complainant has time to go to the paramount chief's or district chief's headquarters to institute suit. Secondly, the hearing takes place in the familiar surroundings of a home. The robes, writs, messengers, and other symbols of power which subtly intimidate and inhibit the parties in the courtroom, by reminding them of the physical force which underlies the procedures, are absent. Thirdly, in the courtroom the conduct of the hearing is firmly in the hands of the judge but in the moot the investigatory initiative rests much more with the parties themselves. Jurisprudence suggests that, in such a case, more of the grievances lodged between the parties are likely to be aired and adjusted. Finally, the range of relevance applied to matters which are brought out is extremely broad. Hardly anything mentioned is held to be irrelevant. This too leads to a more thorough ventilation of the issues.

There is a second surface difference between court and moot. In a courtroom hearing, the solution is, by and large, one which is imposed by the adjudicator. In the moot the solution is more consensual. It is, therefore, more likely to be accepted by both parties and hence more durable. Several features of the moot contribute to the consensual solution: first, there is no unilateral ascription of blame, but an attribution of fault to both parties. Secondly, the mediator, unlike the chief in the courtroom, is not backed by political authority and the physical force which underlies it. He cannot jail parties, nor can he levy a heavy fine. Thirdly, the sanctions which are imposed are not so burdensome as to cause hardship to the losing party or to give him or her grounds for a new grudge against the other party. The gifts for the winning party and the potables for the spectators are not as expensive as the fines and the court costs in a paramount chief's court. Lastly, the ritualized apology of the moot symbolizes very concretely the consensual nature of the solution.[8] The public offering and acceptance of the tokens of apology indicate that each party has no further grievances and that the settlement is satisfactory and mutually acceptable. The parties and spectators drink together to symbolize the restored solidarity of the group and the rehabilitation of the offending party.

This type of analysis describes the courtroom hearing and the moot, using a frame of reference derived from jurisprudence and ethno-law which is explicitly comparative and evaluative. Only by using this type of comparative approach can the researcher select features of the hearings which are not only unique to each of them, but theoretically significant in that their contribution to the social-control functions of the proceedings can be hypothesized. At the same time, it enables the researcher to pinpoint in procedures the cause for what he feels intuitively: that the two hearings contrast in tone, even though they are similar in some ways.

However, one can approach the transcripts of the trouble cases with a second analytical framework and emerge with a deeper understanding of the implications of the contrasting descriptive attributes of the court and the house palaver. Remember that the coercive tone of the courtroom hearing limits the court's effectiveness in dealing with matrimonial disputes, especially in effecting reconciliations. The moot, on the other hand, is particularly effective in bringing about reconciliations between spouses. This is because the moot is not only conciliatory, but *therapeutic.* Moot procedures are therapeutic in that, like psychotherapy, they re-educate the parties through a type of social learning brought about in a specially structured interpersonal setting.

Talcott Parsons[9] has written that therapy involves four elements: support, permissiveness, denial of reciprocity, and manipulation of rewards. Writers such as Frank,[10] Klapman,[11] and Opler[12] have pointed out that the same elements characterize not only individual psychotherapy, but group psychotherapy as well. All four elements are writ large in the Kpelle moot.

The patient in therapy will not continue treatment very long if he does not feel support from the therapist or from the group. In the moot the parties are encouraged in the expression of their complaints and feelings because they sense group support. The very presence of one's kinsmen and neighbors demonstrates their concern. It indicates to the parties that they have a real problem and that the others are willing to help them to help themselves in solving it. In a parallel vein, Frank, speaking of group psychotherapy, notes that: "Even anger may be supportive if it implies to a patient that others take him seriously enough to get angry at him, especially if the object of the anger feels it to be directed toward his neurotic behavior rather than himself as a person."[13] In the moot the feeling of support also grows out of the pronouncement of the blessings which stress the unity of the group and its harmonious goal, and it is also undoubtedly increased by the absence of the publicity and expressive symbols of political power which are found in the courtroom.

Permissiveness is the second element in therapy. It indicates to the patient that everyday restrictions on making anti-social statements or acting out anti-social impulses are lessened. Thus, in the Case of the Ousted Wife, Yua felt free enough to turn to her ousted co-wife (who had been married leviratically) and say:

> You don't respect me. You don't rely on me any more. When your husband was living, and I was with my husband, we slept on the farm. Did I ever refuse to send you what you asked me for when you sent a message? Didn't I always send you some of the meat my husband killed? Did I refuse to send you anything you wanted? When your husband died and we became co-wives, did I disrespect you? Why do you always make me ashamed? The things you have done to me make me sad.

Permissiveness in the therapeutic setting (and in the moot) results in catharsis, in a high degree of stimulation of feelings in the participants and an equally high tendency to verbalize these feelings.[14] Frank notes that:

"Neurotic responses must be expressed in the therapeutic situation if they are to be changed by it."[15] In the same way, if the solution to a dispute reached in a house palaver is to be stable, it is important that there should be nothing left to embitter and undermine the decision. In a familiar setting, with familiar people, the parties to the moot feel at ease and free to say *all* that is on their minds. Yokpo, judged to be the wronged party in the Case of the Ousted Wife, in accepting an apology, gave expression to this when she said:

> I agree to everything that my people said, and I accept the things they have given me—I don't have *anything else* about them on my mind. *(My italics.)*

As we shall note below, this thorough airing of complaints also facilitates the gaining of insight into and the unlearning of idiosyncratic behaviour which is socially disruptive. Permissiveness is rooted in the lack of publicity and the lack of symbols of power. But it stems, too, from the immediacy of the hearing, the locus of investigatory initiative with the parties, and the wide range of relevance.

Permissiveness in therapy is impossible without the denial of reciprocity. This refers to the fact that the therapist will not respond in kind when the patient acts in a hostile manner or with inappropriate affection. It is a type of privileged indulgence which comes with being a patient. In the moot, the parties are treated in the same way and are allowed to hurl recriminations that, in the courtroom, might bring a few hours in jail as punishment for the equivalent of contempt of court. Even though inappropriate views are not responded to in kind, neither are they simply ignored. There is denial of *congruent* response, not denial of *any* response whatsoever. In the *bɛrɛi mu meni saa,* as in group psychotherapy, "private ideation and conceptualization are brought out into the open and all their facets or many of their facets exposed. The individual gets a 'reading' from different bearings on the compass, so to speak,[16] and perceptual patterns . . . are joggled out of their fixed positions. . . ."[17]

Thus, Yua's outburst against Yokpo quoted above was not responded to with matching hostility, but its inappropriateness was clearly pointed out to her by the group. Some of them called her aside in a huddle and said to her:

> You are not right. If you don't like the woman, or she doesn't like you, don't be the first to say anything. Let her start and then say what you have to say. By speaking, if she heeds some of your words, the wives will scatter, and the blame will be on you. Then your husband will cry for your name that you have scattered his property.

In effect, Yua was being told that, in view of the previous testimony, her jealousy of her co-wife was not justified. In reality testing, she discovered that her view of the situation was not shared by the others and, hence, was inappropriate. Noting how the others responded, she could see why her treatment of her co-wife had caused so much dissension. Her interpretation of her new co-wife's actions and resulting premises were not shared by the co-wife, nor by the others hearing a description of what had happened. Like psychotherapy, the moot is gently corrective of behavior rooted in such misunderstandings.

Similarly, Wama Nya, the husband, learned that others did not view as reasonable his accusing his wife of having a lover and urging her to go off and drink with the suspected paramour when he passed their house and wished them all a good evening. Reality testing for him taught him that the group did not view this type of mildly paranoid sarcasm as conducive to stable marital relationships.

The reaction of the moot to Yua's outburst indicates that permissiveness in this case was certainly not complete, but only relative, being much greater than in the courtroom. But without this moderated immunity the airing of grievances would be limited, and the chance for social relearning lessened. Permissiveness in the moot is incomplete because, even there, prudence is not thrown to the winds. Note that Yua was not told not to express her feelings at all, but to express them only after the co-wife had spoken so that, if the moot failed, she would not be in an untenable position. In court there would be objection to her blunt speaking out. In the moot the objection was, in effect, to her speaking *out of turn.* In other cases the moot sometimes fails, foundering on this very point, because the parties are *too* prudent, all waiting for the others to make the first move in admitting fault.

The manipulation of rewards is the last dimension of therapy treated by Parsons. In this final phase of therapy[18] the patient is coaxed to conformity by the granting of rewards. In the moot one of the most important rewards is the group approval which goes to the wronged person who accepts an apology and to the person who is magnanimous enough to make one.

In the Case of the Ousted Wife, Kɔlɔ Waa, the mediator, and the others attending decided that the husband and the co-wife, Yua, had wronged Yokpo. Kɔlɔ Waa said to the husband:

> From now on, we don't want to hear of your fighting. You should live in peace with these women. If your wife accepts the things which the people have brought you should pay four chickens and ten bottles of rum as your contribution.

The husband's brother and sister also brought gifts of apology, although the moot did not explicitly hold them at fault.

By giving these prestations, the wrongdoer is restored to good grace and is once again acting like an "upright Kpelle" (although, if he wishes, he may refuse to accept the decision of the moot). He is eased into this position by being grouped with others to whom blame is also allocated, for, typically, he is not singled out and isolated in being labelled deviant. Thus, in the Case of the Ousted Wife, the children of Yokpo were held to be at fault in "being mean" to their stepfather, so that blame was not only shared by one "side," but ascribed to the other also.

Moreover, the prestations which the losing party is asked to hand over are not expensive. They are significant enough to touch the pocketbook a little; for the Kpelle say that if an apology does not cost something other than words, the wrongdoer is more likely to repeat the offending action. At the same time, as we noted above, the tokens are not so costly as to give the loser additional reason for anger directed at the other party which can undermine the decision.

All in all, the rewards for conformity to group expectations and for following out a new behaviour pattern are kept within the deviant's sight. These rewards are positive, in contrast to the negative sanctions of the courtroom. Besides the institutionalized apology, praise and acts of concern and affection replace fines and jail sentences. The mediator, speaking to Yokpo as the wronged party, said:

> You have found the best of the dispute. Your husband has wronged you. All the people have wronged you. You are the only one who can take care of them because you are the oldest. Accept the things they have given to you.

The moot in its procedural features and procedural sequences is, then, strongly analogous to psychotherapy. It is analogous to therapy in the structuring of the role of the mediator also. Parsons has indicated that, to do his job well, the therapist must be a member of two social systems: one containing himself and his patient; and the other, society at large.[19] He must not be seduced into thinking that he belongs only to the therapeutic dyad, but must gradually pull the deviant back into a relationship with the wider group. It is significant, then, that the mediator of a moot is a kinsman who is also a chief of some sort. He thus represents both the group involved in the dispute and the wider community. His task is to utilize his position as kinsman as a lever to manipulate the parties into living up to the normative requirements of the wider society, which, as chief, he upholds. His major orientation must be to the wider collectivity, not to the particular goals of his kinsmen.

When successful, the moot stops the process of alienation which drives two spouses so far apart that they are immune to ordinary social-control measures such as a smile, a frown, or a pointed aside.[20] A moot is not always successful, however. Both parties must have a genuine willingness to cooperate and a real concern about their discord. Each party must be willing to list his grievances, to admit his guilt, and make an open apology. The moot, like psychotherapy, is impotent without well-motivated clients.

The therapeutic elements found in the Kpelle moot are undoubtedly found in informal procedures for settling disputes in other African societies also; some of these are reported in literature and others are not. One such procedure which seems strikingly parallel to the Kpelle *bɛrɛi mu meni saa* has been described by J. H. M. Beattie.[21] This is the court of neighbors or *rukurato rw'enzarwa* found in the Banyoro kingdom of Uganda. The group also meets as an ad hoc assembly of neighbors to hear disputes involving kinsmen or neighbors.[22]

The intention of the Nyoro moot is to "reintegrate the delinquent into the community and, if possible, to achieve reconciliation without causing bitterness and resentment; in the words of an informant, the institution exists 'to finish off people's quarrels and to abolish bad feeling.'"[23] This therapeutic goal is manifested in the manner in which the dispute is resolved. After a decision is reached the penalty imposed is always the same. The party held to be in the wrong is asked to bring beer (four pots, modified downwards according to the circumstances) and meat, which is shared with the other party and all those attending the *rukurato.* The losing party is also expected to "humble himself, not only to the man he has injured but to the whole assembly."[24]

Beattie correctly points out that, because the council of neighbors has no power to enforce its decision, the shared feast is *not* to be viewed primarily as a penalty, for the wrongdoer acts as a host and also shares in the food and drink. "And it is a praiseworthy thing; from a dishonourable status he is promoted to an honourable one . . ."[25] and reintegrated into the community.[26]

Although Beattie does not use a psychoanalytic frame of reference in approaching his material, it is clear that the communal feast involves the manipulation of rewards as the last step in a social-control measure which breaks the progressive alienation of the deviance cycle. The description of procedures in the *rukurato* indicates that it is highly informal in nature, convening in a room in a house with everyone "sitting around." However, Beattie does not provide enough detail to enable one to determine whether or not the beginning and intermediate steps in the Nyoro moot show the permissiveness, support, and denial of reciprocity which characterize the Kpelle moot. Given the structure and outcome of most Nyoro councils, one would surmise that a close examination of their proceedings[27] would reveal the implicit operation of therapeutic principles.

The fact that the Kpelle court is basically coercive and the moot therapeutic does not imply that one is dysfunctional while the other is eufunctional. Like Beattie, I conclude that the court and informal dispute-settlement procedures have separate but complementary functions. In marital disputes the moot is oriented to a couple as a dyadic social system and serves to reconcile them wherever possible. This is eufunctional from the point of view of the couple, to whom divorce would be dysfunctional. Kpelle courts customarily treat matrimonial matters by granting a divorce. While this may be dysfunctional from the point of view of the couple, because it ends their marriage, it may be eufunctional from the point of view of society. Some marriages, if forced to continue, would result in adultery or physical violence at best, and improper socialization of children at worst. It is clear that the Kpelle moot is to the Kpelle court as the domestic and family relations courts (or commercial and labour arbitration boards) are to ordinary courts in our own society. The essential point is that both formal and informal dispute-settlement procedures serve significant functions in Kpelle society and neither can be fully understood if studied alone.[28]

## NOTES

1. The fieldwork on which this paper is based was carried out in Liberia in 1957 and 1958 and was supported by a grant from the Ford Foundation, which is, of course, not responsible for any of the views presented here. The data were analyzed while the writer was the holder of a pre-doctoral National Science Foundation Fellowship. The writer wishes to acknowledge, with gratitude, the support of both foundations. This paper was read at the Annual Meeting of the American Anthropological Association in Philadelphia, Pennsylvania, in November 1961.

   The dissertation, in which this material first appeared, was directed by Philip H. Gulliver, to whom I am indebted for much stimulating and provocative discussion of many of the ideas here. Helpful comments and suggestions have also been made by Robert T. Holt and Robert S. Merrill.

   Portions of the material included here were presented in a seminar on African Law conducted in the Department of Anthropology at the University of Minnesota by E. Adamson Hoebel and the writer. Members of the seminar were generous in their criticisms and comments.
2. Paul J. Bohannan, *Justice and Judgment among the Tiv,* Oxford University Press, London, 1957; Max Gluckman, *The Judicial Process among the Barotse of Northern Rhodesia,* Manchester University Press, 1954; P. P. Howell, *A Handbook of Nuer Law,* Oxford University Press, London, 1954.
3. Cf. George P. Murdock, *Social Structure,* Macmillan, New York, 1949, p. 74.
4. James L. Gibbs, Jr., "Poro Values and Courtroom Procedures in a Kpelle Chiefdom," *Southwestern Journal of Anthropology* (in press) [1963, 18:341–350]. A detailed analysis of Kpelle courtroom procedures and of procedures in the moot together with transcripts appears in: James L. Gibbs, Jr., *Some Judicial Implications of Marital Instability among the Kpelle* (unpublished Ph.D. Dissertation, Harvard University, Cambridge, Mass., 1960).
5. What follows is based on a detailed case study of moots in Panta Chiefdom and their contrast with courtroom hearings before the paramount chief of that chiefdom. Moots, being private, are less susceptible to the surveillance of the anthropologist than courtroom hearings; thus I have fewer transcripts of moots than of court cases. The analysis presented here is valid for Panta Chiefdom and also valid, I feel, for most of the Liberian Kpelle area, particularly the north-east where people are, by and large, traditional.
6. This simple distilled rum, bottled in Monrovia and retailing for twenty-five cents a bottle in 1958, is known in the Liberian Hinterland as "cane juice" and should not be confused with imported varieties.
7. American currency is the official currency of Liberia and is used throughout the country.
8. Cf. J. F. Holleman, "An Anthropological Approach to Bantu Law (with special reference to Shona law)" in the *Journal of the Rhodes-Livingstone Institute,* vol. x, 1950, pp. 27–41. Holleman feels that the use of tokens for effecting apologies—or marriages—shows the proclivity for reducing events of importance to something tangible.
9. Talcott Parsons, *The Social System,* The Free Press, Glencoe, Ill., 1951, pp. 314–319.
10. Jerome D. Frank, "Group Methods in Psychotherapy," in *Mental Health and Mental Disorder: A Sociological Approach,* edited by Arnold Rose, W. W. Norton Co., New York, pp. 524–535.
11. J. W. Klapman, *Group Psychotherapy: Theory and Practice,* Grune & Stratton, New York, 1959.
12. Marvin K. Opler, "Values in Group Psychotherapy," *International Journal of Social Psychiatry,* vol. iv, 1959, pp. 296–298.
13. Frank, op. cit., p. 531.
14. Ibid.
15. Ibid.
16. Klapman, op. cit., p. 39.
17. Ibid., p. 15.
18. For expository purposes the four elements of therapy are described as if they always occur serially. They may, and do, occur simultaneously also. Thus, all four of the factors may be implicit in a single short behavioural sequence. Parsons (op. cit.) holds that these four elements

are common not only to psychotherapy but to all measures of social control.

19. Parsons, op. cit., p. 314. Cf. loc. cit., chap. 10.
20. Cf. Parsons, op. cit., chap. 7. Parsons notes that in any social-control action the aim is to avoid the process of alienation, that "vicious-cycle" phenomenon whereby each step taken to curb the non-conforming activity of the deviant has the effect of driving him further into his pattern of deviance. Rather, the need is to "reach" the deviant and bring him back to the point where he is susceptible to the usual everyday informal sanctions.
21. J. H. M. Beattie, "Informal Judicial Activity in Bunyoro," *Journal of African Administration,* vol. ix, 1957, pp. 188–195.
22. Disputes include matters such as a son seducing his father's wives, a grown son disobeying his father, or a husband or wife failing in his or her duties to a spouse. Disputes between unrelated persons involve matters like quarrelling, abuse, assault, false accusations, petty theft, adultery, and failure to settle debts. (Ibid., p. 190.)
23. Ibid., p. 194.
24. Beattie, op. cit., p. 194.
25. Ibid., p. 193.
26. Ibid., p. 195. Moreover, Beattie also recognizes the functional significance of the Nyoro moots, for he notes that: "It would be a serious error to represent them simply as clumsy, 'amateur' expedients for punishing wrong-doers or settling civil disputes at an informal, sub-official level." (Ibid.)
27. The type of examination of case materials that is required demands that fieldworkers should not simply record cases that meet the "trouble case" criterion (cf. K. N. Llewellyn and E. A. Hoebel, *The Cheyenne Way,* Norman, Okla., University of Oklahoma Press, 1941; and E. A. Hoebel, *The Law of Primitive Man,* Cambridge, Mass., Harvard University Press, 1954), but that cases should be recorded in some transcript-like form.
28. The present study has attempted to add to our understanding of informal dispute-settlement procedures in one African society by using an eclectic but organized collection of concepts from jurisprudence, ethno-law, and psychology. It is based on the detailed and systematic analysis of a few selected cases, rather than a mass of quantitative data. In further research a greater variety of cases handled by Kpelle moots should be subjected to the same analysis to test its merit more fully.

# 47

# Army Enlists Anthropology in War Zones

*David Rohde*

In 2007 the U.S. military launched a $41 million project called the Human Terrain System. In hopes of helping U.S. soldiers better understand the cultural landscape in Iraq and Afghanistan, this project places anthropologists in combat zones to advise and help develop counterinsurgency operations.

Each Human Terrain System team consists of a team leader, an area specialist, a social scientist, and a research manager. The only civilian member of the team is the social scientist, typically an anthropologist with specialized knowledge on the region and its people. The team conducts original ground-level research and consults existing documents before presenting their conclusions and counsel to military commanders.

The use of anthropology in war zones is not a novel idea; it has created controversy in previous conflicts including World War II and the Vietnam War. In 1964, for example, a U.S. military project named CAMELOT was ostensibly organized to apply social science research to better understand the conditions which lead to military conflict; critics, however, believed that the military would use the project to destroy populist movements in Latin America, Asia, and elsewhere.

Today, anthropologists from the American Anthropological Association debate the ethics of civilian anthropology in Afghanistan and Iraq. Opponents of the Human Terrain System project argue that collaboration with combat operations violates the association's Code of Ethics which mandates that anthropologists do no harm to the subjects of their research. Advocates, on the other hand, counter that if anthropology can reduce combat casualties and assist civilian victims caught up in the destruction of war, anthropologists should apply their methods and training to reduce human suffering if they can. In this selection, David Rohde portrays both sides of this heated debate.

***As you read this selection, ask yourself the following questions:***

- What is mercenary anthropology?
- Why do many anthropologists object to using anthropologists in military operations?
- Why do military officials collaborate with anthropologists in combat operations and war zones?
- Is it ethical for professional anthropologists to work in combat operations?

***The following terms discussed in this selection are included in the Glossary at the back of the book:***

*Human Terrain Team* | *mercenary*
*jirga* | *Operation Khyber*

## SHABAK VALLEY, AFGHANISTAN

In this isolated Taliban stronghold in eastern Afghanistan, American paratroopers are fielding what they consider a crucial new weapon in counterinsurgency operations here: a soft-spoken civilian anthropologist named Tracy.

Tracy, who asked that her surname not be used for security reasons, is a member of the first Human Terrain Team, an experimental Pentagon program that assigns anthropologists and other social scientists to American combat units in Afghanistan and Iraq. Her team's ability to understand subtle points of tribal relations—in one case spotting a land dispute that allowed the Taliban to bully parts of a major tribe—has won the praise of officers who say they are seeing concrete results.

Col. Martin Schweitzer, commander of the 82nd Airborne Division unit working with the anthropologists here, said that the unit's combat operations had been reduced by 60 percent since the scientists arrived

Rohde, David. "Army Enlists Anthropology in War Zones." From *The New York Times*, October 5, 2007. 

in February, and that the soldiers were now able to focus more on improving security, health care and education for the population.

"We're looking at this from a human perspective, from a social scientist's perspective," he said. "We're not focused on the enemy. We're focused on bringing governance down to the people."

In September, Defense Secretary Robert M. Gates authorized a $40 million expansion of the program, which will assign teams of anthropologists and social scientists to each of the 26 American combat brigades in Iraq and Afghanistan. Since early September, five new teams have been deployed in the Baghdad area, bringing the total to six.

Yet criticism is emerging in academia. Citing the past misuse of social sciences in counterinsurgency campaigns, including in Vietnam and Latin America, some denounce the program as "mercenary anthropology" that exploits social science for political gain. Opponents fear that, whatever their intention, the scholars who work with the military could inadvertently cause all anthropologists to be viewed as intelligence gatherers for the American military.

Hugh Gusterson, an anthropology professor at George Mason University, and 10 other anthropologists are circulating an online pledge calling for anthropologists to boycott the teams, particularly in Iraq.

"While often presented by its proponents as work that builds a more secure world," the pledge says, "at base, it contributes instead to a brutal war of occupation which has entailed massive casualties."

In Afghanistan, the anthropologists arrived along with 6,000 troops, which doubled the American military's strength in the area it patrols, the country's east.

A smaller version of the Bush administration's troop increase in Iraq, the buildup in Afghanistan has allowed American units to carry out the counterinsurgency strategy here, where American forces generally face less resistance and are better able to take risks.

## A NEW MANTRA

Since Gen. David H. Petraeus, now the overall American commander in Iraq, oversaw the drafting of the Army's new counterinsurgency manual last year, the strategy has become the new mantra of the military. A recent American military operation here offered a window into how efforts to apply the new approach are playing out on the ground in counterintuitive ways.

In interviews, American officers lavishly praised the anthropology program, saying that the scientists' advice has proved to be "brilliant," helping them see the situation from an Afghan perspective and allowing them to cut back on combat operations.

The aim, they say, is to improve the performance of local government officials, persuade tribesmen to join the police, ease poverty and protect villagers from the Taliban and criminals.

Afghans and Western civilian officials, too, praised the anthropologists and the new American military approach but were cautious about predicting long-term success. Many of the economic and political problems fueling instability can be solved only by large numbers of Afghan and American civilian experts.

"My feeling is that the military are going through an enormous change right now where they recognize they won't succeed militarily," said Tom Gregg, the chief United Nations official in southeastern Afghanistan. "But they don't yet have the skill sets to implement" a coherent nonmilitary strategy, he added.

Deploying small groups of soldiers into remote areas, Colonel Schweitzer's paratroopers organized jirgas, or local councils, to resolve tribal disputes that have simmered for decades. Officers shrugged off questions about whether the military was comfortable with what David Kilcullen, an Australian anthropologist and an architect of the new strategy, calls "armed social work."

"Who else is going to do it?" asked Lt. Col. David Woods, commander of the Fourth Squadron, 73rd Cavalry. "You have to evolve. Otherwise you're useless."

The anthropology team here also played a major role in what the military called Operation Khyber. That was a 15-day drive late this summer in which 500 Afghan and 500 American soldiers tried to clear an estimated 200 to 250 Taliban insurgents out of much of Paktia Province, secure southeastern Afghanistan's most important road and halt a string of suicide attacks on American troops and local governors.

In one of the first districts the team entered, Tracy identified an unusually high concentration of widows in one village, Colonel Woods said. Their lack of income created financial pressure on their sons to provide for their families, she determined, a burden that could drive the young men to join well-paid insurgents. Citing Tracy's advice, American officers developed a job training program for the widows.

In another district, the anthropologist interpreted the beheading of a local tribal elder as more than a random act of intimidation: the Taliban's goal, she said, was to divide and weaken the Zadran, one of southeastern Afghanistan's most powerful tribes. If Afghan and American officials could unite the Zadran, she said, the tribe could block the Taliban from operating in the area.

"Call it what you want, it works," said Colonel Woods, a native of Denbo, Pa. "It works in helping you define the problems, not just the symptoms."

## EMBEDDING SCHOLARS

The process that led to the creation of the teams began in late 2003, when American officers in Iraq complained that they had little to no information about the local population. Pentagon officials contacted Montgomery McFate, a Yale-educated cultural anthropologist working for the Navy who advocated using social science to improve military operations and strategy.

Ms. McFate helped develop a database in 2005 that provided officers with detailed information on the local population. The next year, Steve Fondacaro, a retired Special Operations colonel, joined the program and advocated embedding social scientists with American combat units.

Ms. McFate, the program's senior social science adviser and an author of the new counterinsurgency manual, dismissed criticism of scholars working with the military. "I'm frequently accused of militarizing anthropology," she said. "But we're really anthropologizing the military."

Roberto J. González, an anthropology professor at San Jose State University, called participants in the program naïve and unethical. He said that the military and the Central Intelligence Agency had consistently misused anthropology in counterinsurgency and propaganda campaigns and that military contractors were now hiring anthropologists for their local expertise as well.

"Those serving the short-term interests of military and intelligence agencies and contractors," he wrote in the June issue of *Anthropology Today*, an academic journal, "will end up harming the entire discipline in the long run."

Arguing that her critics misunderstand the program and the military, Ms. McFate said other anthropologists were joining the teams. She said their goal was to help the military decrease conflict instead of provoking it, and she vehemently denied that the anthropologists collected intelligence for the military.

In eastern Afghanistan, Tracy wanted to reduce the use of heavy-handed military operations focused solely on killing insurgents, which she said alienated the population and created more insurgents. "I can go back and enhance the military's understanding," she said, "so that we don't make the same mistakes we did in Iraq."

Along with offering advice to commanders, she said, the five-member team creates a database of local leaders and tribes, as well as social problems, economic issues, and political disputes.

## CLINICS AND MEDIATION

During the recent operation, as soldiers watched for suicide bombers, Tracy and Army medics held a free medical clinic. They said they hoped that providing medical care would show villagers that the Afghan government was improving their lives.

Civil affairs soldiers then tried to mediate between factions of the Zadran tribe about where to build a school. The Americans said they hoped that the school, which would serve children from both groups, might end a 70-year dispute between the groups over control of a mountain covered with lucrative timber.

Though they praised the new program, Afghan and Western officials said it remained to be seen whether the weak Afghan government could maintain the gains. "That's going to be the challenge, to fill the vacuum," said Mr. Gregg, the United Nations official. "There's a question mark over whether the government has the ability to take advantage of the gains."

Others also question whether the overstretched American military and its NATO allies can keep up the pace of operations.

American officers expressed optimism. Many of those who had served in both Afghanistan and Iraq said they had more hope for Afghanistan. One officer said that the Iraqis had the tools to stabilize their country, like a potentially strong economy, but that they lacked the will. He said Afghans had the will, but lacked the tools.

After six years of American promises, Afghans, too, appear to be waiting to see whether the Americans or the Taliban will win a protracted test of wills here. They said this summer was just one chapter in a potentially lengthy struggle.

At a "super jirga" set up by Afghan and American commanders here, a member of the Afghan Parliament, Nader Khan Katawazai, laid out the challenge ahead to dozens of tribal elders.

"Operation Khyber was just for a few days," he said. "The Taliban will emerge again."

# 48

# Moral Fibers of Farmer Cooperatives

## *Creating Poverty and Wealth with Cotton in Southern Mali*

*Scott M. Lacy*

When the imminent threat of Civil War in the United States threatened to disrupt cotton exports to textile mills in France, French entrepreneurs and government officials sought alternative cotton sources in their African territories and colonies. Counter to the ambitions of the French, cotton production in African territories like the French Soudan was geared toward local consumption not export. To feed the demand of domestic textile mills, the French coerced West African farmers to increase cotton production through taxation and technological inputs. The intensification of cotton production established a cash crop, which to this day, serves as a foundation of the economy of West African nations like Mali and Burkina Faso.

Development officials promote cotton production as a means to combat endemic poverty in rural Malian communities, but cotton farming can create poverty as well. When world cotton prices are high, cotton-producing countries like Mali may reap financial benefits, but when prices fall, small-scale cotton farmers pay the price. Mali ranks as one of the poorest countries in the world, and historically low cotton prices make this country's strength its weakness. In this selection, Scott Lacy examines some of the ways Malian officials have tried to assist family farmers. For decades, communities in Mali organized cotton production through farmer collectives, one per village, but starting in 2003 the government gave farmers a new option allowing the formation of smaller sub-village collectives. The freedom to choose the membership and size of one's local cotton grower association may lift some producers out of poverty, but this freedom may further complicate the economic and social viability of other producers and communities in crisis.

***As you read this selection, ask yourself the following questions:***

- What is the difference between cotton produced in the United States and cotton produced in Mali?
- How did colonization transform cotton production in rural Malian communities?
- How do decentralized farmer collectives (CPCs) help some farmers but harm others?
- What is the difference between the memberships of Dissan's two cotton collectives (CPCs)?
- How do fluctuations in global cotton prices impact the lives of small-scale family farmers in rural Mali?

***The following terms discussed in this selection are included in the Glossary at the back of the book:***

*brain drain* | *cooperative*
*cash crop* | *subsidy*

For several centuries, cotton has been a critical component of the agricultural economy of Mali, West Africa. In fact, presidents, economists, and contemporary development officials have long promoted this cash crop as "white gold" with the potential to lift Mali from its status as one of the poorest countries in the world. After all, Malian farmers grow some of the world's highest quality cotton, and at a fraction of the cost of international competitors; U.S. cotton growers, for example, produce lower-grade cotton and they spend nearly three times as much to produce each harvested kilo. To capitalize on this rare market advantage, in 2002 Malian officials modified national policies

This article was written especially for *Applying Anthropology: An Introductory Reader*, 9th ed.

governing rural cotton production based on the idea that decentralizing local farm collectives would encourage farmers to bolster domestic harvests. Initially production statistics confirmed this theory, but the positive effects were short-lived. In the following pages, I describe how farmers from a village in southern Mali adapted to the decentralization of community cotton collectives, and I explore the roles of cotton and cash cropping in rural subsistence economies.

## METHODS

This chapter is based on a long-term study in southern Mali starting with fifteen-months of fieldwork in 2001/2 and annual follow-up studies from 2004–2008. While living and working with family farmers in the village of Dissan (11°36N, 7°31W, 344 masl), I conducted two extensive surveys in 2001/2 to learn about household agricultural production, including farmer practices and knowledge of local crops and growing environments, household economies, and community-based farm collectives. In 2001 I surveyed all sixty-six Dissan households and conducted a comprehensive census of the community to acquire baseline data on household farm production and resources. Before the planting season, in March and April 2002, I interviewed a stratified sample of Dissan households ($n$ = 20) to further investigate farmer knowledge and production practices. After completing these first two surveys, I spent a full growing season apprenticing with four households to actively learn about the resources and annual production cycle of Dissan farmers. Since 2004 I have returned to Dissan to conduct annual follow-up studies focused on crop choices, seed systems, and household farm production. Qualitative data used in this chapter come from ethnographic field notes, individual interviews, and a series of informal group interviews recorded between 2001 and 2008.

## STUDY COMMUNITY

I was introduced to Dissan when I arrived there in 1994 as a Peace Corps volunteer. Dissan is a rural farming community that traces its origins back to the seventeenth century (Lacy 2004:83–85). In December 2001 there were 881 people living in sixty-six households in Dissan. The household (*du*, in Bamanakan) is an extended family that lives, eats, and works together using common resources. Depending on its size, a household either shares a single compound or a conglomeration of adjacent compounds composed of shaded sitting areas, sleeping quarters, cooking huts, and various storage constructions. According to my 2001 census, the mean number of people per household was thirteen (SD = 8.9). Bamanakan is the primary language spoken in Dissan, however, some community members speak other languages including Arabic, French, Fulani, and Wolof.

Though Dissan is in a relatively wet region of Mali sometimes referred to as the cotton zone, even in good years when many households harvest enough grain to last the year, other households suffer food shortages. Annual rainfall throughout Mali is low and extremely variable, making rain-fed agricultural production a complex and risky enterprise. Nonetheless, every family in Dissan depends on rain-fed agriculture for subsistence, including the teachers of the village primary school who farm to supplement their salaries.

In 2007/8, Dissan households used handheld hoes, collective labor, and animal-traction plows to cultivate a combined total of 282 hectares of field crops (not including secondary plots of peanuts and rice), including 21.5 hectares of cotton and 161 hectares of sorghum (Table 1). Farmers typically produce sorghum for household consumption and grow cotton as a cash crop or as a means for procuring agricultural inputs and short-term credit (or both). Data from the 2001 survey show that households who acquire credit and inputs through cotton production are the households that plant the most sorghum; they also are more likely to have expensive farm equipment like cultivators, seeders, plows, donkey carts, and sprayers for applying chemical pesticides and herbicides (Table 2). Despite the fact that cotton opens farmer access to

**TABLE 1 Dissan agricultural production, 2002 vs. 2007**

| | | 2002/3 | 2007/8 |
|---|---|---|---|
| Total hectares planted: | | | |
| | Sorghum | 155 | 161 |
| | Millet | 20.5 | 57 |
| | Maize | 89.4 | 42.5 |
| | Cotton | 31 | 21.5 |
| Number of HHs growing: | | | |
| | Sorghum | 58 | 57 |
| | Millet | 14 | 30 |
| | Maize | 54 | 34 |
| | Cotton | 37 | 15 |

**TABLE 2 Sorghum cultivation and ownership of farm equipment by household, Dissan, 2001**

| | Mean sorghum hectares/HH | Percentages of households owning: | | | | |
|---|---|---|---|---|---|---|
| | | Plow | Cultivator | Seeder | Donkey cart | Spray pump |
| Cotton credit HHs, n = 41 | 2.8 | 88 | 71 | 46 | 61 | 49 |
| Other HHs, n = 25 | 1.7 | 36 | 12 | 4 | 8 | 0 |

small loans and agricultural inputs, cotton production has declined sharply since 2001. In the 2007–8 growing season, only 15 Dissan households grew cotton, in contrast to the 37 households who grew this cash crop in 2002/3.

## HISTORICAL OVERVIEW OF COTTON PRODUCTION IN RURAL MALI

Before the French-led intensification of cotton production in colonial West Africa, family farmers in southern Mali grew regional varieties of cotton for a strong domestic market and for self-sufficient household consumption (clothing, blankets, fishing nets, string, etc.). Starting in the 1890s, commercial and colonial interests worked for decades shaping Malian cotton production in an attempt to capture cotton harvests for French textile mills. By 1950 the colonial state was spending approximately 70 percent of its resources on the intensification of cotton production, targeting southern Mali through the introduction of new varieties, agricultural extension, price subventions, and support for rural investment in machinery and fertilizer (Roberts 1996:280). Prior to the introduction of incentives like agricultural extension and credit for purchasing plows and agrochemicals, family farmers in Mali resisted expanding household production beyond local needs.

Dissan elders explained that cotton cash cropping came with plows; widespread extrahousehold cotton production and farmer credits followed the installation of a regional cotton processing facility in the 1960s. Local farmers first acquired plows in the 1960s from the Compagnie Malienne pour le Développement des Fibres Textiles (CMDT), a state agency created by the government of Mali's first president, Modibo Keïta. In the 1970s the CMDT worked with villages to organize cotton producer collectives and began transferring to these village associations production responsibilities such as ordering and distributing inputs, and managing credits and payments (Bingen, Serrano, and Howard 2003:410–411). The efficacy of the village association strategy developed by the CMDT in the 1970s eventually transformed this once regional program into a national one. Today the CMDT remains the primary agency for agricultural extension services and credit in many southern Malian communities.

### CMDT and Collective Cotton Production in Dissan, 1974–2002

In 1974 the CMDT started the process of transferring to villages responsibility for cotton grading, weighing, orders for equipment and inputs, and credit management (Bingen 2000:357). At first, the CMDT appointed existing village social organizations as the body responsible for such tasks, but by the late 1970s it had established an AV ("Village Association") system for southern Mali managed by community officers, including president, treasurer, and secretary. With World Bank financing, the CMDT organized literacy and numeracy programs in Bamanakan to teach farmers skills for effectively managing village cotton production. The AV program proved to be so efficient by CMDT standards that it eventually became national policy.

As the AV system took hold in southern Mali, many Dissan farmers began acquiring more household money through cotton production. The AV merged all Dissan farmers into a single cooperative for organizing local production, spreading individual responsibility and risk among all village cotton farmers. From the CMDT perspective, this system consolidated fiscal accounting and responsibility into manageable units; every year, after receiving one lump sum for the entire village's cotton harvest, the AV distributed crop payments to individual members. When poor harvests or household crop failures led any number of producers to default on their individual loans, the AV absorbed those debts. In 2001, for example, two Dissan households defaulted on their loans and although both households repaid over half their debts, an outstanding balance of roughly US $300 remained. Although $300 accounts for only 2.5 percent of all Dissan loans in

2001, it is substantial debt for a rural farming family in a country like Mali where annual per capita income was a mere $239 for that same year (World Bank 2003). Furthermore, these economic indicators fail to capture the social discord or peripheral economic hardships endured by individuals and communities as a result of loan defaults.

Once established, the AV system provided farmer access to credit, it established de facto community security nets for cotton farmers and gave rural populations a formidable voice in regional and national agricultural policy. Siaka Sangare, long-standing secretary of Dissan's AV, explained that in 1989, when the CMDT attempted to restructure the AV credit system, producers across the country, including Dissan, used their AVs to organize a cotton strike. Through AV leaders, the CMDT brokered a deal that was acceptable to farmers, and the strike was averted (USAID-Mali 2003). However, in 2000 many Dissan farmers joined a national cotton strike in protest of unpaid harvests and low purchase prices. The CMDT typically set purchase prices after the planting season for cotton, forcing farmers to purchase inputs on credit and organize production without any certainty of returns on their investments. Largely due to a saturated global market, not to mention enormous U.S. subsidies for industrial U.S. cotton producers, international prices for cotton fell significantly in 1998 and 1999. Falling prices translated into significant operating deficits for the CMDT, which meant farmers in Dissan and elsewhere had to bear the brunt of these economic losses. In 1998 the CMDT purchase price for cotton was 185 CFA francs (FCFA) per kilogram, and the price dropped to FCFA 150 in 1999 (USAID-Mali 2003). Secretary Sangare noted that unexpectedly lower prices in 1999 put some Dissan farmers in debt, leading many to abandon the crop the following year. However, in 2001, when the CMDT guaranteed a good purchase price before planting (FCFA 200/kg), many farmers returned to cotton production. The national cotton strike certainly influenced the favorable price of cotton in 2001, but rippling effects of the strike extended further; in late 2002 the CMDT announced the AV system would undergo major organizational changes.

### The Meeting

In November 2002, shortly after most households had harvested their cotton, the CMDT extension agent who works in Dissan, visited the AV to call an important meeting. The extension agent is an agricultural engineer trained in Katiabougou, Mali, and at the University of Dijon in France. The meeting was one of thousands throughout Mali, organized to familiarize farmers with fundamental changes to the organizational structure of cotton collectives in Mali (Diallo 2004). Though renamed, the AV could still serve as a villagewide cooperative, but under the new system, the AV could be composed of any number of independently organized, subvillage collectives. Using diagrams on the chalkboard of a dilapidated one-room schoolhouse, the extension agent explained in Bamanakan how the new system would empower farmers.

With children peeking in windows and with the sounds of chickens and donkeys in the background, the extension agent sat at a table in front of thirty-five farmers seated on weathered desktops. The CMDT representative began with an announcement: after the 2002 harvest, the CMDT would encourage Malian cotton farmers to establish new collectives that permit members to associate themselves at the subvillage level. According to the agent, villagewide associations reduce incentives for skilled, large-scale producers, because these producers bear financial liability for the catastrophic crop losses and irresponsible credit management of other farmers. The agent occasionally looked down at his notes as he discussed the regulations for forming the new cotton collectives. Farmers listened patiently, a few with modest disinterest, as the agent described eight new rules.

- Each group will be called a CPC (*coopératif pour les producteurs cotonnière*).
- Each CPC must have at least five producers and/or a minimum of ten separate cotton fields.
- Each CPC must produce an annual minimum of 30 metric tons of cotton (slightly less than half of Dissan's combined total of 70.7 metric tons produced in 2002).
- CPC members must be from the same village (associations with people from multiple villages are prohibited).
- Every CPC member must have a certificate of residency (obtainable for a small fee from a regional administrator).
- Each member must sign an official document containing CPC bylaws, organizational structure, and a description of responsibilities for each CPC officer. The document, written in Bamanakan, is made official with the approval

and signature of all CPC members and a CMDT officer.

- Each CPC operates for three years, after which it must be renewed as is, modified and renewed, or disbanded.
- All Dissan CPCs collectively constitute the Union des Coopératifs de Dissan.

The extension agent reinforced several CPC policies before taking questions from farmers. First, he explained some of the benefits of the new CPC system. For example, if someone in a CPC turns out to be a poor associate or a bad worker, at the end of the three-year term of the CPC, members can vote to expel the underperforming associate. Meanwhile, CPC members must pay the debts of fellow members in default, but as CPC members they would have recourse. If necessary a CPC can take legal action against members in default using a CMDT legal service available to all CPC members. Some farmers raised their eyebrows when the agent described how the CPC system deals with chronic debtors and rule breakers: in the worse cases, a judge will dispatch gendarmes to claim payment or in-kind restitution. The agent also said that the CPC system will equate to money for community improvements and projects. Under the former system the AV received from the CMDT a sum equal to 2 percent of the gross price of all Dissan cotton delivered to the CMDT scales. These funds were used according to AV bylaws for: operational costs (20 percent), officer stipends (30 percent), and community development projects (50 percent). The extension agent explained that under the CPC system, defaulted loans would no longer drain funds earmarked for community service.

Throughout the meeting, the CMDT representative focused on a central theme, the power of a strong collective voice. Farmers in attendance nodded their heads as the agent recalled how AVs unified farmers during the cotton strike of 2000. Using an intricate diagram of circles within circles, the extension agent demonstrated that the work and efforts of each CPC will have a single, strong voice, while the village collective—the Union des Cooperatives de Dissan—will have an even stronger voice to represent all Dissan CPCs. Although this well-worn selling point may sound trite, there is no doubt that AVs helped farmers organize and amplify their voices en masse in 1989 and 2000 when they successfully convinced CMDT authorities to address farmer concerns regarding AV policy and cotton prices (Lacy 2004:107–108).

From my perspective as an observer, perhaps the most salient yet understated point raised by the extension agent during the meeting was that farmers could use the management skills they develop as members of CPCs to form cooperatives for other crops or animal husbandry. As the meeting drew to a close, some of the biggest cotton producers in Dissan voiced skeptical interest and tacit approval for the new system, but a few producers—one of whom with considerable, old cotton debts—expressed concern about the potential difficulties they may face if they hope to join a CPC to obtain credit.

### Farmer Perspectives of the CPC System

The freedom to choose the membership and size of one's local cotton grower association may help some producers prevent monetary losses stemming from the crop failures of other village producers, but this freedom may further complicate the economic and social viability of producers and communities in crisis. Following the meeting I asked several farmers to describe their reactions to the new CPC program. Although most farmers voiced cautious or little interest in the new CPCs, two of them held starkly opposite opinions. The first farmer, an elder named Sidike Sangare said he was suspicious of the new system. During the meeting Sangare remarked that farmers who default on loans eventually pay their debts, and should not be expelled from a group, chased by gendarmes, nor excluded from cotton production, particularly when their households may be in crisis. Under the CPC system the de facto safety net provided by the AV would be transformed into several smaller nets, spreading larger risks among smaller groups of producers. After the meeting Sangare predicted he would not grow cotton the following year. True to his word, elder Sangare abandoned cotton production and focused on grain for future harvests; he eventually repaid his cotton debts, but he passed away a few years later.

On the other side of the spectrum, AV officer Burama Tarawele expressed great optimism about the CPC system. Tarawele was visiting Dissan from Bougoumbala, a neighboring village, and was present at the Dissan meeting. Immediately following the meeting Tarawele said he was pleased the CMDT was finally addressing the problem he termed, "the politics of CMDT." Echoing the extension agent's words, from Tarawele's point of view, the former AV system was counterproductive for large-scale cotton producers like him. Before the formal initiation of the CPC program in the region, Tarawele had already brokered a special arrangement to create a proto-CPC in his village; he and two other farmers decided to create a subvillage collective to independently procure credit and inputs through the CMDT. Though leaving their villagewide cotton association created some quarreling in the village, Tarawele believes people now understand why he and his two partners left the Bougoumbala AV (*decentralization* was the term Tarawele used). He said that the CMDT cooperated with this decentralization because he and his cohorts—all large-scale producers—threatened to abandon cotton. Tarawele said the CPC program will be good for Mali cotton farmers, but admitted that many farmers do not have the skills to apply for, acquire, and effectively manage independent loans. He acquired his banking and management skills in CMDT workshops and as the former secretary of his village AV. Tarawele's ultimate goal is to intensify his cotton production in order to invest in cattle and animal husbandry.

### Dissan Creates Two CPCs

Even though Dissan farmers were free to create their first CPCs in 2003, they chose to preserve their villagewide collective. For 2004, however, after several quarrels related to a confidential financial dispute, farmers made a decision that would not have been possible two years earlier. Because the new CPC system encouraged subvillage collectives, farmers resolved their dispute with the dissolution of the villagewide AV. Then the former AV leader formed a CPC with seven other households, while all other cotton-producing households banded together to form a second, much larger CPC. The larger of the two groups built a separate storage shed, and by the start of the 2004 growing season both CPCs were operational. Though factors like rainfall and pest control have plenty to do with successful cotton farming, they alone do not explain why aggregate Dissan cotton harvests almost doubled in one year under the stewardship of two independent subvillage collectives (Table 3). Following wildly successful harvests, Dissan farmers reported positive initial experiences with both CPCs, but the enthusiasm of the first two years of the new system has waned.

**TABLE 3 Aggregate Dissan cotton harvests recorded at CMDT facility, Bougouni, 2003–7**

| | Cotton collective system in use | Number of cotton households | Aggregate harvest (kg) | Households making $0 or debt from cotton harvest |
|---|---|---|---|---|
| 2001/2 | 1 AV | 41 | N/A | 4 (10%) |
| 2002/3 | 1 AV | 50 | 70,740 | N/A |
| 2003/4 | 1 AV | 23 | 39,750 | 2 (9%) |
| 2004/5 | 2 CPCs | 47 | 98,521 | 3 (6%) |
| 2005/6 | 2 CPCs | 38 | 86,989 | 2 (5%) |
| 2006/7 | 2 CPCs | 26 | 58,987 | 6 (23%) |
| 2007/8 | 2 CPCs | 15 | 14,285 | 9 (60%) |

The financial dispute that split Dissan's villagewide collective may have inspired a short-lived competition between the two CPCs which emerged from the conflict. This competition may have bolstered local harvests temporarily, but Dissan cotton production has since declined as most small-scale producers have adopted alternative cash crops such as cereals, peanut, and sesame. Per CPC rules, Dissan cotton growers re-established their CPCs in 2007/8, but many producers chose to abandon cotton. In short, all eight of the former AV leader's CPC members renewed their cooperative and grew cotton, but the second CPC membership decreased from 37 households in 2004 to seven households in 2007. The divergent fates of the two Dissan CPCs are rooted in the unique memberships of both collectives. The former AV leader's CPC attracted large-scale producers with production goals similar to Burama Tarawele, but membership was not directly based on production levels; family alliances and social relationships also played a major role. A cursory look at some of the characteristics of the CPC households indicates that the bifurcation of Dissan's AV consolidated some of the village's more wealthy households, leaving the others to fend for themselves (Table 4). Likewise, in other villages across southern Mali, cotton cultivation has been shown to exacerbate economic disparity among households (Moseley 2005:46–49).

### Do Subvillage Collectives and Cotton Increase Poverty, Wealth . . . or Both?

Every year after the CMDT has collected cotton harvests from villages all across the region, farmers listen intently as radio stations announce final production totals for local villages. Cotton is undeniably a major focus of household agricultural production in southern Mali, and transforming the AV system with subvillage cooperatives (CPCs) affects different farmers in different ways. Depending on the resources, skills, and experience of individual producers, the CPC system equates to new opportunities for some farmers, and exclusion from cotton production and farmer credit for others.

In the short term, successful cotton farmers capable of acquiring and managing credit stand to gain more autonomy over production choices. Furthermore, provided they associate with other stable

**TABLE 4 Smaller CPC households versus all other households, Dissan, 2001**

| | Small CPC HHs | Other HHs |
|---|---|---|
| Number of: | | |
| Households | 8 | 58 |
| People per HH | 23 | 12 |
| Field hectares cultivated, 2001 | 10.3 | 5 |
| Percentage of households owning: | | |
| Plow | 100 | 65 |
| Cattle | 100 | 58 |
| Cultivator | 100 | 46 |
| Donkey cart | 100 | 42 |
| Seeder | 83 | 25 |

producers, these farmers may reduce the risk of losses from cotton profits due to crop failures or mismanagement by others. Farmers known to have defaulted on previous loans, whose households may be in crisis (labor shortage, debt, chronic crop loss), face potential difficulties if they seek CPC membership. Just as elder Sidike Sangare abandoned cotton farming because his old cotton debts made him an undesirable associate, Burama Tarawele formed his own CPC to avoid associating with unreliable or crisis-prone farmers. Cotton may not be an equally appealing nor accessible crop choice for farmers of different means.

Elder Sangare was not the only farmer to question whether cotton farming was a worthwhile endeavor. Even before the CMDT announced the changes for cotton collectives, Dissan farmers debated whether or not cotton was "worth it." The Dissan *ton* (a villagewide collective labor organization) decided in 2002 to grow peanuts instead of cotton to raise group funds. This decision was based on the idea that peanuts were a less risky crop and would not require nearly as much labor, in contrast with cotton. Equally important, peanut crops do not require major investment costs for fertilizer, herbicide, and insecticide.

As it evolves, the CPC system will generate new debates and questions about the social, ecological, and financial ramifications of household cotton production in southern Mali, but exactly how these subvillage collectives may or may not transform local production and socioeconomic dynamics has yet to be fully determined. In the long term, three critical issues will determine the success or failure of the CPC system: the exclusion principle, the efficacy of CPCs in expanding the idea and benefits of cooperatives beyond cotton fields, and the strengthening of individual and collective voices of cotton farmers. In southern Mali, responsibility for household cotton production typically excludes women and poorer households, who, as a result, have limited access to extension services and inputs (Moseley 2001:187).

On the one hand, CPCs may lead farmers to exclude crisis-prone producers like elder Sidike Sangare, but CPCs could have the potential to open new opportunities for formerly excluded farmers. Investing in human capacity in terms of ensuring farmers who want to create a cooperative have the financial and literacy skills necessary to protect their own interests could also, with no small effort, bring women and poorer farmers into their own credit-worthy collectives, particularly if the CPC cotton model is successful in encouraging the formation of new cooperatives for other crops and animal husbandry. After all, if literate farmers with proven track records and strong financial management skills (acquiring and managing credit) break off into subvillage collectives, as they have done in Dissan, they might be less able or less willing to assist those farmers with different skill sets and resources. This new, localized manifestation of brain drain and wealth consolidation has the potential to exacerbate social and financial inequality, rendering cotton as a crop for relatively wealthier households. In the recent past, producer organizations like cotton collectives have been shown to amplify the voices of farmers in southern Mali (Bingen, Serrano, and Howard 2003:407). In the end, what may determine the success or failure of the CPC program is whether or not it bolsters or diminishes the voices and opportunities of all farmers.

## REFERENCES

Bingen, James R. 2000. Prospects for Development and Democracy in West Africa: Agrarian Politics in Mali. In *Democracy and Development in Mali*, ed. James R. Bingen, David Robinson, and John M. Staatz, 349–368. East Lansing: Michigan State University Press.

Bingen, Jim, Alex Serrano, and Julie Howard. 2003. Linking Farmers to Markets: Different Approaches to Human Capital Development. *Food Policy* 28: 405–419.

Diallo, Madou. 2004. Situation scolaire: L'heure de vérité à Koulouba. *Le républicain*, December 8. http://www.planeteafrique.com/Web/LeDiplomate/Index.asp?affiche=newsdatabase_show.asp&cmd=articledetail&articleid=252.

Lacy, Scott M. 2004. One Finger Cannot Lift a Stone: Family Farmers and Sorghum Production in Southern Mali. PhD dissertation, University of California, Santa Barbara.

Moseley, William G. 2001. Sahelian 'White Gold' and Rural Poverty-Environment Interactions: The Political Ecology of Cotton Production, Environmental Change, and Household Food Economy in Mali. PhD dissertation, University of Georgia.

_____. 2005. Global Cotton and Local Environment Management: The Political Ecology of Rich and Poor Small-Hold Farmers in Southern Mali. *Geographic Journal* 171 (1): 36–55.

Roberts, Richard. 1996. *Two Worlds of Cotton: Colonialism and the Regional Economy in the French Soudan, 1800–1946.* Stanford, CA: Stanford University Press.

USAID-Mali. 2003. Production and Export Opportunities and Constraints for Coarse Grains. www.usaid.org.ml/mes_photos/production_and_e.

World Bank. 2003. World Development Indicators 2003. Washington, DC: World Bank. CD-ROM.

# 49

# Do Muslim Women Really Need Saving?

## *Anthropological Reflections on Cultural Relativism and Its Others*

*Lila Abu-Lughod*

Religious differences, including the moral and sociocultural assumptions subsumed by religion, are extremely important for understanding our globalizing world. After September 11, 2001, the United States went to war in Afghanistan to fight the Taliban, the ruling group in that country, who were believed to be harboring al Qaeda operatives. In addition to the search for Osama bin Laden, a major rationale for going to war was to "liberate" Afghani women from the Taliban. In U.S. political and media discourses, the *burqa*, a black head-to-toe cotton veil mandated by the Taliban for women in public places, became a symbol of women's oppression in Afghanistan.

Prior to invasion by the United States, Afghanistan had a difficult and war-torn history. For years the country was wracked with civil wars, which were made worse by the fact that the United States and the USSR armed rival Afghani factions as pawns in the cold war. (The Taliban became a powerful group during that period in part because of American financial support for the Islamic radicals.) When the Taliban took control of most of Afghanistan in the late 1990s, many Afghans were cautiously optimistic, hoping that the country might finally experience some peace after years of civil war.

In this selection, anthropologist Lila Abu-Lughod argues that the "liberation of women" rationale for going to war was ethnocentric, and that the focus on the *burqa* ignored issues that may be more important to Afghani women, such as living in an area free from war. Important historical and political connections were ignored by U.S. political leaders, she argues, in favor of the simplistic East–West dichotomy that was used to justify invasion. American cultural beliefs about the "other" can be exploited in attempts to sway public opinion.

Although it has largely fallen from the headlines, the United States has continued to maintain a significant military presence in Afghanistan. Poor security and lack of basic infrastructure have remained pressing problems in most of the country. A positive future for Afghani—women and men—is far from assured.

***As you read this selection, ask yourself the following questions:***

- What is "colonial feminism"? Why was it problematic?
- Why might some women choose to wear a veil?
- In this selection, Abu-Lughod asks, "Can we only free Afghan women to be like us, or might we have to recognize that even after 'liberation' from the Taliban, they might want different things than we would want for them? What do we do about that?" How would you answer this question?
- Why is it problematic to associate feminism with the West?
- How might Americans try to help Afghani women in ways that do not involve "saving" them?

***The following terms discussed in this selection are included in the Glossary at the back of the book:***

| | |
|---|---|
| *burqa* | *ethnocentrism* |
| *colonialism* | *Islam* |
| *cultural relativism* | *Muslim* |

What are the ethics of the current "War on Terrorism," a war that justifies itself by purporting to liberate, or save, Afghan women? Does anthropology have anything to offer in our search for a viable position to take regarding this rationale for war?

Abridged from Abu-Lughod, Lila. "Do Muslim Women Really Need Saving? Anthropological Reflections on Cultural Relativism and Its Others." Reproduced by permission of the American Anthropological Association from *American Anthropologist*, Volume 104, Issue 3, pp. 783–790, September 2002. Not for sale or further reproduction.

I want to point out the minefields—a metaphor that is sadly too apt for a country like Afghanistan, with the world's highest number of mines per capita—of this obsession with the plight of Muslim women. I hope to show some way through them using insights from anthropology, the discipline whose charge has been to understand and manage cultural difference.

The question is why knowing about the "culture" of the region, and particularly its religious beliefs and treatment of women, was more urgent than exploring the history of the development of repressive regimes in the region and the U.S. role in this history. Such cultural framing, it seemed to me, prevented the serious exploration of the roots and nature of human suffering in this part of the world. Instead of political and historical explanations, experts were being asked to give religio-cultural ones. Instead of questions that might lead to the exploration of global interconnections, we were offered ones that worked to artificially divide the world into separate spheres—recreating an imaginative geography of West versus East, us versus Muslims, cultures in which First Ladies give speeches versus others where women shuffle around silently in burqas.

Most pressing for me was why the Muslim woman in general, and the Afghan woman in particular, were so crucial to this cultural mode of explanation, which ignored the complex entanglements in which we are all implicated, in sometimes surprising alignments. Why were these female symbols being mobilized in this "War against Terrorism" in a way they were not in other conflicts? Laura Bush's radio address on November 17 reveals the political work such mobilization accomplishes. On the one hand, her address collapsed important distinctions that should have been maintained. There was a constant slippage between the Taliban and the terrorists, so that they became almost one word—a kind of hyphenated monster identity: the Taliban-and-the-terrorists. Then there was the blurring of the very separate causes in Afghanistan of women's continuing malnutrition, poverty, and ill health, and their more recent exclusion under the Taliban from employment, schooling, and the joys of wearing nail polish. On the other hand, her speech reinforced chasmic divides, primarily between the "civilized people throughout the world" whose hearts break for the women and children of Afghanistan and the Taliban-and-the-terrorists, the cultural monsters who want to, as she put it, "impose their world on the rest of us."

Most revealingly, the speech enlisted women to justify American bombing and intervention in Afghanistan and to make a case for the "War on Terrorism" of which it was allegedly a part. As Laura Bush said, "Because of our recent military gains in much of Afghanistan, women are no longer imprisoned in their homes. They can listen to music and teach their daughters without fear of punishment. . . . The fight against terrorism is also a fight for the rights and dignity of women" (U.S. Government 2002).

These words have haunting resonances for anyone who has studied colonial history. Many who have worked on British colonialism in South Asia have noted the use of the woman question in colonial policies where intervention into sati (the practice of widows immolating themselves on their husbands' funeral pyres), child marriage, and other practices was used to justify rule. As Gayatri Chakravorty Spivak (1988) has cynically put it: white men saving brown women from brown men. The historical record is full of similar cases, including in the Middle East. In turn-of-the century Egypt, what Leila Ahmed (1992) has called "colonial feminism" was hard at work. This was a selective concern about the plight of Egyptian women that focused on the veil as a sign of oppression but gave no support to women's education and was professed loudly by the same Englishman, Lord Cromer, who opposed women's suffrage back home.

Sociologist Marnia Lazreg (1994) has offered some vivid examples of how French colonialism enlisted women to its cause in Algeria. She describes skits at awards ceremonies at the Muslim Girls' School in Algiers in 1851 and 1852. In the first skit, written by "a French lady from Algiers," two Algerian Arab girls reminisced about their trip to France with words including the following:

> Oh! Protective France: Oh! Hospitable France! . . .
> Noble land, where I felt free
> Under Christian skies to pray to our God: . . .
> God bless you for the happiness you bring us!
> And you, adoptive mother, who taught us
> That we have a share of this world,
> We will cherish you forever! [Lazreg 1994: 68–69]

These girls are made to invoke the gift of a share of this world, a world where freedom reigns under Christian skies. This is not the world the Taliban-and-the-terrorists would "like to impose on the rest of us."

Just as I argued above that we need to be suspicious when neat cultural icons are plastered over messier historical and political narratives, so we need to be wary when Lord Cromer in British-ruled Egypt, French ladies in Algeria, and Laura Bush, all with military troops behind them, claim to be saving or liberating Muslim women.

## POLITICS OF THE VEIL

I want now to look more closely at those Afghan women Laura Bush claimed were "rejoicing" at their liberation by the Americans. This necessitates a discussion of the veil, or the burqa, because it is so central to contemporary concerns about Muslim women. This will set the stage for a discussion of how anthropologists, feminist anthropologists in particular, contend with the problem of difference in a global world. In the conclusion, I will return to the rhetoric of saving Muslim women and offer an alternative.

It is common popular knowledge that the ultimate sign of the oppression of Afghan women under the Taliban-and-the-terrorists is that they were forced to wear the burqa. Liberals sometimes confess their surprise that even though Afghanistan has been liberated from the Taliban, women do not seem to be throwing off their burqas. Someone who has worked in Muslim regions must ask why this is so surprising. Did we expect that once "free" from the Taliban they would go "back" to belly shirts and blue jeans, or dust off their Chanel suits? We need to be more sensible about the clothing of "women of cover," and so there is perhaps a need to make some basic points about veiling.

First, it should be recalled that the Taliban did not invent the burqa. It was the local form of covering that Pashtun women in one region wore when they went out. The Pashtun are one of several ethnic groups in Afghanistan and the burqa was one of many forms of covering in the subcontinent and Southwest Asia that has developed as a convention for symbolizing women's modesty or respectability. The burqa, like some other forms of "cover" has, in many settings, marked the symbolic separation of men's and women's spheres, as part of the general association of women with family and home, not with public space where strangers mingled.

Twenty years ago the anthropologist Hanna Papanek (1982), who worked in Pakistan, described the burqa as "portable seclusion." She noted that many saw it as a liberating invention because it enabled women to move out of segregated living spaces while still observing the basic moral requirements of separating and protecting women from unrelated men. Ever since I came across her phrase "portable seclusion," I have thought of these enveloping robes as "mobile homes." Everywhere, such veiling signifies belonging to a particular community and participating in a moral way of life in which families are paramount in the organization of communities and the home is associated with the sanctity of women.

The obvious question that follows is this: If this were the case, why would women suddenly become immodest? Why would they suddenly throw off the markers of their respectability, markers, whether burqas or other forms of cover, which were supposed to assure their protection in the public sphere from the harassment of strange men by symbolically signaling to all that they were still in the inviolable space of their homes, even though moving in the public realm? Especially when these are forms of dress that had become so conventional that most women gave little thought to their meaning.

To draw some analogies, none of them perfect, why are we surprised that Afghan women do not throw off their burqas when we know perfectly well that it would not be appropriate to wear shorts to the opera? At the time these discussions of Afghan women's burqas were raging, a friend of mine was chided by her husband for suggesting she wanted to wear a pantsuit to a fancy wedding: "You know you don't wear pants to a WASP wedding," he reminded her. New Yorkers know that the beautifully coiffed Hasidic women . . . are wearing wigs. This is because religious belief and community standards of propriety require the covering of the hair. They also alter boutique fashions to include high necks and long sleeves. As anthropologists know perfectly well, people wear the appropriate form of dress for their social communities and are guided by socially shared standards, religious beliefs, and moral ideals, unless they deliberately transgress to make a point or are unable to afford proper cover. If we think that U.S. women live in a world of choice regarding clothing, all we need to do is remind ourselves of the expression, "the tyranny of fashion."

What had happened in Afghanistan under the Taliban is that one regional style of covering or veiling, associated with a certain respectable but not elite class, was imposed on everyone as "religiously" appropriate, even though previously there had been many different styles, popular or traditional with different groups and classes—different ways to mark women's propriety, or, in more recent times, religious piety. Although I am not an expert on Afghanistan, I imagine that the majority of women left in Afghanistan by the time the Taliban took control were the rural or less educated, from nonelite families, since they were the only ones who could not emigrate to escape the hardship and violence that has marked Afghanistan's recent history. If liberated from the enforced wearing of burqas, most of these women would choose some other form of modest headcovering, like all those living nearby who were not under the Taliban—their rural Hindu counterparts in the North of India (who cover their heads and veil their faces from affines) or their Muslim sisters in Pakistan.

Even *the New York Times* carried an article about Afghan women refugees in Pakistan that attempted to educate readers about this local variety (Fremson 2001). The article describes and pictures everything from the now-iconic burqa with the embroidered eyeholes, which a Pashtun woman explains is the proper dress for her community, to large scarves they call chadors, to the new Islamic modest dress that wearers refer to as *hijab*. Those in the new Islamic dress are characteristically students heading for professional careers, especially in medicine, just like their counterparts from Egypt to Malaysia. One wearing the large scarf was a school principal; the other was a poor street vendor. The telling quote from the young street vendor is, "If I did [wear the burqa] the refugees would tease me because the burqa is for 'good women' who stay inside the home" (Fremson 2001:14). Here you can see the local status associated with the burqa—it is for good respectable women from strong families who are not forced to make a living selling on the street.

The British newspaper *The Guardian* published an interview in January 2002 with Dr. Suheila Siddiqi, a respected surgeon in Afghanistan who holds the rank of lieutenant general in the Afghan medical corps (Goldenberg 2002). A woman in her sixties, she comes from an elite family and, like her sisters, was educated. Unlike most women of her class, she chose not to go into exile. She is presented in the article as "the woman who stood up to the Taliban" because she refused to wear the burqa. She had made it a condition of returning to her post as head of a major hospital when the Taliban came begging in 1996, just eight months after firing her along with other women. Siddiqi is described as thin, glamorous, and confident. But further into the article it is noted that her graying bouffant hair is covered in a gauzy veil. This is a reminder that though she refused the burqa, she had no question about wearing the chador or scarf.

Finally, I need to make a crucial point about veiling. Not only are there many forms of covering, which themselves have different meanings in the communities in which they are used, but also veiling itself must not be confused with, or made to stand for, lack of agency. As I have argued in my ethnography of a Bedouin community in Egypt in the late 1970s and 1980s (1986), pulling the black head cloth over the face in front of older respected men is considered a voluntary act by women who are deeply committed to being moral and have a sense of honor tied to family. One of the ways they show their standing is by covering their faces in certain contexts. They decide for whom they feel it is appropriate to veil.

To take a very different case, the modern Islamic modest dress that many educated women across the Muslim world have taken on since the mid-1970s now both publicly marks piety and can be read as a sign of educated urban sophistication, a sort of modernity (e.g., Abu-Lughod 1995, 1998; Brenner 1996; El Guindi 1999; MacLeod 1991; Ong 1990). As Saba Mahmood (2001) has so brilliantly shown in her ethnography of women in the mosque movement in Egypt, this new form of dress is also perceived by many of the women who adopt it as part of a bodily means to cultivate virtue, the outcome of their professed desire to be close to God.

Two points emerge from this fairly basic discussion of the meanings of veiling in the contemporary Muslim world. First, we need to work against the reductive interpretation of veiling as the quintessential sign of women's unfreedom, even if we object to state imposition of this form, as in Iran or with the Taliban. (It must be recalled that the modernizing states of Turkey and Iran had earlier in the century banned veiling and required men, except religious clerics, to adopt Western dress.) What does freedom mean if we accept the fundamental premise that humans are social beings, always raised in certain social and historical contexts and belonging to particular communities that shape their desires and understandings of the world? Is it not a gross violation of women's own understandings of what they are doing to simply denounce the burqa as a medieval imposition? Second, we must take care not to reduce the diverse situations and attitudes of millions of Muslim women to a single item of clothing. Perhaps it is time to give up the Western obsession with the veil and focus on some serious issues with which feminists and others should indeed be concerned.

Ultimately, the significant political–ethical problem the burqa raises is how to deal with cultural "others." How are we to deal with difference without accepting the passivity implied by the cultural relativism for which anthropologists are justly famous—a relativism that says it's their culture and it's not my business to judge or interfere, only to try to understand. Cultural relativism is certainly an improvement on ethnocentrism and the racism, cultural imperialism, and imperiousness that underlie it; the problem is that it is too late not to interfere. The forms of lives we find around the world are already products of long histories of interactions.

We need to look closely at what we are supporting (and what we are not) and to think carefully about why. . . . I do not know how many feminists who felt good about saving Afghan women from the Taliban are also asking for a global redistribution of wealth or contemplating sacrificing their own consumption radically so that African or Afghan women could have some chance of having what I do believe should be a universal human right—the right to freedom from the structural violence of global inequality and from the ravages of war, the everyday rights of having enough to eat, having homes for their families in which to live and thrive, having ways to make decent livings so their children can grow, and having the strength and security to work out, within their communities and with whatever alliances they want, how to live a good life, which might very well include changing the ways those communities are organized.

. . . For that, we need to confront two more big issues. First is the acceptance of the possibility of difference. Can we only free Afghan women to be like us or might we have to recognize that even after "liberation" from the Taliban, they might want different things than we would want for them? What do we do about that? Second, we need to be vigilant about the rhetoric of saving people because of what it implies about our attitudes.

Again, when I talk about accepting difference, I am not implying that we should resign ourselves to being cultural relativists who respect whatever goes on elsewhere as "just their culture." I have already discussed the dangers of "cultural" explanations; "their" cultures are just as much part of history and an interconnected world as ours are. What I am advocating is the hard work involved in recognizing and respecting differences—precisely as products of different histories, as expressions of different circumstances, and as manifestations of differently structured desires. We may want justice for women, but can we accept that there might be different ideas about justice and that different women might want, or choose, different futures from what we envision as best (see Ong 1988)? We must consider that they might be called to personhood, so to speak, in a different language.

Reports from the Bonn peace conference held in late November to discuss the rebuilding of Afghanistan revealed significant differences among the few Afghan women feminists and activists present. RAWA's position was to reject any conciliatory approach to Islamic governance. According to one report I read, most women activists, especially those based in Afghanistan who are aware of the realities on the ground, agreed that Islam had to be the starting point for reform. Fatima Gailani, a U.S.-based advisor to one of the delegations, is quoted as saying, "If I go to Afghanistan today and ask women for votes on the promise to bring them secularism, they are going to tell me to go to hell."

One of the things we have to be most careful about in thinking about Third World feminisms, and feminism in different parts of the Muslim world, is how not to fall into polarizations that place feminism on the side of the West. I have written about the dilemmas faced by Arab feminists when Western feminists initiate campaigns that make them vulnerable to local denunciations by conservatives of various sorts, whether Islamist or nationalist, of being traitors (Abu-Lughod 2001). As some like Afsaneh Najmabadi are now arguing, not only is it wrong to see history simplistically in terms of a putative opposition between Islam and the West (as is happening in the United States now and has happened in parallel in the Muslim world), but it is also strategically dangerous to accept this cultural opposition between Islam and the West, between fundamentalism and feminism, because those many people within Muslim countries who are trying to find alternatives to present injustices, those who might want to refuse the divide and take from different histories and cultures, who do not accept that being feminist means being Western, will be under pressure to choose, just as we are: Are you with us or against us?

My point is to remind us to be aware of differences, respectful of other paths toward social change that might give women better lives. Can there be a liberation that is Islamic? And, beyond this, is liberation even a goal for which all women or people strive? Are emancipation, equality, and rights part of a universal language we must use?

Might other desires be more meaningful for different groups of people? Living in close families? Living in a godly way? Living without war? I have done fieldwork in Egypt over more than 20 years and I cannot think of a single woman I know, from the poorest rural to the most educated cosmopolitan, who has ever expressed envy of U.S. women, women they tend to perceive as bereft of community, vulnerable to sexual violence and social anomie, driven by individual success rather than morality, or strangely disrespectful of God.

## BEYOND THE RHETORIC OF SALVATION

Let us return, finally, to my title, "Do Muslim Women Need Saving?" The discussion of culture, veiling, and how one can navigate the shoals of cultural difference should put Laura Bush's self-congratulation about the rejoicing of Afghan women liberated by American troops in a different light. It is deeply problematic to construct the Afghan woman as someone in need of saving. When you save someone, you imply that you are saving her from something. You are also saving her *to* something. What violences are entailed in this transformation, and what presumptions are being made about the superiority of that to which you are saving her? Projects of saving other women depend on and reinforce a sense of superiority by Westerners, a form of arrogance that deserves to be challenged. All one needs to do to appreciate the patronizing quality of the rhetoric of saving women is to imagine using it today in the United States about disadvantaged groups such as African American women or working-class women. We now understand them as suffering from structural violence. We have become politicized about race and class, but not culture.

Could we not leave veils and vocations of saving others behind and instead train our sights on ways to make the world a more just place? The reason respect for difference should not be confused with cultural relativism is that it does not preclude asking how we, living in this privileged and powerful part of the world, might examine our own responsibilities for the situations in which others in distant places have found themselves. We do not stand outside the world, looking out over this sea of poor benighted people, living under the shadow—or veil—of oppressive cultures; we are part of that world. Islamic movements themselves have arisen in a world shaped by the intense engagements of Western powers in Middle Eastern lives.

A more productive approach, it seems to me, is to ask how we might contribute to making the world a more just place. A world not organized around strategic military and economic demands; a place where certain kinds of forces and values that we may still consider important could have an appeal and where there is the peace necessary for discussions, debates, and transformations to occur within communities. We need to ask ourselves what kinds of world conditions we could contribute to making such that popular desires will not be overdetermined by an overwhelming sense of helplessness in the face of forms of global injustice. Where we seek to be active in the affairs of distant places, can we do so in the spirit of support for those within those communities whose goals are to make women's (and men's) lives better (as Walley has argued in relation to practices of genital cutting in Africa, [1997])? Can we use a more egalitarian language of alliances, coalitions, and solidarity, instead of salvation?

Even RAWA, the now celebrated Revolutionary Association of the Women of Afghanistan, which was so instrumental in bringing to U.S. women's attention the excesses of the Taliban, has opposed the U.S. bombing from the beginning. They do not see in it Afghan women's salvation but increased hardship and loss. They have long called for disarmament and for peacekeeping forces. Spokespersons point out the dangers of confusing governments with people, the Taliban with innocent Afghans who will be most harmed. They consistently remind audiences to take a close look at the ways policies are being organized around oil interests, the arms industry, and the international drug trade. They are not obsessed with the veil, even though they are the most radical feminists working for a secular democratic Afghanistan. Unfortunately, only their messages about the excesses of the Taliban have been heard, even though their criticisms of those in power in Afghanistan have included previous regimes. A first step in hearing their wider message is to break with the language of alien cultures, whether to understand or eliminate them. Missionary work and colonial feminism belong in the past. Our task is to critically explore what we might do to help create a world in which those poor Afghan women, for whom "the hearts of those in the civilized world break," can have safety and decent lives.

## ACKNOWLEDGMENTS

I want to thank Page Jackson, Fran Mascia-Lees, Tim Mitchell, Rosalind Morris, Anupama Rao, and members of the audience at the symposium "Responding to War," sponsored by Columbia University's Institute for Research on Women and Gender (where I presented an earlier version), for helpful comments, references, clippings, and encouragement.

## REFERENCES

Abu-Lughod, Lila. 1986. *Veiled Sentiments: Honor and Poetry in a Bedouin Society*. Berkeley: University of California Press.

———. 1995. Movie Stars and Islamic Moralism in Egypt. *Social Text* 42: 53–67.

———. 1998. *Remaking Women: Feminism and Modernity in the Middle East*. Princeton: Princeton University Press.

———. 2001. Orientalism and Middle East Feminist Studies. *Feminist Studies* 27(1): 101–113.

Ahmed, Leila. 1992. *Women and Gender in Islam*. New Haven, CT: Yale University Press.

Alloula, Malek. 1986. *The Colonial Harem*. Minneapolis: University of Minnesota Press.

Brenner, Suzanne. 1996. Reconstructing Self and Society: Javanese Muslim Women and "the Veil." *American Ethnologist* 23(4): 673–697.

El Guindi, Fadwa. 1999. *Veil: Modesty, Privacy and Resistance*. Oxford: Berg.

Fremson, Ruth. 2001. Allure Must Be Covered. Individuality Peeks Through. *New York Times*, November 4: 14.

Global Exchange. 2002. Courage and Tenacity: A Women's Delegation to Afghanistan. Electronic document, http://www.globalexchange.org/tours/auto/2002-03-05_CourageandTenacityAWomensDele.html. (Accessed February 11).

Goldenberg, Suzanne. 2002. The Woman Who Stood Up to the Taliban. *The Guardian*, January 24. Electronic document, http://222.guardian.co.uk/afghanistan/story/0,1284,63840.

Hirschkind, Charles, and Saba Mahmood. 2002. Feminism, the Taliban, and the Politics of Counter-Insurgency. *Anthropological Quarterly*, Volume 75(2): 107–122.

Lazreg, Marnia. 1994. *The Eloquence of Silence: Algerian Women in Question*. New York: Routledge.

MacLeod, Arlene. 1991. *Accommodating Protest*. New York: Columbia University Press.

Mahmood, Saba. 2001. Feminist Theory, Embodiment, and the Docile Agent: Some Reflections on the Egyptian Islamic Revival. *Cultural Anthropology* 16(2): 202–235.

Mir-Hosseini, Ziba. 1999. *Islam and Gender: The Religious Debate in Contemporary Iran.* Princeton: Princeton University Press.

Moghissi, Haideh. 1999. *Feminism and Islamic Fundamentalism.* London: Zed Books.

Najmabadi, Afsaneh. 1998. Feminism in an Islamic Republic. In *Islam, Gender and Social Change*, eds. Yvonne Haddad and John Esposito, 59–84. New York: Oxford University Press.

———. 2000. (Un)Veiling Feminism. *Social Text* 64: 29–45.

Ong, Aihwa. 1988. *Colonialism and Modernity: Feminist Re-Presentations of Women in Non-Western Societies. Inscriptions* 3–4: 79–93.

———. 1990. State Versus Islam: Malay Families, Women's Bodies, and the Body Politic in Malaysia. *American Ethnologist* 17(2): 258–276.

Papanek, Hanna. 1982. Purdah in Pakistan: Seclusion and Modern Occupations for Women. In *Separate Worlds,* eds. Hanna Papanek and Gail Minault, 190–216. Columbus, MO: South Asia Books.

Safire, William. 2001. "On Language." *New York Times* Magazine, October 28: 22.

Spivak, Gayatri Chakravorty. 1988. Can the Subaltern Speak? In *Marxism and the Interpretation of Culture*, eds. Cary Nelson and Lawrence Grossberg, 271–313. Urbana: University of Illinois Press.

Strathern, Marilyn. 1987. An Awkward Relationship: The Case of Feminism and Anthropology. *Signs* 12: 276–292.

U.S. Government. 2002. Electronic document, http://www.whitehouse.gov/news/releases/2001/11/20011117. (Accessed January 10).

Van Sommers, Annie and Samuel Zwemer. 1907. *Our Moslem Sisters: A Cry of Need from Lands of Darkness Interpreted by Those Who Heard It.* New York: Fleming H. Revell Co.

Walley, Christine. 1997. Searching for "Voices": Feminism, Anthropology, and the Global Debate over Female Genital Operations. *Cultural Anthropology* 12(3): 405–438.

# 50

# The Price of Progress

*John H. Bodley*

Anthropologists are not against progress: We do not want everyone to return to the "good old days" of our Paleolithic ancestors. On the other hand, the discoveries of cultural anthropologists have made us painfully aware of the human costs of unplanned social and economic change. Anthropologists do not want our society to plunge blindly into the future, unaware and unconcerned about how our present decisions will affect other people or future generations. Cultures are always changing, and the direction of that change is toward a single world system. Cultures change because a society's economy is pulled into the world economy. "Progress" is a label placed on cultural and economic change, but whether something represents "progress" or not depends on one's perspective.

In this selection, John Bodley reviews some of the unexpected consequences of economic development in terms of health, ecological change, quality of life, and relative deprivation. We have seen this same theme in several previous selections—the invention of agriculture, for example. The benefits of economic development are not equally distributed within a developing society. In this selection, we see the relative costs and benefits of economic progress for some of the most marginalized people of the world—the tribal peoples who have been the traditional focus of cultural anthropology research. We believe that the problems detailed here should make our society think about the way cultural change can make people's lives worse; these are issues of social justice.

Anthropologists have been active in seeking solutions to many serious problems. At the same time, most anthropologists believe that tribal peoples have a right to lead their traditional lifestyles and not to be forced into change. In this regard, an organization called Cultural Survival has been active in the international political arena in protecting the land and rights of native peoples.

***As you read this selection, ask yourself the following questions:***

- What is meant by quality of life? Why might it increase or decrease for a population?
- What are the three ways in which economic development can change the distribution of disease?
- Why do people's diets change? Do people choose diets and behaviors that are harmful to them?
- What is meant by relative deprivation? Can you think of other examples of this process?
- Are tribal peoples more vulnerable to the negative impact of social and economic change than larger industrial societies?

***The following terms discussed in this selection are included in the Glossary at the back of the book:***

| | |
|---|---|
| *dental anthropology* | *relative deprivation* |
| *ecosystem* | *self-sufficient* |
| *ethnocentrism* | *swidden cultivation* |
| *nomadic band* | *tribe* |
| *population pressure* | *urbanization* |

*In aiming at progress . . . you must let no one suffer by too drastic a measure, nor pay too high a price in upheaval and devastation, for your innovation.*

—Maunier 1949:725

Until recently, government planners have always considered economic development and progress beneficial goals that all societies should want to strive toward. The social advantages of progress—as defined in terms of increased incomes, higher standards of living, greater security, and better health—are thought to be positive, *universal* goods, to be obtained at any price. Although one may argue that tribal peoples must sacrifice their traditional cultures to obtain these

Bodley, John H. "The Price of Progress." From *Victims of Progress*, 4th ed., 1999. Reprinted by permission of Rowman & Littlefield Publishers, Inc.

tribal peoples. Urban health standards are abysmally poor and generally worse than in rural areas for the detribalized individuals who have crowded into the towns and cities throughout Africa, Asia, and Latin America seeking wage employment out of new economic necessity. Infectious diseases related to crowding and poor sanitation are rampant in urban centers, while greatly increased stress and poor nutrition aggravate a variety of other health problems. Malnutrition and other diet-related conditions are, in fact, one of the characteristic hazards of progress faced by tribal peoples and are discussed in the following sections.

### The Hazards of Dietary Change

The traditional diets of tribal peoples are admirably adapted to their nutritional needs and available food resources. Even though these diets may seem bizarre, absurd, and unpalatable to outsiders, they are unlikely to be improved by drastic modifications. Given the delicate balances and complexities involved in any subsistence system, change always involves risks, but for tribal people the effects of dietary change have been catastrophic.

Under normal conditions, food habits are remarkably resistant to change, and indeed people are unlikely to abandon their traditional diets voluntarily in favor of dependence on difficult-to-obtain exotic imports. In some cases it is true that imported foods may be identified with powerful outsiders and are therefore sought as symbols of greater prestige. This may lead to such absurdities as Amazonian Indians choosing to consume imported canned tunafish when abundant high-quality fish is available in their own rivers. Another example of this situation occurs in tribes where mothers prefer to feed their infants expensive and nutritionally inadequate canned milk from unsanitary, but *high status,* baby bottles. The high status of these items is often promoted by clever traders and clever advertising campaigns.

Aside from these apparently voluntary changes, it appears that more often dietary changes are forced upon unwilling tribal peoples by circumstances beyond their control. In some areas, new food crops have been introduced by government decree, or as a consequence of forced relocation or other policies designed to end hunting, pastoralism, or shifting cultivation. Food habits have also been modified by massive disruption of the natural environment by outsiders—as when sheepherders transformed the Australian Aborigine's foraging territory or when European invaders destroyed the bison herds that were the primary element in the Plains Indians' subsistence patterns. Perhaps the most frequent cause of diet change occurs when formerly self-sufficient peoples find that wage labor, cash cropping, and other economic development activities that feed tribal resources into the world-market economy must inevitably divert time and energy away from the production of subsistence foods. Many developing peoples suddenly discover that, like it or not, they are unable to secure traditional foods and must spend their newly acquired cash on costly, and often nutritionally inferior, manufactured foods.

Overall, the available data seem to indicate that the dietary changes that are linked to involvement in the world-market economy have tended to *lower* rather than raise the nutritional levels of the affected tribal peoples. Specifically, the vitamin, mineral, and protein components of their diets are often drastically reduced and replaced by enormous increases in starch and carbohydrates, often in the form of white flour and refined sugar.

Any deterioration in the quality of a given population's diet is almost certain to be reflected in an increase in deficiency diseases and a general decline in health status. Indeed, as tribal peoples have shifted to a diet based on imported manufactured or processed foods, there has been a dramatic rise in malnutrition, a massive increase in dental problems, and a variety of other nutrition-related disorders. Nutritional physiology is so complex that even well-meaning dietary changes have had tragic consequences. In many areas of Southeast Asia, government-sponsored protein supplementation programs supplying milk to protein-deficient populations caused unexpected health problems and increased mortality. Officials failed to anticipate that in cultures where adults do not normally drink milk, the enzymes needed to digest it are no longer produced and milk *intolerance* results (Davis and Bolin 1972). In Brazil, a similar milk distribution program caused an epidemic of permanent blindness by aggravating a preexisting vitamin A deficiency (Bunce 1972).

### Teeth and Progress

> There is nothing new in the observation that savages, or peoples living under primitive conditions, have, in general excellent teeth. . . . Nor is it news that most civilized populations possess wretched teeth which begin to decay almost before they have erupted completely, and that dental caries is likely to be accompanied by periodontal disease with further reaching complications (Hooton 1945:xviii).

Anthropologists have long recognized that undisturbed tribal peoples are often in excellent physical condition. And it has often been noted specifically that dental caries and the other dental abnormalities that plague industrialized societies are absent or rare among tribal peoples who have retained their traditional diets. The fact that tribal food habits may contribute to the development of sound teeth, whereas modernized diets may do just the opposite, was illustrated as long ago as 1894 in an article in the *Journal of the Royal Anthropological Institute* that described the results of a comparison between the teeth of ten Sioux Indians and a comparable group of Londoners (Smith, 1894:109–116). The Indians were examined when they came to London as members of Buffalo Bill's Wild West Show and were found to be completely free of caries and in possession of all their teeth, even though half of the group were over thirty-nine years of age. Londoners' teeth were conspicuous for both their caries and their steady reduction in number with advancing age. The difference was attributed primarily to the wear and polishing caused by the traditional Indian diet of coarse food and the fact that they chewed their food longer, encouraged by the absence of tableware.

One of the most remarkable studies of the dental conditions of tribal peoples and the impact of dietary change was conducted in the 1930s by Weston Price (1945), an American dentist who was interested in determining what caused normal, healthy teeth. Between 1931 and 1936, Price systematically explored tribal areas throughout the world to locate and examine the most isolated peoples who were still living on traditional foods. His fieldwork covered Alaska, the Canadian Yukon, Hudson Bay, Vancouver Island, Florida, the Andes, the Amazon, Samoa, Tahiti, New Zealand, Australia, New Caledonia, Fiji, the Torres Strait, East Africa, and the Nile. The study demonstrated both the superior quality of aboriginal dentition and the devastation that occurs as modern diets are adopted. In nearly every area where traditional foods were still being eaten, Price found perfect teeth with normal dental arches and virtually no decay, whereas caries and abnormalities increased steadily as new diets were adopted. In many cases the change was sudden and striking. Among Eskimo groups subsisting entirely on traditional food he found caries totally absent, whereas in groups eating a considerable quantity of store-bought food approximately 20 percent of their teeth were decayed. The figure rose to more than 30 percent with Eskimo groups subsisting almost exclusively on purchased or government-supplied food, and reached an incredible 48 percent among the Vancouver Island Indians. Unfortunately for many of these people, modern dental treatment did not accompany the new food, and their suffering was appalling. The loss of teeth was, of course, bad enough in itself, and it certainly undermined the population's resistance to many new diseases, including tuberculosis. But new foods were also accompanied by crowded, misplaced teeth, gum diseases, distortion of the face, and pinching of the nasal cavity. Abnormalities in the dental arch appeared in the new generation following the change in diet, while caries appeared almost immediately even in adults.

Price reported that in many areas the affected peoples were conscious of their own physical deterioration. At a mission school in Africa, the principal asked him to explain to the native schoolchildren why they were not physically as strong as children who had had no contact with schools. On an island in the Torres Strait the natives knew exactly what was causing their problems and resisted—almost to the point of bloodshed—government efforts to establish a store that would make imported food available. The government prevailed, however, and Price was able to establish a relationship between the length of time the government store had been established and the increasing incidences of caries among a population that showed an almost 100 percent immunity to them before the store had been opened.

In New Zealand, the Maori, who in their aboriginal state are often considered to have been among the healthiest, most perfectly developed of peoples, were found to have "advanced" the furthest. According to Price:

> Their modernization was demonstrated not only by the high incidence of dental caries but also by the fact 90 percent of the adults and 100 percent of the children had abnormalities of the dental arches (Price 1945:206).

## Malnutrition

Malnutrition, particularly in the form of protein deficiency, has become a critical problem for tribal peoples who must adopt new economic patterns. Population pressures, cash cropping, and government programs all have tended to encourage the replacement of traditional crops and other food sources that were rich in protein with substitutes high in calories but low in protein. In Africa, for example, protein-rich staples such as millet and sorghum are being replaced systematically by high-yielding manioc and plantains, which have insignificant amounts of protein. The problem is increased for cash croppers and wage laborers whose earnings are too low and unpredictable to allow purchase of adequate amounts of protein. In some rural areas, agricultural laborers have been forced systematically to deprive nonproductive members (principally children) of their households of their minimal nutritional requirements to satisfy the need of the productive members. This process has been documented in northeastern Brazil following the introduction of large-scale sisal plantations (Gross and Underwood 1971). In urban centers the difficulties of obtaining nutritionally adequate diets are even more serious for tribal immigrants, because costs are higher and poor quality foods are more tempting.

One of the most tragic, and largely overlooked, aspects of chronic malnutrition is that it can lead to abnormally undersized brain development and apparently irreversible brain damage; it has been associated with various forms of mental impairment or retardation. Malnutrition has been linked clinically with mental retardation in both Africa and Latin America (see, for example, Mönckeberg, 1968), and this appears to be a worldwide phenomenon with serious implications (Montagu 1972).

Optimistic supporters of progress will surely say that all of these new health problems are being overstressed and that the introduction of hospitals, clinics, and the other modern health institutions will overcome or at least compensate for all of these difficulties. However, it appears that uncontrolled population growth and economic impoverishment probably will keep most of these benefits out of reach for many tribal peoples, and the intervention of modern medicine has at least partly contributed to the problem in the first place.

The generalization that civilization frequently has a broad negative impact on tribal health has found broad empirical support (see especially Kroeger and Barbira-Freedman [1982] on Amazonia; Reinhard [1976] on the Arctic; and Wirsing [1985] globally), but these conclusions have not gone unchallenged. Some critics argue that tribal health was often poor before modernization, and they point specifically to tribals' low life expectancy and high infant mortality rates. Demographic statistics on tribal populations are often problematic because precise data are scarce, but they do show a less favorable profile than that enjoyed by many industrial societies. However, it should be remembered that our present life expectancy is a recent phenomenon that has been very costly in terms of medical research and technological advances. Furthermore, the benefits of our health system are not enjoyed equally by all members of our society. High infant mortality could be viewed as a relatively inexpensive and egalitarian tribal public health program that offered the reasonable expectation of a healthy and productive life for those surviving to age fifteen.

Some critics also suggest that certain tribal populations, such as the New Guinea highlanders, were "stunted" by nutritional deficiencies created by tribal culture and are "improved" by "acculturation" and cash cropping (Dennett and Connell, 1988). Although this argument does suggest that the health question requires careful evaluation, it does not invalidate the empirical generalizations already established. Nutritional deficiencies undoubtedly occurred in densely populated zones in the central New Guinea highlands. However, the specific case cited above may not be widely representative of other tribal groups even in New Guinea, and it does not address the facts of outside intrusion or the inequities inherent in the contemporary development process.

## ECOCIDE

> "How is it," asked a herdsman . . . "how is it that these hills can no longer give pasture to my cattle? In my father's day they were green and cattle thrived there; today there is no grass and my cattle starve." As one looked one saw that what had once been a green hill had become a raw red rock (Jones 1934).

Progress not only brings new threats to the health of tribal peoples, but it also imposes new strains on the ecosystems upon which they must depend for their ultimate survival. The introduction of new technology, increased consumption, lowered mortality, and the eradication of all traditional controls have combined to replace what for most tribal peoples was a relatively stable balance between population and natural resources, with a new system that is imbalanced. Economic development is forcing *ecocide* on peoples who were once careful stewards of their resources. There is already a trend toward widespread environmental deterioration in tribal areas, involving resource depletion, erosion, plant and animal extinction, and a disturbing series of other previously unforeseen changes.

After the initial depopulation suffered by most tribal peoples during their engulfment by frontiers of national expansion, most tribal populations began to experience rapid growth. Authorities generally attribute this growth to the introduction of modern medicine and new health measures and the termination of intertribal warfare, which lowered mortality rates, as well as to new technology, which increased food production. Certainly all of these factors played a part, but merely lowering mortality rates would not have produced the rapid population growth that most tribal areas have experienced if traditional birth-spacing mechanisms had not been eliminated at the same time. Regardless of which factors were most important, it is clear that all of the natural and cultural checks on population growth have suddenly been pushed aside by culture change, while tribal lands have been steadily reduced and consumption levels have risen. In many tribal areas, environmental deterioration due to overuse of resources has set in, and in other areas such deterioration is imminent as resources continue to dwindle relative to the expanding population and increased use. Of course, population expansion by tribal peoples may have positive political consequences, because where tribals can retain or regain their status as local majorities they may be in a more favorable position to defend their resources against intruders.

Swidden systems and pastoralism, both highly successful economic systems under traditional conditions, have proven particularly vulnerable to increased population pressures and outside efforts to raise productivity beyond its natural limits. Research in Amazonia demonstrates that population pressures and related resource depletion can be created indirectly by official policies that restrict swidden peoples to smaller territories. Resource depletion itself can then become a powerful means of forcing tribal people into participating in the world-market economy—thus leading to further resource depletion. For example, Bodley and Benson (1979) showed how the Shipibo Indians in Peru were forced to further deplete their forest resources by cash cropping in the forest area to replace the resources that had been destroyed earlier by the intensive cash cropping necessitated by the narrow confines of their reserve. In this case, a certain species of palm trees that had provided critical housing materials were destroyed by forest clearing and had to be replaced by costly purchased materials. Research by Gross (1979) and others showed similar processes at work among four tribal groups in central Brazil and demonstrated that the degree of market involvement increases directly with increases in resource depletion.

The settling of nomadic herders and the removal of prior controls on herd size have often led to serious overgrazing and erosion problems where these had not previously occurred. There are indications that the desertification problem in the Sahel region of Africa was aggravated by programs designed to settle nomads. The first sign of imbalance in a swidden system appears when the planting cycles are shortened to the point that garden plots are reused before sufficient forest regrowth can occur. If reclearing and planting continue in the same area, the natural pattern of forest succession may be disturbed irreversibly and the soil can be impaired permanently. An extensive tract of tropical rainforest in the lower Amazon of Brazil was reduced to a semiarid desert in just fifty years through such a process (Ackermann 1964). The soils in the Azande area are also now seriously threatened with laterization and other problems as a result of the government-promoted cotton development scheme (McNeil 1972).

The dangers of overdevelopment and the vulnerability of local resource systems have long been recognized by both anthropologists and tribal peoples themselves, but the pressures for change have been overwhelming. In 1948 the Maya villagers of Chan Kom complained to Redfield (1962) about the shortening of their swidden cycles, which they correctly attributed to increasing population pressures. Redfield told them, however, that they had no choice but to go "forward with technology" (Redfield 1962:178). In Assam, swidden cycles were shortened from an average of twelve years to only two or three within just twenty years, and anthropologists warned that the limits of swiddening would soon be reached (Burling, 1963:311–312). In the Pacific, anthropologists warned of population pressures on limited resources as early as the 1930s (Keesing 1941:64–65). These warnings seemed fully justified, considering the fact that the crowded Tikopians were prompted by population pressures on their tiny island to suggest that infanticide be legalized. The warnings have been dramatically reinforced since then by the doubling of Micronesia's population in just the fourteen years between 1958 and 1972, from 70,600 to 114,645, while consumption levels have soared. By 1985 Micronesia's population had reached 162,321.

The environmental hazards of economic development and rapid population growth have become generally recognized only since worldwide concerns over environmental issues began in the early 1970s. Unfortunately, there is as yet little indication that the leaders of the now developing nations are sufficiently concerned with environmental limitations. On the contrary governments are forcing tribal peoples into a self-reinforcing spiral of population growth and intensified resource exploitation, which may be stopped only by environmental disaster or the total impoverishment of the tribals.

The reality of ecocide certainly focuses attention on the fundamental contrasts between tribal and industrial systems in their use of natural resources. In many respects the entire "victims of progress" issue hinges on natural resources, who controls them, and how they are managed. Tribal peoples are victimized because they control resources that outsiders demand. The resources exist because tribals managed them conservatively. However, as with the issue of the health consequences of detribalization, some anthropologists minimize the adaptive achievements of tribal groups and seem unwilling to concede that ecocide might be a consequence of cultural change. Critics attack an exaggerated "noble savage" image of tribals living in perfect harmony with nature and having no visible impact on their surroundings. They then show that tribals do in fact modify the environment, and they conclude that there is no significant difference between how tribals and industrial societies treat their environments. For example, Charles Wagley declared that Brazilian Indians such as the Tapirape

> are not "natural men." They have human vices just as we do. . . . They do not live "in tune" with nature any more than I do; in fact, they can often be as destructive of their environment, within their limitations, as some civilized men. The Tapirape are not innocent or childlike in any way (Wagley 1977:302).

Anthropologist Terry Rambo demonstrated that the Semang of the Malaysian rain forests have measurable impact on their environment. In his monograph *Primitive Polluters,* Rambo (1985) reported that the Semang live in smoke-filled houses. They sneeze and spread germs, breathe, and thus emit carbon dioxide. They clear small gardens, contributing "particulate matter" to the air and disturbing the local climate because cleared areas proved measurably warmer and drier than the shady forest. Rambo concluded that his research "demonstrated the essential functional similarity of the environmental interactions of primitive and civilized societies" (1985:78) in contrast to a "noble savage" view (Bodley 1983) which, according to Rambo (1985:2), mistakenly "claims that traditional peoples almost always live in essential harmony with their environment."

This is surely a false issue. To stress, as I do, that tribals tend to manage their resources for sustained yield within relatively self-sufficient subsistence economies is not to make them either innocent children or natural men. Nor is it to deny that tribals "disrupt" their environment and may never be in absolute "balance" with nature.

The ecocide issue is perhaps most dramatically illustrated by two sets of satellite photos taken over the Brazilian rain forests of Rôndonia (Allard and McIntyre 1988:780–781). Photos taken in 1973, when Rôndonia was still a tribal domain, show virtually unbroken rain forest. The 1987 satellite photos, taken after just fifteen years of highway construction and "development" by outsiders, show more than 20 percent of the forest destroyed. The surviving Indians were being concentrated by FUNAI (Brazil's national Indian foundation) into what would soon become mere islands of forest in a ravaged landscape. It is irrelevant to quibble about whether tribals are noble, childlike, or innocent, or about the precise meaning of balance with nature, carrying capacity, or adaptation, to recognize that for the past 200 years rapid environmental deterioration on an unprecedented global scale has followed the wresting of control of vast areas of the world from tribal groups by resource-hungry industrial societies.

## DEPRIVATION AND DISCRIMINATION

> Contact with European culture has given them a knowledge of great wealth, opportunity and privilege, but only very limited avenues by which to acquire these things (Crocombe 1968).

Unwittingly, tribal peoples have had the burden of perpetual relative deprivation thrust upon them by acceptance—either by themselves or by the governments administering them—of the standards of socioeconomic progress set for them by industrial civilizations. By comparison with the material wealth of industrial societies, tribal societies become, by definition, impoverished. They are then forced to transform their cultures and work to achieve what many economists now acknowledge to be unattainable goals. Even though in many cases the modest GNP goals set by development planners for the developing nations during the "development decade" of the 1960s were often met, the results were hardly noticeable for most of the tribal people involved. Population growth, environmental limitations, inequitable distribution of wealth, and the continued rapid growth of the industrialized nations have all meant that both the absolute and the relative gap between the rich and poor in the world is steadily widening. The prospect that tribal peoples will actually be able to attain the levels of resource consumption to which they are being encouraged to aspire is remote indeed except for those few groups who have retained effective control over strategic mineral resources.

Tribal peoples feel deprivation not only when the economic goals they have been encouraged to seek fail to materialize, but also when they discover that they are powerless, second-class citizens who are discriminated against and exploited by the dominant society. At the same time, they are denied the satisfactions of their traditional cultures, because these have been sacrificed in the process of modernization. Under the impact of major economic change family life is disrupted, traditional social controls are often lost, and many indicators of social anomie such as alcoholism, crime, delinquency, suicide, emotional disorders, and despair may increase. The inevitable frustration resulting from this continual deprivation finds expression in the cargo cults, revitalization movements, and a variety of other political and religious movements that have been widespread among tribal peoples following their disruption by industrial civilization.

## REFERENCES


Ackermann, F. L. 1964. *Geologia e Fisiografia da Região Bragantina, Estado do Pará.* Manaus, Brazil: Conselho Nacional de Pesquisas, Instituto Nacional de Pesquisas da Amazônia.

Allard, William Albert, and Loren McIntyre. 1988. Rôndonia's settlers invade Brazil's imperiled rain forest. *National Geographic* 174(6): 772–799.

Bodley, John H. 1983. The World Bank tribal policy: Criticisms and recommendations. *Congressional Record,* serial no. 98-37, pp. 515–521. (Reprinted in Bodley, 1988.)

Bodley, John H., and Foley C. Benson. 1979. Cultural ecology of Amazonian palms. *Reports of Investigations,* no. 56. Pullman: Laboratory of Anthropology, Washington State University.

Bunce, George E. 1972. Aggravation of vitamin A deficiency following distribution of non-fortified skim milk: An example of nutrient interaction. In *The Careless Technology: Ecology and International Development,* ed. M. T. Farvar and John P. Milton, 53–60. Garden City, N.Y.: Natural History Press.

Burling, Robbins. 1963. *Rengsanggri: Family and Kinship in a Garo Village.* Philadelphia: University of Pennsylvania Press.

Crocombe, Ron. 1968. Bougainville!: Copper, R. R. A. and secessionism. *New Guinea* 3(3): 39–49.

Davis, A. E., and T. D. Bolin. 1972. Lactose intolerance in Southeast Asia. In *The Careless Technology: Ecology and International Development,* ed. M. T. Farvar and John P. Milton, 61–68. Garden City, N.Y.: Natural History Press.

Dennett, Glenn, and John Connell. 1988. Acculturation and health in the highlands of Papua New Guinea. *Current Anthropology* 29(2): 273–299.

Goldschmidt, Walter R. 1952. The interrelations between cultural factors and acquisition of new technical skills. In *The Progress of Underdeveloped Areas,* ed. Bert F. Hoselitz, 135–151. Chicago: University of Chicago Press.

Gross, Daniel R., and Barbara A. Underwood. 1971. Technological change and caloric costs: Sisal agriculture. *American Anthropologist* 73(3): 725–740.

Gross, Daniel R., et al. 1979. Ecology and acculturation among native peoples of Central Brazil. *Science* 206(4422): 1043–1050.

Hooton, Earnest A. 1945. Introduction. In *Nutrition and Physical Degeneration: A Comparison of Primitive and Modern Diets and Their Effects* by Weston A. Price. Redlands, Calif.: The author.

Hughes, Charles C., and John M. Hunter. 1972. The role of technological development in promoting disease in Africa. In *The Careless Technology: Ecology and International Development,* ed. M. T. Farvar and John P. Milton, 69–101. Garden City, N.Y.: Natural History Press.

Jones, J. D. Rheinallt. 1934. Economic condition of the urban native. In *Western Civilization and the Natives of South Africa,* ed. I. Schapera, 159–192. London: George Routledge and Sons.

Keesing, Felix M. 1941. *The South Seas in the Modern World.* Institute of Pacific Relations International Research Series. New York: John Day.

Kroeger, Axel, and Françoise Barbira-Freedman. 1982. *Culture Change and Health: The Case of South American Rainforest Indians.* Frankfurt am Main: Verlag Peter Lang. (Reprinted in Bodley, 1988: 221–236).

Maunier, René. 1949. *The Sociology of Colonies.* Vol. 2. London: Routledge and Kegan Paul.

McNeil, Mary. 1972. Lateritic soils in distinct tropical environments: Southern Sudan and Brazil. In *The Careless Technology: Ecology and International Development,* ed. M. T. Farvar and John P. Milton, 591–608. Garden City, N.Y.: Natural History Press.

Mönckeberg, F. 1968. Mental retardation from malnutrition. *Journal of the American Medical Association* 206: 30–31.

Montagu, Ashley. 1972. Sociogenic brain damage. *American Anthropologist* 74(5): 1045–1061.

Price, Weston Andrew. 1945. *Nutrition and Physical Degeneration: A Comparison of Primitive and Modern Diets and Their Effects.* Redlands, Calif.: The author.

Prior, Ian A. M. 1971. The price of civilization. *Nutrition Today* 6(4): 2–11.

Rambo, A. Terry. 1985. *Primitive Polluters: Semang Impact on the Malaysian Tropical Rain Forest Ecosystem.* Anthropological Papers no. 76, Museum of Anthropology, University of Michigan.

Redfield, Robert. 1962. *A Village That Chose Progress: Chan Kom Revisited.* Chicago: University of Chicago Press, Phoenix Books.

Reinhard, K. R. 1976. Resource exploitation and the health of western arctic man. In *Circumpolar Health: Proceedings of the Third International Symposium, Yellowknife, Northwest Territories,* ed. Roy J. Shephard and S. Itoh, 617–627. Toronto: University of Toronto Press. (Reprinted in Bodley, 1988.)

Smith, Wilberforce. 1894. The teeth of ten Sioux Indians. *Journal of the Royal Anthropological Institute* 24: 109–116.

TTR: TTR, United States, Department of the Interior, Office of the Territories. 1953. Report on the Administration of the trust territories of the Pacific Islands for the period of July 1, 1951 to June 30, 1952.

United States, Department of State. 1955. *Seventh Annual Report to the United Nations on the Administration of the Trust Territory of the Pacific Islands* (July 1, 1953, to June 30, 1954).

______. 1959. *Eleventh Annual Report to the United Nations on the Administration of the Trust Territory of the Pacific Islands* (July 1, 1957, to June 30, 1958).

______. 1973. *Twenty-Fifth Annual Report to the United Nations on the Administration of the Trust Territory of the Pacific Islands* (July 1, 1971, to June 30, 1972).

Wagley, C. 1977. *Welcome of Tears: The Tapirape Indians of Central Brazil.* New York: Oxford University Press.

Wirsing, R. 1985. The health of traditional societies and the effects of acculturation. *Current Anthropology* 26: 303–322.

# Glossary

**aboriginal** A descriptive term pertaining to artifacts, lands, or populations (deceased or living), that are indigenous to a particular geographic region.

**acculturation** The process of extensive borrowing of aspects of another culture, usually as a result of external pressure, and often resulting in the decline of traditional culture.

**action anthropology** Applied anthropological research combined with political advocacy and planned social change in cooperation with the group studied; associated with Sol Tax from the University of Chicago.

**adaptation** The process by which an organism or a culture is modified, usually through selection, enhancing the ability of individuals to survive and reproduce in a particular environment.

**adaptations** Heritable structures or behaviors of an organism that improve chances of survival and reproduction in a particular environment.

**adipose tissue** Fat. A physiological mechanism of energy storage; some adipose tissue, especially when deposited on the central body, is associated with chronic diseases.

**adjudication** A process of handling disputes in which the ultimate decision is made by a third party appointed by the legal system.

**affinal kin** A kin relationship created by marriage.

**affines** Individuals related to one another because of marriage between their families; related through marriage rather than birth.

**African Eve** The common maternal ancestor of all anatomically modern human beings.

**African survivals** Knowledge, skills, beliefs, and cultural traditions transplanted directly from Africa to other parts of the world through the Atlantic slave trade.

**Afrocentric** An explanation based on African origins.

**age grade** A social category of people who fall within a particular culturally distinguished age range; age grades often undergo life cycle rituals as a group.

**agency** The means, capacity, condition, or state of exerting power.

**agency detection** An evolved tendency to presume the intervention of intelligent agents to understand natural beings, which may have led to human tendencies to presume the intervention of supernatural beings.

**aggression** A forceful action, sometimes involving physical violence, intended for social domination.

**agnates** Individuals sharing a patrilineal kinship tie; people related through the male line.

**agnatic** Related through the male kinship line.

**agrarian** Relating to agriculture.

**agricultural development** Changes in agricultural production intended to improve the system by producing more harvest per unit of land.

**AIDS** Acquired immune deficiency syndrome, a fatal disease caused by the human immunodeficiency virus (HIV) and usually transmitted through semen or blood.

**altrical** An infantile trait of helplessness, as in infants that require long-term parental attention; opposite of precocious.

**Amerindian** Native American populations.

**anorexia nervosa** An eating disorder characterized by extreme dieting and a feeling of being fat even though one is underweight.

**anthropology** The systematic study of humans, including their biology and culture, both past and present.

**anthropometry** Science of the measurement of the human body, including measurement of bones, muscle, fat, and other body tissues.

**applied research** Study directed at gaining valid knowledge to help in the solution of human problems.

**arable land** Land suitable for cultivation.

**arbitration** The hearing and determination of a dispute by a person chosen by the parties or appointed by the legal system with the consent of the parties.

**archaeology** The field of anthropology concerned with cultural history; includes the systematic retrieval, identification, and study of the physical and cultural remains deposited in the earth.

***Ardipithecus kadabba*** A bipedal human ancestor with a body size and brain size similar to the modern chimpanzee. *Ardipithecus kadabba* pre-dates *Ardipithecus ramidus* by 1 million years, and pre-dates the *Australopithecus* remains named Lucy by 2 million years. In conjuction with the *Ardipithecus ramidus* discovery, the fossils of these early human remains support the theory that humans did not evolve from chimpanzees, but rather we share a common ancestor with chimpanzees. Paleoanthropologists discovered fossilized remains of *Ardipithecus kadabba* in present-day Ethiopia.

***Ardipithecus ramidus*** One of the earliest known hominid ancestors of *Homo sapiens*, which dates back to 4.4 million years ago. The discovery of *Ardipithecus* skeletal remains show that this early human ancestor may have combined bipedal locomotion with tree-climbing. *Ardipithecus ramidus* predates the *Australopithecus* remains named Lucy by 1 million years. Paleoanthropologists discovered the fossil remains of *Ardipithecus ramidus* in present-day Ethiopia.

**argot** A specialized, sometimes secret, vocabulary peculiar to a particular group.

**artifact** An object manufactured and used by human beings for a culturally defined goal.

**Aryan** Member of a prehistoric people of northern India who spoke an Indo-European language.

**asexual** Without sexual desire, or in terms of sexual identity, someone with no apparent sexual drive.

**assemblage** In archaeology, a patterned set of artifacts making up one component of a site and usually representing a social activity.

**asylum** The process by which immigrants are allowed to remain legally in their host country because of "persecution or a well-founded fear of persecution" in their country of origin.

**australopithecine** A member of the genus Australopithecus, the hominid ancestors of humans.

**Australopithecus** A bipedal primate; an extinct grade in hominid evolution found in the late Pliocene through the mid-Pleistocene in eastern and southern Africa; an ancestor of humans.

**Australopithecus afarensis** A bipedal hominid that lived in Africa about 3–4 million years ago, discovered by Johansen and White in the Afar triangle of Ethiopia, and exemplified in the "Lucy" specimen.

**Australopithecus anamensis** An early Australopithecine species from sites in northern Kenya that are about 4.2 million years old.

**Australopithecus robustus** See Paranthropus robustus.

**AZT** An antiviral drug used to slow down the replication of HIV, the human immunodeficiency virus that causes AIDS; AZT is very expensive.

**Babel** An incoherent collection of speech or noise. In the Bible, Babel was the place where Noah's descendents attempted to build a tower that would reach up to heaven; the project was unsuccessful because God caused the builders to speak different languages, making it impossible for the builders to communicate.

**baby boom** Population surge in the immediate post–WWII period; the television generation.

**basic research** Study directed toward gaining scientific knowledge primarily for its own sake.

**Bedouin** A term used to denote Arabic-speaking desert nomads in the Sahara, Syrian, Arabian, or Nubian deserts. Many Bedouin have adopted sedentary lifestyles, but traditionally the Bedouin were nomads who made a living through animal husbandry.

**berdache** An anthropological term which refers to ,"two spirit," Native Americans (Native Americans who fulfill mixed gender roles).

**big men** Political leaders in tribal-level societies whose status has been achieved and whose authority is limited.

**binocular vision** Overlapping fields of vision, characteristic of primates, which gives depth-perception.

**biogenetic** Genetic.

**biological anthropology** Subfield of anthropology that studies the biological nature of humans and includes primatology, paleoanthropology, population genetics, anthropometry, and human biology.

**biomedicine** Modern medicine as practiced in the United States and Europe; emphasizes the biological causation and remedy for illness.

**biophysical diversity** Outward biological appearance resulting from interaction of genes and environment; phenotype.

**biotic community** Plants and animals sharing a niche within an ecosystem.

**bipedal** Having two feet. In humans, the ability to walk upright on two legs.

**bipolar knapping** A method for making stone tools in which the tool maker strikes one stone with another that is placed firmly on a flat stationary object.

**blade** A stone tool similar to a knife and having one or more sharp cutting edges.

**blood relatives** A folk term referring to consanguineal kin, that is, kin related through birth.

**bonobo** Pygmy chimpanzees, more gracile in morphology than common chimpanzees and exhibiting more casual and varied sex than any other non-human primate species.

**brain drain** The out-migration of highly skilled and educated people from economically marginalized communities and countries to economically advanced areas and countries.

**brideprice** See bridewealth.

**bridewealth** The presentation of goods or money by the groom's family to the bride's family at the time of marriage; an economic exchange that legitimates the marriage and offspring as members of the father's patrilineage.

**burqa** A head-to-toe veil common in Afghanistan, often made of cotton and covering most of the body, including the face.

**bush-fallow** A technique used by horticulturalists that allows a garden plot to return to the wild state after a period of cultivation.

**cadastral** A government survey and record-keeping system for recording land ownership and property boundaries.

**canton** A small territorial division of a country.

**capitalism** An economic system characteristic of modern state societies where land, labor, and capital all become commodities exchanged on the market and in which socioeconomic inequality is a constant feature.

**carrying capacity** The maximum population size that can be maintained in a given area without causing environmental degradation of the ecology.

**cash crop** An agricultural product grown for money instead of food or subsistence.

**caste** A ranked group, sometimes linked to a particular occupation, with membership determined at birth and with marriage restricted to others within the group.

**ceremony** Public events involving special symbols that signify important cultural values of beliefs.

**chalcedony** A category of durable crystalline quartz stones that early humans used to make weapons, tools, and ceremonial objects.

**chief** The political leader of a society that is more complex than a tribal society and is characterized by social ranking, a redistributive economy, and a centralized political authority.

**chiefdom** A society more complex than a tribal society, characterized by social ranking, a redistributive economy, and a centralized political authority.

**CITES** Convention on International Trade and Endangered Species. An international agreement to limit the capture of endangered animals, including whales, and regulate the market for endangered species; related to the International Commission for the Conservation of Atlantic Tunas (ICCAT) that assigns quotas for tuna fishermen.

**civilization** The culture of state-level societies characterized by the following elements: (1) agriculture; (2) urban living; (3) a high degree of occupational specialization and differentiation; (4) social stratification; and (5) literacy.

**clan** A kinship group whose members assume, but need not demonstrate, descent from a common ancestor.

**class** An economically, socially, and politically similar group of people, e.g., middle class.

**clavicle** The collar bone.

**clines** A gradient of morphological or physiological change in a group of related organisms, usually along a line of environmental or geographic transition.

**clitorectomy (clitoridectomy)** Removal of the clitoris.

**Clovis point** A large lancelike projectile fluted at the base and flanked at both sides.

**clustering** In epidemiology, the concentration of cases by place of residence and time of diagnosis.

**code-switching** A linguistics term that refers to the simultaneous use of more than one language or dialect in a single conversation. A simple example of code switching is the interjection of a Spanish term in the middle of an otherwise all-English conversation: "What's wrong amigo?"

**cognates** Words that belong to different languages but have similar sounds and meanings.

**cognatic kin** Kinship traced simultaneously through the male and female lines in a nonunilineal pattern of descent.

**cognitive empathy** The ability to understand another being's state of mind.

**collective behavior** Patterns of social action.

**colonialism** The establishment of government of sovereign rule in a territory through political, social, economic, and cultural domination by a foreign power.

**commodification** The transformation of a good or service into something that can be bought and sold with money.

**communal** Shared with a group.

**community archaeology** Also known as public- or post-colonial archaeology, practitioners of this collaborative approach to archaeology emphasizes mutual research priorities, participation, and benefit sharing between local communities and the scientific community. Some community archaeology projects are initiated by local communities, while others may focus on external interests such as academic publishing.

**comparative framework** An analytical approach in anthropology using the comparison of cultures across time and place.

**complementary schismogenesis** Forms of social interaction between people or groups that complement or "feed into" one another. Complementary schismogenesis occurs when language and/or cultural differences become exaggerated when two cultures, languages, or personalities come into contact.

**computational linguistics** A multidisciplinary subfield of linguistics that combines computer science with linguistics to analyze and generate models of the structure of human language.

**constructions of femininity** The ways in which a given culture defines appropriate ways of thinking and acting for women. See gender roles.

**consumable commodity** Something that can be bought or sold and then used up.

**consumer society** A characteristic of modern capitalist societies in which the purchase of non-essential material goods and services is an important marker of social status and identity.

**contingent truths** Truth based upon the best scientific evidence available at the time and subject to revision as knowledge expands.

**contract archaeology** Archaeological survey or excavation, usually before a construction project; cultural resources management.

**conversational analysis** A technique in sociolinguistics that focuses on the social and symbolic attributes of verbal interactions.

**cooperative** An organization or enterprise assembled for the production and marketing of goods, and for mutual support, benefits, and the distribution of risk.

**corporate culture** The cultural characteristics of a workplace.

**corporate kin groups** Social groups, like lineages, that share political responsibilities and access to land; characteristic of tribal societies.

**correlate** A variable that stands in a consistent observed relationship with another variable.

**correlation** A statistical relationship between two variables.

**cortical surface** The surface of the cortex, in the brain.

**corvée** A system of required labor; characteristic of ancient states.

**cranium** The skull, excluding the jaw.

**creationism** An ideology, usually based on a literal interpretation of the Bible, that argues against evolution.

**creole** A type of language that results from the widespread adoption of a pidgin language as the primary language of a group.

**Cro-Magnon** A term broadly referring to the first anatomically modern humans, from roughly 40,000 to 10,000 B.C.; named after a site in southwestern France.

**cross-cultural** A standard form of anthropological analysis using the comparison of traditions and practices from different societies.

**cross-cultural research** The exploration of cultural variation by using ethnographic data from many societies.

**cross-cutting ties** Affinal or trading relationships that serve to counteract the political isolation of social groups in tribal societies.

**cross-sectional** Research done across different geographic locales.

**cultural anthropology** A field of anthropology emphasizing the study of the cultural diversity of contemporary societies, including their economies, sociopolitical systems, and belief systems.

**cultural construction/cultural construct** An idea that characterizes people according to categories that are socially or culturally defined.

**cultural dissonance** A situation arising from the incompatibility of two or more interacting cultural systems.

**cultural evolution** The process of invention, diffusion, and elaboration of the behavior that is learned and taught in groups and is transmitted from generation to generation, often used to refer to the development of social complexity.

**cultural ideals** A valued characteristic or belief of a society.

**cultural materialism** The idea, often associated with Marvin Harris, that cultural behaviors are best explained in relation to material constraints (including food, producing technology) to which humans are subjected.

**cultural mediation** The social processes through which someone learns or acquires the normative, shared behaviors and knowledge of a particular group or population.

**cultural pluralism** The simultaneous existence of two or more cultural systems within a single society; multiculturalism.

**cultural relativism/cultural relativity** The principle that all cultural systems are inherently equal in value and, therefore, that each cultural item must be understood on its own terms.

**cultural reproduction** The process by which cultural behaviors and beliefs are regenerated across generations or spread among people of the same generation; cultural construction creates reality.

**cultural resources** Archaeological, traditional, and constructed environments, buildings, or artifacts that are representative of a specific culture.

**cultural resources management** Preservation of the historical and prehistorical heritage; protection of archaeological sites from destruction.

**cultural validators** Actions or performances that enhance a sense of identity and belonging within a community or organization.

**cultural values** Ideas, beliefs, values, and attitudes learned as a member of a social group.

**culture** Learned patterns of thought and behavior characteristic of a particular social group.

**culture area** A largely outmoded idea that the world can be divided into a limited number of geographical regions, each defined by a certain set of cultural features that result from common ecological adaptation or history and are shared by all groups in the region.

**culture broker** An individual who attempts to negotiate and translate between two cultural groups, particularly in contexts of miscommunication or potential miscommunication.

**culture shock** The experience of stress and confusion resulting from moving from one culture to another; the removal or distortion of familiar cues and the substitution of strange cues.

**debt peonage** A system of involuntary servitude based on the debt of a laborer to his or her creditor.

**decoction** The extraction of flavor by boiling.

**Defense of Marriage Act** A federal U.S. law that states that: (a) the federal government may not recognize same-sex or polygamous marriages for any purpose, and (b) no state is obliged to recognize a same-sex marriage conducted or recognized in another state. This law was passed by the U.S. Congress and signed by President Bill Clinton on 21 September 1996.

**demography** The statistical study of human populations, including size, growth, migration, density, distribution, and vital statistics.

**dental anthropology** A specialization within biological anthropology; the study of the morphology of teeth across time and populations.

**dependency** A theory of international economic relations in which an economically powerful nation creates ties with other nations in ways that reduce the possibility of economic independence of the poorer nations.

**dependent variable** The resultant phenomenon that is explained by its relationship with an independent variable.

**diachronic** The comparative study of social and cultural history in a specific culture area.

**dialect** A regional or class-based version of a spoken language, although the difference between dialect and language can be influenced by historical and political considerations.

**diffusion** A process of cultural change by which traits of one society are borrowed by another; the spread of cultural traits.

**diffusion theory** A theory that cultural change occurs through a process by which traits of one society are borrowed by another.

**diseases of civilization** Chronic diseases, such as cardiovascular disease and obesity, that characterize the epidemiological profile of modern capitalist societies and are the result of infrequent exercise and high fat diets.

**divergence** The acquisition of dissimilar characteristics by related organisms, generally due to the influence of different environments and resulting in different evolutionary paths.

**dividual** As opposed to "individual," someone whose identity or selfhood is tied to his or her relationships with other people.

**DNA** Deoxyribonucleic acid; the long-stranded molecule that is the hereditary material of the cell, capable of self-replication and of coding the production of proteins for metabolic functions; most DNA is found on the chromosomes of the cell nucleus, but a small amount is located in the cell mitochondria.

**domestic labor** Work performed in the home, such as cooking, cleaning, and taking care of children.

**domestication of plants and animals** The invention of farming.

**dominance** The principle behind the social ranking hierarchy characteristic of terrestrial primate species.

**dowry** Presentation of goods or money by the bride's family to the bride, the groom, or the groom's family.

**Ebonics** The rule-based and pattern dialect of English spoken by many working-class urban African Americans; black English vernacular.

**economy** The production, distribution, and consumption of resources, labor, and wealth within a society.

**ecosystem** A community of plants and animals, including humans, within a physical environment and the relationship of organisms to one another.

**ecotourism** General term referring to travel experiences that adhere to one or more ecological and educational principles: conservation, scientific research, cross-cultural awareness, advocacy for local populations, and human rights-to name a few. Ecotourism also refers to a type of travel that minimizes the traveler's impact on local ecosystems and communities.

**edutainment** A marketing technique in consumer-oriented societies in which consumerism and education are simultaneously valued.

**egalitarian** A society organized around the principle of social equality; characteristic social formation of food foraging groups.

**egalitarian society** A society that emphasizes the social equality of members and makes achieved statuses accessible to all adults.

**embodiment/embodied** Human experience inside an individual body and the expression of culture through the body.

**embodied knowledge** Knowledge that seems to reside "in the body" and does not require conscious thought (for example, riding a bike).

**emic** Describing or understanding a specific culture from the subjective point of view of someone living within that culture.

**empirical** A terms that describes knowledge that can be verified by observation as opposed to theoretical logic.

**engineering anthropology** Collection of anthropometric data for a population to be utilized in technological design for improved efficiency and safety. See ergonomics.

**epidemic** Higher than normal occurrence of a disease in a particular area.

**epidemiological methods** The methods used in epidemiology.

**epidemiology** A science that studies the incidence, distribution, and control of disease in a population.

**epistemology** The study of the nature of knowledge and its limits.

**ergonomics** Human engineering; an applied science concerned with the anthropometric characteristics of people in the design of technology for improved human-machine interaction and safety.

**essentialist** A view of reality based on single inherent facts rather than a socially constructed reality.

**essentialize** The assumption that all individuals of the same social category (for instance, class, caste, race, gender) have the same beliefs, values, experiences, and other characteristics.

**estrus** The phase of the female mammalian cycle during which the female is receptive to males and encourages copulation.

**ethnic groups** Groups of people within a larger society with a distinct cultural or historical identity; ethnicity is a common mechanism of social separation in complex, heterogeneous societies.

**ethnic markers** Specific artifacts associated with and indicative of certain peoples or ethnicities.

**ethnocentrism** The assumption that one's own group's lifestyle, values, and patterns of adaptation are superior to all others.

**ethnocide** The attempt to exterminate an entire ethnic group (similar to genocide).

**ethnographic methods** The research techniques of cultural anthropology based on long-term participant observations, yielding a description of another culture.

**ethnography** An anthropological method that generally involves living in a place for an extended period of time, participating in and observing daily life, and then writing about the culture or the place.

**ethnology** The study and explanation of cultural similarities and differences.

**ethnomedicine** The medical theories, diagnosis systems, and therapeutic practices of a culture or ethnic group.

**ethnopediatrics** The study of how differing parenting styles affect infant health and growth.

**ethnoscience** A methodological approach in cultural anthropology that attempts to derive native patterns of thought from the logical analysis of linguistic data.

**ethology** The systematic study of animal behavior.

**ethos** The world view of a particular society, including its distinctive character, sentiments, and values.

**etic** Describing or understanding a specific culture from an outsider/external (sometimes neutral) point of view.

**etiology** The theory of causation of a disease or illness.

**eugenics** The genetic improvement of the human race through control of breeding.

**Eurasia** The continent of Europe and Asia.

**Eurocentric** Interpreting the world in terms of Western and especially European values and experiences.

**evaluation researcher** A researcher who assesses the impact or outcome of a treatment or program.

**Eve** In evolutionary studies of mitochondrial DNA (inherited through the maternal line only), refers to a hypothetical female ancestor of all anatomically modern humans.

**evolution** The process of change in the genes or culture of a species or group over time.

**evolutionary medicine** An anthropological approach to disease, symptoms, and medical care based upon our evolutionary heritage.

**exaptations** A novelty arising from features acquired in one context long before being coopted in another context; for example, hominids had essentially modern vocal systems for hundreds of thousands of years before the probable beginning of language.

**excavation** The stage in the process of archaeology in which data are collected.

**exchange** A social system for the distribution of goods; reciprocity is a widespread system of exchange between social equals while markets act as a mode of exchange between strangers.

**excision** One of three forms of female circumcision; includes clitoridectomy and removal of some or all of the labia minora and labia majora.

**exogamous** Relating to a custom that forbids members of a specific group from selecting a spouse from within that group.

**extended family** A domestic unit created by the linking together of two or more nuclear families.

**extinction** A part of the process of evolution in which a species completely dies out, leaving no direct progeny (in the past 300 years, more than 150 mammal species and several hundred species of plants have become extinct; this is the fastest rate of extinctions in the history of the planet).

**facultative biped** An animal that normally uses four limbs to walk or run but is capable of walking upright or running on two legs for a limited time.

**fallow** The period during which a unit of agricultural land is not cultivated so that nutrients can be restored to the soil.

**family of origin** Nuclear family into which an individual is born and in which he or she is reared.

**faunal region** A geographic region with its own distinctive assemblage of animal life.

**fecundity** A demographic characteristic of a society referring to its overall capacity for reproduction.

**feral** Living in, or pertaining to, the wild; without the benefit of society or culture.

**feud** A pattern of reciprocal hostility between families or kin groups, usually involving retribution for past wrongs or deaths; such as blood feud.

**FGM** Female genital mutilation or female genital modification. See sunna circumcision, excision, infibulation.

**fieldwork** The hallmark of research in cultural anthropology, it usually involves long-term residence with the people being studied.

**fission** The splitting of a descent group—a residential unit based on shared kinship—into two or more new descent groups or domestic units.

**fitness** The ability to reproduce viable offspring.

**focus groups** A research strategy in which an investigator leads a small group in discussion on a particular topic; frequently used in market research.

**folk taxonomy** A culture's system of classification or grouping of objects, which can reveal the cognitive categories of that group.

**food foragers** People living in a society with an economic pattern of harvesting of wild food resources, usually by gathering plants or hunting animals; hunting and gathering.

**food loss** Food that is not eaten due to systemic inefficiencies, surpluses, or other types of waste.

**food scarcity** The lack of sufficient food to meet the energy requirements of a population; may be the result of failed food production or a socially unequal distribution system.

**foraging** Hunting and gathering; the original human economic system relying on the collection of natural plant and animal food sources.

**forensic anthropology** A subfield of applied anthropology that uses techniques from biological anthropology and archaeology to help resolve legal matters.

**founder effect** A force of evolutionary change resulting from the nonproportional contribution of genes by a founding member of a small population.

FOXP2 A gene that facilitates understanding grammar and speech in humans.

**fraternal polyandry** An uncommon form of plural marriage in which a woman is married to two or more brothers at a time.

**French Neandertal Mask** A small 35,000 year-old flint rock that archaeologists and paleontologists argue is a crudely manufactured face sculpted by Neandertals who lived along the banks of what is now called the Loire River in France.

**garbology** The systematic study of current household refuse.

**gender** The social classification of masculine or feminine.

**gender dimorphism** Physical and physiological differences between males and females; sexual dimorphism.

**gender roles** Accepted models of behavior, thoughts, and emotions associated with masculinity and femininity that are culturally defined and learned over the course of one's upbringing and socialization.

**genealogy** The systematic study of the consanguineal and affinal kin of a particular person, including his or her ancestors; a common method used in anthropological field studies.

**gene pool** The range of variety of genes within a given breeding population.

**genetic drift** The evolutionary factor that accounts for random shifts of gene frequencies as a consequence of small population size.

**gestation** The carrying of young in the uterus from conception to delivery.

**ghetto** A subsection of a city in which members of a minority group live because of social, legal, or economic pressure.

**globalization** A contemporary cultural, political, and economic process involving world capitalism by which production and consumption are expanded to be worldwide in scope or application.

**Gordian knot** A highly intractable problem or impasse; in Greek legend, a knot tied by King Gordius of Phrygia and cut by Alexander the Great after an oracle said it could be untied only by the next ruler of Asia.

**grooming** A typical social interaction between primates involving the search for and removal of debris and ectoparasites from the fur of another animal.

**hallucinogen** A substance that induces visions or auditory hallucinations in normal individuals.

**hearth** The floor of a fireplace.

**heterozygous** Having different genes or alleles in corresponding locations on a pair of chromosomes.

**hierarchy** The categorization of a group of people according to status, whether it be ascribed at birth or achieved. A hierarchy refers to a group organized in this way.

**historical archaeology** A subfield of archaeology that studies the material remains of past societies that had systems of writing. Historical archaeologists are primarily concerned with human societies after 1500 CE.

**HIV** The human immunodeficiency virus that causes AIDS.

**holistic** Refers to viewing the whole society as an integrated and interdependent system; an important characteristic of the anthropological approach to understanding humans.

**homesigns** A system of communicative gestures created by deaf children who are not exposed to established, widespread sign languages such as ASL (American Sign Language).

**hominid** A broad category that consists of all modern and extinct Great Apes and their direct ancestors (modern humans, chimpanzees, gorillas, orangutans and their direct ancestors).

**hominin** An erect-walking bipedal primate that is either human or an extinct, direct ancestor to present-day humans (includes members of the genera *Homo, Australopithecus, Paranthropus,* and *Ardipithecus*).

**Homo erectus** An extinct, direct ancestor of modern humans; situated on the evolutionary line between Homo habilis and Homo sapiens; first appeared about 1.8 million years ago and could be found throughout the Old World until about 200,000 years ago; associated with the first use of fire; similar to modern humans in all body proportions except cranial capacity.

**Homo ergaster** A hominid that lived in many of Africa's harshest environments between 600,000 and 1.7 million years ago and had a brain almost two-thirds the size of modern humans.

**Homo floresiensis** A species of dwarf human first discovered on Flores, an Indonesian Island. This dwarf human had a small cranial size (417cc), was approximately one meter tall and bipedal. The fossil record dates H. floresiensis from 13,000 to 38,000 years ago. Paleontologists debate whether this dwarf human is in fact a distinct human species or a pathological H. sapiens.

**Homo habilis** An extinct hominin thought to be the earliest member of the genus Homo; situated on the evolutionary line between the australopithecines and Homo erectus; associated with the use of stone tools.

**Homo neanderthalensis (Neanderthals)** A close relative of modern humans that lived from about 200,000 years ago to about 30,000 years ago in Europe and Western Asia. Neanderthals had short, muscular bodies, adapted to cold climates, and had larger brains than modern humans. They were skilled toolmakers and buried their dead.

**Homo sapiens** Hominin species including modern humans and Homo sapiens (archaic); Homo sapiens (archaic) are also known as Homo heidelbergensis.

**homozygous** Having the same allele (form of a gene) at a certain locus on homologous (matched pair) chromosomes.

**horticulture** A plant cultivation system based upon relatively low energy input, like gardening by using only the hoe or digging stick; often involves use of the slash-and-burn technique.

**human rights** Related to a post–WW II international movement begun by the United Nations and associated with the 1948 International Declaration of Universal Human Rights. The rights enumerated include: equality before the law; protection against arbitrary arrest; the right to a fair trial; freedom from ex-post-facto criminal laws; the right to own property; freedom of thought, conscience, and religion; freedom of opinion and expression; freedom of peaceful assembly and association; also included in the document are economic, social, and cultural rights as the right to work and to choose one's work freely, the right to equal pay for equal work, the right to form and join trade unions, the right to rest and leisure, the right to an adequate standard of living, and the right to education. During the 1990s, human rights efforts often emphasized women's rights.

**Human Terrain Team** An experimental and controversial U.S. military program that assigns anthropologists to work with American combat units in Afghanistan and Iraq.

**human universal** A trait or behavior found in all human cultures.

**hunter-gatherers** Peoples who subsist on the collection of naturally occurring plants and animals; food foragers.

**hyperkinetic** Refers to abnormally increased and uncontrollable muscular movement.

**hypothesis** A tentative assumption or proposition about the relationship(s) between specific events or phenomena, tentatively set forth as a "target" to be tested.

**hypothetico-deductive method** A theory about science, in which a hypothesis is posed from which certain observations are predicted. Observations that agree with those predicted are taken as evidence for the hypothesis, and observations that do not agree with those predicted are taken as evidence against the hypothesis.

**ichthyologist** A specialist in the study of fish.

**ideal body images** Culturally defined standards for attractive body shapes.

**indigenous** A descriptive term that refers to the original or native population of a particular region or environment.

**indigenous archaeology** A form of archaeology in which indigenous populations are collaborative partners and/or supervisors of the excavation, analysis, and care of the material and skeletal remains of their ancestors.

**indigenous people** The original or native population of a particular region or environment.

**indigenized** The reconceptualization of a foreign cultural construct or idea to make it fit within a local/indigenous worldview.

**infanticide** Killing a baby soon after birth.

**infibulation** One of three forms of female circumcision; includes circumcisions and excision, followed by the sewing up of the sides of the vulva so that scar tissue covers the vaginal opening, except for a small gap for urination and menstruation; requiring some surgical opening for first intercourse and birth; also called pharaonic circumcision.

**infidel** A nonbeliever with respect to a particular religion.

**informant** A member of a society who has established a working relationship with an anthropological fieldworker and who provides information about the culture; the subject of intensive interviewing.

**institutions** Formal organizations within a society.

**intelligent design** The theory that aspects of the universe, and in particular living things, can best be explained by an intelligent cause rather than an undirected process.

**intensive interviewing** The ethnographic method of repeated interviews with a single informant.

**rite of passage** Religious rituals that mark important changes in individual status or social position at different points in the life cycle, such as birth, marriage, or death.

**ritual** A set of acts, usually involving religion or magic, following a sequence established by tradition.

**rockshelter** A cave.

**Sahelanthropus tchadensis** A hominin that lived in the Sahel region of Africa (contemporary Chad) nearly 7 million years ago; it is one of the oldest known species on the human family tree.

**salvage archaeology** The attempt to preserve archaeological remains from destruction by large-scale projects of industrial society (such as dam or highway construction).

**sample** A subpopulation that is studied in order to make generalizations.

**sanctions** Generally negative responses by a social group as a consequence of an individual's behavior; used to maintain social control.

**scavenge** To collect and eat carcasses of animals killed by carnivores; thought to be part of the lifestyle of australopithecines.

**scientific theory** A testable, correctable explanation of observable phenomena that yields new information about nature in answer to a set of preexisting problems.

**séance** A ritual, usually held at night, designed to promote direct contact between people and spirits.

**secret society** A social organization or association whose members hide their activities from nonmembers.

**segmentary system** A hierarchy of more and more inclusive lineages; functions primarily in contexts of conflict between groups.

**self-sufficient** Refers to a characteristic of most pre-state societies; the ability to maintain a viable economy and social system with minimal outside contact.

**serial monogamy** The marriage of one woman and one man at a time but in a sequence, usually made possible through divorce.

**seropositive** Testing positive for a given disease (such as HIV infection) based on a blood test.

**seroprevalence** The prevalence (proportion of people infected in a population) of a given disease based on blood tests.

**sex** Determined by biological characteristics, such as external genitalia and having XX or XY chromosomes (contrast with gender).

**sex roles** Learned social activities and expectations made on the basis of gender.

**sexual dimorphism** A condition of having the two sexes dissimilar in appearance.

**sexual selection** A type of natural selection resulting from higher reproductive success of males with particular inherited traits that are chosen by females; for example, the male peacock's tail.

**shaman** A part-time religious practitioner typical of tribal societies who goes into trance to directly communicate with the spirit world for the benefit of the community.

**shards** An archaeological term that refers to a broken piece of ceramic, metal, glass or rock. Also known as "sherd."

**shifting agriculture** A form of cultivation (horticulture) with recurrent, alternate clearing and burning of vegetation and planting of crops in the burnt fields.

**sickle-cell anemia** An often fatal genetic disease caused by a chemical mutation that changes one of the amino acids in normal hemoglobin; the mutant sickle-cell gene occurs with unusually high frequency in parts of Africa where malaria is present.

**SIDA** The Spanish, French, Italian, and Haitian Creole acronym for AIDS.

**SIDS** Sudden infant death syndrome—the sudden and unexpected death of an infant, also known as crib death.

**single-interest relationship** A relationship based solely on one connection, such as landlord-tenant.

**site** The location for an actual or potential archaeological excavation; a concentration of the remains of human activities or artifacts.

**situated** Formed by a given person's experiences, based on context.

**skewed** Biased.

**slang** A small set of new and usually short-lived words in the vocabulary or dialect of a language.

**slash-and-burn techniques** Shifting form of cultivation (horticulture) with recurrent, alternate clearing and burning of vegetation and planting in the burnt fields; swidden.

**social class** In state-level societies, a stratum in a social hierarchy based on differential group access to means of production and control over distribution; often endogamous.

**social cohesion** The process by which a social group binds itself together, producing greater cooperation and conformity.

**social construction** A reality that is created and agreed on by interpersonal interaction and discourse; opposite of essentialist.

**social control** Practices that induce members of a society to conform to the expected behavior patterns of their culture; includes informal mechanisms, like gossip, legal systems, and punishment.

**social mobility** The upward or downward movement of individuals or groups in a society characterized by social stratification.

**social networks** An informal pattern of organization based on the complex web of social relations linking individuals; includes factors like kinship, friendship, economics, and political ties.

**social organization** A culturally inherited system that orders social relations within social groups.

**social reproduction** A process through which cultural practices and rituals perpetuate existing social structures and cultural hierarchies.

**social status** A person's level of prestige in society. Social status is associated with factors like education and employment as well as higher and lower levels of wealth or power. In the United States, for instance, doctors tend to have higher social status than cooks at McDonald's.

**social stratification** An arrangement of statuses or groups within a society into a pattern of socially superior and inferior ranks; based on differential access to strategic resources.

**socialization** The development, through the influence of parents and others, of patterns of thought and behavior in children that conform to beliefs and values of a particular culture.

**socially validated** Approved or recognized by the culture of a particular social group.

**society** A socially bounded, spacially contiguous group of people who interact in basic economic and political institutions and share a particular culture; societies retain relative stability across generations.

**sociobiology** The study of animal and human social behavior based on the theory that behavior is linked to genetics.

**sociocultural** Refers to the complex combination of social and cultural factors.

**sociolinguistics** A subfield of anthropological linguistics emphasizing the study of the social correlates to variations in speech patterns.

**soil analysis** Detailed description of the chemical characteristics of a sample of soil that can be used as a "fingerprint" to match stolen artifacts with their location of origin.

**solidarity** Unity based on community interest, objectives, and culture.

**Solutrean** Of or relating to an Upper Paleolithic culture characterized by leaf-shaped finely flaked stone implements.

**sorcery** The use of supernatural knowledge or power for purposes of evil, for example causing sickness; used to further the sorcerer's individual social goals.

**speciation** The formation of biological species or the process that leads to this end.

**species** The largest naturally occurring population that is capable of interbreeding and producing fully fertile offspring.

**speech event** A unit of analysis in linguistics that is defined by the speech occurring within said unit, such as an invitation versus an announcement or an apology.

**spurious** Not an actual or causal relationship, as in the correlation between the number of storks and birth rate.

**states** A complex society characterized by urban centers, agricultural production, labor specialization, standing armies, permanent boundaries, taxation, centralized authority, public works, and laws designed to maintain the status quo.

**stature** Height; can be used as an indirect measure of the health of a population.

**status** Position in a social system that is characterized by certain rights, obligations, expected behaviors (roles), and certain social symbols.

**stigma** Socially constructed shame or discredit.

**stratified societies** A society in which groups experience structured inequality of access not only to power and prestige but also to economically important resources.

**stratigraphic level** In an archaeological excavation, a level of occupation at which artifacts may be found; important for relative dating techniques.

**stroll** A street where prostitution activity is concentrated.

**structure** In anthropology, generally referring to social institutions and patterns of organization.

**subculture** The culture of a subgroup of a society that has its own distinctive ideas, beliefs, values, and worldview.

**subordinate** Submissive to or falling under the control of higher authority resulting in an inferior position in a social group.

**subsidy** Financial aid given by a government to a person or group to support an enterprise deemed essential to the public interest. The U.S. government, for example, provides subsidies to farmers and transportation businesses like Amtrak because they provide essential public services which otherwise may not be profitable.

**sunna circumcision** One of three forms of female circumcision; this procedure includes clitorectomy (removal of clitoris and hood) and sometimes refers only to the cutting of the hood (prepuce); the name Sunna relates the practice to Islamic traditions, although most Muslim scholars and theologians deny any Koranic justification for female circumcision.

**superstructure** In the theory of cultural materialism, refers to a society's ideology.

**sushi** A traditional Japanese food of rice and thinly sliced raw fish and other ingredients rolled in seaweed and artfully presented to the diner, eaten with a horseradish sauce.

**suture line** In osteological studies, the joints between bones, for example in the cranium.

**swidden cultivation** A tropical gardening system, also known as slash-and-burn horticulture in which forest is cleared, burned, cultivated, and then left for bush fallow.

**symbol** A sign that consistently but arbitrarily represents an object or meaning; the basis of communication within a culture.

**synchronic** The analysis of a culture at a single point of time.

**syntax** The word order or pattern of word order in a phrase or sentence.

**taboo** A supernaturally forbidden act as defined by a culture, violation of which can have severe negative consequences.

**technology** The application of science to a practical purpose.

**territoriality** Laying claim and defending a territory; tends to be a characteristic of arboreal primate species.

**TFR (total fertility rate)** The average number of children born to a woman during her lifetime.

**Thalassemia** A hereditary disease that causes a malformation of hemoglobin in the red blood cell, somewhat like sickle-cell anemia; has a high frequency in the Mediterranean region and south Asia, areas with a history of much malaria.

**third/fourth gender** Third gender typically refers to male and sometimes female berdaches, while fourth gender only refers to female berdaches.

**time-allocation study** A quantitative method that identifies what people do and how much time they spend doing various activities; useful for cross-cultural comparison.

**totem** A symbolic plant or animal associated with a social group (clan) used for identification and religious expression.

**transmission** Passing of an infectious agent to an uninfected person from an infected group or individual.

**transnational culture** A pattern of cultural beliefs and behaviors characteristic of elites throughout the world and often spread through mass media.

**tribe** A relatively small, usually horticultural, society organized on principles of kinship, characterized by little social stratification and no centralized political authority, and whose members share a culture and language.

**trophic exchanges** Relationships between organisms having to do with food; eating or being eaten.

**United Nations World Heritage Site** A historical construction or natural site determined to have outstanding universal value as determined by the United Nations Educational, Scientific, and Cultural Organization (UNESCO). There are 851 World Heritage Sites, 20 of which are in the United States.

**universalism** The understanding that certain beliefs, values, rights, or conditions are or should be universal.

**universal grammar** A linguistic theory stating that all humans share an innate and unconscious set of rules that allow us to learn languages and determine whether a sentence is correctly formed.

**urbanization** The worldwide process of the growth of cities at the expense of rural populations.

**urban villages** Small (usually segregated) communities of minorities or rural migrants located in cities.

**usufruct rights** The legal right of using land (or resources on land) that is not one's private property.

**validity** The quality of a measurement tool or variable actually measuring what is intended.

**vanua:** A traditional Fijian concept of community which seeks balance between the ecological, cultural, and spiritual dimensions of daily life.

**values** The ideas of a culture that are concerned with appropriate goals and behavior.

**verb-second structure** A grammar system which dictates a sentence structure in which the verb always follows the subject (also known as SVO structure, i.e. subject-verb-object).

**vertebrate** An animal with a spinal column.

**virilocal residence** Patrilocal postmarital residence.

**walkabout** A custom of Australian aborigines involving a long circular journey to sacred places and a return to home.

**war** Violence between political entities, such as nations, using soldiers; to be distinguished from the smaller scale feud.

**waste behavior** The behavior and practices of people related to the excess remains of human consumption.

**weaning** Acclimating someone (as a child) to take food other than by nursing.

**Western culture** A generic term referring to the common beliefs, values, and traditions of Europeans and their descendants.

**worldview** The particular way in which a society constructs ideas of space, time, social relationship, and the meaning of life.

**woodhenge** A circle of wooden posts arranged to make astronomical observations to chart the passing of the seasons.

**Yerkish** An artificial language using a computer that has been taught successfully to great apes at the Yerkes Regional Primate Center.

**zeitgeist** The general intellectual, moral, and cultural climate of an era.

**Zinjanthropus** The original name given to a 1.75-million-year-old Australopithecine fossil (Australopithecus boisei) found in Kenya by Louis and Mary Leakey.

# Index

## H



## I